Controversies in

SOCIOLOGY

A CANADIAN INTRODUCTION

Controversies in SOCIOLOGY

A CANADIAN INTRODUCTION

Sylvia M. Hale
St. Thomas University

Copp Clark Pitman Ltd.
A Longman Company
Toronto

© Copp Clark Pitman Ltd., 1990

ISBN 0-7730-4770-0

Executive editor: Brian Henderson
Editor: Barbara Tessman
Photo research and permissions: Melanie Sherwood
Design: Catherine Aikens
Typesetting: Carol Magee
Printing and binding: John Deyell
Cover: Miller Gore Brittain (Canadian 1912–1968) *Sing-Song*, 1938 oil on masonite 55.9 x 45.9 cm. Art Gallery of Ontario, Toronto. *Sing-Song* reproduced by permission of Jennifer Brittain, copyright owner.

Canadian Cataloguing in Publication Data

Hale, Sylvia Marion, 1945–
   Controversies in sociology
Includes bibliographical references.
ISBN 0-7730-4770-0

1. Sociology – Canada.   2. Canada – Social conditions.
I. Title.

HM22.C3H34 1990   301'.0971   C89-090687-4

Copp Clark Pitman
2775 Matheson Blvd. East
Mississauga, Ontario
L4W 4P7

Associated companies:
   Longman Group Ltd., London
   Longman Inc., New York
   Longman Cheshire Pty., Melbourne
   Longman Paul Pty., Auckland

Printed and bound in Canada

Table of Contents

Acknowledgements

Peter Weeks, a colleague and associate professor of sociology at St. Thomas University, contributed his special expertise in ethnomethodology to the text. He wrote the extensive review of ethnomethodology for chapter 4, "The Microsociology of Everyday Life," and he cheerfully co-operated with me in three successive drafts to ensure that the completed chapter merged smoothly into the book as a whole. Peter's extensive knowledge of feminist research and the social construction of reality approach contributed much to other chapters as well. Special thanks are also due to Peter for contributing his collection of cartoons and for taking some of the photographs that illustrate the text.

In the preparation of the text, I owe a considerable intellectual debt to Roberta Hamilton, professor of sociology at Queen's University. She undertook a comprehensive review of the first draft and suggested multiple ways in which it might be strengthened. Her suggestions were especially valuable in introducing contemporary feminist research in many areas. I would also like to acknowledge my intellectual debt to David Lee and Howard Newby, the authors of *The Problem of Sociology* (1983).

Colleagues in sociology at St. Thomas University, Michael Clow, Abdul Lodhi, Marilee Reimer, John McKendy, and Peter MacDonald, and also William Dunn, a former colleague, offered valuable help in developing sections of the text concerned with the free trade debate, race and ethnic relations, Marxist feminism, functionalism and microsociology, critical perspectives on education, and Marxist research on rural communities. I am grateful for the support and encouragement that they have given me. Special thanks are also due to William Dunn for helping to research and illustrations for the text and for preliminary work on the glossary.

In closing, I would like to express my appreciation to Barbara Tessman of Copp Clark Pitman in Toronto. Her meticulous editing contributed greatly to the overall coherence and readability of the text. As editor and principle critic of successive drafts, she constantly drew attention to weak sections in the analysis or coverage of issues and drew on her extensive knowledge of current affairs and feminist issues to develop points raised in the text. Barbara Tessman and Brian Henderson, also of Copp Clark Pitman, gave me enthusiastic support and expert advice and help at all stages in the preparation of the text. They taught me much about the social construction of textbooks.

Sylvia Hale
St. Thomas University
Fredericton

Preface

The initial impetus for this text came from a plan to develop a Canadian edition of a British text, *The Problem of Sociology* by David Lee and Howard Newby (Hutchinson 1983). The Canadianization seemed warranted by the outstanding qualities of the original British text. In many ways, it represented a radical departure from the traditional format of North American introductions to sociology. Gone were the token chapters on "great names" and the ubiquitous lists of social institutions. Instead, students were introduced to sociology as a theoretical discipline, grounded in a long historical and intellectual tradition in which controversies and empirical research are fundamental.

Each section of the British book presented a sophisticated, in-depth treatment of theory. Institutions such as education, family, religion, bureaucracy, deviance, and so on, were all represented, but as empirical tests of theory rather than as specialized entities within a structural model of society. The major achievement of the text was that it systematically applied sociological theory to the analysis of contemporary industrial capitalist society. The consistently high quality of Lee and Newby's book, their organizing focus around theories of industrial society, and their empirical testing of theories with contemporary data, all provided a challenging framework for an introductory course.

Using this text for an introductory sociology course in a Canadian University, however, proved frustrating. The historical order of the presentation of theories, combined with their complexity and the absence of specifically Canadian data, made it difficult for the average Canadian student to absorb the material. The historical framework that was used by Lee and Newby meant that contemporary theories came last. We thought it desirable to engage students in actively debating the comparative merits of different perspectives right from the beginning. Not only was it necessary to introduce structural functionalism—which has long dominated North American sociology and introductory sociology texts—right at the outset, but feminist and social constructionist theories had to be presented as well. In this way, students could relate their immediate personal experiences to what they were studying because these interactive perspectives in effect bridge the gap between micro- and macrosociological theory.

These changes, combined with the need to include Canadian data, were too far-reaching to be accomplished by a cut-and-paste Canadianization. Hence, *Controversies in Sociology*. Even the chapters on classical theorists such as Durkheim, Marx, and Weber, which still bear some structural resemblance to the corresponding chapters in Lee and Newby, had to be substantially altered. They had to reflect the present text's concern with integrating the four theoretical approaches of structural functionalism, Marxism, feminism, and social constructionism into each section of the book.

The data that we present in this book are not treated as "facts," but as tests of different sociological theories. Throughout this text, students are encouraged to develop their critical skills instead of passively absorbing material. We believe that such a goal constitutes a striking difference between *Controversies in Sociology* and other Canadian sociology textbooks. It is in this regard that the book remains true to the fundamental conception of Lee and Newby that students should be introduced to sociology as the study of a body of theory, rather than as a collection of rapidly changing descriptive data.

Introduction

This text present sociology as a way of questioning experience rather than as an accumulation of factual knowledge. The objective is to stimulate discussion and to assist students in developing their capacity to think critically about society rather than simply to memorize facts. Theory is accorded central importance and is utilized throughout the text as the basis for exploring all substantive issues.

The text is organized around the comparative application of a range of contemporary theories to problems of industrial capitalist society, with special reference to Canada. It introduces the four broad theoretical perspectives of functionalism, Marxism, the social construction of reality, and feminism, tracing their roots in the works of Durkheim, Marx, Parsons, and Weber. We study the founding fathers' contribution to, and continuing relevance for, a variety of contemporary theories and analyses. The main body of the text combines theory, methodology, and evidence throughout and tries to explain the basis of controversies in sociology. Different chapters present a comparative application of the four major theoretical approaches to the substantive issues of the microsociology of everyday life, community life in rural and urban contexts, religion, suicide, crime and industrial conflict, political economy, stratification, family, education, racial and ethnic relations, development and change, and bureaucracy. Each of these topics is studied as an arena for debate between competing theories rather than as a body of factual knowledge that can be taken as given. The text has no chapter devoted exclusively to women's issues. Such issues are treated as an integral part of human concerns and are given systematic attention in each chapter.

Each substantive chapter illustrates the close relationship between theory, method, and what is taken to be factual information. The theoretical perspectives focus on different aspects of a problem or conceptualize the nature of the problem in very different ways. Hence, the major critique of one approach or one body of data is to juxtapose it systematically with constrasting theories that search for different kinds of data. Throughout the text, the critique of ethnomethodology—that there can be no such thing as disembodied facts separate from the interpretive frameworks that give them meaning—is taken seriously. Feminist theory is similarly critical in showing that much that has been taken for objective information about humanity is in reality ideological, serving to cover up the experiences of half of humanity and to distort the experience of the other half. The goal of the text is not to propound one theoretical perspective over others.

Rather, the text presents substantive material in such a way that students can see how sociologists use their theories and their research techniques to investigate topics. It shows how the assumptions that underlie these different approaches systemtically influence how questions are asked and what kind of data is sought. The ultimate aim is to challenge students to debate competing explanations and theories and so to encourage them to participate actively in sociology as critical readers of theory and research.

Part I of the text introduces the problem of sociology as a discipline and the controversies in theory and research methods that pervade it. Chapter 1 explores the nature of the sociological imagination, defined by C. Wright Mills (1959) as the ability to use information in a critical way to achieve an understanding of what is going on in the world and what may be happening within one's own life experience.

Chapter 2 presents an overview of major theoretical approaches in sociology, outlining their key assumptions, the similarities and differences among them, and how they both complement and challenge each other. The goal is to encourage students to develop a critical comparative approach from the very beginning of the course. This makes possible a flexible order in the presentation of material in the text. Teachers may opt to juxtapose this overview chapter with any of the substantive problem areas explored in later chapters and so engage students in debate over comparative approaches to problems in the first weeks of the class. They can then return to questions of method or to specific theories in more depth without affecting the continuity of the text.

Chapter 3 on methodology stresses that there is no definitive method for doing research in sociology. The appropriateness of the approach is determined by the theoretical perspective and the major questions that are the focus of the study. The objective of this chapter is not to teach students how to do research, but rather to alert them, as critical readers and consumers of research, to the strengths, weaknesses, and blind spots of each technique.

Part II of the text consists of four chapters that explore fundamental questions on the nature of social cohesion and order in industrial society. Chapter 4 on the microsociology of everyday life is in many ways pivotal for the text. It encourages students to relate sociological inquiry to their immediate experience of interpersonal relations, exploring how different perspectives relate the microworld of everyday interaction to the macrolevel of social structures. It introduces ethnomethodology, which lies at the foundation of the social construction of reality perspective. Chapter 5 on rural and urban communities is also designed to relate directly to students' personal experience and

to challenge common assumptions concerning the ideals of rural life and the loss of community spirit in urban or metropolitan centres. The chapter demonstrates how the folk/urban thesis implies certain assumptions that, in turn, imply consequences that can be tested against evidence. The general conclusion, that the evidence falsifies the assumptions, places in doubt the pervasive notion of contrasts between rural and urban life and emphasizes the general need to question taken for granted assumptions about society.

The subsequent two chapters on cohesion and morality, and their breakdown in anomie, disorder, and conflict, are oriented around Durkheim's analysis of social order. They introduce the notion of anomie and the constrasting, and yet closely related, concept of alienation, suggesting that anomie, or the breakdown of moral order, may be generated by alienating, unjust social structures. The discussion of suicide and religion, two central topics in Durkheim's work, facilitates a critical introduction to the social construction of reality perspective. We learn that what Durkheim took to be factual data—suicide rates—are themselves socially constructed through the decision-making processes of coroners, Catholic priests, and bureaucrats who kept the records of deaths in various communities. Feminist theory similarly challenges the interpretations based on data that show relatively high suicide rates by males compared to females. Feminist theory also challenges Durkheimian and Marxist theories of the nature of religion in society.

Chapter 7 examines deviance and crime, an area of study fraught with controversy and unanswered questions. Anomie theory, focussing on morality and the breakdown of values, is pitted against Marxist theories of alienation and exploitation, in attempts to account for the higher rates of crime among the lower classes. Labelling theory and related social constructionist approaches question whether evidence on differential crime rates by social class is factual or is merely an artifact of how labels are applied and who is picked on by law enforcement officers. Current feminist theory casts in doubt almost the entire range of theories of crime—conservative, radical, and social constuctionist—because they fail to account for the vast differences in criminal behaviour between women and men.

Part III of the text focusses specifically on Marx's theory of capitalism. By this stage in the text, readers will already be familiar with the problems of inequality, exploitation, and alienation associated with Marxist interpretations of capitalism. This section explores in more detail the theory of the contradictions of capitalism developed by Marx and current efforts to reformulate classical structuralist–Marxist theory. Social constructionist theory explores how the social reality of structures of capitalism is actually produced through the everyday activities of people in their working lives. Marxist-feminist and radical-feminist theories raise the challenge that relations of reproduction and patriarchy need to be integrated into the study of class and gender-class relations. Chapter 9 systematically tests the predictions based on Marx's theory of the contradictions of capitalism against evidence of the political economy of Canada. It points out both the powerful explanatory utility of the model and its ultimate limitations.

Part IV of the text begins with a detailed exposition of Parsons' model of a social system. The next five chapters all have the same format, exploring research on the specific subjects of family, stratification, education, race and ethnic relations, and development and change. In each chapter, the classical functionalist approach developed by Parsons is pitted against structuralist–Marxist theory that relates the same substantive issues to the workings of capitalism. Both these macrosociological perspectives are then challenged and modified by contemporary theories that look at how this macro reality is socially constructed in the intimate, everyday activities of people. Feminist theory focusses on the relations of patriarchy that pervade these institutions.

Part V of the text is qualitatively different. It is organized around the critical issues of rationality and bureaucracy that are central to Weber's work. Weber merges the interpretive perspective with a macro-historical analysis and critical appraisal of capitalism and bureaucratic organizations. The final chapter presents a synthesis of various approaches. The conceptual boundaries between systems theory and Marxism, interpretive perspectives and feminism, break down as we analyse bureaucracy, which is pervasive in both capitalist and communist societies. This analysis raises multiple questions about whether rationality and the associated values of science and technology are fundamentally irrational. It leaves us with a host of questions that sociologists are only beginning to formulate.

Part I

An Overview of Sociology

Chapter 1

The Sociological Imagination

The Promise of Sociology

In broad terms, **sociology** seeks to investigate the happenings of human society. A basic question immediately arises from this definition: what is **society**? It is not a tangible entity, a **system** that exists independently of the behaviours of the people who constitute it. Rather, it is the set of forces "exerted by people over one another and over themselves" (Elias 1970, 17). Sociology is concerned with the source and form of these forces. During certain periods, as when countries go to war, or when the economy collapses, leaving hundreds of thousands of people adrift without jobs, forces may seem overwhelming, sweeping people along as helpless victims. Yet these are still human forces, pressures that people in groups bring to bear upon each other. Sometimes people resist, fighting back against such pressures and forcing changes. People continue to assert themselves, even within the most oppressive **social institutions**. Goffman (1961a) describes how a patient, stripped of almost all autonomy in a large, closed ward

of an asylum, still managed to assert himself against the system by urinating on the radiator—an ideal location for the act to produce maximum effect.

In a brilliant essay, C. Wright Mills (1959, chap. 1) expresses the sense of ambivalence that people feel given their positions as both victims and creators of society. Mills observes that people often feel as if they are in a series of traps in their personal lives. They feel that they cannot overcome their personal problems, and in this they are often correct. Individuals do not generally control the forces that affect their lives. These forces are socially located far beyond the immediate, personal settings in which people live, and it is difficult for people to see beyond their own private reality: their jobs, their neighbourhoods, their families. The more that threatening forces transcend their direct experience, the more trapped people feel. How do steel workers in Cape Breton feel when foreign companies stop building supertankers and the world market for steel founders? Or Alberta oil workers when the price of oil collapses? Or residents of a small town when its major employer, a **multinational corporation**, closes local operations and moves to the United States? Or parents who see their children's lives bombarded by war toys, pornography, drugs, sex, the threat of AIDS? All these forces are more or less beyond the immediate control of the people who are affected by them. Personal successes and failures occur within definite social situations and reflect the effects of modern historical changes.

The information revolution in the media has increased people's awareness of world events. Anyone who reads newspapers or watches the news on television cannot help but be aware that we are living in the middle of upheaval everywhere: in the Middle East, Latin America, Afghanistan, Northern Ireland, and even at home in Canada. International terrorism has spread to Canada in the form of bombings, skyjackings, and assassinations. Every time we catch an international flight, we are reminded that someone might want to blow it up. People fleeing from civil war, dictatorship, and persecution abroad seek refugee status in Canada almost daily. Still more come seeking to escape grinding poverty at home, only to be faced with Canada's own unemployment problem. The British like to think of their island as democratic and civilized, but this idealized vision is torn apart by racial riots in London and the North, the insurgency of the Irish Republican Army, the rise of aggressive neo-Nazi youth groups, the violence of football fans killing foreign spectators in mass brawls. All this and more is brought into our livingrooms each night as we watch television.

While the media increase our awareness, they do not necessarily increase our understanding of events. When we are unable to understand what is happening or why, we desperately try to interpret these events in individual, personal terms. For example, British Prime Minister Thatcher blamed the participants' parents for the London riots,

suggesting that the youths had been badly brought up and should have been spanked when they were younger. Others believe that the street people huddling over heating grates and lining up outside soup kitchens are inadequate or lazy or alcoholic and could pull themselves up if they wanted to. They believe that riots are caused by a few troublemakers, outside agitators who should be put in prison. But these individual explanations are inadequate.

When we as individuals are faced with forces that we do not understand and cannot control, we often react by withdrawal. We retreat into our private lives, tell ourselves that the problems are not our responsibility, and try to forget them and get on with our own lives. When we cannot avoid the threats, we tend to react with fear, resentment, and hostility. Moral insensitivity can result from people's sense of being overwhelmed by historical changes that they do not understand and that may challenge cherished values. This may help to explain the report carried by the *Globe and Mail*, in December 1986, about a homeless old man who was set ablaze as he slept on a bench in an affluent Chicago neighbourhood. Middle-class residents had apparently become exasperated with having to face this dishevelled man every day and, unable to understand the forces that foster such poverty amid such affluence, they eventually reacted to his presence with violence. In other neighbourhoods, people cover hot air gratings with barbed wire to stop derelicts from huddling over them. People do not want shelters for the homeless, young delinquents, or the mentally retarded built in their neighbourhoods. Fear of unemployment or inflation threatening a tenuous hold on a middle-class lifestyle makes people easy prey for get-tough policies and glib political slogans that promise easy answers.

People need much more than information to overcome their sense of being trapped. We live in the age of the information revolution, with satellite printing of national newspapers, instantaneous around-the-world coverage of events on radio and television, and a plethora of magazines. The media flood us with information, but they do not ensure that we have the capacity to handle it, make sense of it, and distinguish the reliable information from that which is misleading. For C. Wright Mills, the special promise of sociology as a discipline is its capacity to process information. He uses the term the **sociological imagination** to describe "a quality of mind that will help [people] to use information and to develop reason in order to achieve lucid summations of what is going on in the world and of what may be happening within themselves" (Mills 1959, 5).

The basic assumption of sociology is that an individual's life chances are understandable only within a historical situation, through comparisons with the life chances of others in similar situations. One's chances of getting a job, of getting rich, of dying from cancer, going to war, being a Catholic or a Protestant or an atheist, are socially situated. Sociology as a discipline tries to grasp the nature of this relationship between individual biography and social-historical forces within society. The way in which people tend to answer the question, "who are you?"—in terms of their sex, age, profession, **ethnicity**—situates them on a social map. Given information about a couple's occupations and income, one can predict a great deal about them: where they live, what kind of home and furnishings they have, what they read, what music they listen to, how they speak, how they vote, even whether they prefer sex with the light on or off (Berger 1963, 80–81).

According to Mills (1959, 6–7), the sociological endeavour entails three fundamental kinds of questions, which focus on the structure of society, the patterns of social change, and the characteristics of the people who constitute the society. The first category includes such questions as, What is the structure of this society? What are its major parts? How are these—education, church, polity, economy—interrelated ? How does Canada differ from other societies and why? All of us have immediate experience of how different elements of society affect each other. We know that the economy affects education, influencing decisions about whether to go to university or to take a job and about what course of studies to follow. Religion affects voting patterns, the numbers of children people have, the chance that one will commit suicide. Work life affects family life, dictating the standard of living and also the time available for parenting. As a total **social system**, Canada differs from other societies in multiple ways. Some of these are immediately tangible, like the dependence of our economy on what happens in the United States. Others, such as attitudes toward multiculturalism, social security, and federalism, are intangible. The elements of our society interact in different ways from those of the rest of the world. Exploring how these relationships work is a major concern of sociology.

The second type of question is, Where does our society stand in human history? How did Canada get to be this way and how is it changing now? How does any particular feature or episode of Canadian history fit into the present situation? To answer such questions, one needs to dig deep into Canada's past as a colony of France and Britain to explore the kinds of people who settled here, the values that they brought with them, their relations with the old countries and with their neighbours in the more recent past. It also entails trying to understand the forces for change in contemporary Canada: the impact of the baby boom, feminism, increasing numbers of elderly people, and so on. Sociology looks both backwards and forwards in an effort to understand contemporary society.

The third type of question is, What kinds of women and men make up our society? How are people selected and formed? How are they liberated and repressed? How are they made sensitive or blunted? What does the experience of years of unemployment do to young people who are out of work, and what does the constant fear of possible layoffs do to people who are working? The 1960s were known for hippies, flower power, and campus radicalism, but students of the 1980s seemed more conservative and conformist than their earlier counterparts. Why? People fear that the sensitivities of children are being blunted by violence on television or excited in negative ways by war toys or pornography. The **feminist movement** seems in some respects to be radically altering the lives of women and men but, on the other hand, there are signs that schoolgirls do not identify with the movement. Is this because feminism is only a passing fad, or because sensitivity to its message only comes with age? Sociology explains the multiple ways in which social experiences structure the characteristics of individual people.

The student of sociology has to be able to shift perspectives in imagination, to switch from looking at politics to looking at the family, the economy, or war, and to see their interconnections. It is not an easy discipline. The sociological imagination frequently makes the ordinary world look incredible. We commonly think of family relations, for example, as part of our uniquely private lives. It comes as a shock to see how deeply these intimate relations are shaped by wider social forces.

The basic message of sociology is that our society has not always been the way it is, nor is it inevitably this way, and it probably will not be so in the future. It can be different. For this reason alone, the critical eye of sociology can often provoke opposition from powerful groups in contemporary society who benefit from the status quo and who do not want change or want it only in a particular direction.

An important distinction drawn in sociology is between **personal troubles** and **public issues** (Mills 1959, 8–10). Troubles stem from private matters that lie within an individual's character and immediate relations with friends and family. Issues, by contrast, go beyond the personal, local setting, to broader social forces that affect the life experiences of many people. An important part of learning to do sociology is learning to generalize from personal experience to broader social forces that this experience reflects. Consider unemployment. When only a few individuals are unemployed in a large city, it can reasonably be viewed as a private trouble, reflecting the particular problems of the unemployed individuals, and it can perhaps best be dealt with using an individual casework approach. But when fifteen million people are unemployed out of a nation of fifty million, for example, unemployment is a public issue. It cannot be solved by helping individual cases. The structure of opportunities has collapsed.

Similarly, one or two homeless people living on park benches can perhaps be seen to reflect personal trouble. But when an estimated 32 000 to 50 000 such people live on the streets in Los Angeles (*Globe and Mail*, Nov. 21 1986), and there are thousands more in Canada, helping individuals will not solve the problem. Something in the structure of the economy, or of families, or of mental health services has broken down. It becomes a social issue requiring changes in relations between elements of society.

Mills argues that the sociological imagination, the capacity to understand the relationships between elements of society and their impact on individual life chances, has become the central feature of modern society. It dominates how people think, how histories are written, the kinds of art we view and literature we read. Science and

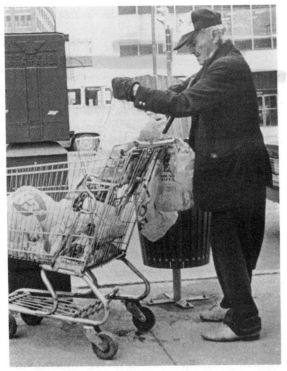

One homeless person may reflect private troubles.

technology remain powerful forces in society, but they are no longer central to how people think, because they have failed us in important ways. In many respects, technology has conquered nature. We know how to get to the moon and beyond, how to grow food artificially, how to transmit thousands of conversations simultaneously on optical fibres, yet we are in a worse mess than ever. Technology has not solved our problems, but has become, instead, part of what traps us. Contemporary literature and art express the uneasiness that people feel, but they cannot provide answers, except insofar as they may suggest new ways of seeing. It is the sociological imagination that seeks to explain social processes, the nature of our traps, and the underlying structural factors that give rise to them (Mills 1959, 14–15).

Sociological explanations are more difficult and more elusive than explanations in the physical sciences because society is not a tangible, fixed entity ready for **objective** experimental research. The very sociological

When thousands of people in Canada are homeless, or depend on food banks and soup kitchens to survive, this becomes a public issue.

knowledge we generate is likely to alter the sets of relationships we are trying to study. In another sense, however, sociology may be easier and more rewarding than the physical sciences in that we ourselves are part of it, creators of the societies in which we live, able to understand social processes subjectively as participants in their production.

Sociology and the Scientific Ideal

As a science, sociology is concerned fundamentally with the search for knowledge about society, but this search is both difficult and dangerous. It involves the study of people who, as members of a society, generate their own sense of truth about the social world. Socially generated ideas can be grouped into two categories. First, they take the form of **common-sense understandings**, or assumptions about how things work, and why, based upon immediate experience. Secondly, they involve more coherent **ideologies**, or systems of values that justify certain kinds of actions or ways of life, sometimes to the detriment of the interests of other people. These ideologies strongly influence the way we see social reality. They tend to sensitize us in certain ways and to blind us in others.

Sociological analysis must typically confront and challenge ideologies. A critical problem is that sociologists may be as blinded by ideologies as are other people, since they are themselves part of the society that they study, and they tend to accept the assumptions of people like themselves. Smith (1974a, 40) has conceptualized ideology, not as specific beliefs, but as a biased form of *method* of inquiry about society, a method that entails in its effects a systematic means *not* to know and *not* to see the situations of others. Given that sociologists are predominantly well-educated, reasonably well-paid professionals, and until recently were predominantly male, it should

come as no surprise that the values of such people tend to be represented in sociology to a greater extent than those of less privileged people. Poorly educated women living on welfare or people working in unskilled jobs, for example, do not tend to publish much in sociology journals. The scientific search for knowledge in sociology entails a major struggle to see past the taken-for-granted understandings and justifications of the professional middle-class world.

It is always easier to see through the ideologies of other groups than to see through one's own. The Nazi ideology of the superiority of the Aryan race has been discredited, but the ideology of **capitalism** and the work ethic are harder for most Canadians to see through. The ideology of "free market" and "free trade," for example, implicitly justifies price wars to crush small competitors; the ideology of profit justifies charging higher prices to poor people who often do not have access to alternative markets; it justifies laying off employees when the going gets tough and charging high interest rates on money that poor people have to borrow. The ideology that effort and ability lead to success justifies labelling the unemployed as lazy or stupid. The Christian ideology that "man" was made in the image of God and given dominion over the beasts justifies the exploitation by humans of everything on the planet, and so on. It is important to remember, however, that we are not merely blind victims of ideologies. We are also their creators and interpreters, and we can learn to analyse them, to challenge them, and to change them.

The major problem with common-sense interpretations of the world, and with most ideologies, is not that they are totally wrong, but that they can be biased and partial. Common-sense knowledge is inevitably self-centred. It tends to deal with very narrow individual concerns, not with the broader interests of other people in other situations. Common sense is incomplete, based on

limited personal experience with only a hazy idea of what other people's lives are like. Ideology, too, has its limitations and can lead to intolerance. We often have a great deal invested in our beliefs, and it can be difficult to question and to change them, especially when change can have disturbing consequences. If we abandon the ideology that effort and ability lead to success, for example, it changes our responsibilities to the poor and the disadvantaged. We begin to feel uncomfortable about our own wealth and about the system that allows such discrepancies to exist.

Science, as a search for knowledge, attempts to provide explanations based upon impartial evidence. Impartiality is particularly difficult in the social sciences because people who are the subjects of research react to findings in a conscious way, and the theories themselves affect their behaviour. Even the physical sciences do not escape this social imprint because human society itself reacts with and alters the physical world. Socially learned values and ways of thinking also profoundly influence how research questions come to be asked.

In sociology, the problem of **objectivity** lies, in part, in the fact that sociologists cannot be impartial to what they study. Our own preconceptions and biases are hard to break. For example, part of the problem for prostitutes is that sociologists define them as a problem. There are alternative ways of looking at the subject. Perhaps the "real" problem is the sexual frustration of the men who seek out prostitutes, or the fact that soliciting is illegal, which makes the prostitutes prey to protection rackets and pimps. Perhaps the problem is the double standard, which leads to the arrest and prosecution of prostitutes while their customers go free. Perhaps there is no problem at all. Perhaps prostitution should just be seen as a service industry like any other and be left to operate freely as in the red light district of Amsterdam.

Notwithstanding the values of researchers, a measure of objectivity is possible in social science. At root, it is not the values that matter so much as the research methods used to collect the evidence. There are many different techniques, some of which are discussed in chapter 3. None of them are foolproof in completely avoiding bias, but there are important principles of research that can reduce it.

The underlying philosophical assumption of all science is that it is relatively easy to find evidence to support an argument. Even stupid theses can usually be backed up by some examples. It is important, therefore, to test an argument by deliberately searching for information and evidence that, if found, would show the argument to be wrong. Consider, for example, a researcher who is interested in studying divorce because she strongly disapproves of it and feels that it harms children. Such a researcher could still provide impartial evidence by deliberately allowing for the reverse data, the possibility that dissolution of an unhappy marriage is a good thing for the children involved. A minimum requirement for such a study would be comparative data from four types of families: those where the parents describe themselves as happily married; those where the parents describe their marriage as unhappy but say that they intend to stay together for the children; divorced families that describe themselves as happier since the divorce; and divorced families that describe themselves as unhappier since the divorce. If data are gathered concerning children in all these sorts of families, the researcher allows for the possibility that children of divorced parents turn out to be happier and healthier than children living with parents in stressful, unhappy marriages. Useful research tests for the possibility that the researcher's starting assumptions might be wrong.

The critical element here is reasoned procedure, the disciplined, rigorous collection of evidence that deliberately tests for the opposite of the initial assumptions. Good research, of course, will attempt much more than this. Given that divorce, like marriage,

does not always bring the same results, it is important to explain the conditions under which different outcomes are likely. Again, the ideal is that explanations will be tested, rather than assumed and supported with only selective examples.

In all scientific practice, regardless of the particular theories and methodologies adopted, three general principles are involved. The first is the need for systematic and public accumulation of experience and observations. It involves a search for materials and the incorporation of a variety of people's experiences, not just those of one's own group. It is critical to be clear about how the evidence was collected so that others can do similar research to check or challenge the results.

A second important principle of research is comparative investigation, incorporating data on people in different situations or different societies. A comparative focus is critically important in avoiding ethnocentrism, the tendency to assume that one's own group's way of doing things is more natural and proper than that of others. A sociological study of families, for example, might look at how family life is managed in other countries, other ethnic groups, or at other times in history. Through such comparative evidence, the study might explore the effects that different patterns seem to have on family members.

The third principle, and for philosophers of science the most important, is systematic doubt. Whatever the evidence looks like, it could be false, or misleading, or biased, or badly collected. Key factors may have been overlooked. Assumptions on which the research was based may turn out to be wrong. One may spend decades researching the effects of divorce upon children, only to conclude in the end that divorce is not the key issue at all; it is the poverty that so often accompanies divorce.

It can be very difficult to discover the "real" factors underlying a phenomenon.

Some researchers spent three years studying the effects of illumination, rest pauses, and length of the working day on productivity of workers in a telephone assembly factory, only to conclude that these variables had next to nothing to do with productivity. The "real" factor was the attention that workers were getting from the researchers, which made them feel important and valued instead of just one of a mass on the shop floor (Mayo [1933] 1960). Sceptical researchers later disputed this result. They argued that the "real" factors influencing productivity were the onset of the economic depression of the 1930s and the desperate need of two of the five women in the experimental group for money to support **extended families** when other relatives were unemployed (Carey 1967).

Facts can be elusive things. The ideal approach is to scrutinize the evidence, to question the theories and assumptions of any research, and to ask how the research was carried out and whether alternative strategies or additional data might have made the picture look different. Science is essentially a style of rigorous, systematic, critical thought, not a collection of facts to be memorized.

In sociological endeavour, controversy is critical. Given the biases and blind spots of researchers, the goal of systematic testing for the opposite of one's beliefs is often not attained. Researchers are often more concerned with supporting their theories than with testing them. Scientific journals are reluctant to publish articles that seem to show that starting assumptions were proven incorrect, as if it somehow meant that there must be something wrong with the research. For a long time, the assumption of differences between women and men was so strongly accepted that research that failed to substantiate behavioural differences between the sexes was simply discarded. Nicholson (1984, 4) estimates that for every

published study showing differences between the sexes, six finding no difference remained unpublished. It is important that research that challenges established theories, whether those of the researcher or of larger groups, be conducted and be available to other researchers.

While it is essential that individual sociologists test their own data and theories, it is also important that the discipline encourage controversy among sociologists. When researchers disagree among themselves, it leads to a search for new evidence. New questions that might never have been thought of from one point of view can be brought forward by another researcher who started with different assumptions. Mutually incompatible assumptions provide the best challenge to each other. If your theory says that village life is happier and less isolating, and my theory is that city life is best and villages are stifling, our combined evidence is likely to be the best test of each other's assumptions. This is true of all science, not merely the social sciences. The philosopher Feyerabend (1970) has argued that, whenever strong consensus emerges among a body of scientists that they have found the truth, the likely result will be **dogmatism**. More and more research will be done supporting the same assumptions, and it will be increasingly difficult for anyone to come up with alternative theories. Evidence that might well show the errors in the dominant theory is likely never to come to light because no one will be looking for it. In effect, controversy or lack of agreement over theories in sociology is not a problem, but an asset. For Feyerabend, such controversy is a precondition for creative research.

Current sociology is in no danger of sinking into dogmatic consensus. As will be evident from the next chapter, there is no one theoretical approach that dominates sociological research, but rather a number of schools of thought that begin from very different assumptions and are often very critical of each other's work. To be valuable for science, however, controversy should be organized, not just shouted opinions. Organized controversy entails checking the assumptions of different perspectives and challenging them with alternative evidence. Clarity of basic assumptions is essential.

This textbook sets out to present the controversies of sociology in an organized way. The theories of classical sociologists are presented in detail. We explore their basic assumptions, the logic behind them, and the consequences or predictions to which they give rise. These consequences are then tested by looking at relevant evidence, drawn mostly from contemporary Canadian research. Controversy among different theorists is used to clarify the strengths and the limitations of different theoretical assumptions by comparing the research results from studies based on different perspectives.

As students, you are encouraged to react to, not to accept, the text. You should challenge arguments by examining their underlying assumptions, thinking up alternatives, and exploring counter-evidence. The goal is to develop a capacity to shift perspectives and to question assumptions in a systematic way. Howard Boughey (1978, ix), in the introduction to his delightful little book *The Insights of Sociology*, comments that the beginning scholar in the Sanskrit tradition must have the capacity to be aware of eight things simultaneously. This text attempts the lesser version of exploring four approaches to a problem. The basic philosophy of the text is that it is more important for you to develop the capacity for critical questioning than to amass facts.

Suggested Reading

The best introduction to the study of sociology is still C. Wright Mills' essay "The Promise," found in his book *The Sociological Imagination* (1959). This essay is now three decades old, but it still conveys the conviction that we must first understand society in order to change it. We need to know what our society is like and be aware of the processes that are shaping it. Mills speaks of the promise of sociology to empower people to bring their hopes for a better world closer to reality.

An excellent and concise introduction to sociology, which is inspired by Mills' essay, is Anthony Giddens, *Sociology: A Brief but Critical Introduction* (1982). Giddens begins with an introduction to the sociological imagination and then shows how questions are raised concerning competing interpretations of industrial society or capitalism, and issues of class, the state, the city, family and gender, and capitalism. This short, readable book is a very good place to start in gaining a feel for sociology as a critical discipline.

Another book that gives a succinct, readable introduction to the discipline of sociology is Peter Berger, *Invitation to Sociology: A Humanistic Perspective* (1963). Berger describes how people actively create their social world through interaction. He introduces many of the issues and approaches to sociology that we examine in this text.

Chapter 2

An Overview of Theories

The relationship between individuals and the society in which they are embedded has been conceptualized in diverse ways and has given rise to very different understandings of how social reality is maintained and reproduced over time. This chapter presents an overview of major contemporary approaches to sociology, their assumptions, and the differences and similarities among them. Their comparative strengths and limitations are examined through critical questions that sociologists, inspired by different approaches, have directed toward each other. Different perspectives start with different problems, ask different questions, see and ignore different things. It is important to try to see how they complement each other, to learn to challenge the contradictions, and thus to explore for the truth. However deep the differences between approaches, all share the same fundamental concern with developing our knowledge of the character of social life.

The Origins of Sociology

In one respect, sociology has always been done, since people have always questioned the nature of the social world. But as a separate scientific discipline, sociology emerged in the eighteenth century. Social upheavals that occurred during this era brought such profound transformations that most hitherto taken-for-granted assumptions about society and social relations were thrown into doubt. A democratic revolution occurred in America in 1776 as immigrants to the new world fought for independence from the colonial domination of Britain and then sought to found a society based on new principles of equality. In 1789 the old feudal structures of European society were shaken by the French Revolution. This revolution was especially significant because it represented the deliberate overthrow of a traditional social order. Landless peasants and industrial labourers revolted against the rule of the landed aristocracy and the clergy. Many thousands of people were guillotined before some semblance of a new order was established. These revolutions prompted a new view of society, a secular view. Social order was no longer seen as ordained by God and maintained by divine right of kings. It was structured by people and therefore could be changed by people.

The Rise of Capitalism

The eighteenth century also saw the advent of another form of revolution that was destined to change irrevocably the old order of things. This was the transformation from **feudalism** to **capitalism** in agriculture. These terms refer primarily to how production was organized and to the relationship between people and the land on which they depended for their livelihood.

Under the **feudal system**, which predominated in Europe until around the beginning of the eighteenth century, most people had some direct access to land, either as **lords** or as **serfs** and **peasants**. This relationship to land was established through hereditary right rather than through purchase. The nobility managed the vast estates and directed the work of the labourers. Generations of labourers were tied to the land that their ancestors had worked. They owed their labour to the lord of the estate but were entitled to fixed shares of the harvest to meet their own subsistence needs. In addition, they had plots of land on which to grow vegetables or to raise animals for their personal use. The lords had an obligation to maintain their serfs. Beyond this, the lords extracted what surplus they could, to sell in exchange for luxury items and a limited range of manufactured goods. The system was very inegalitarian, but it did ensure that the majority of people were able to produce most of what they needed to sustain themselves and their families, with relatively limited dependence on the purchase or sale of commodities in markets.

The capitalist revolution in agriculture fundamentally changed this pattern of production. Within a relatively short period of time, the majority of labouring people lost their hereditary right of access to land and, with it, their ability to produce for their own subsistence needs. They had to work for wages in order to purchase what they needed. Land came to be the private property of the lords.

How did this come about?

The impetus for change in Europe came from expanding markets, particularly for wool and meat and some specialized cereal crops. It became advantageous for feudal lords to shift the focus of production from mixed produce for local consumption to sheep for sale in the markets. Huge estates were divided into smaller, enclosed fields, suitable for sheep pastures. But with this change, the labour of serfs on the big estates became superfluous. It takes relatively few people to manage large flocks of sheep. The feudal obligation of the lord to support serfs became increasingly onerous, and so they began to break the serfs' hereditary right to live on the estates. This came about through a long and bitter struggle. Feudal lords, in effect, became private landowners. They forcibly drove the serfs from the land and further undermined their means of livelihood by restricting the serfs' rights to graze animals and to forage for timber on common lands. The few who remained on the estates became hired labourers, paid for their work with wages. Beyond payment of wages, the landowners had no obligations to provide for the subsistence needs of workers or their families. Those who were driven off found themselves reduced to landless labourers, able to survive only by selling their labour power for wages with which to buy food, clothing, and shelter.

Capitalism is the term used to describe this pattern where the means of production are privately owned, where production is for profit rather than immediate consumption, and where workers depend on wage labour and commodity markets for subsistence. Marx describes a particularly vicious example of **enclosure** in Scotland (Clegg and Dunkerly 1980, 48). The Duchess of Sutherland conspired to turn all the lands in Sutherland County into a sheep walk. Between 1814 and 1820, she systematically drove out the 15 000 members of the Gael clan who lived there, burning their villages and turning all the fields into pastures. British soldiers enforced this mass eviction. One old woman who refused to leave was burned to death in her hut. The Duchess appropriated 794 000 acres of land that had belonged to the clan. The land was divided into 29 huge sheep farms, each inhabited by a single family. The evicted people were given a total of only 6000 acres of barren land along the seashore, about two acres per family, and were forced to pay rent. They had to eke out a living on the rocky coastline by fishing. Even this livelihood was later taken away from them as London fishmongers smelled a profit in fishing. The Gaels were driven out again, and the seashore was rented to the London fishmongers. The people were thus forced into Glasgow and other manufacturing towns to take whatever work they could find as factory labourers. Others joined the waves of immigrants who came to Canada.

The Industrial Revolution

The transition from feudal to capitalist agriculture was critically important to the growth of industrialism because it gave rise to a plentiful pool of landless people who flocked to the towns in search of employment as wage earners. These people provided the labour force needed in the expanding manufacturing towns. The **Industrial Revolution** first occurred roughly between 1780 and 1840 in England and rapidly spread throughout Europe, North America, and parts of the colonized world. People who had become wealthy as merchants, land-owners, or adventurers began to invest in manufacturing industries. They purchased machines and factories and hired wage labourers to produce products for sale in the marketplace. This process was essentially capitalist in nature: it was geared to production for profit rather than for personal subsistence, and it presupposed a fundamental division of people into those who owned the machines and factories and those who had to work for wages in order to survive.

The other prerequisite for the Industrial Revolution was the expansion of the physical sciences. During the eighteenth century, intellectuals in search of the truth increasingly turned, not back to ancient scriptures or to the authority of elders, but to science, testing theories about the physical world against observations by using experimental methods. In essence, scientific method seeks to establish arguments on the basis of factual knowledge that can be verified by others and that is potentially refutable by contradictory observations. In the late eighteenth century, this scientific approach began to be applied systematically to society. This application was not easy, but the first important step had been taken with the assumptions that the scientific study of society and people was possible and that science rather than theology held the key to understanding.

Early theories of society were inspired by the idea of progress. If society was created by people, it was therefore changeable and could be made better. In principle it was perfectible yet, at the same time, industrialization and political revolt spread disruption, misery, and terror. Revolution was both destructive and creative, both feared and welcomed. People trying to come to terms with the social upheaval were forced to grapple with basic questions concerning the nature of humankind.

Thomas Hobbes (1588–1679).

Thinkers who feared the revolutions tended to focus on the uglier aspects of unrestrained human nature and to stress the **conservative** values of maintaining law and order. They drew upon the classical work of the British philosopher Thomas Hobbes (1588–1679) in his famous treatise *Leviathan*. Hobbes focussed on the fundamental question of the basis of order in society. He reasoned that order is possible only because society constrains nature. Life in the state of nature, Hobbes surmised, might well be nasty, brutish, ugly, and short, degenerating into a relatively permanent state of aggression among people. Life as we experience it is not generally like this because **social structures** impose order. In their own self-interest and in return for social protection from others, people come to accept constraints upon their own selfishness and aggression. Society therefore becomes crucial for individual happiness, crucial for life itself. Society regulates relations and disciplines individuals and so makes people "social."

Conservatives saw the violent excesses that characterized the French Revolution as an expression of life in the state of nature. People had suddenly been freed from the traditional controls of church and nobility, and the result was chaos and violence. Conservatives argued that the restoration of order in social life required a renewed emphasis on morality, discipline, and obedience. The primary mechanism had to be teaching children to want to be obedient through a system of programmed learning. Society was possible only when people internalized social discipline from a very young age.

Jean Jacques Rousseau (1712–78).

But there was another view of the French Revolution and of industrialization, one that saw them as liberating forces that would shatter an oppressive feudal order. Advocates of such a view drew their inspiration from the writings of the French philosopher Jean Jacques Rousseau (1712–78). Rousseau had a more benign view of the state of nature than did Hobbes. He surmised that people were naturally peace loving and were inclined to go about their own business and not bother others provided they were left alone. In Rousseau's philosophy, the complicating question was to explain the evidence of conflict and aggression between people. Rousseau argued that this did not arise automatically, from the state of nature. It arose because people were aggravated by inegalitarian and repressive social relations. Social harmony could best be sustained, not by subjugating children to programmed learning and discipline, but by giving them freedom to develop their natural talents and inclinations with a minimum of frustrating restrictions.

Radical thinkers adapted Rousseau's philosophy as a basis for a favourable interpretation of the French Revolution. Revolutionaries were no longer seen as rabble who needed the discipline of the feudal order, but as oppressed serfs rising up against the nobility who had exploited them and driven them into destitution as landless labourers. From this perspective, the restoration of peace depended upon establishing a new order based on principles of liberty, equality, and fraternity.

The philosophical assumptions concerning human nature and society expressed by Hobbes and Rousseau are still reflected in contemporary sociological theories. Emphasis upon one view rather than the other influences the kinds of questions that sociologists ask, what they tend to focus on, and what they ignore. The Hobbesian view promotes concern with the maintenance of order within society, while those who espouse Rousseau's view are concerned with social conflict and revolt.

Controversies in Sociological Thought

As we saw in chapter 1, current sociology is in no danger of sinking into dogmatic consensus. There are strikingly different schools of thought that begin from very different assumptions and generate very different kinds of research. This chapter's overview of approaches to sociology begins with a consideration of the notion of **historical sociology**. This type of sociology offers a way of understanding how human actions generate social structures over time. While this is among the most recent of theoretical perspectives, it will be discussed first because it helps to pull together the other approaches and shows how they are interrelated as aspects of the same complex process, however different they might seem from each other at first reading. Next we examine the classical theoretical approaches of **structural functionalism**, or **systems theory**, which focusses primarily upon the problem of order. The third approach we examine is **conflict theory**, or **political economy**, which challenges the notion of equilibrium and order in society. The next broad perspective, which is loosely called **interpretive sociology**, encompasses various approaches that focus less on the system and structures of society than on how individuals create their social reality in ongoing interaction. The last perspective, **feminist theory**, offers a radical critique of the male-centred biases built into virtually all existing approaches to mainstream or "male-stream" sociology.

Sociology as History

The historical origins of sociology as a discipline have much more than passing relevance to contemporary sociological theory. For Abrams (1982, 2), sociological explanation itself is necessarily historical in character. We cannot address serious questions about the contemporary world without historical responses (Abrams 1982, 1). By historical sociology, Abrams does not mean imposing grand schemes of evolutionary development on the relationship of past to present. What is involved, he argues, is the attempt to understand the relationship between individual personal activity and experience on the one hand, and social organization on the other, as something that is continuously constructed in time (Abrams 1982, 16).

A perennial problem in sociology is reconciling two seemingly contradictory views of people. Proponents of one perspective see people as agents who purposely choose between different courses of action and so consciously create their social world. Advocates of the other approach see people as part of a **social system**, an existing set of structures that constrains and in many ways determines their actions. We have a sociology of *action* and a sociology of *systems* and tend to shuffle uneasily between the two. Some theorists stress free human actions and choice, while others stress how the structures of society determine people's lives. When these alternative views are pushed to their extremes, they appear to be so different that it is hard to see how they could be reconciled or even how they could be part of the same discipline of sociology. Even words like *society*, *social structure*, and *social system* are used in such different ways that definitions favoured in one approach are hotly disputed in the other.

The goal of theorists such as Abrams and Giddens is to bridge these two extremes by reconceptualizing the relationship between human agency and deterministic social systems. They do so by focussing on time. Abrams (1982) refers to the concept of "processes in time" while Giddens (1979) refers to the "*dureé* [continuance] of human agency." They both argue that human actions produce the **structures** of society that people later experience as constraining or determining their actions, and that theorists later identify as "entities" like "the capitalist system." Abrams and Giddens accept the classical Marxist notion that we make our own history, but not in circumstances of our own choosing. They emphasize the critical point that these circumstances were produced by other people, or perhaps even by ourselves, through choices made at earlier points in time. When social theorists focus on a particular, fixed period of time, it seems to make sense to analyse how human actions are constrained by social structures. But, given a longer time frame, we see that these structures were themselves produced by human actions. The dilemma of whether to conceptualize human actions as free or as determined is thus resolved by recognizing that, within historical time, human actions are shaped by prior human actions. In the same way, what we choose to do now will shape the circumstances that our children inherit.

Seen from this perspective, the analysis of social structures as the embodiment of past human actions necessarily entails a historical analysis of human agency. Both Abrams and Giddens criticize much contemporary sociological theory for failing to see the relevance of time and, hence, for failing to understand the mutual dependence of structure and action. Theorists tend to discuss these as if they were very different kinds of phenomena. On the one hand, some theories focus on structures, which have concreteness and act as constraints on people. History is reduced to grand evolutionary schemes or laws, which seem to have occurred by themselves and to which people must adapt. On the other hand, there are theories that focus on people taking action, as if social constraints could be ignored. However, when the notions of time and the *dureé* of human agency are introduced, the artificial distinction between structures and actions disappears. Structures comprise actions taken collectively in the past. Actions produce structures for the future.

Consider the example of the transition from the feudal system of production to the capitalist system. People did not wake up one day, notice that the era of capitalism had begun, and so decide they had better start looking for wagework or wool merchants. Rather, people in a position to decide how to dispose of large areas of land started keeping more sheep to take advantage of new opportunities to sell wool for money. Labourers began to find that they had more free time on their hands; landlords began to speculate that they might be further ahead to feed fewer peasants, and so on. The very long-term outcome of such actions over time produced the pattern of production that theorists subsequently refer to as the rise of capitalism.

This focus on human agency over time as the core of sociological explanation holds for all levels of analysis. It applies both to momentous historical changes such as the rise of capitalism or industrialization and to **microhistory** involving the study of interactions at the level of factories, schools, families, and friendships. Abrams argues that any relationship that persists in time has a history. Individual actions are moments in a sequence of actions, never isolated events. Communities in which people find themselves at any one time do not simply exist. They are continually being constructed and coped with. Modern families are microcommunities that people are born into, grow up in, and transform in the process of living out their personal relationships. Conversations are likewise microhistorical processes in which what one person says only makes sense in terms of what someone else previously said.

This vision of sociology as the study of human agency in time is emerging particularly as a challenge to the traditional sociological perspective of structural functionalism or systems theory, which tends to be both static and **deterministic**, and the alternative Marxist approach, which incorporates historical change but often in a deterministic form. These two major perspectives in sociology are outlined next.

The Problem of Order: Systems Theory and Structural-Functionalist Analysis

Classical structural-functionalist analysis in sociology is modelled on biology. A society is viewed as a **system** of interrelated parts analogous to a biological organism. A society, like an animal, can be studied as an operating system at one point in time, without concern for evolution, origins of parts, or even developmental processes. People in a social system are analogous to cells in a biological system. It is possible to study a single cell operating in a localized environment in a body. Likewise one can study single people or types of people operating in localized social roles.

Of particular interest in biology is how groups of cells develop specialized structures that perform specific **functions** for the biological system as a whole. The cells in the retina of an eyeball, for example, have a highly specialized structure that makes them particularly sensitive to light. Their function is to transmit impulses of light to the brain. Other cells located within the kidneys have a very different structure, adapted to the specialized function of removing waste matter from the blood, and so on. A biological organism as a whole can be conceptualized as made up of a series of specialized structures with distinct functions that maintain the whole body. Groups of specialized cells can be studied as collectivities or organs, like the eye, the heart, the kidney. Collections of specialized organs can also be analysed in terms of integrated functions or subsystems of a body. Biologists study the respiratory system, the circulatory system, the reproductive system, and so on. There are also other less familiar systems, like hormones and enzymes, that function to regulate and harmonize these different subsystems and parts. The same part of an organism often performs multiple functions and so can be studied as part of different functioning subsystems.

Classical sociology studies parts of society in a way analogous to biological analysis. Hence the terms **systems theory** or **structural functionalism**. People, like cells, are specialized to play distinctive **roles** in the social system. Roles and sets of roles can be analysed in terms of how they perform their functions. Organized collections of interacting roles can be studied as organs or **institutions** of society: a university, a school, a family, a church. These organized relations can also be analysed more abstractly in terms of integrated functions or subsystems of society: the educational system, the child-care system, the economic system, the administrative system, the political system, and so on. Particular institutions may have multiple functions in different subsystems. Schools are part of the child-care system, the education system, and the economic system. The same is true of families.

The terminology here is somewhat imprecise. Some theorists talk about *institutions* while others talk about *structures*. Some may use the term *structure* in a broad sense to refer to *functioning subsystems*. Most theorists refer simply to *systems* rather than *subsystems*, unless they are talking in very general terms about an entire society, as we are here. So long as you keep in mind the biological analogy of organs working together in functioning subsystems of the body, like the parts of a reproductive system, the ideas should not be too confusing.

A central concern of biology is how the multiple parts of a body are made to function together so as to maintain the whole body in a state of normal healthy balance or **equilibrium**. Deviations from this are seen as illness in need of special explanation and corrective action. Systems theory in sociology has the same overriding concern with how various parts of society are regulated so as to ensure a stable state of order in the society as a whole. Hence, systems theory is also referred to as **order theory**.

This approach to sociology as analogous to biology has a long history. It is particularly associated with Comte and Spencer and, to a lesser extent, with Durkheim. Its development in contemporary theory is identified with Talcott Parsons. The distinctive contributions of these theorists are explored in later chapters, particularly chapter 6 on cohesion and morality and chapter 10 on Parsonian **functionalism**. Here we will give only brief summaries of their basic ideas and an overview of systems theory.

Auguste Comte (1798–1857) lived and worked in Paris just after the French Revolution. He shared with Hobbes a concern with the need for order and structure. He is widely regarded as the father of sociology. He first coined the term *sociology* and tried to establish it as an independent science of social systems. He viewed sociology as the last great science developed after biology. Comte originated a model of the evolution of societies in which he argued that a society passes through theological, military, and industrial stages much as biological organisms passed through evolutionary stages from fish and reptiles to birds and mammals.

Herbert Spencer (1820–1903), writing in the very different context of capitalist expansion following the American Civil War, carried Comte's early ideas on the evolution of social systems much further. He analysed the development of industrial society in terms of evolutionary processes of adaptive selection and the **survival of the fittest**. Because business people liked to think of themselves as the best adapted members of the human species, dominating the social world because they were the fittest to do so, Spencer's ideas made him extremely popular with the emerging business class.

Emile Durkheim (1858–1917) shared this fascination with the scientific study of the evolution of industrial society and its special characteristics as a system. He was especially concerned with understanding the moral basis of order in industrial society. He viewed morality as the essential mechanism that maintained the equilibrium of a social system. His work has had a much more profound impact on contemporary sociology than either Comte or Spencer.

Within systems theory, however, it is undoubtedly Talcott Parsons who ranks as the central figure, sometimes described as the high priest of American sociology. Born in 1902, Parsons spent most of his career at Harvard University. He systematized the work of many early sociologists in his *Essays in Sociological Theory* (1948) and *The Structure of Social Action* ([1937] 1968) and then went on to develop his own abstract model of society as a functioning system.

Basic Assumptions of Systems Theory

Central concerns for systems theory include how large numbers of individuals can be organized to function in ways analogous to cells in a biological system, and how this organization can be smoothly perpetuated from one generation to another so that order is maintained. The twin concepts of **roles** and **socialization** provide the key. Social order is maintained primarily because people internalize appropriate behaviour patterns and the desire to conform to them.

The model of society presented by systems theory begins with the conception of an individual person as an **actor** or role-player within a system of roles. The actor's position or **status** is set by the social context. The important feature of social roles in systems theory is that they exist independently of any single actor. They are predefined, and new generations of role-incumbents are trained to fit them. This does not mean that all people play the same role in exactly the same way, but rather that the role itself has typical aspects that are common to all incumbents, regardless of individual idiosyncrasies. It is this typicality that makes social order possible and ensures continuity from one generation to another.

Roles vary in the degree of detail with which they are laid down. Bureaucratic work roles are generally defined in the highest detail and require exact conformity. A job description, for example, sets out what the incumbent must do. If he or she does it willingly, all is well, but if not, then rules are invoked to force compliance. The role of motherhood is much vaguer, but there are still set minimums. A mother must clean, feed, and clothe her children and get them to school every day. If not, social workers will intervene to force closer compliance with society's minimum expectations. The role of professor includes expectations that the incumbent will arrive on time, come prepared, lecture for set periods of time, and not be drunk. Students are expected to attend classes, not to talk privately during the lecture, or at least not loud enough for others to hear them, and so on. The **norms** or standards associated with being a student are much more flexible than those required of a professor. Role interactions between professors and students are also defined very differently from those among students themselves. Sexual advances between professor and student, for example, are proscribed, while flirting among students is permitted and even expected.

Sets of roles constitute the sum of the roles with which one actor interacts. For example, a school teacher, in the performance of the teacher role, interacts with students, the school principal, other teachers, the school board, and parents. All have expectations of the teacher role, and one can locate the job in the centre of these overlapping expectations. The sum of all the patterned role interactions constitutes the **social system**. At the other extreme, the **personality system** comprises the system that integrates the different roles that one persons plays, both simultaneously and throughout life. Research into this system is the proper domain of psychology.

Society must motivate people to play their alloted roles and to meet the typical expectations for minimal role performance. Berger (1963, 68–78) refers to "**circles of social control**" to describe the mechanisms by which such conformity is produced. The innermost circle, and probably the most powerful, is guilt. We come to want to conform, to see conformity as morally proper, and nonconformity makes us feel guilty. For most of our social roles, most of our lives, this internalized sense of guilt may be all that is necessary to ensure conformity. Closely supporting these innermost feelings are our relations with family and friends, our primary group. Because our relationships with these people matter to us, we usually want to conform to their expectations. We feel unhappy if we disappoint them by not playing our roles in relation to them in ways that they have come to expect. Only when these intimate pressures fail, or in more impersonal aspects of our lives where friendship ties are not involved, do more formal societal sanctions come into play. These may be economic sanctions, in that we may risk losing our jobs or not being hired if we do not conform at least minimally to the expectations that employers have of us. Students who do not do assignments or perform in class as expected will not pass the course and will face sanctions of not being eligible for promotion or for jobs that require such courses. In such cases we conform out of economic self-interest, meeting role demands so that other needs of our own are met. As a last resort, formal sanctions and laws punish those who refuse to conform minimally to the expectations of others as to how roles must be played.

The process by which people in society learn new roles is called **socialization**. As children, we learn primarily by watching and emulating our parents. Later we learn by watching and playing teacher and the many other roles that we encounter. Because we want others to approve of us, we come to want to behave in ways that earn their approval. Reciprocally, we tend to give approval to others who behave in their roles as we expect them to. This learning and **internalization** process is most intense during childhood, when almost all roles are new, but it continues throughout life. As adults, we learn our job roles both by formal training and by on-the-job learning through watching

Figure 2-1 Circles of Social Control

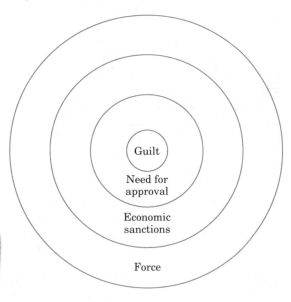

Source: Adapted from Berger (1969).

and emulating others. Even in old age we learn to retire, sometimes taking courses on retirement in which we are trained in what to expect and how to cope. In the final analysis, what we are as people is constituted by the sum of all the social roles we play.

Certain roles are more important in defining our identity than others. Traditionally, men have been defined by their work roles, and women by their wife-mother roles. We all play many other roles simultaneously, but they are tailored to fit these dominant roles.

Through internalization, we become the role, and it becomes part of us, part of our identity. Playing a role becomes not merely a set of learned behaviours or doing what is expected of us. It becomes a duty. If we fail in our performance, we fail to meet not only the expectations of others but our expectations of ourselves. It upsets our sense of our own identity if we fail in major roles. Approval of others whose roles overlap with our own is a central element in our sense of self. It is very upsetting if others convey the impression that they see us as failures in the roles we play. Such feelings are important in social control. We conform because we want to, because we attain a sense of self-identity and belonging by identifying with and performing the roles that we play throughout life.

People develop a sense of duty toward work roles, to their job as teacher, secretary, soldier, police officer, manager, and so on. Being a good doctor, a good mechanic, or a good student becomes central to our sense of ourselves. Our body image, our **presentation of ourselves**, is intimately tied to the jobs we do. It is frequently possible to tell what work people do just by looking at them. There are student types and business types. Students may turn up for a first-year law school class wearing jeans and sweaters and carrying book bags, but they come out after three years wearing tailored suits and carrying leather briefcases. Teachers tend to look like teachers and to talk like teachers even when they are not on the job.

The centrality of jobs to self-identity is especially apparent when we change work roles. People who change their jobs tend to change their personalities as well to better conform to new role demands. This process is what underlines the common practice of co-optation of troublesome subordinates or outsiders into insider roles. In business this may take the form of promoting a good union person or good worker leader into the role of supervisor. It takes a very strong commitment indeed to resist identifying with the new role and eventually coming to act as management over workers who were once one's colleagues. Those who cannot fully identify with the supervisory role are likely to quit or to be fired quickly and returned to the ranks.

The changed expectations of others are central to new role socialization. Lieberman (1956) gives the example of a private who is newly promoted to the rank of officer. At first he is likely to feel sheepish and embarrassed before his old peers and not want them to treat him any differently. But every response of the other privates, their changed reactions to him, their salutes, their obedience, their deference to his orders, all reinforce his new status. New clothing, new terms of address, new expectations of others, all work toward the individual coming to see himself as an officer. It will not be long before he not only comes to expect a salute from former friends, but to become angry and resentful if such deference is not shown.

Stages in life that entail major changes in role sets are often marked by public ceremonies. Marriage ceremonies, baby showers, graduation days, ceremonial investitures into higher ranks, all mark role transfers and serve as rites of passage into new lifestyles. New clothes frequently serve as symbolic external indications of role

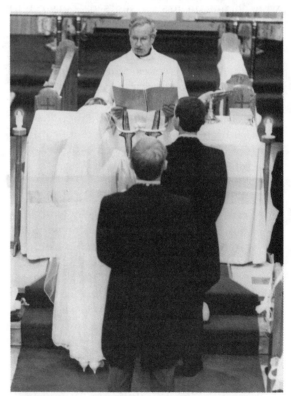

Events such as wedding ceremonies serve as rites of passage into new lifestyles.

changes, signalling to the rest of society that one must now be treated in a new way, subject to new expectations. As they get older, girls begin to wear make-up, high-heeled shoes, and nylon stockings to signal that they are young women who should be treated as such by young men. Boys sport mustaches and perhaps their first tailored suit. Employees in positions of authority over the public typically wear uniforms to signal to others exactly what role they are authorized to perform.

Over a lifetime, a person performs a series of roles that mark the passage of time. You may begin life within your family as a baby, but very quickly you become younger sibling, older sibling, child-minder, daughter or son, spouse, parent, breadwinner, grandparent, retiree. We play multiple roles that overlap, such as career and family roles. The sum of all these roles together constitutes the social self. Research in the **role-theory** tradition studies individual role sets, the expectations associated with roles, systems of roles as they interrelate, and the socialization processes by which roles are learned and internalized throughout life. Another area that is studied by role theorists is **role strain**. Role strain can occur when different actors in a system of roles have conflicting expectations of what a particular role entails or when an individual experiences conflict within personal roles, such as between career and parental roles.

Culture and Role Integration

Each social role is recognizable as a set of unique behavioural expectations or norms, but there are also broader patterns of expectations that many roles have in common. The overarching **values** of a society or collectivity of people constitute a **culture**, the set of shared ideas about what comprises ideal behaviour within a given society. People may not always live up to these ideals, but they generally know what they are and tend to use them to evaluate their own behaviour and the behaviour of others. Through internalizing the generalized culture of a community, actors are already oriented toward appropriate patterns of behaviour even before learning details of specific roles.

A culture serves to integrate roles within a society and to minimize friction between them. When roles have very different values, such as work roles requiring aggressive, competitive behaviour, and family roles requiring supportive and co-operative behaviour, they are typically separated both in time and space. People perform work roles at one time of day in one context and family roles at another time and in another place. Alternatively, mothers with young children at home may give up paid work altogether to devote themselves full-time to nurturing roles while fathers devote the major part of their days to earning money.

A culture typically includes ideals concerning appropriate masculine and feminine behaviour, ideals that tend to circumscribe behaviour from early childhood through to old age. Such ideals can become an influential part of our self-concepts. We deviate from these generalized values only with difficulty and with considerable insecurity and fear of disapproval and/or sanctions from friends and elders.

Consider a few examples. Try to imagine how people might react if your father were to go to work wearing a dress. Males who want to become ballet dancers or nurses, or who would like to be full-time homemakers, tend to face considerable ridicule from other males and indeed from females as well. Young boys who like to play with dolls may be ridiculed so harshly by other children that they at least publicly abandon dolls for more "masculine" toys. In North America, girls can often get away with adopting dress codes and behaviour typical of males. But there are still many subtle pressures to conform. Girls who do not follow accepted rules for dress and make-up may be shunned and taunted as lesbians. Women who do not want to become mothers often face strong criticism from relatives.

Subgroups within a society tend to develop distinctive subsets of values or **subcultures**, typically related to the dominant roles that they play. Durkheim argued that occupational specialization necessarily produces cultural diversity, even without major differences in ethnic background. As societies become more complex and differentiated in terms of occupational roles, so subcultural differences become more common. Members of such occupational subcultures share **dominant values** with the rest of society but differ on important subsets of values.

Jazz musicians, for example, develop a jazz-linked subculture of values. Within this subculture, musicians value spontaneity, reject the 9-to-5 work ethic, wear unconventional clothes, have an intense commitment to playing music, and sometimes take illicit drugs (Becker 1963, 85–100). Such values set the musicians apart from the rest of society and help to confirm their identity as a distinct subgroup. Outsiders tend to expect them to behave differently from the average person. These expectations help to reinforce distinctive behaviour.

It can take a long time to learn the elements of a subculture. First-year students who live in residence, for example, may spend more time learning the student subculture than learning coursework.

A particular form of subculture is that associated with **ethnic minorities**. Typically, such subcultures share a dominant set of values with the wider society and share norms concerning public work roles. But they have distinctive subcultural values in terms of the family and religion, and perhaps in dress and food habits. The degree

Subcultures associated with ethnic minorities often have distinctive religious, familial, dress, or food habits.

of subcultural differences may vary from minor aspects of private life to broad patterns of private and public behaviour that serve to set one group of people apart from the majority. The term **assimilation** denotes the process of change as individuals or groups of people lose their distinctive minority group patterns of behaviour and adopt the norms and values of the majority. Learning a new language or a new jargon is a major step in this transition, which might also include changes in dress, family relations, and so on.

Individual roles constitute the lowest or most personal level of the social order. At a higher level, sets of rules combine into **institutions**, or established patterns of action organized around a central function. Institutions in a sociological sense constitute typical ways of structuring social relations. The institution of the family, for example, constitutes the typical role relations between relatives. In some instances, family boundaries may take in "adopted" aunts and uncles who are treated as kin. The institution of a university comprises a set of roles including those of professors, students, secretaries, administrators, cooks, and caretakers. It is embedded in a broader set of roles that constitutes the education system.

Sets of institutions and the normatively regulated relations between them constitutes the social system as a whole. Each member institution has a distinct set of social functions and together they fulfil the overall system requirements. The institution of the family produces and nurtures young people and socializes them into adult roles. Economic institutions produce and distribute goods and integrate occupational roles. Political institutions set common beliefs in the legitimacy of power structures and organize collective goals. Religious institutions reinforce moral values, which integrate roles. The education system builds on the specialized role of family by socializing young people, teaching adult role

skills, and reinforcing collective values. Administrative and legal systems serve to integrate institutions and to discourage non-compliance with collective values.

Institutions change primarily by becoming more specialized and differentiated from each other. In simple societies, the family may perform almost all social functions but, in complex industrial societies, families specialize in nurturing roles while most other functions are performed by specialized institutions outside the family.

The functions of some institutionalized patterns may not always be immediately obvious (Merton 1967, 73–138). Largely unrecognized or **latent functions** may occasionally be more important than the more obvious or **manifest functions**. Veblen (1928, 25), for example, has pointed out that the manifest functions of buying Cadillacs, caviar, and rare art works are mobility, satisfaction of hunger, and ornamentation. But the latent reason why certain people buy such goods is **conspicuous consumption**: not direct gratification, but a desire to demonstrate their wealth to others and so enhance their social status. The manifest function of funerals is to bury the dead, but their more important latent function is to bring family members together to reinforce the identity and solidarity of the family in the face of loss that might otherwise tear it apart. The manifest function of magic rituals is to appease the gods, but their latent function may be to relieve anxiety (Merton 1967, 88).

In summary, the systems approach to sociology sees society in a form analogous to an organism, comprising interrelated parts that perform specialized functions for the whole. These parts, or institutions, in turn are made up of interrelated sets of roles, or pre-established patterned expectations for behaviour, that are learned through socialization. Social order requires that most actors within the society be motivated to fulfil their roles adequately and that they share a culture that defines the minimum expectations for proper behaviour. The reactions of others, of approval or disapproval, and an internalized sense of guilt, serve to keep most people conforming most of the time. Harsher control mechanisms of force and coercion are used only as a last resort. Social systems are normally in a state of **dynamic equilibrium**; that is, a state of orderly self-regulation and replication in relatively stable form over generations.

The systems perspective is the dominant approach to sociology in North America. The major kinds of research done in this tradition tend to centre around the study of specialized institutions such as family, education, religion, ethnic relations and so on. Research is strongly empirical and is particularly associated with a survey approach and with the analysis of cultural norms and values as they influence social behaviour. The research also tends to emphasize **positivism**, a scientific approach that bases conclusions upon evidence that is taken to be **objective**, factual, and subject to statistical testing.

The Problem of Conflict: Conflict Theory and Political Economy

The dominant approach in European sociology begins from very different assumptions than systems theory. It is strongly identified with the work of Karl Marx (1818–83). Although born in Germany, Marx did most of his writing in England. His first-hand observation of the suffering of working-class people in nineteenth-century London inspired him to write *Capital*, his famous critical analysis of capitalism. Marx characterized capitalism as an inherently exploitative economic system that divides people into antagonistic social classes. The umbrella labels of **conflict theory** or **political economy** now include a diversity of theorists who share the basic assumption that the analysis

of class division is fundamental to the understanding of social order.

For the most part, conflict theorists accept the systems theory model of society as a system of interrelated parts, but they conceive of these parts as held together in a very different way from **normative consensus** or shared expectations governing the performance of predefined roles. The crucial explanatory variable becomes, not internalized values and norms, but organized relations of power, which determine access to and control over the important resources of a society. This focus leads to the study of asymmetrical relationships and **hierarchies** of power and dependency. People who control essential resources exploit those who lack such resources. Inequality, injustice, and the resulting conflict, competition, aggression, and war, are as much features of society as is peaceful co-operation. To the extent that there are shared values and expectations in an unequal society, **consensus** is likely to be manipulated rather than freely adopted. Values are seen more as the effect of people's class location in society than as the cause of behaviour. For example, business people tend to have very different values and to vote in different ways from working-class people because any given policy option or social change will affect them in distinct ways.

Like systems theorists, conflict theorists see interrelated sets of roles at the level of interpersonal relations. But conflict theorists draw attention to the inequality in prestige and social and financial rewards that accrues to different roles. They also point to the frequently forced character of role incumbency. For example, factory workers often find themselves trapped in dull, routine work that offers little intrinsic interest and few other rewards. Worse still, they may find themselves trapped in unemployment, their energies and skills not wanted by local employers. Young women in small mining towns, where there are few jobs for women, are forced into marriage and the role of dependent wife because nothing else is available. Internalization of the values and expectations of roles seems at best inadequate to explain the behaviour of such people. At worst, such an explanation constitutes a cruel distortion of these people's situations in life. It functions as an ideology that covers up what is really happening to people. The fact that people have few if any viable options in life can be masked by the argument that they do what they do because they have internalized the appropriate values.

The concept of **alienation** is central to conflict theory. People experience alienation when they feel powerless to control central aspects of their lives, such as how to make a living; when they are forced into work that is demeaning or is meaningless to them; when what they produce is owned or controlled by someone else; and when they are exploited by being paid less for their labour than the true value of what they produce. At the individual level, this alienation is experienced as a sense of entrapment. The central question in conflict theory concerns how such inequalities of power and alienation arise and are perpetuated.

Unequal power relations are evident even in intimate interpersonal relations. A wife who is economically dependent upon her husband may find herself constantly deferring to his wishes over her own. Girls may defer to the wishes of their boyfriends because the boys have more money to pay for a night out. In our society, young people remain under the authority of their parents until well beyond puberty because our economy is not set up in a way that allows adolescents to provide for themselves.

It is not just money, however, that can provide the basis for unequal power relations. Blau (1967, 76–84) describes the effects of asymmetry in a love relation where the less interested or less committed lover has the advantage. The partner who most wants the relationship must compensate by greater willingness to defer to the other's wishes. In theory, the exchange is balanced because greater dependence is compensated for by greater deference. This is but one example of unequal exchange relations. In any exchange, it A needs resources that B controls, A can either reciprocate with other resources wanted by B, use force to compel B to give the resources needed, do without, or act in a subordinate manner to B, complying with B's wishes in return for the needed resources. The ideal of reciprocal exchange of equally valued resources, creating genuine social equality, is rarely attained.

Like systems theory, the conflict theory perspective notes the existence of subcultural values, but it tends to analyse them differently. Poor people may well have different subcultural values from wealthy people in the same society, but such values may reflect more a rational *response* to the situation, and an effort to cope psychologically with limited opportunities, than a voluntary choice of different lifestyles inspired by distinct values.

Conflict theory acknowledges a functional interrelation among the institutions that make up the social system but with the important qualification that such functions are not necessarily equally beneficial to all sectors of society. The critical question that conflict theorists raise is, functional for whom? The answer, invariably, is that existing institutions are more beneficial for powerful groups or classes of people than they are for the powerless.

For example, unemployment is functional for depressing wage demands and thus for increasing profits and competitiveness on international markets, but it is painfully **dysfunctional** for unemployed people and for their families. Unemployment is psychologically damaging and deprives people of sufficient money to exchange for the goods and services that they need. Similarly, pornography may be functional for providing profits to those who manufacture or sell it, and for the release of sexual tension of frustrated males, and for controlling women, but it is dysfunctional for women who feel victimized by it. At the level of the whole society, systems theory sees the legal system as functional for upholding shared values and expectations for appropriate behaviour and thus ensuring order in the society as a whole. But, when society is viewed as inherently inegalitarian, this same system of laws can be analysed for its function of protecting the property of the haves from the have-nots. Quinney (1975) argues that laws serve the primary function of defending the interests of the ruling class, usually the owners of property, discouraging the behaviour of those who act against its interests. In Canada, laws to protect property, for example, are more prolific and are enforced to a far greater degree than are laws to protect the environment or workers' health.

For conflict theory, the question of how order is maintained, or why the disprivileged classes do not rebel against the social order, becomes problematic. There appears to be so much injustice and exploitation in society that it is hard to believe that people conform simply because they have internalized the appropriate values. Conflict theorists criticize systems theory for assuming an **over-socialized** conception of people (Wrong 1961). The idea that individuals are taught the proper ways of behaving, internalize them, and then never want to behave any differently, seems altogether too simplistic. If people's behaviour were indeed totally shaped by norms, then the problem of order would disappear. Wrong asks the question, "How is social order possible in an anthill?"

Laws to protect the environment or workers' health lag behind those protecting private property.

His answer is, because any other way of behaving is inconceivable. This is certainly not the case for people in society. The psychoanalytic theories of Freud draw attention to strong rebellious forces deep within the human personality, which are at best only partially restrained by internalized social values.

The question of why rebellions do not constantly occur has prompted concern with the psychology of domination, the mechanisms by which our sensitivities can be stunted such that we do not perceive alternative forms of social order or we lack the will to fight for them. One line of argument at the critical edge of this approach is that traditional sociological theory itself, in the form of systems analysis, has proven a powerful intellectual tool in promoting **one-dimensional thought**. Traditional sociology views the current order as an integrated, functional system. Critics argue that the broad acceptance of this view has dulled our capacity to perceive alternatives.

Evidence of a consensus of values supporting existing institutions cannot simply be accepted on face value as support for the system. Such consensus may be more a reflection of manipulated public opinion than values that are genuinely felt by the majority of people from among the disprivileged classes.

A major concern within conflict theory, therefore, is the mechanisms by which such manipulated consensus might be achieved. A central tenet of Marxist thought is that the **dominant culture** of a given society is the values of the dominant class. Stinchcombe (1968, 108–17) points to a number of mechanisms through which people in powerful positions perpetuate their values among succeeding generations with more success than their opponents. Members of the dominant class may control the socialization process by influencing both school curricula and the appointment of teachers, clergy, and other influential people. They may be able to

determine not only the rules governing how subsequent incumbents must perform in prescribed roles but also the kinds of people who will or will not be permitted to take up important jobs. As successful figureheads of society, they are likely to attract hero worship and serve as **role models** for the younger generation. They are in a better position than others to influence the content of mass media, either because they own media outlets directly or because they control the advertising revenues on which such outlets depend.

As we noted in chapter 1, disprivileged people such as the ill-educated and the unemployed rarely write books. They may well have conflicting values concerning what is functional or dysfunctional for the mass of people, but they are scarcely in a position to shape the knowledge and values of many other individuals. Similarly, those people who are busy in other jobs simply do not have the same amount of time to propound their values in public as those who can afford to pay public relations personnel to do so full-time. It follows, therefore, that some groups in society are more influencial than others in the creation of ideas.

As we noted in the discussion of sociology as history, human agency produces social structures; but not everyone's actions are equally significant. The powerful pepole, at any given time, are those whose actions can determine the kind of structures that a society will have. The more powerful a class, the more influencial that group is as a cause of social structures (Stinchcombe 1968, 94).

The principle basis of power is control over economic resources; the capacity to influence values is secondary. People who lack the means to produce subsistence for themselves are at the mercy of those who own the means of production. In agricultural societies, the primary resource is land. In an unequal exchange relation, landless people have little choice but to labour for those who own land, and on terms largely determined by the will of landowners. In modern industrial societies, those who control capital—the factories, machinery, and raw material needed for manufacture—can exact an unequal contract for labour from those who lack such resources to produce for themselves. In the classical Marxian formulation of the concept of **class**, people are divided into two opposing classes: those who own the means of production and those who do not. In industrial capitalist societies, these two great classes are the **bourgeoisie**, the owners of industrial resources, and the **proletariat**, the workers who must sell their labour power. A smaller intermediate **petit bourgeois** class comprises those who have sufficient means of production to work for themselves but who hire few employees beyond their own family members.

In more recent formulations, the concept of class has been modified to take into account other kinds of resources, including specialized skills that give people more bargaining power in the exchange relationships of the marketplace. Middle-class professionals have very different life experiences from unskilled manual workers when they seek employment, but the underlying power relations remain. Even professionals are still at the mercy of employers using their services. In the 1980s, as the big oil companies curtailed their activities, Canada saw the crisis of unemployment hitting professional workers such as geologists, scientists, and managers in the oil industry. In the crunch, class differences based on skills may be more apparent than real and more tenuous than many middle-class people care to think.

Another recent modification to the concept of class within the conflict theory tradition has been to take into account a group's generalized capacity to control the allocation of resources within a society. Elites within the **bureaucracies** of socialist countries, for example, can be seen as a class, or a collectivity of people who can wield political influence. The fundamental basis of power, however, still remains economic resources, and sociologists who do research in the conflict theory tradition focus primarily upon political economy. The central questions they ask concern the workings of industrial capitalism, the international relations of capital, and how particular societies such as Canada fit into this world system. The new reality of late twentieth-century capitalism is that the world economy is dominated by **multinational corporations** that may actually control more resources than do nation-states. In the light of this new reality, contemporary theorists are having to re-evaluate their notions of nations, states, and politics.

A central assumption of conflict theory is that social order is inherently unstable. Unequal and consequently exploitative relations between classes produce a situation where disprivileged participants have a permanent reason for pressuring for change. When this observation is projected onto the societal level, it challenges the assumption of systems theory that societies, like organisms, tend towards equilibrium. Class conflict appears as a major force for change throughout history. Indeed, Marxists believe that the history of all societies has been the history of **class struggle**. Those who do not own the means of production struggle to take them away from those who do. From this perspective, the French Revolution can be understood as the struggle of landless peasants to take land away from the nobility. Many **Third World** countries are engaged in similar struggles today. In industrial societies, the class of propertyless labourers has most to gain from the overthrow of the owners of capital, the bourgeoisie. Marx suggested that this might be the final battle of history. With the collective ownership of all means of industrial production, the last major source of class conflict would be eliminated, and social equilibrium based on genuine consensus might be possible. Contemporary theorists, trying to understand and explain strife in communist societies, are not so sure. Ownership of capital is one basis for power, but bureaucracy and political influence need to be examined as alternative bases for control over resources.

Currently, systems theory remains the dominant form of sociological analysis within the Soviet Union and the United States, but conflict theory, with its particular focus on political economy and class analysis, is fast gaining ground in Canadian sociology. Richardson and Wellman (1985, 774) suggest that the visible dependency of Canada on the American economy may be largely responsible for the emergence of a strong political economy tradition among Canadian academics. Americans, at the centre of international capitalism, have tended to ignore the power links that bind others to them and to stress instead the estimable traits of their own society. The powerful influence of American sociological traditions on Canadian academics can be explained by the major influx of Americans into expanding Canadian universities in the 1960s and by U.S. domination of the publishing industry. The pattern of American sociology may change if the thesis proves correct that the American economy is losing its pre-eminence in international capitalism, as multinational corporations pull their investments out of the United States and direct capital to other parts of the world where labour is cheap and taxes and environmental controls are minimal (Marchak 1985, 694–96).

Interpretive Sociology: Symbolic Interaction and Ethnomethodology

Interpretive sociology focusses on different kinds of questions from either systems theory or political economy. Theorists in this tradition also conceive of people as playing roles and reacting to each other's expectations. But interpretive sociologists do not assume that such roles are preprogrammed, available independently of role-incumbents. Instead, the patterns of behaviour that people come to interpret as roles are actively created and negotiated, sustained or abandoned, in on-going interaction. These patterns are constantly subject to reinterpretation by the role-players involved as well as by onlookers. From this perspective, the fundamental problem for sociology is to understand how people actively produce their social world as a mutually comprehensible reality. Terms such as *roles* and *reality* are frequently placed in quotation marks by interpretive theorists to emphasize that they are not seen as factual entities but as interpretations that people use to make sense of what they perceive to be happening.

It may take only a small shift in perspective for one's entire sense of what is going on to change. Take, for example, the kinds of words that different people use to talk about those who are fighting against government authority. They may be "terrorists," "freedom fighters," "bandits," "vandals," or "members of . . . ." The nature of the reality that is being talked about is fundamentally altered by the choice of words. Terrorists are evil people who terrorize the innocent for illegitimate reasons; freedom fighters are good people striving to liberate others who are wrongfully oppressed; bandits are simply out to rob people for private gain; vandals are people who irrationally damage the property of others for no clear motives; members of implies an organized group of people acting upon orders rather than individuals acting on frustrations or motivations of their own, and so on. The reality behind the words is by no means obvious.

"What is going on" is the outcome of people's efforts to make collective sense of their perceptions and to influence the perceptions of others. Consider a simple situation. A woman wearing spike heels steps on your toe. What actually happened depends upon

*"Good news. The 'Times' has upgraded us from a
'junta' to a 'military government.' "*

Drawing by Joe Mirachi; © 1984 The New Yorker Magazine, Inc.

your interpretation—whether you see your-self as the deliberate target of an angry woman, or the victim of someone who has a careless disregard for others, or an unfortu-nate participant in a totally chance, unin-tended event. Perhaps you are being warned of some social blunder she feared you were about to make or she created the incident in the hope of getting your attention and a chance to talk to you. What happened could be literally anything imaginable.

Theorists in the interpretive tradition fault much of the analysis of systems theory and conflict theory for the unwarranted **reification** of "society," as if it were some entity existing over and above relations be-tween people. Interpretive sociologists argue that sociology begins with people as active producers of social reality.

The interpretive approach to sociology as the study of systems of meanings has a long tradition. Its founder was Max Weber (1864–1920). Weber was a philosopher, sociologist, and historian who lived in Germany at a time when it was becoming unified and con-solidated as a powerful industrial state. One of his central concerns was to develop a mode of historical and social analysis that would be scientific and yet at the same time would have as its core assumption a view of people as unique individuals endowed with free will, freely choosing their actions. For Weber, the central method of sociology was **Verstehen**, the process of meaningful understanding. *Verstehen* involves the interpretation of behaviours as actions by attributing goals, motives, and intents.

The concern of interpretive sociology is with the analysis and explanation of socially meaningful actions. Understanding entails making motives, the meaningful subjective bases of actions, intelligible. Unless we, as sociologists, can so empathize with the behaviour of another person that we come to feel that if we had been in the same situation, with the same background experiences and the same values, we might have behaved the same way, we do not truly understand that person's behaviour. We have explained the rise of Nazism in German, for example, only when we have come to understand how, given the appropriate circumstances and experiences, we might have taken part ourselves.

A common assumption among North Americans after the Second World War was that there must be something uniquely evil about German culture for Nazism to have arisen there. They believed it could not happen in the United States because of strongly internalized cultural values of freedom and democracy. However, experiments carried out by Stanley Milgram in the U.S. between 1960 and 1963 suggest that the average American might be just as prone to obey cruel orders as the average German had been. People were asked by a psychologist in a laboratory to give electric shocks of increasing intensity to another person every time that person made mistakes in a memory test. The frightening part is that close to half of all the people who took part were willing to obey orders to the point of administering electric shocks that they thought were severe enough to be potentially life threatening (Milgram 1974). Many people got upset and pleaded that the experiment be stopped, but most participants continued as long as they were told to do so. Researchers interested in the social psychology of domination cite such experiments as evidence that factors promoting unquestioning obedience to clearly cruel commands from authority figures are prevalent in American society as well as in more overtly **authoritarian** regimes.

One possible explanation for the behaviour observed in Milgram's experiments might be that many subjects simply disbelieved that the experiment was real, correctly guessing that the so-called shocks were faked (Boughey 1978, 76–77). However, similar experiments have been carried out in Australia, supposedly to test fear reactions. In these experiments, people obeyed orders to pour water into a drum that had a kitten

tied to the bottom. They could not avoid knowing that the kitten was being drowned. Apparently, also, people were less likely to agree to continue with the experiment when they were offered payment than when asked to participate without pay in a scientific experiment. Something in the definition of the situation appeared to have been changed by the offer of money (William Foddy, personal observations).

These experiments raise serious questions about ethics for sociological research. Do researchers have the right to use persuasion or other pressures to get people to take part in experiments that could well cause them emotional stress and humiliation? Do researchers have the right to torment animals just to carry out a study of patterns of obedience? Professional ethics committees associated with the Canadian Sociology and Anthropology Association have generally concluded that they do not and have recommended quite stringent controls to protect the rights of potential subjects of research. The issue of ethics will be raised again in chapter 3, which focusses more directly upon techniques of research.

Symbolic Interaction Theory

Early approaches to interpretive sociology, which can loosely be referred to as **symbolic interaction theory**, tend to complement rather than challenge systems theory by developing a deeper understanding of the socialization processes involved in role playing. This approach explores the **reflexive** character of all interaction, as people respond to their interpretation of the meaning of the actions of others. Advocates of symbolic interaction theory argue that behaviour is fundamentally symbolic. A major proponent of this theoretical approach, Charles Horton Cooley (1864–1929), promoted the sociological technique of **sympathetic introspection**, an approach that involves putting oneself in another's position. He popularized the concept of the

looking-glass self to describe the dependency of self-conceptions upon the reactions of others. Even as tiny infants, he suggests, we learn that we can influence other people, and we are also deeply concerned with how others see us. We learn to see ourselves as objects through the eyes of others. This reflected image invokes feelings of pride or shame. Some people are more significant to us than others in this development of self. People such as our family and friends, whom we know on an intimate level, are most important initially, but later in life a variety of other people take on significance. The process is flexible in that we can to some extent choose our **significant others**; that is, those who are most important to us. People frequently change their friends when they change their beliefs, seeking out people who support them and avoiding those who are overly critical.

George Herbert Mead (1863–1931), one of the early sociologists at the University of Chicago, greatly influenced the development of symbolic interactionism as a discipline in North American sociology. He developed the concepts of the **self** and **other**, arguing that they were inseparable parts of the same concept. Children acquire self through learning a language and thus learning to see themselves as objects. The self comprises both the **I** and the **Me**. The latter is the internalized other and is formed through the common set of attitudes and definitions of our significant others. The I, on the other hand, represents the uniqueness of the individual, the impulsive, spontaneous, and reflective aspects of the person.

Personality develops in stages. At first young children imitate the behaviour of others without understanding it, as when they pretend to read. Later, they begin to take on a role, as when they play at being mothers and fathers. **Role taking**—"taking the role of the other toward self," as Mead says—involves imagining and trying to empathize with the experience and expectations of others. More complicated forms of role taking involve assuming a number of roles together. In team games, for example, a player must be able to imagine the expectations of all the others in the game so that she or he can act accordingly. Eventually, in an even more complicated form of role taking, we develop a sense of a **generalized other**, which is the synthesis of expectations and attitudes of the group or community.

Sometimes we imagine future roles to play. This is known as **anticipatory socialization**. It is perhaps strongest when we are children and most roles are unexplored, but it continues into adult life. People imagine themselves in different roles and try to select ones that they are comfortable with. For example, students trying to decide on a career may read accounts of people in a variety of jobs and try to imagine themselves in these people's shoes.

These early theories of symbolic interaction, involving ideas of anticipatory socialization and role taking, are compatible in some aspects with systems theory. We have already examined the idea that people learn the behavioural expectations associated with different roles. But interpretive sociology has developed in ways that go well beyond these simpler notions of role playing. In particular, theorists emphasize the need to break free from the systems theory image of roles as preprogrammed and deterministic and to recognize that roles are fluid and continually subject to reinterpretation and renegotiation (Heritage 1984, chap. 3). Roles are not just adopted, they are actively created by participants. Alfred Schutz explored how the philosophical approach of **phenomenology** could be used to develop our understanding of how our social world comes to be meaningfully understood by us as made up of roles. Phenomenology studies the ways in which sensory information becomes meaningful.

Sensory experience means nothing until it is interpreted. A classic example of this is the picture that looks like either a white vase on a dark background or the silhouette of two dark faces on a white background (see figure 2-2). Another example comes from the children's book *The Little Prince*, by Antoine de Saint-Exupéry, in which the hero laments that he has drawn a picture of a boa constrictor that has swallowed an elephant, but people keep mistaking it for a picture of a hat (see figure 2-3). The difference lies not in the sensory experience but in what is attended to.

The social world is vastly more complex than the physical in that we experience it from the outset as subjectively meaningful. Actions and reactions are seen to reflect the motives and goals of others. In Schutz's view, the problem of **intersubjectivity**, of knowing what the other person actually intended, is solved for all practical purposes by **recipe knowledge**; that is, by reference to typical patterns of actions learned through socialization. Berger and Luckman (1967) use this Schutzian approach to develop a model of how social reality is constructed, in which they attach particular importance to

Figure 2-2 Interpreting Sensory Experience

Figure 2-3 Interpreting Sensory Experience

Source: Adapted from Saint Exupéry ([1943] 1971, 3–4).

language and symbols in the development of shared meanings. Two actors in isolation, such as Robinson Crusoe and Man Friday, may first watch each other, looking for patterns. Actions soon become **typified** ("there he goes again") and routinized ("this is the way we do things"). When such patterns are transmitted to a second generation, they acquire legitimation and are accepted as rationales for why people like us do things in a particular way. Eventually such patterns and legitimations become reified and objectified, as if they existed independently of people. Yet this social reality remains, at root, nothing more than patterns of behaviour that people justify to themselves. Interactions with others may reaffirm this reality, or may change it by objectifying doubts. Social reality is inherently unstable, open to change whenever its justifications are called into question.

The essentially creative aspects of role playing are emphasized in Erving Goffman's **dramaturgical model** of society. Seen from this perspective, roles are not so much learned as created and negotiated by people. The bare outlines of the script in the form of minimum expectations for compliance with the role's demands may be typified and interchangeable between actors, but the details are not. Moreover, many social interactions do not take the form of pre-defined roles at all. Goffman's work provides fascinating glimpses into how people manage interactions. Using the theatre as a metaphor, he points out the importance of a backstage region where one can drop the act and check the performance, rehearse, and repair appearances. Dressing rooms can be of strategic importance as places in which to disappear while avoiding or recovering from social blunders. Frequently we invoke the aid of a team in giving a performance. We seek the help of others who can be trusted to support the image, who share the backstage of a particular performance. The membership of such teams varies with the situation; the audience for one performance may be backstage for another. Information control is crucial in maintaining the act, but total control is difficult to achieve. For example, unintended gestures, signs of tension, fumbling, sweaty palms, and so on, convey to others the message that one is ill-at-ease.

Most of the examples of interaction in Goffman's writing take place in informal settings of parties and social gatherings, but wider structures are still apparent in some of his studies in the form of power relations that set boundaries or constraints on individual performances. In his famous study of asylums (1961a), Goffman shows us doctors, nurses, and patients in a total institution playing out their roles in positions of very unequal power. This aspect of Goffman's work parallels another important branch of the symbolic interaction perspective, that of **labelling theory**. This explores the power of people, often those in authority positions, to impose labels upon others in certain situations. In the context of the asylum, doctors have the power to label others as mentally ill or not, a decision that has momentous consequences for the ways in which the person so labelled will be treated. Labelling theory has been especially significant in exploring aspects of **deviance**. It argues that deviant behaviour lies as much in the perception of the onlooker as in the actual behaviour.

Deciding that someone is mentally ill is a negotiated process. Consider Daniels' (1972) example of an army doctor faced with a soldier whose marriage has just broken up. The soldier appears depressed, marginally suicidal, delusional, and is drinking heavily. If the doctor decides that the behaviour is a reaction to a stressful situation, he is saying in essence that the soldier is not mentally ill. If he decides that the problems stem from the soldier's character, then he is laying the blame on the man. But if he labels the behaviour psychotic, then it indicates that he is worried about the soldier, but not holding him responsible for the behaviour. The consequence of each label is very different. In the first instance, the soldier may get an honourable discharge on compassionate grounds; in the second case, a dishonourable discharge or other punishment, including loss of a pension; in the third case, specialized care and a disability pension. The label chosen depends more on what the doctor wants to happen to the man, how long he has been in the army, what he is perceived to deserve, and what facilities exist for treating someone labelled psychotic, than on what the symptoms are. Once labelled, however, the person is typified in a way that will strongly influence how others react to him. The very expectations that others have of the mentally ill may pressure the person so labelled to act in ways that confirm their impressions. Deviant behaviour will be the effect rather than the cause of the deviant label.

Official statistics on such matters as the proportion of soldiers discharged for mental illness, or rates of illness in the armed forces, are compiled on the basis of just such ad hoc decisions. Given that the availability of services to treat the mentally ill comprises an important element in whether a doctor decides to designate a would-be patient for treatment, the statistics on rates of mental illness may reflect the number of hospital beds more than the number of people with symptoms. Similarly, crime statistics may be more indicative of the politics of police staff and workload decisions than the numbers of crimes actually occurring.

Ethnomethodology

How MUCH ?

The symbolic interaction perspective offers valuable insights into the nature of the social world and its symbolic and negotiated character, but important questions remain unanswered. If social reality comprises only actors' recipe knowledge and typifications, then what is the role of sociology as the scientific study of social structures? What is the status of the sociologist's perception, as distinct from the perceptions of the actors involved? How can indeterminate networks of typifications be studied? More importantly, the problem of how social order is possible still has to be addressed. Symbolic interaction theory moves away from the image of people as "cultural dopes" acting out internalized roles like puppets, but it still does not explain what motivates compliance, or how the world, made up of mundane **typifications**, actually exerts itself upon the perceptions, actions, and interactions of people (Heritage 1984, 74).

Ethnomethodology, a relatively recent perspective in sociology, is associated with the founding work of Harold Garfinkel and a large group of associates working at the University of California. His path-breaking book, *Studies in Ethnomethodology*, was published in 1967. Garfinkel was a student of Talcott Parsons, but he broke with systems theory because he felt that, in starting with the notion of pre-existing sets of roles, systems theory was guilty of taking for granted the very subject that had to be researched. Ethnomethodology asks the basic question, how do social actors come to know, and to know in common, what they are doing and the circumstances in which they are doing it? How do you come to know what

Reprinted by permission of United Features Syndicate, Inc.

role I am playing? How do I know that you know it? How do we both know that each of us shares and will sustain the definition of reality that we are trying to produce?

Garfinkel designed **breaching experiments** to expose the rules underlying familiar everyday activities and to show how these rules and activities are mutually sustained. His students were asked to disrupt the taken-for-granted order in ostensibly very simple ways and to describe what happened (Garfinkel 1967, 41–49). In one case, simply asking for clarification of a routine question like "How are you?" was sufficient to destroy the entire interaction. When the student asked, "How am I in regard to what? My health, my finances, my school work, my peace of mind, my . . . ," the other person lost his temper and shouted back, "Look! I was just trying to be polite. Frankly I don't give a damn how you are." A bus driver exploded with anger when asked if he were sure he knew where the bus was going. One father flew into a rage and all but ordered his son out of the house when the son spoke politely to him as would a boarder, for fifteen minutes.

These experiments reveal the inherent fragility of **social order**. The moral outrage that these breaching experiments engendered reveals also the power of sanctions sustaining that order. Garfinkel argues that the threat to people's sense of reality, not the actual behaviour, invoked the indignation. People calmed down as soon as they could find some alternative set of motives to make sense of what was going on. Clearly, for any sense of social reality to be sustained, we have to rely upon assumptions that other people will use their **background understandings**, will trust appearances as corresponding to intentions, will be willing to anticipate the sense of conversations, using future remarks to clarify what is being talked about, and so on. Otherwise interaction is impossible.

Another experiment showed just how much and what kind of work people do to create a sense of what is happening (Garfinkel 1967, 79–94). Students were asked to participate in what they thought was an experiment in alternative methods of counselling in a psychiatry department. They were asked to describe a serious situation for which they were seeking advice and then ask ten questions. The counsellor could answer yes or no to the questions but could not offer further advice. In fact the answers were entirely random. The counselling was literally nonsense. Yet students stayed for the entire "counselling" session, made sense out of each of the yes or no answers, even when they were blatantly contradictory, interpreted the counsellor's reasoning, and came away for the most part actually thinking they had received sage advice. Sense was imposed entirely by the students' imagination. They interpreted random **utterances** as meaningful conversation because this was what they were expecting.

These experiments have far-reaching implications for sociology as a scientific discipline. They raise the very real possibility that the order that sociologists purport to describe may be nothing more than the one that sociologists themselves impose. The methods that they use and the theories they invoke to make sense of the data actually create the order that they describe. How do we know whether the order that sociologists describe constitutes an order inherent in the reality being observed or an abstract order produced by sociologists themselves as they try to make sense of the random utterances they gather? There is no easy answer.

Ethnomethodological research has increased awareness of the ways in which social scientists and other professionals, in their routine work, actually serve to create the versions of "reality" that they appear to be describing. Research methods definitely do influence the data collected. Questions structure the answers that people give.

Eichler (1980, 62–68) argues persuasively that much of the research data on male/female differences succeeds only in finding the patterns already built into the way the research was done. But as reported "scientific" evidence, it helps to structure readers' expectations or typifications. People who do not fit such expectations come to consider themselves deviant.

Smith (1974b) points out that a great deal of what we think we know about our society comes to us second-hand through reports produced by other people. Through radio, television, newspapers, and various publications and speeches, we come to learn about "facts" such as crime waves, rates of mental illness, unemployment levels, protests, wars, world markets, and the like. These accounts are, in Smith's words, **worked up** by people, usually government bureaucrats. They tell us about features of our society, and we treat the information as our factual knowledge. But how factual are the facts? It becomes critically important to find out exactly how these professionals collect evidence. Their selective attention and their preconceptions help them to impose patterns upon the data and serve to construct what then appears to the rest of us to be evidence of "what is going on." Facts, in other words, are not just sitting out there waiting to be collected. Facts are socially produced. Before we can make sense of them, we need to understand how they are produced. This is the major contribution of the ethnomethodological approach to sociology, and we shall draw upon it a great deal in this text to take a critical look at what sociologists present as evidence for the reality of Canadian society.

Feminist Theory

The **feminist perspective** in Canadian sociology is quite recent, beginning only in the 1970s, although it has a much longer history in the struggles of individual women to challenge the **sexism** and the social rigidities of their time. It has strong roots in both Marxism and ethnomethodology. It shares with Marxism a central concern with structures of power and inequality, although feminist theorists examine not only the relations of capitalism and production, but those of **patriarchy**, or male power over women, and of reproduction. Feminism shares with interpretive theory, and especially with ethnomethodology, a sensitivity to the ways in which intimate personal relations create the social world and continually reproduce male dominance within the workplace, the family, the kitchen, and the bedroom. Feminist theory, by its very existence, has drawn stark attention to inadequacies in other branches of sociology, especially to the omission of perspectives on social reality that begin from the standpoint of women.

As Dorothy Smith (1975) expresses it, women in general, along with other disprivileged people, have been systematically excluded from the creation of culture. Historically, women have played little part in the creation of dominant ideas in society. Nor have they played much part in their transmission, with the exception perhaps of the socialization of children.

A complex industrial society such as Canada is organized by written texts—books, newspapers, regulations, forms, laws—as well as other documentary modes such as radio, television, and film. In order to function, the government or management of our society depends on such texts and media. The media and advertising also influence how we come to think about ourselves, our body image, what our homes should look like, and so on. Women and other disprivileged groups have been largely excluded from the occupations in which such texts and documents are produced. It is predominantly white, middle- and upper-class males who are directly involved in producing, debating, and developing ideas. Their perspectives prevail in devising medical, psychological, and sociological theories and educational curricula and in framing laws and evaluating creative arts. The issue here is not simply the tendency to value men's work and men's concerns more highly than those of women. The issue is women's exclusion from the formation of the dominant culture. Their perspectives are not even present.

An illustration of how their exclusion works is provided by Sharon Fraser (1987; 1988) who describes the rejection of women and women's issues by the CBC. She describes a meeting between staff writers and a producer when she worked at CBC radio. Three staff writers suggested stories about such issues as a new potash mine, rising mortgage rates, and changes in the downtown traffic patterns, and they made plans to talk to the Minister of Natural Resources, the president of a financial institution, and the mayor. Fraser suggested a very different kind of story about some female bank tellers who were being cut from full-time to part-time hours with loss of all benefits and with a 50 percent cut in pay. Her proposed story was rejected, amid stifled yawns and such comments as, "Oh no, not that women stuff again" and "We've already done women stuff this week." Significant topics are determined according to a male agenda. Women's issues are afterthoughts and fillers at best and can be treated with journalistic contempt. These issues are the first to be cut when editors and producers lack time and space (Fraser 1987).

At one point, Fraser was invited to apply for the position of producer of a CBC radio show. She decided that, during the interview, she would say what she really felt rather than what she knew the CBC executives would want to hear. She argued that it was important for the issues of the day to be dealt with regularly from the point of view of those people who were most affected by them. Commonly, all we hear is how selected issues will affect white, middle-class males, like how a downturn in the market affects men who trade shares. In contrast, Fraser

wanted to cover how rising interest rates affect single mothers, pensioners, and disabled people on fixed incomes, or how increases in transit fares affect customers, 80 percent of whom are women and children. In 1988, the issue of free trade was extensively covered, but overwhelmingly from the perspective of how it would affect male workers and businessmen. What about how it would affect immigrants, women, people on the fringes, everyone, in fact, but white, middle-class males? Fraser did not get the job with the CBC. The official reason she was given was that she lacked experience in selecting music for the show. When Fraser asked what the real reason was, the CBC official replied that she was "ideologically incompatible with the CBC." The CBC, Fraser concludes, is ideologically oriented to serving the interests of white, middle-class males, with everything else treated as fringe topics. She sees this as a violation of Canadian women's fundamental right to free speech.

Smith (1987a) cites evidence of how the biases of beginning from the experience of men pervade the social sciences. Freud's theory of psychoanalysis, for example, starts from a man's experience of his body and his sexuality. Women are conceptualized as suffering traumas because they are "missing" a penis. There is no suggestion that men might suffer traumas because they are "missing" a uterus or are unable to become pregnant.

Historically, a primary mechanism for excluding women from the creation of culture has been their exclusion from higher education. Women were sometimes taught to read and write, but there was little provision for women to be taught philosophy, hard sciences, or mathematics. The very few women in the past who became mathematicians did so typically through some accident, such as gaining access to their brothers' notes. When women have contributed major intellectual work, this has typically been appropriated by men. Caroline Herschel did extensive work in astronomy with her brother William, but all this research is attributed to him. Also, because male critics have controlled the principles used to judge art, the beautiful work produced by women in the form of quilts, embroidery, or tapestries was not seen as "real art" until the modern women's movement demanded a reassessment of aesthetics.

In the same way, women have only begun to gain a written history as feminist historians search for women in the past, often outside formal political, military, religious, and educational institutions. Women's historians use sources such as letters, diaries, and crafts to document the rich history of women. The search for women in history has revealed instances where women's contributions have not simply been ignored, but brutally repressed. In the late fifteenth century, women were forbidden to preach the scriptures, and some women were persecuted, imprisoned, and even martyred as heretics for continuing to preach. In the mid-nineteenth century in the United States, a Mrs. Packard was committed to an insane asylum by her Calvinist husband simply for disagreeing with him on theological matters. The male medical establishment systematically barred midwives from practising their profession. Women were also systematically excluded from universities and medical and law schools. The first woman was admitted to the University of New Brunswick in 1886, one hundred years after it was founded. Even in the 1980s women are not equally represented at all levels of higher education. As figure 2-4 illustrates, the proportions of women fall lower and lower as one moves up the educational hierarchy. They are especially underrepresented in administrative positions of professional leadership.

These patterns are changing. Women scholars are entering the professions in

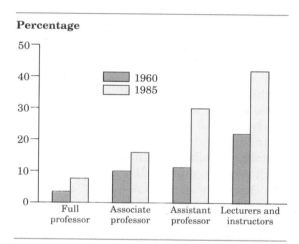

Figure 2-4 Women as a Percentage of Full-Time University Teachers by Academic Rank, 1960 and 1985

Source: Statistics Canada, Cat. 81-241.

increasing numbers, especially in the humanities and social sciences, and also in the information professions such as journalism and film. But the pre-established patterns within these disciplines, which reflect male interests and concerns, have not necessarily changed. Fraser (1987) points out that so long as the white, middle-class male agenda prevails in the CBC and in mass media generally, it is of little consequence whether the person filling a position is a man or a woman. Women, she suggests, have been socialized to believe that their concerns are not very important and that they should not whine so much about such issues as domestic violence and sexual assault when there are really important things happening, like wars and strikes and uprisings. As consumers of the media, we have been conditioned to believe that some things are more important than others. Now the media maintain that, in order to keep our attention and respect, they must not spend too much time on "women's issues."

In the humanities and social sciences similarly, the dominant **paradigms**, the analytical frameworks, and the major questions have already been set up from male perspectives. What junior women scholars write is evaluated, approved of, or ignored in terms of what their work adds to existing bodies of knowledge and theory. The dominant perspectives of the social sciences can thus serve as an ideology that blinds us to the reality of the situation of women as they directly experience it.

By the late 1980s, the majority of Canadian universities had begun to develop women's studies programs, but these still tend to be marginalized. It is not atypical for a department with ten faculty members, offering between fifty and sixty courses in an academic year, to offer only one course dealing specifically with women. Even this may be perceived as somehow detracting from the main business of the discipline. The era when the perspectives and contributions of women automatically receive half the attention in any course dealing with people is still a very long way off.

Margrit Eichler (1988b) has prepared a guide to nonsexist research methods in which she draws attention to multiple ways in which the social sciences reflect male perspectives to the exclusion of women, even when research is written up as if it included everyone. An example from social anthropology describes how intergroup warfare is a rational means of gaining livestock, women, and slaves. Within this image of society, women appear only as property. Discussions of hunting and gathering societies typically give central attention to how male-dominated hunting parties are organized, and how these may determine the evolution of community structures. The potential importance of how women organize to gather food is ignored. This is despite evidence that gathered food may comprise close to 80 percent of what is eaten in hunting and gathering societies. The practice of **polygyny** is generally described in terms of one man having several wives. It could as appropriately

be described as husband-sharing, but the male viewpoint takes precedence. In sociology, studies of stratification focus on the relative statuses of father and son, or maybe father and daughter. The role of mothers in family stratification and status mobility is simply subsumed under the status of her husband.

In virtually every subfield of sociology, with the possible exception of research on families, women tend to be invisible or are noticed only as they deviate from the male norm. Even in the area of the family, where women have been the centre of attention, their contribution has been downplayed or trivialized as relevant only to the "private realm." Only recently has housework come to be thought of as work at all. Meanwhile, it is men who are seen as active in the public realm, the realm where "important things" happen. This sexist stereotyping also distorts our understanding of male roles. Men are pervasively portrayed only as breadwinners, rather than as co-parents who may be fully involved in day-to-day caring and nurturing work with their children. It is a rare children's book that shows fathers competently cooking dinner, cleaning the house, washing clothes, and taking care of babies and toddlers. Feminist theory is inspiring a growing movement toward **men's liberation**, which is also working to challenge stereotyped thinking.

Eichler (1985a, 629–31) defines certain guiding principles of feminist contributions to sociology. The first principle is that knowledge is socially constructed. As we have seen above, women's systematic exclusion from the professions where books, legislation, media, art, history, and religion are produced has had a profound impact on the culture of our society. From this recognition comes the second principle of feminist theory: what is accepted as a dominant ideology is the ideology of the ruling group, the people whose opinions count, who are quoted as authority figures, and who formulate policies. Only a tiny minority of these people have been women. The third principle is that there is no such thing as a value-free social science. The knowledge we create is human knowledge and stems from our position within our social world. Much of what passes as gender-neutral or objective social science is written from the standpoint of one gender, with the other one silenced. The fourth principle is that perspectives vary systematically with location in society. What it means for a man to have more than one wife is not the same as what it means for a woman to share her husband. What it means for a man to work for wages while his wife remains at home is not what it means for a woman to work at home, without directly earning any money, while her husband is away all day.

Applied to sociology, these principles imply that much of our sociological knowledge has been constructed for men, in male interests. The discipline helps to bolster and maintain patriarchy by reinforcing the notion that what men do is more important and central to society than are the activities associated with women. Feminist theory seeks to reverse this priority. It begins from the assumption that women's perspectives are at least as valuable as those of men and may be even more so since people in inferior positions often tend to have keener insight into society's workings than do dominant groups.

Developing sociology from the standpoint of women entails much more than adding a variable to some existing list of topics. It involves a new way of looking. It may also involve changing much of the taken-for-granted language of sociology because the reality described in feminist sociology is different than that in other perspectives. Smith (1979a, 16) gives the example of members trying to analyse problems experienced in a trade union local that includes both women and men. People are complaining that women who are on the executive never seem to do anything and that women members never come to meetings. Women, it seems, are apathetic about the union. They are not interested in its affairs and prefer to leave men to run things. But when the women begin to talk among themselves about what they feel is happening on the executive and to the female members, a very different reality emerges. Women speak of meetings being held at times and in places where it is hard for them to attend when they also have to care for children. Women go home from their paid jobs to take up their other responsibilities for preparing dinner, giving time and attention to children, bedding them down, and cleaning the house. It is precisely because women are shouldering primary responsibility for domestic work that men are free to go to union meetings after working hours. Moreover, when women attend union meetings and speak out, they find that they are commonly not listened to at all, or that what they say is not taken seriously. The sense of reality that emerges from this discussion centres on the organized exclusion of women from influence within the union, not upon apathy. It is important to recognize that the dominant sociological explanation—that of female apathy—contributes to women's oppression by rendering it invisible.

Traditional Marxist theories of political economy, in which class is defined solely with reference to ownership or non-ownership of the means of production, similarly require radical changes in language and definitions of reality in order to take account of **gender**. Marxist analysis ignores the social organization of reproduction. The existing patterns of division of reproductive labour between women and men are taken as natural, rather than as socially constructed. Hence the ongoing struggles between women and men for control over their reproductive lives remain outside traditional Marxist class analysis. The reorganization of relations of economic production under communism seems to leave the inequalities between women and men virtually intact. House-wives are not conceptualized as members of the working class. This traditional class analysis cannot account for the evidence that women comprise more than one-half of the world's population, do an estimated two-thirds of all labour, but earn only a small proportion of gross income and own a miniscule amount of total property (Sen 1985; Sivard 1985).

A basic assumption of the feminist perspective is that *the personal is political*. The concept of the *political* is used here in its broadest sense to refer to relations of authority and control. Feminist theory recognizes that these relations are struc-tured at the level of intimate personal interaction. As we saw above, even the issues of when and where to hold a meeting, whose opinion is responded to, or who talks with whom during the coffee break, are critical factors in silencing women and promoting policies favoured by male leaders. Within a household, the issue of who will do the dishes or clean the bathroom demarcates important lines of authority. An abstract language that tries to separate the public political sphere from the supposedly private and interper-sonal relations of families is a distortion, not a description, of reality.

Feminist research that explores the dynamics of sexual behaviour between women and men powerfully illustrates that even such intimate relations are through and through political. In theory, the state has no business in the bedrooms of the nation. Sex is supposedly a private biological act. But in reality there is a strong link between sex and politics. Sexuality is directly connected to the distribution of resources and power in society. In order to understand how women and men experience and express their sexuality, we need to understand the political economy of sex (Frank 1987).

Steedman (1987) examines the relation-ship between sexual behaviour and the per-petuation of masculine dominance in society. She argues that sex is political in that it reflects a social system of male power, a system that rewards and encourages certain forms of sex and discourages others. These patterns begin early in life in the ways in which girls and boys are socialized. Women are expected to be standard-bearers of morally correct behaviour. They are to hold back sexually until the "right man" comes along and then immediately throw off all reserve on the honeymoon. It is considered feminine for a woman to accommodate her-self to male sexual arousal rather than to experience her own. Women who are sex-ually assertive may find themselves per-ceived as "cheap" by other women as well as by men. Steedman (1987, 99) comments that this good girl/bad girl dichotomy perpetuates the ideal of innocence and restraint as a component of femininity, and that such behaviour is a powerful way of suppressing sexual pleasure. The perpetuation of this vision of womanhood is tied to male domi-nance in the wider economy. To the extent that women are economically dependent on men, it is risky to challenge or to threaten their masculinity in the bedroom. Masculine control over sexuality is exercised in law, in language, and in symbols.

From this perspective, the most intimate experiences of being male or female cannot be separated from the wider context of capitalism within which they occur. The practice of traditional masculinity, the orga-nization of masculine personality in industrial societies around aggression, com-petition, rationality, objectivity, and lack of emotion, corresponds precisely to the values demanded by and produced within the corpo-rate organizations of advanced capitalism. People, predominantly men, who work in such corporations are forced to set aside their own consciences, their cares and concerns, and subordinate themselves, their work, and their efforts to corporate objectives and interests over which they have no control

(Smith 1975). Theories assuming that this is all it is to be male distort reality and reinforce the oppression of men by making it invisible.

The purpose of feminist theory, as with political economy, is to understand the workings of society in order to bring about change. Both of these paradigms see people as creators of social reality, not merely its victims. **Critical sociology** has been defined as any sociological activity that grounds theoretical work in a normative diagnosis of the fate of humankind in a technocratic society or as any sociological methodology that explicitly distances itself from its own social present (Morrow 1985, 712). According to this definition, feminist theory is pre-eminently critical sociology, challenging both the social psychology and the political economy of domination, with the hope that new perceptions of social reality will foster new alternatives.

Conclusion

Important philosophical and methodological differences clearly separate the major theoretical perspectives in sociology. Philosophically, the theories assume either that the social world comprises a factual, objective, external system that can be known through the scientific study of facts, or that it is at root merely a construct of individual cognition, and can be analysed through subjective experiences. Human nature is conceptualized either as determined by environmental stimuli or as autonomous, with people able to think out new alternatives. One assumption about the nature of society is that it is characterized fundamentally by consensus and equilibrium. This assumption promotes concern with regulation and with the study of stability, integration, and functional co-ordination. The opposite assumption is that society is characterized fundamentally by conflict and injustice. This viewpoint promotes concern with disintegration, coercion, and movements for social change.

Burrell and Morgan (1979, chap. 1) plot these assumptions to give a four-fold typology of theories as either subjective or objective and concerned with either regulation or with change. This way of thinking about theories is represented in figure 2-5. Systems theory is characterized by concern with objective reality and regulation, while political economy or Marxist theory is concerned with objective reality and radical change.

Figure 2-5 Typology of Sociological Theories

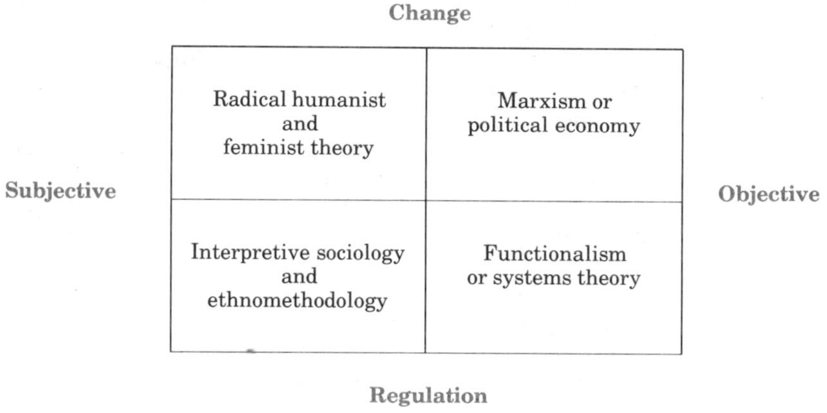

Change

Radical humanist and feminist theory	Marxism or political economy
Interpretive sociology and ethnomethodology	Functionalism or systems theory

Subjective   Objective

Regulation

Source: Adapted from Burrell and Morgan (1979).

Interpretive perspectives are characterized by concern with subjective reality and regulation or social order, while the feminist or radical humanist approach is concerned with subjective reality and radical change. Having drawn these divisions, however, it is important to soften the boundaries, to recognize that theories merge into each other rather than maintaining rigid demarcations. Whatever their differences, they remain united as part of the same discipline of sociology, concerned with the same goal of the scientific understanding of the social world.

Fournier (1985, 794–96) points out that any review of a discipline involves a political dimension, in that it consolidates and legitimizes certain theoretical streams rather than others and aggravates the conflicts that divide the scientific community. Even the demarcation of major theoretical movements is political since it creates inevitably arbitrary classifications. In reality, sociologists do not work within exclusive categories. Consensus about where to draw the boundaries is weak, and any original theoretical process usually develops through confrontations with and interpenetration of different theoretical perspectives. Good research is often eclectic, borrowing from several traditions. The theories of Durkheim, Marx, and Weber have elements of each of the perspectives outlined above. Marx, for example, is pre-eminently a systems theorist but is also a leading political economist. In addition, he is a forerunner of ethnomethodology and feminism in that he drew attention to socially constructed meanings and to how ideologies can distort people's understanding of what is happening to them.

It is important, then, not to reify the perspectives outlined in this chapter but to try to borrow from each of them and to see how they challenge and complement each other. When this becomes frustrating and confusing, as it inevitably will, it is important to remember that a variety of conflicting theoretical approaches is the best. This eclecticism is perhaps the only safeguard against doctrinaire assumptions about "reality" supported by selective evidence and closed off from criticism by the suppression of alternative reasoning.

Suggested Reading

There are many books available that give detailed summaries of each of the approaches outlined in this chapter, but at this stage the goal is to give you a feel for the variety of theories and the controversies in sociology. Particular approaches are studied in later chapters in more depth.

A simple but lively and critical introduction to three perspectives in sociology—order theory, conflict theory and interpretive theory—is Harold Boughey, *The Insights of Sociology: An Introduction* (1978). Boughey continually pits the different approaches against each other, encouraging his readers to take sides and join the fray. Sociology for Boughey is not for people who like to sit passively on the sidelines and collect facts. Boughey has a large blind spot, however, in that he gives no attention to feminist theory. Margrit Eichler fills this gap with her book *The Double Standard: A Feminist Critique of Feminist Social Science* (1980). She shows how many theories in sociology have to be revised to take into account the situation of women.

The best way to get a feel for sociology in practice is to read some studies. Below is a list of material that you might browse through. Most are designed for the general reader rather than the specialist.

Among the finest works in the functionalist tradition are studies of community life. They show how the various institutions of society, economy, family, education, and religion are integrated into a total system. A series that includes many studies of communities in eastern Canada is published by the Institute of Social and Economic Research, Memorial University of Newfoundland. Selected titles include T. Philbrook, *Fisherman, Logger, Merchant, Miner: Social Change and Industrialism in Three Newfoundland Communities* (1966) and N. Iverson and R. Matthews, *Communities in Decline: An Examination of Household Resettlement in Newfoundland* (1968).

Holt, Rinehart and Winston have produced a series of short community studies. Some of the studies that are of particular interest to Canadian readers are N. A. Chance, *The Eskimo of North Alaska* (1966); E. A. Hoebel, *The Cheyennes: Indians of the Great Plains* (1960); and J. A. Hostetler and G. E. Huntington, *The Hutterites in North America* (1965).

An old but excellent functionalist study of a work situation is William Foote Whyte's *Human Relations in the Restaurant Industry* (1948). Whyte describes in intimate detail how all the different employees' roles function together to make up the food-delivery system.

Jean Briggs' *Never in Anger: Portrait of an Eskimo Family* (1970) describes how the Eskimo build a satisfying system of life centred around a subsistence hunting and gathering economy in a harsh environment.

For a critical approach, which focusses particularly on the effects of economic relations on people's lives, a valuable and very readable collection of articles is by Gary Burrill and Ian McKay, *People, Resources, and Power: Critical Perspectives on Underdevelopment and Primary Industries in the Atlantic Region* (1987). These articles look at life in the Atlantic region of Canada, organized around the four issues of agriculture, fishing, forestry, and mining and energy. They speak with anger of how deeply the communities within Atlantic Canada are being damaged by corporate capitalist business practices over which they have no control. The publication *This Magazine* also provides general interest articles on contemporary

issues, mostly from a critical perspective. The study by Joan Kuyek, *The Phone Book: Working at the Bell* (1979), provides a worker's view of life in the Bell Telephone Company and how the class relations of capitalism work.

Meg Luxton's *More Than a Labour of Love: Three Generations of Women's Work in the Home* (1980), is both Marxist and feminist in orientation. Luxton describes life in the single-industry town of Flin Flon, Manitoba. In one sense Luxton's book is a community study like those suggested above, but the kind of questions she raises about how the lives of people are integrated around the mining economy are very different from traditional functionalist studies.

The many studies by Erving Goffman of everyday interaction and how people create and negotiate definitions of themselves, provide an excellent introduction to interpretive sociology. Some of his smaller and very readable books include *The Presentation of Self in Everyday Life* (1959); *Interaction Ritual: Essays on Face-to-Face Behavior* (1967) and *Stigma: Notes on the Management of Spoiled Identity*. When reading studies by Goffman, try to place yourself in the situations of his characters and see how you would have negotiated similar interactions.

Ethnomethodology is an approach that many people initially have difficulty understanding. One fascinating essay is by Harold Garfinkel, "Passing and the Managed Achievement of Sex Status in an Intersexed Person" in *Studies in Ethnomethodology* (1967). Garfinkel describes how a person who was born biologically male, but who chose to be a female, manipulated the entire range of her adolescent relationships to maintain the status of a female. Garfinkel uses the study to show how definitions of masculine and feminine identity are socially constructed in everyday life.

An excellent collection of articles by ethnomethodologists is Roy Turner, ed., *Ethnomethodology* (1974). Part Three, "Practical Reasoning in Organizational Settings," is particularly useful in providing examples of how ethnomethodologists do their research.

Chapter 3

A Critical
Look at Methodologies

Given the variety of theoretical perspectives in sociology, it should come as no surprise that there are also a great many research techniques to choose from. These can be used individually or in combination. No one technique is either better or worse than any other. They are rather more or less appropriate for different kinds of research contexts and different theoretical questions. No fixed correspondence exists between theoretical paradigm and type of methodology, although there is a tendency for certain combinations of theory and methods to be more common than others. Systems theory, for example, is widely associated with a positivist approach that, in principle, emulates approaches of the physical sciences, stressing quantitative, objective data rather than subjective or impressionistic research. Those who turn a critical eye on systems theory tend to accuse such sociologists of being "number crunchers," of creating the social world out of surveys, census data, and statistical analysis of trends. Yet, ironically, systems theory is

also associated with the very different approach of **participant observation** in anthropology in which researchers try to live as participants in another culture, learning from the inside how the complex web of social institutions comes together as a total culture of a people.

Certain writers in the feminist tradition have argued that feminist research necessitates a new and qualitatively different approach in order to get beyond the abstractions of mainstream theory to uncover the intensely personal, intimate experience of women (Duelli Klein 1980). This need may simply reflect a stage in the development of feminist research (Eichler 1985a, 632–33). Early in the development of a discipline, when little is known about a phenomenon, the best method is one that allows exploration, imposing the minimum of prior expectations. In feminist sociology, such methods include listening to women, watching them in their intimate daily lives, and learning to see them from their own standpoint and experience. Later, the discipline matures as we learn more and begin to make generalizations, to see patterns, and to formulate hypotheses. At this point, different techniques may be needed that allow us to test the generalizations in relation to very large numbers of women, to document how their experiences fit into the dominant institutions and political economy of a society, and how their position has changed historically. For such research, techniques such as surveys, questionnaires, census data, and content analysis of historical documents may be more appropriate.

The important question is not which method one might prefer, but which is more appropriate for the particular kinds of evidence one is trying to get. As you will see, no method is foolproof. Each has its particular strengths and utility and its particular weaknesses and blind spots. The ideal, therefore, is to have a number of researchers coming at similar issues from different perspectives and starting points. Hopefully their studies will not only complement each other and increase our overall understanding, but will reveal the limitations and blind spots of specific approaches.

This chapter surveys a variety of techniques and gives brief examples of the kinds of research topics that have used them. It examines the value of techniques for gaining knowledge of the social world, and the problems to which each approach is prone. Techniques can be loosely divided into quantitative and qualitative methods. **Quantitative methods** try to establish generalizations that apply to large numbers of people. **Qualitative methods** explore smaller settings in depth with the goal of gaining insight that may subsequently form the basis for broader generalizations.

The objective of this chapter is not to teach you how to do research, but rather to convey a sense of how to be intelligent readers of research. You should not just passively absorb "facts." Rather, it is important to learn to be constructively critical of research findings by developing an awareness both of the strengths of good research and of the inevitable limitations of knowledge.

Experiments

For researchers in the physical sciences, **experiments** are virtually the defining characteristic of "scientific" method. There is no better technique for testing precise causal relationships. The ideal experiment controls, or holds constant, everything that could possibly influence the phenomenon of interest, then allows one **variable** to change. If there is a change in the phenomenon, and the experiment was done properly, one knows that the manipulated variable, and only that one, could have caused the change.

One interesting experiment began with the observation that students who habitually sat near the front of classrooms tended to get higher marks on average than students who habitually sat near the back (Dooley 1984, 20–23). Two plausible hypotheses were suggested. The phenomenon could be due to "self-selection"; that is, that the more interested and able students chose to sit near the front. Alternatively, it could be that increased interaction and eye contact with the professor stimulated higher performance from students at the front.

An experiment was designed to test these theories. The professor let students choose where to sit on the first day of classes, then asked them to stay in that place for the next three weeks until he gave the first test. Then he randomly mixed everybody up, with some of the back-row people moving to the front and some of the front-row people sitting at the back. Three weeks later he tested the students again. The theory was that if self-selection caused the association, then making some of the better students sit at the back would make no difference to their test results. But if sitting at the front under the close eye of the professor was the real cause, then there should be noticeable changes in test results after students were moved.

The results supported the self-selection hypothesis, showing that randomly moving people seemed to make little difference to test results. Good students choose to sit at the front and poor students at the back. It was interesting to note, however, that the level of participation, measured by their asking questions and getting involved in class discussions, did change as students were moved from back to front and vice versa. Closeness to the professor rather than personality characteristics of the students seemed to be the major factor in class participation.

This study has all the elements of a true experiment. It includes a clear theory that either self-selection or proximity to professors causes grades to be higher among students who sit near the front. Two logical predictions are derived from this theory. If the theory of self-selection is correct, then moving the students will make no difference to their marks. If proximity to the professor is the correct theory, then moving students will make a clear difference. The researcher changes one variable—where people sit—and everything else is held constant. All students receive the same lectures and tests. The researcher observes what happens and decides which theory is correct on the basis of whether the results were as predicted.

Other experiments can be more exploratory, investigating how people react to very controlled situations or stimuli. Such experiments are frequently used in the area of social psychology. Researchers often make use of **small groups laboratories** for such experiments. These are specially equipped rooms designed so that researchers can control all key variables such as seating arrangements, lighting, noise, whether subjects in the experiment can or cannot communicate with each other, and so on. The room may be equipped with a one-way mir-

ror so that subjects in the experiment can be observed without being distracted by the visible presence of the researcher.

An example of this kind of experimental research is the study of coalitions and bargaining in competitive games. One of the simplest such games is "Prisoner's Dilemma," a game that involves two players and two choices, X or Y. If both players choose X, they both win a small amount, while if they both choose Y, both lose heavily. But if one chooses Y while the other chooses X, then the person choosing Y stands to win a large amount while the other loses. It is in one's self-interest to be unco-operative and choose Y if the other player can be relied upon to be nice and choose X. But if the other player chooses Y, both will lose far more than if they co-operated (figure 3-1 shows the possible outcomes for players A and B). Each player knows the rules of the game but does not know what the other player is going to choose. The game is repeated a number of times. Each player tries to guess whether the other will be co-operative (i.e., choose X) or competitive (choose Y) in the next game. On that basis the player decides whether to be co-operative or to risk taking advantage of a co-operative partner to make a large gain.

Experimental results, based mostly on American college students, show that couples make mutually co-operative choices—that is, both choosing X—only about 45 percent of the time. The majority of American subjects were competitive in spite of the fact that they then consistently lost money. They continued to choose the Y option even when they had seen the previous outcome. Knowing that an opponent is co-operative does not increase the likelihood that a player will also co-operate. People are more likely to take advantage of the other's co-operation.

More complex three-person games study coalition behaviour. Other experiments showed that two partners are more likely to choose the coalition that brings them the

Figure 3-1   Prisoner's Dilemma

highest individual outcome than the coalition that would make the outcome more equal and yet still permit the coalition to be a winning one. In games with two women and one man, or with two men and one woman, the two members in the majority sex appear to compete for the member of the opposite sex. Each of the two men, for example, would try to get the women on his side against the other man. All-female groups tended to be less egoistic than men in coalition formation games and were more likely to form a three-way rather than a two-against-one coalition, dividing the outcomes equally (Archibald 1978, chap. 7).

Archibald suggests that the competitive behaviour revealed in these games may not necessarily hold as a universal human trait, but may be more a characteristic of people who live in competitive capitalist societies rather than ones based on co-operative forms of economy.

Experiments have one major advantage over other forms of research in that they provide clear tests of theoretical predictions. Their limitation as a tool in sociological research is that it is rarely possible to control all the variables in a social situation. Experiments can only be done under very particular circumstances. Results may be fas-

cinating, but the question always arises whether it is valid to generalize from what people do in artificial and simplified contexts to how they will behave in complex social institutions in the wider society. The results of experiments that use as their subjects the predominantly male undergraduates in Harvard University psychology courses cannot necessarily be generalized to the behaviour of others. Feminists in particular have argued that serious distortions are introduced when conclusions from experiments using male subjects are applied as explanations for the behaviour of women.

Another problem peculiar to social science experiments is that of the subjects guessing the purpose of the experiment and accommodating their responses to what they think the experimenter wants. As Boughey (1978, 77) points out with respect to experiments where participants administered "electric shocks" to another person, once subjects even tentatively guess that the shocks might not be real, the experiment fails. Garfinkel's breaching experiments, where he tried to disturb the taken-for-granted rules of behaviour, also fail once too many people have heard of ethnomethodology. A student in Vancouver who nervously tried to breach customary rules for privacy and public space by sitting right next to a stranger on a nearly empty beach was taken aback when the stranger smiled and said, "You must be taking the ethnomethodology class." The stranger's new set of accounting procedures made perfect sense out of the behaviour and robbed it of the bizarre element that the student was trying to create.

Part of the problem of subjects guessing the intent of the experiment stems from the impressions that experimenters themselves can unwittingly give off. A self-fulfilling prophesy can come about whereby people act in such a way that they produce the expected results. This is graphically illustrated by one experiment where psychology students were asked to do learning experiments with rats.

Six students were told that they had "maze-bright" rats—that is, rats genetically bred to be particularly bright—while six had "maze-dull" rats. True to expectations, the maze-bright rats learned much faster and made fewer mistakes than the dull ones (Rosenthal and Fode 1963). What is curious is the fact that the animals were randomly distributed: no one set of rats was brighter than the other. The performance differences stemmed entirely from the students' expectations, not from the abilities of the rats. Somehow when students thought they had bright rats, they related to them in ways that stimulated the curiosity of the rats, while those who thought they had stupid animals actually depressed them. In the case of the experiment with student performance and seating arrangements, the professor may also have contributed to a self-fulfilling prophecy by modifying—whether consciously or unconsciously—the way he interacted with his class after he had moved the good students to the back of the room.

It is clear that caution must be exercised in interpreting experimental data. There are also ethical questions to be considered. Do researchers have the right to perform experiments on students when there is at least some risk that certain students may get lower grades because they were made to sit at the back of the classroom? Can people be treated like rats? This, of course, raises the issue of whether rats should be made to live out their lives in psychology laboratories just so students can experiment on them.

Non-scientific factors also come into play in influencing which experiments get published and which are disregarded. Experiments that disprove accepted theory are likely to be dismissed as invalid. A music student taking a biology elective described carefully controlled experiments that seemed to demonstrate that plants not only can hear music, but actually have preferences and are particularly attracted to Beethoven and Ravi Shankar (Tompkins and Bird 1972, 168–75). Standard biology journals refused to publish the results on the grounds that the experiments must be rubbish because plants cannot hear.

Experiments clearly can provide a valuable tool for social research, especially in the interdisciplinary area of social psychology, but they have limited applicability in sociology. The majority of issues that are central to sociological theory are not amenable to experimental testing, although they may draw on some of the insights of experimental results in psychology.

Survey Research

Survey research is so commonly associated with sociology as to be virtually synonymous with the discipline in the minds of many people. Typically, surveys involve the use of **questionnaires** or structured interviews in which a series of questions is asked of large numbers of people. In theory, one could approach every person in a population when doing a survey, as when a census is taken. But in practice this is so expensive and time consuming that usually only a **sample** of people is used. A sample comprises a small proportion of people carefully selected from a wider population. On a university campus with 30 000 students, for example, a researcher might interview a selected sample of 300 students (a one percent sample) to study aspects of student life. The goal is to use information gained from the sample to generalize to the wider population it represents.

It is very important that the sample be selected carefully so that it fairly represents the range of experience and characteristics in the population. The data garnered from a survey of 300 students in a local pub, for example, would not be representative of the student body as a whole since these students differ in important respects from others who rarely or never go to pubs and hence would not be included in the sample.

Surveys are a research method almost synonymous with sociology.

The ideal way to select a sample is through a random process. A random sample is one in which every member of a population has an equal chance of being selected, leaving no possibility that researchers can select their friends or particular types of people who might be easily available. To draw a random one percent sample of university students, we might get the university registrar's list of students, close our eyes and stick a pin in the list to choose the first person for our sample, and then select every hundredth name thereafter, until we had the number of names we wanted for our survey.

One important advantage that surveys have over experiments is that they permit **multi-variate analysis**. As we have seen above, an experiment works by studying the effect of change in one variable while all others remain the same. Surveys, in contrast, can gather information about a number of variables at the same time and explore how combinations of variables influence the issue of interest to the researcher. In a survey of students, for example, we might be interested in finding out why some maintain a high grade point average while others fail or barely scrape by. We have good reason to believe that no single variable can explain this. Multiple variables may be involved. We might want to find out not only about students' IQs but also about how many classes they attend, how many hours a week they study, how often they visit a pub, what kind of family background they have, and so on. With the aid of computers and statistical techniques it is possible to see how sets of variables interact in combination. Do less intelligent students who study long hours do better or worse on average than highly intelligent students who spend more time socializing than studying? What difference does it make if we also take into account that some students come to university straight from school while others have not been in full-time education for years?

One example of large-scale survey research explored patterns of immigrant settlement and race relations in an English city (Richmond et al. 1973). It used a questionnaire with 172 questions, covering such topics as housing conditions and overcrowding, social and economic status, local slang and idioms, work experience, including discrimination in getting a job and possible prejudice experienced from fellow workers, satisfaction with the neighbourhood, interaction between residents of different ethnic origins, and continuing relations between immigrants and people in their country of origin. The survey also covered the topic of **acculturation**, or the extent to which immigrants have adopted the culture—lifestyle, behaviour patters, values, and attitudes—that prevails among local people.

Responses to a range of questions provided a wealth of material for understanding the life experiences of immigrants and their neighbours and allowed researchers to explore a multitude of hypotheses concerning how variables might relate to each other.

Do relations with neighbours improve with acculturation? Are immigrants measurably worse off than indigenous people with respect to housing? Does the level of co-operation or conflict with neighbours vary with ethnic group, social class, or family size and structure? Does it vary in terms of whether immigrants keep their houses in good repair?

Since a complete **enumeration** of the 2633 households in the chosen area was used as the basis for the sample, one can be confident that the results give an accurate picture of the community, free from the biases that would occur if any volunteers or personal friends and contacts of the researchers had been used as sources of information. This particular study was carried out by a team of researchers who went door-to-door, called back many times, took great pains to encourage people to be interviewed because it was so important to learn how everyone felt, and arranged for foreign language interviews whenever necessary. Virtually no other research technique could have provided the quality of information derived from this survey. Even living within the area as a member of the community would have been less effective, since friendship pattern and acquaintances are invariably limited and selective. Mailed questionnaires or forms that people are left to fill in themselves also could not have achieved this very high level of coverage.

Not all survey research is conducted like this. Such exhaustive surveys take a great deal of time, skill, and money. Under the broad term *survey*, there is a wide variety of techniques that can be used to contact people. At one extreme, tightly structured questionnaires can be mailed out for people to fill in themselves and post back to the research headquarters. Such an approach may be particularly valuable for collecting data on topics that are sensitive or embarrassing. People may feel more comfortable answering questions about their sexual behaviour, for example, in an anonymous questionnaire than with an interviewer facing them. Mailed questionnaires are also quick, relatively cheap to administer, and can be mailed out to very large numbers of people simultaneously.

There are problems, however, that make questionnaires unsuitable for many kinds of research. Clearly they cannot be sent to illiterate people. They are also unsuitable for many less-educated people who, while able to read and write, may have difficulty understanding the language of the questionnaire and expressing themselves in writing. More importantly, if the questions are the least bit vague or ambiguous, there is no way for the recipient to ask for clarification. Another common problem is inappropriate answer categories that do not fit the person's peculiar circumstances so that she or he is unable to answer accurately. Since recipients cannot explain to the researcher what the problem is, they are likely to answer randomly or pick an inappropriate response and leave it to the researcher to work out what they meant. In addition, the researcher has no way of knowing what people answering the questionnaire meant by their answers and can only assume that what they meant is what the researcher would have meant. If you recall what happened in the experiment described in chapter 2, in which students made sense of the random utterances of a counsellor, you can see why the major critique of survey research raised by ethnomethodologists is that researchers are simply reading into the answers the patterns that they are determined to find. In reality, these patterns might not be there at all. There is much evidence that the wording of the questions themselves can determine, at least in part, the kind of answers given.

Researchers can influence the answers given in surveys in other ways. To oblige the researcher, subjects have been known to rank what, unbeknownst to them, were fictitious television programs. The resulting order is entirely the product of the researcher's question. It is possible that other rank orders, such as ethnic preferences, may be equally artificial, with people actually having no particular preferences, just obliging the researcher. Other questions distort reality by imposing false answer categories. Consider a question on the quality of relations between siblings, which provides the following answer categories: (a) warm, co-operative, supportive relations; (b) helpful and co-operative much of the time; (c) strained, mildly competitive relations; (d) much competition and tension. The problem is that answer categories do not allow for the possibility that people may have very warm and supportive relations that are also very competitive, or tense relations that are not competitive. Competition is bad by definition, whatever the respondent might think.

Another problem with questionnaires is that the meaning of answers to questions is commonly context-dependent. For example, attitudes toward the desirability of large families depend heavily on whether one is thinking about family parties or education costs. The coded answer may be meaningless if interpreted out of context (Cicourel 1974).

The distortions that can arise when researchers assume they know what the respondent meant by an answer to a particular question are illustrated by Eichler's (1988a, 82–88) studies of **sex-role** stereotyping. One question asked the respondent to agree or disagree with the following statement: "If a married woman has to stay away from home for long periods of time in order to have a career, she had better give up the career." More working-class people responded by agreeing with this statement than did middle-class people. This was interpreted as greater sex-role stereotyping among the working classes. However, when a second statement was added, "If a married man has to stay away from home for long periods of time in order to have a career, he

had better give up the career," more working-class than middle-class people also agreed with this. The two questions together suggested that what working-class people really meant by their "yes" response was not sex-role stereotyping of women's work in the home, but rather a generalized sense that family life is more important than jobs for both men and women. In contrast, middle-class people were more inclined to put jobs before family. The interpretive pattern was imposed by the researcher and did not reflect the values of the people being studied.

Surveys are only as useful as the quality of the questions asked. A critical reading of research must involve taking a hard look at the questions used to see whether the researcher's interpretation of the answers is warranted or whether some other meaning could reasonably be applied. The same question with slightly modified wording can quite easily mean different things to different people. In the previous example, if the word *job* had replaced the word *career*, middle-class people might have reacted to the question differently, since giving up a career does not mean quite the same thing as giving up a job.

In some respects, interviews are better than questionnaires at clarifying meanings because the interviewer is there to correct any ambiguities and misunderstandings. Response rates are also likely to be much higher. People may simply throw a questionnaire into the waste basket, or never get around to answering it, but they will talk to someone standing in front of them, particularly if they get on well with the researcher and actually enjoy the interaction. Researchers can also gather much additional, subtle information by watching the respondents' facial expressions, body language, and so on. People commonly dislike admitting that they do not understand a question for fear of looking stupid. They would rather mutter a vague agreement and let it pass. Vague answers and a confused facial expression may alert the

"Glad you brought that up, Jim. The latest research on polls has turned up some interesting variables. It turns out, for example, that people will tell you any old thing that pops into their heads."

Drawing by Saxon; © 1984 The New Yorker Magazine, Inc.

interviewer to the need for a more detailed explanation of what the questions mean. Likewise, when people avert their eyes while answering a question, it may signal that they are not telling the truth.

The very sensitivity of the interview situation, however, may prove its downfall. **Interview bias** can become a factor. This is particularly true when the interviewer is unskilled or uninterested. Some interviewers show their feelings to the extent that respondents can guess the kind of answers that would please or disappoint them. Respondents may alter their answers accordingly. In extreme cases, answers may tell us more about the attitudes of the interviewer than those of the respondent.

The distortions that can occur between what a person meant and what their com-

ments are interpreted to mean by a researcher is evident in the reaction of one housewife to the race relations survey referred to above. She said that she did not want to be interviewed because she felt researchers always jump to the conclusion that people are prejudiced even if they raise legitimate complaints. She explained carefully that she did not dislike immigrants but hated the way that the immigrant men living in a rooming house on her street would whistle and shout sexual remarks when she walked past them, as if she were one of the local prostitutes. She was also disturbed and intimidated by the noise these men made as they crowded onto the steps outside their house on warm summer evenings. The female interviewer assured the woman that she could understand her feelings. But when the interviewer discussed these remarks with a senior researcher, he responded bluntly that the woman obviously was prejudiced against immigrants and was merely rationalizing her responses. Perhaps he was right. But the problem is that if the woman meant what she said—that she was distressed, not by their racial characteristics, but by the sexual taunts from a crowd of frustrated single men—there was absolutely no way she could say this so that researchers, out to prove their theory that English people are prejudiced, would believe her. There is the risk that researchers' conclusions on the extent of prejudice among the local people stem from the predetermined interpretive scheme used by the researchers rather than from the internally experienced values of the people being studied.

Census Data and Government Records

Census data are immensely valuable for social science research. These comprehensive surveys of the entire population of a country, carried out with government funding, and with the force of law to compel people to answer all the questions, provide a wealth of information about the social, economic, and **demographic** characteristics of a people, which no other form of research can parallel. Since they are carried out every ten years in Canada, and within the vast majority of countries in the world, these government data banks provide comprehensive historical and comparative information that permits analysis of patterns of social change. Armstrong and Armstrong (1984), among others, have used census data to show changes in the economic status of women in Canada during the twentieth century, tracing proportions of women in different occupations. In addition, reports prepared by Statistics Canada include a special labour force study of the relative importance of age, marital status, and education as factors

influencing participation of women in the work force (Report 71-509) and a study exploring patterns of job search and success for persons in the labour market (Report 71-525). Reports under the general heading of education, health, and welfare include vital statistics on births, marriages, and deaths, and causes of death and suicide rates by age, sex, and province, with international comparisons (Report 84-528). Other reports can provide detailed information on home values, rents, household facilities, population distribution, education, ethnic groups, religion, language, migration, occupation, income, and so on (Report 95-703).

Many sociologists use the census as their primary source of data for studies of social change. The comprehensiveness of coverage of the population and the huge numbers involved make possible statistical analysis of the interaction between multiple variables. There is no substitute for these kinds of data, and it is consequently a matter of great concern to social scientists what kinds of questions are included in the census. The omission of a simple question such as ethnic origin of parents, for example, would greatly hamper the study of assimilation, migration, and discrimination in the labour market. When one Canadian prime minister even hinted at not carrying out the regular census in order to save money, it was sufficient to have all associations of social scientists start lobbying efforts to retain it. Luckily for sociologists, the business community also wanted the census since demographic data help them in deciding market patterns. The census survived.

Other less comprehensive sources of information are government agency statistics including, for example, crime statistics from the Department of Justice or poverty statistics from the Department of Health and Welfare. These statistics are often released as annual reports.

A famous classical study based entirely upon decades of government statistics is

Emile Durkheim's analysis of *Suicide* ([1897] 1951). As we will see in more detail in chapter 6, he showed that suicide rates per 100 000 people varied markedly for different groups. Catholics, for example, had a much lower rate than Protestants, and Jews lowest of all. Married people and those with children had lower rates than single or childless people. From these patterns, Durkheim supported his thesis that human happiness depends upon social cohesion: the more cohesive the group, the lower the proportion of people too unhappy to live. Low suicide rates suggested that people were, on average, happier when living in families and as members of cohesive religious communities or villages. They were likely to be less happy living alone or in the anonymity of large cities or when their religious values stressed individualism over community. Such a study would have been impossible without access to decades of suicide statistics kept in comparable ways across a wide variety of regions.

As with any other data, the problem with using census data and government statistics for sociological research is that the results are only as good as the methods used to collect the original statistics. If statistics are gathered in a sloppy or biased manner, then the resulting research will also be inaccurate and biased, no matter how carefully the researcher tries to handle the data. The social world comes to us already worked up by somebody else for certain specific purposes, usually those of a bureaucracy (Smith 1974b, 257). We have access to the end product of the statistical rates but not normally to the procedures by which the rates were counted up in the first place. Even census data is not necessarily "factual." During the 1975 mini-census, I was asked how many hours a week I worked. Since this was my first year of university teaching, I estimated it to be about 120 hours a week. The interviewer smiled and said, "For professors, we always put 60 hours." If this was indeed common practice, then any research that correlates hours of work by profession will be invalid. The data might not be any more correct if the estimates given by professors themselves were recorded at face value. Those professors who actually do no more than the minimum nine hours of formal lectures per week are unlikely to admit that they are so lazy, even in a census!

Census data are inadequate in other respects in that the categories used to collect the information may not be those appropriate for the research interests. The census, for example, records the total number of marriages for the period under consideration, but does not indicate whether a given marriage is a first or a subsequent one for the persons involved. It thus becomes impossible to determine how many **reconstituted families** may exist within a community. Similarly, the census records the number of single parents who have children living with them, but does not record the number of men who have fathered children without a long-term attachment to the mother. Records of family income as units give no information on how much money the wife might actually have to call her own. Hence, many interesting questions about family life simply cannot be answered using census data because the recording categories do not permit it (Eichler 1988a, 21–23).

Worse problems can arise, in that it is by no means always obvious how particular experiences are coded into categories used for the statistics. Different record keepers may make these decisions quite differently. Suicide rates for a particular region jumped by fifty percent in one year when government bureaucrats replaced Catholic priests as keepers of the rates (Douglas 1967). Douglas suggests that, because suicide is a mortal sin for Catholics, the priests tended to give almost every ambiguous case the benefit of the doubt and label it an accidental death. Bureaucrats were more inclined to label such deaths suicides. Researchers who mistake the apparent increase in counted suicides as evidence of a real increase in the numbers of people choosing to kill themselves may be building up complex explanations for something that never happened. The statistical "facts" are socially constructed by the people doing the original counting. It thus becomes important to study exactly how the data are collected, in order to interpret what the resulting categories actually mean.

As with questionnaires, the actual definitions of categories used by people doing the counting fundamentally determine the resulting rates. The Badgely report on child abuse in Canada (1984, 116) concludes bluntly that it is simply impossible to determine the actual rate or incidence of abuse because different methods of counting have produced huge variations in estimates. Reports that state that X percent of children are abused, without indicating precisely the methods used for counting, may be seriously distorting people's grasp of what is actually going on.

Statistics on emotional issues such as child abuse or wife battering are particularly prone to distortion. This distortion can take the form of under-reporting, with people trying to keep such behaviour secret, or over-reporting, with people using such accusations as powerful mechanisms for social control over others, ammunition in child custody cases, or justification for professional intrusion upon families. Premarital sex was once such a **taboo** practice that people were reluctant to mention it. Now, in order to appear sophisticated, high school students may even brag about sexual experiences they have not had. Incest rates might well shoot up in the next few years as this once taboo topic emerges from the closet. The increase may partly reflect increased willingness of victims to talk about their experience, but one cannot rule out the possibility that it might be happening more often. People with such inclinations might interpret the increased

discussion of the act as a sign that it is becoming more widespread and thus more acceptable. Or increased publicity may influence an impressionable mind. Publishing the rates might change the rates, which is one reason why the Toronto Transit Commission never publishes statistics on the number of people who commit suicide by jumping in front of trains.

Statistical Analysis

Statistical analysis in sociology has reached a high level of sophistication with the aid of computers. It is possible to model sets of data to explore the relative impact of many variables upon each other. Such analyses, particularly when based upon large amounts of data, are important tools for exploring social reality, but like all other forms of research, the results are only as valuable as the quality of the original data. As computer analysts are fond of saying, "garbage in, garbage out." It is important to gain some understanding of statistics and how useful they can be, but at the same time to avoid the trap of assuming that, just because evidence is presented in numerical form, it is somehow any more scientific or rigorous or objectively true than any other form of presentation. Darrell Huff, in his book *How to Lie With Statistics* (1954), gives many examples of how numbers can be deliberately used to convey false impressions, particularly in advertising. "Four out of five doctors. . ." gives the impression that one is talking about 80 percent of the medical profession, when in fact one may be discussing only four hand-picked quacks.

Correlations also do not prove **causality**. It may be possible to show that two variables are correlated, in that as one variable increases so does the other, without there being any casual relationship between them. There is a strong association, for example, between increases in the price of rum and increases in the incomes of Presbyterian ministers. Does this mean the ministers are rum-running? Not necessarily. It may reflect merely that both salaries and prices of liquor are affected by inflation in the economy. Bernard Shaw pointed out a strong correlation between age of British men at death and what type of hat they wore. Men who wore top hats seemed to live much longer than men who wore cloth caps. Does this mean we should all start wearing top hats if we want to live longer? Of course not. The association reflects the fact that top hats were worn largely by upper-class men who had much better living conditions and healthier diets than the working-class men who generally wore cloth caps. To help ensure that they lived as long as upper-class people, working-class men would have needed a higher standard of living, which itself would have required changes in the distribution of incomes and access to resources within society.

The important point with statistics, then, is to read them critically and to question how they have been manipulated from the original counting and what they mean. Numbers do not mean anything in themselves. They have to be interpreted, and this involves crittical reading.

Participant Observation

Participant observation involves varying degrees of personal involvement in the everyday lives of the people being studied. Through intimately sharing in their activities on a face-to-face level, observing, questioning, and learning how to participate in their world, the researcher is in a uniquely valuable position to develop a sympathetic understanding of social reality from the perspectives of the people themselves. This is pre-eminently the methodology of anthropology, since it is ideally suited to developing an understanding of the total culture of a people who live in a different society from one's own.

This form of research takes a great deal of skill and commitment on the part of researchers. It entails systematic observation guided by theory. As such, it is far removed from the casual observations that a tourist might make.

An instruction like "go and observe" immediately raises the question, "Observe what"? The "what" is supplied by theory. Even when approaching an alien culture for the first time, anthropologists begin with a conception of society as a system, the parts of which are functionally interrelated in patterned ways. As outsiders coming into the new society, they learn by a process of self-conscious socialization the patterns of behaviour and values of the people. This technique is especially valuable in exploratory research; that is, research into the lives of people about whom relatively little is known beforehand. Unlike surveys, where questions are necessarily structured in advance, the participant observer is more flexible, more open to chance and to the unfolding of formerly unknown and unthought of patterns of interaction.

In sociology, which can be seen as the anthropology of industrial societies, this form of total immersion is less common, primarily because social institutions are so much more differentiated and specialized and people's lives are more segmented than in pre-industrial societies. However, participant observation has been adapted to the study of distinctive subgroups or interaction within specific social locations or activity groups such as work groups, churches, group homes, and the like. This technique enables sociologists to study the patterns of socialization involved in membership in these subcultures.

The observer can adopt different methods, from concealing the research to openly playing the researcher role. One example of concealed research is Hochschild's (1973) study of old people in a senior citizens' housing project. Hochschild did the research while working as a reporter for the project's monthly newsletter. Through regular involvement in the daily activities of the old people, she was able to gain intimate insights into the complexity of their lives, as no survey or questionnaire could have done. Other sociologists have researched the groups of which they were active members. Becker, for example, studied the lives of jazz musicians in the band in which he himself played. His book, *The Outsiders* (1963), provides a fascinating account of the sub-cultural values of the musicians who perceived themselves as deviants, set apart from the squares. Through Becker's study we come to see how the musicians view us as audience, and the mechanisms by which they protect themselves and their musical forms from the demands of non-musicians who hire them to play.

In the case of both the musicians and senior citizens, the people being studied were unaware that they were actually subjects of research. This minimized the likelihood that their consciousness of being observed would influence their behaviour. Other researchers have openly revealed their research interests, trading the value of anonymity for the advantage of being able to question people more directly for insider information. A classic study of this type is Whyte's analysis of *Street Corner Society* (1943). Whyte joined a group of unemployed Italians in Boston, hanging around with them on the streets and participating in their daily activities. His intrusion into their group undoubtedly influenced behaviour initially, but the experience of most researchers is that, as time passes and friendships develop, people soon forget about the fact that they are being researched, and the pre-established routines of behaviour re-emerge. Jules Henry (1971) was able to attain this level of acceptance as an unobtrusive observer while actually living with the families of disturbed children.

Within a very short time, family members seemed to fall back into the routines of everyday behaviour with its intimacies, bickering, and fights, as if oblivious of the quiet observer.

Participant observation has the potential, unmatched by any other research technique, for providing a depth of understanding of social reality as the lived experience of the people being studied. But it also has its limitations. For a start, it requires a special form of dedication on the part of researchers to be willing to disrupt their own lives in order to immerse themselves in the lives of others. It is immensely time consuming. Learning by participating takes many months. In anthropology it typically takes two years or more of fieldwork to feel close to achieving competent membership knowledge of another culture.

Participant observation can take a tremendous psychological toll on researchers. Jean Briggs' account of her anthropological fieldwork, *Never in Anger* (1970), describes the emotional stress she experienced while living through one winter with an isolated Inuit community. She recounts her at times desperate efforts to protect her own privacy from the intensely curious and sometimes reproachful gaze of all the members of the community as they, in their turn, studied her.

There is also the risk that the presence of the researcher may alter the interaction being studied. Within the Inuit community, for example, it subsequently became clear to Briggs that the people accommodated to her presence in a number of ways in order to protect her. They left women behind in the camp so that she would not be alone, shortened the distances they travelled so that she could keep up, and hid from her their growing resentment at some of her own behaviour, such as hoarding food supplies, which was anathema to the Inuit.

The biases that result from interaction

between researcher and respondents are not peculiar to participant observation but what is problematic, especially given the public character of scientific knowledge, is that participatory research is very difficult to replicate. The complex sets of experiences through which a researcher gains insight into the group that she or he is studying are essentially unique, and the quality of the final analysis depends very heavily upon the personal resources and sensitivities of the individual researcher. Another researcher, joining the group at another time, may draw very different conclusions or impressions of its social reality. The question then arises whether one researcher is correct and the other mistaken, or whether the group culture itself has changed in the meantime.

When Oscar Lewis (1949) did a repeat study of the village of Tepoztlan, which had previously been studied by Robert Redfield (1930), he did not find the peaceful, smoothly running, cohesive community described by Redfield, but rather a community riven by conflicts. His conclusion was that village society had always been divided and that Redfield's theoretical convictions—that village life was more harmonious than city life—had seriously biased his perceptions. In effect, he accused Redfield of finding what he was looking for while ignoring contrary evidence. Margaret Mead has been similarly accused of painting an overly harmonious picture of adolescent life in Samoa, failing to see the teenage strife, delinquency, and illegitimacy that actually occurred (Mead 1928; Freeman 1983). The people themselves may have gone out of their way to hide this seamier side of Samoan life from the gaze of a stranger.

Margaret Mead's work in Samoa is a famous early example of the research method of participant observation.

In summary, then, participatory research has both strengths and weaknesses. As a technique, it offers unparalleled depth of insight, but it lacks some of the systematic controls and potential for replication and checking of other techniques. It greatest strength lies in exploratory studies that open up new areas of knowledge. Subsequent testing of these insights may benefit from more structured approaches. Participant observation is often combined with elements of survey research to provide quantifiable measures of early insights.

Like some other types of research, participant observation studies raise difficult ethical questions. Do sociologists have the right to conduct research on or in a group of people without their prior consent or knowledge? Is it very different if people know that the research is going on but do not understand exactly what it is that the researcher is looking for? If we conclude that people should always be told everything, and that their consent should be obtained beforehand, how do we get around the problem that all research would be biased in favour of the kind of people who like the idea of being researched and against the many other kinds of people who, for whatever reason, may decide not to participate? If we are researching an entire village community, whose consent should we obtain? Practical and political considerations usually dictate that we get the permission of the leaders or elders. But it is hard to argue on moral grounds that such people can legitimately speak for everyone else in the community. There are no easy answers to such questions, but we still have an obligation to raise them and to deal with them as best we can. We can state that, at the very least, research should not be carried out in ways that might reasonably be expected to harm the subjects. We will return to this question again at the end of this chapter where we discuss research ethics.

Unobtrusive Measures

In the arsenal of social science research techniques, there are a few that avoid the risk of interaction biases between researcher and subjects by focussing upon traces or records of events that have already been completed. Very occasionally some of these **unobtrusive measures** have found their way into sociological studies (Webb et al. 1966). A survey of community tombstones may reveal much about migration patterns, ethnic mix, and relative wealth or poverty of families in different communities, and some hints as to the status of women through the size of lettering accorded to them on family gravestones. A study of janitors (Gold 1951–52) revealed how they sometimes amused themselves by drawing inferences about the lives of tenants from the composition of their garbage. One can potentially learn quite a lot about people from what they throw out. Unopened mail may indicate financial difficulty or unpaid bills, torn letters suggest thwarted love affairs, empty bottles a secret alcoholic, and pet food tins, in the absence of pets, indicate severe poverty.

Other simple research devices have included counting the height and number of nose prints on the glass surrounding museum exhibits to determine the relative popularity of different exhibits and the age range of those most interested. In much the same way, the grubbiest sections of bound journals in a library indicate where the most useful articles are located. Advertisers may survey the dials on car radios in a parking lot to determine which radio station people listen to on the way to work. All such techniques have the value of being unobtrusive, of not disturbing the interaction or the behaviour that is being studied, and of providing rough quantitative data on incidence. Their limitations include the selective survival of traces and sometimes a considerable element of guesswork as to what the traces mean.

Other techniques, which focus on written documents, provide much greater scope for unobtrusive research into the social reality of the writers. Writing is in essence an intentional form of communication of facts or records and impressions by the authors, often for specific audiences. The social scientist is frequently as interested in reading between the lines to explore the underlying assumptions of the authors as in reading the overt text. An early study by Thomas and Znaniecki, *The Polish Peasant* ([1919] 1971), used the letters and diaries written by Polish immigrants to America to piece together what life was like for these people. The problem, however, is that one cannot be certain that what the immigrants wrote was, or was intended to be, an accurate description of their experience. Immigrants may feel under pressure not to worry family members left behind, to make their accounts more rosy than their experiences really were, and to leave out references to activities of which relatives might disapprove. In the same way, letters that students write home may not be accurate accounts of what they have actually been doing at university. What written records do provide, however, is evidence of the patterns that the authors themselves chose to impose upon their social reality as they tried to make their experiences accountable to others. It is frequently this aspect, as much as factual data, that interests the social science researcher.

A specialized research technique known as **content analysis** has been developed to aid this kind of study of written materials. In such analysis, the content of samples of written material is counted in predefined categories determined by the theoretical hypotheses. Depending on the researchers' interests, this may involve counting the number of times particular topics are raised in newspapers, or in letters and diaries, within a given time frame, the number of column inches devoted to these topics, the number of positive or negative adjectives used to convey approval or disapproval of the topic, and so on. This technique has been used very effectively to study sex **stereotypes** in children's picture books. Researchers count the numbers of stories devoted to activities by girls versus boys, active and passive characters by sex, and the variety of roles in which characters are displayed (Weitzman et al. 1972). The general pattern has been that girls are referred to less often and are usually in passive roles or in situations where they need to be helped by a boy. Similar studies have been done of ethnic and racial stereotypes in literature. The technique can also be adapted to analyse television programs for cultural content and biases.

Textual analysis involves a more sophisticated study of the form, as distinct from the content, of particular pieces of writing, to reveal in detail how meaning is constructed by the text. As it concerns the manner in which documents, including written accounts by sociologists, serve to construct definitions of social reality, this method is associated particularly with the theoretical approach of ethnomethodology.

Smith (1974b, 258–59), for example, analyses the way in which texts convey to readers that certain statements, and not others, are to be taken as facts. The factual property of a statement is not intrinsic but is conveyed by the social organization of the text. If a statement is prefaced by the words "in fact" or "the fact of the matter is" or is bluntly stated without qualification—"X is a conservative"—then the statement comes across to the reader as unarguably factual. If the same statement is prefaced by "I think," "I believe," or "she said that X is a conservative," then it comes to the reader as an opinion that can be subject to questioning and interpretation. These subtle changes fundamentally alter the relationship between the reader and the text. The factual form conveys the impression that the statements are fixed and eternal, the same for everyone, while the non-factual form invites the reader to participate in questioning the underlying social reality.

Smith demonstrates other techniques by which different versions of reality are textually constructed. A powerful tool is the location of "brackets," or the cutting-off points that one chooses to take as the beginning and end of an account of an event. For example, if brackets are placed at one time frame, a confrontation between police and street people may appear as an instance of people throwing rocks at police who then have to defend themselves. But if the brackets are expanded to include events several days earlier, then the same event may appear as police harassment of people who eventually fight back. Police accounts are likely to be presented in factual form as depersonalized aggregate knowledge of what happened. Accounts from other bystanders will be presented in the "I saw" or "it seemed to me" form. Given that most of our knowledge of our social world comes to us in the form of documents, either written or spoken on radio or television, textual **analysis** has critically important implications for our understanding of how we come to think about our society.

The development of **conversation analysis** is currently at the leading edge of ethnomethodological research, exploring at the most intimate level of interaction how people construct and maintain definitions of social reality. This research examines in minute detail the shape of conversations or sequences of **adjacency pairs** of utterances produced by different speakers. The basic assumption is that conversations are structurally organized so that no order is accidental or irrelevant. One example of this type of research is the analysis of the invitation and acceptance/denial sequence (Heritage 1984, 260–79). Acceptance of an invitation is usually immediate, with no delay in response. Rejections usually involve a pause before delivery, use of a preface such as

"well," and other displacement and postponement strategies such as appreciations, apologies, qualifiers, and hesitations. The decline component is usually mitigated, qualified, or indirect. The very fact that a pause is associated with a probable refusal allows the first speaker to add a comment to embellish the invitation or to suggest acceptable excuses such as, "If you have time."

Conversation analysis relies on tape recordings of brief conversations occurring in natural settings. The detail of the analysis is so precise that researchers could not rely simply on memory or re-enactment. Conversation analysts regard the fragments of the conversations they study as the foundations of social order.

It is fitting that this brief survey of research techniques concludes with content, textual, and conversation analysis. Textual analysis alerts us to the fact that sociology texts, like other forms of writing, are socially constructed. Intelligent reading requires analysis of the bases of factual assertions and the mechanisms by which accounts of social reality are put together. There are multiple techniques for gaining insight into social reality, and they are often used in combination in particular research projects. Each approach has its own validity and is appropriate in different contexts for researching different issues. None are foolproof. What is critical for social science is that, whatever methodology is adopted, the bases for statements should be sufficiently clear that readers can make reasonable judgments for themselves as to their credibility, and future researchers can either replicate the study or evaluate its insights through alternative procedures. The ideal is to compare multiple sources of data generated through different perspectives and different research techniques, and to explore systematically where and why accounts differ. Different findings may reveal limitations or biases in the original research or may mean that the situation itself has changed. For this reason alone, sociological research needs to do more than take snapshots. We need to know the shifting, evolving contexts in which the events we study are taking place.

Reading sociology is itself a form of research requiring an active interaction with the text. You cannot simply treat everything you read as factual. What appears as factual is always socially constructed. Accounts are always written to persuade readers to come to certain conclusions. You, as active readers, complete the research process by the responses that you have to these accounts.

Ethics of Research

The responsibility of the researcher to protect informants or subjects of research constitutes the basic ethic of sociology. The Code of Ethics of the Canadian Sociology and Anthropology Association emphasises that informants should not be damaged by research. In addition, subjects' anonymity must be protected; they have the right to refuse to participate in the research; they should be informed as clearly as is possible of the objectives of the research; and they should have access to the results. The code insists that students in particular should be protected and should not be forced to be subjects of research against their will as a condition of passing their courses.

These basic ethics are largely adhered to, although the discipline is not without its horror stories of researchers who have shown callous disregard for the well-being of their informants. One piece of research that was considered ethically borderline was a study of homosexuality where the researcher posed as a look-out for men meeting in a public washroom. He then used his vantage point as an opportunity to take down the licence plate numbers of the men in order to learn their identity and to do follow-up interviews with them (Humphreys 1970). There was some

debate at the time whether the researcher's doctorate should be withheld, although it was eventually accepted that he had scrupulously protected the anonymity of the men involved. If his research files had come into the wrong hands, however, the men could have been seriously hurt. All research in Canada that is carried out with the aid of university or government funding now has to receive prior approval from a research committee indicating that the techniques proposed are ethically acceptable.

Ethical issues for sociology, however, do not stop at consideration of the well-being of informants. They also include responsibility for the consequences of the final report. All social science research has political implications because of the central role that such research plays in structuring perceptions of social reality of the people being studied. Sociological research is capable of fundamentally influencing the choices people make, the alternatives they perceive, and their understanding of how others relate to them. At the macro level, it makes people aware of how changes in major social institutions affect behaviour in other sectors of the social system. No sociology is entirely politically neutral and, as a consequence, researchers have an ethical responsibility for the uses to which their results may be put. This was emphasized in a striking way during the survey research on race relations in Britain, referred to earlier in this chapter. One West Indian man commented that, while he had not directly experienced racial prejudice, he felt that British people were racist because of an incident he knew about. He described the event in some detail, indicating how much it had upset him. Only later did it become apparent that he was quoting from a book that was a sociological study of immigrants carried out several years earlier in another part of the country. This man's understanding of the attitudes of white Britons towards West Indians, and hence how he conducted his own relations with them, was based as much on this book as on his own direct experience, and perhaps more so since the book conveyed the impression of scientific accuracy.

Sociological reports are capable of generating self-fulfilling prophesies if sufficient numbers of people come to believe the analysis and orientate their behaviour in accordance with it. White home-owners are liable to react to non-white neighbours quite differently if sociological reports convince them that other people are open-minded and tolerant, than if such reports suggest that other people are sufficiently prejudiced for property values to fall when non-white neighbours move in.

A deeper ethical problem concerns the possible uses to which the results of research might be put, particularly by people who have the power to influence social policies. A proposed study of political insurgency in Latin America, known as Project Camelot, was halted on precisely the grounds that such knowledge, in the wrong hands, could be dangerous (Horowitz 1968). The project had been conceived as large-scale, fundamental research into social conflict, designed to "predict and influence politically significant aspects of social change, to assess the potential for internal war, . . . and to assess government actions to relieve this." The problem was not that such a topic was not valuable social science, but that the U.S. Army wanted to fund the project and to have access to the results. Mounting political protest halted the study on the grounds that the Army wanted to use the information to crush opposition groups. Closer to home, research into worker satisfaction and productivity in factories has provided management with valuable information on how to manipulate workers to increase their output. Given that managers are in a better position to manipulate the mechanisms for controlling social structures than are workers, it is more likely that managers will benefit from the information than that workers will.

Certain radical and critical social scientists have taken the stand that they have an obligation to redress this imbalance by directing their work toward empowering subordinate groups in society to understand and to manipulate social structures in their own interests. Feminist scholars make this commitment when they strive for a sociology for rather than *of* women, a sociology that will expose the roots of women's subordination in society as a first step toward changing it.

Early in the 1980s, the ethics committee of the Canadian Sociology and Anthropology Association grappled explicitly with the problem of the rights that subjects who participate in research have with respect to the knowledge generated through their co-operation. The concern was to try to overcome the tendency for sociological research to be a parasitic exercise in which subjects are used to further the academic careers of researchers without gaining anything themselves. The general ethical guidelines adopted by the association include the recommendation that, wherever possible, researchers should offer to provide subjects with the results of their study.

I personally felt very uncomfortable with this recommendation. On the one hand, I agreed with the sentiments behind it: researchers do not have the right to use people without giving anything in return. But, on the other hand, my own research on development projects in Indian villages made the recommendation problematic for several reasons. First, I write in English, and academic English at that. The vast majority of villagers, with the exception of a handful of elites and officials, only understand Hindi. My scholarly papers would mean nothing to them. More importantly, much of what I wrote could get individuals into serious trouble if they were ever identified. Small villages being what they are, identification would not be too difficult. My solution was to publish a series of articles that I hope may sensitize policy makers to problem areas and so potentially improve the quality of future development programs. But I am painfully aware that it is wishful thinking to expect that what I write will have much impact on what goes on in rural India. The village people who taught me so much have definitely helped my career far more directly than I have helped them.

In this research experience I also confronted another aspect of exploitation: that of relatively affluent Western researchers who employ assistants from Third World countries at low wages to help with their projects. During my doctoral research, my Indian assistant complained vehemently that I was exploiting him financially. As a far from affluent graduate student myself, I felt I was paying him quite well, particularly as he was earning four to five times the weekly income of his previous job, and far more than local Asian researchers could pay. On the other hand, I would have had to pay a student in Canada several times more money. We parted company after an argument over quality and quantity of work expected. The more I paid him per interview, the faster and the sloppier he seemed to work—a classic problem, incidentally, with research assistants. I still have not resolved for myself the issue of who was exploiting whom in that arrangement.

There are no easy answers to ethical questions. They constitute an on-going personal and professional struggle.

Conclusion

Is it all worthwhile? Susan Clark, one of the members of the Fraser Commission on Pornography and Prostitution, asked this question when assessing the outcome of the commission's long study. Few of the recommendations in the final report had been adopted by the Canadian government a year or more after the report was published, but Clark concluded that nonetheless, the answer must be yes, it is worthwhile. Research to increase our understanding of our social world has to be the first base for informed social policy. As C. Wright Mills concluded more than twenty-five years ago, people need the sociological imagination now more than any other form of knowledge in order to make sense of and to control the social realities of twentieth-century industrial society. The ultimate truth may be unknowable, but we have a responsibility at least to struggle to root out falsehoods.

Suggested Reading

This chapter is not designed to teach you how to do research. The goal is only to convey a feeling for the variety of research techniques available and the limitations associated with each of them.

There are many textbooks available on research methods in sociology. Some of them are referred to in this chapter, but they tend to be technical and difficult to read. One book stands out as a very readable and straightforward guide to good research practice: Margrit Eichler's *Nonsexist Research Methods: A Practical Guide* (1988). Eichler presents an overview of many kinds of research, showing how the ways in which various studies were conducted have distorted the results. She is particularly interested in sexism, but her insights have much broader relevance. She teaches how to read research in a critical way, rather than taking results for granted.

Part II

Social Cohesion and Order in Industrial Society

Chapter 4

The Microsociology of Everyday Life

by Peter A.D. Weeks

In his review essay entitled "On the Micro-foundations of Macrosociology," Randall Collins (1981) offers the following definitions for two extremes of sociological concern. **Microsociology** comprises "the detailed analysis of what people do, say, and think in the actual flow of momentary experience." **Macrosociology** comprises "the analysis of large-scale and long-term social processes, often treated as self-subsistent entities such as 'state,' 'culture,' and 'society'." Collins also draws attention to the recent upsurge in **radical microsociology**, which refers to the study of everyday life in second-by-second detail. It entails the use of audio and video recordings to permit the close analysis of conversations and non-verbal interaction. Collins argues that these new techniques in microsociology are helping to develop a view of how larger social patterns are constructed out of micromaterials.

Collins advocates a **microtranslation strategy**, which shows how macrosocial structures can be understood as patterns of repetitive micro-interactions. He argues that, strictly speaking, there is no such thing as a state, an economy, a culture, a social class. There are only collections of individual people acting in certain kinds of microsituations. Terms such as *state* or *class* are a kind of shorthand. They are abstractions and summaries of different microbehaviours in time and space. The causal mechanisms or active agents in any sociological explanation of macrosocial patterns must be microsituational. Microsituations make up the empirical basis of all other sociological constructions. Researchers never leave their own microsituations. They compile summaries of microsituations by using a series of coding and translating procedures from which they produce macro-analytical constructs (Collins 1981, 988–89).

If this perspective on the relationship between micro- and macrosociology were generally accepted, we would expect to find extensive research into microstructures. But in fact we find very little. Interest in what Collins calls radical microsociology began to expand only in the early 1970s, building on the pioneering work of Harold Garfinkel. By the late 1980s it was still a fringe discipline. However, if Collins' assessment is correct, and there are growing indications that it is, this relatively low priority could change in the 1990s.

The main reason for the limited attention given to microsociology is that it falls outside the explanatory frameworks of the main sociological perspectives of functionalism and traditional Marxist theory. From the standpoint of functionalism, the micro-events of everyday life can only be understood in relation to the functioning of the macrosocial whole. Similarly, for traditional Marxist theory, it is the structure of the capitalist system that accounts for the experiences of everyday life. Explanations thus work from the top down, from the macrostructures of the social system or the broader forces of capitalism down to the microlevel. The microlevel itself is of little theoretical interest because it is not viewed as causally significant, but only as a reflection of social structures. It is thus not an appropriate level of analysis for finding out what is really going on. Traditional theorists would not accept Collins' suggestion that a microtranslation strategy would be fruitful.

Interpretive perspectives in sociology, which do focus on micro-events, have had to battle for recognition against the flood of mainstream research and writing. As we saw in chapter 2, there are a variety of ap-

proaches under this broad umbrella, including symbolic interaction, phenomenology, labelling theory, and most recently, ethnomethodology. It is ethnomethodology, founded by Garfinkel, that represents the fullest critique of the holistic, top-down approaches of mainstream sociology. This is why it is given central attention in this chapter. Ethnomethodology not only criticizes traditional sociology for overlooking interesting issues in micro-analysis. It questions the validity of the very foundations of conventional sociological knowledge itself. Not surprisingly, it has met with considerable resistance and confusion.

The feminist perspective in sociology has been expanding during roughly the same time period as ethnomethodology. It has strong roots in critical Marxism, but also has a close affinity with ethnomethodology. A central assumption of feminist theory is that the personal is political. In other words, feminists are particularly interested in analysing the intimate personal interactions between women and men through which the relations of patriarchy are expressed and reproduced. Much current research by feminist scholars focusses on the social construction of reality; that is, on the ways in which society, as we experience it, is socially constructed in everyday behaviour.

This chapter presents an overview of diverse approaches to the microsociology of everyday life, with the main emphasis on ethnomethodology. Examples from research in the functionalist and Marxist traditions show how micro-experiences as diverse as professional-client relations or work in restaurants can be explained as reflections of the broader structures in which they play a part. We then switch to the meticulously detailed and critical work of radical microsociology. This markedly different approach seeks to show how the very notion of structures or social classes used in explanations by traditional sociology can be studied as ongoing accomplishments of the people involved, rather than as external entities that direct the interaction. The chapter concludes with selected examples from feminist research to show how this heightened awareness of the social construction of reality can be used to explore how the relations of patriarchy are accomplished in intimate personal behaviour.

Microsociology from the Functionalist Perspective

As seen from the functionalist perspective, behaviour is tied to the social systems in which individuals are enmeshed. These social systems are comprised of various positions, or statuses, organized in relation to each other. Each status carries with it cultural norms that specify the ways in which individuals are expected to behave as they play the roles attached to a position. A person's behaviour—going to work, handing in a term paper, standing in line at a bank—is considered explained when it has been presented as in accord with the norms associated with a particular role. People learn and accept their roles in a social system through the process of socialization.

David Orenstein (1985, 106) illustrates the functionalist approach with an example from his personal experience as a neophyte sociology instructor. He was only twenty-one at the time, and he feared that students, many of them close to his own age, might not respect him. He tried the following experiment. He dressed in denims and a casual shirt, arrived early for his first lecture period, and sat with the students for a few minutes. Students started talking and commenting on the lateness of the professor. Then Orenstein got up, went to the front, wrote his name on the board, faced the class, and spread out his lecture notes. There was an immediate transformation in the behaviour of the students. They stopped talking in mid-sentence, faced the front of the class, and got their pens ready. To an ignorant onlooker it might have appeared that they had rudely stopped talking, turned their backs on each other, and silently stared at this young man in jeans. Why? Were they rude? Was he strange? Were his clothes or his behaviour abnormal? No. The sociological explanation, say Orenstein, is that all the students in the class knew the culturally shared rules for behaviour in a given situation. They knew what to expect and how to act because they had been socialized into North American society. As typically socialized adults, they had shared knowledge of many different social situations and the appropriate behaviours in each. They could differentiate between such situations as cafeteria, bar, classroom, dancehall, library, or grocery store, and alter their behaviour to fit the appropriate expectations.

Orenstein's introductory text is devoted almost exclusively to an elaboration of the process of socialization, the ways in which we learn cultural roles. He refers to the values governing what we should or should not do in different situations as **prescriptive** and **proscriptive norms** respectively. He notes that we also learn emotional behaviour; that is, what to feel and when to feel it. We learn that it is not acceptable to cheer at funerals or to get too ecstatic over an A grade if our friend has done badly. Even the expression of romantic love is learned behaviour. A teenage girl is expected to have a boyfriend. On the other hand, if a girl and boy, aged thirteen and fourteen, were to express undying love for each other and commit suicide if this love were thwarted, we would consider them emotionally disturbed, unless, or course, we were reading *Romeo and Juliet*.

Orenstein's analysis of micro-events in terms of learned expectations for appropriate role behaviour summarizes the dominant American tradition in sociology. In principle, every situation comprises roles with pre-defined expectations that people need to know in order to participate. These expectations include exactly what one has a right to ask of other people, how to judge their performance, who is permitted to play what roles, and whether or not it is appropriate to express emotions toward others in the situation.

Work roles are particularly well-defined because work situations typically entail interaction between a number of specialized roles, oriented to the achievement of specified broader functions. Talcott Parsons' (1951, 454–79) analysis of professional-client interaction, particularly that between medical doctor and patient, in many respects set the standard for such research. In the process of training, a physician learns not only the technical knowledge of medicine, but also a set of attitudes and rules that governs professional interaction with others in related roles as patients, colleagues, nurses, and staff. Above all, doctors must learn to be neutral and objective and to avoid emotional attachment to patients. They must also learn that they are expected to put the welfare of patients above their own interests. Decisions about surgery must be based solely on a medical assessment of the patient's condition and not on a doctor's desire to finance a vacation in the Caribbean.

Clear guidelines establish the limits of any relationship between doctor and patient. Parsons argues that such guidelines or norms are functional, because they facilitate the physician's penetration into the personal affairs of the patient, which is essential for effective treatment, while protecting the patient from exploitation. When people are sick, they are particularly vulnerable to emotional, sexual, and financial manipulation. They must expose private parts of their bodies and divulge information that is potentially damaging. The rules governing the practice of medicine protect the patient from exploitation and also protect the doctor from excessive or inappropriate demands from the sick person.

The doctor-patient relation shows how interaction between two people in the privacy of an office is structured in precise detail by the predefined norms of behaviour for persons playing the roles. Each person enters the setting with clear and mutually shared expectations as to how each is supposed to behave vis-à-vis the other. Deviations will be subject to sanctions, including the threat of formal reprimand for professional misconduct. These predefined rules for behaviour can be directly explained as necessary for the smooth and adequate functioning of the health-care system. Adjacent roles of nurse, receptionist, orderly, and so on, can be analysed in similar ways to build up a picture of the total functioning system.

William Foote Whyte's pioneering study, *Human Relations in the Restaurant Industry* (1948), analyses the micro-interactions between people in all the different roles that make up the functioning system of a restaurant. Whyte begins his study with a description of the functions of waitress, dining-room manager, kitchen worker, and service-pantry worker, beginning well before the restaurant opens its doors to customers. We learn the functional **prerequisites** of the restaurant system: "the food must move, and it must move in the right amounts to the right places at the right time." Delays must be avoided, plates must be clean, customers must be served what they ordered, and so on. We also see how the restaurant business functions to handle feeding and food ceremonials in complex industrial society. The ongoing development of civilization, Whyte argues, requires a corresponding growth and development of the restaurant industry. Centralized means of mass feeding play an important role in keeping the system working when industrialization requires that most people work in factories or offices, often located far from their homes. Indeed, without the restaurant industry, Whyte (1948, 9) argues, our industrial society would cease to function.

Within this functional setting, Whyte describes the human structure of the restaurant, the patterned interactions between people of different statuses, co-ordinated so as to achieve the integration of production with service. Typical of a functionalist approach, he views the relationships between customer and waitress, waitress and supervisor, waitress and service-pantry worker, as interdependent parts of a social system, such that changes in any one part lead to compensatory changes in other areas. The seemingly idiosyncratic behaviours of individuals are explained as examples of threats to the kitchen hierarchy. Occasional frictions are used to illustrate the operation of the supply system—the continual flow of food from pantry through to kitchen workers to waitresses and finally to diners—and the necessity of appropriate role performance by everyone in the supply train. Episodes when waitresses burst into tears are explained by reference to role strains between them and kitchen staff when the supply system is under pressure. The use of written orders placed on spindles facilitates smoother interaction between the two status groups of waitresses bringing orders and countermen filling them. This is particularly important since the situation of females giving orders to males potentially violates wider expectations of interaction norms according to which males are dominant and females subordinate.

Whyte's study gives us an intimate account of the emotional ups and downs of people interacting in the different roles that make up a restaurant. But the overarching interest is how people are moulded into the roles that they play within the social system. Those who cannot make the necessary adjustments, like bad actors in a play, are required to leave the scene.

Limitations of Functionalist Analysis

The central problem with the functionalist approach to microsociology is that it shifts the active agency in social life from living people to inanimate and abstract structures. Functionalists run the risk of **reifying** society when they conceive of social rules as existing outside and above ongoing human activity and what people themselves do. People appear as "cultural dopes," programmed to play their roles as if they were puppets, with social structures pulling the strings. It may be that people often do feel trapped and manipulated in their personal lives, but we still need to explain how these feelings come about. As we shall see below, theorists who adopt the interpretive perspective in sociology argue that functionalism provides only a descriptive account of everyday experience. It does not explain it.

Functionalists describe what people do in a given situation, but not the actual mechanisms that produce and maintain the collective sense of what is going on. It is through continual processes of mutually negotiating the sense of what is happening now, and what will happen next, that people produce the patterns that functionalists subsequently observe as a particular role.

Microsociology in the Structuralist–Marxist Tradition

Analysis of micro-experiences from the structuralist–Marxist or political economy perspective adopts a more explicitly top-down approach than even functionalist theory. The Marxist perspective rejects the basic assumption of functionalism that social systems can be understood by reference to normative consensus, or shared expectations governing the performance of predefined roles. Important explanatory variables are found at the macrostructural level of the capitalist system as a whole. Production for profit, private ownership of the means of production, dependent wage labour, exploitation, and class conflict are the key elements in this system. What happens at the microlevel of interpersonal interaction, including the expressed norms and values of participants, reflects their class position in this system of production. Microlevel interactions are effects, not causes, of how the system works.

The debate over the **culture of poverty thesis**, which will be treated more fully in chapter 15, provides a classic example of the difference between functionalist and Marxist approaches to microsociology. Functionalists direct attention to the attitudes and values of poor people to account for why they are trapped in the roles they play. Such attitudes include: rejecting the value of hard work as a means to getting ahead; spending money or going into debt to get what they want rather than saving for it; seeing whatever happens to themselves or others as based on luck or cheating rather than effort; an inability to imagine themselves in different roles; a tendency to distrust the motives of everyone outside immediate family networks; and a "handout mentality," in which they look to others to solve their problems. In more technical terms, this pattern of values can be described as lack of achievement motivation, limited aspirations, fatalism, lack of **deferred gratification**, **familism**, low empathy, and dependence on and hostility to authority. Such values are appropriate for only the most menial jobs, which have minimal responsibilities and low wages.

In Marxist theory, however, the cause and effect relation between values and social position is reversed. Exploitative relations of capitalism give rise to an underclass of chronically unemployed or underemployed people, with incomes barely meeting subsistence needs. People trapped in the bottom social class develop distinctive values as a means of coping with a reality in which they are denied genuine opportunities to better themselves. Their experience of being cheated and exploited generates their distrust and hostility toward those who have power. A significant transformation in the structure of opportunities open to them is a necessary precondition for changing these adaptive reactions. Hence for Marxist theorists, there seems little point in researching how poor people think or behave. What matters is to research how the structures of capitalism operate to produce and perpetuate the poverty class.

The limited research that has addressed micro-experiences from the perspective of political economy has typically sought to demonstrate how class position and class relations structure personal lives. Archibald (1978) reviews much of this material to show how working-class people cope with and adjust to alienation; that is, to the experience of being powerless to control the conditions of their working lives and of being trapped in meaningless and humiliating jobs. Significantly, Archibald entitles his book *Social Psychology as Political Economy*, suggesting that he views this level of analysis as more appropriate for the discipline of psychology than for sociology. He gives descriptions of people coping with the low self-esteem and misery that come from doing mindlessly boring and routine jobs. The symptoms of reactive depression—daydreaming, withdrawal, and learned helplessness—experienced by many such workers reflect in many respects the symptoms associated with mental illness or schizophrenia (Archibald 1978, 178).

A study of women employed as word processors focusses on the damaging effects of hierarchically ordered and fragmented work roles. The study describes the experience of one woman who paused briefly in her work as the manager walked in. Asked what she was doing, she replied, "Oh, I'm just thinking for a minute." "Well get back to work," snapped the manager, "You're not paid to think. I am" (Gregory 1983, 99). Another woman described her working day as like being in a coma. Such mind-numbing jobs tend to carry over into restricted involvement in social and political activities outside of work.

Occupations such as word processing often reflect fragmented and hierarchical work roles that can result in alienation.

Limitations of Structuralist–Marxist Analysis

The Marxist focus on class structures challenges the simplicity of the functionalist assumption that internalized role expectations can adequately account for everyday behaviour. But it does not resolve the deeper problem of reifying society. Traditional political economy theory is even more dependent than functionalism on holistic explanations of structures being the active agents in

human behaviour. Archibald (1985, 61–62) makes this very clear when he insists that adequate causal explanations in sociology must be at the level of macrostructures because individuals do not act as "free agents." He argues that Marx himself referred to individuals merely as dependants or accessories of their collectivities or class position, and even as "herd animals." Individuals generally do not think or act differently from other members of their class. The few who do, suggests Archibald, are by definition anomalies and are largely irrelevant to our understanding of broader social processes and social change. Hence, he argues strongly for the principle of **methodological holism** rather than **methodological individualism**. The principle of methodological holism asserts that social experiences need to be explained in terms of forces that operate at the level of the social system as a whole. They cannot be adequately explained simply in terms of **psychologism**, or the individual psychology of the participants.

It is important to note that we are painting this picture with a broad brush. Not all theorists who identify themselves with the Marxist tradition feel comfortable with this conclusion. The Marxist historian E.P. Thompson (1963), in particular, has argued that macrostructures such as the system of economic production set the context in which people experience their lives. But reference to such structures is not sufficient to explain the formation of classes. For Thompson, classes are actively produced by working people through the processes of subjective experience, conflict, and struggle, which bring them into active relations with others. His own historical research seeks to understand, through the study of ongoing relations between people, how classes arose. More traditional Marxist critics, however, accuse Thompson of reducing objective structural conditions and economic forces to the level of psychologism, attempting to explain them in terms of subjective personal experiences and individual choices and attitudes (Wood 1982, 64). Thompson denies this, arguing that he sees the patterns of relations between people, which arise in their struggle for shares of material goods, as genuinely social forces, albeit at the microsociological level.

The central problem with the critique of Thompson's analysis as psychologism is that it runs the same risk of reifying society that we encounter with respect to functionalism. People appear as puppets while inanimate structures appear as the agents pulling the strings. Wood (1982, 65) points out the irony that critics of Thompson, who accuse him of trying to reduce history to the level of personal experiences and choices, end up talking about macrostructures as if they were people. The *working class* does things. *It* has interests. *It* sometimes fails to understand what *its* true interests are. Notions of **subjectivism** and **voluntarism** seem to have simply shifted upwards to the aggregate level of the working class, as if "it" were some living entity with subjective feelings and capable of voluntary choices.

In summary, traditional Marxist theory focusses on class relations rather than typical role expectations to explain the micro-experiences of everyday life. But it shares with functionalism the common assumption that critical explanatory mechanisms cannot be found at the level of mundane interactions. Such mechanisms have to be sought in the broader macrostructures of the social system as a whole. It is this fundamental assumption that is challenged by interpretive theory.

Microsociology from the Interpretive Perspective

Interpretive theory shifts the focus of explanation from macrostructures to micro-interactions. This approach developed primarily out of dissatisfaction with functionalism, particularly with the image of people as programmed puppets obedient to predetermined role expectations.

Critics of functionalism suggest that people normally operate with very little conscious awareness of their roles. They tend to take a great deal for granted, performing their routines without having to call to mind at each point what norms they should be following. Sometimes people are aware of the rules, and they attempt to conform to them but, at the same time, they try to indicate their lack of commitment to, perhaps even their disdain for, the role they are playing. This is what Erving Goffman (1961b) calls **role distancing**. Whether committed or cynical, individuals on many occasions improvise their performances, attempting to cope with uncertainty about what is going on, with disagreements about what should be happening, and with competing expectations of their various role partners.

It is too simplistic to try to account for smooth interaction in terms of learned role expectations. A great deal of work—improvising, joking, interpreting, second guessing, and manipulating—must go on for any particular performance to be carried off. What we need to study in any given situation, therefore, is precisely how people collectively accomplish the work of creating and sustaining a particular definition of the situation, so that they perceive each other to be playing a specific role rather than some other possible one.

Emerson's research (1970) on gynaecological examinations illustrates in detail the work that goes into maintaining doctor-patient relations. In Parsons' account, described above, the rules seem non-problematic: the doctor should be emotionally detached, altruistic, and committed to viewing illness in an objective way. Emerson, however, asks how such abstract rules are actually practised. She argues that maintenance of the definition of the situation of a gynaecological examination requires much effort and skill on the part of the doctor and nurse to guide the patient through this precarious scene. In theory, doctors should be able to conduct gynaecological check-ups in the same matter-of-fact manner that they would carry out an examination of the ear. But in the actual microsituation, this is not possible.

Emerson argues that the situation involves several role definitions simultaneously, and they each have to be managed if the encounter is to work. From a purely medical perspective, the woman is merely a gynaecological specimen. But she is also a woman who is striving to retain her personal dignity while having her sexual parts penetrated by metal instruments. If her emotional stress is not attended to, she may become so physically tense that it will be impossible to conduct the examination without causing considerable pain. If pain is added to humiliation, the "specimen" may get up and leave the office.

The woman cannot be treated merely as a specimen. But the sexual aspects of the encounter cannot have prominence either, for this would also jeopardize the exam. It is the task of the doctor, with the active assistance of the nurse, to balance the various interacting roles. These people have to try to reassure the woman that her personhood and her sexuality are being respected and that her embarrassment is quite normal. She must be reassured that, while she is not regarded as a specimen, she is being treated as one in the sense that she is being examined and not sexually violated. These different levels of meaning are active at the same time, and the balance between treating the woman as a medical specimen and as a person is not struck once and for all. Rather, "it is created anew at every moment." It can, and sometimes does, go wrong. In 1988, fourteen women complained to the Nova Scotia Medical Board that a particular gynaecologist had handled them so roughly, and had made sufficiently inappropriate comments, that they had come to feel they were being sexually assaulted rather than examined. The review board's response to the complaints was that there was a communication problem between the doctor and the women (CBC Radio, "Maritime Magazine," 18 Sept. 1988).

Seen from the interpretive perspective, functionalists make the mistake of reifying society when they fail to link their macroscopic concepts of functioning systems to the detailed examination of mundane interaction. They treat social rules as if they existed as factual entities outside of human activity. Interpretive theorists stress that norms do not exist in isolation, to be unambiguously applied when the proper situation presents itself. Instead, norms are produced and reproduced through actual behaviour in particular settings. We are constantly engaged in processes of interpretation, defining and redefining the situations in which we find ourselves. We must constantly ask ourselves questions. Who am I to them? What are we doing together? In effect, we are actively engaged in the construction of reality.

Ethnomethodology

Interpretive perspectives in general explore how the variety of expectations concerning social behaviour are actively negotiated by participants. Ethnomethodology pushes the questioning still further. How does the notion of *role* itself arise? How do participants come to decide collectively that it is this role and not some other possible role that is being played at this particular time? How is it that sociologists as outside observers come to decide that a specific role is or ought to be going on at a particular moment in time?

Ethnomethodology focusses on how members of a given society or community use their common-sense knowledge and their **background understandings** to make sense to themselves, and to one another, of their activities, the situation they are in, and the wider social structure in which any particular activity is embedded. The complexities of the gynaecological examination described above can only occur if all the people present share basic background knowledge about what such an examination is. It is normally taken for granted, for example, that the patient knows more or less what is going to happen and what is expected of her. A routine ten-minute examination would take all day if the doctor had to explain to each patient why she had to go into the examination room, get undressed, lie on the table, place her feet in the stirrups, be examined in a particular way, and so on.

The study of research methods in social science explores how social scientists use their practical research activities to arrive at their conclusions about what is going on. This process often involves asking the participants themselves what they think is happening and accepting the explanations offered. Ethnomethodology seeks to understand ordinary participants' methods for deciding what is happening.

The term *ethnomethodology* is derived from the Greek word *ethno*, referring to people or members of a society, and *methodology*, referring to the methods of reasoning that people use to make sense of the social world around them. Harold Garfinkel (1967, vii) offers the following definition:

> Ethnomethodological studies analyse everyday activities as members' methods for making those same activities visibly-rational-and-reportable-for-all-practical-purposes, i.e., "accountable" as organizations of commonplace everyday activities.

This definition is such a departure from traditional ways of thinking that it deserves further explanation. Garfinkel strings words together with hyphens because he wants to break our usual way of thinking. We are actually being asked to think backwards. The way most of us tend to think is that, first, some activity happens; secondly, we think about it and decide what is happening and

what kind of practical relevance it might have; then, thirdly, we form some account of it such that we can tell an observer "this is what is happening."

Garfinkel argues that the sequence actually works in reverse. It is the process of forming an account that actually produces for us the sense that something is happening. Otherwise nothing much would be happening, or at least nothing recognizable. This is a two-sided process. On the one hand we, as members of a society, have to be able to formulate accounts so that the vague blur of people milling around us becomes recognizable as persons involved in discrete activities. On the other hand, as members we have to know how to behave or to talk in ways that we can reasonably expect other members to recognize.

These are actually very complex processes, and we need a great deal of background understanding about our society or our community to accomplish them successfully. Consider what we need to know in order to carry on an intelligible conversation. Obviously, we need to be able to understand a common language, with a recognizable dialect, accent, and technical jargon. But much more than this is required for us to feel that our utterances are being understood the way we intend and that we also understand what others are trying to say to us.

Ethnomethodologists analyse conversations to discover how people convey such multiple messages as whether an utterance is to be taken literally or figuratively, whether it is a statement or a question that requires a response, whether what one is saying or hearing is comprehensible or requires some qualifiers or additional explanations, when one person's turn is up and another may legitimately take up the conversation, how a topic change or conversation end is signalled. These are only a few of the multitude of questions raised by theorists who focus on conversation analysis, a branch of ethnomethodology that explores the typical ways in which talk is structured by participants. Talk is perhaps one of the most basic building blocks of our intelligible social world. The more closely we look into how talk is collectively structured and managed, the more we come to appreciate how complex it is.

Another deceptively simple example is that of a queue or service line-up. What are members' methods of producing a queue? How do people recognize or signal to each other that they are in a queue and are not just standing around? Perhaps people have simply been socialized to expect queues in certain places, and so they invoke common-sense understandings to recognize them. The notion of queue-forming is certainly more established in some cultures than others. Many a hapless British tourist in Canada has found this out after queuing expectantly to board a bus or train, only to be swept aside as the local people surge forward in a mass. However, even when the common-sense notion of queuing is shared, it is by no means obvious when and where queues do or do not exist. In crowded airports or shops, or in front of busy service counters, for example, people may be spread out sideways as well as in front of and behind each other. Yet this may constitute a queue in that members are collectively aware of the ordering, of who is in front of whom, even when they are arranged in a bunch.

Ethnomethodologists study exactly how we organize the details of what we are doing to create and sustain our collective understanding that this is the distinctive kind of social order we call a queue. This does not mean that people always follow the rules of queuing when there is a line-up. But it does mean that failure to conform, as when someone pushes to the front, is recognizable by the people involved as a violation, and hence as requiring some explanation or **accountability**. Once people have formed the notion that what is going on is queuing,

then just about any behaviour that seems consistent with this is likely to be considered accounted for. You assume, for example, that a man standing behind another in a line-up is himself queuing up. He might actually be lost, or spying on people, or even just standing around waiting to find out what other people are standing around for. But you are unlikely to question his motives, unless you are watching some kind of mystery thriller. However, any behaviour that does not conform to the behaviour of queuing immediately threatens our notion of what is going on, and so requires some account. We tend to search for or to demand some valid excuse that will confirm for us that, yes, this is a queue, but that person is not in it because of some particular reason. Once too many people seem not to be keeping in the proper order, our notion that this is a queue is likely to fall apart.

Ethnomethodologists focus on what they term **practical reasoning**, or the methods by which ordinary people, in their everyday affairs, mutually create and sustain their common-sense notions of what is going on. It is people's capacity to do this that makes it possible for sociologists to talk about the notion of **social structures**. It is pointless for sociologists to discuss roles and social structures as if their existence could be taken for granted before they have understood how ordinary people manage to create and sustain these notions.

In going about our everyday lives, we generally do not reflect upon how we manage to accomplish activities like having a conversation or forming a queue. We tend to adopt what ethnomethodologists refer to as the **natural attitude**. We simply take it for granted that everyone knows how to do such things, unless they are severely mentally handicapped or have suddenly arrived in our milieu from a culture so totally different that we cannot expect them to share even our simplest common-sense understandings. Yet these understandings are absolutely essential if we are to maintain any sense of a meaningful social world in which we can participate. Ethnomethodologists therefore insist that sociologists, in order to study how society works, must suspend this natural attitude and reflect on precisely the processes that ordinary people take for granted. Roles need to be studied, not as social facts that are treated as given, but rather as processes or ongoing accomplishments that emerge through our everyday, practical reasoning.

In summary, ethnomethodology inquires into the methods whereby we, as members of a society or community, organize our activities so that we, as well as sociologists, come to recognize the patterns that we think of as social structures. By suspending the natural attitude and thus viewing ordinary social activities such as talking or queuing as if they were "anthropologically strange" or problematic, we can begin to explore the many taken-for-granted practices and rules for practical reasoning through which our world becomes socially constructed. As we shall see, this kind of research strategy gives rise to a radically different conception of society and very different methods of studying it. Many of the concepts and the terms used in such research appear strange when first encountered. The reason is that we are being forced to think about processes that we never normally reflect upon, processes that seem so mundane we are scarcely aware they exist.

The best way to get a feeling for this research is to get involved in it. In this chapter we review several ethnomethodological studies of how people accomplish everyday activities and what practical reasoning processes they use. These studies should help you to explore how your own everyday activities are accomplished.

Harold Garfinkel is the recognized founder and still a leading proponent of ethnomethodology as an approach to doing sociology. He completed his doctoral studies

at Harvard University under leading structural functionalist Talcott Parsons. But Garfinkel became increasingly disillusioned with the functionalist approach. As we saw earlier in this chapter, functionalism seeks to explain social order from the top down in terms of a pre-existing common culture that defines our norms and social structures. Individuals learn this normative order through socialization and feel committed or pressured to conform to it. Garfinkel advocates a bottom-up approach that studies how people, in their practical everyday interactions, create or build up the patterns that we subsequently come to recognize as distinctive social structures and social activities. A classical statement of the principles of Garfinkel's approach, and his early experiments designed to explore mundane reasoning, are contained in his text *Studies in Ethnomethodology* (1967).

Background Understandings and Indexicality

Garfinkel developed his now famous technique of breaching experiments to explore how people create social order in everyday interaction. The ways in which order is produced are exposed by finding out what would disrupt given social scenes. Experimenters begin with the stable features of the scene and ask what can be done to make trouble. Garfinkel (1963, 187) suggests that

> the operations that one would have to perform in order to produce and sustain anomic features of perceived environments and disorganized interaction should tell us something about how social structures are ordinarily and routinely being maintained.

One procedure for disrupting and thus exposing the practical reasoning that underlies social order is to demand that the meaning of common-sense remarks be explained. In the two examples given below (from Garfinkel 1967, 42–43), (S) refers to the subject trying to have a normal conversation; (E) refers to the experimenter or ethnomethodologist requesting that the subject explain his or her commonplace remarks.

(S) Hi Ray. How is your girl friend feeling?
(E) What do you mean, "How is she feeling?" Do you mean physical or mental?
(S) I mean how is she feeling? What's the matter with you? (He looked peeved.)
(E) Nothing. Just explain a little clearer what do you mean?
(S) Skip it. How are your Med School applications coming?
(E) What do you mean, "How are they?"
(S) You know what I mean.
(E) I really don't.
(S) What's the matter with you? Are you sick?
. . .

On Friday night my husband and I were watching television. My husband remarked that he was tired. I asked, "How are you tired? Physically, mentally, or just bored?"
(S) I don't know, I guess physically mainly.
(E) You mean that your muscles ache or your bones?
(S) I guess so. Don't be so technical.
(After more watching.)
(S) All these old movies have the same kind of old iron bedstead in them.
(E) What do you mean? Do you mean all old movies, or some of them, or just the ones you have seen?
(S) What's the matter with you? You know what I mean.
(E) I wish you would be more specific.
(S) You know what I mean! Drop dead!

In both cases the subjects clearly expected that the experimenters would rely upon common background understandings to make sense of their utterances. Garfinkel suggests that such expectations are essential features of all spoken interaction. When the experimenters did not use their background understandings, the subjects almost immediately expressed anger and indignation. As Garfinkel expresses it, people feel they are morally entitled to have their talk treated as intelligible, and they react with swift and powerful sanctions when it is not.

Another set of experiments explores the **indexical** or context-dependent character of conversations. When we talk, we invariably include only brief references to, or indications of, the context and subject matter. We expect other participants to fill in the rest—the background understandings that make talk possible. Garfinkel illustrated this by asking his students to take a scrap of a conversation in which they had participated and note in the left-hand column what had actually been said and in the right-hand column what they and their partners understood they were talking about. One such analysis is given in figure 4-1.

It is quickly apparent from the fragment of conversation in figure 4-1 that there were many matters that the partners understood but did not mention. These were the

BLONDIE

Reprinted by permission of King Features Syndicate, Inc.

Figure 4-1 The Indexical Nature of Conversation

Husband:	Dana succeeded in putting a penny in a parking meter today without being picked up.	This afternoon as I was bringing Dana, our four-year-old son, home from the nursery school, he succeeded in reaching high enough to put a penny in a parking meter when we parked in a meter parking zone, whereas before he always had to be picked up to reach that high.
Wife:	Did you take him to the record store?	Since he put a penny in a meter that means that you stopped while he was with you. I know that you stopped at the record store either on the way to get him or on the way back. Was it on the way back, so that he was with you or did you stop there on the way to get him and somewhere else on the way back?
Husband:	No, to the shoe repair shop.	No, I stoped at the record store on the way to get him and stopped at the shoe repair shop on the way home when he was with me.
Wife:	What for?	I know of one reason why you might have stopped at the shoe repair shop. Why did you in fact?
Husband:	I got some new shoe laces for my shoes.	As you will remember I broke a shoe lace on one of my brown oxfords the other day so I stopped to get some new laces.
Wife:	Your loafers need new heels badly.	Something else you could have gotten that I was thinking of. You could have taken in your black loafers which need heels badly. You'd better get them taken care of pretty soon.

Source: Garfinkel (1967).

background understandings that both partners required in order to carry on a meaningful exchange. For example, the statement, "Dana succeeded in putting a penny in the parking meter," would hardly be intelligible without the background knowledge that Dana was a young child. Otherwise, we might surmise that Dana was a severely handicapped adult. Similarly, the reference to Dana being "picked up" only makes sense when we have the background understanding that Dana, as a young child, is too short to reach most parking meter slots. In another context, the reference to being picked up might have a totally different meaning, like getting into a vehicle that has stopped, going out on a date, or accepting an offer to go off somewhere, possibly for a sexual encounter.

Conversations are always indexical; their sense is always context-dependent. Actions and words can only briefly refer to the background understandings that participants in the conversation must invoke in order to understand what is being said. If every participant in every conversation insisted on having all elements of that conversation explicated, talk would be impossible.

The mix of background understandings required to carry on conversations is the stuff of which many cartoons and jokes are made. What strikes us as funny is the invoking of meanings and contexts other than the one that we know should be applied. One example is the image of two martians standing at a stop sign, wondering how long they have to wait before it says "go." The cartoon reminds us that, in order to be effective, the deceptively simple device of a stop sign requires complex background understandings from people. Where does one stop when one sees a stop sign? At the point where the sign stands? On the road next to it? On the side of the road directly in front of it? Does one stop indefinitely? If not, when does one start again? Does the sign apply only to cars, or to pedestrians and cyclists as well? Does the sign mean the equivalent of "arrêt" in Quebec or does it stand only as a symbol of Anglophone imperialism that can be ignored by all Francophones? Clearly if a sign had to explicate all possible background understandings, if would be useless. Signs, by definition, stand as indicators for background knowledge that all competent members of a community are expected to have.

HERMAN

We can't stand here all day.
It must have jammed.

Herman copyright 1983 Universal Press Syndicate. Reprinted with permission. All rights reserved.

The recognition that ordinary interaction is indexical, its meaning dependent upon context and upon background understandings supplied by participants, means that no social event can ever be totally unambiguous. The full meaning of any interaction cannot be stated in an objective, factual account, devoid of subjective interpretation. It does not follow, however, that all meaning is therefore subjective, and we can interpret interaction any way we wish. On the contrary, ethnomethodology starts with the observation that most social actions and communications have an orderly character. Members of a community are routinely competent at selecting precisely those aspects of the relevant context required to make sense of the interaction. In the jargon of ethnomethodology, it is **members' competences** that make order possible. If someone says to you, "Mary is out to lunch," you generally know which Mary this refers to, and whether the intended meaning is that she has gone elsewhere to eat lunch or she is showing signs of mental incompetence. You may both grin at the statement to show that you know the alternative meanings, but you nonetheless know, and know in common, what the intended meaning is. The ability to invoke correct background understandings is part of what is involved in being recognized as part of a group. In this sense, meaning is not subjective, but intersubjective, or dependent upon and defined by shared background knowledge.

Indexicality has important implications for research methods in sociology, especially for survey research in which questionnaires are commonly used. Researchers gamble when they assume that respondents all invoke the same context and the same background understandings in answering questions as the researchers intended. Respondents take a similar gamble when they assume the researchers will invoke the appropriate background understanding to know what they meant by their answers. We saw an example of this in chapter 3 when a white English woman refused to answer questions about her relations with black and Asian immigrants living nearby. She feared that, in interpreting her remarks, researchers would invoke the background understanding of racial prejudice rather than the specific context, which she herself experienced, of sexual taunts and propositions from large groups of single men in adjacent houses.

A further implication of indexicality is that researchers who rely on observations to collect their data must first learn a great deal of insider knowledge before they can accurately interpret the meanings of actions. Observed interaction between insiders in an unfamiliar occupational setting, for example, may come across as largely incomprehensible **shoptalk** when one does not have the necessary background knowledge to interpret it correctly. More seriously, researchers in unfamiliar contexts may be routinely guilty of imposing their own irrelevant or incorrect background understandings, and thus producing false accounts of what happened. We saw examples of this in chapter 3 when anthropologists with different theoretical backgrounds were able to produce markedly different accounts of life in ostensibly the same village setting.

The Documentary Method of Interpretation

The search for patterns in the vague flux of everyday interaction is a critical component of members' methods of making sense of what is going on around them. Garfinkel refers to this process of imposing patterns as the **documentary method of interpretation**. In our practical everyday reasoning, Garfinkel suggests, we assume that there is some underlying pattern. Hence we habitually search for such a pattern in any new situation. We know that activities and conversations are indexical. We know that the surface appearance cannot be more than a sign of broader background knowledge to which it refers and which we are expected to know and to use in order to make sense of what we are experiencing. In our ordinary reasoning, therefore, we treat actual

appearances not as all there is to know, but as signalling some presupposed underlying pattern. The surface appearance of the action provides clues to the underlying pattern. Once this pattern is deduced, at least tentatively, it provides clues to the interpretation of other details of the surface appearance. These details appear as instances of the supposed pattern. This reasoning process is thus circular, continually moving between surface appearances and hypothesized underlying pattern. Each becomes defined and redefined in terms of the other. In the jargon of ethnomethodology, the relation between appearances and underlying pattern is *reflexive*, or mutually determining.

Figure 4-2 gives a simple example of this reflexive process. When we notice such an element in a book, we almost automatically assume that it is not some random doodling that is on the page by accident. We assume it is a picture, and a picture of something. One possibility is that the pattern underlying the specific lines of the drawing might be a duck. With this in mind, we interpret the protuberances on the left as the bill and the small indentation on the right of the figure as irrelevant. But if we adopt the idea that

Figure 4-2 The Reflexive Nature of Perception

Source: Adapted from Heritage (1984, 87).

the pattern is a rabbit, then the same features are interpreted differently. The features on the left are ears, and the small indentation on the right now has relevance as the rabbit's mouth. The same surface appearances can thus be seen as instances of totally different features, once a new underlying pattern comes to mind (Heritage 1984, 86–87). If you stare at the pattern long enough, you may be able to come up with other interpretations that would assign yet other meanings to the surface appearances. There is also the possibility that the lines are nothing but random doodling and have no meaning at all, but this interpretation is likely to be the least satisfying. Almost any pattern tends to be more believable than no pattern at all.

A counselling experiment, briefly mentioned in chapter 2, was designed by Garfinkel to illustrate how tenaciously people strive to find underlying patterns and also how they utilize these patterns to reinterpret surface features of their experience. In the experiment, psychiatry students were told that they were trying out a new technique in personal counselling in which the counsellor would give a yes or no answer to any question asked but would not otherwise elaborate. Students were asked to comment on the advice they received. What the students did not know was that the "answers" were simply random. What interested Garfinkel was the practical reasoning that students used to make sense of these utterances and how long it would take them to realize that they were in fact random, or literally senseless. The beginning of one of these interchanges is given below (Garfinkel 1967, 80–81).

> SUBJECT: Ok, this is the situation that I am presented with. I happen to be of the Jewish faith and I have been dating a Gentile girl now for about two months. My dad is not directly opposed to this situation, but I feel at the same time that he is not exactly pleased with it. Mother feels that as long as Dad is not directly opposed to this situation that I should go ahead and continue dating until he makes some direct statement to the contrary. My reason for feeling why he is not too pleased with this is that he has never said don't date her, but at the same time he will come up with digs and sayings that make me feel very ill at ease about dating the girl. My question is, do you feel under the present circumstances that I should continue or stop dating this girl? Let me put that in a positive way. Do you feel that I should continue dating this girl?
>
> EXPERIMENTER: My answer is no.
>
> SUBJECT: No. Well, that is kind of interesting. I kinda feel that there is really no great animosity between Dad and I but, well, perhaps he feels that greater dislike will grow out of this. I suppose or maybe it is easier for an outsider to see certain things that I am blind to at this moment.
> I would like to ask my second question now.
>
> EXPERIMENTER: Okay.
>
> SUBJECT: Do you feel that I should have a further discussion with Dad about this situation or not? Should I have further discussion with Dad over this subject about dating the Gentile girl?
>
> EXPERIMENTER: My answer is yes.
>
> SUBJECT: Well I feel that is reasonable but I really don't know what to say to him. I mean he seems to be not really too understanding. In other words he seems to be afraid really to discuss the situation. I mean at least it appears that way to me so far. But I guess if it is worthwhile to me, if I really want to continue to date her that I will go on and have this discussion with Dad. I really don't know what to say because I mean I am dating her. I am not in love with her or anything but I really never know what is going to come out. I guess we should have a discussion based on what the future possibilities might be and how he would feel about that. He may not be too strongly opposed now because we are only dating, but perhaps he sees future complications that he would really like to get off his chest at the moment. I am ready for my third question now.

If after having my conversation with Dad and he says to continue dating her, but at the same time gives me an impression that he is really not, he really does not want me to date her, but he is only doing it because he wants to be a good Dad, should under these conditions, should I still date the girl?

EXPERIMENTER: My answer is yes.

SUBJECT: Well I am actually surprised at the answer. I expected a no answer on that. Perhaps this is because you are not quite aware of my dad and his reactions and he seems to be the type of person that is sensitive and therefore he is very careful in the way that he will handle things. Even though he might have said go ahead and date her I perhaps would feel guilty in knowing that he really did not want me to continue to date her. Though I don't know that it would actually help the situation any. So, well, perhaps we will look into this further and that is another question.

In practice, all the students managed to get through the nonsensical exchange with the counsellor, to make sense of it, and to reinterpret current and previous answers to give them the appearance of consistent advice even when they were blatantly contradictory. The students typically heard the random utterances as answers that were motivated by their questions. One of the basic principles of any normal conversation, Garfinkel suggests, is that utterances immediately following any question will be an answer to that question. Students applied this practical reasoning by construing whatever followed each of their questions as prompted by the question and as an answer to it.

A second principles of any normal conversation is that people expect that what they say will be treated as meaningful and that other participants will draw upon their background understandings to make sense of what has been said. Remember the earlier experiments in which people rapidly became indignant when the experimenter asked that

common-sense remarks be explained. In the counsellor experiment, student went to great lengths to treat the random utterances as meaningful and were almost always successful, to the degree that they claimed they could see "what the adviser had in mind." Students drew very heavily upon background understandings to infer what the counsellor might have meant. They displayed the basic expectation of normal conversation: that statements are indexical or context-dependent and that the context is inferred but not explicated in the statements. Students went back through the conversation as the context that would make sense of the particular answer received.

Garfinkel further points out how students displayed the retrospective-prospective character of normal conversations. We have already seen that normal conversation becomes impossible if people demand that every statement be fully explicated before the talk continues. In normal conversation we anticipate that a future statement will help to clarify what has previously been said. Hence, rather than stopping to ask for an explanation, we continue to talk on the basis of our working interpretation of what the conversation is about, and we use the next statement to test or to revise our interpretation. Students in the counsellor experiment did this continuously. They thought back over the preceding part of the conversation to come up with working interpretations of what the counsellor might have meant and then formulated their next question on the basis of this. The following yes or no was immediately incorporated in a retroactive reshuffling of plausible interpretations of the conversation to be consistent with the new response. This modified interpretation then set the stage for the next question.

In managing their one-sided conversation with the counsellor, students displayed their competence in applying the documentary method of interpretation, a further basic principle of all normal conversation. They assumed throughout that any utterance by the counsellor signalled an underlying pattern. They searched for the pattern that would be consistent with the surface appearance of what the counsellor had said, referred to the pattern to reinterpret details of the exchange, used it to formulate new questions, revised their working assumptions concerning the underlying pattern as soon as they had the new answer, performed all necessary reinterpretation of details, and carried on.

When Garfinkel spells out for us everything these students had to do in order to carry on a ten-minute conversation, the complexity is staggering. Even the students were amazed when they learned how much and how actively they had contributed to making sense out of the random utterances they had heard. Yet this is what we, as competent members of society, accomplish everyday in ordinary conversations.

Practical Reasoning and the Social Construction of Order

Ethnomethodological research explores how the documentary method of interpretation underlies all sense of order in social life. Order does not exist. It is accomplished by the same kind of practical reasoning processes that the students used to make sense of nonsensical advice. The undefined flux of experience becomes recognizable as instances of underlying patterns and hence is made accountable as certain kinds of events. Actions that appear to us as normal are those that can readily be interpreted as instances of typical underlying patterns. Behaviour that is out of order is problematic until it comes to be reinterpreted as instances of some alternative pattern.

One interpretive scheme that may be invoked to account for a series of actions that otherwise appear as out of order is the act of labelling a particular person as deviant.

Once someone is so labelled, the risk is that, by the same documentary reasoning processes, all other details of that person's life tend to become reinterpreted as instances of the new underlying pattern of deviance. Actions previously accounted for as within the normal range, or as mild aberrations that might result from stress or from too much alcohol, come to be seen as the result of the person's essentially deviant character. Past actions are reinterpreted retrospectively to fit the new pattern of accounting, so as to confirm that this person was deviant all along. At the same time, these accounts have a prospective character in that they shape how the person's future actions will be interpreted. The deviant label provides such an all-encompassing accounting scheme that it is very difficult to break.

Rosenhan (1973) reported the experience of some researchers who faked hallucinations to gain admission to the a mental hospital. It took a significant length of time for their "normality" to be recognized. They behaved normally from the time of their admission to the hospital onwards, but everyone around them, including patients, nurses, and doctors, interpreted whatever they did as what deviants do. Their protestations that they were normal, and that they had merely faked hallucinations to get into the hospital, were not believed. The fact that they took notes was not seen as a research activity but as a symptom of a deviant mental state. The researchers were eventually discharged as schizophrenics in remission rather than as people who were "normal all along."

Other organizational settings concerned with defining and processing deviants rely on similar practical reasoning, in which the underlying pattern or notion of a typical deviant is used to interpret observed details. One study shows how, under pressure of overcrowded courts, public defenders use common-sense stereotypes about who is or is not a "normal" criminal to decide who should be provided with a certain type of defence or who should be offered plea bargaining (Sudnow 1965). Another study describes the on-the-spot interpretive practices used by police officers in skid-row districts to decide who are the trouble makers (Bittner 1967). An extensive study of juvenile justice shows how police draw on their own stereotypes about serious criminals to label some boys as hard-core criminals and others as merely acting out family problems. Boys from lower-class homes, associated with the stereotype of a typical criminal, were likely to be categorized as criminals for relatively minor activities, while boys from more "respectable" social backgrounds were more likely to be classed as having family problems, even when they had committed objectively more harmful deviant acts (Cicourel 1968).

The underlying reasoning processes examined in all of these studies are similar. Hospital personnel, defence lawyers, and police officers all drew on their sense of an underlying pattern of typical deviant behaviour in order to interpret details of surface appearances. Behaviour that might otherwise have passed as within the normal range, or as irrelevant features, became reinterpreted as instances of the underlying "deviant" pattern. In every case, such labelling had critical consequences for the people concerned because the labellers held positions of authority. This meant that their interpretations of surface appearances became translated into the facts of the matter for the practical purposes of administering hospitals and courts.

The sense-making practices of officials and members of organizations are basic elements in the accomplishment of a factual reality on which orderly, everyday administration depends. Zimmerman (1974) conducted a pioneering study of caseworkers in a public assistance agency to explore how they decided matters of fact about applicants for assistance. Caseworkers were required to be sceptical of applicants' stories concerning eligibility and to treat such stories as merely claims that had to be evaluated against relevant documentary evidence. Caseworkers were under pressure to decide such matters quickly since they had heavy caseloads and were expected to dispose of each case within a thirty-day period.

What interested Zimmerman was how certain kinds of records or pieces of paper seemed to be accepted immediately as factual, without further investigation, while other pieces of paper were rejected. When one caseworker recounted an incident where an applicant for old age assistance had told the caseworker that she had lost her citizenship papers stating her age but had copied her birthdate on a piece of paper for the use of the agency, all the caseworkers laughed. Yet no caseworkers laughed when they were handed citizenship papers, birth certificates, bank statements, medical records, and the like, as proof of claims. For practical purposes, any paper that was signed by someone with an official position, and that bore the letterhead of an organization, was treated as an objective, impersonal, and unquestionable statement of fact, while anything stated by a person was merely a claim. Caseworkers refused even to consider the possibility that official papers might themselves be open to doubt or in need of any investigation. To do so would be to risk calling their entire view of an ordered world into question.

Zimmerman points out that the papers that the caseworkers treated as factual were put together by the same kind of reasoning that they themselves used to produce documents attesting that a particular applicant was eligible for assistance. Caseworkers accomplished their own social construction of reality by using selected bits of previously constructed reality.

Much of the surface appearance of social reality comes to us not through direct experience but through documents. These documents, which may be written or on tape or film, are produced by professionals and people in positions of authority within organizations. Ethnomethodological research explores how the manner in which such documents are constructed influences the practical reasoning processes of their audiences.

A study of the news media (Jalbert 1984) draws attention to the morally loaded categories in which various parties to a conflict are presented and particularly to the subtle use of grammatical devices that create the underlying patterns that audiences use in interpreting details of the events. For example, the actions of one party to a conflict may be expressed in the active grammatical voice, while the actions of the other party are expressed in the passive voice. The effect is to convey the impression that responsibility for the conflict rests with the former.

The sense that a particular news report is impartial, and therefore a credible factual account, is similarly created by subtle structuring devices. For example, a typical underlying notion is that there are always at least two parties to a conflict. Reporters may incorporate quotations from two parties to a debate and thus trigger the interpretive response that they have covered the issue. The possibility that there may be many more sides to the issue, or that the two parties quoted may be merely variants of the same side, while the opposing side is unrepresented, disappears from view (Tuchman 1972). The problem is that we, as consumers of the news, see only the final report. We generally know nothing about the various practices, unquestioned assumptions, stereotypes, organizational pressures, and so forth, that influenced the story's production (Smith 1974b).

Margrit Eichler (1988b, 87–88) draws attention to the use of grammatical devices in typical anthropological descriptions of sex roles and social sanctions in primitive societies. Commonly, writers use the passive voice when discussing the behaviour of women. Consider the following example (Ford 1970, 102):

> Most of the restrictions imposed by primitive societies upon a woman's freedom stem from one or another aspect of her reproductive role. Restrictions connected with pregnancy have been noted, as well as those imposed during the period after childbirth and during lactation. Among many people, limitations are placed upon the activities of women during their menstrual periods as well. Societies vary markedly, however, in the degree to which they curtail a menstruating woman's participation in social life. In a few societies, the only restriction placed upon her activities is that she may not engage in sexual intercourse. In a few other societies, menstruation involves strict seclusion and isolation. The majority of primitive peoples surround the woman with specific restrictions, leaving her free to move about with certain exceptions. Always she is forbidden sexual intercourse, frequently she may not go into the gardens, and may not participate in religious ceremonies.

Eichler argues that the passive voice is far from inconsequential in our understanding of what is really going on. The above passage assumes that women are the passive recipients or victims of the restrictions placed on them by society. They are not active agents deciding their own behaviour. The unstated implications are that men order them to behave in these ways and that women comply. Our vision of what is going on changes radically when Eichler (1980, 25–26) rewrites the same passage in an active voice:

> Most of the female taboos in primitive societies are directly related to one or another aspect of woman's reproductive role. Pregnancy taboos have been noted as well as post-partum taboos and taboos concerning lactation. Among many peoples, women refrain from certain activities dur-

ing their menstrual periods as well. Societies vary markedly, however, in the degree to which a woman refuses to participate in social life during menstruation. In a few societies, the only activity she refuses to engage in is sexual intercourse. In a few other societies, menstruation may lead women to completely separate themselves, both physically and socially, from men. In the majority of primitive peoples, women engage only in specific withdrawals and maintain their usual social relations in all other cases. Always, however, the woman refuses to engage in sexual intercourse; frequently, she will not enter the gardens or refuses to cook for men. Her power may be such that, if she touches the man's hunting or fishing gear, calamity may befall him. She will only do so, therefore, if she wishes him ill. Finally, she may refuse to participate in certain religious ceremonies.

This passage conveys the same "facts" but totally different information about the power relations and decision-making processes in the society and the relative position of women. Women are portrayed as active agents in control of their own behaviour.

Eichler (1980, 23–24) rewrites the passage a third time using neutral or passive terminology throughout. In this version we are given no indication of who is acting and who is being acted upon:

Most of the taboos concerning women in primitive societies are related to one or another aspect of woman's reproductive role. Pregnancy taboos have been noted as well as post-partum taboos and taboos concerning lactation. Among many peoples there are menstrual taboos as well. Societies vary markedly, however, in the type of menstrual taboos that are prevalent. In a few societies, the only female taboo is one on sexual intercourse. In a few other societies, menstruation involves strict seclusion and isolation. The majority of primitive peoples have specific taboos for women, leaving them free to move about with certain exceptions. Always, there is a sexual intercourse taboo; frequently, there is a gar-

dening taboo, a cooking taboo or a taboo against touching the male's hunting and fishing gear, and a taboo on participation in religious ceremonies.

This third version conveys the impression of neutrality or objectivity in reporting, but it is not necessarily any more factually correct than the other two versions. If one party is actively imposing its will on others, then reports that convey the information in neutral terms distort what is really going on.

The ideal, suggests Eichler, is that we should write about both sexes in the active voice, to acknowledge that both women and men are subjects in the social world and not passive objects or victims of it. This implies much more than sensitivity to the niceties of the generic *he* versus *he/she*. It requires new forms of data collection. To present the victim's perspective in the active voice, we would need to know much more about what the world looks like from the victim's standpoint, and the "resistance, helplessness, fear, rage, or mute acceptance" of the situation that this person may feel (Eichler 1988, 89).

The Social Construction of Gender

The state of being either male or female is generally taken for granted as a biological fact, although we recognize that the associated attributes of masculinity and femininity may, in varying degrees, be socially constructed. The term *gender* is widely used in social science writing to refer to the socially constructed component of male and female identity, and we will generally use this convention here. Eichler (1980, 12–13), however, cautions against this use of *gender* as distinct from *sex* because it may too readily convey the impression that there are basic biological sex differences that may still be taken for granted. Research in ethnomethodology has called even the notion of a fixed biologically based sex difference into question.

Garfinkel's (1967, chap. 5) pioneering work in this field is based on extensive interviews with a **transsexual** who was born a boy but chose to be a girl. Garfinkel met her when she was nineteen years old and had entered hospital for a sex-change operation. He refers to her as Agnes. Agnes was born and raised a boy and had the normal sexual characteristics of a boy until puberty. At this point she developed the secondary sexual characteristics of a female: female body shape, ample breasts, and an absence of facial hair. Agnes insisted that she had been a girl all along, and that her male genitalia were simply the result of some bio-medical abnormality. She successfully persuaded surgeons to amputate them and to surgically construct a vagina. Some years later, Agnes confided to Garfinkel that she had developed a female body shape at puberty by taking estrogen, which she had obtained by forging her mother's prescription. At the time when he carried out his initial interviews with Agnes, he did not know this.

What interested Garfinkel was how Agnes was accepted by her friends, including her boyfriend, as female, despite her abnormal physical state and her early upbringing as a boy. What he learned from Agnes was how she had deliberately controlled all the surface appearances of her interactions with others to be consistent with the underlying interpretive pattern of a typical female. In a sense, Agnes performed a lifelong breaching experiment, in which she constantly negated what would otherwise be the taken-for-granted assumption that she was a male. In learning how she had done this, Garfinkel could explore how our typical understanding of what it is to be an adolescent female in North American society is socially constructed.

A major problem for Agnes as a young adult was her childhood. She was well aware that boys and girls are typically raised in very different ways in North American society. They are dressed differently, given different toys, encouraged to get involved in very different activities, and expected to learn different skills. Upbringing plays a major role in explaining why adolescent boys and girls think and talk about different things. In order to be accepted by her teenage friends as having been a typical female all along, Agnes had to cover up most of her childhood and invent an appropriate biography. Garfinkel (1967, 148) quotes Agnes as saying:

> "Can you imaging all the blank years I have to fill in? Sixteen or seventeen years of my life that I have to make up for. I have to be careful of the things that I say, just natural things that could slip out. . . . I just never say anything at all about my past that in any way would make a person ask what my past life was like. I say general things. I don't say anything that could be misconstrued." Agnes said that with men she was able to pass as an interesting conversationalist by encouraging her male partners to talk about themselves. Women partners, she said, explained the general and indefinite character of her biographical remarks, which she delivered in a friendly manner, by a combination of her niceness and modesty. "They probably figure that I just don't like to talk about myself."

In her everyday behaviour as an adolescent female mixing with other students at college, Agnes had to monitor every aspect of her activities and her conversations. As Garfinkel expresses it, Agnes, along with other transsexuals, had to earn her right to live in her chosen sexual status, and she lived under the constant fear that disclosure would ruin this. She developed an acutely un-common-sense awareness of social relations and how they were structured to display sexual status as naturally male or female. These structured patterns of behaviour are part of the routinized, "seen but unnoticed" backgrounds of everyday affairs (Garfinkel 1967, 118). These patterns are so familiar to us and so unconsciously part of our everyday behaviour that most of us would find it very

In our society, boys and girls are often dressed differently, given different toys to play with, and encouraged to get involved in separate activities.

difficult to articulate in detail what it is that we notice as typically female or male behaviour. Yet people who choose to adopt a sexual identity different from the one with which they were born and brought up, need to develop an acute awareness of these patterns and how to conform to them.

Agnes was so anxious to pass as a normal female that she became painfully concerned with conforming to all the surface features consistent with being typically female. She felt she had to achieve convincingly feminine dress, make-up, and grooming. She had to manage appropriately feminine comportment—talking, sitting, and walking like a typical woman, and so on. Talking like a woman requires knowing a wide range of issues from the perspective of a typical woman rather than from that of a typical man. Agnes became a "secret apprentice," picking up this detailed knowledge of women's experience through conversations with roommates and other girlfriends, learning how to talk about boyfriends, dates,

clothes, and other topics typical of teenage girls. She dared not risk doing or saying anything that might trigger in an onlooker the thought that she was behaving like a boy, because any detailed questioning might disclose her secret transsexual identity.

Agnes carefully avoided any activities that might expose her anomalous genitalia, and at the same time she developed a set of excuses for not participating, which would sound justifiable or reasonable to others. She refused, on the grounds of modesty, to undress anywhere where she might be seen by others, and she refused, on the excuse of "not being in the mood," to go swimming if there were no private dressing rooms available. She told Garfinkel that she even avoided driving a car lest she have an accident where her secret might be discovered.

In summary, Agnes felt she was always on display in that she had to demonstrate in every detail of her surface appearance that she was as she appeared to be, naturally female. Most of us assume that other people will automatically recognize our appropriate sex. We do not expect to have to prove it or demonstrate it, and we would probably get angry very quickly if anyone challenged us or demanded such proof. In a sense, we have a moral right to have our appropriate sex identity recognized, just as we have a moral right to expect others to understand common-sense remarks in ordinary conversations. Transsexuals cannot automatically claim that right to be recognized; they have to actively earn their sex identity. In accomplishing this, they make visible all the details of everyday behaviour that create and sustain for us our identities as one sex or the other.

This recognition of how fully our sexual identity is socially constructed draws attention to the importance of Eichler's observation that the distinction sometimes drawn between gender and sex is difficult to sustain. In principle, gender refers to differences that are socially constructed while sex refers to differences that are biologically determined. In the story of Agnes it is impossible to draw such a line. In the lives of most of us, it may be much more difficult than we first imagine. Our notion that there are two distinct sexes with distinct behavioural characteristics may be sustained far more by practical reasoning from unexamined assumptions than from any biologically determined reality.

Eichler's response (1980, 75–77) to the issue of transsexuality is that, in behaving as they do, and particularly in going to the extreme of sex-change surgery, transsexuals like Agnes only reinforce the rigid sex-role stereotypes against which they rebel. Eichler argues that we are not destined immutably to behave as one sex or the other; there is no reason why anyone should feel compelled to conform to stereotypes of typical masculine or feminine behaviour. She argues, moreover, that the notion that there are typical masculine or feminine behavioural characteristics is largely a myth. The myth is perpetuated by social psychologists who construct scales purporting to measure masculine and feminine traits on the basis of asking people what their stereotypes are. The scales are then applied to people, and those whose behaviour does not fit the stereotype are analysed as deviants. All they deviate from is an artificial notion of masculinity and femininity that most people do not conform to in any case.

Garfinkel's study of transsexuals was carried out in the late 1950s in Los Angeles. It would be interesting to find out whether transsexuals still feel that they need to conform to the behaviour patterns that Agnes found so compelling, or whether the childhood experiences of male and female children are still sufficiently different that transsexuals would have to blank out their childhood as a member of one sex to pass as a member of the other.

Conversation Analysis

Conversation analysis is a branch of ethnomethodology that focusses on the detailed features of talk and their role in creating and sustaining our sense of social order. Conventional macrosociology tends to ignore talk altogether, or to treat it as a passive medium through which major social structural variables relate to one another. When researchers use questionnaires and interviews, they take for granted the mutual intelligibility of such written and verbal interaction. But, as we have seen in the discussion of indexicality, the achievement of mutual understanding is far from automatic.

Conversation analysis explores in minute detail how talk itself is structured. Typically this involves analysing tape recordings of conversations. Specialized transcripts are made, which are designed to capture hearable details of talk, such as intonation, pauses, the stretching of vowels, and the overlapping of turns, all of which may be significant for making the talk comprehensible. Video recordings are now used to study the non-verbal aspects of talk. The elements of talk are so complex that most researchers still prefer to work only with verbal transcripts, or even with telephone conversations where there is no visible component of interaction. People in everyday life organize their conversations in incredible detail. The use of video tape recordings makes possible repeated and detailed examination and reinterpretation of data while eliminating any risk of distortion arising from the limitations of respondents' memories (Heritage 1984, 238). Tape recordings also avoid the problem, which plagues conventional sociology, that data are coded into preset categories in ways unknown to the researcher.

Conversation analysis focusses on members' methods of producing recognizable forms of talk and understandable utterances. In other words, it analyses how people get their meaning across to others in conversations and how they continually recognize and repair the instances when the meaning has not been completely clear. Transcripts of conversations, interviews, court hearings, lessons, and the like, are analysed to discover the very general features of how talk is structured. Researchers look for the context-free features of these speech-exchange systems. These are features or structures that are common to all conversation, regardless of topic or situation and the age, sex, social class, or ethnicity of the participants. In a sense, these universal features can be viewed as the machinery through which people communicate verbally for all sorts of purposes.

One critical aspect of this machinery is the organization of turn-taking. Generally, in a conversation, one party talks at a time, and the transitions between speakers' turns usually occur with little or no gap or overlap. This is despite the fact that the order in which the participants speak and the length of the conversation as a whole are not preprogrammed. Even where there are violations of these features, such as when two people start to talk at the same time, systematic repair mechanisms come quickly into play to restore order.

This turn-taking machinery is worked out by the participants in the immediate ongoing setting of the talk. Such organization depends on the participants listening carefully to one another so as to figure out just the right moment to start speaking without interrupting. Despite the fact that the alternations of talk are improvised moment by moment, people are able to produce a recognizable order in their talk that can be detected by close listening and analysis (Sacks, Schegloff, and Jefferson 1974). Similar machinery of talk governs the familiar activities of opening up conversations and bringing them to a close. The interpretive practices and improvised manoeuvres involved give a structure to conversations that goes far beyond simply starting to speak or instantly shutting up.

A further common aspect of the machinery of talk is that utterances occur in pairs. Questions, for example, are expected to be followed immediately with answers, summonses are followed with acknowledgements, and greetings with return greetings. These are adjacency pairs; a first pair-part of one type is expected to be followed immediately by a second pair-part of the same type. Hence, the moment that one participant in a conversation says a first pair-part, by asking a question or offering a greeting, the situation of the talk has changed, because the people involved know that they are accountable for coming up with appropriate responses. If they do not do so, their failure will be immediately noticeable and will require some explanation. For example, when A greets B, A's greeting has a prospective character in the sense that it changes how B's next utterance will be heard. If B returns the greeting, then it acts as an acknowledgement that A and B are mutually involved in the interaction. But, if B fails to respond, B's silence will be "hearable" as a silence and will require some explanation. It is not the same situation as silence if A's greeting had not occurred. The silence is out of order and A, together with other listeners, will need to think about whether B's silence is intelligible as, for example, an insult or a failure to hear A's greeting (Heritage 1984, 106–09).

The kind of practical reasoning involved here is essentially similar to that involved in recognizing a queue. So long as we think people are just standing around or milling about, then one person going up to a counter is not significant. But as soon as we formulate the notion that people are standing in a queue, then the same behaviour of going up to the counter becomes noticeably out of order, and requires some explanation. The person may be insulting other people by pushing in front of them, or may not realize that there is a queue, or may be involved in an emergency that overrides the rule of standing in the queue, and so on.

The management of conversations is intimately associated with the social construction of status and power relations. Studies by Zimmerman and West (1975) systematically compare male-female and same-sex conversations to demonstrate how patterns of interruptions, lapses in the flow of the conversation, and grudging support of topic development can be related to issues of power. They illustrate statistically that, while both overlaps and interruptions in same-sex conversations are evenly distributed, in female-male conversations virtually all the overlaps and interruptions are by male speakers (Zimmerman and West 1975, 115–17). In addition, females in cross-sex conversations display silences that are related to males giving delayed and minimal support to what the females are saying. Furthermore, females are found not to complain about being interrupted. The authors conclude from these data that "men deny equal status to women as conversation partners with respect to rights to the full utilization of their turns and support for the development of the topics" (Zimmerman and West 1975, 125). They speculate that male dominance is reflected in the micro-institution of talk, just as it is in the macro-institutions of society.

In another study, West found that male physicians usually interrupt their patients far more than patients interrupt them. Female physicians, however, are interrupted by patients as much or more than vice versa. West concludes from these data that gender can have primacy over the status of physician "when the doctor is a lady" (West 1984, 102). Studies such as these give valuable insight into how the microworld of everyday interaction both reflects and reproduces the wider system of inequality and power.

The techniques of conversation analysis

have similarly been applied to other settings such as courtrooms (Atkinson and Drew 1979), doctor-patient interviews (Heath 1981), service encounters (Merritt 1976), and even the Watergate hearings (Molotch and Boden 1985). These studies give a new perspective on the microsociological bases of control over information, biases in decision making, and the exercise of power.

Ethnomethodological Studies of Work

Recent developments in ethnomethodology are moving beyond the analysis of conversations to explore the intimate details of practical reasoning that make possible the joint activities of people at work. The kinds of work processes studied range from improvised jazz performances (Sudnow 1978) and the order of service in a queue to discoveries in astro-physics (Garfinkel, Lynch, and Livingston 1981) and research in a chemistry laboratory (Lynch 1985).

This research approach is so strikingly different from conventional sociology of occupations that our primary objective here will be to clarify the kind of questions that the ethnomethodology of work raises, rather than to present an overview of findings. The analysis of conversations described above may give you a hint about these differences. Conventional sociology tends to focus on the content of what people say, the answers they give to questions, and what information we might learn from them. Ethnomethodology, in contrast, focusses on the mechanisms that make orderly talk possible, regardless of what people are talking about. Similarly, in the study of work, conventional sociology of occupations tends to tell us a great deal about the occupation in question and the lives of the workers. What we do not learn is exactly how people do what they are doing (Heritage 1984, 293–99). Earlier in this chapter, while looking at functionalist approaches, we learned about people working in restaurants, but we learned almost

nothing about how one does the work of serving. On the basis of Whyte's study we could not apply for a job and claim to be competent waitresses or waiters. What we are missing is the crucial information that might be supplied by someone on the job helping us and saying, "This is what you do. . . .Watch me." Ethnomethodology explores "the missing what."

An excellent example of the contrast between conventional and ethnomethodological studies of work is Becker's (1951) conventional study of professional musicians and Sudnow's (1978; 1979) ethnomethodological studies of jazz improvisation. Becker focusses on musicians' work as a service occupation in which the players have personal contact with members of their audience who exert pressure on how they do their work, particularly on the musical selections they are asked to play. Becker's specific interests are (1951, 249):

1. the conceptions that musicians have of themselves and of the non-musicians for whom they work and the conflict they feel to be inherent in this relation;
2. the basic consensus underlying the reactions of both commercial and jazz musicians to this conflict; and
3. the feelings of isolation musicians have from the larger society and the way they segregate themselves from audience and community.

His analysis is based on eighteen months of interviews and participant observation as a jazz pianist. He describes how musicians think of themselves as artists who possess a mysterious gift that sets them apart from outsiders, whom they regard as "squares." The musicians feel that the audience, who are mostly squares, have no right to dictate what they should play. But since the audience is the major source of their income, they are faced with the dilemma of whether to "go commercial," which implies abandoning the creative principle but making a good living, or to stay with what they consider good jazz but make a precarious living. Commercial musicians look down on the audience, but they choose to sacrifice self-respect and the respect of their peers in order to enjoy the advantages of steady work and higher income (Becker 1951, 254).

In the actual playing situation, the musicians segregate themselves from the audience as much as possible by playing on a platform and positioning the piano to act as a physical barrier that reduces direct interaction with, and therefore undesirable influence from, the audience. Becker concludes that generally musicians are hostile towards audiences and that they tend to associate mostly among themselves.

This study is in many ways a fascinating account of the lives of musicians. But a crucial aspect has been ignored. We learn about the musicians' roles, their relations with the audience, their career choices, and their distinctive subculture, but we learn nothing about their actual musical activities, despite the fact that Becker was a participant musician. We are no more competent to play jazz piano in a band at the end of reading Becker's study than we were at the beginning. We do not learn even the most elementary information, such as how all the members of the band manage to start playing at the same time. Garfinkel (1976, 36) sums up the problems with Becker's study thus:

> We learn from Becker . . . that there are jazz musicians, where they work, whom they work with, what they earn, how they get their jobs, what the audience size and composition is . . . but . . . nowhere in the article can it be read and no interrogation of the article can supply that it is just in those places, with just those persons. . . at just those times, under the circumstances at hand, these parties must in and of their local work make music together. The curiosity of the reportage . . . is that Becker's article omits entirely . . . and exactly what the parties are doing that makes of what they are doing for each other

recognizably, just so, just what, just this that is going on, namely, their making music!

In contrast, Sudnow (1978) raises the question of how jazz musicians actually manage to play. His study focusses on the stages he went through learning to play jazz piano. He also discusses the frantic character of playing with other people when they set the pace at which his hands had to move. Sudnow argues that aspects of tempo and rhythm are integral parts of any social interaction. We have to pay attention to how people notice changes in tempo and how these are accomplished (Sudnow 1979, 117).

Ethnomethodological studies of musicians focus on the practical activity of playing music. In a study of band members, for example, an ethnomethodologist would explore the intimate details of the interaction between members that makes it possible for them to play together, to keep time, to pace their collective movements. One of the basic things we need to know in order to play in a band is how the members jointly manage to keep in time. A conductor might help, provided we know that when he or she lifts the baton and flicks it, some, though not necessarily all, of the musicians start playing. For amateur orchestras, however, simply following the conductor may not be enough, as can be jarringly obvious when they have to start a new piece or change tempo. For a small jazz group or any small musical group without a conductor, the question of when to start and how to keep together is more complicated. As a new band member, we would have to learn what the gestures are, what to watch out for, and how to listen to other players.

Ethnomethodology explores how bands rehearse or prepare for performances, and what their everyday shop practices are (Weeks 1982; 1988). We listen in on their shoptalk and glimpse just what kind of interpretive thinking is required to go from the underlying pattern, that this is the piece being played, to making sense of the surface features of given instructions. We will also learn how musicians fake it when something goes wrong: how they cover for someone who has come in on a wrong note, how they blend in and slur a beat to catch up, and how they make what are initially wrong notes sound intentional and leading to the right notes after all, so that the performance keeps going and the audience does not notice the error.

If we are studying professional musicians, we can usually assume that they have mastered the techniques of how to play their instruments to get the sounds required, once they have understood the instructions. But a band leader in a junior school cannot make such assumptions. Here the shoptalk might be much more explicit, like "Trumpeter, take a big breath right here so you have enough air left for the da-a-a, and that goes for the singers too. Violinist, get your bow right up

so you will have enough of it left to hold the note. Move it slo-o-wly." We might see the trumpeter drawing a balloon shape in the music notebook and the singers writing a large B with an arrow at the same place. The violinist might write "up-sl." If we attend the school performance after reading an ethnomethodological account of rehearsals, we would have a much better idea of just how the band leader and the students together manage to do what they are doing. This is the goal of the ethnomethodology of work studies.

Similar studies of formal talk during classroom reading lessons (McHoul 1978; Heap 1979) give us intimate details of how children organize their turn-taking in round robin reading. We see how teachers strategically time their interruptions, or utterances like "uh-h?" to signal to a child that the previous word was not quite right and that some error repair is needed. The

Ethnomethodological studies of musicians examine the practical activity of making music and ask how jazz musicians actually manage to play together.

student who has made the mistake displays **interactional competence** when she or he takes up this hint and inserts the proper word in the proper sequence in the subsequent reading (Weeks 1985). After reading such studies, we gain a sense of precisely how teachers do their work of teaching, and how children do their work of learning to read.

Ethnomethodological studies of professional scientists at work explore the practical everyday reasoning through which scientists collectively arrive at the belief that they have made a discovery. Garfinkel, Lynch, and Livingston (1981) examined tape recordings and notebooks made by astronomers when they discovered optical pulsars. Conventional accounts of the discovery make no mention of the work that went into it or how the scientists involved managed to convince themselves that they had found something. Garfinkel, Lynch, and Livingston (1981, 139–40) describe what we learn from one conventional account:

a)　the pulsar is depicted as the cause of everything seen and said about it;

b)　the pulsar is described as *existing prior to and independently of* any specific method of detecting it;

c)　the account is in the third person, that is, it is impersonal with nothing of [the scientists'] personal presence included;

d)　the scientists through proper lucid methods came upon the pulsar that was otherwise hidden due to ignorance, sloppy work, etc.

In other words, the report takes for granted that the pulsars were there all along and that appropriate research procedures made their presence obvious.

When ethnomethodologists explore the tape recordings and notebooks made by the scientists involved, however, we get a strikingly different view of the scientists' work. We hear their shoptalk as they discuss among themselves how to interpret the ambiguous readings they were getting from their research equipment. Before the "discovery" was made, it was by no means obvious how to interpret these surface appearances. Many different underlying patterns could be and were proposed to account for these details, with the option of optical pulsars only one among several interpretive schemes. The scientists had to talk themselves into believing that what they were seeing were pulsars. Perhaps if the shoptalk had gone differently, the conclusions drawn about what they were looking at would have been different, and pulsars would not have been discovered at all.

Studies of scientists trying to interpret fuzzy images produced by electron microscopes in a neurosciences laboratory (Lynch, Livingston, and Garfinkel 1983; Lynch 1985) reveal similar practical reasoning processes. We listen in on their shoptalk as they try to figure out what is going on and as they propose or reject interpretive schemes. We watch as they struggle to decide whether an unusual slide under the microscope reflects some mistake in how the slide was made or is potentially some real discovery. The course of such arguments among scientists on a research team, as they try to convince each other that "this is irrelevant" or "that is really something," determines whether their day's work will be seen as resulting in a discovery or in nothing in particular.

Limitations of Ethnomethodology

In summary, ethnomethodology focusses on the ways in which we, in our everyday lives, use our common-sense knowledge and background understandings to make sense to ourselves and to each other of what is going on around us. Our sense of reality, including all the familiar features of our society, is created through such practical everyday reasoning. The vague flux of people milling around us only becomes visible as discrete activities because we actively search for patterns that might account for what we notice. Talk is meaningful only because we continually search for underlying patterns to which utterances might refer. Order is visible in activities and conversations only as a result of such reflexive practical reasoning, which moves continually from experiences to the interpretive schemes that seem to account for them to new experiences and to revisions of the interpretive scheme.

The central contribution of ethnomethodology is its focus on the methods or practices by which people actively create a sense of what is happening in intimate, everyday interactions, and how they actively construct their own actions in order to make what they are doing sensible to others. These sense-making processes form the basis of all social life. The problem that this approach leaves largely unresolved is how to build from micro second-by-second experiences outwards to the broader social structures that people come to experience, somehow, as constraints upon their lives. These constraints are embodied in such notions as *typical expectations*, *power*, and *class*. Collins (1981, 986–89) conceptualizes macrostructures as aggregates of micro-experiences stretched out from seconds to days, months, and years, with the numbers of people involved growing from one or two to increasingly larger groups. He suggests that concepts of physical space, the amount of time that social processes take, and the number of people involved are true **macrovariables**; that is, they are variables that cannot be reduced to micro-elements. But the problem remains that much more than an exercise in addition seems to be needed to get from microsecond, sense-making practices to what people come to experience and to talk about as social structures. Ethnomethodology has uncovered the microfoundations of these macro-experiences, but the linkages and the building mechanisms remain obscure.

What seems to be needed is a theoretical approach that is rooted in ethnomethodology but that works outwards to explore how people bring macrostructures into being. This new approach is loosely referred to as the **social construction of reality**. As a body of theory, it explores how members' methods for making sense of experience continually sustain and reproduce the larger social world. This larger world is experienced as external constraints on people's lives, yet it exists not as a given but as an ongoing accomplishment.

The Personal as Political: Feminist Theory and the Social Construction of Reality

Feminist theory is currently at the forefront of explorations into the social construction of reality. There are important reasons for this. First, the everyday lives of most women are not experienced as embedded in the formal organizations of society—administration, government, and so on—that are the central foci of dominant sociology. Women's lives are experienced as embedded in what Smith (1987a, 7) refers to as the "local particularities of home and family." Smith herself, as a sociology graduate and a mother of young children, found it almost impossible to reconcile the abstract theoretical debates of academic sociology with her local and particular world of feeding, cleaning, bedding down, and playing with small children—the parks they went to together, the friends they had, the neighbours, the children's sicknesses and visits to the doctor, or walks down the road to look at the scenery and at the bugs under the leaves.

This is still the world inhabited primarily, although not exclusively, by women. It is a mode of being that is not readily captured by the abstractions of traditional macrostudies in sociology. Smith herself concluded that there must be something wrong with the academic sociology she was studying and trying to teach if it failed to connect with the world of her own immediate experience. She worked to develop a new way of doing sociology that begins with people in their everyday lives and moves outwards.

As we saw in chapter 2, feminist theory, beginning from the standpoint of women in the particularities of everyday life, emphasizes that the personal is political. Intimate encounters between women and children and men, intimate decisions about who will do what in day-to-day relations, are fundamentally implicated in sustaining and reproducing what feminists refer to as the structures of patriarchy. At the same time, theorists working within dominant sociological perspectives have had considerable difficulty incorporating notions of patriarchal structures into their work or even recognizing that they exist. They have generally not been taken for granted as social facts in the functionalist sense of external constraints. Learning to see them is a struggle.

Dorothy Smith is concerned with showing how micro-experiences, the intimate particularities of everyday life, produce the macrostructures of a patriarchal world. She begins with the insights of ethnomethodology into how talk is put together and the devices used by men, apparently with women's consent, that serve to maintain male control over the topics of conversation (Smith 1987a, 33–36). These devices include not picking up topics raised by women, or re-attributing such topics to a man, and the polite pauses when a woman speaks followed by a swift return to the "real" conversation being held by men. Such micropractices produce a world dominated intellectually by men in which women's experience does not appear as the source of authoritative expression (Smith 1987a, 51). The patriarchal world view is reproduced in what is written about and read, and hence in what becomes part of the formal macrostructures of

academic disciplines. As Smith describes it, men tend to take seriously only what other men say. What other men write becomes established as the standard for the discipline, against which new writing, including that done by women scholars, is evaluated.

Again at the microlevel of sense-making practices, Smith (1987a, 31) describes studies that explore how people accomplish evaluations of other people. Identical descriptions of academic backgrounds and qualifications are evaluated quite differently when they appear to be those of a woman rather than a man. These sense-making practices, in the conversations of people on hiring committees, help to accomplish the macrostructural reality of where women and men come to be located in universities and other organizations. These are part of the active microprocesses that produce the reality of women in junior positions being evaluated by men in senior positions, in terms of standards set in advance by men—a "factual" reality experienced by women as external constraint.

Dixon (1976) uncovers the microlevel sense-making processes through which the social construction of radical professors as "incompetent academics," unworthy of tenure, was socially accomplished in many North American social science departments. These processes are part of the members' practices that socially accomplish what Marxists refer to as the dominance of ideas of the ruling class.

Smith shows how the ways in which academic talk is managed in sociology become built into the dominant ideas and methods of the discipline. Academic sociologists do not write and talk about what they are doing as if they were ordinary people doing their jobs. Instead, they adopt a detached, abstract mode of "professional talk." This is a mode of scientific shoptalk that invokes membership in the particular profession and conveys the image of the scientist as outside any particular location. It serves at the same time to accomplish the reduction of the people being talked about to the level of objects for discussion. In academic sociology, people are thought about as if they were specimens, role incumbents, or instances of abstract models. Smith refers to this as the **imperialism of rationality**.

It is this mode of talking, Smith suggests (1987a, 71–72), that makes it possible for professionals to relate to battered wives as objects for discussion—precisely the mode of relating that makes wife battery possible. It is also the mode of talking that socially accomplishes the perspective that macro-structures are causal agents and that people are objects of them. Earlier in this chapter we saw how this worked in Eichler's illustration of how anthropologists typically use the passive voice to describe what women do. Women thus do not appear as subjects actively creating their social world. They are merely examples of culture at work. Eichler includes stronger examples. An anthropological description of how kinship ties strengthen group cohesion in primitive societies stresses the importance of the genetic interrelatedness among adult males (Shaw 1985, 197–98). In writing in this form, Shaw has conceptualized the group as consisting only of males, with assorted wives who have no effect whatever on group cohesion and solidarity (Eichler 1988, 25). Here we begin to see how functionalism and patriarchy in social science are socially accomplished in the ways in which we do our research and write our reports.

Smith (1987a, 151–80) proposes an alternative way of doing and writing sociology, which she terms **institutional ethnography**. It begins with the particular activities of people in particular localities and explores how these practical activities are co-ordinated to bring our world into being. It shares with traditional ethnomethodology the need to see exactly what work is done to accomplish the accountable order. At the same time, the method draws upon the insights of Karl Marx, who insisted that all social life is essentially practical, and hence that understanding must begin with the study and comprehension of practical human activities. The method goes beyond the boundaries of traditional ethnomethodology in explicating the wider set of social relations in which the local activities of any one participant are embedded and in terms of which they are organized.

As an example of this method, Smith focusses on the social construction of the school system and class differences within it. She begins with the particular situation of mothers describing how their day's work within the home is put together. We see how a child's success in school is socially produced by mothering work, including the "monitoring and repair sequences" by which mothers check on homework and try to fix it after deciding what teachers want. We see the work processes involved in being what teachers mean by "concerned parents." Smith illustrates how the practical work of mothers in the home is organized by relations outside it, the demands of scheduling the departures and arrivals of children and husband to fit the timetables of school and job, the ongoing accomplishment of shopping, cooking, mealtimes, and cleaning children so they will pass the monitoring activities of school health officials.

Smith shows how the monitoring sequences of teachers in classrooms produce the status of particular children as proceeding normally or not. We realize how the teacher's work of managing a classroom and accomplishing a reading lesson is directly related to and dependent upon the ongoing mothering work that accomplishes the readiness of children to act in ways that make possible such activities. Smith also illustrates how relations of class and inequality are socially accomplished in the practical struggles of poor women, living in places without even indoor plumbing, to accomplish the appropriate level of preparedness of their children for school. She discusses the struggles of single-parent women to accomplish the skilled and time-consuming practices of monitoring and repair sequences appropriate for competent mothering. It is through such everyday practices that our world as hierarchically ordered is brought into being. These relations are explored in detail in chapter 13 of this text concerned with education and the social construction of class.

Limitations of Personal Politics

As sociologists, we can explicate how our social world is socially accomplished through the everyday activities of people in local, particular settings. But this cannot work magic. The apparatuses of ruling are still there, even when we see how they are accomplished. Garfinkel's breaching experiments show how our sense of reality is accomplished, but do not thereby change that reality. Smith (1987a) again points to the social organization of talk, which excludes or trivializes what women contribute, the social organization of written talk in texts, which constructs women as objects of study, the social organization of evaluation, which accomplishes how what is written comes to be judged, and its translation into who is appointed to what positions.

Research oriented to explicating the subjectively experienced world of women, to show how schooling is imposed upon mothers, and how they might act collectively vis-à-vis this mode of organizing, is central to Smith's own vision of what a sociology for women might be like. But, speaking from her own experience, she comments that "such bold contravention of professional constraints would be a one-time-only operation" (Smith 1987a, 219). Such research proposals have to be evaluated in order to get funding. In the particular location of government funding agencies, the ongoing accomplishment of evaluation of research proposals is based on very particular standards, not those of feminist sociology. Smith's ideal of a research centre organized to create a sociology from the standpoint of women could not survive, for the very simple reason that it could not get funded. Time and again the social organization of funding, the way in which voluntary organizations are required to act on order to get money, and the forms through which they have to account for what they are doing, make it impossible to do what they intended to do.

Conclusion

The critical value of microsociology is that it provides a means of discovering how social relations are produced through the everyday activities of individual people. Macrostructures comprise collections of individual people acting in certain kinds of micro-situations. What gets done is accomplished by people, not by abstract systems. But the warning sounded by Smith with respect to the feminist exploration of power in personal relationships holds for all forms of micro-analysis. Recognizing the interpersonal foundations of social organization does not make the organization disappear. The apparatus of ruling is still there. People have come to think about society as if it consisted of structures in which they are embedded. This conception expresses their real experience of constraint in their everyday relations with others.

In the following chapters we will be centrally concerned with the patterns of collective organization or macroprocesses of society. But we will try to explore these organizations and write about them in ways that never lose sight of the ongoing practical activities and the micro sense-making processes of people who bring our social world into being.

Suggested Reading

An excellent theoretical analysis of the relations between micro- and macrosociology is provided by Randall Collins in "On the Microfoundations of Macrosociology" (1981). Since this is not an easy article, it is best to read it over for the general ideas without worrying about the details of the debate. Dorothy Smith's work also tends to be highly complex and written for advanced students. A refreshing exception is her book *The Everyday World as Problematic: A Feminist Sociology* (1987a). Smith gives multiple examples of how the everyday lives of women are socially constructed, both in the intimate details of interaction and in relation to wider social organizations in which such interactions are embedded. Her work effectively bridges microfoundations and macrostructures.

David Orenstein's introduction to sociology, *The Sociological Quest: Principles of Sociology* (1985), is limited to the functionalist perspective, but it presents an excellent overview of theories of socialization and role playing. He uses multiple examples that are readily familiar to students.

For a good introduction to a Marxist approach in microsociology, see W. Peter Archibald, *Social Psychology as Political Economy* (1978). He describes with passion how the intimate daily lives of workers are influenced by capitalism. See particularly chapters 7 to 9 in the section entitled "A Political Economic Approach to Some Pressing Social Psychological Problems."

The early text by Harold Garfinkel, *Studies in Ethnomethodology* (1967), provides an excellent introduction to ethnomethodology. Garfinkel's theoretical discussions are complex, but his descriptions of experiments are fascinating and straightforward. See particularly chapters 2 and 3.

For the application of ethnomethodology to practical situations, see Egon Bittner, "The Police on Skid Row: A Study of Peace-Keeping" (1967). Bittner shows how police officers make their everyday decisions about what behaviour will be treated as ordinary and why other similar actions may be treated as reportable offences. Candace West, "When the Doctor is a 'Lady': Power, Status and Gender in Physician-Patient Encounters" (1984), shows how individuals continually negotiate their sense of what is going on in a doctor's office.

Chapter 5

Loss of Community?
The Rural–Urban Debate

The question mark in the title of this chapter is very significant. It is a signal that what you will find here is not a collection of factual knowledge. Rather you will confront evidence and disputed interpretations concerning the nature of rural and urban communities, both now and in the past, and an on-going debate surrounding the patterns of social change. It is a debate that calls into question many fundamental assumptions about the structure and functioning of human communities.

The methodology of social science is a critical issue in this chapter. We will trace the processes of formulating a theory, elaborating it, spelling out its basic assumptions, testing them against evidence, and framing conclusions about whether the original theory worked and how it might be modified or replaced by alternative theories that seem better able to account for the evidence at hand.

The loss of community thesis originated in the ideological perspective of conservatism in the late nineteenth and early twentieth centuries. The assumptions implicit in this world view were spelled out in a theory concerning the fundamental characteristics of community life and how they were being threatened. This theory, in turn, has empirical consequences, and it is these consequences that can be compared with evidence collected through research. In principle, evidence that conflicts with the expected consequences challenges the assumptions on which the initial theory was based and so prompts its revision. In practice, however, this linear progress is complicated by the development of competing theories, which search for very different kinds of evidence. What is particularly problematic is that theories can easily generate blind spots and distortions in the amassing of evidence. As a result, the "evidence" tends to get so stacked in favour of the dominant theory that advocates of competing ones face a major battle in reinterpreting what is perceived as existing "knowledge."

Loss of Community

The loss of community thesis is rooted in the belief that, from the nineteenth century onwards, human communities underwent very profound changes with the development of industrialized, urban centres. This thesis posits a fundamental division between "then" and "now"; it sees a cleft rather than continuity in social history. As the concept of loss implies, this thesis also includes a moral critique of this apparent cleft. The thesis is accompanied by a nostalgia for the past and a vision of a more humane form of community as the focus for harmonious, integrated, and stable relationships and collective sentiments of loyalty and belonging. By contrast, the present world is defined in terms of growing individualism, with concomitant disharmony, disintegration, instability, disloyalty, and lack of a sense of belonging. In effect, the thesis constitutes a basic critique of industrialization and urban life.

Gemeinschaft and Gesellschaft: Community and Association

The German theorist Ferdinand Tönnies was the first major exponent of the loss of community thesis, which was set out in his study entitled *Gemeinschaft and Gesellschaft* (1887). The term **Gemeinschaft** can loosely be translated into English as *community* and **Gesellschaft** as *association*. Tönnies argues that, with the development of modern industrial society, a very distinctive pattern of social life began to emerge, which differed in almost all respects from the kind of society that it replaced. Pre-industrial social life is characterized by what Tönnies refers to as "natural will." Relations between people in pre-industrial society are governed by natural ties of kinship and long-established friendship, by familiarity and liking, and by age-old habit and customary ways of doing things. Industrial society, by contrast, is characterized by "rational will." Relations

between people are governed by careful deliberation and evaluation of means and ends, or the advantages that people expect to gain from others.

The *gemeinschaft* community, as conceptualized by Tönnies, is akin to the natural community of a living organism. It involves an underlying consensus based on kinship, on residence in a common locality, and on friendship. Relations exist for their own sake and cannot be arbitrarily terminated. Tönnies assumes that this pattern of relations is characteristic of pre-industrial society. Social position or status in such a community is clearly defined from birth. It is based on who one is, who one's parents and ancestors were, and one's sex and age. Personal achievements, education, property, and so on, matter little compared with status ascribed by birth. By and large, people in *gemeinschaft* communities are socially immobile, remaining within the same status group, as peasants or nobles, throughout life. People are also geographically immobile, staying in or close by the same locality.

These stable communities are generally homogeneous. People are descended from the same racial stock, and they share the same ethnic identity, religion, language, and way of life, all rigidly enforced by the central institutions of church and family. Both of these institutions derive their strength from the people's unquestioned acceptance of them as natural. Core values within this culture are the sanctity of kinship ties, solidarity as a community, and attachment to the locality. People share a sentimental attachment to conventions handed down through generations of ancestors. Their community operates through dense networks of interaction between people who are highly interrelated through marriage, who know each other well, and who know that they hold cherished values in common.

The *gesellschaft* pattern of relations differs so greatly from this traditional form as scarcely to warrant the term *community*. Tönnies refers to this form as an *association* of people, which is based on principles of contract and exchange. He conceptualized such a society as merely a mechanical aggregate rather than a living organism, an artificial society that is transitory and superficial. It emerges out of competitive struggles between individuals who do not feel themselves bound together by either kinship or religion. People are geographically **mobile** and, hence, tend to be heterogeneous with respect to racial and ethnic origins and religious beliefs. Relations between individuals are impersonal, based on rational calculation of advantage, and they are restricted to definite ends. In such calculations the spirit of neighbourly love and the virtues and morality of community life are lost. People tend to collect in large-scale agglomerations rather than in small local groups.

Tönnies' vision of *Gesellschaft*—the collapse of community life into merely an association of individuals motivated by calculated self-interest—was intended as a critique of the whole order of society underlying industrialization. The fundamental value of competitive capitalism, the rational pursuit of profit and individual advantage, generates dehumanized and artificial relations.

George Simmel, a German theorist who was a contemporary of Tönnies, modified Tönnies' ideas to apply more specifically to rural versus urban settings. Simmel identified *gemeinschaft* patterns with rural communities and *gesellschaft* trends with urban settings. He proposed further that a unidirectional process of change was occurring from rural to urban type. Urban life appeared essentially rational, with only weak emotional attachments. Diverse interests further weakened local controls. Simmel feared that this weakening of communal solidarity in urban areas would lead to the collapse of a stable social order. Rural community life appeared to be superior to urban lifestyles.

Early American sociology drew heavily on the work of Tönnies and Simmel in developing classifications of rural and urban forms of society. Sorokin and Zimmerman (1929) highlighted nine orders of difference between rural and urban life, based largely on common-sense comparison:

1. The primary occupation in rural communities is agricultural, while in urban areas it is non-agricultural.
2. The rural environment is "natural," while the city environment is "artificial," comprising structures of concrete and steel.
3. Rural communities are small in size, while urban ones are large.
4. Rural areas are characterized by low-density residence, with people thinly spread over wide geographic areas. Urban people have high-density residence.
5. Rural communities are homogeneous, urban communities heterogeneous.
6. Social mobility, in the sense of changing one's status or rank, is minimal in rural areas. Urban people experience considerable status mobility, especially between generations.
7. Geographic mobility is restricted in rural areas, common among urban people.
8. Social stratification in rural areas in restricted with respect to specialization, differentiation, and hierarchy. There is only a limited number of occupations. These do not differ greatly from each other, they are not highly specialized, and there are relatively small status differences among them. Stratification in urban areas is high in all three of these dimensions. There is considerable occupational specialization, with marked differences among jobs and in relative status and power.

9. Lastly, in the important area of social interaction, rural people are confined to a few contacts dominated by family and friends. Relations are generally permanent, strong, and durable. Social networks are overlapping and many-faceted, in the sense that any one person interacts with the same people for a wide variety of purposes, and all these people also have relations with each other. Urban social interaction, by contrast, is characterized by many contacts that are spatially spread out. These take place between strangers and involve relatively few contacts between family and friends. Most contacts are casual, superficial, and short-lived. Social networks are complex, segregated, and standardized, in that each different purpose or function may entail contact with a different person, and such persons will not normally know each other. It is the function rather than the person that shapes the interaction, so everyone tends to be treated in a uniform manner for a uniform function.

The Chicago School

The **Chicago School** of urban sociology, which emerged at the University of Chicago in the late 1920s and 1930s, built on this earlier work, with the goal of elaborating a general theory of urban life. Chicago School theorists accepted the basic classification of rural and urban types and tried to develop them further into theories of change.

One such theorist, Louis Wirth, in his essay "Urbanism as a Way of Life" (1938), set out a formal theory in which he suggests that the characteristics of the city as a city explain the patterns of culture identified by Tönnies and others. Wirth identified three critical variables as causal determinants of the *gesellschaft* type of community: size, density, and heterogeneity.

The large *size* of urban centres inevitably gives rise to differentiation between people. It becomes impossible to know and to interact with everyone over a wide variety of concerns. Hence, the interactions inevitably become limited and specialized, and therefore superficial, transitory, and anonymous. The result, suggests Wirth, is the experience of individual loneliness within the urban crowd.

The second key variable is *density*. People are concentrated in a limited space, where they experience overcrowding and pollution. Like rats artificially crowded together in laboratories, people are forced into a competitive struggle for space. Laboratory rats, housed in a spacious cage, tend to live peacefully together. But as more and more

Chicago School theorists argue that high density is one factor that characterizes *gesellschaft* communities.

animals are crowded into the same space, their behaviour changes. They become increasingly aggressive and more likely to inflict injuries on each other. The Chicago School theorists reasoned that overcrowding in cities would tend to generate similar antisocial behaviour among people.

The third variable is *heterogeneity*. People with different racial and ethnic backgrounds and different occupations and statuses are mixed together. In the face of such heterogeneity, people have divided allegiances and hence cannot form a secure sense of belonging, either to their locality or to the people around them.

In this model, the relation between urban setting and values reverses the original association proposed by Tönnies. For Tönnies, the values of rational, calculated self-interest led to the break-up of community life and to the impetus to gather in cities that offered economic advantages. In the Chicago School model, the gathering in cities led to the loss of community values and their replacement by calculations of individual advantage.

Robert Redfield (1947), another contributor to the Chicago School, elaborated an **ideal-type model** of a rural or **folk society** to contrast with urban society. An ideal-type model, as a research tool, is designed to highlight the typical features of the kind of society or social institution being studied, so as to guide research. Any particular example may not have all the features listed in the model, but the broad characteristics should be visible. Redfield was particularly interested in the folk communities typical of relatively isolated rural areas. In his model he highlighted five key features.

1. Folk communities are familial. They are organized around kinship ties and descent groups.
2. They involve intimate face-to-face relations, where people know each other on personal terms.
3. Folk societies have minimal specialization or division of labour. Most people are occupied in farming or related activities.
4. They manifest intense cohesion, with people united together by strong bonds of local identity and loyalties and mutual obligations.
5. Folk societies are characterized by traditionalism, a deep commitment to shared cultural values and ways of behaviour, which takes on a religious or sacred character.

The ideal-type model of an urban society incorporates the opposite of these key features of a folk society, namely, weak family ties, superficial relations between strangers, a high degree of specialization of occupations, limited cohesion, and readiness to adopt new and changing values and ways of behaving. Redfield utilized these ideal-type models in his research on social change in Mexico. He suggests that the typical differences between a hamlet, a village, a trading centre, and a city, can be described in terms of a systematic and linear process of change from folk to urban characteristics.

The Urban Agglomeration

These theoretical models of folk versus urban society, both in Tönnies' original conception and in its subsequent modification and incorporation into the Chicago School theory of rural-to-urban transition, reflect a strong conservative ideology. Folk society or village life, with its stress on family, church, and tradition, seems more natural and more stable. Proponents of this theory view the passing of village life with concern, anticipating the breakdown of social cohesion in cities.

The overwhelming impression that comes through these theories of urbanism is a sense of loss and of regress rather than positive change for the better. The term *loss of community* expresses dissatisfaction with the quality of life in the contemporary world and a desire to return to a more humane society where individuals were integrated into a stable and harmonious community of family, friends, and neighbours. The concept of *community* symbolizes a desire for security and certainty in life, and for identity and belonging. While the past may well not have been as rosy as the idealized image of integrated community life, the feeling of loss cannot be dismissed as merely misguided nostalgia. It carries an implicit criticism of the present and articulates the private troubles that people feel. In this sense it must be taken seriously by sociology.

A public opinion survey conducted in Toronto by the Minister of Justice in July, 1982, found Canadians "in the grip of fear": fear of losing their jobs or their homes, and above all, fear of crime (Taylor 1983, 1–6). The survey revealed that the average Canadian believes that 40 to 55 percent of crimes reported to the police involve violence, that prison inmates released on parole were almost certainly going to continue to act violently, and that the number of murders had risen. While these beliefs can be shown statistically not to be correct, the strength of the fear is real. Generalized fear is also shown in the growth of private security agencies, the sale of crime-prevention devices, and insecurity in new housing developments. Town planners in the 1940s and 1950s assumed that when people were relocated from slums into new developments, community life would improve, but this rarely happened. Crimes against property increased by over 34 percent between 1976 and 1981. In 1981 one in every thirty-nine houses was burglarized, compared with one in fifty-one in 1976. People's sense of security within their communities has declined and is combined with a deeper fear that police are incapable of protecting them on the streets (Taylor 1983, 47).

Given this sense of insecurity, it is perhaps not surprising that people mourn the loss of community. However, what people mean by the term **community** is vague, and frequently contradictory. Lee and Newby (1983, 57–58) suggest that in sociology it has come to have two broad meanings. First, sociological research broadens the geographic sense of community, that of a particular territory, to refer to a *local social system*, the set of social relations in a particular bounded area. Research in this tradition has focussed on the decline of **localism**—the tendency toward communities that are relatively self-contained and self-sufficient—and its replacement by **mass society** in which decisions are increasingly centralized in federal or international economic and political centres. Localities are progressively losing control over their own affairs. Twentieth-century town planners, particularly those in Britain, have deliberately tried to recreate community neighbourhoods or "garden cities" within subdivisions of cities. This includes promoting neighbourhood stores and amenities in the hope that they would encourage local loyalties and face-to-face interaction. The underlying assumption, that this focus on locality will invigorate community feelings, remains largely untested (Lee and Newby 1983, 55).

The second, broader meaning of *community* in sociological research is a *type of relationship*, a sense of identity, communality, or spirit among a group of people. This approach has tended to incorporate both a critique of industrial society and an implicit moral claim that human relationships ought to be of a certain kind. Again, however, there are many untested assumptions in such an approach. People may not, after all, want the kind of relations that proponents aim for.

The focus in this chapter is on testing theories in rural and urban sociology. We explore the predictions or consequences that can be logically derived from traditional theories and compare them with the predictions that can be derived from alternative systems of explanation. You should keep in mind that plausible arguments, however convincing they might sound, are not necessarily correct. They need to be tested in a systematic way against evidence, and the evidence itself has to be scrutinized for the biases and distortions that preconceived notions can impose.

The main theory we will test here is that of the Chicago School, particularly as expressed by Louis Wirth. In this formulation, large cities are seen as unnatural ecological environments for people and hence as putting great strain on social relationships. As stated in the argument proposed by Wirth, there are three problematic characteristics of cities: size, population density, and heterogeneity. Each is responsible for producing specific negative features of social life in cities. The large size of cities promotes compartmentalized and segmented relationships that are impersonal and superficial rather than intimate. Population density or overcrowding promotes aggressiveness, competitiveness, and generalized friction. Heterogeneity promotes rootlessness and insecurity as people lose their sense of identity. Wirth's theories are backed up by studies of animal behaviour that have shown that rats housed under overcrowded conditions develop behavioural disorders, with an abnormally high incidence of infant neglect and mortality, a constant turnover of leadership accompanied by violence, and the occurrence of promiscuous and bisexual relations among males (Hall 1966, chap. 1; Calhoun 1963; Michelson 1970, 6–7).

A central prediction of Wirth's theory is that, where population settlement is small in size, of low density, and relatively homogeneous, as in rural areas, one can expect the sense of community to be strong and characterized by intimacy, co-operation, and a clear sense of security and personal

identity. Alternatively, in large cities such as Toronto and Montreal, and more so in metropolises such as New York, London, and Tokyo, relationships will be superficial and competitive, with limited sense of belonging to a cohesive and satisfying community. In effect, one can expect to find a rural-to-urban continuum with the sense of community being strongest in the smallest settlements and steadily weaker as the size of the city and overcrowding increases.

As we argued in chapter 2, the most useful and productive way to test a theory is to compare it with an alternative theory that begins from different assumptions and makes different predictions. It is the contrast of predictions that helps to draw attention to problem areas and to types of data that we need to look for and that might be overlooked if we only begin with one perspective. It also helps to guard against distortions that can arise when researchers come to see the evidence in a way that makes it appear to support their theory. The same evidence can look very different if viewed from another perspective.

In this chapter the most important alternative theory to the Chicago School is the Marxist or political economy perspective. It starts out from different assumptions and makes different predictions about the changing quality of rural and urban community life. This theory finds the same evidence of dehumanization—loss of community and dissatisfaction among people in contemporary industrial society—but explains it in terms of different causes. The dehumanizing effects of capitalism are seen as crucial, with insecurity stemming from poverty, inflation, and unemployment, and exploitation at work. This theory does not predict that people living in small towns or rural areas will be any more or less happy than people in urban areas. It predicts rather that people who have economic security, and who control their own means of production, will develop satisfying social relations with others, while this sense of community will collapse when fundamental economic security is undermined. To the extent that villages are comprised of farmers or small producers who have both security and independence, such communities are likely to be contented and cohesive. But economically insecure rural poor are as likely as the urban poor to experience a breakdown in sense of community. Political economy theory is closer than the Chicago School model to the original ideas of Tönnies. It implies an indictment not of cities as such but of the values of rational, calculated self-interest that pervade industrial capitalist society at all levels.

Later in the chapter, we explore the perspective of feminist urban geography, a theoretical orientation that emerged during the 1980s. It challenges both the traditional Chicago School and the Marxist alternative for neglecting a critical dimension of urban community life, namely the networks established by women. Patterns of home life and working life, and the relations between them, appear in a very different light when viewed from the standpoint of women. Generalizations formed on the basis of male experiences distort in important respects the patterns of life and social relations established by urban women, especially in response to recession in the labour market. To the extent that earlier theories cannot account for this female experience, they need to be substantially revised.

In the following review of research in rural and urban sociology in Canada, we explore first the contribution of traditional theory to the analysis of folk society or pre-capitalist rural life in Quebec. This is followed by studies of contemporary rural and urban communities. With respect to each broad area, we draw attention to evidence that seems to contradict the basic assumptions of the Chicago School model. Similar research contexts are re-examined from the perspective of Marxist theory to test the extent to which it can account for these apparent contradictions. Feminist research adds its own unique contribution in each area, by offering a critical re-assessment of available data and by generating different kinds of evidence.

Folk Society: A Test of the Chicago School Thesis

The thesis that rural communities are more cohesive than urban centres initially found strong support from Redfield's (1930) pioneering study of life in Mexico in the 1930s. Redfield cites evidence that the small village of Tepoztlan was a homogeneous, smoothly functioning, well-integrated, contented, stable, and harmonious community. He compared it favourably with a neighbouring town, which he characterized as heterogeneous and faction-ridden.

However, this apparently powerful support for his folk society model was not to go unchallenged. A study of the same village by Oscar Lewis (1949), conducted less than twenty years later, shattered the harmonious image and, with it, some of the credibility of Redfield's thesis. Lewis argues that Redfield biased his research by focussing only on co-operative and unifying factors. He charges Redfield with glossing over evidence of violence, cruelty, disease, suffering, poverty, economic and social maladjustment, and political schisms. Redfield later attempted to defend himself by arguing that Lewis had imposed his own value judgments on his research. Lewis wanted to find support for the Marxist argument that the low material standard of living in Tepoztlan gave rise to social maladjustment. Hence he went out of his way to look for evidence of suffering and stress in the community, and then overemphasized the problems that he found. Whatever the validity of this response by Redfield, Lewis's work did challenge the image of the village as an ideal-type *gemeinschaft* community.

In Canadian research, studies of the folk society of rural Quebec offer powerful and convincing descriptions of life that accord closely with the *gemeinschaft* image. But these studies too have been subject to the criticism that researchers found just what they were looking for, rather than what was actually there.

A widely cited study of French-Canadian folk society is that by Horace Miner (1939) on the parish of St. Denis. Robert Redfield wrote the introduction to the book, and he leaves no doubt that he views St. Denis as the epitome of a folk society: "Habitants live in terms of common understandings which are rooted in tradition. . . .Fundamental views of life are shared by everyone, and these views find consistent expression in the beliefs, institutions, rituals, and manners of the people" (Redfield 1964, 58). Sanctions have a strongly sacred character in St. Denis. The way of life of the people is endorsed by the priest, but followed because of deeply felt convictions of the people themselves rather than due to any pressure from outside authority. The family system is also strong, pervasive, and certain in its effects. Almost all aspects of life—work, getting married, finding a career, politics—are largely determined by position in a family. There is minimal social disorganization. The strongly competitive behaviour of the two political parties in St. Denis affairs is likened to "the dual divisions common among simpler folk."

Redfield and Miner acknowledge that the fact that St. Denis is not an isolated peasant community, but part of a modern urbanized world, cannot be ignored. But it can be discounted in large measure. While people do have connections with the city, and even relatives who live there, this exposure to alien influences is mediated by the Catholic Church, which "has stood between the changing world and the habitant, preventing admission of elements which she [the church] condemns and interpreting admitted elements in accordance with the faith and

with the local culture" (Redfield 1964, 60). When local ways are threatened, the church minimizes the influence of outside forces and so helps to preserve the folk character of the community.

The only threat to this way of life has come from the structural problem of land pressure (Miner 1964, 66), a consequence of traditionally large families, indivisible small farms, and limited supply of land. Farmers needed money to educate sons for alternative city jobs or to buy farms for them. The result suggests Miner, was the gradual erosion of independent subsistence farming as a way of life. Farmers slowly became more dependent on the outside economy. The only other solution to the land pressure problem would have been to cut the birth rate, but Miner argues that this was strongly opposed by the Catholic Church, which has always played a vital role in the rural parish. Birth rates declined rapidly in urban areas during the interwar years, but not in the villages, suggesting to Miner that the old culture of religion and **familism**—or life centring on the family—was not disrupted.

Hubert Guindon (1964) and Marcel Rioux (1964) similarly defend the appropriateness of the folk society model as applied to rural Quebec until well into the twentieth century. They cite evidence of strong family ties, low geographic and social mobility, the central importance of inherited land, and the powerful moral leadership of the clergy in perpetuating the folk character of communities such as St. Denis. Rioux characterizes rural Quebec as made up of small communities, with few outside contacts, and with people bound together by organic ties of family, culture, and church. It is this folk cultural identity, Rioux suggests, that underlies, and is in turn reinforced by, contemporary Quebec nationalism and sense of French-Canadian identity. While Quebec has an urban population, Rioux argues that the province can still be characterized as essentially a rural folk culture.

It is Philippe Garigue (1964) who plays the role of Oscar Lewis in challenging the validity of this folk society thesis in the context of rural Quebec, notwithstanding the wealth of data in its support. Garigue, like Lewis, argues that the model has led researchers to overemphasize evidence that supports it, and to minimize the relevance of empirical data not related to the definition. He suggests that the concept of *folk society* is not valid in French-Canadian history nor is it appropriate for contemporary rural Quebec. Historically, he argues, there never were the equivalent of close-knit, self-contained, traditionalist, organic communities in rural Quebec. The land was colonized by a process of ribbon development out from small towns, which acted as colonial trading posts. Individual farms were established in parallel rows, first fronting a river and then on an interior road built for the purpose.

This pattern of settlement militated against the development of close-knit communities, suggests Garigue. Farmers were fiercely individualistic. They built houses in the middle of their own individual plots about three miles away from neighbours in either direction. Only much later did communities or villages begin to emerge once a church was built in the district. The church provided an initial gathering place around which other buildings were established. Old people tended to move near the church when they retired, and the locality slowly began to function as a service centre for the district. Only at this stage could a village be said to exist. But the development of such a village centre did not substantially alter the private family individualism of independent farmers. In 1663 Louis XIV of France tried, for administrative convenience, to force settlers or habitants to build houses in village groups rather than on their own land (Falardeau 1964, 20). But such edicts were strongly resisted. Farm families refused to move. People maintained social relationships with the families living on neighbouring plots, but

had no desire to form village communities. Parishes were not formed until long after colonial settlement, and they constituted only huge administrative areas. Throughout most of Quebec's history, they could not be equated with rural communities.

Tenancies were frequently bought and sold (Garigue 1964, 126). This too challenges the notion of cohesive, long-settled folk communities. In addition, one researcher found that entire families had moved away from parishes to seek their fortune elsewhere. Nobody seemed to find this unusual or regrettable (Gérin 1964, 36).

The structural constraints of large families, indivisible farms, and limited land meant that the majority of children in any large family could not settle near home. They had to seek a livelihood elsewhere. Thus, there was considerable geographic mobility within families, contradicting the folk society model, despite the near truism that there was low mobility among the people who stayed behind. Usually only the youngest son would inherit the family farm when the parents where too old to farm it themselves. Older sons left. Only the lucky ones among them got farms in neighbouring parishes. This accounts for the observation that rural families in the 1950s were not usually centred in one community but were spread all over the province of Quebec and beyond (Garigue 1964, 134).

Garigue challenges even the notion of an all-embracing church with a subservient flock of parishioners. He cites evidence of widespread accounts of lay persons who refused to obey their priests, or even the bishop, over such matters as building a church and paying dues (Garigue 1964, 129–30).

Hence, in multiple ways, Garigue argues that rural settlement in Quebec does not conform to the folk society model. The concept, he suggests, is a myth, an ideology imposed on the data by the researchers. The intensely individualistic, independent farmers that Garigue found have more in common with the image of nuclear family individualism, characteristic of urban life, than with the Chicago School caricature of people embedded within an organic folk society.

Advocates of the folk society model have only partially responded to Garigue's challenge. Guindon, for instance, suggests that inheritance of land was still the norm and the stabilizing feature of rural life. Yet, hypothetically, if 70 percent of farms were inherited, this would mean that over three generations only about 34 percent of farms around a village would remain in the hands of the original family, a proportion close to that observed in St. Denis. Proponents of the folk society theory claim that these figures demonstrate a high level of stability. Critics, however, argue that this interpretation glosses over the considerable amount of geographic mobility that took place. Two-thirds of the land around St. Denis was not in the hands of the original families. Moreover, even when farms were inherited, there was considerable family mobility because there was not sufficient land for all the sons to settle locally. People tended to have large families, and yet the size of the village population remained relatively stable. Hence, the majority of children in large families must have moved away (Hughes 1964, 78).

Critics of the folk society model argue that such large families were not as common among French Canadians as the myth of the fertile Québécoise would suggest.

The fact that almost all village families would have close relatives living in other districts, and in towns and cities across Quebec and beyond, may help to account for the rapidity with which farms were abandoned after World War II. People sought higher standards of living in the urban areas and had family members who could help them to resettle (Fortin 1964, 1–2). Rioux tries to counter the claims of Garigue and others primarily by arguing that urban areas of Quebec were largely rural in character, hence accounting for the limited cultural differentiation found between urban and rural areas. If this is the case, it suggests that urban areas do not fit the folk-urban model any more than the rural areas seem to.

A strong challenge to the notion of folk culture in Quebec comes from an unlikely source, a re-evaluation of fertility data. Marie Lavigne (1986) questions the image of the fertile French-Canadian mother, dominated by the Catholic clergy and local political elites advocating a large French-speaking population. Québécois women have been portrayed as fertile mothers, responding not only to Catholic admonitions to have as many children as possible but also to nationalistic propaganda exhorting "the revenge of the cradle." Lavigne questions how we can reconcile this image with the history of the women's movement in Quebec from the nineteenth century onwards. Her answer is that this fertile mother image is largely a myth, applying at best to about one-fifth of all Quebec women from the 1850s onwards, when her data begin. Folk culture values, admonitions from the clergy, lack of access to modern contraceptives, and their illegality prior to 1968 notwithstanding, the birth rate in Quebec fell steadily every decade between 1850 and 1961.

As table 5-1 shows, of the women born during the years 1887, 1903, and 1913, at least 25 percent never became mothers. Most of these childless women remained unmarried, and only a small minority of them

became nuns. A further 15 to 25 percent of women made only a minimal contribution to fertility rates by having one or two children. At the other extreme, the ideal-typical large family of ten or more children was produced by less than one-fifth of the 1887 **cohort**. This ratio dropped to about one in fifteen women by 1913. The percentage of women having six or more children also dropped from almost 40 percent to just over 20 percent in the same period. This sharp drop indicates that many girls whose mothers had large numbers of children did not see this model of motherhood as one they wanted to copy.

Table 5-1 Birth Cohorts of Women by Marital Status and Number of Children, Quebec

| Number of Children | Birth Cohort | | |
	1887	1903	1913
0	10.8	13.7	11.9
1–2	15.8	21.2	25.2
3–5	21.9	22.8	27.4
6–9	19.7	16.3	14.7
10 or more	17.7	11.0	6.5
Unmarried women	14.1	15.0	14.3
Total	100	100	100

Source: Lavigne (1986). Calculations based on Henripin (1968).

Clearly, large numbers of women did practise contraception, regardless of the church's teachings on the subject. Interviews in 1960 with elderly women who had had their families at the turn of the century, indicated that they had not been particularly influenced by church doctrine, despite outward conformity. They practised contraception and still went to church. Lavigne argues from these data that we have to revise our view of the influence of religion on family life in Quebec. It appears to have been considerably shallower than the folk culture model would lead us to believe. We only have to compare these data with Redfield's commentary at the beginning of the study of St. Denis—with his references to the sacred character of sanctions, the deeply felt convictions of the people, and the family system as "strong, pervasive, and certain in its effects"—to realize how significant a challenge Lavigne's work presents to taken-for-granted theories.

We still need to ask where the image of fertile French-Canadian women comes from, if the majority of women did not conform to it. Lavigne points out that the collective memory that all Québécois ancestors had large families derives from the fact that most people remember the same minority of women. For example, if, hypothetically, ten women have one child each and one woman has ten children, half of the resulting 20 children in the second generation will have grown up in a large family, even though 90 percent of families did not conform to this pattern.

From Lavigne's article we learn that strong convictions, even when they appear well substantiated by evidence, may still give a false overall picture. The folk society concept of large families, inherited land, and overarching religious control by the Catholic Church is not wholly false, in that it does apply to a portion of people. The problem is that it may not fit more than half the members of the community. The majority of women and men made decisions about their family size that conflicted with the teachings of the church. It cannot even be assumed that women with large families were mindlessly following church edicts. Lavigne suggests that economic factors, like the usefulness of child labour on farms and in textile mills or the disadvantages of large families once schooling became compulsory, played a role in decisions about family size. Women make rational choices in historical-economic circumstances, Lavigne suggests, rather than conforming unquestioningly to cultural norms. It would seems, then, that the folk culture model obscures more than it reveals about life in rural Quebec.

Contemporary Rural Communities

The second stage of our critical review of rural-urban sociology in Canada turns from historical research to more contemporary studies of village communities. The main questions are the same. Do the characteristics described by researchers fit the Chicago School model? Is there sufficient contradictory evidence to suggest that the basic assumptions of the model are false?

In this section we will focus on Louis Wirth's causal model of the determinants of *gemeinschaft* and *gesellschaft* communities. As we saw earlier in this chapter, Wirth argues that three critical variables—large size, high density, and heterogeneity—generate *gesellschaft* types of association. *Gesellschaft* patterns include superficial, anonymous, and transitory relations, competitive struggle, divided allegiances, and limited sense of belonging, either to a locality or with the neighbouring people. The logical obverse of Wirth's three variables—small size, low density, and homogeneity—should maximize the probability of *gemeinschaft* relations. These are characterized by close-knit communities based on the sanctity of kinship ties, solidarity, attachment to the locality and to the core of shared cultural values. How well does this model stand up to contemporary research on rural communities?

Samuel Clark's study of four selected villages in the Miramichi and Bathurst areas of New Brunswick, conducted during 1972–73, found very little to support the image of *gemeinschaft* communities. The villages have the characteristics of small size, low population density, and homogeneity, but the social life described by Clark (1978, chap. 3) is anything but well-integrated and cohesive. Instead he gives a picture of rural society in a state of deterioration, with little evidence of any rich social life. The impression is one of people shut in on themselves. Not only did residents have little contact with the outside world, many of them indicated that they did scarcely any visiting among neighbours. "No one ever visits," said one respondent. "Television ruined that," said another. "People visit less now, got no reason to visit. . . . I'm not one for visiting." Many residents complained about the lack of social activity in their area, yet they gave no indication of any inclination to do anything about it. "There's not much social life here. People don't try to get together," was a typical response.

Two sets of ties did have some meaning: kinship and church. Almost everyone in the communities was either a relative or a neighbour of a relative of someone else in the community, and few new people moved in. Yet Clark found that kinship obligations appeared shallow and rarely extended beyond the immediate family circle. A sense of obligation between mothers and daughters was evident, but extended obligations tended to be accepted only if reciprocal. If they became a burden, they were likely to be repudiated. A son in jail in central Canada could be quietly forgotten. In the Catholic communities, virtually everyone went to mass but, apart from this obligation, there was no clear indication how meaningful church was to the people. In Protestant communities, church attendance tended to be associated with higher status, but the church otherwise seemed to have little influence over village life. It did not form the focus of much active social life.

Apart from what limited social life developed around kinship and church, the communities appeared to lack anything in the character of a social structure. A few residents in these villages indicated that they belonged to clubs or bought a newspaper, but most did not. Clark concludes that what generally obtained was "what might be described as a state of social anomie." **Anomie** is a state of social breakdown, characterized by weak bonds between people, a limited sense of meaningful relations, and the lack of any strong commitment to shared norms and regulations guiding interactions. Most residents appeared to have little feelings for their social obligations; that is, what they owed to their local community or to the society at large. There was nothing to support the view of idyllic contentment. Mostly people gave vent to their grievances, discouragement, and at times despair. The dominant attitude was a fatalistic acceptance of things as they were.

In general, the two subsistence farming communities in Clark's study were described as socially and culturally impoverished. Families turned in on themselves for material, social, and cultural wants. People lacked interest in music or literature and were ignorant of the outside world and indifferent to politics. Their religion was reduced to an elementary form of belief and organization.

The two other communities in the study, located on the outskirts of large towns, showed similarly impoverished social life. There was evidence of a good deal of animosity and little visiting among neighbours. One person described her neighbours as "a God-damned bad crowd—from way back in the woods where they never see no people, only bear and fox. Maybe is good people. We can't tell" (Clark 1978, 92). Insecurity and fear of crime were widely felt in these communities. Interviewing was actually cut short because "the fieldworkers had reason to fear for their physical safety had they attempted any extensive interviewing in the more congested parts of the inner area" (Clark 1978, 73). People were suspicious that interviewers on the project might be government agents, checking on them with the intention of cutting off their welfare payments.

Something clearly is wrong. According to Louis Wirth's theory of causality, these small, low-density, and homogeneous kinship-related areas in New Brunswick ought to be harmonious and integrated communities. But they are not. Clark's study is not alone in finding that small size, low-density living, and homogeneity do not ensure close community ties. The image of idyllic rustic communities may be part of our collective cultural mythology, but it is not part of the contemporary reality of village and small-town life. A 1983 study of towns and villages in Canada concludes that, while Gallup polls may show that people still express consistent preferences for farm and small community living, citing the appeal of peace and friendliness and simplicity of life in the countryside for city-weary, ecology-conscious, and independent urbanites, there is little evidence to support these images (Hodge and Qadeer 1983, 131). The study suggest that, while individual towns and villages differ widely from each other, patterns of daily life show minimal differences between rural and metropolitan centres.

Small communities are not necessarily safer places than big cities. The per capita incidence of crimes of violence may actually be higher in small towns than in cities. The residents of the small Miramichi communities studied by Clark learned in 1986 that they were not immune to violent crime when local people were charged in two separate cases of assault and murder. In the same vein, a report of the Advisory Council on the Status of Women indicates that the incidence of wife battery is as high in rural areas as it is in cities. This is especially serious because there are fewer facilities in rural areas for dealing with wife abuse. Indian reservations are typically small, ethnically and socially homogeneous, and have low-density populations, yet they experience far more than their share of social anomie. Reserves are

often wracked by alcoholism, high suicide rates, crime, and violence. In 1974, native Indians comprised less than 2 percent of the Canadian population, but nearly 20 percent of the people convicted of homicide (Taylor 1983, 102). Discrimination against native Indians in the courts, such as that experienced by Donald Marshall in Nova Scotia, exacerbates these problems.

To the outside world, small towns and villages may present a face of serenity, but internally they are communities with a fair degree of individualism and social division (Hodge and Qadeer 1983, 143). Smallness results in high visibility, and hence familiarity between residents, but this does not necessarily lead to sociability and friendliness. Often small towns harbour a hard core of poverty that is combined with a general indifference toward the poor. Prejudice is also often present. Racial and ethnic minorities may be tolerated, but they are often made to feel unwelcome.

These negative accounts of social disorganization in rural communities should not be taken to imply that all or even most rural communities are characterized by social anomie. Towns and villages vary widely. There are innumerable small settlements that provide satisfying community life for the residents. The critical point here is that smallness and homogeneity by themselves do not guarantee integrated community spirit. To explain such patterns we need more complex explanations than the Chicago School model provides.

Urban Communities: The Myth of Anomie

If many rural communities do not fit the folk image, can it be argued that the metropolitan environment, characterized by large size, high-density living, and heterogeneity, necessarily results in a loss of community? Evidence from McGahan's (1982) extensive research in urban sociology in Canada leads to a convincing "no." The Chicago School theory predicted that local neighbourhoods would decline in significance in urban centres. Nuclear families would be mobile and hence isolated, detached from strong allegiance to kinship ties beyond those of husband, wife, and dependent children. Social disorganization would increase with the demise of traditional bases of social solidarity.

Research in the Metropolitan Toronto borough of East York did not bear out these predictions (Wellman 1978; Shulman 1976). A study of a small sample of young, native-born, Anglophone, lower middle-class couples found that these people did not live isolated lives. Geographic integration between generations was quite high. People valued being near to other family members and wanted frequent interaction with them. Three-quarters of the sample visited kin in the metropolitan area at least once a week. The minority whose parents lived further away saw them less frequently. Couples expressed a sense of obligation to keep in contact with other family members. They regularly initiated contacts and participated in common ritual activities such as birthdays and anniversaries. Almost one-third saw their parents more than any other persons. The telephone was also a common means of contact.

The study also hints at interesting differences between women and men in their social relationships with kin and neighbours, although this was not itself a central focus of the research. Wives telephoned their parents more frequently than did their husbands. Most of the emotional contacts and interaction were organized by women. This finding suggests a certain sex bias in theories of urbanism. Generalizations prompted by research in the Chicago School tradition tend to be based on expectations about the behaviour of urban male workers. Female networks, and how these might vary for housewives compared

with employed women, receive little attention. But current research in urban geography by feminist theorists suggests that this is a critical blind spot in traditional and Marxist theory and has resulted in distorted perceptions of urban social relations.

The studies of East York note that mutual aid was very important between young couples and their parents. Almost half the young couples lived with one set of parents during the early years of marriage, before they could afford a place of their own. Common forms of aid included young people caring for sick parents, and grandparents babysitting their grandchildren. Parents also gave financial aid in crises, while young adults helped their parents with house repairs and with other needs of older people. The prediction that urban life would result in the breakdown of kinship ties was not substantiated in East York.

The prediction that high mobility would result in social isolation was similarly not supported by the data from studies in Fredericton and Montreal (McGahan 1982, 239–41). Geographic mobility did not reduce the size of the **kin universe**. The average number of kin contacted did not differ between the mobile and non-mobile urbanites. The non-mobile people had more face-to-face contacts, while the others used letters and telephones to keep in touch with relatives. There was no difference between them in the importance that they accorded to the kinship bond. The death of central connecting relatives was more important than geographic mobility in terminating kin ties.

Because of the strength of the image of large, traditional, rural families, French-Canadian families provide a particularly valuable test of the thesis that family ties decline with urban residence. One would expect city families to present a very different picture from rural ones, but in fact we do not find this. The data totally contradict the prediction that **nuclear family** isolation would be evident in urban areas.

People in the Montreal sample were able to name, on average, 215 relatives. Women were generally able to name more relatives than could men in the sample, and wives could often name more of their husbands' relatives than the husbands knew themselves (Garigue 1956). Women had much greater knowledge of the affairs of the kin group and interacted with the group more frequently. Contact with both parents and siblings was sustained regardless of geographic location. In the French-Canadian community in St. Boniface, Manitoba, mobility also did not disrupt kinship bonds (Piddington 1965). Instead, migrant kin tended to cluster together, and chain migration was common. Intermarriage among distant kin was not unusual.

In a study of Chicago, the sense of locality and identification with one's own small neighbourhood within a larger city was evidenced by the sustained interest in community newspapers. In 1952 there were eighty-two such local newspapers in Chicago, a seven-fold increase from 1910 (Janowitz 1967). Readership was concentrated among those closely tied to the local area, such as women, married couples, households with children, and long-time residents, and also those whose social class paralleled that of the neighbourhood. The local newspapers appeared to augment rather than compete with the city-wide media. People who bought local papers were more likely to participate in politics. Local neighbourhood involvement thus did not discourage a broader orientation. Those with the greatest political knowledge and competence were also highly attached to the local neighbourhood.

The Inner City

The strongest predictions of urban anomie and blight in the Chicago School thesis are directed at the **inner city**, seen as the locality with the highest density and the most mobile and heterogeneous populations.

The term *inner city*, referring to the central areas of old properties within large cities, actually encompasses a wide variety of neighbourhoods, including the commercial core of office blocks, stable working-class areas, slums, and "skid row." The inner city has increasingly come to include revitalized areas where more affluent middle-class people have bought up and renovated old properties. Clearly these different neighbourhoods vary widely in community character.

Stable working-class areas in large cities show a consistent pattern of close identification with neighbourhood and kin. McGahan (1982) cites the example of Toronto's Cabbagetown, a locality then inhabited predominantly by Anglo-Saxon, blue-collar, semiskilled or unskilled workers with below average incomes (Lorimer and Phillips 1971). Family roles were very traditional and were segregated along age and sex lines, but family ties were strong, with mutual support and obligations. Circles of close friends commonly included kin, often parents and adult children.

This pattern confirms what many other studies have found. A famous one is Young and Willmott's study (1957) of the working-class area of Bethnal Green in East London. In the heart of one of the largest cities in the world, they found not an anonymous *Gesellschaft* but a stable, homogeneous, and very close-knit community. On a shopping trip, for example, one of their respondents met sixty-three people in all, thirty-eight of whom were relatives. Herbert Gans (1962) found a similar pattern in the Italian neighbourhood in Boston.

Over the past decades in many cities in Canada and the United States, the cohesiveness of these old working-class communities has been disrupted by middle-class renovators looking for the convenience of downtown residence. This influx can erode the cohesiveness of the inner-city working-class and ethnic communities. Tensions in Cabbagetown in Toronto have resulted as middle-class renovators buy up neighbourhood houses. Relations between the long-term residents and the renovators are described as cautious but edgy, with a mutual recognition that they are quite different types of people. The newcomers tend to be less noisy and "troublesome" than some working-class residents, but on the other hand these newcomers cause more annoyance by making a fuss about such things as the congestion created by neighbours parking on the street (McGahan 1982, 273). Nonetheless, the impression from the research is that the working-class residents derive much satisfaction from living in Cabbagetown, and have a sense of identity with the neighbourhood. This is shown in their organized opposition to the city's urban renewal plans.

Affluent middle-class people are moving into previously working-class areas, such as Cabbagetown in Toronto, and renovating older houses.

Their middle-class neighbours may think them disorganized, but the image they give of themselves is one of strong community cohesion.

A central presumption among town planners is that physical deterioration goes with social deterioration and that urban slums are dangerous areas that should be avoided. Yet even in the slums one can find some evidence of integrated social order based on loyalties to ethnic group and to territory. One famous study was conducted in the mid-1960s in the Addams area in Chicago. This area comprised half a square mile and had a population of 20 000 people including Italians, blacks, Mexicans, and Puerto Ricans (Suttles 1968, 1972). Even in this area of high density, heterogeneity, and poverty, an underlying social order existed with territoriality and ethnicity providing bases for association and integration. A certain mutual trust and predictability developed among the various groups, which were subdivided by ethnicity, territory, age, and sex. Sectors opposed each other at times but were also able to co-operate against a common enemy from outside the neighbourhood. Street life was critical for forming personal acquaintances. People got to know each other as they lounged on street corners or met informally in local businesses and corner stores. In effect, the middle-class view of the slums was not supported by the residents themselves. For most it was a viable community with which they could identify.

A study of hobos, or the men on skid row, reflects the same discovery that, behind the appearance of destitution and personal disorganization, there is nonetheless a recognizable and, in some measure, supportive social organization (Harper 1979). When the researcher spent two weeks living and travelling with a hobo companion, he found that the man had a network of lifelong friends, and that together they had their own complex system of stratification and moral obligations.

An important word of caution here is that, just as Redfield found what he was looking for in describing harmonious village relations, so other researchers may be overemphasizing the sense of social organization to the exclusion of tensions and hostilities. In an effort to counter the middle-class bias that too easily equates poverty with disorganization, they may be overstating the opposite image. Nonetheless, these studies demonstrate that, just as a village environment does not guarantee cohesive community relations, neither does a densely populated, mobile, and heterogeneous urban environment preclude integrated community relations, local loyalties, and strong kinship ties. The predictions of the Chicago School theory are not borne out.

There are two kinds of locality for which there is a certain amount of consensus in applying descriptions such as urban anomie and social disorganization. The first is the area to which people have been relocated after slum clearance programs. The second is the concentrated area of subsidized housing, particularly where the housing takes the form of highrise apartment blocks. The objective of city planners is usually to improve the lot of the residents, but rarely does this seem to have worked. More commonly, the forced relocation destroys the existing networks and support mechanisms within the slum areas and moves isolated and impoverished people in among strangers. As in Clark's description of the lives of rural migrants who settled on the outskirts of Bathurst and Newcastle, isolation and shallow, distrustful relations, bordering openly on fear, seem to characterize many such resettlement zones. People have been unable to reproduce the cohesiveness of old slum communities (McGahan 1982, 278–82).

Public housing projects constructed to replace the slums appear to offer few advantages. They are still overcrowded, the noise level is intense, and services and facilities

Concentrated areas of subsidized housing, particularly when they are made up of highrise apartment blocks, seem to bear out predictions of urban anomie and social disorganization.

are not maintained. The stigma of public housing creates a negative stereotype that is internalized by residents. Tenants have improved accommodation, but they mostly view it unfavourably, complaining of swearing, drinking, fighting, noisy and destructive people, and few social controls, particularly over children. Controls are imposed from outside the area, by police and social workers. Thus, in the public housing projects "extensive solidarity is inhibited by mutual distrust, inability to co-operate, and subordination to external authorities" (McGahan 1982, 281). Residents still lack control over their total life situations. This sense of powerlessness, of being pawns in a game played by impersonal government agents in the housing office, or in the social work department, may well be the most important

element in the fatalism or "welfare mentality" often associated with residents in subsidized housing.

Suburbia: The Gender Ghetto

Suburbs provide an intermediate environment between low density, long-settled rural
areas and high density, heterogeneous city
centres. Suzanne Mackenzie (1986b, 87)
describes them as the late nineteenth-century and early twentieth-century solution to
the problem of co-ordinating production and
reproduction in the industrial city. City
planners, who were strongly influenced by
Chicago School theories, argued that the
high density and artificial environment of
industrial city centres were not conducive to
stable community life. Inner cities seemed no
place to raise children. But workers still had
to live within commuting distance of the factories and offices where they were employed.
Suburban housing developments seemed to
provide the solution. They offered relatively
low density, single-family homes, with open
spaces and parks, and with transportation
routes that would service commuters in the
mornings and evenings.

This kind of city planning assumed as its
basic premise the segregation of gender
roles, with women as housewives and
mothers working full-time in the suburban
home while the husband-father commuted to
the city each day as the family breadwinner.
Suburbia was the geographic and physical
expression of this **gender-role segregation**,
based on the spatial, temporal, and functional separation between home and work
and, concomitantly, between the gender
categories of woman and man. Suburbs
worked, suggests Mackenzie, so long as this
assumption held.

As places to live, suburbs have earned a
mixed reputation. While they provide
spacious family homes, they exact mindless
conformity. As we shall see later in chapter
11 on the sociology of the family, "homes"

may be intentionally separated from the
workplace, but jobs still influence in major
ways the quality and patterns of home life.
This is particularly true for corporate professionals where image is important.

Whyte's book *The Organization Man*
(1956) contains a section on "the organization man at home" that closely conforms to
the stereotype that suburban housing
estates represent vast transit camps for
upwardly mobile middle-class executives
concerned only with the conspicuous consumption of consumer durables and with
keeping up appearances. Whyte emphasizes
the homogeneity of suburban life: the ranks
of identical housing contain lifestyles of
similarly relentless conformity.

A study of the upper middle-class suburb
of Crestwood Heights in Toronto describes a
similar concern with attainment and maintenance of social status and the importance
of material affluence as a basis for judging
the status of others (Seeley, Sim, and Loosley
1956). The type of house owned, and its
specific location in the suburb, together with
membership in the proper clubs and associations, formed an important basis for social
esteem.Outside institutions, particularly
schools, came to dominate family life while,
within the home, furnishings were dictated
by the latest fashions presented in decor
magazines.

Other studies, however, serve to emphasize that not all suburbs are alike. Clark's
(1966) study of the suburbanization process
in Toronto during the 1950s suggests that
the character of the suburbs depends much
upon self-selection. Some suburbs may
attract professional families, while others
may attract low- or middle-income families,
and yet others appeal to older, retired people.
In cosmopolitan cities, different suburban
areas may attract people from distinct ethnic
backgrounds. In Clark's study, the main
reason why most residents moved to the
suburbs was to have adequate living space,

not to escape from the city. They were mostly young middle-class families with children, and they focussed on home and family rather than on neighbourhood participation. Unlike those in Whyte's study, Clark's families tended to want to be left alone. Neighbourhood associations were casual and ephemeral.

Differences between wives and husbands in their response to suburban living have received incidental attention in these studies. One year after settling in the suburbs, wives tended to be less satisfied than their husbands with the way they spent their time. They complained about not being employed and about the distance they had to travel to various activities, which discouraged their involvement in organizations located outside the suburb. The primary benefits seemed to accrue to husbands. It was men who believed most strongly in the desirability of a suburban location for the family. At the same time, they suffered the fewest obstacles in daily escaping this location for their place of employment, leaving wives to encounter the negative aspects of suburbia.

The most important negative aspect of the suburban setting for women is that it makes their dual roles as domestic worker and wageworker difficult. Suburbs worked well, Mackenzie suggests, for the brief period between 1930 and the mid-1950s, when the common pattern was single income families and wives as full-time homemakers. But this started to break down in the 1960s as the costs of purchasing and maintaining suburban houses rose to the point where they were beyond the reach of average middle-class incomes. Families required two incomes to keep up a suburban lifestyle. The cost of housing in the Toronto area in the 1980s, for example, is so high that it takes almost all of one average income just to meet the rent or mortgage payments. The family lives on what the second parent earns. Mackenzie

gives examples of single parents having to double up with other single parents just to keep a house.

Once women began to seek paid employment in large numbers, the disadvantages of suburban living became increasingly evident. Suburbs were not designed to accommodate the dual roles of houseworker and wage earner. The layout assumes that workers have minimal domestic responsibilities. Public transit routes, for example, are radial; that is, they are arranged like, spokes of a wheel, going into the downtown centre from outlying suburbs. Bus time-tables are geared to "business hours," with the majority of vehicles going from suburb to city centre in the mornings and from city centre to suburb in the early evenings. This arrangement of bus routes is often very inconvenient for women. Their income-earning activities often require lateral movement from one suburban district to another at irregular hours. Women who earn money by selling cosmetics or clothing or other home-produced goods, or who do domestic work or child care in other people's homes, or who tutor in the evenings, for example, may find the bus service extremely inconvenient if not useless. Transit systems also tend not to be geared to women's erratic and multi-stop movements between child care, shops, children's teachers, and so on (Mackenzie 1989).

The entire pattern of a private family, **dormitory suburb** style of living, with male workers sleeping in the suburbs and commuting downtown to work while their wives stay home all day keeping house, has begun to change in radical ways. More and more women have set up networks to assist them in their dual homemaker/income-earner responsibilities (Mackenzie 1986b, 92). Networks among friends and neighbours have been redesignated as working networks, sources of contact, advice, and assistance. Such networks disseminate information about the quality of goods and services provided by homeworkers, and also operate as referral systems, linking child-minders with mothers needing the service, and knitters and dressmakers with their clientele. Mutual aid networks among women have also developed facilities such as drop-in centres and playgrounds to support their "domestic-community work" (Mackenzie 1986b, 93).

Mackenzie points out that the traditional distinction between domestic work in the home and community work outside it does not apply to these women. Their homes function as their work station, factory, or office, in which they manufacture crafts, food, or other goods for sale, or organize play centres, tutorial classrooms, drop-in centres, and the like. Industrialization is associated with the transfer of work from home to factory, and hence with the separation of domestic work, usually done by women, from factory work, usually done by men. But the women living in the suburbs studied by Mackenzie are reversing this pattern. In a sense, they are recreating a pre-industrial pattern of economy in which the distinctions between homemaking, housework, employment, and work cannot be drawn.

This very recent research into the working lives and the "hidden economy" of women accomplishes two things. First, it shows how different the experience of suburban living can be for men and women. Most men leave the suburb to go to work in the morning and return at night, while most women spend their working day in the suburb. Men may thus find the suburb a convenient place to relax after work and play with the children, while women may find it a frustrating and restricting place in which to make a living. On the other hand, people who work elsewhere may develop few social ties within the suburbs, but people who are trying to transform them into work centres may find them teaming with networks of support services and clientele.

A Re-orientation of Theory: Political Economy and Feminism

This overview of the findings of rural-urban research—into the "folk" society of Quebec, contemporary life in villages and small towns, and conditions in different urban areas, including settled middle-class and working-class districts, the inner city, and the suburbs—points to the general failure of the Chicago School thesis. The model predicts that small and homogeneous villages will function as integrated and cohesive communities. Loneliness, isolation, and social disorganization will increase steadily as size, density, and heterogeneity increase, and will reach their worst extreme in the centre of metropolitan cities. No doubt instances can be found to fit the model, but these are not sufficient for the theory to be retained. What matters is that there is clear evidence that these predictions have failed in many instances. We have examples of villages where residents described their lives in terms of loneliness, isolation, and distrust; alternatively we have examples of residential areas in the heart of some of the largest metropolitan centres in Canada where people describe their lives in terms of integrated, cohesive neighbourhood ties and strong kinship links. The theoretical model that has guided a great deal of this research cannot account for such results.

Political Economy Analysis

The dominant alternative perspective of Marxism, or political economy theory, is beginning to fill this theoretical vacuum. Researchers working in this tradition are offering new insights into the economic determinants of "loss of community" and why it seems much more in evidence in some contexts than in others. They focus not on the demographic characteristics of different localities, but on the surrounding economy and the destructive impact of economic insecurity, poverty, and exploitation. Political economy theory predicts that, regardless of size or location, the communities that will show the most evidence of social disorganization and demoralization will be in areas of relatively severe poverty or, more importantly, where people are losing their basic sense of economic security and control over their life situation.

The study of villages in the Miramichi region of New Brunswick in the early 1970s gives ample evidence of prolonged economic decline, which is consistent with the conditions of social anomie found by researchers. Clark suggests that the poor quality of farmland, with the exception of isolated pockets of fertile soil near the river valleys, meant that many farms in the region could support only a **subsistence** level of living. In other words, the farms might provide sufficient food, fuel, and building materials to meet the basic necessities of life for a family, but they provided little surplus produce that could be marketed. Most farmers depended on supplementing their farm income with part-time work as woodsmen, fishermen, or labourers. Some farms became more prosperous as the opening of nearby urban markets promoted commercial farming, but success was not possible for all, and many were ruined by debt (Clark 1978).

Clark himself tends to blame impoverishment, minimal levels of education, or the experience of industrial work for the apparent inability of many Miramichi residents to move in search of better opportunities. A few of the more enterprising people did get out, but the remainder are trapped by cheap housing, unemployment insurance or welfare payments, and the absence of any social or educational skills that might equip them to survive in a city such as Toronto.

William Dunn, a sociologist who worked directly with Clark on the study, and who is himself a native of this area, disagrees

Studies have argued that residents of inpoverished villages in some areas of the Maritimes are trapped by cheap, substandard housing, unemployment payments, and lack of skills.

strongly with the historical-cultural perspective adopted by Clark. While he supports all the quotations in the book and the experience of anomie that the people expressed, Dunn argues strongly for a more critical neo-Marxist perspective to analyse the findings. In particular he stresses the high level of poverty and welfare that the researchers found in three of the four villages studied. He comments, "that the very poor should lack interest in literature is not surprising. When one struggles day by day to survive, there is not time for literature, or other interests that middle-class folk take for granted" (*Miramichi Leader*, 9 March 1988, 5). Dunn notes further that research data may exaggerate the small proportion of Maritime natives who went to Toronto but failed to integrate, because it is precisely these people who tend to be concentrated in low-income housing projects where they can be readily identified and contacted for research. The majority who succeeded bought homes and are scattered all over the city.

The Marxist theorist James Sacouman (1980; 1981) goes beyond Clark in his analysis of the economic and social impoverishment of rural areas in the Maritimes. He rejects the notion that poverty might be accounted for by an inadequate rural culture, arguing instead that the uneven development of farming, fishing, and forestry in the Maritimes was the result of organized capitalist policies. This process he terms the **semi-proletarianization** of the domestic mode of production. What he means by this is that people who once worked for themselves as small farmers, woodlot owners, or small fishermen, or some combination of these activities, have been pushed into a situation where they have to take part-time wagework to survive. The jobs made available to them are seasonal, insecure, and at the bottom of the wage scale, so that it is impossible to survive on wages alone. The fact that people in the region could provide for themselves, at least in part, through subsistence farming has meant that employers in big corporations have been able to exploit them ruthlessly, paying below **subsistence wages** or extremely low prices for the raw materials. Merchants also benefitted from unequal exchange: they bought products from rural producers at low prices and sold supplies at high prices. The result was that merchants always came out on top, and the rural population was effectively unable to accumulate any wealth.

Clark notes that the inevitable results of such an economic trap are fatalism and the "depletion of social stock," or the tendency for the most able and ambitious young people to leave such an economically depressed area. Less able and less motivated people are overrepresented among those who remain.

A collection of articles on farming, fishing, forestry, mining, and energy in the Atlantic region (Burrill and McKay 1987) documents the extensive destruction of the rural

maritime economy to the state of near catastrophe for many communities. Between 1941 and 1981, for example, 87 percent of New Brunswick farms disappeared as highly mechanized corporate capitalist farming took over the potato industry. During the same period, the number of farms in Nova Scotia dropped by 85 percent and on Prince Edward Island by 74 percent. In human terms, there were 6000 farmers in New Brunswick in 1951; in 1981 there were just over 4000 (Burrill and McKay 1987, 16, 20). What happened to the 22 000 displaced farmers and their families? Where did they go? Many of the young people with options migrated from the region, going to Alberta and Toronto. Others went to Moncton and Saint John. Many more people, who lacked the financial and educational resources to move long distances, drifted into the outskirts of smaller towns in the Miramichi area, forming the settlements described in Clark's study. They survived as best they could on intermittent, low-wage work and welfare. Thousands of families lived below the poverty line in the substandard housing that still dots the area.

People on welfare, people who have lost their means of independent subsistence, do not tend to give generously to the local United Way or the Red Cross. Nor do they generally show much interest in literature and the arts. They cannot. They are victims of the system. From this perspective, the "social anomie" described by Clark has little to do with the culture of the people, or with "a few bad apples." The quality of community life suffers through no fault of the people themselves. Powerlessness, dependency, and loss of hope for the future breed anger, frustration, and sometimes violence. The underlying factor is fear. It was precisely such feelings that led residents in one community to threaten researchers, for fear that they might be collecting evidence that could be used to cut welfare cheques, the only source of meagre economic security for many local families in the early 1970s. These people had already lost their dignity as independent farmers and farm workers. The probably could not take much more.

A large number of Indian reserves in Canada are similarly so poor that they cannot provide a standard of living above welfare for the residents. Welfare dependency, loss of dignity, and the absence of hope for the future manifest themselves in exceptionally high rates of alcoholism, glue and gasoline sniffing, suicide, and violence. Kellough (1980, 352) describes Indians as "a permanent underclass of unemployed people within capitalism." This situation too is not due to the culture of the Indian people. One does not have to dig far into Canadian history to find the evidence of a multitude of Indian bands driven from their land by white settlers and forced back onto the poorest quality land, which white settlers did not

want. Indians were cheated repeatedly out of the lands they did possess, and their capacity to run their own affairs was constantly undermined by the patriarchal powers vested in agents from the Department of Indian Affairs.

The same explanatory model linking economic collapse to loss of community can be applied to urban contexts where social anomie is most in evidence. Under clearance projects, economically disadvantaged people are uprooted and bundled together into subsidized housing complexes, under the patriarchal authority of government agencies. It may well be that this uprooting from the slum districts, while it gives people better quality housing, also destroys the existing community support and working networks that made it possible for people to make a living in the inner city. City planners are generally not trained to notice or to look

High levels of poverty among native peoples are partly due to government policies that herded native bands onto the poorest quality land.

favourably on such networks. More precisely, with respect to the Chicago School theory, they are actively trained *not* to look for and *not* to see such networks, especially among dependent women. In an effort to help, planners may have destroyed the people's means to help themselves, made them "grateful" recipients of welfare housing, and actually produced the social collapse that they then blame on the character of the residents.

Another context in which the impoverishment of community life tends to be reported is in the many single-industry, non-renewable resource extraction towns in Canada. These are town that on the surface may look prosperous, but they share relative powerlessness and long-term economic insecurity, particularly for young people. This is the central theme of Lucas' study *Minetown, Milltown, Railtown* (1971). The majority of people who live in these single-industry towns work for one company, and many live in company houses. They want their children to be employed locally but invariably one company cannot absorb all school leavers. Young people are forced to leave the area to find work, resulting in communities of elderly people in many one-industry towns in northern Canada. Many of these towns face uncertain futures because mines particularly depend upon the extraction of a non-renewable resource. Eventually the mines will close down and the town will die. Nova Scotia, British Columbia, and Alberta are dotted with ghost towns deserted after coal seams ran out. The result is that the towns always have a finite life expectancy, with no long-term prospects for children.

Single-industry towns rarely expand and are particularly vulnerable to any change in technology or markets. They are also subject to the total control and paternalism of the companies. This control is evidenced in the comment of one company executive concerning why there were few women working in the town. In the early days, the company had both husbands and wives working, but the children were running wild and the police were moving in. So the company laid down new rules by which married women were not permitted to work (Lucas 1971). Meg Luxton (1980) describes in depth the entrapment experienced by women in the northern Manitoba town of Flin Flon, where early marriage and dependence on a male breadwinner offer virtually the only option for adult women in the town. Even elite members of these towns are powerless to influence major decisions concerning the future economy since these decisions are made by head office, by government policies, and by international trading agreements, all subject to impersonal forces outside the community.

Class and ethnic divisions split the towns internally. The normal pattern is that top jobs are held by the British ethnic group while French-Canadians and native Indians work in the lowest levels, if at all. Senior jobs within the companies tend to go to young executives brought in from headquarters. Local people are trapped in a low-mobility system. It is little wonder that a sense of fatalism and apathy pervades such towns. It is neither locality nor small size, but wider economic forces that shape small towns and the people in them.

Seen from the political economy perspective, the major problem with theories that focus on urbanism is that they deflect awareness from the wider societal forces shaping communities. Town planners may try to build "garden-cities" for people to live in, but they cannot influence the structure of industrial capitalism that results in major economic decisions being made at company headquarters, far outside the sway of the communities concerned. Evidence may be found of expressions of apathy, fatalism, and low community spirit within impoverished and uprooted rural communities or subsidized housing estates, but analysis cannot stop there, with the implication that culture is the cause of the problem. We need to press further, to explore the workings of an economic system that reduces large numbers of people to an impoverished, semi-proletarian existence, or that creates the unemployment and insecurity that undermine independence.

A Challenge from Feminist Theory

Political economy theory goes considerably beyond traditional theories of the Chicago School in accounting for patterns of rural and urban community breakdown. Yet this perspective also is coming under increasing criticism for presenting too simplistic a picture. It tends to imply **economic determinism**, at least in the negative sense of predicting that all economically insecure or impoverished localities will be characterized by social anomie. But this is too rigid. This pattern does not accurately describe all communities experiencing economic stress. It underestimates the capacity of people to fight back and to maintain viable social communities in spite of such problems. As Dunn points out, the study of New Brunswick villages in the early 1970s uncovered an appalling amount of rural poverty, but it also indicated that some people wished to remain where they were, not because they could not leave, but because they did not want to (*Miramichi Leader*, 9 March 1988, 5). This attachment is itself a measure of the resilience of community spirit. Such spirit cannot be reduced to economic variables, even as we acknowledge that economics has a role in its perpetuation.

A particularly important blind spot in political economy theory concerns the roles that women play in the life of communities and in the hidden economy of domestic-community work. Mackenzie (1987a, 248–49) criticizes the pervasive assumption that contemporary industrial society can be understood as comprising an economic sector that is distinct from a home and community sector. Traditionally, political economy assumes that the home and community sector is dependent upon the public sector, and hence that it can be ignored in research on the determinants of community survival.

Another aspect of political economy theory that Mackenzie challenges is the **core-periphery model**. This model implies that innovation is centred in the *core*—the large industrial centres that are the homebase of multinational corporations. It is here that new ideas, new technology, and new kinds of economic relations are assumed to emerge. They then diffuse slowly to the *periphery*—the outlying areas that provide raw materials and cheap labour to the core. The result of these two assumptions regarding women's role and the core-periphery model is the notion that the home and community sector of peripheral areas must be the most dependent and the least innovative place of all. Hence it is neglected and devalued in research.

Mackenzie's own research on the community of Nelson, in the British Columbia interior, focusses directly on this neglected sector of domestic-community work in a peripheral area. Her work shows how crucial this sector can be in understanding communities that are experiencing economic stress (Mackenzie 1987b). Nelson is a resource-extraction area that underwent severe economic decline in the 1980s. Almost all industrial plants either closed down or "modernized" their operations resulting in significant cuts in their labour force. This occurred at the same time as massive cuts in resource extraction and related industries in mining, smelting, and forestry.

Secure, highly paid, unionized jobs for men disappeared. What remained were the once economically marginal activities largely done by women, such as caring for children, maintaining homes, cooking meals, growing food, and manufacturing goods and crafts in the home. It was this informal economy that was galvanized into action by the collapse of the formal economy of wagework for men. As unions, employers' groups, and chambers of commerce contracted, women's networks expanded. The local Doukhobour community revived its farming and food processing co-operatives, largely inactive since 1940. They joined forces with two groups to generate small businesses based on skills and existing resources. These two groups were the politically active and articulate feminist movement and the back-to-the-landers, or relatively well-educated people, formerly from the cities, who were attracted to a self-sufficient rural lifestyle. Woodworking, home renovation, machinery maintenance, food processing co-operatives, artisans' co-operatives, home child-care services, and related nursery education classes all sprang up to provide alternative employment. Deserted university buildings were used to house a Summer School of the Arts and to promote tourism and the sale of artwork.

In this process of developing a home and community sector economy, old networks among women were strengthened and restructured, and community spirit was stronger than it had ever been. Under the umbrella of the West Kootenay Women's Association, various groups worked together to provide support and resources for small enterprises, holding seminars on business management and grant applications, sharing employment grants, and holding skill-development seminars. They also worked actively with what was left of the men's union groups to sponsor projects.

The outcome, suggests Mackenzie, was a radical transformation of the formerly gender-segregated, resource-based, male-working-force town. The definitions of public and private locations, and of what constitutes unskilled and private activity versus marketable and public skills, broke down. The informal economy became the public economy, and with it women gained prominence in community activities.

This did not happen smoothly or without a struggle. Mackenzie (1987b, 8) notes that local conservative groups contested these changes in gender definitions and stressed that attention should be focussed not just on job creation but on the creation of *men's* jobs and other conditions for the re-establishment of "normal" family life, by which they meant the male-breadwinner–female-homemaker pattern. The politics of recovery, Mackenzie suggests, are being cast in terms of gender roles and conflict between conservative and feminist strategies. Regardless of the nay-sayers, however, it seems to have been the feminist strategies that kept the community going when the formal economy pulled out.

Existing theoretical frameworks in urban geography and sociology, both traditional and Marxist-inspired, have been designed primarily to explore men's relations to their environment. They have been adapted only with difficulty to the analysis of gender-based differences in the use of urban resources and urban networks. At first they attempted merely to "add on" women without otherwise changing any research methods (Mackenzie 1989, 4). At the end of his 1980 paper on semi-proletarianization in the Maritimes, Sacouman has a paragraph noting that women lost their jobs in the fish-packing plants as freezer trawlers were introduced. This addendum is an advance over women being ignored altogether, but they are still marginal to the analysis of community life and restructuring.

A second attempt to include gender in urban studies has been to develop the analysis of women as a separate subfield, as if they were a subgroup deviating from the male norm. Women appear as a valid topic— mostly for women to do research on—but are still marginal to the discipline. Only very recently have feminist questions begun to shift into the centre of the theoretical debates in the social sciences, not as a subtopic, but as a central part of the process of theorizing itself. There is still a long way to go to accomplish this integration within urban sociology, or indeed within any branch of sociology.

An Integrated Political Economy

Mackenzie's research on women's response to economic recession in Nelson offers an important qualification to predictions from political economy theory concerning loss of community. But, as she herself acknowledges, women's response has its limits as a steady means of holding a community together. It may not be sustainable in the long term. The informal economy offers work only for a few people and entails working long and irregular hours for low income. Nelson may have been particularly well suited to the development of such locally based survival strategies because of its long history of self-sufficiency prior to the influx of the resource-extraction industries and also because its university centre attracted a core of skilled artists who could set up new businesses. The town also has potential as a tourist centre for summer and winter sports and has been used for location shooting by Hollywood filmmakers. Not many of the peripheral areas experiencing economic recession will have such resources.

The presence of such an informal economy was not evident in Clark's study in the Miramichi. The critical difference from Nelson is that many of the people Clark interviewed had been self-sufficient producers in family enterprises in the past, and it was precisely this self-sufficiency that was broken by corporate capitalist farming, fishing, and forestry. Few other self-help options are open, beyond the great panacea of tourism. Sacouman has said that this emphasis on tourism promises to reduce the Maritimes to a zoo.

Yet the Miramichi villages studies by Clark have survived as viable, if not prosperous, communities. The description of social disorganization and anomie cannot be applied to them in an unqualified way. Indeed, several local people wrote spirited defences of their communities to the local newspaper, the *Miramichi Leader*. They insisted that they enjoyed their communities and did not find them anomic. But it is to the wider economy of the Maritime region that we need to look for an explanation for these feelings. There has been a great deal of change in some or in all of the Miramichi communities since 1972–73 when the study was conducted (*Miramichi Leader*, 9 March 1988, 5). Federal and provincial support for the Chatham Air Base, the expansion of jobs in the pulp and paper industry around Newcastle, increased mining activities around Bathurst, and government subsidies to small fishermen along the North Shore have all helped to provide a viable economic base in the area. With this support the small communities have pulled through.

Is their future secure? There are important questions hanging over the future of the regional economy, and consequently over the small communities in the region. Their future will depend heavily upon monopoly capitalist practices and upon politics. In its 1989 budget, the federal government announced plans to cut its military spending. The Chatham Air Base, which employed 700 to 800 civilian and military personnel in 1989, must cut 40 to 50 percent of its staff by the end of 1990. A nearby base, St. Margaret's, which in 1989 employed 40 military personnel engaged in satelite identification and tracking, is scheduled to close down by 1993. Technological development in the pulp and paper industry carries the possibility that crushed sugar cane residue may soon provide a cheap alternative to pulp wood. New Brunswick could end up with an oversupply of trees good only for pulp with nowhere to sell them (Schneider 1987, 122).

Government support for factory freezer trawlers already threatens to destroy the means of livelihood for small inshore fishermen in the Atlantic region. One of the implications of the free trade deal with the United States is that processors in the U.S. would have unlimited access to unprocessed Canadian fish, with serious consequences for people all along the North Shore who make their living in fish packing and processing. Women stand to be particularly hard hit by such changes. As Sacouman has pointed out, the advent of freezer trawlers has already cost many women their jobs in fish packing. So long as the packing plant was near where they lived, women could juggle the dual demands of domestic work and wagework. But this is no longer possible when freezer trawlers require that they be away at sea for forty days at a stretch. Families that survived on a semi-proletarian lifestyle may fall back onto welfare without the added income that women brought home. New Brunswick miners may find themselves competing with operations—often Canadian-owned—in the Third World where the base pay for miners may be one-tenth of New Brunswick wages. If all these things should come to pass in the next thirty years, the suffering of Miramichi people may well be worse than what their grandparents went through with the collapse of their farms.

The central message of political economy theory, which is not contradicted by feminist perspectives, is that people need a secure economic base on which to build viable and vital community life. They do not need wealth, but rather basic confidence that they can provide for themselves and their children. Without this, families break up as children leave, and people become demoralized, fatalistic, depressed, and afraid. In this respect, political economy theory is much closer to the original explanation of *gemeinschaft* and *gesellschaft* communities offered by Tönnies than is the classical Chicago School model. In mourning a loss of community, Tönnies did not blame urbanism or the size of the community, but the basic value system that places rational calculation of economic gain over social and cultural values. It is the values of the capitalist system itself that are in question.

Conclusion

The folk-urban thesis popularized by Chicago School theorists has been largely discredited. Rural communities are not uniformly or even generally characterized by the close-knit, integrated social life envisioned in the notion of folk society. Neither do urban communities fit the image of shallow and detached associations between strangers. The three key factors of size, density, and heterogeneity do not turn out to be good predictors of the quality of community life. Marxist predictions based on economic security as the foundation of community integration are stronger. This approach suggests that Tönnies' model of *Gemeinschaft* and *Gesellschaft*, based on a generalized critique of industrial society, was more accurate than the Chicago School's distinction between rural and urban settings. However, Marxist theory generally fails to take account of the tenacity with which people fight to hold viable communities together in the face of economic hardship. The role of women in these processes of community integration had been overlooked before recent feminist research began to change how questions are asked.

The most valuable lesson to be learned from this loss of community debate is the importance of subjecting evidence to a critical evaluation. The folk-urban model sounds convincing. It fits the preconceptions that most of us have about simple rural life, where people care about each other, and about anonymous crowds in the city, where self-interest prevails. But however convincing this argument sounds, when the assumptions are systematically tested against the evidence, they do not hold up. It is essential to adopt the same critical approach to all other theories in sociology and, indeed, in all other fields of study.

Suggested Reading

Two short essays that give a good introduction to the Chicago School approach to rural-urban sociology are Louis Wirth, "Urbanism as a Way of Life" (1938), and Robert Redfield, "The Folk Society" (1947). Both authors support the theory that rural community life will be highly cohesive and integrated around shared values and commitments of kinship and religion. Urban life, in contrast, is characterized by shallow associations between strangers.

The collection of articles edited by Marcel Rioux and Yves Martin, *French-Canadian Society* Volume 1 (1964), provides an excellent overview of the folk-society thesis as applied historically to rural Quebec. Articles by Guindon, Rioux, and Redfield strongly support the folk-society argument, while the article by Garigue and, to a lesser extent, those by Falardeau and Gérin, challenge it. A contemporary challenge to the folk-society thesis is provided by Marie Lavigne in "Feminist Reflections on the Fertility of Women in Quebec" (1986). Lavigne questions whether Quebec women as a whole ever internalized the traditional Catholic emphasis on large families and the church's opposition to contraception.

The study by Samuel D. Clark, *The New Urban Poor* (1978), provides a largely functionalist view of community life in rural New Brunswick in the early 1970s. Clark explores the problems of social and economic decline associated with widespread, if temporary, migration from New Brunswick to Toronto and the West.

The text by Peter McGahan, *Urban Sociology in Canada* (1982), provides an excellent and comprehensive overview of research on urban communities in Canada. Different sections of the book cover such topics as the inner-city areas, middle-class and working-class suburbs, and comparisons between Toronto and Montreal.

A political economy perspective on life in single-industry towns is provided by Rex Lucas in *Minetown, Milltown, Railtown* (1971) and Meg Luxton in *More than a Labour of Love* (1980). Lucas shows how all aspects of life in small Canadian towns are dictated by the policies of major corporations that dominate the local economies. Inhabitants are relatively powerless to influence the future of their town. Many of these towns, especially those that rely on extraction industries, have an uncertain future, and that insecurity carries over into community life in a sense of fatalism and dependency upon the corporation. Luxton focusses particularly upon the lives of women in such towns.

A series of articles by Suzanne Mackenzie explores how women, both in suburbs and economically declining small towns, actively create new social and economic relations of community life. Her articles include "Women's Response to Economic Restructuring: Changing Gender, Changing Space" (1986) and "Neglected Spaces in Peripheral Places: Homeworkers and the Creation of a New Economic Centre" (1987).

Chapter 6

Cohesion and Morality: A Critical Look at Durkheim

The development of sociological theory in the eighteenth and nineteenth centuries was powerfully influenced by belief in the inevitability of progress and in the evolution of social and biological forms from simpler to more advanced states. From these perspectives, the industrial and political revolutions occurring in Europe and North America reflected not the breakdown of social order but the emergence of a new and potentially better order, one based on science and reason and the liberation of individuals from the crushing yolk of superstition and feudalism.

The Emergence of the Scientific Study of Society

The idea of social progress found philosophical roots in the work of the German philosopher G.W.F. Hegel (1770–1831). Hegel reasoned that people have an innate capacity to plan for the future, to imagine what the future might be like, and to strive to bring their visions to reality. Human history comprises the collective human struggle to mould the future into closer conformity with a shared vision of an ideal world. Humans are unique in the animal kingdom in their capacity to have visions and to project themselves actively into the future. Humans are not stuck in the present, or biologically programmed to behave in certain ways, as squirrels are programmed to hoard nuts in the fall. Humans are able to reason, to evaluate their social world, to be aware that the world could be better than it is. Hence, they can never be totally content with things as they are. To be human is to have plans or projects for the future and to strive, at both the individual and collective level, toward perfection. The human spirit or essence is embodied in this striving for a perfect state. Hegel refers to this vision, at its highest level of abstraction, as *The Idea*. For Hegel, this is ultimately what we mean by *God*.

The idea of progress also found support in the biological sciences, which were revolutionized by the theory of **evolution**. This theory accounts for diversity in the natural world in terms of systematic development from simple, single-cell organisms to progressively more complex life forms, with humans the most advanced. Society is seen to follow an analogous course of change from simple, undifferentiated hunting and gathering societies, comprising only a few families relating together, into highly complex industrial society.

The challenge for early theorists of society was to account for cultural diversity, for the spectacular advance of science, and for its corollary, the Industrial Revolution, in European societies. The theories of progress that emerged focussed on stages through which societies pass in a struggle to survive and adapt. The comparative study of contemporary non-industrial societies, conceptualized as being at earlier stages of development than western European cities, promised to yield insights into the origins and course of development of technologically advanced societies.

Such theories gathered momentum under the impact of **colonialism**. Following the European conquest of Africa and Asia, and of the native peoples of America, the colonizers and missionaries began to study these societies. The superiority of European societies tended to be taken for granted, and other peoples were seen as more "primitive" or "uncivilized."

Auguste Comte and Positive Society

The system of sociology developed by Auguste Comte (1798–1857) represents one of the earliest and most famous theories of societal progress. Comte wrote during the period of French history following the revolution, the final defeat of Napoleon in 1815, and the return of the Bourbon

G.W.F. Hegel (1770–1831).

Auguste Comte (1798–1857).

monarchy. Despite the restoration of the Bourbons, there was not a return to the order that had prevailed before the revolution. Comte sought to understand the basis of this new order, in which he saw that the old powers of absolute monarchy, military, and church had become bankrupt.

Comte's fundamental argument is that changes at the societal level reflect fundamental changes in forms of thought or stages in the search for understanding. He proposed a law of three stages in which the development of distinctive types of knowledge and belief is associated with typical forms of organization of society and social institutions.

The **theological stage** is a form of society dominated by primitive religious thought. People seek to explain events and phenomena in terms of supernatural forces such as gods or spirits. Such a society is based on intuition, sentiment, and feelings. It is ruled by priests and by military personnel, and its moral structure is centred around blood ties.

The **metaphysical stage** of society is associated with a limited development of critical thought. It is marked by a transition to belief in a single deity and the search for some kind of ultimate reality. Phenomena come to be explained in terms of abstract forces rather than irrational spirits. Such forms of thought are conducive to a unified concept of society. The notion of the state and its defence are central principles of social organization.

The third stage is **positive society** based on scientific **empiricism**. Explanations take the form of regular law-like connections between empirically observable phenomena (Keat and Urry 1982, 72). Science seeks to establish such relations through the accumulation of factual knowledge derived by means of observation, experiment, comparison, and prediction. It involves the rejection of the religious search for final ends and reasons. Scientists, not priests, become the

new intellectual and spiritual leaders. This mode of thought is associated with industrial society.

Changes in patterns of thought are thus mirrored in changing social structures. Social organization changes from a military state, where progress is based on conquest and plunder, to an industrial state where wealth is generated by rational, scientific organization of work. Comte hypothesized that war would have no place in industrial societies where plunder was no longer the basis of wealth. For Comte the decisive characteristics of progress include the scientific character of industry, especially the way in which labour is organized, the unparalleled development of wealth and resources arising from scientific applications, and the new social phenomenon of large-scale organization of work in factories.

Progress had begun with the overthrow of the old religious order during the French Revolution. What was needed to complete the transition to a positive society was a science of society itself—*sociology*. Sociology would complete the study of **natural laws**, which had begun with the physical world. It would have a critical role in the reorganization of society in more rational ways through the scientific study of the laws of society. Comte is credited with being one of the first exponents of **positivism** as an approach to the study of society. This is an approach to knowledge through the search for law-like relations between observable phenomena established through empirical and experimental research. For Comte, the tremendous value of such an approach lay in its practical applicability. Sociology held the promise of providing a factual basis for controlled change of social organization.

Problems with Comte

There are many limitations to Comte's system of sociology. As a theory of progress it provides a fascinating classification of stages of intellectual and social development, but it does not explain the mechanisms behind such changes or account for why either reason or society itself should develop in the observed direction. Comte is vague not only as to what he means by "observables" but also as to how one might distinguish between empirical regularities and the unobservable scientific laws hypothesized to explain them. The main value of his thought lies in his insistence that the extent and form of variations in human nature and social organization are empirical questions that can in principle be settled by scientific investigation.

Herbert Spencer and Social Evolution

Herbert Spencer (1820–1903) was a British philosopher who was strongly influenced by Comte's classification of stages in the development of societies and by his positivist approach to the study of social organization. He went beyond Comte's descriptive model to explore the mechanisms behind the phenomenon of progress. Spencer's theory of evolution involves a grand scheme that unifies all realms of the universe, inanimate and animate, biological and social (Keat and Urry 1982, 80).

All matter, he argues, tends to move from a state of disorganized flux to one of order and relative stability. In the course of this movement, simple forms and structures give rise to more complex ones by means of two simultaneous processes: **differentiation** and **integration**. **Differentiation** refers to the breakdown of simple, unspecialized structures into many separate specialized part. **Integration** means the development of a specialized function, organ, or bond preserving unity among the differentiated parts. Social evolution conforms to the same principles of differentiation and integration. Societies evolve toward even greater institutional complexity based on greater specializ-

ation of tasks or division of labour. With this complexity comes the development of some central co-ordinating agency, such as the modern state.

Herbert Spencer (1820–1903).

Spencer drew close analogies between biological and social systems to demonstrate his theory of unifying processes of change. Both systems grow in size, unlike physical objects. Both also increase in complexity and differentiation. Differentiation in structure accompanies differentiation in function in both systems. The parts and the whole are interdependent: change in one part affects all the others. At the same time, however, each part is also a microsociety or organism in itself. In a biological organism, single cells can be separated out, each with their own functioning internal systems. In society, each individual is similarly capable of free, spontaneous life, although integrated with others in the social system as a whole.

Just as organisms are bounded, self-maintaining systems, which tend toward equilibrium, so societies develop analogous self-regulating mechanisms. Organisms operate as self-maintaining systems that have basic needs that must be met. Likewise, a society has basic needs that have to be met for it to continue. Hence, like organisms, societies develop progressively more specialized structures to meet these functions. Societies, for example, need an energy supply (the economy), a circulatory system (administration), and a head or organizing body (government). The key characteristics of most advanced societies are their increasingly specialized parts, which are integrated through an increasingly more complex central co-ordinating body.

For Spencer, the fundamental mechanism governing this evolutionary change in both organic and social systems is competitive struggle. This struggle encourages more complex and specialized forms to emerge out of simpler ones. The chances of survival in a highly competitive environment are enhanced if an organism can adapt to a specialized niche that few other organisms inhabit, or if it can develop specialized ways of obtaining food and other scarce resources that give it a competitive edge. Such specialized adaptation requires great flexibility over a wide range of activities. Competitive struggle between social groups similarly heightens the degree of differentiation and intensifies the need for regulation and integration. Groups that cannot make the necessary adaptations will be eliminated in favour of those who can. It was Spencer, not Darwin, who first coined the phrase "survival of the fittest" to describe this process.

From this idea of competitive adaptation, Spencer developed the notion of **function**. To judge whether an adaptation is successful, one needs to evaluate it in relation to essential conditions or functions that must be met if the social system is to survive. Three crucial functions include: the *sustaining system*, which comprises economic arrangements, such as agricultural and industrial production, that provide a means of livelihood for members of society; a *distribution system*, which allocates products and services between members; and the *regulation system*, which manages and co-ordinates these separate activities. More advanced societies are those with more voluntary, less compulsive systems of regulation since they allow the greatest flexibility.

The impact of Spencer upon the society of his time was enormous. His ideas won widespread acclaim, and when he travelled through the United States in 1882 he was welcomed by leading industrialists such as the Carnegies and the Rockefellers. His model of competitive advantage fit perfectly with their liberal philosophy of laissez-faire individualism and the survival of the fittest in the market. If unbridled competition leaves some individuals worse off than others, this is merely the price of allowing the struggle for survival to perform its progressive function.

Problems with Spencer

There are a number of problems with Spencer's system of sociology that limit his influence on contemporary theory. The biological analogy that permeates Spencer's thought is at root only superficial. The differences are in many ways more crucial than the similarities. It may make sense to talk about the survival and healthy functioning of an organism, but it is by no means simple to make such judgments about societies. Did feudal France "die" with the French Revolution, for example, or simply adapt? How should one judge the survival of the fittest in a social context? Is the fitter society one that crushes another militarily, or one that extracts riches from another? In biology the bases for judgment are relatively clear. Organisms live in environments with limited food supplies and, by processes of accidental mutations and natural selection, some organisms are better able to exploit niches in the environment than others. But no such clear bases for judgment exist when comparing societies. Societies differ further from animals in that they modify their environments rather than simply adapting to them. Spencer is also somewhat vague about just what is doing the adapting in social evolution. Is it the whole social system or individual human nature? Moreover, while Spencer seems to have believed that men were evolving into increasingly more intelligent, rational beings, he was not prepared to apply this generalization to women. In fact, he argued that too much thinking makes women infertile (Nicholson 1984, 74).

His grandiose system of classification of societies along an evolutionary continuum has also come under criticism. Other theorists have challenged his idea of an unvarying sequence of development, suggesting that different societies may take different paths, and that convergence of social forms is not inevitable. Spencer's comparative method, which assumes that the prehistory of all societies was the same, is particularly suspect. Anthropologists have pointed out

that supposedly "primitive" societies themselves have long histories. Impoverished societies may have regressed into that state due to exploitative colonialism rather than weak adaptation mechanisms.

In summary, then, Spencer's main contribution to the development of sociology lies in his biological analogy, which conceptualizes society as a functioning system. He is notable for his elaboration of processes of differentiation and specialization in societal development, his analysis of specialized functions, and his comparative analysis of social forms. He had a major influence on the development of structural-functionalist theory, which is explored in chapter 10. Other offshoots of his thought can be traced in contemporary theories of **sociobiology**, which explore the role of inherited racial and sexual differences in social behaviour, and the study of the impact of changing technology as a determinant of a society's character.

Durkheim's Theory of Morality and Cohesion

Emile Durkheim (1858–1917) shared with Comte and Spencer a concern with the comparative evolution of societal forms and a commitment to a positivist methodology, which seeks to identify and to establish law-like relations of cause and effect within the sphere of social behaviour (Keat and Urry 1982, 81–82). He rejected the notion that metaphysical forces could be responsible for the character of the empirically observable social world. At the same time, however, he acknowledged the importance of the internal mental states of individuals, their states of consciousness, their moral beliefs and values, and their motives and reasons for acting, in the structuring of social order. His influence upon the subsequent development of sociology far exceeds that of Comte and Spencer.

Emile Durkheim (1858–1917).

Details of Durkheim's personal life give valuable insights into his sociology. He was born a Jew in the Rhineland province of Alsace, a territory that was the focus of prolonged disputes between France and Prussia during the nineteenth century. Durkheim's family moved to France and became French citizens but, as a Jewish immigrant, Durkheim always felt himself to be a somewhat marginal member of French society. France at that time was just emerging from a long period of political instability that had begun with the French Revolution of 1789. This was followed by the rise of Napoleon and the Napoleonic wars, the restoration of the Bourbon monarchy, further revolutions in 1830 and 1848, followed by the coup d'état of Napoleon's nephew Louis Napoleon. Two events of 1870 ended this period: a crushing military defeat by Prussia and the last brief flowering of the Parisian insurrection known as the Paris Commune, which Marx regarded as a true proletarian uprising. The Third Republic, inaugurated in 1871, was to last until the German invasion of 1940. Durkheim strongly supported the Third Republic and the promise of stability that it brought. He saw himself as a socialist but rejected revolutionary politics in favour of a more administrative form of socialism.

As a Jew in predominantly Catholic France, Durkheim experienced **prejudice** and oppression at first hand. Although an atheist himself, he understood the intense commitment of Jews to their community and the power of the religion of Judaism as a social force. He was very concerned with religious tolerance, and he insisted that in a highly diversified, multi-racial, and multi-ethnic society, such tolerance for individual differences was essential. This belief motivated his political involvement in the Dreyfus case in 1894. Dreyfus, an Alsatian Jew like Durkheim, was a French army officer. He was falsely accused of selling information to the Germans and was con-victed on the basis of minimal evidence. After a counter-intelligence review concluded he was innocent, it was a full two years before his case was re-opened and he was pardoned. All France took sides in what came to be seen as a blatant case of **anti-semitism**. Durkheim's argument was that anti-semitism threatened the cohesion of modern multi-ethnic society, directly undermining social solidarity.

The themes of intense commitment to community, and the religious character of this commitment, together with his insistence on the sanctity of the individual person and individual rights, and the necessity of tolerance for diversity, are central to all of Durkheim's sociological writings. Each of his major works addresses the question of the origins and nature of **morality** as the expression of the relationship between individuals and society. In his first major work, *The Division of Labour in Society* ([1893] 1964), Durkheim develops his theory of the evolution of society from relatively simple, undifferentiated, small-scale communities to complex and heterogeneous industrial societies. His central theme traces the evolution of a new form of social cohesion.

The Scientific Study of Morality

The first premise of Durkheim's methodological approach to the study of society is that social forces exist as a distinctive level of reality. Sociology, which takes these forces as its subject matter, is therefore a legitimate and meaningful scientific discipline. The guiding rule of his methodological teachings is that the sociologist must treat **social facts** as if they were things ([1895] 1964, 14). By this rule, Durkheim does not mean that aspects of social life can literally be observed in the same way as physical objects can in the natural sciences. But they nonetheless have the characteristics of things in two crucial respects: they are external to individuals, and they exercise constraint over individual behaviour. Social facts comprise anything that people experience as external constraints on their behaviour. The sense of being constrained provides a sign of the presence of social facts. These facts, or external constraints, cannot be understood in terms of individual personality and circumstances alone, nor will wishful thinking make them disappear.

In biology, certain combinations of molecules produce a new emergent level of biological organism that for certain purposes need not, and cannot, be studied in terms of molecules at all. A grain of wheat, a loaf of bread, a flower, can in principle be studied as collections of molecules. But they can also be studied as distinct entities in their own right. Moral authority of society over individuals is similarly a product of an emergent level of facts. The intercommunication of minds, which forms a society, is never a wholly individual matter, but rather extends beyond individuals in both time and space. In this sense, social facts can be studied as it they were things.

In the preface to *The Division of Labour in Society* ([1893] 1964, 32), Durkheim proposes to "treat the facts of moral life according to the methods of the positive sciences." His goal then, is to study the facts of moral life scientifically and to look for the laws explaining them. His central argument is that the conditions under which people live give rise to moral rules, and these rules change when society changes. The nature of morality underlying complex industrial society is necessarily very different from the morality of simpler societies, but it nonetheless does have a moral base. He totally rejects the utilitarian view that industrial society could develop from purely self-interested behaviour in the marketplace. The doctrine of **utilitarianism** holds that rational human action entails the selfish or self-interested pursuit of satisfaction and happiness. Relations between people are based on the calculation and exchange of advantages or utility. In economics, for example, the theory states that all people seek to maximize benefits to themselves: sellers to get the maximum price for their goods, buyers to give the minimum. Provided all buyers and all sellers are free to compete, the outcome should be beneficial to all and should lead to the greatest good for the greatest number. Durkheim argues that the basic assumption of utilitarianism is false. Society could never be held together by selfishness. For Durkheim, human nature is fundamentally social, and morality is the expression of that social nature.

The moral order, for Durkheim, refers to two central aspects of society. The first is a sense of **solidarity** with others or the achievement of cohesiveness and integration. The second is **regulation**, which involves restraint—including self-restraint or **altruism**—upon the pursuit of self-interest. Durkheim's basic thesis in *The Division of Labour in Society* is that there are two fundamentally different kinds of solidarity and therefore of morality. First, there is **mechanical solidarity**, which is based on sameness and shared conditions. Durkheim illustrates this form with reference to the saying that "birds of a feather flock together." People feel closer to others who share very similar backgrounds and experiences than to people who seem very different. The other form of solidarity is **organic solidarity**. This is based on recognition of differences that complement and complete us and that are experienced in exchange and mutual dependence. Durkheim gives the example of the bonding between a woman and a man in marriage, where their differences and resulting dependence unites them. Durkheim argues that, ultimately, organic solidarity based on complementary differences is stronger than the simpler mechanical solidarity based on sameness.

The fundamental character of solidarity or moral order of a society can be studied objectively through the ways in which members of the society intervene to regulate each other's behaviour. For Durkheim, any form of behaviour that threatens the solidarity of a community will be experienced as immoral and will be subject to sanctions. Law constitutes the codified morality of a society, and hence the study of law provides for Durkheim an objective basis for the scientific study of the underlying moral life of the society.

Durkheim argues that the two kinds of solidarity are reflected in two very different kinds of law. Mechanical solidarity based on sameness promotes penal or **repressive law**. Such law is essentially concerned with the punishment of offenders who have transgressed the shared values of the community. He uses the French words *conscience collective* to refer to this sense of collective moral awareness and mutual obligation. He defines *conscience collective* as "the totality of beliefs and sentiments common to the average citizens of the same society" (Durkheim [1893] 1964, 79).

There is some dispute as to whether *conscience collective* should be translated into English as "collective conscience"—referring to people's sense of what is right or wrong— or as "collective consciousness"—referring to people's sense of involvement in a community. The French term implies both meanings. Many sociologists who write about Durkheim's work prefer to use the French form to alert readers that the term has this dual meaning.

Durkheim emphasizes that the totality of beliefs and sentiments associated with the *conscience collective* forms a determinant system that has its own life and that exists independently of the particular conditions in which individuals are placed. Any one member of a society encounters these beliefs and sentiments as social facts, as constraints upon behaviour that are above and beyond individual whims or feelings. Repressive law is oriented toward behaviour that violates the collective conscience of the community of people. The societal function of punishment is not primarily to take revenge against the perpetrator of crime, but to publicly reaffirm collective values and thus to strengthen the collective conscience itself. This is what is codified as repressive law.

Organic solidarity, based on differences and mutual dependence, promotes **restitutive law** or contract law. This is exemplified by civil law, encompassing commercial, contractual, constitutional, and administrative regulations. Restitutive law is less concerned with punishment than with the return of things as they were or with the reestablishment of reciprocal obligations between members of a society. As such, civil law presupposes a division of labour among people who have specialized functions and who therefore depend upon each other to perform these functions in definite, reciprocal ways.

Durkheim uses these two models— mechanical solidarity and repressive law versus organic solidarity and restitutive law—to develop a theory of evolution in forms of society from simple agricultural to complex industrial patterns.

Societies Based on Mechanical Solidarity

Durkheim argues that simpler, pre-industrial societies are characterized by mechanical solidarity, the form of cohesion that is based fundamentally on sameness. Most of the members of such societies live very similar lives, with little specialization or division of labour beyond that associated with age and sex. Members feel bonded together essentially by their shared beliefs and sentiments, their common conscience and consciousness. The stronger the uniformity of beliefs and practices in such communities, the stronger the social solidarity will be. Hence the intensity with which these beliefs and practices are defended against diversity.

For Durkheim, any strong convictions that are shared by members of a community take on a religious character because they inspire reverence. Violation of these convictions is sin. The system of law associated with such intensely felt values is essentially repressive. Religion is critically important and tends to regulate all details of social life. Repressive or penal law is thus, at root, religious law. Nonconformity in such communities constitutes a threat precisely because uniformity of beliefs is the basis of solidarity. If such beliefs are allowed to weaken through tolerance for nonconformity, then the very cohesion of the community itself is threatened.

Transition in Forms of Society

Mechanical solidarity could be very powerful in relatively isolated and homogeneous communities, but it could not retain its hold over individual consciousness in the face of rapid social change or in the context of heterogeneous, multi-ethnic, and multi-religious societies such as the France of Durkheim's time. The erosion of mechanical solidarity as a unifying force was the inevitable result of the cultural, demographic, and economic changes that preceded industrialization.

Durkheim follows Spencer in proposing a detailed theory concerning the mechanisms that generated the transition to industrial society. Three factors are accorded paramount importance. The first is the development of communication over vaster areas, which allows information to reach previously isolated segments. Geographic barriers had allowed distinct cultures to develop but, as communication expands, local territories lose significance, distances decrease, and contacts between cultural groups are heightened. The second critical factor is demographic: an increase in population size.

If all people continued to eke out a living in the same way while encroaching upon each other's territories, the result would inevitably be violent conflicts, with people fighting over the same limited resources. Hunting and gathering societies, for example, require large territories to support small numbers of people. As population pressure increases, people are forced to diversify in order to survive. This necessity gives rise to the third major factor: division of labour. Durkheim likens this process to biological evolution where plants and animals adapt so as to occupy different niches. As population density increases, people are pressured to develop in increasingly divergent directions, which allows them to co-operate rather than compete.

The combined effects of these three factors upon the social order are very far reaching. The common consciousness of shared beliefs and sentiments becomes more abstract as it rises over local diversities. The God of humanity is necessarily less concrete than the god of an individual clan. As Durkheim expresses it, "the gods take leave of space." This process in itself makes possible individual emancipation. There is more room for variation and for diversity of beliefs and sentiments. Durkheim argues that, once experienced, liberty becomes increasingly more necessary and inevitable. There can be no turning back. The social basis of individual emancipation is division of labour. As people develop specialized functions, they have different life experiences, and so develop different perspectives on life.

Societies Based on Organic Solidarity

Durkheim argues that complex, industrialized societies are characterized by organic solidarity, the form of social cohesion that is based on division of labour and the resulting interdependence. As people become more specialized, they also become more dependent upon each other. A homesteading family engaged in subsistence farming, for example, may survive with little or no help from similar homesteaders, but specialized workers in a garment factory cannot survive without a host of other specialized workers supplying their basic needs. Members of a society characterized by advanced division of labour are united by mutual obligations, and not merely by sentiments of sameness. Their ties to each other are based on co-operation that cannot be neglected.

Some of the theories of urbanism that we explored in chapter 5 saw size, density, and heterogeneity as negative features of society, leading to the breakdown or weakening of social cohesion. Durkheim rejects this interpretation. He argues in contrast that the earlier homogeneous forms of society, made up of relatively undifferentiated family groupings, were actually more fragile. The parts, or family groupings, that made up such societies, could break away from each other and remain relatively independent on their homesteads, or in their small villages or kin communities. But modern, heterogeneous, urban societies, while they foster a far greater degree of individualism, are also more interdependent. The specialized parts need each other and cannot break away. Heterogeneity thus presupposes differences and specialization. These differences give rise to ties of mutual obligation and co-operation that grow progressively stronger as specialization increases.

In such societies, repressive or religious law necessarily declines because the core of common beliefs and sentiments declines. Restitutive or contract law expands in its place. Restitutive law regulates the rules of justice that cannot be violated by individual contracts. Respect for the individual and for individual rights constitutes the fundamental ground of justice, or what Durkheim calls the **pre-contractual basis of contract**, that expresses morality in highly specialized societies. Respect for the individual and for

individual rights is not merely "good." It is essential for solidarity in modern society.

The grip of religious dogma on everyday life declines, and the *conscience collective*— the shared beliefs and sentiments—becomes more abstract. What replaces it is the religion of individualism, or **humanism**. Such moral individualism is not to be equated with selfish self-interest, but rather with reciprocal obligations and mutual respect. This recognition of the fundamental moral role of the division of labour in society is Durkheim's most important theoretical contribution. He totally rejects the arguments of Spencer and utilitarian economists who suggest that a stable society could be based upon unbridled self-interest. Durkheim ([1893] 1964, 204) argues that "there is nothing less constant than interest. Today it unites me to you; tomorrow it will make me your enemy. Such a cause can only give rise to transient relations and passing associations." Even purely economic contracts presuppose a pre-contractual basis of moral standards that underlies and regulates the agreements between people and determines standards of justice.

Problems with Durkheim

Durkheim's analysis of division of labour and moral order was an important advance over theories that viewed this division as entirely negative and destructive, but in turn it is open to a number of criticisms. His early formulation of the transition from mechanical to organic solidarity as a unilinear process is seriously overdrawn. Anthropological studies have shown that there is much division of labour and contractual obligation in non-specialized, simple societies. Similarly, mechanical solidarity is still deeply embedded in industrial societies, manifested in strong identification with religious and ethnic groups. A related point is that repressive, penal law has by no means disappeared in modern societies. It is not difficult in the late twentieth century to point out authoritarian regimes that demand conformity to dominant political doctrines. Many such regimes are arguably the direct result of the exploitative economic interest of advanced industrialized nations.

The first criticism based on the transition from mechanical to organic solidarity can be deflected if one measures the type of solidarity in terms of relative preponderance rather than in an absolute either/or manner. As a member of the Jewish community in France, Durkheim was certainly well aware of strong religious and ethnic affiliations, and he probably never intended his formulation to be interpreted rigidly. Specialization and differentiation certainly exist in non-industrialized societies, but not to the same extent as in industrial societies. In Canada in the 1980s, even rural areas are totally tied to specialized mono-crop production, and farmers are as dependent as industrial workers upon the market economy for their subsistence needs.

Restitutive or contract law impinges on almost every aspect of market transactions. In China, for example, economic reforms under Deng Xiaoping permit peasant farmers to sign contracts in which they agree to deliver fixed amounts of produce to the state in return for the right to farm a plot of land for themselves. One result of this policy has been an explosion in the number of restitutive laws, just as Durkheim predicted. It has been followed by an explosion in the number of lawyers needed to handle contracts and disputes. Law schools in China are booming. In 1984, 9500 students started law training, three times the number in 1980. Since 1978, two hundred new economic laws have been promulgated. Some people argue that China is now on the road to Western "rule of law" and is experiencing a rapid expansion of legal rights for individuals and families, as newly wealthy peasants seek legal ways to protect their property (*Globe and Mail*, 13 Nov. 1985).

The second criticism, that repressive law has not disappeared, is harder to deal with. Division of labour has the potential for sustaining organic solidarity based on mutual obligation and duty, with humanism as the supreme religion. Yet this state is far from being realized. The struggle to establish a universal commitment to human rights is one of the most pressing international moral issues of our time. The recognition of basic human rights is an important requirement for political stability in the interdependent world community, but it is not yet achieved. Like the Marxist vision of a socialist utopia, Durkheim's vision of a cohesive, co-operative world community has nowhere been realized.

Demonstrators protesting human rights abuses in Chile are confronted by police.

Anomic Division of Labour

Durkheim's lasting contribution to sociology has been his development of the concept of **anomie** as an explanation for the moral ills of contemporary industrial society. Anomie is a complex concept, not easily defined. In general, it refers to a relative absence or confusion of values and to a corresponding lack of clear regulations or norms for behaviour. People feel lost, disorganized, unsure of how to behave or what to believe in, so that their lives come to feel meaningless or purposeless.

Durkheim struggled to explain the prevalence of anomie in the industrial society of his time. He recognized that industrial and commercial crises were becoming more frequent, and the conflict between labour and capital more apparent. But he argued that these were not a necessary result of industrialized society, nor could they be resolved by a retreat to the mechanical solidarity of nationalism. One cannot force moral uniformity in the face of functional diversity. The key problem, he argues, is lack of regulation. At the societal level, the absence of necessary regulation means that the parts of the social order are insufficiently co-ordinated. The consequence of this for the individual is a sense of isolation and meaninglessness of life and work. The economic structure of a **laissez-faire** society, with its powerful inducements to self-interested behaviour, hurts people. They lose a sense of being tied to others in ongoing relations and so feel separated and alone.

A major cause of anomie is a forced or unjust division of labour. To be just, division of labour or specialization must fit natural talents. People must be able to choose their occupations freely. This sense of natural co-operation is destroyed when rules constrain people by force. Fair contracts require that both parties be equal so that both may freely enter the contract. This basis for justice is violated by inherited wealth; hence hereditary privilege should be abolished. There cannot be rich and poor at birth, Durkheim argues, without there being unjust contracts (Durkheim [1893] 1964, 384).

A further cause of anomie is fractionalized work. This is precisely the kind of work pattern produced by **scientific management**, which aims to maximize control and productivity of labour for the benefit of management. Under scientific management, operations are broken down into their separate components. Workers specialize in a discrete task rather than following the operation through. Labour becomes fragmented, lacking unity, co-ordination, and coherence. As a direct result, workers lose the feeling of the solidarity and continuity of work essential to the sense of organic community. They also lose their sense of pride in their own contribution. Work becomes meaningless when individual workers are reduced to machines, subjected to monotonous routines without intrinsic interest. Normal specialization does not require this level of **fragmentation**.

In his analysis of **anomic division of labour**, Durkheim anticipates much modern writing on the meaninglessness and routine character of industrial work and on the moral breakdown that threatens to occur because of the hierarchical nature of factory life. One possible solution suggested by Durkheim is the establishment of associations representing each specialist occupation. These associations would be responsible for regulating contracts and would provide an intermediate focus for identification between the individual and the state. Durkheim had in mind professional associations akin to a national association of anthropologists and sociologists or a college of physicians and surgeons. Trade unions might also provide a focus for identification and belonging for non-specialist workers, but the problem is that they tend to divide groups of workers from each other and from managers rather than uniting all members of an occupation.

Durkheim concludes that the objective of ensuring justice in the treatment of workers in industrial society is a critical task facing most technologically advanced societies. Liberty for individuals can only be attained through just regulations. It is not enough that there be rules governing contracts; the rules must be just. The basic question that Durkheim does not address, however, is whether such justice would ever be possible within a capitalist economic structure. It is at this juncture that Marxist theorists diverge from Durkheim. While Durkheim describes the factors that give rise to "abnormal forms" of division of labour, Marxists seek to examine the origins of these forms within the exploitative structures of capital-ism. The Marxist thesis is that justice in impossible within a profit-motivated system where a small class of people control the means of production upon which others depend. From this perspective, capitalism itself creates the lack of regulation, the **egoism**, and the immorality in collective life that Durkheim identifies as abnormal.

Chapter 7 explores at more length the concepts of anomie and alienation in the study of social disorder and conflict within industrial society. We now turn to two major studies that Durkheim himself undertook as a test and elaboration of his conception of the nature of social solidarity and of anomie: *Suicide* ([1897] 1951) and *The Elementary Forms of Religious Life* ([1915] 1976). Both of these studies have had a seminal influence on sociological study in these two areas.

Suicide

Suicide and the Loss of Social Cohesion

Durkheim's study of suicide is fundamentally a test of his central hypothesis that human happiness depends upon social cohesion. The corollary of this assertion is that, whenever social solidarity weakens or breaks down, the level of unhappiness among members of that community will rise. The critically difficult task for Durkheim as a positivist was to find some scientifically acceptable, objective method for studying essentially intangible and subjective states such as cohesion and unhappiness. Durkheim's brilliantly innovative proposal was to use data on suicide rates to measure the level of unhappiness within a society. He defines suicide as "intentional self-death by any action known to have that effect" (Durkheim [1897] 1951, 44).

The act of committing suicide is a supremely individual and private act, but suicide rates are social facts. The suicide rate is the actual number of people per 100 000 population recorded as having intentionally killed themselves. It is regularly published by government agencies. Suicide, thankfully, occurs relatively rarely, and it is almost impossible to observe directly. But when statistics are kept for large populations, and over long periods of time, it becomes possible to study patterns and to compare differences in rates among nations and among subgroups. For Durkheim, therefore, officially recorded suicide rates provide objective facts that can stand as indicators of the general level of happiness of members of different communities.

As a sociologist, Durkheim is not interested in the precipitating factors for each individual suicide. He is interested in the conditions that would increase the general level of unhappiness and hence increase the proportion of people unhappy enough to consider killing themselves. He carefully examines individual factors such as mental illness, but argues that such factors tend to occur randomly and do not explain differences in rates of suicide between social groups. One needs more than individual explanations to account for these differences. Durkheim's theory is that specific kinds of social conditions that lead to a weakening of social solidarity generate increasing unhappiness and hence higher suicide rates.

Durkheim outlines three categories of suicide: egoistic, anomic, and altruistic. **Egoistic suicide** occurs when society is poorly integrated; that is, when people lack a sense of strong social bonds linking them to each other. To test this hypothesis, Durkheim needed **indicators** of the strength of social bonding. A series of comparisons based on religious affiliation and marital status provided just such indicators. Durkheim first compares Catholics and Protestants. He argues that Catholics have a ready-made faith and relative certainty of beliefs, while Protestants emphasize free inquiry by individuals. Hence Catholics would appear to have greater social cohesion than Protestants. Durkheim predicted that Catholics should have lower suicide rates than Protestants. Official suicide rates kept for Catholic and Protestant administrative areas, over many decades, confirmed this prediction. In Catholic areas the recorded suicide rates were much lower than in Protestant areas.

Secondly, Durkheim argues that marriage and children tie people into social life and reflect greater social bonding than the state of being single or childless. Almost all the comparative data on rates of suicide confirmed his predictions that suicide rates would be lower when people are married and have children. Married men committed suicide less often than single men, married men with children less than husbands without children, widowers with children less than widowers without children.

Similarly, he argues that rural communities are more cohesive than urban areas because people know each other more. Again his prediction was supported: rural communities did have lower rates of suicide than urban ones.

A particularly significant comparison is between Jews and gentiles. Jews are predominantly urban dwellers and are highly educated. Both factors are associated with higher suicide rates in general. However, as a persecuted religious minority they tend to be intensely cohesive. Durkheim hypothesizes that the internal cohesion would counteract the divisive forces of urbanism and education. The data confirm his prediction that Jews would have lower suicide rates than non-Jews.

There is only one statistic that goes against Durkheim's predictions. Women had higher suicide rates when married than when never married, although the rates were lower when they had children than when they were without children. Durkheim concludes that marriage benefits men more than women. Men, he suggests, need restraints more than women. Divorced men are more prone to go on drunken sprees, consort with many different women, and then fall into despair and suicide. The explanation is only guesswork on Durkheim's part, but the statistical difference has stood the test of time. Jessie Bernard, writing in 1972, found that single women described themselves as considerably happier than married women (Bernard 1972, 28). In general, however, the recorded suicide rates were strongly consistent with Durkheim's theoretical prediction that, under conditions where bonds of social cohesion are relatively weak, suicide rates are relatively high.

Anomic suicide is closely related to egoistic suicide and occurs when people experience a loss of regulation. When people have a clear sense of their position in life, have meaningful goals and realistic expectations as to what they should be and should become, then they are contented and happy. But when these constraints are vague, and the limits unclear, people tend to become dissatisfied with their lot, unhappy, and frustrated. Durkheim predicts that the suicide rate, as the proportion of people too unhappy to live, will increase as social regulation declines.

The main data with which he tests this prediction are periods of economic boom or bust compared with periods of relative stability. One might expect that people may become depressed during periods of economic collapse, but Durkheim shows that boom times are equally disturbing. The scales are upset, regulations are lacking, goals appear limitless and hence meaningless. Enough is never enough; people cannot stop running. During such times, Durkheim shows that suicide rates go up.

A comparable source of stress is family disruption. Divorced people have a four to five times higher rate of suicide than do married people. Again, divorced men seem to suffer more than divorced women, judging from their higher propensity to commit suicide.

Altruistic suicide is qualitatively different from the other two forms. It is associated with too much cohesion or overly strong social bonds, rather than with the weakening of such bonds. In this extreme situation, society is so tight and cohesive that individuals are totally obedient to it and are willing to die for the honour of the group. Altruistic suicide is thus voluntary death as an obligation to one's group. Old or sick Inuit people would walk out of the camp to die rather than be a burden on younger people during periods of famine. Japanese kamikaze pilots during World War II flew their planes directly into their target, knowing that they would die, but willing to do so for the success of their country in war. In

India, the tradition of *suttee*, in which a widow threw herself on the funeral pyre of her husband, was once widespread. This practice is now outlawed but it still happens occasionally. There is some dispute, however, whether such widow-burning is or was always voluntary. More recent examples of altruistic suicide include hunger strikers in the Irish Republican Army who chose to die for their cause rather than bow to the will of the English government, and Palestinians who drove trucks loaded with bombs into American military camps.

Durkheim suggests that altruistic suicide is comparatively rare in modern society because individualism is valued more intensely than religion. Hence, egoistic or anomic suicide is more likely. The only context where he finds rates of altruistic suicide to be quite high is in the army. He found that army men have higher suicide rates than civilians, volunteers more than conscripts, officers more than privates, and re-enlisted men more than newcomers. If the hard life of the army were the main explanation for suicide, one would expect all these rates to be reversed. Durkheim concludes that higher rates for volunteers, officers, and re-enlisted men reflect their greater subordination of their individuality to the group. They are willing to die for their country.

This study of suicide rates has had a tremendous impact upon sociology. Durkheim demonstrated conclusively the relation between intensely individual acts and social conditions. He also showed the critical importance of treating societal forces as a distinct level of reality. He pioneered the methodological approach of using statistical data as objectively visible indicators of abstract concepts such as happiness and cohesion, thus opening them to empirical research. The work is now dated, and subsequent researchers have shown flaws in his analysis. Pope, in particular, has used more sophisticated statistical analysis to show that some of the relationships claimed by

Durkheim are suspect. The association between bankruptcy and suicide and between relative severity of economic crisis and suicide has been shown to be a small negative rather than positive relationship. In other words, suicide rates decline somewhat as the crisis period worsens. Pope also points out that the theoretical distinction between egoistic and anomic suicide is vague. Suicide rates among divorced people can readily be classified under either type, suggesting that the differences between them are a matter of emphasis rather than clear-cut distinctions (Pope 1976, 116–17). The high rates of suicide in the army would also seem to contradict Durkheim's own predictions that strong cohesion would reduce the rates. That scholars can find flaws in Durkheim's work nearly a century after he completed it, however, does not detract from its brilliance as a pioneering analysis of its kind.

The Marxist Critique

The political economy or Marxist approach to the study of suicide has added a new dimension to Durkheim's research. Boughey (1978, chap. 1) contrasts the two approaches in the following ways. Both make use of statistical rates in their analyses, but they focus upon different underlying factors. While Durkheim stressed the breakdown of moral order, Marxists emphasize the underlying exploitative relations of capitalism, which may precipitate such breakdown. Their first impulse is to examine the class position of the deceased and relate this to injustices and oppression that may stem from an inegalitarian economic system. From this perspective, the cause of the problem is the lack of revolutionary social change rather than the upheaval of the moral order.

The kinds of data to which Marxists draw attention are the social problems associated with poverty. We saw in chapter 5 how crime, depression, and defeatism were high in the impoverished regions of northeastern New Brunswick and among low income and unemployed people living in subsidized housing in pockets of Canada's large cities. The central prediction of Marxist theory is that poverty and unemployment will correlate positively with suicide rates and also with marital stress and divorce. Class oppression causes the anomie that drives people to despair.

Current data bear out this prediction. Horwitz (1984) finds a consistent association between economic deprivation and psychological distress. Unemployment ranks among the most stressful of events. People who have experienced a period of unemployment are far more likely to report feelings of unhappiness, dissatisfaction with life, and high levels of personal strain. Studies of unemployed workers show that this experience is associated with many forms of distress such as depression, fear, loneliness, anxiety, insomnia, headaches, and stomach problems. Unemployment rates correlate positively with mental hospital admission rates. There is a consistent association between economic decline and a subsequent rise in suicide rates in five separate studies cited by Horwitz (1984, 102).

The relationship between economic prosperity and suicide rates, first noted by Durkheim, is an ambiguous one. Several studies using aggregate data suggest that rising per capita income rates are related to long-term increases in suicide, homicide, rates of imprisonment, and alcohol consumption. At first glance it seems that people who get richer must also experience anomie and be prone to suicide. But this conclusion does not follow from the data. Such reasoning involves what is called an **ecological fallacy**. In other words, one cannot argue from aggregate data on rates to individual inferences. The apparent association between generally high levels of affluence and suicide may be the result of the great strain upon and misery of the poorest people who do not share the prosperity. Their sense of **relative deprivation** gets worse as they have to watch other people enjoying luxuries that they cannot afford for themselves or their families. They also experience a sense of personal failure and blame because they are not "successful."

Studies based on individual-level data support this interpretation. A study of lottery winners failed to support Durkheim's contention that sudden prosperity would generate anomie. The lottery winners did not score high on a series of questions designed to measure anomie (Abrahamson 1978). On the other hand, a study of unemployed workers indicates that they have a suicide rate thirty times higher than the national average (Stillman 1980). More microstudies are needed to inspect which groups are affected by suicide in times of unemployment: whether it is the unemployed person directly, immediate family members, those who fear losing their jobs, or new entrants and re-entrants to the labour force who cannot find good jobs (Stack 1982). Aggregate census data showing rates of employment and suicide rates cannot answer such questions.

Suicide Among Women

Data that show lower rates of suicide for women generally, compared with men, are also ambiguous in their meaning. The differences in themselves are impressive. Suter (1976, 129) indicates that males commit suicide about three times more frequently than females. Others confirm this pattern, suggesting that it holds for all age groups, from approximately one woman to every two men at age twenty to twenty-five, to one woman to every ten men in the group sixty years or older. The gap is so large that suicide has been called "a masculine behaviour" (Neuringer and Lettieri 1982, 14, 15). The difference in suicide rates between men and women in Canada is shown in figure 6-1.

Are we to conclude from these rates that women are much happier than men? That men's lives in the rat race of industrial society are more anomic than the lives of housewives protected within their homes? Not necessarily. The catch is that women *attempt* suicide far more frequently than men. Suter suggests that females attempt suicide two to three times more often than males. Suicide attempts generally are six to

Figure 6-1 Suicide Rates in Canada, by Sex, 1921–86

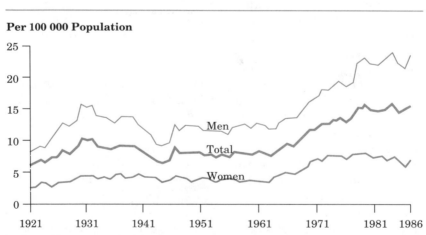

Per 100 000 Population

Source: Statistics Canada, Cat. 84-202, 84-206, and 84-528.

ten times more frequent than completions. Altogether, women seem considerably more suicidal than men, although they are less likely to complete the act. One straightforward explanation for this difference may be that men are trained to be more aggressive than women and have easier access to the favoured technique of using a gun. Women are more likely to use barbiturates or poison, methods that have a greater margin of error.

The explanation as to why women in general appear more suicidal than men remains unsatisfactory. From the Marxist-feminist perspective, however, the generalized subordination of women to men, their relative poverty and powerlessness, and their entrapment in marriages that they lack the economic resources to leave, would go far toward explaining these patterns. Many of these issues will be explored in subsequent chapters. For now, the most important message is methodological. Statistical rates, treated in isolation, can lead to erroneous conclusions.

In summary, there are important parallels between the Durkheimian and

Table 6-1 Suicide Rate by Age and Sex, Selected Provinces, 1981 (per 100 000 Population)

	15-19 Years			20-24 Years		
	Male	Female	Total	Male	Female	Total
Nova Scotia	11.4	9.6	10.5	33.1	--	16.6
Manitoba	39.0	2.1	20.8	44.5	10.7	27.7
Saskatchewan	41.4	17.1	29.5	42.3	15.9	29.2
Alberta	32.8	3.8	18.7	34.3	3.1	19.3
British Columbia	22.9	4.3	13.8	33.6	7.9	20.7

Source: Lapierre and Aylwin (1985, 87).

Table 6-2 Hospital Separation Related to Attempted Suicide or "Self-inflicted Injuries" by Age and Sex, Selected Provinces, 1980–81 (per 100 000 Population)

	15-19 Years			20-24 Years		
	Male	Female	Total	Male	Female	Total
Nova Scotia	22.4	35.2	28.6	27.8	38.7	33.1
Manitoba	148.9	243.3	195.5	154.7	167.4	161.0
Saskatchewan	53.1	90.5	71.5	80.2	86.4	83.2
Alberta	98.5	211.7	154.1	125.0	191.8	157.1
British Columbia	161.5	303.7	231.2	212.7	272.2	231.5

Source: Lapierre and Aylwin (1985, 87).

Marxist approaches to the study of suicide. Essentially, while Durkheim describes the symptoms of anomic division of labour, the approach of political economy explores the origins of these symptoms in the capitalist mode of production. This is a system of production in which the mass of workers are exploited by a minority of **capitalists**, or those who own the means of production. This system produces anomie by reducing human relations to the level of inhuman cash payment. Workers are hired when their labour power is useful to the capitalist, and fired when it is no longer needed. In a society in which division of labour provides the central social and moral bond between people through a sense of mutual obligation and interdependence, unemployment does not merely produce financial difficulties for the victims. It deals a devastating blow to one's sense of self-worth and belonging to a society. The right to work has become a fundamental human need, a moral obligation of society. But under the capitalist mode of production, when the rate of profit falls, workers are laid off. Women especially find themselves shut out at such times. Typically, women are the last hired and first fired when the job market is tight.

The Ethnomethodological Critique

The approach of ethnomethodology to the study of suicide raises questions of a qualitatively different kind from either Durkheim or the Marxist theorists. It has prompted the most far-reaching and, in some respects, devastating critique of Durkheim's study. Theorists in this tradition challenge the basic assumption that statistical rates produced by government agents can be unambiguously treated as a factual counting of the actual incidence of suicides among different groups and societies. They point out that such rates are in fact socially constructed. They are the result of a large number of coroners' decisions about whether to classify a particular death as suicide, accident, murder, or resulting from natural or unknown causes.

It may seem simple and unambiguous enough at first glance to make such decisions, but consider some of the following situations. A man dies by crashing his car at high speed into a tree; another apparently gets heavily drunk, falls asleep in the car with the engine running in a closed garage, and dies from carbon-monoxide poisoning; a women takes an overdose of sleeping pills; an old woman is found dead in her room with the doors and windows stuffed shut and the gas coming from an unlit heater.

A coroner who assigns the label *suicide* to such cases is, in effect, assigning responsibility for the death to the individual who has died. It becomes an excuse for no further action by the law. But how does one make such decisions? Was the car crash just an accident, or was the person driving full speed into a stationary object on the very realistic expectation that this would end it all, while still permitting the family to claim his life insurance? Did the woman take an overdose of pills deliberately in order to die, or did she simply wake up in the night confused and half-drugged and take some more pills without being conscious of what she was doing? Did the old woman intend to gas herself, or had she simply stuffed the cracks to keep out the cold and become a victim when the gas fire did not ignite properly or blew out? Suicide, by definition, means intentional self-death, but did these people intend to die? We can never know because we cannot ask the dead.

The label *suicide* imputes motives after the fact, and coroners can only do this by guesswork, by asking witnesses or close family members, or looking for suicide notes, and then coming to a decision whether it was likely that this person might have wanted to die. This procedure leads to other questions.

How many witnesses were consulted? Who was consulted with respect to assumed motives? One might get different answers from an estranged wife or from a Catholic priest. Suicide rates are the outcome of decisions such as these. Their "factual" character is much more problematic than the neat tables in Statistics Canada reports would have us believe.

Douglas's (1967) ethnomethodological critique of Durkheim's study challenges all the evidence that Durkheim used. As a first step, Douglas shows conclusively that huge changes in suicide rates occur when the method of counting changes. In Prussia in 1868, for example, Catholic priests kept the records of suicides. The rate jumped 50 percent in one year when the methods were reformed and civilian officials began keeping the rates. Similar jumps occurred in the official statistics in Austria, Hungary, and Italy when methods of record keeping changed. Douglas concludes that changes of between 10 and 50 percent were due to methods of collection alone. Durkheim's tests of his theory rely on smaller differences than these and so might be due to nothing more than differences in how rates were counted.

Douglas goes on to show that all the reasons hypothesized by Durkheim as causes of low social cohesion, and hence higher suicide rates, are the same reasons that influence coroners to make their decision one way rather than the other. During the period in which Durkheim did his study, suicide was considered a mortal sin for Catholics and was sufficient grounds for denying them a Christian burial. One can realistically expect that when Catholic priests kept the rates, they would go to great lengths to give the benefit of the doubt to the deceased and list the death as accidental, and that Catholic family members would do likewise. Protestant record keepers and witnesses would not be under such pressure. Douglas shows that Catholic cantons in Switzerland recorded fewer suicides than did Protestant cantons, but more accidents. Douglas concludes that different rates may reflect different concealment and not real differences in the propensity of Catholics and Protestants to kill themselves.

He suggests, similarly, that all the conditions of higher social integration listed by Durkheim are associated with a higher propensity, and ability, to cover up a suicide. When a person is married and has children, these family members are likely to want to influence a coroner to see the death as accidental, while a divorced person living alone has no one to speak for him or her. A small rural community is more likely to close ranks and cover up damning evidence of a suicide in their midst than are neighbours in a loosely integrated city area. Durkheim was correct in claiming that the number of deaths officially classified as suicides is lower among Catholics, married people, and villagers, but differences in rates may be solely an artifact of how coroners were influenced to make their decisions.

Smith (1983a) goes further than Douglas in demonstrating the essential circularity of theory and data in studies of suicide. She cites work to show that not only coroners, but witnesses and family members themselves, rely upon theories about motives for committing suicide when they produce accounts of what happened. Consider the man who crashes his car into a tree. People generally believe that a married man with children is unlikely to commit suicide, but that a divorced man who keeps to himself might well be miserable and potentially suicidal. Thus if the victim were a married man, friends might well comment, when questioned by a coroner, that he was a happy man, a bit reckless with the car, perhaps, and so assure themselves and the coroner that it was an accident. If the victim were divorced, friends would be much more likely to comment that they had always feared that he would do something terrible to himself, poor man, how miserable he must have been, and thus convince themselves and the coroner that his death was probably a suicide.

All that is needed for people to become convinced of the truth of their speculation is for like-minded people to reinforce their interpretation. People tend retrospectively to pick out the incidents that support their emerging theory, and they downplay evidence to the contrary. Experts who analyse such accounts for features of suicidal behaviour are likely to discover in them the theories that people use when they put the accounts together.

Smith presents several analyses of written texts to show how their authors selectively structure details of events into accounts that are consistent with their interpretation of what happened. It is not a question of lying or deliberate falsification, but rather of selective sensitivity toward what seems to be important. One account describes a mother who worked hard and consistently to provide for her children, keeping them neat and healthy and taking them for long walks in the park every day, even though the woman lived in great poverty that was exacerbated by the oppressive and irresponsible behaviour of her husband. The family was crammed in a room that offered no space for privacy. Sometimes the mother would sit behind the door in a corner and stare vacantly across the room.

Smith herself presents this account to us in a way that leads us to feel that this is a normal, healthy woman living under appalling conditions, and that it is these conditions that cause her at times to become depressed. A psychiatrist's clinical report, however, presents the particulars of the case in a different way and diagnoses the onset of psychotic depression. In this account, prominence is given to the woman's abnormal behaviour of sitting behind the door staring vacantly into space for long periods of time, not responding to anyone. These accounts are both honest, in the sense that both Smith and the psychiatrist believe what they are saying. The

psychiatrist believes that the patient is psychotic. The other details in her family life may be considered, but they are essentially irrelevant to her medical treatment. Smith believes that the medical profession generally is far too prone to impose a medical diagnosis of mental illness on depressed women. Women are then prescribed mood-changing drugs when the real problem of oppressive living conditions is ignored.

For our purposes here, what is significant is how the accounts are structured by the authors' different conclusions. In Smith's words, the accounts *intend* their own conclusions. The intentions of the author structure how the details of each account are presented so that any reader is likely to come to the same conclusion as the author. It is only when we as readers are faced with two different accounts of the same set of events that we realize how our feelings have been structured by the way the accounts were written, rather than purely by "the facts of the matter."

Smith gives the example of two different accounts of the suicide of Virginia Woolf, one written by her nephew Quentin Bell, the other by her husband Leonard Woolf. Bell's account gives considerable attention to the conditions under which Virginia was living, which might have precipitated her suicide. During the summer of 1940, after the collapse of France and the evacuation of the British army from Dunkirk, both Virginia and her husband feared a Nazi invasion of Britain. Given that they were socialists and that Leonard was a Jew, they feared they would be tortured by the Nazis if they were caught. Hence they made plans to commit suicide in the event of an invasion. Virginia also lived through a painful quarrel with her sister and the bombing of her family residence in London, among other agonizing events. It is not surprising in such circumstances that Virginia would feel depressed. Leonard became anxious that this might portend the severe depressive illness that

Virginia had had in the past, so he arranged for her to see a physician friend of theirs. In Bell's account, when Virginia, already in a depressed state, came to believe that both Leonard and the physician feared she might again be on the verge of psychotic illness, she killed herself. She would rather die than go through such misery again.

As readers of this account, we are led to see Virginia's suicide as a rational and fully reasonable act of a sane women trapped in an unbearable situation. She has coped with the war, the threat of Nazi invasion, and the probability that she and her husband would be targets for torture if this invasion succeeded. She has coped with her home being bombed and with the family quarrel. In fact, she has coped with circumstances that would have defeated many of us. But she could not bear the suggestion that her husband and her friend thought she was sinking into psychotic depression.

The alternative account given by Leonard Woolf is closer in form to a psychiatrist's clinical report. In this account, it is Virginia's earlier psychotic illness that has prominence rather than the external conditions of her life in wartime England. The external events that make it reasonable that she might feel depressed without being psychotic are glossed over. We learn that she openly talked of suicide, but we miss the fact that both she and Leonard had a suicide pact. We learn that Virginia was manifesting cyclical mood swings, but we are not led to make the connection between these moods and her home being bombed or her quarrel with her sister. Hence, in Leonard's account, we are drawn into seeing Virginia as psychotic and her suicide as the foreseeable and probably unavoidable act of a mentally ill woman.

The issue here is not which account is the correct version. What is significant is the way in which the author's interpretive scheme or theory directs how each account is put together such that we as readers will come to the conclusion that the author intended. The account, or text, *intends* the interpretive schema that has entered into its creation (Smith 1983a, 322). We have no possibility of knowing "the facts of the matter," listed in some uninterpreted form, on the basis of which we might draw our own independent conclusions. We only have access to the facts as the tellers of the tales recount them to us. So it is with coroners, or anyone else trying to find out what might have happened. The facts come to us already worked up, already organized in a certain way. The patterns that we find in them are not the patterns necessarily inherent in the occurrences. They are the patterns that the tellers unavoidably impose in the effort to make the vague flux of experience accountable, to themselves and to others, as what happened.

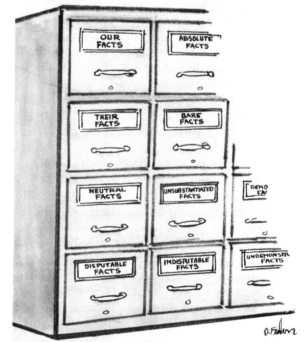

Drawing by D. Fradon; © 1977 The New Yorker Magazine, Inc.

These ethnomethodological critiques do not necessarily mean that Durkheim's conclusions about propensity to suicide being associated with egoistic or anomic social circumstances, or Marxist conclusions about poverty and exploitation as precipitating suicides, are wrong. But they do show that neither case is proven because what these theorists take as factual statistics are no more than coroners' biased interpretations of shaky evidence. Ethnomethodologists insist that we need detailed observational studies of exactly how coroners do their work of classification of deaths before we can draw any firm conclusions about what suicide rates actually mean.

Religion

Elementary Forms of Religious Life

Durkheim's last major work, *The Elementary Forms of Religious Life* ([1915] 1976), still represents a milestone in the sociology of religion. In this study he ties the analysis of religion intimately to his conception of the nature of social cohesion and, in effect, to the foundations of society itself. His first premise is that something like religion, which people of virtually all societies on earth have accepted, could not be based on illusion or superstition. It is not merely a response to the unknown or to fear of the unexpected, or it would never survive discovery of the truth. Like magic, it would be replaced by science.

Many theorists predicted that religion would lose its hold over people in the modern, industrial world. In some senses it has. Churches have become less dogmatic, adherence to religion has declined, and the church has lost its power to prohibit people from doing such things as opening stores, gambling, or going to ball games on Sundays (Collins 1982, chap. 2). Religious organizations such as the Lord's Day Observance Society seem to function as anachronistic voices in the wilderness against the secular mass.

Yet the predictions of a steady trend toward total secularism and rationalism are clearly false. In the United States, a country with one of the highest levels of education, science, and technology in the world, religion

Many theorists predicted that religion would lose its hold over people in the modern, industrial world.

has not only not disappeared, it has gained in strength and has become a powerful influence in politics. There are religious groups of many kinds, including fundamentalist sects that take the Bible as literally true, and evangelical programs on radio and television. Oriental religions have made a greater influx into Western societies than at any previous time, with Hindu gurus,

Buddhist monks, and followers of Krishna appearing in large numbers (Collins 1982, 31). Religion is clearly not a spent force, although the forms that it is taking may differ from the past.

Durkheim demonstrates through a comparison of major religions that there is no one doctrine that all have in common. Some religions believe in a single god, but many others believe in a multiplicity of gods and goddesses. Nor do all religions share the concept of god. Buddhism is a religion, but its basic concept of Enlightenment is completely atheistic. In many tribal religions there are no gods, only **totem** animals, plants, or rocks that constitute cult objects.

Yet there are central characteristics that all religions have in common. Firstly, they all comprise certain shared beliefs that are held by all adherents, and secondly, they all have certain rituals that all believers collectively perform (Collins 1982, 33). From these characteristics Durkheim derives his fundamental definition of **religion**: "Religion is a unified system of beliefs and practices, relative to sacred things, which unite into a single moral community called a church, all those who adhere to them" (Durkheim [1915] 1976, 10). A central element of all religious thought is the distinction drawn between the **sacred** and the **profane** or worldly. The distinction is absolute and is manifest in ritual prescriptions and prohibitions surrounding the sacred realm. All religions have a church, in the sense of an organization that performs rituals and ceremonies on a regular basis for a particular group of worshippers (Giddens 1971, 107).

What does this sacred realm refer to? What is it in people's normal, everyday experience that is so powerful that it could give rise to the sacred? For Durkheim, the one reality that has all the characteristics people attribute to the divine is society itself. Society is a force far greater than any individual. It brought us to life, and it can kill us. It has tremendous power over us.

Everyone depends on it. Our sense of ourselves and the concepts and the language through which we think and communicate come to us through society. The community, omnipresent and omnipotent, comprises an anonymous, impersonal force to which all belong. *God* is the symbolic expression of the intensity of our feeling of community with others. It is this human community that arouses in us the sense of the divine and that has moral authority over us. The duality of the human person and the *soul* is, like religion, found everywhere, and so cannot be illusory. For Durkheim, the concept of soul symbolizes the force of the group within the self, the duality of human nature as both individual and social.

Collins (1982, 39–41) describes the tremendous force of emotional energy that we derive from a sense of belonging with a group. It gives us courage beyond any level that we could muster alone. It makes us capable of heroism and sacrifice and gives us confidence to achieve things we could not otherwise reach. Such energy can also become fanatical, powerful, and potentially dangerous. These intangible but very real forces are part of what religion expresses. Religious rituals have a special power to draw us together. The sacred **taboos** and ceremonials reinforce the sense of cohesion with others in the moral community. Rites such as Communion reinforce the bonds of kinship between us. *Representative rites—* the dramas and myths that repeat the actions of our ancestors—perpetuate tradition and reinforce a sense of belonging to the past and to the future of our community. Other rites such as funerals draw us together in grief to reaffirm the continuity of the group beyond the life of the individual. All religious rites draw people together and so reaffirm consciousness of our moral community.

If religion and the concept of God do indeed reflect society, then different types of societies should have different types of gods, reflecting their own unique structures (Collins 1982, 47). Durkheim's own study focusses on the most primitive form of religion—totemism among the aboriginal hunting and gathering societies of Australia—to show how the concepts of their religion intimately mirror the structure of their clan communities. They have no wealth and no hierarchy, and the different clans that make up the tribe are equal. Each clan has a sacred totem that gives the clan its name and is the centre of its special rituals and beliefs. The totem is the emblem of the clan and has sacred force because it transcends the individual in representing the group. The sacred force is not intrinsic to the animal or plant selected as a totem, any more than a Christian cross is sacred. The sacredness resides in its nature as a symbol. Just as all clans within the hunting and gathering society are equal, so all the totems of the different clans are religiously equal (Collins 1982, 47–48).

Collins goes on to note that in agricultural communities, which are larger than hunting and gathering societies and have some accumulated wealth, the nature of religious belief is different. In particular, he argues, the role of kinship ties and inheritance and, hence, the position of women is more important, and this is reflected in fertility rites and the worship of goddesses. As societies become more hierarchically organized, the gods are likely to be thought of as arranged in a hierarchy as well. Finally, in literate, cospolitan civilizations, the concept of God as a single, transcendent reality emerges. This type of religion aims to be universal. It reflects a rationalized, literate society with sufficient political power that it can foster the idea of a universal state (Collins 1982, 48–50).

Durkheim's anthropological data with respect to aboriginal social structures and religious practices were somewhat limited, and a number of his specific descriptive claims have been criticized. But his overall conception of the nature of religious experience and its grounding in the everyday experience of communal life still stands as a seminal argument in the sociology of religion.

Durkheim and Contemporary Functionalist Theory of Religion

Durkheim's analysis of rituals remains central to the functionalist theory of religion. Functionalists do not concern themselves with the question of whether religious ideas represent reality, but with the more immediate practical issue of what consequences religion has for human society and for individuals. Like Durkheim, they argue that a phenomenon such as religion, which is universally present, must be crucial for the maintenance of society; it must have some indispensable function. That primary function is the integration of society in the face of the suffering and death of its members (Yinger 1957, 7–12). Society, they argue, requires a unifying value system to legitimate social order. At the individual level, all human desires—for power, love, knowledge, consolation—find expression in religious beliefs. Above all, religion helps people to grapple with death. The hope of salvation eases suffering while the rituals surrounding death draw people together.

The implicit assumption in functionalist theory is that somehow religion was invented because people or society needed it, and that it must be maintained because it is necessary for social cohesion. A detailed examination of the logic of functionalist theory is reserved for chapter 10, but it is worth noting here that it reverses Durkheim's original thesis about the relationship between religion and cohesion.

According to Durkheim, religion does not produce cohesion, it expresses it. It reflects, in symbolic form, the deep emotional awareness of belonging to a human community, which is fundamental to the human condition. Rituals objectify and thus strengthen community bonds.

Durkheim was aware that, as social life becomes more diversified, the shared values of mechanical solidarity are no longer the central unifying force. Religion, he suggests, must take a very different form, the religion of humanism. The core experience of belonging to the human community is manifest through the awareness of mutual interdependence and moral obligation—despite, or in fact because of, the tremendous diversity of lifestyles and values in the world community. For Durkheim, only the unity of the religion of humanism could ultimately express this experience, a unity in which tolerance for diversity would be a basic premise (Neyer 1960).

Religion and Class

The functionalist perspective, which posits that religion expresses and reinforces social cohesion, has been extensively criticized. Critics maintain that the functionalist argument's weakest link is its underlying view of society itself as a unified, cohesive system. This view might be valid for the very small-scale hunting and gathering societies associated with Durkheim's study of elementary forms of religion. But complex industrial societies are ethnically heterogeneous and riven with class divisions and conflict. Fundamental divisions of power and inequality cannot be glossed over by Durkheim's appeal to humanism. In industrial societies, critics suggest, religion functions primarily to reinforce the values of the dominant class. The shared beliefs and sentiments of established religion tend to reflect an artificial or manipulated consensus that does not give full expression to the values of subordinate classes.

Marxist Theory

The Marxist approach to the study of religion gives fullest expression to this perspective. Marx himself addressed the issue of religion only in a fragmentary way. Much of what now stands as the Marxist theory of religion was not actually written by Marx himself and was developed by later theorists. Marx characterized religion as a powerful form of ideology that legitimates and strengthens class domination by inculcating among subordinate people an acceptance of subordination. In the Marxist critique of functionalist theory, religion functions as an "opiate of the masses." Religions that stress acceptance of suffering, with reward in the life after death, drug people into passivity and submission. As we shall see below, **puritanism** which prevailed in nineteenth-century England during the period when Marx was writing, was a particularly notorious target for such criticism. It was an ethic that justified the wealth and power of capitalists as somehow ordained by god or merited on the basis of holy grace, while poor people were enjoined to endure suffering or hardship as trials that would prove their worthiness for ultimate salvation in the life beyond death.

Marx did not entirely discount the radical potential of religion. However distorted its particular message might be, Marx recognized that "religious distress is at the same time real distress and the protest against real distress" (Baum 1979, 30). The problem for Marx was that religion was all too often a powerful force that prevented people from recognizing their real situation and rebelling against it.

Engels ([1894] 1978), a close confederate of Marx, explicitly recognized the affinity between the ideas underlying communism and Christianity, particularly as reflected in early Christian communities. Christianity appeared as a religion of slaves and emancipated slaves, of poor people deprived of all rights. Like **socialism**, it promised forthcoming salvation from bondage and misery. The major difference between them was that Christianity did not want to accomplish the transformation in this world, but beyond it, in heaven, in eternal life after death. Engels accounts for this difference by reference to the historical condition of slaves and to the absence of a strong working-class structure that would have made the socialist revolution possible at the time that Christianity first took hold. Christianity subsequently became the dominant religion of the Roman Empire, and its promise of salvation after death was tied to a message of passivity and submission to earthly rulers.

Despite his generally negative orientation toward religion, Marx's ideas are compatible with the theories subsequently developed by Durkheim and particularly by Max Weber. He shared with them the underlying notion of an affinity between systems of ideas and the actual material situation in which people find themselves.

Max Weber's Contribution

Much of Weber's work was acknowledged to be a conversation with the ghost of Marx, an effort both to elaborate Marx's ideas and to go beyond them. Weber's contribution was to undertake a historical, comparative study of world religions and of the varied forms of religious expression among different social classes within Western industrial societies. Weber documents how closely the patterns of religious expression reflect diverse life experiences. The road to salvation varies markedly with social position (Weber [1922] 1964, chaps. 6 and 7). People who do different kinds of work and who occupy different places within a society, whether as warriors, peasants, intellectuals, or business people, have very different religious tendencies,

even within the same overarching religious tradition such as Christianity. People whose work exposes them to the cycles of the seasons tend to develop a very different view of the ultimate meaning of life than those confined to the routines of offices and factories or those whose life's work centres around raising children.

The religion of the disprivileged tends to be inclined toward magic and toward salvation in the hereafter. The self-esteem and honour of such people rest on a promise for the future and on their significance in the eyes of a divine authority who has values different from those of the world. For such people, breakaway sects and cults of heroes and saints have special appeal. Peasants have a secure relation to the land but experience the vagaries of weather and unpredictable natural forces. They have little interest in rationalized theology and are more inclined toward magic. The ethic of warriors, on the other hand, is not compatible with a kindhearted divinity. Concepts of an otherworldly god with systematic ethical demands have little or no appeal. Warriors are drawn toward an image of a god of power and toward a religion that allows them to view their adversaries as morally depraved. Weber traces such themes in the origins of Christianity. The Old Testament god Yahweh is essentially a god bent upon war, revenge, and punishment. The New Testament religion of Jesus is, in contrast, the religion of slaves, of a subordinate people under the Roman Empire. Here the salvation ethic rather than justification of war is paramount.

Burridge (1969) describes the transition from the ethic of warriors to the religion of a disprivileged people among the Plains Indians of North America with the coming of white settlers. These tribes ruled the great plains, braves on horseback hunted wild buffalo, and the values of warriors were paramount. Great esteem was accorded the dashing fighter who could get horses by stealth or war, execute successful moves in battle, gallop in amongst a herd of buffalo, and face extremes of physical pain in stoic silence (Burridge 1969, 77). The warrior ethic found religious expression through such rituals as the Great Sun Dance. The Sun Dance was a political occasion when nomadic bands of Indians gathered together to dance, feast, resolve their disputes, compete in games and ritual exercises of self-torture, and renew their common allegiance to an overall political order (Burridge 1969, 80).

The warrior culture collapsed as white settlers took over the plains for farmland and cattle pastures and drove the Indians onto small reservations. Those who died fighting the whites at least earned a traditional redemption, Burridge suggests, but there could be no redemption for the remnant people who lived through the end of the Indian wars in reservations, without horses, without buffalo, without war, dependent upon handouts from the government. Their

situation found a form of religious expression in the new Ghost Dance religion, which spread among the Indian communities. It prophesied a general catastrophe that would herald a new millennium where the whites would be destroyed, or all racial differences would disappear, and the boundless plains would re-emerge. Prophets preached a new philosophy in which people must not quarrel or fight or shoot one another but wait for the renewal projected in dreams and visions.

The rites of the Ghost Dance involved singing and chanting, falling into trances, stripping naked, and torturing oneself, all of which promoted union with the glorious dead. Ceremonies also included opening graves to communicate more closely with ancestors. Rites involved enjoying in trance what in the past had been fully realized (Burridge 1969, 79–80). The rites of the Ghost Dance were thus in many ways heir to the Sun Dance, expressing a new focus for reintegrating communities. The Ghost Dance

Canadian native people continue to participate in such rites as the Ghost Dance, which recalls native peoples' proud past.

had definite political overtones: the communal dance—in which participants could escape the mundane world, speak in tongues, have visions, and gain inspiration—was the seed of future political organization.

For Burridge, all religions are concerned fundamentally with principles of power and the moral basis of people's obligations toward society. New religions, he suggests, emerge during periods of social unrest, when these principles are called into question (Burridge 1969, 4–7).

The Distinctive Religion of the Capitalist Class

Weber's most famous study in the sociology of religion, *The Protestant Ethic and the Spirit of Capitalism* ([1904] 1930), explores in depth the ethic of the business class in Europe. The disprivileged seek redemption and salvation in the **millennium**—the anticipated thousand years of Christ's reign on earth predicted in the Book of Revelation. The religions favoured by the privileged classes, however, tend to be oriented much more toward worldly success, and its moral justification, rather than other-worldly concern with judgment hereafter. Weber argued that bureaucrats and business people in general evidence a profound dislike of all "irrational" emotionally based religions and are not the types to go to evangelical revival meetings. The more privileged the class, the less inclined are its members to follow other-worldly religious doctrines.

Weber observed that members of the business class in Europe were disproportionately adherents of a puritanical Calvinist form of Protestantism, even though the dominant religion of Europe at that time was Catholicism. The religious dogma of **Calvinism** advocated a sober, frugal style of living, and prohibited alcohol, dancing, and luxuries. It also stressed a disciplined obligation to work as a means to serve God. The Calvinist conception of God was of a harsh, all-knowing, all-powerful being, incomprehensible to

humans. From the assumption that God knew in advance who would be damned, and who saved, came the doctrine of **predestination**. There could be no salvation through the church or magical sacraments or human actions, only through grace. An important feature of this deterministic philosophy was the belief that success in the world was a sign of God's grace, while poverty or failure was a measure of lack of moral fervour and of damnation.

Such ideas, Weber argues, provided unique encouragement to capitalism. Work was a duty, and amassing wealth a sign of grace. At the same time, however, there was a puritanical edict against spending such wealth upon idle consumption. Unemployment, even among the wealthy who had no need to earn money, was seen as slothful and immoral, a sign of damnation. Hence, the only moral option was to invest wealth in expanding business. The Catholic Church of the period forbade usury, or lending money with interest, as profiting from the distress of others, but Calvinism supported it as morally proper business behaviour.

Weber never addresses the issue of whether Calvinist religion promoted capitalism or capitalism promoted Calvinism. Rather, he speaks of an *elective affinity* between the two. By elective affinity, Weber means the mutual attraction between the business lifestyle and the Protestant ethic, the tendency for this kind of ethic to promote behaviour and values conducive to good business practices, and the propensity for people who spend their lives in business to be attracted to this kind of moral teaching. Business people were drawn to, and stimulated by, the ethic of worldly work as a duty and a sign of grace. This ethic provided a moral justification for wealth and also for poverty. The Elizabethan Poor Law Act, which was passed in England in 1601, regulated the treatment of paupers for almost three centuries. The Act advocated extremely harsh and punitive treatment of destitute people as a way of forcing them to become more industrious and self-sufficient. It found its justification in the Calvinist belief that poverty was a sign of moral depravity. The poor were poor through their own fault, and to help them was to help the devil.

"Where in heaven's name does he get these bizarre 'left wing' notions? 'The meek shall inherit the earth,' indeed."

Puritanism and the Working Class

Calvinist doctrines interpreting wealth and success as signs of grace held little appeal outside the business class. It was the rise of **Methodism** in Europe that spread the puritan message to the workers. Puritanism as a general philosophy advocated scrupulous moral behaviour and extreme strictness in adherence to details of religious practice. Many forms of spontaneous enjoyment and leisure, including parties, dancing, and especially sex, were seen as sinful and were either banned or very strictly controlled. E.P. Thompson (1963, chap. 11) leaves no doubt that the puritanical doctrines embodied in Methodism fit the Marxist vision of religion as imposing on the masses the values of the dominant capitalist class.

Methodism gained strength in England during the Napoleonic Wars, which closely followed the French Revolution. The doctrine was profoundly anti-revolutionary in its stance. It stressed submission and obedience to authority and zeal in combatting enemies of the established order. A Methodist text written at the end of the eighteenth century stressed that "God would prefer to suffer the government to exist, no matter how evil, rather than allow the rabble to riot, no matter how justified they are in doing so" (Thompson 1963, 399).

Methodism was remarkable in appealing simultaneously to the industrial bourgeoisie and to wide sections of the working class (Thompson 1963, 391). Methodist doctrine incorporated the poor through its stress on spiritual egalitarianism and religion of the heart rather than the intellect. The simplest and least educated might attain grace through sincere repentance and forgiveness of sin. This forgiveness, however, was always conditional and provisory, lasting only so long as the penitent went and sinned no more. Grace could be attained in several ways: by perpetual service to the church itself as a leader or preacher; through personal tract-reading and repeated emotional frenzy associated with conversion, penitence, and visitation by grace; and, most importantly, by methodical discipline in all aspects of life. God's curse over Adam and Eve when they were thrown out of the Garden of Eden provided the doctrinal support for the emphasis on the blessedness of hard work, poverty, and sorrow "all the days of thy life" (Thompson 1963, 401). Methodist tracts stressed the sinfulness of youth, the threat of death, and the state of humans as poor, blind, fallen, wretched, and (without divine grace) helpless sinners. Sinfulness was especially associated with sexuality. These doctrines translated into an extremely harsh edict of repression and inhibition: " 'A more appalling system of religious terrorism, one more fitted to unhinge a tottering intellect and to darken and embitter a sensitive nature, has seldom existed" (Thompson 1963, 410, quoting Lecky 1891).

The utility of religious discipline for controlling the industrial working class was indisputable. The major problem for employers during the early stages of industrialization was the immense resistance of workers to the unnatural and hateful restraints of machine-paced work. What was needed, from the employers' viewpoint, was education not only in methodical habits, but also in punctilious attention to instructions, fulfilment of contracts on time, and the sinfulness of embezzling materials. The discipline of an overseer might be sufficient to control child labour in factories, but not "bad-tempered, intractable, and cunning" adults. Mere wage payment could never secure "zealous service." An inner compulsion was needed, and this is what Methodism provided.

The question still to be answered is why such a repressive doctrine as Methodism should have appealed to such large numbers of working-class people. Unlike the business people attracted to Calvinism, workers stood to gain little from such dedication to their employers. Thompson (1963, 415–18) suggests that three factors were important. The first was the power of indoctrination, especially over children in Sunday schools. Methodism stressed the inherent sinfulness of children and the need to break their will in order that their souls might live. Secondly, membership within the Methodist Church provided a kind of community for people uprooted by the Industrial Revolution. The church offered much mutual aid, some recognition for sobriety, chastity, and piety, and could contribute to family stability. The third reason for its appeal was that it provided an emotional opiate, not unlike the real opiates that were widely consumed during this period. Methodism offered religious consolation to people oppressed by war and the wretched conditions of industrial working-class life. Thompson (1963, 428) argues that Methodism gained its greatest converts precisely during the periods when "political or temporal aspirations met with defeat."

Methodism, with its emphasis on the afterlife, brought the promise of ultimate salvation to the defeated and the hopeless. People were drawn to its message of the millennium precisely when life on earth was becoming unbearable.

Conversion, however, was not necessarily or even usually permanent. People who turned to Methodism for consolation during times of hopelessness could be readily lured into political activism when times changed. Given the right stimulus, the sexual repression and the hostility that were pent up in the puritanical zeal of Methodism might explode into spontaneous and irrepressible social and political revolt.

Methodism, despite itself, contained the dormant seeds of political radicalism, perhaps much as the Ghost Dance heralded the possibility of concerted political action among native Indians in North America. In a number of ways it unwittingly contributed to working-class political movements. Rural Methodist chapels, by their very existence, tended to assume a class-conscious form. The chapel was an affront to the traditional authority of the vicar and the squire. Nonconformity to the established Church of England also meant nonconformity to the local political authority associated with the established church. The chapel functioned as a centre in which labourers could gain independence and self-respect. Field labourers who converted to Methodism were accused of all kinds of seditious intentions, including claims to equality with their superiors (Thompson 1963, 437).

The official Methodism of the bureaucracy of ministers who received church stipends was very different from the "Primitive Methodism" of lay preachers in the countryside, so much so that the official Methodist Conference and circuit superintendents from 1812 onwards actively tried to stamp out Primitive Methodism. It was feared that its tumultuous Bible camp meetings might serve as political precedents.

The Methodist doctrinal emphasis on spiritual egalitarianism carried the constant risk of spilling over into demands for political rights. When this did happen, it was likely to be characterized by the same kind of passionate moral commitment that the religion itself engendered. When committed Methodists turned to political action, they could find doctrinal justification in the allegory of the Children of Israel, which had many parallels with their own tribulations. The Old Testament contains more than the message of a vengeful, authoritarian God. It also includes tales of the release of the Israelites from bondage and of the punishment of corrupt governments in the cities of Sodom and Gomorrah.

Methodist lay people were particularly well trained in practical ways for political action. The emphasis on lay preaching, self-education, and self-government within each church actively promoted self-confidence among working people. Those who first learned to read in Sunday schools could read the Bible for themselves, but they could also read radical political tracts. The organization of the Methodist Church provided working-class people with experience in how to organize meetings on a regular basis, including the collection of penny subscriptions and the centralized administration at district and national level. Such techniques were frequently borrowed by radical and trade union organizations.

In summary, while the official doctrines of the Methodist Church preached repression, obedience, discipline, and submission to authority, the underlying message was of passion, egalitarianism, and self-reliance. It was this very mixed message that Methodist immigrants brought with them to Canada.

The Social Gospel in Canada

Methodism in Canada at the beginning of the twentieth century reflected a similar dichotomy between a puritanical, pro-business establishment church and an egali-tarian, social-justice fringe that could provide the basis for socialism (Smillie 1979, 35–37). Mainstream Canadian Methodism encouraged financial aristocrats in the industrialized West. When J.S. Woodsworth, a socialist-Methodist, tried to intercede in the Winnipeg General Strike of 1919, he pleaded with the strikers that Winnipeg businessmen were not hard-hearted hypocrites, or men who led self-indulgent lives, but hard-working, self-made men who were as much victims of the social and economic system as were the workers themselves.

Appalled by the effects of industrial capitalism on the poor, J. S. Woodsworth became a prominent advocate of the Social Gospel in early twentieth-century Canada.

Yet notwithstanding close sympathies with the entrepreneurial class, Methodists, along with other radical Christian groups and labour churches, provided leadership for the labour and agrarian protest movements. Woodsworth himself conducted extensive research into the conditions of the poor in Winnipeg. The appalling conditions that he found convinced him that the Christian churches had to become involved in the struggle for social justice. The churches could not hope to minister to the spiritual needs of the working classes without also caring for the physical conditions of their lives. The movement reflecting this idea became known as the **Social Gospel**.

The Social Gospel movement in Canada was strongest during the period between 1880 and the 1920s (Allen 1975). Inspired by the implications of spiritual egalitarianism, the movement stressed the links between Christianity and socialism and the doctrine of collective social responsibility. The meaning of sin and salvation was translated in social rather than individual terms, so that social justice became central to the Christian message. Under the leadership of radical ministers from Methodist, Anglican, and Presbyterian churches, adherents of the Social Gospel rejected the earlier stand of the establishment churches that trade unions should be condemned for usurping the rights of employers. They also argued that neither unions nor socialist groups threatened the church. A church union movement, initiated in 1902, won the Lord's Day Observance Act, granting Sundays off for workers. By 1913, the church union became the Social Services Council of Canada, which was active in the provision of schools, libraries, savings banks, nurseries, and clubrooms for the working classes. The church union movement was also a powerful force behind prohibition during World War I.

By 1920, however, the Social Gospel movement was in decline. Orthodox sectors of the churches withdrew their support, especially after the Russian Revolution and Winnipeg General Strike. They feared growing labour power and strikes. Methodists as a whole grew richer and tended to place more stress on individualism and entrepreneurship than collective responsibility. The spirit of the movement found more direct political expression on the prairies in the formation of the Co-operative Commonwealth Federation (CCF) led by Woodsworth and Tommy Douglas, a Baptist minister turned political reformer. The CCF later became the New Democratic Party.

Methodism was certainly not alone in carrying a mixed message of individualism and Social Gospel. Such a dichotomy is perhaps unavoidable in any religious movement in capitalist societies. A similar division has been traced in the history of the United Church of Canada, which has provided a forum for radical groups to exist alongside the conformist mainstream church (Smillie 1979, 36).

The Catholic Church worldwide has also manifested this internal struggle with a radical Social Gospel movement known as **liberation theology**, which has emerged as an important fringe group. Liberation theology seeks to integrate the radical social theory of Marxism with the central Christian message of God's love for humanity. The lived experience of Catholics in Latin America, struggling against repressive political regimes, has been an extremely powerful force for radical theology within Catholicism. The efforts of liberation theologists to recover and reinterpret the social dimension of the Christian message found a sympathetic response in the work of German theologians such as Ernst Bloch and in the radical Catholicism of Antonio Gramsci, one of the founders of the Italian Communist Party (Baum 1979; 1981).

Gregory Baum, a Catholic priest, theologian, and sociologist in Canada, takes pains to emphasize that this radical Social Gospel is a liberation *theology*, and not merely, or even primarily, a secular political movement. Concern with spirituality and the concept of divinity is at the heart of this Catholic message. Liberation theology seeks, above all, to deprivatize the Christian message. In other words, it rejects the interpretation of salvation, sin, and conversion in individual terms. In contrast, it emphasizes the social dimension of the Christian message and the social covenant of the Old Testament between God and the people of Israel in which God fulfills the promise to deliver the Israelites, as a nation, from bondage. It implies also what Baum calls "the preferential option for the poor," which reveals God as one who takes the side of the oppressed, the excluded, the outcasts, the Hebrew slaves.

This is a spiritual commitment which, in Baum's view, goes far beyond the Marxist focus on the industrial proletariat as the revolutionary force in economic change. It gives primacy to action over the search for abstract knowledge as the basis for learning the truth about society. It stresses a transformation and liberation of human life that comprises both action and theory, both practical struggle and spiritual, cultural transformation. Liberation theology is thus "this-worldly" in Weber's sense, but also transcendent, a Christian mystical, divine call for justice (Baum 1981). Baum argues that Pope John Paul II's encyclical on labour and the dignity of human work, together with the Catholic bishops' pastoral letters on the economy and social justice, express a Christian option for the poor that integrates the one-sided Marxist emphasis on economic infrastructure with an essential spiritual and cultural dimension, working together for the transformation of society.

The problem is that the Social Gospel message remains as ephemeral and as marginal to the establishment churches now as during the last century. It exists on the fringes of the Christian community, vulnerable, occasionally isolated and attacked. At worst, liberation theology has been reduced to just another consumer item for intellectuals (Green 1979, 38–39), a program filler for organizations whose comfortable middle-class patrons do penance merely by listening to the hard words of the activists. At best it constitutes small radical groups engaged in relatively low-profile action and research, including such groups as GATT-fly (concerned with injustices in international trade regulations), the Task Force on the Church and Corporate Responsibility, Project Ploughshares, and Project North.

Project North was established in 1975 to help Canadian churches address the issues of massive resource development projects in northern Canada and to side with the native peoples in their push for self-determination. It incorporates recognition of and an attempt at atonement for the church's integral role in the colonization of native peoples (McCullum and Hatton 1979). This project in particular has been attacked by the conservative Coalition of Church and Business People (CCBP) for contributing to strife and unemployment in the North and undermining the economic philosophy of free enterprise. In 1978 the CCBP had offices in Toronto and a budget reported to be $100 000, and it had hired a full-time director. The aim of the coalition is to discredit radical interchurch projects as sponsored by small groups of activists who do not represent the majority of church people across Canada.

In Latin America also, the establishment church largely supports the repressive governments, while movements such as Christians for Socialism now exist only in exile. Baum concludes that there is no clear, definable Christian Left in North America. He fears that as class conflict becomes more intense, the churches may cease to be permissive of left-wing members and push them out altogether (Baum 1979, 34).

Yet the radical fringe remains, its voice heard, and its influence felt in proportion far beyond its numbers. Its very existence within all the established churches is a reminder that culture is not a monolithic, nor a fixed, unchanging entity, and that wherever there is repression there will also be resistance. As E.P. Thompson (1963, 431) acknowledges, no ideology is wholly absorbed by its adherents: it breaks down in practice in a thousand ways under the criticism of impulse and of experience. The contemporary struggle within the United Church of Canada over the ordination of practising homosexuals is part of this long history of the struggle to assert the Christian message of radical social justice within the established churches. Another example is the long and often bitter struggle for the incorporation of women as equals at all levels of the church. The United Church of Canada, after a long and often bitter debate, now officially incorporates women as equals with men at all levels of the church ministry. Within the Anglican and Catholic churches, however, the feminist movement still represents a radical fringe.

Lois Wilson became the first female moderator of the United Church of Canada in 1980.

Feminist Critiques of Religion

The **radical feminist** critique has been strongly influenced by the Marxist thesis that dominant ideas and values within a society provide a justification for the ruling-class position. Feminists break with classical Marxist theory over their focus, which is not upon economic classes, but upon patriarchy, or male dominance, and the low **sexual-caste** status of women. They see the position of women in society as analogous to that of a caste in the sense that it is assigned by birth. Engels ([1884] 1978) defines the male subjugation of women as the first oppressor-oppressed relation and the foundation of all other class and property relations. It is also the last inequality to be challenged by established religions, after racism and slavery (Ruether 1975, 3). As Mary Daly emphasizes, the exploitative sexual-caste system could not be perpetuated without the consent of its victims as well as of the dominant sex, and such consent is obtained through **sex-role socialization**; that is, through a conditioning process in which the dominant religion is a potent force (Daly 1973, 2). Religious doctrine concerning the appropriate behaviour and responsibilities of women functions as an opiate for the mass of women, dulling the pain of subordination and the capacity to rebel and change things.

Feminist theologians stress that the fundamental symbolic systems of Judaic and Christian religions, and the conceptual apparatus and linguistic instruments for communication that go with them, have been male creations, formulated by men under the condition of patriarchy. Hence, they inherently serve the purposes of a patriarchal social order (Daly 1973, 7, 20). The dominant symbol of God as male—as Father—makes societal oppression of women appear right and fitting. It renders it "natural" and according to divine plan. The husband dominating his wife represents God

"Himself" (Daly 1973, 3, 13), and the husband's authority over his wife is sanctioned by God's command in the Book of Genesis.

The roots of this symbolism lie deep in Greco-Roman philosophy. A fundamental element of this heritage is the philosophical separation of mind and body. Rational powers, associated with men, are seen as superior to the faculties of the body and nature, associated with women (Kolbenschlag 1979, 183). Within this intellectual system, even the myths of primitive **matriarchy**—where women commanded the highest authority by virtue of being the only known parent—and the mother goddess associated with mother nature do not promote female equality. They serve rather as a stage in the co-optation of the female into a male-defined power system (Ruether 1975, 6–14).

As men sought to free themselves from dependence on nature, they downplayed not only the generative aspects of women as mothers but the overall position of women as well. Men developed a philosophy that males were created from above, and were identified with intellectuality and spirituality, while femaleness was identified with the bodily world and was seen as dependent upon, and inferior to, maleness. The myth of the creation of woman through Adam's rib is a classic portrayal of this. The male, Adam, is the human prototype, and he "gives birth" to the woman with the help of a father God. Similarly, in Aristotle's theory of biology, women are denied all generative potency. They are not seen as actively contributing anything to the creation of a baby; they are merely the passive carriers or incubators of male seed.

Women were denigrated in other ways. Although old tribal taboos treated menstrual blood as the blood of life and a dangerously sacral substance, menstruating women later came to be seen as "unclean" as maternal power was undercut and suppressed culturally. Canon law in the fourth century cited the uncleanliness of women as a major reason for eliminating the office of deaconess. Even lay women were advised to stay away from Communion during menstruation (Ruether 1975, 16, 70). These old ideas linger on, manifest in the 1980 edict of Pope John Paul II banning altar girls. This edict has been quietly ignored in many Catholic churches but, in June 1987, an eleven-year-old girl who had served as altar girl at Sacre Coeur Church in Toronto for four years was banned from a special mass to mark the hundredth anniversary of the parish, on the orders of Emmett Cardinal Carter (*Globe and Mail*, 19 June 1987, A1).

Ruether argues that Christianity has a dual view of women, represented by the Virgin Mary, who symbolizes sublimated spiritual femininity, and the Fallen Eve, who symbolizes the actual fleshy woman. Mariology, or the love of the Virgin Mary, presupposes that real women are feared and hated (Ruether 1975, 18–19). If real women can only be loved when they have no sexual desires of their own and remain chaste virgins, except for submitting to pregnancy through some form of artificial insemination, then no real woman would ever be loved. To be a normal, fleshy woman, with normal sexual desires and sexual attractiveness, is to be a failure, a fallen woman. When Uta Ranke-Heinemann, the world's first female Catholic theology professor, challenged this vision of the pure, holy, asexual Virgin Mary by daring to dispute the virgin birth, the church withdrew her authority to teach theology (*Globe and Mail*, 20 June 1987, A10).

When, in 1971, the Episcopal bishop of California denied the capacity of women for ordination on the grounds that only males possess the capacity for "initiative" that represents the "potency" of God, he had a long history of clerical **misogyny**, or woman hating, behind him. He could cite the lines of 1 Timothy 2:13–14 that women are "to learn in silence with all submissiveness. I permit no woman to teach or to have authority over men; she is to keep silent." One could recite a litany of antifeminism in Christian history. One of the church fathers, Tertullian, wrote "Women, do you not know that you are Eve? You are the devil's gateway." Saint Augustine opined that women are not made in the image of God, and the Decretum of Gratian in 1140, the first enduring systematization of church laws, assumed this with impunity (Kolbenschlag 1979, 183). St. Thomas Aquinas defined women as misbegotten males who do not possess the image of God by themselves, but only when taken together with the male who is their "head" (Ruether 1975, 72). Martin Luther held that God created Adam lord over all living creatures, but Eve spoiled this early idyll. John Knox composed a "First Blast of the Trumpet against the Monstrous Regiment of Women." The theologians Barth and Bonhoeffer insisted that women should be subordinate to their husbands (Daly 1973, 5). The list goes on and on.

What angers Daly most is that it is possible for scholars to acknowledge the blatant misogyny of these theologians and at the same time to treat their unverified opinions on far more imponderable matters with the utmost reverence and respect (Daly 1973, 20). They do not seem to see any serious credibility gap. Daly rails against scholars who persistently deny the evidence of patriarchy within the church and refuse to see the sexual-caste problem against which women struggle. Devices for this refusal include trivializing the issue, dismissing it as merely "a Catholic problem," as if it did not exist elsewhere, and spending time on pseudo-problems that are not what women are really concerned about. Theologians spend time arguing whether Paul was really the author of the objectionable passages against women or claiming that "in Christ there is neither male nor female." Such arguments do not alter the fact that the Christ image is male; nor do they do anything to alleviate the deep injustice that is being per-petuated against women in the church (Daly 1973, 5).

Ruether (1979, 64) notes that Jesus himself can be seen, in some respects, as a feminist, challenging the stereotypes of his time. He had close female friends who accompanied him on his preaching and teaching trips, including Mary Magdalene, Joanna, and Susanna. He praised the faith of poor widows and outcast women against the faithlessness of the religious establishment. He performed his first miracles for women, and women were the first witnesses of his resurrection. Women also seem to have been prominent as teachers in the early period of the church. However, by as early as the fourth century A.D., things changed. Women were excluded from any teaching or leadership roles within the church, and the misogyny of the early church fathers became deeply entrenched in the dogma and practices of the church.

The period from the fifteenth to the seventeenth centuries was marked by the systematic persecution and slaughter of women as witches, with the authority of the church. The *Malleus Maleficarum* (*The Hammer of Witches*), written in 1486 by two Dominican inquisitors, was used as a guide for witch hunters. This document makes very clear the perceived link between witchcraft and sex. It claims that "All witchcraft comes from carnal lust, which is in women insatiable. . . . Wherefore for the sake of fulfilling their lust they consort even with devils" (Jong 1981, 69). According to Jong, the book gave credence to every misogynist myth: women cause impotence; women are weak-willed, weak-minded, carnal temptresses; women are unfit to rule or to have professions; midwives kill babies, and so on.

There were some male witches, but the notion *witch* is still synonymous with woman. The proportion of women to men slaughtered as witches throughout Europe was about 80 percent, and as high as 95 to

100 percent in England and Russia (Larner 1984, 85). Conservative estimates of the numbers of people burned as witches are in the hundreds of thousands, but overall figures are unknown because many records were lost or destroyed, and many archives are still unexplored. Some chroniclers estimate that the total was as high as nine million, more than all the Jews murdered during the Nazi holocaust (Gardiner 1954).

Theological foundation for witch hunts came from the Lateran council decree of 1215 that all heretics should be punished with death (Jong 1981, 51). Typically, "confessions" were extracted through torture: "arms came out of sockets and trysts with the Devil came out of the unlikeliest mouths" (Jong 1981, 43–46). The women most at risk of being targeted as witches were those who did not conform to the male idea of proper female behaviour; assertive, independent women, particularly those who did not nurture men or children, were particularly in danger (Larner 1984, 84). There is some evidence

By conservative estimates, hundreds of thousands of women were executed for witchcraft in Europe.

that homosexual men were also disproportionately likely to be targeted as witches.

The established Christian churches no longer engage in witch hunts or inquisitions, but the basic structure of male dominance within the churches remains largely unchallenged. Women are still banned from all but the lowest rungs of the Catholic Church hierarchy. Some Protestant churches are, in theory, more open and permit the ordination of women, but women are far from achieving equal stature.

During the 1980s, there was a slow but steady increase in the number of women ordained to the ministry (McAteer 1989). Churches that refused to ordain women were still in the majority; of the eighty denominations surveyed in Canada in 1987, only twenty-nine ordained women to the full ministry. But where women are admitted, their numbers are rising. The United Church of Canada leads the way. In 1989 15.4 percent of its ministers were women, and women comprised over half of the students studying for the United Church ministry at theological colleges. The Reverend Lois Wilson became the first female head of the United Church in Canada when she was elected to a term as moderator in 1980.

Numbers, however, do not tell the full story of women's struggles for acceptance in the churches. Most ordained women are still concentrated in administrative posts rather than in the ministry. Those who aspire to the ministry itself have to battle discrimination and sexism. A survey of ordained women in Canada reported widespread bitterness, unhappiness, and anger in women who were trying to find a place in the ministry. Fully one-third of the women surveyed in the United Church said they had been sexually harassed in their ministry.

Women ministers continue to face an uphill struggle. They tend to minister to very small congregations. They tend to experience the exodus from their congregations of a number of people who dislike women in leadership positions. Most of the liturgy, hymns, rituals, and symbols of the churches still remain sexist. The battle for **inclusive language** has yet to be won in most churches. The United Church of Canada is making more headway than most in this respect with the publication of a language manual to guide the introduction of non-sexist terms.

For Madonna Kolbenschlag, the most important of all the misogynist pronouncements of the church is the mutilation of the spirit that the image of God as Male has wrought in the lives of women. Woman, she says, has adapted herself to a relationship with a transcendent Being who is radically Other than herself. The closer she comes to this God, the more she loses her own soul. She concludes that "a woman has no choice but to be an atheist" (Kolbenschlag 1979, 184). Kolbenschlag herself means this statement in a positive sense. For her, the rejection of the image of God as Father is a necessary prelude to spiritual maturity and to the rediscovery of an autonomous image of God that is experienced as transpersonal and as a ground of personality. She chooses to continue to live as a nun and to work for change within the Catholic Church.

Mary Daly takes the much more radical option of leaving the established Christian churches altogether. In a lecture at the University of New Brunswick in 1984, she commented that, while she would not oppose the ordination of women in the Catholic Church, she would not recommend it, since it would be like inviting blacks to join the Ku Klux Klan. She prefers to explore the realms of *Gyn/Ecology*, the ancient sciences of womankind, rejecting the phallo-centric value system imposed by patriarchy, a value system that glorifies the power of male sexuality and that ultimately threatens to rape the earth of its life. She writes a "crone-ology," "dis-covering" the hidden history of thought of her foresisters, the Great Hags or witches "who the institutionally powerful

but privately impotent patriarchs found too threatening for co-existence and whom historians erase" (Daly 1978, 14). The word *Hag* comes from an old English word meaning "an evil or frightening spirit," but frightening to whom? These are women who frighten the patriarchs. Hags are often "haggard," in the sense of the word's ancient meaning of "intractable, wilful, wanton, unchaste," and especially "a woman reluctant to yield to wooing." The Great Hags live to be Crones, or the "long-lasting ones."

Daly defines herself as a revolting hag and a *spinster*, meaning one who spins complex webs of thought in new directions, participating in the whirling movement of creation. One example of her journey of "discovery" and "re-membering" of the ancient religions of women concerns the antecedent myths and symbols that underlie the Christian concept of the Holy Trinity. These are the symbols of the Triple Goddess, which are omnipresent in early mythology (Daly 1978, 75). Kolbenschlag (1979, 187) also notes that in the Gnostic or mystical tradition of early Christianity, the Holy Spirit was equated with god the mother. The suppression of these heretical scriptures is linked more to the ecclesiastical suppression of women than to dogmatic interpretation.

Kolbenschlag and Daly are far apart in their level of tolerance for existing Christian churches, but both concur in seeing the emergence of feminism as a critical turning point for civilization. The feminist movement challenges the entire culture and the religious expressions of our social order.

Conclusion

Durkheim's insight that religion fundamentally expresses our deepest experience of our human community, and reflects in its dogmas the deepest values of that community, has stood the test of nearly a century of sociological theory. In future decades we can expect radical changes in our faith as the changing status of women transforms our society, and as global pollution, starvation, and the threat of nuclear war force us toward a more Durkheimian conception of an all-inclusive humanism.

Many of those who study the sociology of religion are themselves deeply religious people. Critical sociology, like liberation theology, may challenge many taken-for-granted assumptions of traditional teaching. But ultimately there is no conflict between faith and sociological analysis for they are concerned with different, although related, levels of human experience. Sociology does not seek to provide answers to ultimate ques-tions of value or the meaning of life. What it reveals is that the ways in which people all over the world struggle with such questions are grounded in their human experience, which is through and through social. As Durkheim acknowledged, all churches are, by definition, communities of believers, and all religions comprise a shared social experience. The sociology of religion explores the relation between forms of thought and religious expression and the grounds of human experience in social life. For those who are willing to share in this exploration, the sociological imagination is not a threat but a gift.

Suggested Reading

Durkheim's first major work, *The Division of Labour in Society* ([1893] 1964), provides the theoretical foundation for his later studies. In this text he develops his ideas concerning the transition from traditional society based on mechanical solidarity to modern society based on organic solidarity. This is a large and complex book. For an excellent introduction to Durkheim's work see Robert Bierstedt, *Emile Durkheim* (1966). Bierstedt provides an overview of Durkheim's life, followed by selections from each of his major works: *The Division of Labour*; *The Rules of Sociological Method*; *Suicide*; and *The Elementary Forms of Religious Life*.

Jack Douglas's study, *The Social Meanings of Suicide* (1967) revolutionized the analysis of suicide rates. Douglas systematically challenges each of Durkheim's conclusions on the grounds that the patterns that Durkheim found in the data on suicide rates reflect, not concrete evidence, but the outcome of coroners' decisions. Durkheim discovers the theories used by coroners to decide how to classify suspicious deaths.

Two short essays by Garfinkel and Sudnow that show how ethnomethodologists approach the study of suicide are in the edited collection by Roy Turner, *Ethnomethodology: Selected Readings* (1974).

An article by Dorothy Smith, "No One Commits Suicide: Textual Analysis of Ideological Practices" (1983a) explores how people necessarily impose patterns on evidence in the process of accounting for what they think happened.

With respect to religion, Durkheim is best known for his study of The *Elementary Forms of Religious Life* ([1915] 1976), in which he discusses aboriginal society and religion. Durkheim's view of the nature of religion in complex societies is discussed by J. Neyer in "Individualism and Socialism in Durkheim" (1966). Neyer explores Durkheim's argument that in complex industrial societies religion must rise over all ethnic diversity. The most all-encompassing religion is humanism, with respect for human rights at its central principle.

A functionalist perspective on religion as providing an integrative force in society can be found in J.M. Yinger's *Religion, Society and the Individual: An Introduction to the Sociology of Religion* (1957). The first chapter presents a useful overview of this approach.

A famous and controversial thesis on the relation between social class and religion is Max Weber's *The Protestant Ethic and the Spirit of Capitalism* ([1904] 1930). Weber argues that the Calvinist doctrine of individual salvation by the grace of God, manifest through worldly success, is ideally suited to capitalist enterprise. This is not, however, an easy book to read. A valuable selection from Weber's work on religion is provided by Stanislav Andreski, ed., *Max Weber on Capitalism, Bureaucracy and Religion: A Selection of Texts* (1983). See particularly chapters 6 and 7 on "Protestantism and the Spirit of Capitalism" and "Religion and Other Factors in the Development of Modern Capitalism."

A radical Marxist perspective on religion is provided in a special edition of *Canadian Dimension*, "The Left Hand of God" (Jan.–Feb. 1979). Articles by Baum, Green, Jungueira, and Smillie argue that a living religion does not merely function to provide social integration. The radical gospel message of social justice implies that religion must be at the centre of revolutionary movements to change societies in which justice is not respected.

Radical feminist writers apply this social justice message to women. They challenge traditional forms of Christianity, along with other world religions, for fostering a patriarchal ideology. Studies by Mary Daly, *Beyond God the Father* (1973), and Rosemary Ruether, *New Woman New Earth* (1975), explore new forms of religious expression inspired by feminism.

Chapter 7

Anomie: The Roots of Industrial Conflict and Crime

Durkheim's Theoretical Legacy

To summarize from chapter 6, the central focus of Durkheim's theoretical work concerns the moral basis of social cohesion. In its simpler form, this cohesion rests on sameness or mechanical solidarity. It is supported by the totality of beliefs and sentiments held in common by members of a society, which comprises the *conscience collective*. This collective conscience or collective consciousness is reflected in and reinforced by repressive or penal law, which is fundamentally religious in character. Violation of shared values threatens the cohesion of the community and hence is met with outrage and repression. In complex industrial societies, characterized by extensive division of labour, an alternative form of moral order, which has its roots in interdependence, gains prominence. Organic solidarity presupposes not sameness, but diversity and specializa-tion. The essential moral precondition for contracts between specialized and interde-pendent people is respect for human rights and the sanctity of the individual. Interde-pendence creates mutual obligations, which are reflected in and reinforced by restitutive laws. These laws regulate contracts, and their transgression is met by a demand for restitution rather than punishment. It is the violation of underlying respect for human rights that generates outrage.

Durkheim's major theoretical contribu-tion to sociology lies in his analysis of the moral division of labour. Ideally, indus-trialized societies, characterized by exten-sive division of labour and specialization, allow greater individual freedom and yet at the same time involve greater dependence on others. The bonds of social cohesion based on mutual obligations are potentially far stronger than those based upon shared senti-ments alone.

The moral order breaks down, however, under conditions of anomic division of labour. This occurs when the division of labour is not based upon the different interests and abilities of the people concerned, but is forced upon them and is therefore experienced as unjust. It also occurs when work becomes so fractionalized that all sense of meaningful co-operation in the work process is lost. Under these conditions, people become isolated from each other rather than integrated. Unhappiness increases when people lack social ties with others and become egoistic or when peoples' lives are anomic and lack a sense of meaningful values and moral regulation. In extreme cases, such unhappiness can lead to suicide.

Marxist analysis focusses upon the specific characteristics of division of labour within the capitalist system of economic production. When a minority of people own the means of production upon which others depend for their livelihood, the result is class conflict, exploitation, and alienation. Alienation refers to the dehumanizing character of social relations under capitalism. When the majority of people are denied access to any means of producing for themselves, they are reduced to a state of chronic insecurity and powerlessness. They survive by selling their labour power for wages, but there are no further obligations between workers and employers. Workers are laid off whenever their labour power is no longer useful or profitable for employers, such as when new technology makes their labour redundant. It is in the interests of employers to minimize labour requirements and to routinize and simplify tasks so that they can be done by unskilled, and therefore cheap, easily replaceable workers. Work is reduced to a meaningless, demoralizing activity. From the Marxist perspective, the capitalist system itself precludes justice and creates the selfish egoism and fractionalized work that give rise to anomie.

Businesses can be closed up and workers laid off when profits fall or new technology makes workers redundant. Government promises for job retraining can be hollow.

The concepts of anomie and alienation thus have complementary aspects, notwithstanding the very different concerns of Durkheimian and Marxist analyses. Durkheim was concerned primarily with social order and the foundations of cohesion and morality, while Marx focussed upon conflict and the foundations of revolution. But these can be seen as two sides of the same issue: the factors that threaten social cohesion are also those that promote conflict. This chapter explores the relevance of these theories of social cohesion and conflict in the analysis of industrial unrest, deviance, and crime in contemporary Canadian society.

Disorder and Conflict in Labour Relations

The Human Relations School of Management

The early application of Durkheim's ideas to the study of industrial relations was decidedly conservative in orientation, focussing upon the human need for social ties and ignoring the concern with social justice implied in Durkheim's own analysis of anomic division of labour. Elton Mayo ([1933] 1966) pioneered this approach in his lengthy study of the Hawthorne Electrical Company in Chicago from 1927 to 1932. The focus of the study was how to improve productivity of workers engaged in the assembly of telephone relays. The researchers' initial experimental interest was on fatigue and monotony and how they affected production. A series of experiments, carried out over two years, systematically varied rest pauses, hours worked per day, provision of free lunches, and intensity of lighting. Five young women were selected from the factory floor and set to work in the experimental test room. Their output had been measured without their knowledge for two weeks prior to the experiment. This provided the base line for measurement of subsequent changes in productivity.

To the surprise of the researchers, output increased with every change. With shorter hours, more rest pauses, more lunch breaks, output went up. Then, when they returned to the original working conditions, output went up higher than ever before. The researchers concluded that increased output was not due to the experimental variables at all. They theorized that it was due to changes in the social situation of the workers. Instead of being part of an anonymous mass of workers on the factory floor, they had become the centre of attention in a small work group. They were also directly consulted and involved in organizing the various changes in work schedules that took place during the years of the study.

Mayo's research is frequently referred to as the origin of the **human relations school of management** theory. The basic assumption of this theory is that workers are happier and thus more productive when they belong to small cohesive, family-like work communities and when they are consulted by management and are encouraged to participate in decisions affecting their working lives.

A second influential study, conducted in 1948, was of young women in a pajama factory, doing the routine work of sewing, folding, and packing pajamas. The management noticed that even small changes in job specifications resulted in marked resentment and lost productivity among the workers. However, when they experimented with **participatory management** styles, allowing the women to be involved in planning the changes in work patterns, the result was a rapid increase in productivity, with no signs of aggression or labour turnover (Coch et al. 1949). The researchers concluded that the original problem was anomie. The workers were suffering from non-involvement in their work community and a lack of group cohesion. Again the thesis is that a human relations approach to management, which encourages democratic involvement, would resolve industrial conflicts and create a productive work community.

Such research appeared to take all the teeth out of Marxist analyses of capitalism. No fundamental changes in the social order seemed to be required to resolve industrial conflicts and anomie. Only a more humane, participatory style of management seemed necessary. Theorists concerned with order and consensus latched onto these and similar studies as providing empirical justification for conservative theoretical models concerned with the maintenance of existing institutions. Durkheimian analysis came to be seen as radically different from Marxist analysis.

These early experimental data, however, turned out to be flawed. Subsequent **secondary analyses**, especially of Mayo's Hawthorne study, led to the conclusion that both the data and the theoretical conclusions reached by the researchers were erroneous (Landsberger 1958; Carey 1967). Carey convincingly argues that change in **piece-rate payments**, and not the move to smaller work groups, was the major factor behind the initial rise in productivity among the five women selected for participation in Mayo's experiments. When they were paid on the basis of the average output as a group of five workers, their own personal productivity could directly affect their wages. This was not possible when their pay was calculated on the basis of the average output of the entire shop floor of over one hundred workers. When other workers not in the experiment heard about the change in piece-rate payments, they began to demand that they also be paid on the basis of small-group or individual output.

Carey also shows that the participatory supervision and the family-like atmosphere within the experimental work group was a myth. The experimenters had selected five highly co-operative women in the first place. When two of the women talked too much and did not work hard enough, they were reprimanded and then fired. They protested that they had been told to "work as they feel," but they learned to their cost that this was not the case. The two women who replaced them in the experimental group were both desperate for money. One was the sole supporter of a large family after her father had lost his job. She drove the other women to work harder and cursed them when they seemed to

ease up and so threaten the group's average productivity rate, which determined her wages. Carey also noted that Mayo's research took place during the early years of the depression of the 1930s when workers feared losing their jobs. Mass layoffs from the Hawthorne works occurred in 1932, which was the point when the Mayo study finished. Carey's general conclusion is that the Hawthorne experiments are scientifically worthless since too many variables were not controlled.

The study of change in the pajama factory was likewise suspect in that it focussed on young female workers from rural Virginia who had no industrial work experience. Later, when a union organizer illustrated how exploited and underpaid the women were, labour unrest escalated and management became more harsh. When a similar experiment in participatory management was tried among male workers in a Norwegian shoe factory, it had no effect (French, Israel, and As 1960). These male workers were already unionized and had some experience of bargaining over working conditions. They were not impressed by the invitation from management to participate in minor decisions about work tasks. They perhaps understood better than did the young women in the pajama factory that true industrial democracy would require a much more radical sharing of power between management and workers.

These critiques raise some basic questions. How did the original researchers draw such erroneous conclusions from their data? Why were these studies so readily accepted by later sociologists? Carey argues that the studies served the ideological interests of management and perhaps also of sociological theorists committed to the order perspective.

Durkheim's analysis of anomic division of labour draws attention to political issues that human relations theory ignores. Durkheim's fundamental premise is that social cohesion presupposes distributive justice as a precondition of contractual relations. Friendly supervision without such justice cannot allay conflicts indefinitely.

The Synthesis of Alienation and Anomie

A valuable synthesis of the concepts of anomie and alienation is developed in Blauner's thesis on alienation and freedom among factory workers. Blauner (1964) combines the ideas of emotional detachment and a loss of commitment to core values, which are central to Durkheim's concept of anomie, with the experience of economic oppression and powerlessness, which is central to the Marxist concept of alienation. He defines these abstract concepts in practical terms so that he can measure the degree of alienation and anomie experienced by workers in different work settings.

Blauner enumerates four situations in which alienation develops. It can be found when workers are unable to control their immediate work processes; when they cannot develop a sense of purpose and function connecting the work they do with the work done by others; when they lack a sense of belonging to an integrated industrial community; and when they cannot achieve a sense of personal self-expression or pride in their work (Blauner 1964, 15). He attributes the identification of only the third element—lack of an integrated work community—to Durkheim, but the elements of injustice and fractionalized, meaningless work included in Durkheim's discussion of the anomic division of labour are also present in Blauner's definition.

In his comparative study of work settings, Blauner develops measures of degree of alienation with respect to four elements that derive from the work situations in which anomie develops. **Powerlessness** involves job insecurity, fear of unemployment, and lack of control over the task itself. **Meaninglessness** derives from overly fragmented jobs where the individual worker's contribution is so small that the worker loses any sense of co-operating meaningfully with others in a total product. Social **isolation** may result from workers being alone on the job but, more importantly, Blauner links it to absence of a sense of loyalty and commitment to the workplace. A critical aspect of this is the breakdown of normative integration, when workers no longer accept the rules that govern the relations between employees and employers. These rules include practices for disciplining and laying off workers, assigning wages relative to the earnings of others, and awarding promotions (Blauner 1964, 25). When these are perceived as fundamentally unjust, social integration breaks down. The last element, **self-estrangement**, occurs when jobs are so monotonous and boring that workers cannot develop a sense of personal involvement or pride in what they do. This again is directly related to Durkheim's conception of a forced and fragmented anomic division of labour.

The epitome of alienating work, for Blauner, is labour on car assembly lines. Technology is limited to a conveyer belt that carries car bodies from one end of the factory floor to the other. Workers stand on either side of the belt, performing highly repetitive, mechanical tasks that are paced by the speed of the belt. Workers are little more than appendages to the machine. This situation results in total monotony and self-estrangement. Moreover, because workers are tied to a noisy assembly line, camaraderie while on the job is precluded. The only plus is that the pay is generally good.

Some see little wrong with this particular organization of work. Such theorists describe automobile workers as relatively contented with their lot, arguing that they find solace in high wages and life outside working hours (Goldthorpe 1966). Others see precisely this reduction of people's primary life's work to solely extrinsic rewards as itself a symptom of deeply alienating lives. The workers' resignation to their dull jobs reflects the experience of self-estrangement and failure to live up to deeply internalized values of the American dream (Chinoy 1955).

Blauner suggests that **automation** might reduce alienation at work. The highly automated technology in a chemical plant, for example, is very different from the assembly lines in a car plant. Complex machines do all the mechanical work associated with the manufacture of the chemicals. People are needed only to watch the dials on the computers regulating the production process, and they have to intervene only when there is a malfunction in the system. Hence, Blauner reports, workers in the chemical plant that he studied enjoyed more control over their own tasks, less fragmented work, more freedom of movement and interaction, and also better promotion prospects than car assembly workers. Other researchers dispute these claims. For many workers, automation has brought only isolation as a result of greatly reduced work forces, chronic job insecurity, and shift work, which interferes with family life and leisure activities.

Automation and computers may have the potential to enrich the lives of workers and reduce drudgery, but frequently such technology has served only to intensify managerial control. Bell Telephone workers, for example, find themselves totally monitored by machines, which record the number of seconds they take to respond to incoming calls and the amount of "downtime" workers take (Kuyek 1979, 18). Computer operators find that every keystroke and every error can be counted and recorded. Such close monitoring results in near intolerable levels of stress for employees. Under such working conditions, anomie takes a new form as old norms of regulative justice and old concepts of humane working conditions are undermined.

The most far-reaching effect of automation for the mass of workers has been chronic job insecurity. There is an ever-present threat that labour-saving technology will make old jobs redundant, and there is no guarantee that new types of jobs will replace them. Given the moral basis of division of labour in interdependence, the issue of unemployment has become a major moral concern. An unemployed worker's loss of a sense of integration with others in a productive community may generate a deeper experience of emotional stress than does lack of money, difficult though this is.

Anomie and Unjust Contracts

Anomie, for Durkheim, has its roots in the breakdown of social regulations. Anomie does not simply mean a lack of rules. Rather, it is the state that results when the moral preconditions for contracts have been undermined and thus when the rules that regulate the division of labour are experienced as fundamentally unjust. Flanders and Fox (1969, chap. 15) argue that anomie in industrial relations occurs when two types of norms—procedural and substantive—are undermined. **Procedural norms** include legal provisions for negotiations and dispute settlements, while **substantive norms** regulate the content of collective bargaining such as standard wage rates, working hours, and so on. Fox and Flanders argue that in Britain there has been a steady erosion of national consensus on both types of norms in recent years.

Marxist analysts link the escalation of conflicts in industrial relations to economic factors, particularly to the effects of labour-saving technology, rising unemployment, inflation, declining markets, and declining profit margins. The emotional consequence of cycles of boom and bust within capitalist economies is anomie. Anomie also results from the profound weakening of consensus concerning the rules that govern the distribution of wealth. This lack of consensus stems not simply from disagreement as to whether the distribution of wealth has become more or less unequal in recent years. The issue is whether people see the degree of economic inequality—and the reasons for that inequality—as fair. For Durkheim, when inequality of wealth appears unjust, it promotes dissatisfaction and conflict between classes. Within the working class itself, different levels of bargaining power create inequalities. Rising frustration and resentment among workers who lack the power to pressure for their demands in wage disputes split them from more powerful workers.

Canadian Labour Relations

In Canadian labour relations, as in those of many other industrialized countries, both procedural and substantive norms have come under increasing criticism. Provincial and federal governments have been directly drawn into the resulting conflicts.

Procedural Justice

Jamieson (1968) draws attention to a basic contradiction in ideology and policy in Canadian labour relations. Both employers and union spokespersons express a shared **liberal** ideology, demanding maximum freedom for free enterprise and free collective bargaining. But, on the other hand, a rigid and highly complex system of laws and administrative procedures has come to govern relations between the two classes. Business enterprises want maximum freedom of competition and freedom to determine investments, prices, and output policies, including the freedom to close down plants and lay off workers when business is unprofitable. Ironically, such freedom has led employers to depend upon government to enact and enforce laws to protect them against organized labour. On the other hand, unions uphold the freedom of workers to organize into unions, to strike, to picket, and

to boycott. They depend upon government to enact and enforce laws to protect them against employers and anti-union policies and practices. But such protection has been accompanied by laws on behalf of employers, which sharply restrict unions' freedom of action. Pressure from both sides has resulted in such an extremely complex system of laws, suggests Jamieson, that violations and recourse to illegal actions are frequent and unavoidable.

Warskett's (1988) study of the largely failed attempt to unionize bank workers in Canada throughout the 1980s is particularly insightful in this regard. She demonstrates how the labour laws restricted the freedom of action of union organizers and effectively shifted the locus of struggle from workers themselves to a team of legal experts. A seemingly endless series of litigations, challenges, appeals, and counter-accusations of unfair labour practices was sufficient to tie up the certification procedures for years.

Warskett argues that the labour relations system was introduced primarily as a response to the unprecedented labour unrest in the 1930s, which directly threatened capitalist interests. Laws governing certification of unions, arbitration, and protection against unfair labour practices were all established in return for labour's agreement to limit the use of the strike weapon to specified moments in the collective bargaining process. Such laws are thus the outcome of a compromise between what labour agitators wanted and what industry and government would concede. The contradictions of the class struggle are built into the labour laws themselves. On the one hand, workers look to these laws for protection but, on the other hand, the laws encircle and restrict every action they wish to take.

The centrality of law to the class struggle has far-reaching effects on union ideology and practice. It creates dependency on legal experts and serves to obscure the basis of union power, making it appear as if this power derived from legal processes rather than from the unity of union members. The right to strike appears to have been granted to workers by the liberal-democratic state, instead of being the outcome of long historical struggles. The laws appear to be neutral, but in fact they are profoundly political, and their ultimate intention is to ensure the smooth working of capitalism.

Warskett argues that this appearance of neutrality is not merely a distortion. Workers are inclined to obey labour laws, partly because their repressive aspects are relatively hidden behind claims to neutrality and equality of treatment, but also because the laws embody gains won by subordinate classes over time. Workers can look to the laws to protect their rights to unionize, to bargain, and to arbitrate grievances without being threatened with dismissal or other reprisals. But in return, workers' potential for political action is blunted by the requirement that they obey the laws or be punished by the state. Control is taken from the workers and vested in legal experts in the hearing rooms of the Labour Relations Board and the courts.

The succession of bitter and occasionally violent confrontations between labour and management, both in private and government enterprises in Canada, can be understood as the expression of deep-rooted

Major demonstrations in Alberta protested against what workers saw as draconian anti-labour legislation and the intransigence of Gainers owner Peter Pocklington.

anomie in industrial relations. Procedural laws regulating strikes, lockouts, and strikebreakers are the formal expression of fundamental moral questions concerning legitimacy of power relations in society. It is the legitimacy of these procedural laws that is challenged by workers. In 1986 workers protested what they saw as draconian anti-labour legislation in Alberta with a protracted and very bitter strike at Gainers meat packing plant. The company was able to hire strikebreakers during a period of high unemployment, leaving former workers with little or no leverage in contract negotiations and with a very real threat that they would permanently lose their jobs. In Ontario, newly unionized workers at Eatons stores faced similar risks and had to settle for a poor contract. In British Columbia, in the late 1980s, a coalition of workers tried to organize a challenge to Premier William Vander Zalm's Bill C-19, which workers felt undermined the precontractual basis for future negotiations in the province. Nationally, post office workers walked picket lines during the summer of 1987 and 1988, attempting to intimidate the busloads of strikebreakers who were themselves unemployed and frequently desperate to earn money or to take over the stable jobs that the postal workers seemed unhappy with.

In all these disputes it is much more than money that matters. National consensus on the issue of procedural justice is at stake. The moral dilemmas are real. Employers feel that their rights to run their own businesses in a free market are being undermined by powerful unions and efforts to establish closed shops in which employers are prohibited from hiring anyone who is not a union member.

Employed workers feel that their right to bargain collectively for terms and conditions of employment is being undermined by laws that weaken their limited means to apply pressure during negotiations with vastly more powerful employers. During the nine-month strike of INCO workers in Sudbury in 1978, for example, workers found themselves unable to get management to negotiate seriously because the market for nickel was weak, and the company had been stockpiling supplies for several months before the strike began (Clement 1981, chap. 9). Striking newspaper workers at the *Times* in London, England, found themselves up against the Thomson corporate empire, which, during the strike, made the biggest profits in its history from its diverse holdings.

People other than employers and workers are affected by labour disputes. Unemployed people feel that their rights to bargain for work are being undermined by the unions from which they are excluded. Police become targets for frustration and anger when they are called in by governments to keep the peace on picket lines. Lastly, people who are dependent upon the services once provided by the striking workers pressure for their rights to transportation, educational, postal, or medical services.

Industrial anomie in Canada has at times reached the level of pitched battles between opposing forces with mass arrests of strikers by police. More than a decade of labour unrest, punctuated by increasingly violent strikes, preceded the Winnipeg General Strike of 1919. Mounted police were used to quell strikers during this major confrontation. Panitch and Swartz (1988) indicate that coercion against strikers was the norm in Canada prior to the 1940s. The right of workers to free collective bargaining was only recognized by the Canadian state in 1945. This was precipitated by the unprecedented expansion of trade unions during World War II and the increasing militancy of workers, bolstered by war mobilization and full employment. The authors argue, however, that during the 1980s collective bargaining rights eroded. The right to strike was conspicuously not enshrined in the

During the Winnipeg General Strike of 1919, the RCMP were brought in to dispurse strikers, resulting in dozens of casualties and one death.

Charter of Rights and Freedoms of 1982. Since then, both federal and provincial governments have frequently passed anti-strike and back-to-work legislation. The trend is toward increasing state coercion of unions through both the police and the courts.

Substantive Justice

Like those governing procedural justice, the norms for judging the merits of claims to financial and other rewards are in dispute, creating further divisions within Canadian society. Durkheim argued that, to avoid anomie, it is not sufficient that there be rules; the rules must be accepted as just. For example, it has been the norm throughout Canadian industrial history that women receive less pay than men for comparable jobs, but this is no longer perceived as just, at least by the majority of women. Women's groups have become increasingly active in pressuring for **pay equity**. This began with

the demand for *equal pay for equal work.* Women are now legally guaranteed the right to equal pay when they do the same work that men do. The problem is that very commonly women do not do the same kind of work as men. They are concentrated in different kinds of jobs. The demand for *equal pay for work of equal value* brings to the fore the contentious issue of just how the value of different work is assessed. Is "men's work" so much more valuable than "women's work" that it warrants 40 percent greater pay? Should groundskeepers at a university be paid more or less than its secretaries? What criteria are used to make such judgments? Questions such as these are disturbing to the status quo.

Breckenridge (1985) argues against equal pay for work of equal value legislation on the grounds that it would weaken Canada's competitive position abroad. Supporters of the equal pay approach argue that Canadian society has a moral imperative to end the discrimination by which women earn on average only 60 percent of what men earn. Breckenridge counters that this would be disastrous for Canada's economy since it would result in higher prices and reduced profits and hence would stall foreign investment. She warns that firms will do everything possible to avoid pay equity laws, including refusing to hire women. In effect, Breckenridge admits that the market is not concerned with justice. Competitive advantage in world markets is accorded greater importance than is the morality of equal pay.

Other income policies in recent years have included the wage and price controls attempted by the Trudeau government. The objective was to control inflation by holding average wage and price increases to within 6 percent and 5 percent, respectively, of those of the previous year. Claims for additional increases or "catch-up pay" had to be based on explicit arguments about relative merit, judged against comparable job categories. Such claims bring issues of justice right out in the open, since they publicize the principles of comparisons between jobs.

Inequalities in rewards, according to Durkheim, are justifiable only in a **meritocracy**; that is, in a system where inequalities directly reflect the natural capabilities and interests of different people. Marxists dispute this, arguing that hours of labour time expended should be the primary criterion for rewards. People should not expect a higher standard of living simply because they happen to have more intelligence or stronger bodies than others. From this perspective, moral justice dictates that people should work according to their abilities and be rewarded according to their needs. This is a fundamental difference in basic moral principles that cannot be resolved by logical arguments alone. In Canada, the prevailing consensus is that the principle of meritocracy provides the moral basis for differential rewards within the economy. But people remain deeply divided on the

question of how merit should appropriately be judged and on the relative importance to be accorded to training, skills, responsibilities, personality, seniority, and such factors as the danger or inconvenience of the job.

There are many problems with the merit principle. The first difficulty is methodological: how do we measure and compare the qualities of different jobs? It is no easy matter to identify or to quantify skills. Gaskell (1986) argues that what counts as a skill is socially constructed. Organized workers are continually engaged in the political process of defining what constitutes a skill. A deceptively simple measure used in many studies is length of training: the longer the training, the more skilled the job. But the time and form that training takes reflect politics and power more than job characteristics. Well-organized workers will go to great lengths to prevent attacks on traditional apprenticeship systems. Long apprenticeships serve to create a shortage of licensed workers and so enhance their bargaining power and wages and provide a means of exploiting young workers at low wages. But employers have an interest in circumventing these training programs, especially when there is a labour shortage. What happens is the outcome of the relative power of employers and workers.

Gaskell describes how training for clerical work, by the twentieth century a predominantly female occupation, shifted from employer apprenticeship schemes to the public school system, where it became a part of the vocational education curriculum. One result is that the long, arduous training period becomes disguised as schoolwork. Skills come to be taken for granted as part of every young woman's education and thus are not seen as skills at all. In contrast, training in business skills, such as bookkeeping, accounting, and managing and administering a business, is still conducted outside the regular public school system. It is thus considered postsecondary education, akin to an apprenticeship. Such trainees are therefore considered to be "skilled."

The difference in perceptions of clerical and business skills, Gaskell argues, reflects the greater political clout of male over female workers. Clerical workers were—and are—predominantly non-unionized and fragmented and hence were unable to defend their trade skills. Additionally, employers were reluctant to invest in training females, who were perceived as temporary workers. Hence, the public school system was pressured to take over this training, and women workers were not organized to resist this pressure. Male workers have tended to be better organized to defend traditional apprenticeship schemes, although many male trades have been unable to withstand the concerted efforts of employers to fragment and deskill the work.

A change in focus from training time to actual job characteristics only shifts the locus of the methodological problems associated with quantifying job skills; it does not resolve them. Ethnomethodological research has demonstrated that even "factual" elements of job requirements are socially constructed. Like coroners' decisions on whether particular deaths were or were not suicides, judgments of skill level are the outcome of specific actions taken by members of organizations.

Reimer (1987) describes how the skills needed by advanced clerical staff, almost all of whom are women, in government bureaucracies are systematically undervalued and even rendered invisible by a series of organizational practices. Bureaucratic job classifications define clerical work as comprising routine, delegated tasks. The comprehensive knowledge, initiative, and decision-making responsibilities that these women require in order to do their jobs are obscured by the terminology used to describe what they do, by the format of job interviews that never question them on their knowledge outside of routines, and especially by the manner in which the end product of advanced clerical work is appropriated by the predominantly male managers.

Reimer describes an example of discriminatory terminology and classification that arises with respect to the same objective task of searching through files for information. This is described as "research" when done by a manager or professional, but as "routine getting files" when done by a secretary. In another instance, a clerical worker put together the annual budget estimates for her ministry, but it was her superior who was officially credited with it. He, and not the secretary, got the better pay and promotion prospects as a result. This process of systematic undervaluation and underremuneration of the work of subordinates is not confined to positions occupied by women, but historically they have certainly suffered disproportionately from the effects.

Of all the jobs predominantly done by women in Canada, the work of homemaking ranks as the most systematically undervalued. Luxton (1980) demonstrates the complex and multidimensional aspects of domestic labour, including financial management, household maintenance, and the care of adults and children. But the woman displaying these skills is belittled—even by the woman herself—as "just a housewife."

Durkheim himself would probably never have thought of applying his concept of anomie to the situation of housewives. He tended to share the prevailing view of his time that what women did as wives and mothers was somehow natural. But the feminist movement has challenged the notion that it is natural to expect women to bear the full responsibilities of the housewife-mother role. The central driving force behind the feminist movement is a sense of anomie; that is, a sense that the prevailing values of our society as they apply to women are profoundly unjust and unacceptable. Feminists argue that the norms governing the distribution of both tasks and rewards, including income, prestige, and leisure time, systematically discriminate against women and devalue their work.

Patterns of Labour Unrest

Jamieson (1968), in his analysis of labour unrest in Canada between 1900 and 1966, notes that strike waves coincided with periods of economic upheaval when the terms of **distributive justice** were being challenged. These included the postwar periods 1919–20 and 1946–47 and the decade of unrest from 1955 to 1965. This pattern can be explained in terms of traditional class analysis. Strike activity declines during recessions and high unemployment periods when unions are weak, and it rises during boom times when there are alternative jobs and fewer strikebreakers. But more than this is involved. During periods of inflation, Jamieson points out, the high profits of leading corporations are publicized in newspapers, together with accounts of huge profits made in real estate or on the stock market and evidence of conspicuous expenditures by the nouveau riche. The injustice of vastly different levels of income becomes more obvious to people.

During the period from 1957 to the mid-1960s, economic growth was declining in Canada relative to other western countries, technological unemployment as a result of automation was rising, and employers were taking an increasingly tough stance in the face of high costs and lagging sales. Workers, therefore, faced wage restraints, tough management, job insecurity, and restrictive legislation. Then hundreds of millions of dollars were spent on Expo '67 in Montreal. Construction workers were in high demand and their wages rose. Longshoremen, who had been suffering the insecurity of pronounced seasonal and cyclical fluctuations in their work, began to compare themselves with construction workers

and went out on a long, bitter, and often violent strike to gain similar wages. The wave of strikes then spread to seaway and railway workers and then into the public sector with strikes among aircraft workers, liquor control board employees, and postal workers.

During this period, there was an unusually high incidence of wildcat strikes— illegal strikes that occur while a contract is still in operation. Jamieson explains this pattern in terms of factors that challenge the legitimacy of procedural rules governing labour relations. These include technological unemployment, job insecurity, repressive labour legislation, and especially the increasing scale of industry and management, which makes grievance procedures increasingly impersonal, drawn out, and complex. Frustrations build up to the boiling point.

Gouldner's (1965) study of a wildcat strike at a Gypsum plant similarly concludes that fundamental issues of injustice were at its root. Workers deeply resented the heavy-handed and punitive discipline of a new supervisor, compared with the easy-going atmosphere of friendship and trust that had formerly prevailed. The strike focussed on wages and not on discontent with patterns of supervision. The reason for this displacement of concerns was legislative restrictions on the content of contract negotiations. Workers are legally entitled to negotiate wages and benefits, but not styles of supervision and the special privileges that the more indulgent supervisor had permitted.

There has been a breakdown of social cohesion in business enterprises that no amount of human relations management can gloss over. In an article entitled "Losing Often and Losing Badly to Japanese," Cook (1987), perhaps unwittingly, uses a very Durkheimian analysis to account for why the Japanese electronics industry is outstripping the American. He cites arguments by American political scientist Robert Reich that U.S. companies lack flexibility and are too frequently embroiled in competitive lawsuits that take years of costly litigation to resolve. The article compares these trends with Japan's team culture, which typically places high value on loyalty and seniority. Salaries directly reflect length of service. Newcomers start at the bottom of the pay scale regardless of prior experience or qualifications. Companies also stress team decision making rather than a hierarchy of command that isolates one executive at the top as key decision maker. The major disadvantage of the system for workers is that it demands lifelong, workaholic loyalty to one firm, but the benefit is lifelong job security, at least as long as the firm itself survives.

The pattern in U.S. companies is very different. In many large companies, managers and workers have little or no sense of loyalty. On average, an executive will change jobs every four years. Workers are disaffected by how they are treated and especially by lack of job security. Meanwhile managers look after themselves with contracts that assure them of rich retirements no matter what happens to the company and regardless of how incompetently they perform. Rules of work and labour codes

multiply because of lack of faith in the system, and so do lawsuits. Cook estimates that in the United States between 1970 and 1985, the number of private contract disputes that had to be decided by federal courts tripled to 35 000. Reich is cited as concluding that "organization for the common good [Japanese-style] wins and the pursuit of self-interest [American-style] loses" (Cook 1987). His solution is employee ownership or collective entrepreneurship so that people can pool their efforts, insights, and enthusiasm without fear of exploitation.

Summary

Anomie is a result of an alienating industrial order in which profits take precedence over justice in economic relations. As Durkheim foresaw, when inequality lacks a moral base, social cohesion weakens and people become egoistic and preoccupied with individual grievances rather than co-operation for the collective good. The demoralizing effects of anomie also weaken working-class solidarity, generating a more privatized and fragmented political consciousness.

Deviance and Crime

The sociological study of deviant behaviour and crime has been profoundly influenced by Durkheim's theoretical analysis of the relationship between law and social structure. Durkheim argues that law expresses the moral basis of social cohesion, the core of shared values, and the fundamental rules of orderly contractual relations that are essential for the maintenance of industrial society. Crime, as the violation of law, challenges the foundations of the social order itself. Crime rates, much like suicide rates, reflect the level of anomie or moral breakdown within

any given society. Variation in these rates between subgroups within society reveal the stress points in the social system.

In this section we will first examine functionalist theories of crime and deviance, which are drawn directly from Durkheim's work. Then we explore how these ideas are being modified and challenged by interpretive, Marxist, and feminist perspectives. Each perspective can be assessed for its usefulness in accounting for data concerning crime rates in Canada. Among these data is evidence that people in trouble with the law are disproportionately drawn from the lower class and have below average levels of education and income. Members of economically disprivileged minority groups, such as native people and blacks, are especially over-represented among those charged with offences, as are young people between the ages of fifteen and twenty-five. Criminals are also overwhelmingly male, notwithstanding evidence that crime rates among women have been rising in recent years. This pattern differs little from the patterns found in the United States, Britain, and other industrialized societies.

Functionalist Theories of Deviance and Crime

Functionalist theories focus on socialization and consensus with reference to the values and behavioural norms of society. Learned consensus is seen as the central mechanism assuring the maintenance of stability and order within any social system. The purpose or role of the criminal justice system, which includes the framework of laws, the police, the courts and prisons, is to protect the members of society from the minority of deviants who might otherwise threaten this order. Various theoretical approaches to the study of deviance and crime within this broad perspective include **anomie theory of crime**, **differential opportunity theory**, **differential association theory**, and **deviant subculture theory**. These are discussed below.

The Anomie Theory of Crime

As we have seen, the concept of anomie, as developed by Durkheim, refers to a relative absence or confusion of values and a corresponding lack of clear regulations or norms for behaviour. People feel lost and unsure of what to believe in or how to behave. Robert Merton (1968) systematizes this broad con-

cept into a general model, **the anomie theory of crime**, which focusses upon the discrepancy between aspirations and achievements in society. All societies, Merton argues, teach culturally valued goals and socially approved means or behaviour to achieve them. Strains develop in such value systems because not everyone has access to the means needed to attain valued goals. Merton's central hypothesis is that deviance is a symptom of the dissociation between the goals that people are taught to aspire to and the means through which they can be achieved.

Table 7-1 Typology of Modes of Adaptation

Mode of Adaptation	Culturally Valued Goals	Socially Approved Means
Conformist	accept	accept
Innovator	accept	reject
Ritualist	reject	accept
Retreatist	reject	reject
Rebel	replace	replace

Source: Merton (1968, 194).

Merton has developed a typology of possible responses to goals and means (see table 7-1). In this typology, **conformists** accept cultural values and are able to achieve them by socially acceptable means. Such people must constitute a majority in any given society for that society to be stable or orderly. **Innovators** accept cultural goals such as material success and money, but they lack legitimate opportunities to attain them. Hence they seek alternative, illicit means such as theft, prostitution, or drug trafficking. Merton suggests that this category best accounts for the relatively high crime rates found among the poor. **Ritualists** are people who give up on cultural goals, no longer even trying to attain them. They ritualistically obey the rules and conform to outward behaviour patterns, but they have no motivation to succeed. This category includes people who live as petty cogs in the bureaucratic machine. **Retreatists** reject both goals and means. They essentially withdraw into a form of apathy. Merton suggests that hobos, dropouts, skid row alcoholics, and drug addicts fit into this category. Finally, **rebels** are people who generate new goals and new means. They are the revolutionaries and political activists who aspire to a new social order. They reject the value placed on money, individualism, and competition in North American society and favour new values such as co-operation, communal welfare, and equality.

The value of Merton's typology is that it focusses directly upon social-structural variables and not on individual pathology. By drawing attention to unequal opportunities and the strains that such inequality generates, it also incorporates an implicit criticism of industrial society. It suggests that lower-class people and members of disadvantaged minority groups seem particularly likely to engage in deviant or illegal behaviour, not because they have innately criminal characters, but because they face more obstacles to achieving the success goals of the dominant culture.

The **differential opportunity theory** of delinquency developed by Cloward and Ohlin (1960) modifies Merton's formulation to take account of illegitimate as well as legitimate opportunities in explaining why members of one group rather than another are more likely to turn to crime. People who can get what they want legally have little incentive to turn to crime. They are likely to be the conformists. But for potential nonconformists to become deviant innovators, rather than ritualists or retreatists, they have to have criminal opportunities. It helps, when embezzling funds, for example, to be a bookkeeper or an accountant.

Merton's formulation of the anomie theory of crime has been criticized for a number of flaws that limit its usefulness in analysing deviance. Boughey (1978, 112) in particular criticizes the model for treating everything but the successful achievement of socially acceptable goals as deviant. If you play by the rules and do not succeed, you are a ritualistic deviant. If you change the rules in order to succeed, you are a disreputable innovator, while if you refuse to play the game, you are a pathological retreatist. If you reject the rules and formulate new ones, you are still a deviant from your own society. In addition, the five categories are vaguely defined and difficult to apply. Rebellion and innovation, for example, are very similar. Merton lists such groups as hippies within the category of retreatists, but they might equally well be categorized as rebels, rejecting both the goals and the means of a consumer-oriented society. Marxists criticize Merton for a superficial treatment of rebellion. His model avoids the issue of an alienating social order that should be overthrown. Feminists argue that the categories cannot be unambiguously applied to crimes commonly committed by women. Are prostitutes retreatists who reject the goals and means thought appropriate for women, or are they rebels whose primary goal is money (Leonard 1982, 61)? Alternatively, are they innovators who accept financial success goals but have unorthodox means to achieve them?

Merton's model assumes that deviance can be clearly recognized against the background of a basically stable and homogeneous community with clearly defined goals and means. The model focusses on opportunities without questioning the goals themselves. Nor does it allow that goals might differ between subcultures. Indulgence in drugs or alcohol, for example, may be deviant for people in certain social groups, but may represent conformity to peer group norms for others. The focus upon lack of legitimate opportunities as the explanation for crime also takes it for granted that most crimes are committed by disadvantaged or lower-class people. Marxist critics agree that the majority of people in prisons are lower class, but they suggest that this reflects not the absence of crime among the middle and upper classes, but the tendency for such crimes to go unpunished.

Leonard (1982, 57–62) argues that Merton's theory does not adequately account for the significantly lower rates of crime among women. According to Merton, all forms of deviance will be highest among people with the least access to legitimate means to achieve culturally valued goals. Women face multiple barriers to career success and are more likely than men to live in poverty. Yet women as a whole are responsible for very little crime.

A modification of anomie theory, proposed by Ruth Morris (1964), is that women may experience less anomie than men because they have different success goals. Women may focus primarily on relational goals rather than economic achievement. She suggests that success for women means getting married and having children. Since such goals are easy to achieve, the argument goes, women suffer less frustration and hence commit less crime. A woman may be very poor, but if she has successfully raised children she will not feel a failure. The growing influence of the women's movement in recent years may encourage more women to aspire to economic success goals, and hence frustration levels and crime rates among women may rise. Indeed, Adler (1975) argues that feminism may account for rising crime rates among American women.

Feminist theorists challenge the assumptions underlying such arguments as unsubstantiated by evidence and as distorting reality for many women. Even if it were to be shown that women have primarily relational goals, it is by no means obvious that such goals are easily achieved. Children may grow up to be delinquents; marriages may be miserable. Conservative estimates of wife abuse in Canada suggest that 10 percent of women are beaten by their mates (Canada 1982). Between 30 to 40 percent of marriages end in divorce. The modified anomie theory of crime would predict very high crime rates for women in these circumstances, but statistics do not bear this out (Morris 1987, 7; Leonard 1982, 57).

In order to fit in with Merton's theory, the relatively low crime rate among women should reflect extremely low aspirations among women (Leonard 1982, 62). But an adequate theory of crime would have to account for such low aspirations. Allison Morris (1987) argues that, despite the fact that they are more likely than men to live in poverty, women do have economic success goals.

A final criticism that can be offered against Merton's theory is that cultural goals are socially learned, and they vary widely over time and between groups. They cannot simply as assumed as given for the purpose of developing theories about crime.

Subcultural Variations in Crime

Alternative theories developed within the broad functionalist perspective suggest ways in which Merton's model can be adapted to better account for subcultural variations in crime rates. They share the basic assumption that socialization and value consensus are critical mechanisms explaining behaviour, but they focus on distinctive subgroups and subcultures rather than assuming a uniform pattern of values.

Sutherland's theory of **differential association** developed out of his attempt to explain the culture of professional thieves (Sutherland 1937; Sutherland and Cressey 1960). Rather than analysing professional thieves as deviants from a broader system, he analysed their lifestyles in terms of a cohesive cultural system, much as an anthropologist might study a tribe. In his differential association model, he suggests that deviant behaviour is socially learned in interaction with close associates. Deviants learn both the motives and the techniques of crime; in Merton's terms, they learn both deviant goals and deviant means. From Sutherland's perspective, however, deviants appear as normal conformists; the only difference is that they are conforming to an unusual minority group culture.

A criminal lifestyle, suggests Sutherland, presupposes specific values and attitudes. People who are surrounded by others who violate the law tend to copy them. Sutherland concludes that early childhood experiences are likely the most significant factor in developing an allegiance to a criminal lifestyle. Children who live in areas with a high delinquency rate are particularly likely to conform to such behaviour patterns and so become delinquents themselves. This, he argues, might explain the perpetuation of high crime rates in certain areas.

Sutherland ([1949] 1961) also applies the model to **white-collar crime**; this is crime among people in business, professional, and managerial roles. He suggests that business people often learn contempt for legal regulations that restrict misleading advertising, infringing patents, unfair labour practices, and the like. Hence, they can engage in such practices without feeling like deviants. Even prosecution for such acts is unlikely to result in loss of status among corporate associates.

The general model of differential association has not been widely adopted. The situations in which it might be usefully applied to explain crime rates seem very limited. Leonard (1982, 91–105) argues that the view of crime as merely like any other form of learned behaviour is too deterministic. It leaves unanswered the basic question of how and why people choose the associations they do. By no means all people in high crime areas adopt criminal lifestyles. This fact discounts the assumption that deviant lifestyles can be viewed as a form of minority group cultural variation. The differential association model also offers little to the explanation of white-collar crime beyond giving some insight into how people are able to rationalize self-serving behaviour. Further, the theory offers little insight into the relatively low crime rates among females, even in high crime areas. It might be argued that females have very different patterns of association from males, even while living in the same families. But this observation, if true, raises the question of why males and females choose different patterns of association and why the male pattern is linked with so much more crime than the female pattern.

Gang Subculture

Alternative versions of a **subcultural theory of deviance** growing out of Merton's anomie theory have been developed specifically to account for behaviour of members of working-class gangs found in many large urban centres in North America (Cohen 1955; Thrasher 1963; Miller 1958). The motivation for youths to join gangs is seen to stem from the status frustration of lower-class males who are exposed to middle-class expectations they cannot hope to achieve. The gang culture turns traditional cultural values such as ambition, responsibility, skills development, and respect for property upside down. Gang culture grants prestige to whose who rebel, get into trouble, outsmart others, take risks, and are tough and autonomous. Violation of legal norms for its own sake is a respected part of gang culture, and to gang members it represents conformity rather than rebellion. Descriptions of gang life tend to read like studies of exotic tribes with their own internal social organization, moral codes, and sanctions.

This model is appealing. It has the advantage of offering some explanation for the pattern of values found in street gangs by rooting these values in lower-class status frustration and reversal of unattainable middle-class success goals. But there remain serious flaws in the use of subculture theory as an explanation for such behaviour patterns. The concept of value inversion is based largely on speculation, with little evidence to support it (Leonard 1982, 124–28). Much gang culture seems to reflect an exaggerated emphasis on masculine values of power and autonomy rather than a reversal of dominant cultural values. Gang members, moreover, clearly know that their behaviour is deviant, and they can experience guilt as well as defiance when caught. The notion of conformity to alternative cultural values does not adequately explain this sense of guilt. The theory seems to function primarily as a rationalization and neutralization of behaviour that frequently has clear victims and is rational, calculated, and utilitarian. Leonard sees gang behaviour as an innovative way of achieving the goals of money and power rather than as the expression of exotic cultural diversity.

The strongest argument against the subcultural model as an explanation for gangs is the extremely restricted and temporary character of their membership. Gangs are composed overwhelmingly of adolescent males. Greenberg (1981b) focusses on this problem when he raises the following questions. If gang behaviour reflects conformity to lower-class subculture, why do only adolescents conform? Why do members stop conforming to this lower-class culture by about the age of twenty-one? Why do lower-class residents generally fear attacks from teenage gangs if they are or were part of this culture themselves? Why do violent offences occur later than juvenile offences such as theft and joy-riding in stolen automobiles? The answers, he suggests, may be found by paying closer attention to the structural position of juveniles in North American urban society. Merton's anomie theory, in its simpler version, focusses only on the attainment of adult goals through illegitimate means. This will not explain behaviour, such as joy-riding, burglary, and taking drugs,

that appears to be largely unrelated to adult goals.

Greenberg suggests that teenagers have very specific aspirations, and thwarted expectations lead many of them, temporarily, into deviant behaviour. Adolescents are denied the prerogatives of adulthood even while they are admonished to act like adults. Excessive drinking, promiscuous sex, and wild car rides provide symbolic substitutes for adult rights and privileges, and they are generally abandoned once the real things are available. Teenagers are excluded from adult work and leisure activities but, at the same time, they are becoming less involved in parentally supervised family activities. The result is that they spend their time in virtually exclusive association with other adolescents until they leave school and find work. This adolescent period has become greatly extended with changing patterns of work and education. Young people have to stay in school much longer than did previous generations if they hope to attain even entry-level jobs. Vandalism, risk taking, and other visible displays of autonomy in gangs may be explained as rebellion against an authoritarian school system that continues to treat adolescents as children when they feel like adults.

Participation in teen social life requires financial resources. Teenagers want money for clothes, cosmetics, cigarettes, cars, motorbikes, records, and often liquor and drugs. Those without jobs may feel pressured to steal to support their group-centred social activities. A study of teenage gangs in Toronto (*Globe and Mail*, 30 Jan. 1989, A1-5) reports that some teenagers are accosting well-dressed youths on the streets to steal their jewelry, leather jackets, and so on.

Greenberg further suggests that masculine status anxiety may account for the disproportionate involvement of males in teenage gangs and for their exaggerated masculine posturing. A boy may doubt his ability to fulfil traditional male sex-role expectations of finding work and supporting a family, particularly if he lives in a neighbourhood where many men are unemployed or if he has an ineffectual father. He may compensate for such anxiety by exaggerating traditional male traits. Compulsive concern with toughness, violence, and domination over women provides a sense of potency denied in other spheres of life. Smoking, sexual conquests, joy-riding, vandalism, and fighting are common among boys, but such behaviour tends to peak between the ages of fifteen and sixteen, and drop off just before school-leaving age. Older youths who fail to resolve masculine status anxiety after they leave school gravitate toward more serious crime. The incidence of homicide, rape, assault, and narcotics offences peaks among males between the ages of nineteen and twenty-one and falls off more slowly then delinquent behaviour among younger adolescent boys.

This modified theory of anomie and teenage culture proposed by Greenberg provides a valuable framework for explaining adolescent gang behaviour among males. But as Leonard (1982, 130–37) points out, all the theories about youth gangs have one serious omission. They do not account for the virtual absence of girls from gangs. All-female gangs are very rare and nowhere do they reach the intensity of emotional involvement or level of criminal behaviour of the male gangs. Most often girls are only peripherally involved in gangs, as the girlfriends of male members. In order to accept the explanatory models proposed for male gang behaviour, we would have to conclude that girls do not experience thwarted aspirations and expectations during adolescence, that they are not compelled by the same needs for money to participate in their peer culture, and that they do not experience female status anxiety either as younger teenagers in school or as young adult school leavers. We must further conclude that when

young women fail to get jobs, when sexual relationships break down, and marriages fail, they do not experience the level of sex-role status anxiety that supposedly drives young men to commit homicide, rape, and assault.

If we reject such arguments and concede that girls and young women do indeed experience all these frustrations and anxieties, then we are faced with an unanswered question. Why do so many adolescent boys turn to gangs, violence, and sexual aggression when girls do not? Typical explanations offered are that, compared to boys, girls are socialized to stay home more, are more closely supervised and chaperoned, and are more oriented toward families. Does this mean that if boys were more closely supervised and encouraged to be nurturing fathers rather than breadwinners, then adolescent male problems would be resolved? Greenberg's argument that male status anxiety is related to securing a job assumes that such anxiety, and the exaggerated masculine posturing that goes with it, should be concentrated among lower-class and unemployed males. But there is evidence that crimes of rape and assault occur among all social classes. Such behaviour might be more prevalent among unemployed males, but it by no means disappears once men secure stable jobs. We still have much to learn about adolescent delinquency and the factors that account for differences in female and male behaviour.

In summary, the critical explanatory mechanisms in functionalist theories of conformity and crime are socialization and consensus around success goals and the means to achieve them. Deviance is accounted for primarily as the effect of unequal opportunities, which compel disadvantaged individuals to adopt illegal means to achieve their goals. Alternatively, deviance is seen as reflecting socialization and conformity to subcultural goals that are perceived as deviant from those of the wider society. The perspective incorporates an implicit critique of an inegalitarian social order, but this critique is not developed into any broader analysis of the social structures that generate crime. Differences between males and females with respect to crime rates are either ignored or dismissed under the argument that the two sexes are socialized into different roles and values and that only male roles are sufficiently problematic to generate much deviance. Definitions of what constitutes consensus and deviance are treated as common-sense matters that need not be questioned.

Marxist Theories of Crime

The Marxist perspective places the structure of capitalism at the centre of the analysis of law and the criminal justice system. The central assumption is that crime reflects contradictions or irresolvable problems within the capitalist economic system. The functionalist emphasis on individual pathology or deviant socialization at best touches only on the symptoms, not the causes of crime. Human action, including criminal behaviour, is shaped by the socially structured inequalities of wealth and power. Under capitalism, which is discussed in more detail in chapters 8 and 9, capitalists strive to beat competitors in the market. **Labour-saving technology** serves to boost productivity, reduce labour costs, and so raise profits. But such competition generates exploitation, unemployment, continuous cycles of booms and slumps in the economy, and misery for the mass of workers who sell their labour power. An underclass of chronically unemployed or temporary and **marginal workers** bears the brunt of this exploitative system. This class is disproportionately composed of racial and ethnic minorities. People from this underclass also predominate among the prison populations in capitalist countries.

Marx and his colleague Engels, in their descriptions of early industrialization in England, argue that workers were demoralized and dehumanized by the brutally unhealthy conditions in the factories and factory towns. A high crime rate among these people was not evidence of any inherent degeneracy or antisocial culture, but was an understandable reaction to social conditions. Engels argues that immorality is fostered by the conditions of working-class life. Workers are poor; life has nothing to offer them; they are deprived of virtually all pleasures. Under such conditions, they have no reason to restrain their impulses to steal property from the rich (Greenberg 1981a, 48).

Marxism and Anomie

Marxist theorists argue that the anomie at the centre of functionalist explanations for crime is directly produced by capitalism. Even those workers who escape the grinding poverty and insecurity of the underclass of marginal workers still commonly suffer the alienating effects of fragmented, meaningless jobs under conditions that give the majority little scope for pride or fulfillment in work. Most adolescents grow up to a future in which they can expect to spend eight hours a day doing pointless work and to come home afterwards to be entertained by mindless television. Goodman (1956) suggests that crime and delinquency among adolescents do not reflect merely transitory problems of adjustment to adult role responsibilities. They express the pervasive moral emptiness of capitalist society, which adults only partially manage to push from their thoughts when coping with the routine of earning a living. Adolescents grow up into a world that is absurd. Few jobs are intrinsically worth doing in the sense that they provide goods or services that people need or that improve the quality of life.

In the contemporary North American economy, jobs are often worse than useless.

They involve products designed to harm people. As many as one-third of all jobs in the United States are, directly or indirectly, connected to the military. Military funding is a significant source of university research grants, both in the United States and in Canada.

Since 1986 the Nova Scotia government has been seriously considering a proposal by a German armaments company to build tanks in Cape Breton for export to Saudi Arabia. German laws prohibit the sale of armaments made in Germany to any foreign government that potentially might use them against Israel. Editorials in Maritime newspapers, however, scoffed at the argument that Cape Bretoners might also view such trade as morally repugnant. All that counted was that Cape Bretoners needed the four hundred jobs the tank factory might provide. An editorial (*The Daily Gleaner* (Fredericton), 28 Feb. 1986) pointed out that Canadians had benefitted from thousands of jobs, and had made millions of dollars in profits selling armaments to the Americans, during the Vietnam War. Why, then, should they be concerned about making tanks destined to be used in the Arab-Israeli conflict or any other theatre of war? The editorial concluded that "to moralize on the backs of the jobless is unconscionable."

In September 1989, after years of negotiations between the company and the Nova Scotian and Canadian governments, it was announced that the plant will go ahead (*Globe and Mail*, 25 Sept. 1989, A1–5). This decision was reached in spite of fierce opposition and intense lobbying by the Canadian Jewish community, which believes that the military equipment will eventually end up in the Middle East. The Canadian government has controls on arms sales to countries where there is an imminent threat of hostilities. But the new company will have unrestricted access to U.S. defence markets under the Canada–U.S. Defence Production Sharing Agreement. The company plans to sell its goods through a U.S. intermediary, and the United States routinely supplies arms to both the Israelis and the Arabs.

The project will receive extensive financial backing from both the federal and provincial governments. The incentive is the promise of 500 jobs, plus another 800 spin-off jobs in related industries. Dependence on the military for jobs is likely to increase in poorer regions of Canada as a result of the free trade deal with the United States. Defence spending is the only form of government investment in industry that is explicitly exempt from rules restricting subsidies. The basic message behind the editorials and the positive response of the business community generally to the prospect of armaments factories is that concern with moral issues has no place in capitalist business deals. Wars are welcome when they provide opportunities for jobs and profits.

If this argument is accepted, it would seem that anomie, or the undermining of moral order, occurs at the heart of the capitalist system. The origin of this immorality lies not with the workers but with capitalism itself. When the economy is based on competition, and workers are exploited to make profits, everyone comes to see everyone else as a potential competitor, an enemy. The consequence is social war (Greenberg 1981a, 40). Capitalism reduces altruism and compassion and promotes a spirit of domination and insensitivity to others that is conducive to crime (Leonard 1981, 146).

Laws for the Capitalist Class

The link between capitalism and crime goes much deeper than generating an atmosphere in which moral issues have low priority. Capitalism originated in larceny of the largest scale imaginable (Greenberg 1981a, 39). As we saw in chapter 2, the feudal system with its mutual responsibility between lord and serf ended when it became profitable for large landowners to raise sheep for market. Landowners converted croplands into pasture and drove peasants off the land. Laws were pushed through the British parliament to deprive villagers of their customary rights to use common lands to graze their own livestock, gather wood, and so on, so that the big landowners could use the land to graze sheep. Church lands were confiscated, depriving paupers of their legal right to share in the harvest or rental incomes from these lands. In effect, common lands were stolen from peasants to enlarge the estates of rural landlords.

Comparable processes took place in Canada and the United States. Huge land grants were given by government decree to businessmen, railway tycoons, politicians, and loyalists, with scant regard for the rights of native peoples. Indigenous peoples were driven from their traditional hunting grounds to make way for white settlers, and these settlers in turn were exploited by bankers and landowners who speculated on

real estate for huge profits. The process continues in Canada as capitalists seek to exploit minerals and timber on land occupied by Indians and Inuit peoples. In the 1980s, the Lubicon in Alberta, the Haida Nation in British Columbia, and the Dene in northern Quebec found themselves fighting to defend their traditional land-use rights and means of livelihood against logging firms, the oil industry, and hydro-electric companies.

The important point for Marxist criminology is that laws were enacted almost entirely to protect the interests of the people who were stealing the lands, not the people who had traditional use-rights. Law within capitalist societies is thus rooted in **class struggle**. The Marxist historian E.P. Thompson (1975) analyses the use of law in the class struggle that marked the transition from feudal to capitalist forms of property ownership in eighteenth-century England. One such law was called the Black Act. Passed in 1723, it imposed the death sentence for the seemingly innocuous act of

The Lubicon Nation protest in Alberta by blocking access to disputed land.

blacking one's face. The reason behind the penalty was that such blacking was widely used by peasants as a disguise while hunting deer in the king's forests and other lands that had been enclosed. The death sentence also covered such acts as poaching, hurting cattle, cutting down trees, and burning haystacks or barns on the estates.

On the surface, the laws imposed an unbelievably harsh sentence for minor felonies, but they reflected a class struggle of profound importance. The new estates enclosed vast acres of common lands that earlier generations of village people had had the right to use. The common lands were decreed to be the private, inalienable property of the nobles, politicians, and other favoured persons. One legal decision after another emphasized the absolute property rights vested in the big estate owners over the coincident use-rights of local people. The laws appeared, in their wording, to be neutral and impartial. They merely protected property held by one individual against damage or theft by another. Yet underneath this neutral terminology was class war. The laws simultaneously created and defended two classes: people who owned no property and those who owned the means of production.

Marxist theory holds that the rule of law in a capitalist society is never neutral. The power and vested interests of the elite class, and not the collective morality of the community as a whole, determine the character of laws. Laws are mechanisms by which the dominant class exercises control over subordinate classes.

Quinney (1975) proposes four hypotheses in which he juxtaposes the Marxist view of law with the functionalist interpretation developed from Durkheim's work.

1. Acts are labelled as criminal, not because they offend morality, but because they offend the interests of the ruling class.

2. Acts are labelled deviant, not when they are beyond public tolerance, but when they threaten the interests of the ruling class.

3. Lower-class people are arrested more, not because they commit more crimes, but because middle-class people control law enforcement.

4. Contractual law protects, not justice in contracts, but capitalist property interests.

Quinney argues that the processes that favour the interests of the dominant class within the criminal justice system work at the stage of enactment and enforcement of legislation. Laws protecting property owners are the most prevalent and tend to be diligently enforced with strong penalties. Conversely, laws to protect workers against the capitalist class are few, they are laxly enforced, and their infringement generally results in lenient penalties, with little regard for the level of harm involved. Criminal behaviour by the powerful is likely to be lightly punished, if punished at all.

Defining Crime: Illegal Behaviour or Social Harm?

This radical reinterpretation of law calls into question the legal definition of what constitutes crime and, with it, the very scope of the field of criminology (Greenberg 1981a, 5). If laws are commonly class-biased, serving the interests of capitalists rather than the moral values of the community as a whole, then the violation of such unjust laws can no longer be regarded as the violation of morality. Similarly, behaviour that the community might regard as immoral may not be illegal. Marxists argue that the traditional functionalist approach to criminology, which defines crime as the violation of state legislation, constitutes an ideology that serves to legitimate an often unjust and fundamentally class-biased system of laws. The functionalist perspective also excludes from scrutiny many forms of harmful behaviour by members of the propertied class because they are not defined as against the law. Analysis that accepts official statistics on people in prison as a measure of the number of criminals in society perpetuates the myth that lower-class people are bad or anti-social, while middle-class people are good, law-abiding citizens.

Marxists challenge the traditional definition of crime and propose an alternative meaning in terms of violation of human rights. One definition of human rights includes the right to well-being; to food, shelter, clothes, and medicine; to challenging work; and to social, sexual, and economic equality. It also includes freedom from predatory and repressive social elites (Schwendinger and Schwendinger 1975). When crime is defined as a violation of these human rights, it is clear that state agencies are guilty of much criminal behaviour. Green-

berg (1981a, 6) points out that the overwhelming majority of murders in this century have been carried out by governments during wartime. To such deaths can be added killings by police that go unprosecuted. In North America the largest forcible plunder of property has been the government-sanctioned takeover of Indian lands. The largest mass kidnapping in Canada was the government internment of Japanese Canadians during World War II; these people were also robbed of their property. More recently, hundreds of innocent people in Quebec were arrested under the War Measures Act in 1970. None of these actions fall within the scope of traditional criminology because they are not technically in violation of the law.

Some radical criminologists broaden the definition of crime to include corporate behaviour that clearly harms the well-being of workers, consumers, and other members of

Under the War Measures Act, declared in response to the October Crisis of 1970, civil liberties were suspended and hundreds of people were arrested without charges.

society, even though such behaviour may not be prohibited under the criminal law (Greenberg 1981a, 9). A list of such behaviour includes polluting the environment, failing to improve hazardous working conditions, profiteering, marketing unsafe products, or taking advantage of professional status and expertise to cheat clients.

We owe the limited research that has been done on white-collar crime primarily to Marxist criminologists. Such violations of the law tend to be committed by professional people and rarely find their way into official statistics. Practices include misappropriating public funds, padding expense accounts, bribery, influence peddling, tax fraud, insider trading, and illegally acquiring funds through padding payrolls or through kickbacks from appointees. Labour union bosses may likewise misappropriate union funds, act in collusion with employers to the disadvantage of members, or engage in fraudulent means to maintain control.

People who commit such offences tend to see themselves as respectable citizens rather than common criminals, and they are able to rationalize their behaviour as smart business practice (Sutherland [1949] 1961). The dollar figures involved in such illicit activities may vastly exceed the amounts stolen by poor people during break-and-enter offences, yet the perpetrators tend to be treated more leniently. A welfare recipient who fails to disclose additional income is far more likely to go to prison than is a professional person who cheats on an income tax return.

White-collar crime is often not punished or is dealt with by civil and administrative action rather than criminal prosecution. Those who are convicted tend to get small sentences, served under relatively good prison conditions. John Dean, convicted of playing a leading role in the Watergate affair during the Nixon administration in the United States, was sentenced to five years, but he served only eighteen months, and this in a small, comfortable institution

that he shared mainly with Mafia figures.

The Amway Corporation pleaded guilty in 1983 to a criminal charge of evading customs duties and taxes by falsifying invoices between 1965 and 1980. The company was fined $25 million. No one was sent to prison. A federal lawsuit estimated that Amway's outstanding taxes were $148 million, but the Canadian government settled out of court in September 1989 for $45 million (*Globe and Mail*, 23 Sept. 1989, B1–3). If these figures are accurate, they indicate a net profit from Amway's income tax evasion of $78 million.

Companies convicted of major pollution offences routinely meet with only token fines while taxpayers cover the costs of the cleanup. In March 1989, the supertanker *Exxon Valdez* ran aground, spilling 38 million litres of crude oil into Prince William Sound, off the coast of Alaska. After the accident, an Exxon spokesperson confidently announced that the cleanup would not cost the company anything because all costs could be written off against taxes as legitimate business expenses. No one contradicted him.

Offences committed by police officers are routinely forgiven as errors of judgment when similar behaviour by anyone else would be considered a serious crime. Two Quebec police officers who killed an innocent man by opening fire with a machine gun through a hotel door, before checking who was inside, were not convicted of any crime. They were actually promoted. Police in Ontario who kill people during high speed chases need fear no more than a symbolic rap on the knuckles.

Boughey argues that the biggest crooks and swindlers may be found at the top of society's power ladder. People most often labelled deviant are those powerless to assert their respectability. He concludes that, "in an age that exposed the crookedness of former President Richard Nixon and Vice-President Spiro Agnew, and proved the top officials of the largest corporations guilty of multi-million-dollar bribery and other scandals, to continue to study petty thieves, vandals, and pot smokers as social deviants is an absurdity" (Boughey 1978, 107).

Crime and Politics

From the Marxist perspective, both crime and crime control in capitalist societies are political acts. Criminal behaviour constitutes a form of protest against oppressive social conditions, a refusal to play the game by the established rules or to accept the unjust distribution of property and the spoils of capitalist social war (Greenberg 1981a, 9). Individual crimes are the rudiments of what might one day culminate in universal revolution. Crime prevention cannot be viewed as a socially neutral, technical function, for it is an integral part of the class struggle. This does not imply that all criminal acts are self-conscious acts of rebellion against unjust authority. The majority of offences involve selfish behaviour such as stealing and breaking and entering other people's homes. Nonetheless, the incarceration of such people is a political act in the sense that it is the end-product of decisions to treat some social harms as deserving of penal sanctions and others as not, with little regard for the actual extent of social damage (Smith and Fried 1974, 140).

Seen in this light, the reformist goal of rehabilitating individual prisoners makes no sense. Vocational training for prisoners does nothing about the capitalist processes that generate unemployment and a permanent underclass of marginal workers. Rehabilitation easily becomes an instrument of oppression because it justifies the expansion of administrative powers of the state that are used to control inmates (Greenberg 1981a, 8).

Critique of Marxist Theory

The main criticism of the Marxist theory of crime is not that it is wrong, but that it suffers from tunnel vision. It overgeneralizes from some valid observations to propose an all-encompassing theory that seriously distorts the complex reality of criminal behaviour and the legal system. The central notion that all crime can be attributed to capitalism is not persuasive (Greenberg 1981a, 11–14; Leonard 1982, 161–75). Quinney presents a grand scheme of law as defined and enforced in the interests of capitalism, but his hypotheses are too vague to be tested. Almost any findings can be construed somehow or another as in the interests of capitalism. His assumption that crime will disappear under socialism is particularly unconvincing. The persistence of criminal behaviour in non-capitalist communities forces recognition that Quinney's spotlight is too narrowly focussed to provide a general theory of crime.

Marxist theory is more broadly criticized for romanticizing crime and for seeing deviants as rebels engaged in purposeful and rational behaviour. As Currie (1974, 139) expresses it, "an approach to deviance that cannot distinguish between politically progressive and politically regressive forms of deviance is not much of a basis for real understanding of political action." This tendency to view deviance as a progressive force grew out of the cultural milieu of the late 1960s and early 1970s in the United States when Black Power and the hippie **counterculture** were prominent. But such a view cannot readily be applied to vicious, racist, ultra-right-wing forms of deviance such as neo-Nazi groups, skinheads, and gangs that take sadistic pleasure in attacking immigrants and non-whites. What is needed is a theoretical framework that will help to explain the conditions under which deviance is or is not politically progressive.

A further criticism of Marxist criminology concerns its characterization of law and law enforcement as nothing more than a weapon used by the capitalist class to preserve its domination over workers. The extreme version of this argument dismisses fear of crime and popular support for law enforcement as the distorted thinking of people duped by capitalist propaganda. The notion that all law is merely manipulation with no legitimacy among the mass of working-class people is untenable. Their fear of crime is based in real experience and not illusion.

E.P. Thompson (1975, 258–66) argues that the rule of law is not the same as rule by naked force. In order to function as support for ruling-class power, law has to be seen by subordinates as legitimate. In order to retain this aura of legitimacy, the law must be experienced as just, at least a significant part of the time. Laws may well be devised by members of the propertied class to defend their interests and property against other people, but law is also used by others to limit the arbitrary power of property owners. Common people fought tenaciously for their legal rights to use grazing lands, and not without effect. Native Indians in Canada have similarly used aboriginal treaties to fight a long and bitter but not entirely hopeless battle for land claims. Law, argues Thompson, is not an instrument of class power so much as the central arena of class conflict. Law cannot be reserved for the exclusive use of the powerful. They are also bound by the rules.

Marxist criminology has also been faulted for lack of attention to the issue of women and crime. Women are almost totally ignored in major collections of writings on critical criminology (see Taylor, Walton, and Young 1975; Greenberg 1981a). It is assumed that theories that apply to men can be generalized to women, but the variation in experience of crime by gender cannot be ignored. Marxist theory argues that the demoralizing conditions of the working masses, including brutalizing poverty and severe competition, reduce people to the level where they have no reason not to steal. But this does not explain the significantly lower crime rates among women.

Another line of theory is that women are spared the most directly harmful influences of capitalism because they largely work at home rather than in the labour force. But Leonard (1982, 170) argues that the prevalence of wife abuse, child abuse, and incest undermines the notion that women are spared the conflicts of the larger society by being at home. She also rejects the notion that the relative non-criminality of women implies the absence of suffering or conflict in their lives. If crime rates are seen as reflecting incipient rebellion and its suppression by the ruling elite, then one would have to assume that women are more compliant and more easily controlled than men. But Marxist theory offers no explanation for why this might be so. Nor does Marxist theory offer any explanation for the prevalence of crimes committed by men against women. The crime of rape, Leonard observes, is an expression of the exploitative system that oppresses women. It cannot be romanticized as a form of struggle against the capitalist system. Class analysis does not explain women's oppression, which cuts across class lines. The dynamics of patriarchy cannot be subsumed under relations of capitalism.

In conclusion, Marxist criminology is valuable in that it exposes the capitalist underpinnings of demoralization that foster criminal behaviour among the underclass of marginalized workers. It also exposes the class-biased character of many laws and law-enforcement policies. What is needed is a broader approach to criminology that retains these insights while breaking out of the tunnel vision of cruder versions of Marxist theory. In particular, we need to explore the processes through which definitions of crime are socially constructed and how they are challenged and changed over time.

Interpretive Theories of Deviance and Crime

The interpretive perspective shifts the ground of the debate. Rather than asking why certain people behave in deviant ways, these theorists focus on the problematic meaning of concepts such as *deviance* and *crime*. They question why certain acts are labelled deviant or criminal while other actions, which might be equally benign or injurious to others, are not so labelled. They explore the dynamics of how consensus about definitions is negotiated in social interaction. In particular, they question how the police and others come to categorize certain behaviours in particular ways so as to produce the statistics on crime rates that other theories try to explain.

Crime as Defining Group Boundaries

The origins of interpretive theories of crime can be found in Durkheim's observation ([1893] 1964, 102) that crime is a natural social activity that will be found in all healthy societies. He argues that crime constitutes a violation of the collective conscience of the community. It is functional—even necessary—for society in that it draws people together in their unified reaction against it. The vehemence of the collective reaction to crime serves to reinforce the values that underlie social cohesion.

Erikson (1962; 1966) develops these insights in his study of deviance among members of the extraordinarily law-abiding and puritanical community that settled in Massachusetts in the 1630s. One would expect to find little or no crime in such a setting, and yet Erikson finds a strong preoccupation with it. He argues that this preoccupation served an important function for members of the community. The Puritans labelled activities that were commonplace among other people, including playing card games and dancing, as deviant for people like themselves. In doing so, they effectively drew **symbolic brackets** around their community, defining the behavioural boundaries between themselves and others and thus identifying their group as distinct.

To the extent that definitions of crime serve to mark the boundaries between members and non-members of a community, they must necessarily be different for each community. Each society has its own unique identity and hence its own types of deviant behaviour. It is often hard for members of one society to comprehend why certain behaviour is seen as deviant in another. The fine distinctions that the Puritans of Massachusetts drew between orthodoxy and heresy are hard for us to see now. Non-Moslems remain largely mystified by the outrage with which Moslems reacted to Salman Rushdie's novel *Satanic Verses* and by the Ayatollah Khomeini's call for the author's death. Nor do westerners generally comprehend the Moslem dress code for women, which decrees that they wear veils and loose clothing to cover their hair and

Strict dress codes for women in Islamic countries can be seen to mark group boundaries.

bodies. Non-Catholics find it hard to understand why the Catholic Church insists on the celibacy of priests and refuses to ordain women. Yet such distinctions make sense if their intended function is to define the boundaries between members of one group and another and so strengthen in-group identity.

Erikson argues that definitions of crime commonly involve picking out details of behaviour that often may appear to be relatively trivial. Most people who are labelled deviants are conformists most of the time. Even the details picked out may only be defined as deviant for individuals with a specific social status. Behaviour that constitutes a crime for a juvenile may be acceptable for an adult. What makes an act deviant is the threat to group identity posed by nonconformity. The irony is that crime tends to occur precisely where members most fear it. When a community feels most threatened by particular behaviour, members spend more time and energy rooting it out and punishing it. The emphasis placed on such violations precipitates nonconformity in precisely these areas. Thief and victim, for example, share the same high value on private property; the heretic and the religious fanatic relate to the same sensitive points of religion (Erikson 1966, 20).

Labelling deviant behaviour can fulfil the underlying function of defining group boundaries and strengthening group identity only if the labels are continually reaffirmed. Boundaries are never static. They change as the situation of group members change. They also have to be taught anew to each generation. Hence, the work of labelling and punishing crimes entails a continuous process of testing and redefinition. Any crime that goes unpunished loses its efficacy as a boundary definition. Acts of censure reinforce norms and restate group identity. To serve this role, censure must be public. In earlier times, great publicity was given to punishment. Witches were publicly tortured and executed in Europe, providing a very powerful statement of the limits of acceptable female behaviour. People who challenged the monarch's authority might be executed in a public square. Foucault (1977, chap. 1) suggests that public executions were abandoned in Europe only when it became clear that onlookers sometimes were so horrified by the cruelty of the punishment that they sided with the criminal against the authorities and could be incited to revolt. Punishment now occurs in private, behind prison walls. The public censure of crime takes place through the media.

Erikson carries the argument that crime is functional for reaffirming group identity to the extreme of suggesting that agencies of social control may actively recruit offenders and may take steps to ensure that crime rates remain roughly stable over time. Prisons, for example, are ideal institutions for gathering marginal people together where they can learn both the skills and motives for crime. Judges help to stabilize crime rates by tending to give harsh sentences when rates are high and lighter ones when they are low. Erikson concludes that, in principle, even if a community were to lop off all marginal people and expel them, as when Britain banished prisoners and heretics to the colonies, the size of the deviant population would not diminish. People would merely draw the boundaries closer and look for new examples of deviant behaviour. A society of cloistered nuns or monks, for example, is prone to magnify trivial faults into major sins.

Deviance as the Product of Labelling

Erikson's research is narrowly focussed on the maintenance of moral order in a puritanical community, but his insights into the nature of crime and control have far wider implications. He suggests that, in order to understand crime, one must study the agents of social control and the people who formulate the laws rather than the people who become labelled as deviants. He draws attention to the arbitrary character of much of the labelling that selects details of behaviour for punishment. In Erikson's model it is not the presence of criminals that gives rise to laws and agents of control. Rather, the agents of control seek out people to label and to punish. Marginal people are targets for the censure that reinforces the identity and security of the dominant community. The labelling theory of deviance centres attention on processes of labelling, censuring, and controlling marginal people and the effects these processes have on their victims. Becker (1963, 9) sums up the approach in this way: "Social groups create deviance by making the rules whose infraction constitutes deviance and by applying those rules to particular people and labelling them outsiders."

Early work in labelling theory focussed on the interaction processes involved in the transition from labelling specific acts as deviant to labelling the individual who committed the act a deviant. One deviant act does not automatically produce a deviant person. A youth might steal a car once for a joy-ride, for example, but otherwise remain a conformist. This is particularly likely if there is no appreciable reaction to the act. But if the youth is caught and punished, a cycle of reaction and counteraction may develop. After once being publicly charged for a deviant act, it becomes easier for that person to feel like "someone who does deviant things," and so commit a second deviant act. When the second act meets with harsher reactions and punishment, feelings of hostility and resentment build up, promoting further **secondary deviance** and further punishment and **stigmatization**. Strong reactions to the sense of being stigmatized by others push the youth into the final stage of personal acceptance of deviant status. The youth has been transformed from a normal person who occasionally did wrong things into a deviant or criminal person (Lemert 1951). Interactions are not always so unidirectional (Lemert 1972; Leonard 1982, 69), but the basic premise remains that societal reactions to some initial detail of deviant behaviour generate the process of self-definition as a criminal, which precedes a life of crime.

Labelling theorists are particularly concerned with the effects of stigmatization on individuals who engage in **victimless crimes**. These are transactional crimes where the persons involved in exchanging goods and services do not see themselves as either criminals or victims and are very unlikely to complain to the police. Such offences include buying and using marijuana and other banned drugs, illegal gambling, prostitution, and virtually all proscribed sexual behaviour involving willing adult partners, homosexual activity being the most notable (Schur 1965; 1971; Schur and Bedau 1974). Participants in such activities are harmed, not by the offence, but by the legal system that brands them as criminals and by the feelings of humiliation and degradation that result from this label. In Ontario, a family man arrested after a homosexual encounter in a public washroom committed suicide rather than face the shame of a conviction, which would probably have resulted in a minor fine (*Globe and Mail*, 8 Jan. 1985). Such law enforcement also has important consequences for others who must adopt the furtive lifestyles of deviants in order to avoid arrest or censure.

Research into the lives of people who are labelled **outsiders** in such ways documents the damage done to otherwise ordinary, law-abiding people (Becker 1963, 33–34; Schur 1971, 69–81). They become engulfed by the deviant label. Their self-confidence and self-esteem are lowered. They face discrimination in many aspects of their lives, including restricted job opportunities. They are systematically depersonalized by the process of **retrospective reinterpretation** through which other people "reread" their character and redefine them in ways that fit the stereotyped images of typical deviants. Processes of arrest, criminal trial, and mental competence hearings function as **status degradation ceremonies** (Garfinkel 1956) and signal a fundamental change in social status from that of normal citizen to criminal. There are no corresponding ceremonies to re-elevate the status of degraded people once they have paid their fines or served their sentences.

The process of retrospective reinterpretation of the character of stigmatized people within the legal system is extreme. But such reinterpretation goes on in other ways as well. A study of students' reactions to acquaintances they discovered or suspected were homosexuals showed how students typically reviewed all past interactions with the people in question, searching for clues and nuances of behaviour that might give further evidence of the alleged deviance (Kitsuse 1962, 253). Kitsuse suggests that such retrospective reading generally provided students with the evidence they were looking for to support the conclusion that the person in question was deviant all along. Negative social reactions toward stigmatized people are important mechanisms propelling, rather than inhibiting, the development of deviant careers (Schur and Bedau 1974, 29).

So far we have assumed that people labelled as deviants clearly engaged in proscribed behaviour. The decision that a person has violated a rule is the first step in the labelling process. Labelling theorists examine how this decision is made. The ways in which decision processes work depend very much on what kinds of people are involved, where they are, and who is doing the observing. Police officers, for example, identify and apprehend deviants by referring to practical notions of what actions seem to be "suspicious for this time and place" (Boughey 1978, 116; Bittner 1967; Sacks 1972). Even such ostensibly innocuous actions as standing on a street corner or sitting on a park bench, when performed by

certain types of people at certain times of day, may be sufficient grounds for these people to be picked up and taken in for a police check.

Ethnomethodologists insist that, in order to understand what deviance means in practice, we have to study how the people who enforce the rules make decisions about what to react to and what to ignore. Studies of how police carry out patrol work suggest that they routinely react to situations in terms of their stereotypes about the kinds of people who constitute typical criminals. The police are most likely to view the actions of certain types of people as suspicious and warranting further investigation. Young males from lower-class areas of town, particularly those from visible minority groups, are common targets for suspicion. Ontario police also stop bikers and hippies for identity checks with far greater frequency than people who fit the conventional middle-class stereotype (Ericson 1982). Ericson suggests that the primary objective of such identity checks is not to catch criminals. The vast majority of routine checks do not find anything, and police officers do not appear to expect that they should. The purpose of the exercise is to control marginal people, to put them in their place. When police officers stop such people, make them get out of their vehicles, surrender their wallets, and submit to identity checks, they visibly display and achieve intimidation and submission to police powers. Any resistance on the part of such people might be defined as "obstructing an officer in the exercise of his duty," which is an offence for which they could be formally charged.

John Sewell (1985) suggests that police in patrol cars largely kill time, burn gas, and harass marginal people. The time and resources of the police service might be better spent with officers waiting at the police stations for calls or perhaps walking local beats where they might be more effective and actually get to know people.

Racism and the Policing Process

From the perspective of labelling theorists, marginal people are criminalized not because they commit more crimes than anyone else, but because they are more often labelled as deviants. They fit the criminal stereotypes that guide police in the apprehension of offenders. They are more often stopped, searched, checked, caught, and charged. Consequently, they are more often subject to the cycle of negative reactions and counteractions that transforms them from normal people, who might occasionally do something wrong, into criminal personalities. They are least able to withstand the status degradation ceremonies that destroy self-respect and self-esteem.

Their punishment as outsiders confirms the security and identity of the majority and visibly displays the forces of law and order policing the boundaries of the community. The price that marginalized people pay for this control is very high.

In Canada the position of a visible criminalized marginal group has been filled overwhelmingly by native people and, to a lesser extent, by blacks in the areas of Nova Scotia and Toronto where they are concentrated. The proportion of native people who are in trouble with the law is six to ten times higher than their proportion in the population at large. Table 7-2 shows the overrepresentation of native people in federal prisons. Table 7-3 shows the overrepresentation of native

Table 7-2   Overrepresentation of Native Peoples in Federal Prisons, June 1989*

Province	All Inmates	Native Inmates	Percent Natives Inmates	Natives as Percentage of Total Population
Newfoundland	204	8	3.9	0.8
Prince Edward Island	39	1	2.6	0.5
Nova Scotia	551	10	1.8	0.9
New Brunswick	365	15	4.1	0.8
Quebec	3 888	29	0.7	1.3
Ontario	3 454	165	0.5	1.9
Manitoba	689	241	35.0	8.1
Saskatchewan	584	286	49.0	7.8
Alberta	1 462	359	24.6	4.4
British Columbia	1 840	260	14.1	4.4
Yukon	18	9	50.0	21.4
Northwest Territories	60	54	90.0	58.7
Outside Canada	48	2	4.1	--
Missing data	22	1	4.5	--
Total Canada	13 224	1 440	10.9	2.8

* There are no accurate figures available concerning the overrepresentation of natives in provincial prisons because local prison officials do not collect data on the ethnic background of inmates. However, many informal surveys suggest that the rates are much higher. In Saskatchewan, for example, natives are estimated to comprise fully 70 percent of inmates in provincial prisons. See LaPrairie (1984).

Source: Management Information Services, Correctional Services Canada. Population Profile Report and Native Population Profile Report. Population on Register 30/06/89, p. A002; Department of Indian Affairs customized census count 1986. Figures provided by Indian and Inuit Affairs Atlantic Region, 6 Oct. 1989.

women in provincial and territorial correctional institutions.

In Nova Scotia in 1988, a public inquiry was set up to explore why Donald Marshall, a Micmac Indian, was imprisoned for eleven years for a murder he did not commit. The inquiry heard evidence that the police may have bullied witnesses into perjuring themselves in order to secure the original conviction. Subsequent evidence pointing to Marshall's innocence was covered up. People who gave testimony before the inquiry spoke of a litany of abuses that native peoples routinely experience at the hands of police.

In Ontario in 1988 a similar public inquiry into **racism** in the police force was set up in response to the fatal police shootings of two Toronto-area blacks. The inquiry heard testimony of beatings and racial slurs directed by the police against native people.

It heard of depression and suicide among native people who felt they were victims of the police. Some members of the inquiry suggested that the only solution might be a separate native justice system set up on the reserves, with native police, native courts, and even native jails (*Globe and Mail*, 20 Feb. 1989, A1, A9).

An inquiry into aboriginal justice in Manitoba heard essentially the same kinds of testimony. One native chief spoke of an incident when he was stopped by Winnipeg police and ordered to get out of the car with his hands up, to put his hands on the roof of the car, and then to put his wallet on the roof. He was convinced that, had he made any sudden movement, he would have been shot. His "crime" was that there was dirt on the licence plate and tail lights of the car (*Globe and Mail*, 9 Feb. 1989, A5).

Table 7-3 Overrepresentation of Native Women in Provincial and Territorial Correctional Institutions

Province	Percent native in general population 1981	Number non-native women inmates 1982*	Number native women inmates 1982*	Percent native in female inmate population
Yukon Territory	18	0	3	100
Northwest Territories	58	3	9	75
British Columbia	3	52	13	20
Alberta	3	99	41	29
Saskatchewan	6	14	46	77
Manitoba	6	11	27	71
Ontario	1	232	46	17
Quebec	1	143	2	1
New Brunswick	1	15	2	12
Nova Scotia	1	20	0	0
Prince Edward Island	1	2	0	0
Newfoundland	1	0	8	100
Canada	2	591	197	25

* One day snapshot.

Source: Johnson (1987); Misch (1982); Statistics Canada (1984).

While natives are harassed for petty or non-existent offences, crimes against natives often go unpunished. The Manitoba inquiry heard testimony that, over the past fifteen years, at least eight Indians have been killed on the road but no charges have been laid (*Globe and Mail*, 19 Jan. 1989, A1-2). The RCMP always assumed that the Indians had been drinking even when the victims had clearly been seen sober before they died. Native witnesses were convinced that some of these deaths constituted murder. They spoke of being afraid to walk beside the roads because cars routinely come so close that it appeared that the drivers actually intended to hit them. In Toronto in January 1989, a semi-conscious native woman, lying on the road after being hit by a car, was taken by police to a detoxification centre rather than to a hospital. The stereotype of drunken native peoples was so powerful that police ignored their own regulations requiring that people found unconscious be taken to a hospital. The woman died from head injuries ten days after the incident.

Perhaps the most horrific example of the lack of punishment for offences against natives is the case of Helen Betty Osborne. Osborne, a native woman living in a small town in Manitoba, was abducted in 1971 by four young white men. She was beaten, sexually assaulted, and brutally murdered. More than fifteen years later, the murder was still unpunished, despite the fact that many of the people in the community— including the sheriff—knew who had committed the crime: those responsible did not even feel compelled to keep their involvement a secret. A trial was held eventually, but only one man was imprisoned. Of the other three, one was acquitted, one was granted immunity, and one was never charged. Formal protests over the investigation and the verdict led to the establishment of a public inquiry on justice and native peoples (Priest 1989).

Labelling Women Offenders

Stereotypes of the typical criminal largely exclude women. Excepting offences such as shoplifting and prostitution, women have significantly lower crime rates than men. Labelling theory suggests two explanations for this pattern. There may be a direct connection between lower crime rates and lack of criminal stereotyping of females. It is possible that females may simply commit fewer crimes. Alternatively, they may commit as many initial offences as men but escape the labelling that leads to a cycle promoting secondary deviance and a criminal self-image. Another possibility is that women who do something wrong are subject to negative labelling. However, they may be labelled as sick or mentally disturbed individuals, rather than as criminals. The cycle of response to the mentally disturbed label is different from the criminal label and results in very different overall outcomes for women and men.

Early theoretical speculation about the character of female offenders leaves little doubt that women were stereotyped in very negative ways (Smart 1977, 91). These stereotypes were used to supply evidence for either greater or lesser involvement of women in criminal behaviour, depending on the biases of the writer. Caesar Lombroso (1895), basing his conclusions on interviews with prostitutes, argued that women were inherently evil and prone to crime, but that their criminal potential was generally kept in check by their natural passivity, lack of intelligence, and especially by their "maternal instincts." Lack of maternal instinct in a woman was a sure sign of a criminal character. Otto Pollak (1950) similarly believed that women were naturally criminal, prone to lying, deceit, and trickery. Women instigated crimes and manipulated gullible males into enacting them. Women had lower crime rates only because of their success at concealment. Women were as

Figure 7-1 Percentage of All Offences Committed by Men and Women 1985

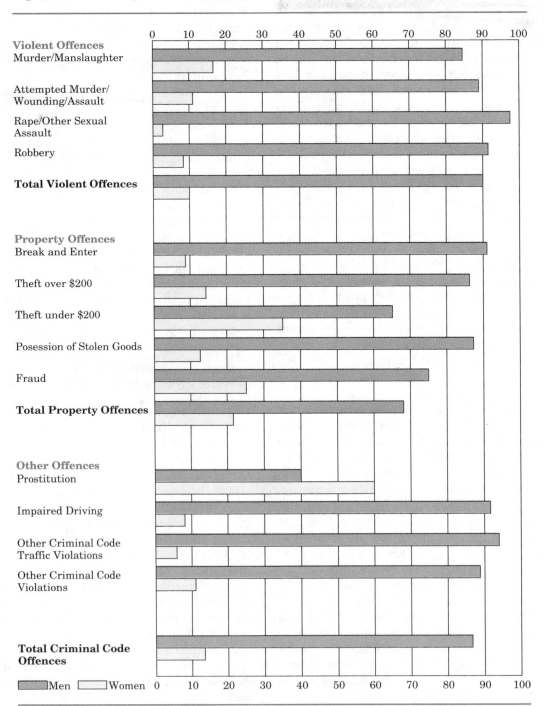

Source: Adapted from Johnson (1987); Statistics Canada (1986).

murderous as men but were caught less often because they tended to use poison, which is harder to detect than the use of a weapon. Not surprisingly, the evidence for these pronouncements was thin indeed.

These early theories of covert criminal dispositions in women gave way to more explicitly biological explanations for female crime rates. Female crime, it is argued, is linked to hormonal imbalances associated with menstruation, pregnancy, childbirth, and menopause (Cowie, Cowie, and Slater 1968; Smart 1977, 91). The illness label functions as an alternative to a criminal label and implies a different kind of treatment. Females are far more likely to be remanded for psychiatric evaluation before sentencing than are men (Morris 1987, 53). Morris concludes from a review of psychological studies that there is little reliable data to support the notion that premenstrual tension is a significant factor in mood fluctuations; but

she notes that courts are still receptive to arguments positing such tension as a mitigating circumstance in crimes of violence committed by women (Morris 1987, 46–51).

The different stereotyping of female and male offenders makes official statistics very difficult to interpret. Differences in crime rates for women and men may reflect biases in how statistics were collected, different socialization of women and men and hence real differences in predispositions for behaviour, different opportunity structures, different expectations and labelling, or some combination of all of the above.

Morris (1987, 52–53) cites data that indicate that, while male criminals outnumber females by five to one, females labelled mentally ill outnumber men so labelled by three to one. One reason for this latter pattern, she suggests, is that the typical standard of mental health is male. The model for a healthy

Table 7-4   Males and Females Admitted Under Federal Sentence, 1975–84*

Year	Total	Male	Female	Percent Female
1975	3 923	3 834	89	2.3
1976	3 941	3 820	121	3.1
1977	3 974	3 873	101	2.5
1978	4 175	4 055	120	2.9
1979	3 966	3 846	120	3.0
1980	3 981	3 884	97	2.4
1981	4 317	4 237	80	1.9
1982	4 556	4 455	101	2.2
1983	5 158	5 041	117	2.3
1984	5 362	5 263	99	1.8
Total	43 353	42 308	1 045	2.4
Percent Increase 1975–84	—	+37.3	+11.2	—

* Excludes re-admissions by straight revocation of parole and mandatory supervision. Includes admissions to federal institutions and transfers to provincial institutions.

Source: Johnson (1987); Solicitor General Canada, Correctional Services Canada, Offender Information System.

adult is a healthy male. A healthy female is typified as excitable, submissive, emotional, and dependent. Such characteristics are the opposite of those attributed to healthy adults. Women tend to outnumber men mostly in the vague categories of mental illness such as "neurotic" and "depressed."

The tendency to label female offenders as sick or mentally disturbed rather than as criminal does not necessarily result in greater leniency toward them. Females may actually be subject to more stringent controls. Smart (1977, 96–98) found that **double standards** regarding appropriate sex-role behaviour frequently result in girls being punished for behaviour that is not considered deviant for boys. For example, girls who display promiscuous behaviour are considered to be in need of treatment and control; boys displaying similar behaviour are considered to be normal. Girls are also more likely to be punished for being "incorrigible" or "out of control" than are boys. Smart cites evidence from Britain that girls are far more likely to be incarcerated in reform schools for being found "in need of care and protection" or "in moral danger" than boys. Government statistics for 1960 revealed that 95 percent of boys sent to reform schools had committed some offence. The corresponding figure for girls was 35 percent (Smart 1977, 98). In other words, two-thirds of all girls sent to the equivalent of prison for children had committed no criminal offence. Benevolent paternalism toward females provides justification for stringent controls over their behaviour, including imprisonment.

In Canada, under the Juvenile Delinquents Act, which was in force from 1908 to 1984, adolescents could be brought to court for numerous offences that were not crimes for adults. These juvenile offences involved violations of parental or adult authority and included such behaviour as truancy from school, running away from home, sexual immorality, and incorrigibility—a catch-all category for juveniles considered unmanage-able or very badly behaved. Self-report studies suggested that boys were more sexually active than girls. Truancy and running away from home were offences committed by girls about as often as by boys. But girls were far more likely to be charged with such offences and sent to training schools (Geller 1987, 114-17).

The Young Offenders Act, which came into force in 1984, promised to change such practices. Under the new act, young people can only be charged with offences for which adults can be charged. The act also stresses alternatives to taking juveniles before the courts for minor infractions. In principle, it should be harder for police and judges to continue to treat boys and girls differently, but stereotyped views and practices are strongly entrenched. Female adolescents are still being controlled indirectly. They are more likely than boys to be charged with a trivial criminal offence, enabling authorities to gain power over them and to deal with other problem behaviour such as promiscuity and running away from home. Child welfare, drug and alcohol, and mental health legislation is also being used to punish girls who are considered unmanageable (Geller 1987, 119–23).

Smart argues that belief in chivalry and leniency acts as an ideology that distorts understanding of how the legal system actually operates. This ideology conceals not only the unfavourable attitudes toward female offenders but also the real injustice often meted out under the guise of humanitarianism. Behind the notion of chivalry is the unequal distribution of power between the sexes. A woman must depend on a man for her protection and must be deserving of such protection. Women who are labelled as having bad moral character are open to the full force of outraged male morality. Women from visible minority groups are particularly likely to be targets for harsh treatment (Leonard 1981, 86). Smart concludes that the theoretical analysis of female criminality in terms of individual pathology, hormonal imbalance, and mental illness, carries an inherently political message. Such analysis locates the causes of the problem within the individual and the solution in technical controls and psychiatric treatment programs in prisons, rather than in the social emancipation of women.

In summary, the labelling process is fundamentally about power. Deviance is the result of processes of social definition and reaction. Social groups create deviance by making the rules whose infraction constitutes deviance and applying those rules so as to label particular people as outsiders. Deviants are those to whom such labels have successfully been applied (Schur 1980, 9; Becker 1963, 9). Schur speaks of the **deviantizing process** as essentially a political issue involving the exercise and distribution of power in society.

The Limitations of Labelling Theory

The central Marxist critique of labelling theory is not that it is wrong, but that it does not carry the analysis far enough. It fails to study the structures of power that underlie the labelling process. Marxist theorists argue that this structure is capitalism. They suggest that the problem populations that are labelled deviant and so controlled under capitalism are those whose behaviour or position threatens the interests of capitalists in accumulating profits (Spitzer 1975, 642; Schur 1980, 77). Labelling theorists respond that capitalism may well be centrally involved in certain aspects of the labelling process: economic factors influence the vested interests of agencies of control, and socio-economic factors influence the selection and processing of people labelled deviant. But this is a far cry from proving that capitalism causes or directs all labelling processes. The routine stigmatization of so many types of people occurs far beyond the realm of what can be attributed to the

interests or efforts of the capitalist class. Extreme versions of Marxist analysis assume that labelling would not occur under socialism, but this is not supported by evidence. Homosexuality continues to be rigidly stigmatized in postrevolutionary Cuba, but on the grounds that such behaviour is tied to "counterrevolutionary sentiment" (Schur 1980, 78).

Schur concludes that there is nothing distinctive about capitalism or the interests of the capitalist class that dictates the labelling process. While groups that threaten capitalist interests are especially likely to be harassed within capitalist societies, it is nonetheless the case that most of the people who are viewed as problems and stigmatized at any given time pose no such threat. It is hard to see how the interests of capitalism require the harassment of homosexuals or prostitutes or native people, or how capitalism is threatened by promiscuous girls or by

The stigmatization of prostitutes cannot be explained solely with reference to capitalism.

people growing marijuana in their backyards. Schur does not carry the argument further to explore other bases of power and control in racism and patriarchy. But labelling theorists might justifiably respond that such broader structural analysis lies beyond what the perspective sets out to do.

A more decisive critique of labelling theory is that it fails to address critical aspects of the labelling process itself. Labelling theory focusses almost entirely on how certain behaviours are labelled as offences and on how secondary deviance can be caused by the processes through which offenders are stigmatized, degraded, and humiliated. One problem with this approach is that the original behaviour is ignored or treated as unimportant (Leonard 1982, 77).

Labelling theory does not consider the question of why the offender committed the initial offence that attracted the attention of the labellers. The theory applies only at the stage of reaction to the offence. This focus may be valid for analysing victimless crimes or offences against morality, when what needs to be explained is why labellers stigmatize relatively innocuous behavior. But not all crimes are of this kind. Most behaviour that is labelled criminal clearly involves victims. Offenders know in advance that the behaviour is wrong, that it will damage other people, and that they will face sanctions if they are caught. The critical question must be why certain people engage in such criminal behaviour. Their reaction to subsequent labelling, if caught, is of secondary interest.

The labelling theory perspective is weak in another critical regard. It assumes in advance that crime comprises only behaviour that is labelled deviant and therefore is condemned. It is impossible by definition to have crimes that are not labelled. There is virtually no consideration within labelling theory of selective failure to impose criminal labels on behaviour for which there clearly are innocent victims. In an effort to break the assumption that crimes consist only of acts that violate state statutes, Marxist theory stresses the need to redefine crime in terms of the violation of human rights. In Marxist theory such crimes include all practices that damage workers and the environment in the interests of increasing profits. Feminist theory pushes this criticism in a different direction, to explore how pervasively women and children are victimized by behaviour that the criminal justice system consistently trivializes or refuses to label as a crime, and how the perpetrators of such acts escape stigmatization.

Victims of Crimes Without Labels

When criminologists study crime, particularly crimes of violence against individuals, what they typically have in mind is street crime. This is the kind of crime in which people are victimized by strangers in public places. Surveys designed to measure the incidence of crime and fear of crime within a population use questions concerning how safe people feel on the street, or after dark, or when they are out alone in their neighbourhood (Stanko 1988, 76–79). Typical victims of such crimes are males who are under thirty years of age, tend to go out several nights a week, drink heavily, and assault others (Morris 1987, 161). Women tend to have more fear of crime than men but appear less likely to be victims. Stanko criticizes such research for being inherently sexist because it ignores private violence and, in so doing, it bypasses the reality of women's experience of violence. Women are far more likely to be victimized at home, in private, than on the streets. They are most likely to be attacked by a member of their own family or someone they know, someone who has access to them in their own home. The fear generated by being attacked within this supposedly safe place and by someone familial and familiar is worse than fear of attack by strangers, because the victims have literally no safe place to go.

Interpersonal violence against women involves battery and sexual assault by partners and intimate companions. Historically, wife beating was approved by the church and the state in Britain and North America. Until the end of the nineteenth century, a husband could beat his wife for her own spiritual and moral benefit, provided the stick he used was no bigger in width than his thumb. In Canada, before changes in the sexual assault legislation in 1983, it was legally impossible for a wife to be raped by her husband. Most sexual violence is still not considered a crime unless the resulting injuries are so severe that the victim requires hospitalization. Even then the batterer is not automatically charged with a criminal offence.

A crucial mechanism inhibiting the recognition of sexual and domestic violence as crime is the lack of names to apply to such acts. Terms like *battered women* and *sexual harassment*, for example, did not exist before the 1960s. As a result, these experiences remained amorphous and unnamed, felt but not seen for what they were, and women were silenced (Kelly 1988). Kelly explores the power of naming what is happening in her study of how women define sexual violence. She obtained in-depth interviews with sixty women, focussing on events experienced as very distressing but not named as a particular form of violence. Previous studies have shown that questions like "have you ever been raped?" versus "have you ever been forced to have sex?" get very different responses. The main reason for this is that "rape" is stereotyped as an act committed by a deranged male stranger in a public place. Hence, forced sex with an acquaintance is not classified as rape, although such experience is extremely upsetting.

In her interviews, Kelly moved chronologically through childhood and adolescence to adulthood, asking the women if they had ever felt pressured to have sex or experienced violence in intimate relationships. What she found was that, in the course of the interviews, fully 70 percent of the women changed their definition of what had happened to them, from initially denying that they had ever experienced sexual abuse, to recognizing that what parents, other relatives, and partners had done to them was indeed abusive. A very common way of coping with such experiences was to repress the memories or to minimize the hurt with flippant comments. The experience of being interviewed on the subject of sexual violence, and the subsequent experience of reading the research report based on the interviews, frequently triggered these memories for the women involved and gave them the means of verbalizing what happened.

Rape, or sexual assault as it is now called, is an offence under the Criminal Code, but it is exceedingly difficult for sexually violent behaviour against women to be recognized and labelled as rape. Powerful non-labelling mechanisms intervene to inhibit such naming (Morris 1987, chap. 7). Evidence from surveys of women's experiences suggests that only a tiny minority of incidents that women themselves name as rape ever get reported. Morris estimates that only about 8 percent of alleged rapes and 18 percent of other types of alleged sexual assault are reported to the police. The main reasons that women give for not reporting such incidents is that they believe that nothing can or will be done; they fear reprisals from the men involved; and they fear, justifiably, that police will not believe them.

When incidents of sexual assault are reported to the police, only a minority of such cases ever result in charges being laid. A study of 116 rape cases reported to the Toronto police in 1970 revealed that the police rejected two-thirds as unfounded

(Clark and Lewis 1977). All the professional women who reported being raped had their allegations treated as founded, but only half the students, and none of the women who were on welfare. Police were especially unsympathetic to black and native women. Police routinely advised victims not to press charges if they were over seventeen, not a virgin, and on the pill.

The labelling process is also inhibited by powerful stereotypes regarding what rape is and who can be raped. The classic believable case is one that is sudden, violent, occurs in a public place, and involves a male stranger and a virgin. The stereotype perpetuated in the media is that the man is unknown to the woman and that he is oversexed, frustrated, or mentally ill. The victim is a virgin who was not voluntarily in the place where it happened and who fought to the end and was physically injured. If a case does not fit this stereotype, it is likely not to be taken seriously.

Sexual assault trials, those few cases that actually do make it past the screening processes into court, are dominated by the same set of assumptions. *No means yes*: most women want and encourage the sexual encounter even though they complain afterwards. *She asked for it*: she was dressed in a seductive way; she was alone in an inappropriate place; she led him on. *Yes to one means yes to all*: a woman who consented to sex before probably consented to the act in question. Such assumptions are so powerful and so pervasive that they discredit the majority of rape charges in the eyes of judges and jury members. One male gynaecologist is cited as saying, "there is one type of woman I would have a hard time believing has been raped; a woman between 16 and 25, on the pill, and no longer a virgin" (Morris 1987, 170). As an expert witness in a trial, or as a jury member, this man would dismiss out of hand the majority of cases he would encounter. A study of 600 Minnesota residents in 1980 revealed that more than half of

these potential jurors held stereotypes about rape that would lead them to dismiss most charges: any healthy woman can resist; a rape victim is usually promiscuous; it is usually her fault for letting things get out of hand.

A consistent pattern in rape trials is that the woman who lays the charge, and not the alleged male offender, is subjected to the processes of degradation and humiliation. It is *her* character that is on trial. Sexual assault legislation generally precludes questions about prior sexual activity, unless the main issue in the trial is whether or not the woman consented to having sex or the man could reasonably assume that she had consented. Since the most common grounds for defence is that the accused believed she had consented, lawyers commonly ask for prior sexual behaviour to be admissible, and most of the time such requests are granted (Morris 1987, 171). Lawyers often do not need to raise the issue of consent directly. Asking the woman if she is on the pill, even if the question is not answered, is often sufficient to discredit a woman in the eyes of jury members predisposed not to believe in rape.

Many parallels can be drawn between the non-labelling processes involved in rape and wife battery. The physical assault of a spouse is an offence under the Criminal Code, but very rarely do such cases ever get to court. When they do, the perpetrators face minimal stigmatization or punishment. The true extent of domestic violence is unknown. Official statistics do not exist in Canada because it is not a reportable offence. Doctors, social workers, or others who may know or suspect that wife battery has occurred, are not under any legal obligation to report such occurrences to the police. Estimates of the true rate of such abuse are thus based on unofficial surveys. A House of Commons report on violence in the home (Canada 1982) conservatively estimates that one in every ten women living with a man as a couple is battered. Morris (1987, 181) puts the rate at between 20 and 33 percent. Wives also attack their husbands, but overwhelmingly in the context of self-defence or retaliation. A few sparse studies on the topic of husband battering suggest women instigate domestic violence in about one-tenth of all cases (Saunders 1988). The people who end up in hospitals and transition houses after being severely beaten are overwhelmingly female. In Ontario alone, in 1981, over 30 000 women sought help from transition houses.

Despite such staggering figures on the prevalence of domestic violence, the perpetrators are only very rarely labelled as criminals. Police in Canada respond to only about half the domestic disturbance calls they receive (Canada 1982, 10), and they are trained merely to calm the situation down and leave rather than to press assault charges. Police typically see such cases as nuisance calls that interfere with their "real work" of controlling crime. Some police lump domestic disputes in with lost dogs, rowdy youths, and bothersome drunks as "rubbish work" (Morris 1987, 185). Responding to a call related to domestic violence is accorded the same level of importance as finding a stray animal.

The physical and sexual abuse of children similarly ranks as a crime where the perpetrators very rarely face public censure. Behaviour that would constitute assault if directed at anyone but one's own child becomes invisible under the rationale of a paternalistic prerogative to discipline children. Incest is a crime that is only beginning to be given a name and a presence in courts. It too is typically rationalized away as not doing any harm to seductive youngsters who participate voluntarily (Morris 1987, 188–91).

It is important to recognize that the physical and sexual abuse of children is not confined to girls. Boys are also victims, although the extent of their victimization only began to come to light in the late 1980s. In 1989, widespread media coverage was given to the alleged sexual abuse of boys in Newfoundland by Roman Catholic priests, former priests, and members of a Roman Catholic lay order of teachers in an orphanage (*Globe and Mail*, 19 April 1989; 26 April 1989, A7). Reports of abuse at the orphanage first surfaced in 1975, but they were apparently hushed up by the combined actions of the church elders, the police, and the Newfoundland Department of Justice and Social Services. Perhaps the success of the feminist movement in exposing the prevalance of the sexual abuse of girls encouraged more young men to reveal their past experiences. Victims and their parents began to speak out publicly about their overwhelming sense of hurt and betrayal and the long-term emotional damage that these boys suffer.

The problem is by no means confined to Newfoundland. A confidential report prepared for the U.S. Roman Catholic bishops in 1985 suggests that the church may have to pay out more than $1 billion (U.S.) over ten years in claims against priests and other church officials for the emotional suffering of the boys they sexually abused (*Daily Gleaner* (Fredericton), 26 April 1989, 1, 12).

Why did these offences happen? Guindon (1989) suggests that the sexual lifestyles of priests make them particularly vulnerable to the commission of sexual offences against underage males. Firstly, as men themselves, priests share in the prevailing aggressive definition of male sexuality, an aggressiveness that threatens all weaker members of society, particularly women and children. Singling out priests for special blame or labelling offenders as homosexuals provides a defence mechanism, a scapegoat that enables men in general not to look at their own aggressive sexuality. The overwhelming evidence is that the typical sex abuser is a heterosexual male.

Secondly, as clerics, priests are particularly vulnerable to the abuse of power because they so often identify themselves and are identified by others with the power structure of the Catholic Church. The laity are too ready to hand over their own responsibility for moral decisions to priests. Such power corrupts. It gives rise to the "father knows best" syndrome: a dangerous mixture of patriarchal sexuality and clerical power and control. Sinclair (1989) argues that sexual abuse is fundamentally an abuse of power. It is fostered by patriarchal structures within the church and the family that bolster the exaggerated image of the priest/father who has absolute authority over his flock/family. Sexual domination is the extreme expression of this sense of absolute authority. *Globe and Mail* columnist Valpy makes a similar point when he suggests that, until very recently, Roman Catholic clergy in rural Newfoundland exercised an almost medieval control over their flock. They acted as lawyers, doctors, administrators, accountants, and letter writers for their often illiterate parishioners. This unhealthy power, Valpy suggests, was exacerbated by the isolation of many priests in the outports (*Globe and Mail*, 26 April 1989, A7).

The third factor stressed by Guindon is the celibate lifestyle of priests. Marriage, of course, does not prevent rape and incest. But the celibate lifestyle can often mean that the emotional and sensual needs of priests, to be loved and touched by others, are unmet. Priests are strongly discouraged from forming friendships with women, lest the community perceive these as sexual relationships. In our society, few men are capable of forming intimate friendships with each other. So, what is left? Only friendships between priests and young males have, at least until recently, received open social approval. Young males want companionship, intimacy, and conversation, and priests are encouraged to get involved with them.

The potential for danger arises from the social isolation of priests. Studies cited by Guindon suggest that only one priest in ten describes himself as having a fulfilling, enriching friendship with anyone. Many live in lonely, barren rectories. Such men do not have to be innately either homosexuals or pedophiles to turn to boys for sexual closeness. The majority are normal, heterosexual males who are isolated, lonely, and desperate for human warmth and closeness in their lives. The enormous public attention given to the sexual abuse of boys by priests in Newfoundland may worsen the problem by increasing the isolation and desolation of priests.

Guindon suggests that the prolonged media attention given to the abuses in the Newfoundland orphanage stem from the fact that boys were involved. The far more widespread sexual abuse of girls within families receives relatively little media attention. It tends to be seen as regretable, but somehow normal.

Whatever the cause or set of causes that promotes the sexual abuse of children, it exacts a heavy toll of suffering that affects the later lives of the victims. The potential importance of child abuse as a factor in adult criminal behaviour is only beginning to gain recognition. It has been estimated that 80 percent of female prostitutes were sexually abused by their father or a father figure when they were young children. An estimated 80 percent of prison inmates, both female and male, were physically abused as children (*Globe and Mail*, 22 March 1988, A13; Martin 1977, 14–15). Other studies show that wife battery is closely associated with physical abuse of children (Bowker 1988). Children who have seen their father battering their mother are very likely to become abusers and batterers in their own adulthood (Shupe, Stacey, and Hazlewood 1987, 36–37; Bowker 1988).

Such trends, taken together, suggest that patriarchy, reflected in the battering of women and abuse of children in the home, may be not only a prevalent source of crime in its own right. It may also rank among the most important causes of secondary deviance and criminal behaviour, through the degradation, humiliation, and chronic emotional insecurity it generates.

Crime and Patriarchy: A Feminist Overview of Criminology

Criminology is fundamentally sexist. This is the main conclusion of feminist theorists such as Leonard (1982) and Morris (1987) in their overview of contemporary literature. None of the major perspectives—functionalist, Marxist, or interpretive—give more than cursory attention to the issue of women and crime. In all the explanations of criminal behaviour that are proposed from these perspectives, the standard is the male.

The problem is that theories designed with reference to male offenders fail conspicuously when they are applied to women. Women do not display the same behaviour patterns as men in comparable situations. Anomie theory, for example, stresses the gap between success goals and legitimate means. This gap is worse for women than for men, yet women's crime rate is markedly lower than men's. The expansion of legitimate opportunities for women should result in declining crime rates, according to the same theory, but in reality the rates go up. Lower-class subculture theories of crime do not explain why girls, growing up in the same neighbourhoods, even in the same families, commit fewer crimes than boys and are markedly less inclined to join youth gangs. Theories that account for crime in terms of poverty and powerlessness cannot explain why women, who are more likely to live in poverty and are manifestly less powerful than men, have much lower crime rates. Interpretive theorists argue that labelling and stigmatizing certain behaviours as crimes generate a deviant self-image and ultimately a criminal lifestyle. They propose that girls and women are less likely to be stigmatized and so less likely to become criminals. But these theories do not explain why women are victims of crimes without names, nor why it has taken the full force of the women's movement during the 1960s and 1970s to have these assaults labelled as crimes and to begin to protect the victim herself from being blamed for the assault.

The analytical weakness of criminology becomes particularly apparent when explanations given for higher crime rates among certain kinds of men are used to predict the opposite rates among women: lower-class men commit crimes because of their sense of powerlessness, their frustrated success goals, and their lack of legitimate opportunities; lower-class women do not commit crimes because they are powerless, learn to fear and abandon success goals, and lack legitimate opportunities to enter positions that facilitate criminal behaviour.

Most criminologists do not even notice the contradictions because they do not notice women. As Adelberg and Currie (1987) express it, women are "too few to count" in criminology. Women may be unnoticed in analysis even when they are central figures in the criminal behaviour. In a study of serial killers, Leyton (1986) uses anomie theory to account for the rising number of multiple murderers in the United States. He estimates the increase to be from about one or two serial murders per decade between the 1920s and the 1950s to twenty-five during the first four years of the 1980s, or one every two months or so. Leyton argues that contemporary multiple murderers are mostly socially ambitious upper-working-class or lower-middle-class workers who feel excluded from the American dream of secure middle-class status. They relieve a burning grudge engendered by their failed ambition by wreaking vengeance on the symbol and source of their exclusion. Their victims are drawn from middle-class neighbourhoods, university students, aspiring models, and pedestrians in middle-class shopping malls.

The questions that remain unasked are

why virtually all serial killers in the twentieth century are males and why the vast majority of their victims are females. Ted Bundy did not merely hunt humans in general. He hunted women, and especially women whose social status was higher than his own. Leyton's theoretical model cannot account for why women do not get involved in serial killings. Neither does it explain why males should choose female victims. He does not ask why it might be that men with acute status anxiety should feel most threatened by women. If he had considered the question, it might have shifted his theoretical analysis toward a study of patriarchy and the women's movement. Leyton is intent upon refuting the arguments that serial killings can be explained by psychiatric disorders, or uncontrollable sexual urges. He completely ignores the dynamics of the gender hierarchy.

Morris (1987, 15) sums up the state of criminology with the blunt conclusion that there is as yet no feminist theory of crime. Her ideal is to develop a criminology that avoids the sexism of conventional wisdom, that makes women visible, and that acknowledges the fear of oppression that women feel. The goal is not to generate a separate theory that applies only to women or to have a "criminology of women" chapter in standard textbooks. The goal is to develop an integrated theory that explains male and female worlds and the connections between them. Any theory that adequately explains male crime rates must necessarily explain the differences between male and female rates. This goal is still a long way off.

Conclusion

Contemporary studies of the breakdown of social order still owe much to Durkheim's original analysis of social cohesion in industrial society. Durkheim insists that justice, based on respect for individual human rights, constitutes the essential moral foundation of social order in societies based on the interdependence and mutual obligations of specialists. This concept of justice must transcend racial, ethnic, and occupational diversity if it is to hold complex societies together in relative harmony. Failure to establish a regulative order that members perceive to be just results in anomie. That anomie is reflected in suicide, conflict, and crime.

The prevalence of industrial conflict in contemporary Canada suggests that this sense of justice is still far from being realized. The central Marxist critique of Durkheim's work is that he gives inadequate attention to the structure of capitalism. Marxists argue that this structure precludes the possibility of social justice. They point to the law as a central arena of class struggle between workers and capitalists, a struggle in which the outcome is heavily biased in favour of capitalists. Marxist analysis itself has been tarnished by the evidence of widespread, if muted, industrial unrest in non-capitalist societies. The rise of the independent union movement Solidarity in Poland during the early 1980s, and its development into a governing party, and the extensive strikes by coalminers in the Soviet Union during the summer of 1989 suggest that conflicts over power, privilege, and injustice plague labour relations in communist economies no less than in capitalist ones. But in such economies blame cannot be assigned directly to profit motives and private ownership of capital. The struggle for distributive justice seems to be an endemic problem in industrialized societies.

Feminist theory is also forcing a reappraisal of justice in labour relations in terms of inequalities associated with gender. In Durkheim's analysis, gendered division of labour is accepted as natural and therefore compatible with principles of justice. But such assumptions of natural order are now being questioned. The contemporary struggle in the arena of labour law focusses on affirmative action for gender equality as well as for distributive justice along class, racial, and ethic lines. More recently activists have recognized the importance of incorporating the demands of handicapped people. These struggles are complicated by the fact that the terms of the debate are not consistently defined. For feminists, justice requires affirmative action to redress systemic inequality. Meanwhile, their opponents see affirmative action as institutionalized discrimination on the basis of sex, and therefore as unjust.

High crime rates in Canada suggest that anomie is prevalent in many other spheres of social life. The functionalist theory of anomie regards crime as the expression of frustration felt by disprivileged groups in society who lack legitimate means to attain socially approved goals. Marxist theory, by and large, views criminals as victims of an intrinsically unjust and inegalitarian capitalist economic system. But it also calls into question the ways in which crime itself is defined and meaured. If crime is defined in terms of such acts as vandalism, theft, and property damage, the disprivileged swell the ranks of criminals. But if the definition of crime is broadened to include acts that result in social harm, then the majority of criminals may well turn out to be members of the business elite and agents of the state itself. In effect, the definition of crime determines the distribution of criminals. Within capitalist society, the elite class have disproportionate power to impose such definitions.

Interpretive theory focusses on the discourse of criminology. It explores the processes through which deviant and criminal labels are applied to actions and the effects such labelling has on the victims. Such research goes beyond the naming of behaviour to question how police, in their routine everyday activities, decide that certain behavior by certain kinds of people fits the category to which criminal labels apply. Disproportionate arrest of members of visible minority groups is arguably as much a reflection of police prejudices as it is of actual variations in criminal activity.

Feminist theory challenges the entire field of criminology for systematic gender bias that undermines the scientific credibility of the field. None of the major explanations for crime proposed by anomie theory, Marxism, or labelling theory adequately accounts for differences in crime rates between women and men. Criminology is also blinkered in virtually dismissing the major problem of domestic violence, especially violence against women, from its concern. The contemporary areas of debate and struggle in criminology thus centre around such fundamental questions as the definition of crime itself and where or if the boundaries should be drawn around the subject matter of criminology.

Suggested Reading

The study by Robert Blauner, *Alienation and Freedom: The Factory Worker and His Industry* (1964), is a classic in the field of sociology of work. In the introductory chapters he develops a research model based on a combination of the Marxist concept of alienation and the Durkheimian concept of anomie. He then systematically applies this model to four kinds of industrial work. He concludes by relating patterns of technology to the relative experience of alienation and anomie.

Alvin Gouldner's study *Wildcat Strike* (1965) explores the frustrations that lay behind a series of strikes in a mine. He warns against the simplistic assumption that formal issues raised in a strike, commonly demands for more money, are necessarily at the root of the strike. A Marxist perspective on labour unrest is provided by Leo Panitch and David Swartz in *The Assault on Trade Union Freedoms* (1988). They argue that the state has systematically broken the power of unions in Canada by repressive legislation.

Rosemary Warskett's article "Bank Worker Unionization and the Law" (1988) explores the contradictory role of labour legislation for unions. In part, the laws protect union rights, but they also constrain and rigidify union actions and remove the locus of class struggle from the workplace to the courts.

Eileen Leonard's *Women, Crime, and Society: A Critique of Theoretical Criminology* (1982) provides a comprehensive and critical overview of criminology theory. She develops a perceptive critique of the entire range of current theories and shows that they cannot account for the marked difference in crime rates between men and women.

A classic presentation of the functionalist perspective on crime is by Robert Merton in chapters 6 and 7 of *Social Theory and Social Structure* (1968). Merton develops a model of types of deviance based on the gap between socially desired goals and socially approved means to achieve them. Also in the functionalist tradition is the work of Mike Brake, *The Sociology of Youth Culture and Youth Subcultures: Sex and Drugs and Rock 'n' Roll?* (1980). Brake describes the deviant subcultural values that integrate different youth gangs from working-class and middle-class backgrounds. His data are drawn mostly from Britain.

The Marxist perspective on crime is well presented by David Greenberg, ed., *Crime and Capitalism: Readings in Marxist Criminology* (1981a). The introduction is particularly useful in giving a critical overview of the approach. Eighteen short articles by different authors provide a valuable overview of the criminal justice system. A particularly useful article on adolescent delinquency and gangs is by Green-

berg, "Delinquency and the Age Structure of Society." The short book by Ian Taylor, *Crime, Capitalism, and Community: Three Essays in Socialist Criminology* (1983), also provides a valuable introduction to the Marxist approach to crime.

An excellent overview of labelling theory is provided by Edwin Schur in *The Politics of Deviance: Stigma Contests and the Uses of Power* (1980). Schur acknowledges the criticisms of earlier formulations of labelling theory but argues persuasively that this approach is valuable, particularly for understanding crime where there is no clear victim and no clear threat to the interests of the capitalist class.

Two useful studies of policing practices in Canada are R.V. Ericson, *Reproducing Order: A Study of Police Patrol Work* (1982) and John Sewell, *Police: Urban Policing in Canada* (1985). Both books describe what police officers do in the routine performance of their jobs and how the labelling processes work in terms of who is singled out for police checks. For a study of racism in the criminal justice system see Michael Harris, *Justice Denied: The Law Versus Donald Marshall* (1986).

An excellent resource book on women and crime is E. Adelberg and C. Currie, eds., *Too Few To Count: Canadian Women in Conflict with the Law* (1987). The chapter by Holly Johnson provides valuable statistical data on changing crime rates and on women in Canada convicted of various crimes. Other articles present case studies of the lives of women in trouble with the law and relate their experiences to patriarchal social institutions. A critical essay showing how criminology theory systematically ignores violent crimes against women is Elizabeth Stanko, "Fear of Crime and the Myth of the Safe Home: A Feminist Critique of Criminology" (1988).

Part III

Political Economy: The Marxist Challenge

Chapter 8

Karl Marx and the Analysis of Capitalism

Karl Marx (1818–83) was a profound thinker whose work has had a phenomenal impact upon the twentieth century. His most famous treatise, the three-volume *Capital*, stands as a monumental study of Western industrial society. It is difficult to overstate Marx's importance. It is also very difficult to condense his prolific writings into one short chapter. Much controversy surrounds the interpretation of his ideas: some theorists see an important break between his early philosophical and later economic works, while others stress the underlying continuity. Some see him as an **economic determinist**, others as the forerunner of the mode of analysis concerned with the social construction of reality. Analysis is made more difficult by the fact that Marx died before the last volume of *Capital*, particularly his section on class analysis, was complete. Much of this work was pulled together by his colleagues from his notes. Marxist thought also stirs up often intense political feelings for or against the communist world society that Marx advocated and

predicted would come to pass with the collapse of capitalism. Such feelings tend to cloud the assessment of his work itself. It is not possible, therefore, to give a definitive summary statement of Marx's work. The presentation here is very much an introduction to his ideas. It is also slanted toward sociological theory. Economists and political scientists would place their emphasis differently.

Historical Materialism

Historical materialism is a theory of history in which the material conditions of life are seen as ultimately determining the course of human history. For Marx, the most fundamental aspect of human existence is the absolute necessity for people to produce the means for their own **subsistence**. In order to survive, people must produce food and process it to the point where it is edible. In all but the rarest conditions of an ideal climate, people need to produce clothing and shelter and heat for warmth and for cooking.

They also need to produce the tools or technology required for such processes. Even the simplest hunting and gathering economies use surprisingly complex implements. People also organize themselves in complex ways to hunt and gather, to process and preserve food, to build shelters, and so on. As the means of providing for material needs become more complex—in herding economies, settled agriculture, trade and industry—so the ways in which people organize themselves around these activities change in both form and complexity.

Marx reasoned that the processes by which people meet their basic subsistence needs constitute the foundation of social organization. Any system of production entails a definite pattern of relations between people. Human production is by nature social. From simple economies to the most technologically complex industrial production, work is a co-operative activity. The way in which people co-operate varies with different **modes of production**, and this affects all other aspects of social life. **Relations of production** directly influence the prevailing family forms, political structures, religious ideas, and modes of thought. People experience social life as it is organized through relations of production. As they reflect on this experience, they generate the patterns of thought and ideas that come to prevail. For Marx, and theorists inspired by him, it makes sense to begin the analysis of economic and social life with the study of the prevailing mode of production and relations of production associated with it. All others aspects of social life can be understood as reflecting and responding to this underlying form of economic organization.

Class Relations and Modes of Production

Marx briefly traces historical changes in modes of production, or ways in which societies transform their material environment to meet subsistence needs. The

Karl Marx (1818–83).

simplest form is **primitive communism**, with production confined to hunting and gathering. Simple hand tools such as weapons, bowls, and digging sticks are easily made and shared. The key means of production—the flora and fauna in the surrounding territory—are accessible to all. No one has ownership rights to the terrain or its resources.

The second stage is ancient society or slavery, which already assumes a higher level of productivity within the society as a whole. There is sufficient surplus production that one class of people, the slave-owners, are supported by the labour of others without producing anything themselves. Slavery is associated with warfare: warring communities capture people from other societies and use them for drudgery and heavy manual labour.

The third stage, **feudalism**, is associated with settled agriculture. Here the predominant means of production are land and the draught animals, machinery, tools, seeds, and so on, required to work it. But this land is not communally shared as under primitive communism. It is owned by a hereditary class of nobles. Peasants or serfs, the people who actually work the land, inherit their position as labourers who are tied to the particular estate on which they are born. They are not free to leave it to work land elsewhere. In a sense, they are part of the property of an estate and are transferred with it when the estate is inherited by a new lord.

In Marxist theory, the two great classes under feudalism are nobles and serfs. Marx suggests that this two-class system tends to develop wherever the land is sufficiently fertile to produce a substantial surplus, over and above the needs of peasant producers. Powerful families gain control over the lands and extract a surplus from labourers in return for protecting them and providing them with whatever is necessary to work the land. Only land that is too poor to bear the double burden of labourers and landlord is likely to remain in the hands of small peasant producers.

Within the feudal mode of production, the majority of people still have direct access to the means of producing for their own subsistence needs. Serfs work plots of land and keep animals for themselves, but they are also required to work on the estates of the nobility. All the surplus production—that is, production over and above the subsistence needs of the labouring families—belongs not to the workers who produce it but to the owners of the estates. Serfs have no choice in this matter and no freedom to move away or to work only for themselves. The land on which they build homes and farm for their own needs is tied to the estates, and so are they themselves.

In the fourth mode of production, **capitalism**, a crucial change occurs in access to land. Serfs lose their hereditary rights to live and work on the land. Land becomes defined as the exclusive, private property of the owners of the estates. It is fenced off and used to produce cash crops, such as wheat and wool, for sale rather than to meet local subsistence needs. The families of serfs who have supported themselves for generations on the land are forcibly pushed off. They lose all direct access to the means of producing for their own subsistence needs. They have nothing left but their capacity to work, their labour power. They can survive only by selling their labour power for wages to whomever will hire them and by using the money they earn to purchase what they need.

This was the case in England on the eve of the Industrial Revolution. Some of the former serfs were able to get work as wage labourers on big farms, tending the cereal crops and the sheep. The rest found themselves destitute. They had no choice but to migrate to the cities and compete with each other to get whatever jobs were available, often working under wretched conditions in the factories that were slowly opening up. Over time, industrial technology and factories became the dominant means of production, with land becoming steadily less important. But the factories and the industrial technology, like the land, were privately owned by a relatively small class of wealthy people. The mass of landless people sold their labour power to the owners of the factories. Marx saw the transition from feudalism to capitalism as the most profoundly important change in the history of society. It brought fundamental changes to the nature of the relationships between people. The term *capitalism* refers to an economic system based on private ownership of **capital**, or the means of production, in the hands of a limited number of people. Capital comprises not only the funds and the stock of land, machinery, and materials with which a company or person enters into business, but also the accumulated wealth that is used to produce more capital. Those who do not own capital have to sell their labour power to survive. As we saw in chapter 2, people who sell their labour power are collectively referred to as the proletariat, or working class, while those who own the means of production and purchase the labour power of others are referred to as the bourgeoisie, or capitalists.

Marx foresaw a fifth stage, which he called **advanced communism**, where all the important means of production in a society—farmland, factories, technology, and so on—would be communally owned. Everyone would share access to them and would labour collectively according to their ability and share the communal produce according to their needs. Ideally, this mode of organizing production would take advantage of all the benefits of technological advances made under capitalism without the devastating costs of inequality, exploitation, and alienation that capitalism entails. But we are getting ahead of ourselves. We need to go back and explore what is so important and distinctive about capitalism as a mode of production, and why it seems in Marxist analysis to be both the key to progress and, at the same time, an inherently destructive system.

Capitalism and Technological Progress

Capitalism, more than any other mode of production, is associated with an ever-accelerating pace of technological change. It is uniquely geared toward the continual re-investment of profits in innovative technology to enhance labour productivity. All types of economies are oriented toward generating surpluses to make life easier or more comfortable for people. Only under capitalism is there a never-ending compulsion to invest the surplus or profit in accumulating productive forces, rather than to consume it in luxuries or leisure. It is this compulsion to invest, to accumulate capital, and to increase labour productivity that is the engine of economic development. But from where does this compulsion come? To

answer this question, we draw upon the work of the contemporary Marxist Robert Brenner (1977) who elaborates the unique relationship between capitalism and modernization.

Brenner begins with a critical look at Adam Smith's famous treatise, *The Wealth of Nations*. For Smith, the expansion of trade relations promotes division of labour, specialization, and hence rising productivity. Increasing food demands of large manufacturing centres stimulate rural production, which in turn induces the expansion of manufacturing to supply the countryside. These processes of self-sustaining growth are fuelled by the central values of capitalism: rational individuals in free competition in the marketplace, each striving to maximize profits.

The problem with this theory, suggests Brenner, is not that Adam Smith was wrong, but that he assumed too much. The core values of competition and profit maximization in the market presuppose structural conditions that Smith ignores. The principle condition is that producers are separated from the means of production; that is, from the ability to produce their own subsistence. Labour becomes a commodity that can be freely bought and sold. Subsistence has to be bought in the market. The means of production themselves, such as land and later factories and machines, have to be bought or rented in the market, for they are also commodities. It is only under these conditions, conditions specific to the capitalist mode of production, that people must trade in order to survive. Only then do money and transactions in the market become crucial. Concerns with competition and profit maximization follow from this. Brenner stresses that the use of money to buy commodities to make more money does not exist under other modes of production, such as slavery, feudalism, or small peasant landholdings.

In feudal economies, the direct producers are still tied to the land. On their own plots they produce crops that have use value for their own subsistence. The landlords can also provide their own means of subsistence through their command of the land and the labourers who work it for them. They market only what is left over after their own needs or wants are filled. The critical difference from capitalism is that neither serf nor lord depends upon markets for survival, and hence at a fundamental level it does not matter whether they beat the competition or maximize profits. There is no immediate pressure to innovate or to increase the productivity of labour.

Under this system, exploitation takes the form of squeezing serfs to extract more **absolute surplus**. In other words, the absolute amount that a particular labourer can produce in a particular period of time remains roughly constant, but more of what is produced is taken for sale in the market. This can be done by cutting the subsistence standards of the workers to have more left over for the market or by cutting the workers' leisure time to extend the length of the working day.

Under both slavery and feudalism, the direct producers themselves have no interest in the productive process. Slaves are maintained by the master; it is not in their interest to produce more for the owner to market. Serfs have their own plots for subsistence. It does not matter to them how much or how little landlords can sell. Under these conditions, when trade expands, it may result only in more intensive squeezing to extract more surplus. The long-term result may actually be a decline in production as serfs lack time to tend their own plots, and soils are exhausted.

Small peasant farmers who own their land are similarly independent of the market. Since they can produce their own means of subsistence, the pressures of competition and profit maximization are largely irrelevant. It is in their own interest to produce a variety of crops and animals to enhance their own sub-

sistence standards of living. They may sell surplus produce in the market to buy luxuries, but they are not dependent upon the market.

Brenner argues that, in order to establish capitalism, it is necessary to break the ability of producers to produce their own means of subsistence. They must be separated from land, so that they have to rent it for cash or buy it in the real estate market. Then they must earn money in the market to survive. Once farmers must pay rent or mortgages, Brenner argues, they must be concerned with competition in the market and with profit maximization. They have to make the average rate of profit on what they produce, because otherwise they will be unable to pay the going rents and will be thrown off the land. Hence, they have to increase their labour productivity to keep up with competitors, which forces them to be concerned with technological innovations.

Large landowners, cultivating their lands with the aid of wage labourers or rent-paying tenants, must also be concerned with labour productivity. They cannot squeeze the workers indefinitely to extract a greater absolute surplus for themselves, because the workers will go elsewhere. Hence, they must focus on **relative surplus**; that is, upon increasing the productivity of workers through **labour-saving technology**. If they do not, they will be unable to pay the going wage rate, and workers will leave. It is actually in the interest of the landowners to invest in their lands so that the tenants or labourers can produce more and pay higher rents.

Brenner concludes that both labour power and means of production must become commodities in the market for market forces to have the impact upon people that they do under capitalism. The ideology of market forces and profit maximization taken for granted by Adam Smith is the *effect* of this capitalist mode of production and not the *cause* of it. Capitalism presupposes some form of class struggle that forcibly separates producers from means of production. The history of capitalism has been, in this sense, the history of class struggle, taking various forms in different times and regions.

In Canada, the emergence of capitalism and the class struggles associated with it took a very different form than in Europe. As we have seen, capitalism presupposes a large class of people who have no direct access to any means of production and who are thus forced to sell their labour power. But such a class of people did not exist in Canada before the 1850s. It took active government policies and a peculiarly Canadian version of the class struggle to produce it.

Indigenous peoples in Canada practised a hunting and gathering mode of production, supplemented by horticulture and trade, including the fur trade with Europeans. They could support themselves and had little interest in becoming permanent wage labourers. They had to be forcibly driven from the land by settlers, the buffalo exterminated, and traditional northern hunting grounds disrupted by mining, exploration, and lumber companies, before they would begin to turn to wage labour for their livelihood.

Attracting immigrants to Canada was not difficult. Masses of displaced and landless people were produced by the enclosure movement and the capitalization of agriculture in Europe, as land belonging to the great estates was fenced off for keeping sheep or growing cereal crops, and the serfs were driven off. These landless people were willing, and indeed desperate, to seek a new life in North America. During the first half of the 1800s, tens of thousands of immigrants came to Canada every year from Ireland alone, fleeing the appalling conditions of enclosures, economic collapse, and famine generated by economic domination from England (Pentland 1959, 459). They joined the multitudes of immigrants leaving similarly wretched conditions throughout Europe. Mass immigration from China and other parts of Asia began toward the end of the nineteenth century. Few European immigrants had any intention of remaining wage labourers if they had any choice. What they found in Canada was a vast and sparsely populated land. So long as free or cheap land was available, the majority of immigrants preferred to acquire land and to work for themselves rather than for employers.

The problem, from the perspective of members of the business class, eager to develop capitalism in Canada, was how to staunch this outflow from the labour pool (Pentland 1959, 458–59). This was at the root of deliberate policies to make land so expensive that immigrants would be forced to labour for many years to earn even a down payment for a farm. Policies included monopolization of land for speculative purposes all across Canada and grants of huge tracts to absentee proprietors (Teeple 1972, 46). In one day in 1767, for example, the whole of Prince Edward Island was granted to a few dozen absentee landlords. Between 1760 and 1773, Nova Scotia had a population of about 13 000, but 5.4 million acres of the best land were given in grants to individuals and land companies based in Britain and the United States. Similar policies were followed in central Canada, sparking riots against land monopolies in 1794 and 1796. On the Prairies there were vast tracts of virgin land, and the Homestead Act granted 160 acres per settler. Yet even here the enormity of land speculation was eventually to stifle settlement and drive land prices far beyond the reach of the average immigrant.

Such policies were far from accidental. The Land Act of 1841 clearly expressed the objective of "creating a labour pool" by the two-pronged approach of promoting massive immigration and making land prohibitively expensive. The land speculators and the class of merchant industrialists who wanted a cheap wage-labour force, to build canals and railways and to work in factories, were the same people, and so indeed were members of the government! The wretched conditions of poverty and unemployment within the developing industrial cities of Canada from the mid-nineteenth century mirrored in many respects the conditions of early industrialization in Britain.

Alienation Under Capitalism

A central unifying theme in Marx's early philosophical writings is the concept of **alienation**. This refers to the dehumanizing character of social relations that emerge in their purest form under the capitalist mode of production. Marx saw people as, by nature, producers, engaged in creative relationship with their physical environment to transform it to their needs. They are also, by nature, social beings, co-operating together in this creative, productive process. People experience alienation from their human nature when this fundamental relationship to production is broken: when they are denied access to the basic means of producing for their own subsistence needs, when they are separated from the products of their labour so that what they create does not belong to them, and when their social relations with other producers are broken.

Life within hunting and gathering societies is often harsh, but it is not alienating. People relate to the natural world and to each other in a direct and immediate way in meeting their collective subsistence needs. Under feudalism, the tied labourers are exploited but are still not alienated in the same way as under capitalism. They still work with the land directly and collectively to produce what they consume. They are exploited to the extent that what they produce as labourers on the estates belongs not to them but to those who control the estates. All the surplus, beyond what is needed for their immediate subsistence, is expropriated. Under harsh landlords, the labourers themselves may be reduced to the meanest level of survival while the leisured, ruling class lives in luxury on what the workers produce. Yet still there is a human relationship between the two great classes of those who work the land and those who control it. Feudal lords acknowledge a hereditary obligation to sustain the families attached to their estates in the bad years as well as the good, and the labouring families have a hereditary right to use that land for their own needs, generation after generation.

It is only under capitalism that alienation is experienced in its fullest and harshest form, pervading every aspect of human relations. The root cause of alienation is separation of the mass of people from the means of production, leaving them unable to provide for themselves. Under capitalism all means of production, first land and then the developing factories and industrial capital, are owned by a tiny minority of people. They become private property, and the mass of people have no direct right to use them. The masses still retain their labour power but not the means to employ it for themselves. In order to survive, they must sell that labour power as a commodity on the labour market to others who will use it in the factories, or on the factory farms, for their own productive purposes in return for a cash wage. Almost everything that workers need to survive must be bought for cash in the marketplace. It is during times of high unemployment, or low demand for wage workers relative to supply, that the alienating character of capitalism is most immediately experienced. People can offer their labour power for sale, but there is nothing to oblige employers to buy it. Unwanted workers cannot use their labour power to meet their own subsistence needs because they have no access to any means of production, and they have no hereditary rights to share in what the society as a whole produces.

Under the capitalist mode of production, the reality of alienation is experienced in multiple ways. Workers are alienated from the products of their labour. Feudal serfs had a right to a share of the harvest, but factory workers have no claims whatever to their products. They are paid a wage, but everything they produce belongs to the factory owner. In effect, the harder they work and the more they produce, the more impoverished they become, because more and more of their creative effort is taken from them. Workers in developing industrial capitalism are also alienated from the work task itself, which has no intrinsic meaning or sense of purpose. Under such alienating conditions, Marx suggests, people avoid work. They are often forced to work under miserable conditions. People are reduced to appendages to machines; the work rhythms are set not by the changing seasons, or by the human body, but by the machines.

Bad as the conditions of work often were during early industrialization, and still are in many industries, they are a reflection rather than the cause of alienation experienced in social relations of production. The underlying problem is that, under capitalism, human relations of production are reduced to inhuman cash payment. Within the labour market, it is not a whole person who is bought and sold, as in slavery, but her or his labour power, the power to produce. Labour power is purchased by capitalists as needed, and laid off when not needed, with no further responsibilities to meet the subsistence needs of those who provide that labour power or of their dependants. The sole obligation of employers is to pay wages for labour power as and when they need it. People no longer co-operate with each other as full human beings in the production process. Marx suggests that in the capitalist exchange of labour power for wages, the employers are themselves as alienated as the workers, for they too are cut off from human social relations. Private property and money dominate their existence.

It is precisely these inhuman relations of production that make possible the classical economics concepts of *economic men, profit maximization*, and *market forces*. In addition, these relations encourage the functionalist conception of human relations as emotionless, narrow, and calculated by market attributes.

The Model of Capitalism as an Economic System

So far in this chapter we have alluded to capitalism or to the capitalist system without describing this system itself in detail. But it is the actual workings of capitalism, its internal dynamics and its contradictions, that occupied Marx's central attention in all his later work. His three volumes on *Capital* comprise an extensive analysis of the capitalist system, and his model still forms the basis of the contemporary theory of political economy. A condensed version of his elaborate model is laid out below.

Certain key terms are useful in understanding Marx's model of a capitalist economy. A **commodity** is anything produced for exchange, and not for use by the producer. The production of commodities presupposes a division of labour. It is only as people become specialized in distinct occupations, and cease to produce everything that they need for themselves, that exchange becomes important. **Exchange value** refers to the amount of human labour time that went into the production of a commodity. It measures a social relation between producers. As people exchange what they have produced, they are exchanging the time and skill that each has contributed to the product. **Abstract labour time** refers to labour in general, to the average amount of time that it takes to produce a given commodity in a society with a given level of technology and knowledge.

The Theory of Exchange

The **theory of exchange** is fundamental to Marx's analysis. He begins from the observation that people in every society must labour to produce goods. Commodities exchange in definite proportions in the market. It is usually possible, for example, to calculate roughly how many pairs of shoes a cobbler would have to sell or barter in order to buy a wool coat or a given amount of firewood. Each such commodity also absorbs a definite amount of human labour time. From these basic propositions, Marx derives his **labour theory of value**. The theory posits that the exchange value or price of a commodity is determined not by the laws of supply and demand proposed by classical economists, but by the amount of labour that goes into the commodity.

For Marx, the exchange ratio between commodities is the labour-time ratio. In other words, in order to calculate the true exchange value of one commodity, such as shoes, for another commodity, such as firewood, one has to calculate how much total time went into raising the cow, getting the hide, tanning it into leather, and fashioning it into shoes, compared with the time it takes to care for trees to the appropriate age, cut the timber, saw it into logs, and take them to market. In using labour time as the fundamental measure of value, Marx is not suggesting that lazy people who take twice as long as others to do something will thereby be able to exchange their production for twice as much, or that people who make things quickly will get less. What counts, over the economy as a whole, is how long it takes, on average, to produce commodities, given the prevailing level of technology and skills. Marx refers to this as **socially necessary labour time**; it averages out lazy, unskilled, and unusually quick people. Skilled labour includes teaching and learning time in the calculation of socially necessary labour time.

Consider a simple example of exchange within a hunting society. Suppose, in a given community at a given time of year, it takes the average hunter one hour to catch a deer and two hours to trap a beaver. Fair exchange would then be two deer for one beaver. This exchange has nothing to do with the nature of the commodities themselves: the size of the animal, the amount of meat, the relative utility of deer skins over beaver pelts. It is based on the amount of human labour time it takes to catch them. If hunters could not get two deer for one beaver, they would pretty quickly stop "wasting time" catching beaver and start catching deer instead. People would start trapping beaver again when they were sufficiently scarce, or people wanted them enough, that the labour time spent would be compensated by what the beaver could be exchanged for. The classical relations of supply and demand are thus balanced by time. Individual producers decide how best to allocate their labour time so that what they produce in the course of a day's labour will exchange for the equivalent of a day's labour by other people.

In the traditional exchange process money may be used, but only as a convenient mechanism for keeping tallies on exchanges between many different people, particularly when spread out over time. The fundamental exchange is still one useful commodity for another.

Capitalist exchange entails a subtle but extremely important difference from this traditional exchange process. The basis of exchange is not one commodity for another, but some money for more money by means of a commodity. The objective is not to trade useful items, but to increase the amount of money one started with. Money as such has no use value. One cannot eat money or dress up in it. We want money because we can exchange it for something else. This fact itself makes the desire for money very different from desire for useful commodities.

There is a limit to our desire for such commodities. We only want so much food, so much clothing, and so on, and we then lose interest in getting any more. Money is not like that. There is no intrinsic limit to how much we want. Desire for money is, in principle, insatiable. It is this desire that drives capitalist exchange.

Labour Commodity and Surplus Value

In capitalist exchange, labour itself is treated as a commodity. As we have already seen, the means of production are owned by a few people, while labour power is owned by others. As a commodity, labour has a value and, like every other commodity, that value is the labour time needed to produce it. This is averaged out as the **subsistence wage**. This value includes not only the cost of maintaining the adult labourer at an acceptable standard of living, but the cost of replacing that labour through raising and educating children. Capitalists use money wages to purchase the commodity of labour power with the objective of using it to make more money.

In Marxist theory, profit comes from surplus value. The only way for the capitalist to make a profit is for labourers to produce goods of more value than the subsistence value of their labour time, for which they are paid in wages. Marx argues that profit cannot arise through dishonest or underhanded practices. Nor does it merely come from charging more for given commodities. If all commodities, labour power included, were sold at double their previous price, nobody would benefit.

The one place in the system where profit can routinely be made is in the use of labour power. Human labour can produce more than its own value. The exchange value of labour power, expressed in the subsistence wage, is the time it takes to produce and maintain the worker. The exchange value of a commodity is the average time it takes a worker, with a given technology, to make that commodity. The goal of the capitalist is to maximize the productivity of labour power for a given subsistence wage; that is, to maximize the gap between the exchange value of the labour power and the exchange value of the commodities produced. This gap constitutes **surplus value**. For example, if in six hours a worker can produce a commodity with an exchange value equivalent to her or his daily wage, then any commodities produced outside of those six hours produce surplus value for the capitalist. The value of the time expended in producing the additional commodities accrues to the capitalist, not to the workers.

The gap between a day's wages and the resale value of all commodities produced by a worker in a day constitutes, in principle, an objective measure of the degree of exploitation of labour. The actual calculation of surplus value is more complicated than this. Capitalists have to spend money to buy or replace machines and materials, to rent the factory, and to satisfy their own subsistence needs. Surplus value arises over and above these socially necessary exchange values.

If the objective of production were solely to provide useful commodities for people, there would be no problem with hiring labour and then distributing everything produced. But this is not the objective of capitalist exchange. The objective is to make money, to maximize surplus value so that the largest possible amount of money comes back to the owner of capital.

Competition is crucial in the process of creating surplus value. Commodities exchange for the average time it takes to produce them in a given market, with a given level of technology. The goal of the capitalist is always to better this average labour time—to get more than the average amount of commodities for a given subsistence wage bill. Those who can better the

average rate can make large profits by having more commodities for exchange at the going rate or by undercutting competitors and controlling the market. Those who only make the average rate may break even, but they will not make much profit. Those whose level of production falls below the average rate will go bankrupt. They will have insufficient commodities to sell at the going price to cover their higher-than-average labour time costs.

How can individual capitalists maximize surplus value? Logically there are only three ways to do so. First, the capitalist can extend the working day, trying to harness more and more of the workers' energy. During the early stages of capitalism in Britain, workdays often extended to sixteen and eighteen hours, work weeks to six or seven days, even for children in factories and coal mines. Ultimately, however, this became self-defeating. Workers reach such a point of exhaustion that they can no longer produce anything. Pushed to the extreme, people die. Long before this point is reached, overworked people become markedly slower and less efficient so that overall production actually falls.

The second possibility is depressing real wages. This can be done either by raising prices while wages stay the same, by reducing actual wages while other commodity prices remain the same, or by some combination of lower wages and higher prices. This process also has natural limits. If wages drop so low relative to prices that workers cannot meet subsistence needs or feed and educate their children, people collapse and the labour power available drops both in quantity and quality. Workers are also not totally passive under such conditions, and employers can expect strikes and sabotage if they push these policies too far. As Marx acknowledged, there tends to be an acceptable minimum standard of living for a particular community of people, and employers cannot easily push workers below this level.

Individual capitalists cannot indefinitely drive their workers harder than the average, or pay them less than the average wage, because workers will quit their jobs and go to work elsewhere. The exception to this rule occurs wherever workers have limited mobility, as in peripheral regions where unemployment is high or in Third World countries. In such locations, workers can be exploited more than the average. But there are still absolute limits on how far even these workers can be pushed.

There is a third option that is much more important than the other two because it is, in principle, limitless. That option is to strive to increase the productivity of labour power through labour-saving technology. Machines are critically important for their usefulness for increasing the productivity of labour power. For a given number of working hours, and at a given level of wages, the proportion of surplus value goes up. In principle, if the introduction of a new machine doubles a worker's output, it would be possible to cut working hours per week by 25 percent and give a 25 percent pay raise to the workers, and still increase profits by about 50 percent once the new machine is paid for.

This process can work in several ways. New technology may speed up production while using the same workers. Alternatively, the technology may simplify the production process so that the training time required to produce workers is reduced, hence reducing the exchange value or wage costs of the labour power needed. Innovations that improve the quality of commodities are another way of improving the average rate of production. Other producers would require far more time to create a product of the same quality without the technology.

At first glance, it looks as though everybody wins under this scenario. Workers get a better standard of living while capitalists make more profits. In the short run this is correct. However, in the long run there is a very serious problem: the process becomes self-defeating. In fact, Marx saw this process as the fundamental contradiction in capitalism and predicted that it would eventually bring about the collapse of the system.

Law of the Falling Rate of Profit

The problem begins from the fact that capitalists are competing among themselves for profits. The first ones to introduce new labour-saving technology can make large profits, for their commodities are cheaper to produce and hence they are able to undersell competitors in the marketplace. Other capitalists must rapidly introduce similar technology to keep their production costs down, or they will go bankrupt. Smaller or less efficient capitalists, who cannot afford to purchase the new technology, find themselves unable to compete in the marketplace. They have to drop their prices in order to sell their commodities, but they are unable to drop their costs of production. Eventually they become uncompetitive, go bankrupt, and drop out of the market. Those capitalists who remain can buy up the bankrupt person's machines and factories cheaply and can expand their market share with their high-volume, low-cost commodities.

Over time, however, profits start to drop. Eventually all the capitalists remaining in the market are using the new technology. They are all achieving the new rate of production. This becomes the standard or average labour time that sets the exchange value of the commodity. The average commodity price drops to this real exchange value, and nobody makes much profit. The economy will stagnate until some new technological breakthrough permits innovative capitalists, once again, to better the average rate of production and raise profits.

A further problem is that, as mechanization increases, capitalists must spend relatively more money on machines than on wages. Since profits are made on the latter, the actual rate of profit starts to fall. The new technology must increase productivity markedly over the older method of production for the capitalist to keep ahead.

Crisis of Overproduction

If this were the only problem with labour-saving technology, it might not be that serious, but there is a more serious problem associated with it. As the technological race increases, machines replace labour at an ever greater rate. The result is unemployment. Unemployed people are not the responsibility of the capitalist. The problem for capitalists is that unemployed people do not have the money needed to purchase the commodities that flood the market. Capitalists find themselves with surplus production that they cannot sell. In this situation, they are forced to operate more and more below capacity but, at the same time, they must make still greater efforts to develop technological innovations that will cut production costs so that they can sell more cheaply. They thus generate still more unemployment.

Labour-saving technology may increase productivity and so make possible an increase in wages in the short run. Expanding production will also give rise to increased demand for labour power, which will work to raise wages above the real subsistence value of labour power. Rising wages, however, reduce surplus value, and so generate a reaction. It becomes potentially more profitable to invest in more labour-saving technology to displace high-priced labour. As unemployment increases, the bargaining power of workers collapses. They start to undercut each other to get jobs, and wages start to fall, either in an absolute amount or relative to rising prices. People displaced by machines form a **lumpenproletariat**, a **reserve army of labour**, and their competition depresses wages still further. In the long run, Marx suggests, these processes work to force down the average wage across the market to subsistence value. Workers may make temporary gains in their standard of living, but these gains will always be insecure and threatened by the prospect of technological change that will make their work obsolete.

Contradictions of Capitalism

When all these processes are combined, the internal contradictions of capitalism look formidable. There is the tendency toward a falling rate of profit, as expensive technology replaces labour. Secondly, there is the tendency toward increasing concentration of capital and the resulting **polarization of classes** as members of the petite bourgeoisie are bankrupted and join the proletariat. Thirdly, there is the tendency toward the increasing poverty of the masses as unemployment forces wages down. Fourthly, there is the crisis of overproduction as unemployed and poorly paid people lack the money to purchase commodities. The remaining capitalists are driven to invent still more labour-saving technology to push down the costs of production in order to undercut competitors in an ever-tighter market. In the process, they produce yet more unemployment, tighter profit ratios, more bankruptcies, and a still bigger glut of commodities that people cannot afford to buy.

In these multiple ways, the competitive relations that develop between the two great classes of workers and capitalists, and among capitalists themselves in the marketplace, fetter the productive potential of new technology. Marx predicted that these internal contradictions within capitalism would generate an endless cycle of crises, of booms and slumps characterized by bankruptcies, unemployment, and overproduction. In the long run, the system would collapse due to its own internal problems. Marx expected, however, that social revolution would forcibly overthrow the system long before it reached this stage. Marx foresaw the possibility of a new form of economic relations that would not be based

on competition for profits and so would avoid all the internal contradictions of capitalism. New technology could be communally owned and worked to full capacity, with the products shared communally. As less and less labour time was needed to satisfy people's desire for useful products, relative to their desire for more free time, the portion of the day spent working could drop. In principle, people could work in the mornings, relax and have fun in the afternoons, and gather for intellectual, creative, or social activities in the evenings.

Counteracting Factors

An unavoidable question arises in relation to Marx's analysis of the capitalist system. If his theories were correct, why have his predictions not come to pass? How is it that capitalism remains the dominant mode of production a century after he predicted its demise?

Critics of Marx's thesis have pointed to extensive empirical evidence that seems to contradict his predictions. Shareholder capitalism appears to have countered the tendency toward the concentration of capital foreseen by Marx. Twentieth-century workers are vastly better off than Marx ever foresaw, in some cases enjoying a standard of living that rivals that of the middle classes. The rise of the middle classes, in particular, appears to contradict Marx's law of the increasing polarization of classes. Democratic politics, the welfare state, and the organization of trade unions have also served to ameliorate the exploitative aspects of capitalism. From this perspective, capitalism appears to have weathered the crises.

Theorists within the Marxist tradition have countered these claims by pointing out that many of the crises that Marx foresaw do plague capitalist economies. The ultimate crisis, they argue, has been avoided so far by a series of counteracting factors. These serve to soften, but do not resolve, the internal contradictions of capitalism.

Central among such factors has been the accelerating rate of technological advance, which has staved off the falling rate of profits. Labour productivity has continued to rise with the aid of computers, robots, fossil fuels, and nuclear energy. An important effect of this accelerated innovation has been the cheapening of the costs of the machines themselves, as labour productivity has risen in heavy industry. Machines can be mass produced in shorter periods of labour time. Some theorists suggest that bankruptcies and mergers have also significantly reduced the costs of heavy industry. Tax write-offs and other state benefits also help. Technological developments have also led to an explosion in the variety of cheap, mass-

produced consumer goods available, which has helped to reduce the intensity of cut-throat competition to sell commodities. In addition, huge military expenditures in the centres of capitalist development have staved off the crisis of overproduction. Weapons constitute a staggering proportion of production. They are bought and blown up or thrown away as obsolete. Newer weapons are then purchased, and production in war industries is maintained.

The worldwide expansion of capitalism, through the economic domination that corporate interests in wealthy countries have been able to exert over underdeveloped countries, has meant that the worst contradictions of capitalism have been shifted from the

Some Marxists argue that the permanent war economy has staved off the crisis of overproduction within capitalist centres.

centres of capitalism to the Third World. Here multinational corporations have been able to protect profits through cheap labour and long working hours. These countries also provide sources of cheap raw materials and at the same time provide expanded markets for manufactured goods.

Within the developed centres, revolt has been held off by the lure of mass produced consumer goods and by a process of legitimation referred to as **ideological hegemony**. This is the capacity of the dominant class to rule not only by control over means of production but also by control over ideas. This control is exercised through such agencies as education, religion, and the mass media. When Marx dismissed religion as the opiate of the masses, he had in mind precisely the ways in which religion has been used to legitimate the social order and gross inequalities in wealth as manifestations of God's will. This legitimation is evident in a verse from the nineteenth-century Anglican hymn "All Things Bright and Beautiful" (Himelfarb and Richardson 1979, 53).

> The rich man in his castle
> The poor man at his gate
> God made them high and lowly
> And each in his estate.

In addition to legitimating extremes of wealth and poverty, religion also encourages the poor to endure earthly misery by focussing on their reward after death. The biblical aphorism that it is easier for a camel to pass through the eye of a needle than for a rich man to enter the kingdom of heaven, for example, helps to make poor people more content with their lot.

God and big business are still closely associated, as we have seen in the discussion of the Protestant ethic and the spirit of capitalism in chapter 6. But as religion loses its hold over everyday life for many people, other powerful influences take its place. The state plays a fundamental role in the legitimation of capital. The political arena

and welfare state policies keep the potential for revolt in check but do not resolve the fundamentally alienating and exploitative character of capitalism. The relations between capitalism and welfare state policies will be explored in greater detail in subsequent chapters.

The Base–Superstructure Debate: Materialism versus Idealism

The implications of the Marxist analysis of capitalism as a mode of production go to the roots of all social science analysis. Marx insists that the prevailing mode of production in a society fundamentally determines the structure of relations between people and the superstructure of prevailing ideas. In effect, Marx argues that in order to understand social relations, ideas, religion, social institutions, indeed all aspects of the culture of a society, we must ground our analysis in the study of relations of production. Theorists in all the subdisciplines of the social sciences have been struggling with or against this challenge ever since.

Marx's early philosophical writings grew out of the philosophical traditions of his day and yet profoundly transformed their meaning. He acknowledged a great intellectual debt to the eighteenth-century philosopher Hegel, and yet at the same time he claimed to have reversed Hegel's idea of the causal relations between social structures and ideas. As we saw in chapter 6, Hegel argues that the human spirit is the guiding force of history. The essence of what it is to be truly human is to strive constantly toward a better future, toward perfection and the ultimate merging of humanity with God. It is this spirit that distinguishes people from other animals. The unified expression of the collective ideal, over and above individual selfishness, is, at any particular stage in history, embodied by the state. For Hegel, the state is the sphere of universal, rational, orderly life.

Marx reverses this causal relation. He argues that it is not human consciousness that determines our existence, but our social existence that determines our consciousness (Marx [1859] 1975, 452). This reversal brought the study of society out of the realm of metaphysics and into the arena of social science. In his study *The German Ideology*, written between 1845 and 1847, Marx develops these insights. He argues that the social relations of production form the **base** that determines the character of all other aspects of culture, including thought itself. Intellectual systems, religion, legal and political structures, all constitute **superstructure**. They develop out of and reflect economic relations and can only be understood by reference to their economic roots.

Marx praised the work of the philosopher Feuerbach for raising a similar criticism against traditional Christian theology. Feuerbach insisted that the starting point in philosophy had to be real people in their material, physical context. He argued that the concept of "god" as the ideal was really the projection of human self-awareness. There is not some pre-existing spiritual entity or god that creates humanity; rather humanity creates god. Feuerbach believed that people become alienated from themselves when their own projected ideal is held over them as if it were some external force, ordering and judging their actions.

Marx agreed, but he went further than Feuerbach. He asked why people came to conceive of god in this alienating form, as something set above and against them. Marx's answer was that people experience alienation in their everyday lives. Powerful forces are indeed set above them, and they are indeed utterly dependent for their very existence on feudal lords or capitalist market forces. It is little wonder that the mass of people would accept such an alienating feudal vision of the "lord god," or that the ruling intelligentsia among the aristocracy and the clergy would propound such doctrines. Marx further emphasized that merely pointing out the relationship between the lord god and feudalism, or the alienating character of the conception of god, as Feuerbach did, would accomplish nothing with respect to changing people's vision. So long as their actual material experience of life was alienating, so too would be their vision of god. One would have to change the material base before one could hope to change the thinking of the mass of people. A few intellectuals might adopt different views, but that was only a reflection of the fact that intellectuals commonly experienced totally different material conditions of existence from the mass of people.

Classical Economics as Ideology

Marx turned the same critical eye on theories of classical economics. He did not so much argue with their ideas as question how the actual material experiences of people in their economic relations would give rise to the kind of ideas promoted by classical economists.

The classical economics of Marx's day, exemplified in the works of Smith, Ricardo, and Malthus, sought to explain the workings of capitalism in terms of abstract market forces. These economists built models of economic systems based on concepts like *supply-demand curves*, *prices*, *wages*, *commodities*, and *markets*. They conceptualized the actions and decisions of "rational economic men" as dictated by the workings of the market. The basic explanatory tools of market-driven capitalist economics are provided by the exchange of commodities in the market and how the balance of supply and demand determines price. These market forces, which govern relations between goods, seem to function in terms of laws of their own. Together these forces make up the

invisible hand of the market, an external reality to which people must adapt.

Marx himself was not concerned with whether classical economics models accurately described market relations. He was well aware that categories such as wages, commodities, capital, profits, and markets were part of real-life relations. The problem with classical economics is that they assume precisely what needs to be explained. We cannot simply take for granted that it is human nature to maximize profit. People only begin to behave like this when they have lost all direct access to the means of providing for their own subsistence needs. They then have to buy and sell labour power for wages and purchase everything they need in the commodity market. It is not abstract market forces that determine such behaviour, but very real relations of class struggle between people. All this gets covered up when we focus on market forces doing things to people.

The classical economists' vision of abstract market forces is very similar to the theological vision of an abstract god that was criticized by Feuerbach. Both are external to the lives of people, acting over them, doing things to them, and punishing or rewarding them depending on their behaviour. Marx dismisses these supposedly explanatory models of market forces and exchange of commodities as **commodity fetishism**. A **fetish** is an inanimate object that is worshipped for its magical powers. Commodities become fetishes in economics. Things appear to rule people instead of people producing things. Exchange is regarded as relations between things, instead of relations between people. Abstract typifications are treated as causal agents while people become objects, their lives determined by the properties of things. Inanimate objects cannot possibly do anything by themselves, and neither can abstract ideas like market forces. Yet people come to think that their human lives are being directed by such forces.

Marx asks why people should create and accept such abstract systems as an explanation for human actions. There are two kinds of answers. The first is that classical economics functions as an ideology for the bourgeoisie, a means not to see what is actually going on. The motions of an invisible hand and market forces offer very powerful legitimation for capitalism as an economic system. It appears to be rational, inevitable, logical. The system works in a certain way, and it is irrational to fight against it or to try to interfere with the invisible hand. All the underlying forces of alienation, exploitation, and class struggle disappear from the model. Capitalists actually look like benefactors.

The second half of the answer concerns why the classical economists' version of the economic system should be so readily accepted. The answer Marx gives is that it completely fits the lived experience of an alienated reality for the mass of people. Their lives are indeed experienced as controlled by abstract forces like labour market supply and demand, and wages and prices. The categories of thought fit the actual social relations of experience. No amount of intellectual argument that this experience is illusory will alter the fact that this is how people experience their lives. It takes a major effort to get underneath this and see the human processes going on. In order to do away with the illusion, we have to change the entire system of the relations of production that produces it. Hence, Marx states that "so far the philosophers have only interpreted the world in various ways. The point, however, is to change it" (Marx [1845] 1975, 5).

In *The German Ideology*, Marx explains at some length what he means by *ideology*. It is not a matter of having opinions or values or class bias. It is the way in which real relations between people, including alienation, exploitation, power, and so on, are covered up by abstract logical models, like abstract notions of god judging people from on high or invisible hands controlling people. The creation of an ideology involves three distortions or tricks. First, real data, real experiences are noted. Secondly, they are embedded in abstract conceptual schemes. Finally, these abstract models are treated as causal forces, and imposed as explanations for behaviour. The original relations between people are mystified, covered up. This is a powerful way of controlling people because the logical models do indeed seem to fit the original data. People believe them and become obedient to them. It is much more effective than if the feudal lords, or capitalists, or members of the ruling class generally, came right out and stated their class bias (Smith 1974a, 45–46).

Marx argues that capitalism, more than any other social form, creates this illusory appearance, because its survival depends on it. Once it becomes really obvious that all the suffering caused by abstract market forces is only a reflection of the concentration of private ownership of the means of production, and the mass of people's forced separation from it, the entire edifice is likely to totter. Marx even goes so far as to suggest that once capitalism is overthrown and replaced by the openly visible, communal sharing of access to the means of production, social science itself will wither away. It would be unnecessary, for people could directly see for themselves what was going on (Cohen 1980).

Dialectical Method

In the meantime, Marx tried to develop a method of research that would help to expose the processes underlying human history and immediate experience. He borrowed the notion of **dialectical method** from Hegel and adapted it to his own purposes. In Hegel's philosophy, the dialectical method is a form of testing and developing logical arguments by first exploring the contradictions that may be present in a particular argu-

ment and then devising solutions. Hegel argues that the advancement of human knowledge reflects the recurrent cycles of **thesis**, **antithesis**, and **synthesis**. The **thesis** consists of any philosophical system or theory. Its **antithesis** comprises the logical inconsistencies, internal problems, and unexplained anomalies within the system of thought. These problems force philosophers to attempt to resolve them. **Synthesis** is achieved with the integration of a new system of ideas that resolves the old problems. This provides a new starting point or thesis, until new problems become obvious. The dialectical processes of antithesis and synthesis continue until perfection is reached.

Marx applied this dialectical method to material conditions to arrive at his theory of **dialectical materialism**. For him the thesis consists of the existing organization of production. The antithesis comprises the internal contradictions. These are the tensions and practical inconsistencies between productive potential of a given means and how people organize their productive relations. The synthesis breaks these contradictions by establishing new forms of organization capable of unleashing the full potential of the emerging means of production.

In relation to the historical processes of his own time, Marx identified feudalism as the original thesis. It is a mode of economic production that endured for centuries and gave basic security of subsistence to all its members. But it was destined to give way under its own internal contradictions. The productive potential of feudalism was stifled by its social relations. Tied labourers, who were responsible for production, had no incentive to produce more than was necessary for their own subsistence, and those who controlled the estates had little incentive to invest in them. The system could only expand by squeezing the absolute surplus, to the point that production itself was threatened.

Capitalism seemed to resolve the contradictions inherent in feudalism. For all its faults, capitalism succeeded in breaking feudal restraints. Productive potential expanded exponentially under competitive capitalism, and labourers were freed from their hereditary bondage. It was because of this tremendous liberating potential of capitalism that Marx believed it was a necessary intermediate step between feudalism and communism.

When Lenin declared the communist revolution a fait accompli in Russia in 1917, a great many committed Marxist revolutionaries had their doubts. Most of what is now the Soviet Union was trapped in a backward feudal mode of production, with only a tiny and mostly foreign bourgeoisie. Lenin's Marxist critics argued that it would be impossible to advance from feudalism to communism without the intermediate stage of capitalism. They were partially right. The struggle toward economic development in the Soviet Union has been long and hard and has involved severe internal repression that Marx had not foreseen. Supporters argue that the system will yet come out ahead, without advanced capitalism's inherent fetters on production. Critics argue that communism has internal contradictions and restrictions of its own, particularly with respect to bureaucracy.

In any case, while capitalism may have broken the fetters of feudalism, it has its own internal problems and contradictions. Like feudalism, its productive potential is stifled by the relations of production. These relations generate the inherent tendencies toward concentration of capital, falling rate of profit, crises of overproduction, and increasing misery among the masses.

The new synthesis that Marx foresaw was advanced communism. Communal, shared ownership of the means of advanced industrial production would finally remove the shackles on the productive potential of capitalism. There would no longer be a class

of economically dependent labourers separated from the means of production and vulnerable to unemployment and poverty with every advance of labour-saving technology. Production could truly take off. There would be no crisis of overproduction until all the wants of all the people had been satiated. Then the system could settle down at this desired production level with the minimum input of labour, using the best labour-saving technology available. According to Marx, perfection would be reached.

The Class Struggle

This perfection, however, would not be achieved automatically. Marx did not posit an abstract evolutionary scheme that would inevitably come to pass. Rather, he saw a dynamic process in which class struggle would necessarily play a central role. As we have seen with respect to both Europe and Canada, the development of capitalism was a violent process in which capitalists overthrew the existing relations of production and asserted their private property rights, which drove producers from the land and into the position where they had to sell their labour power for wages. It would take a similar struggle to break private ownership of the productive forces developed under capitalism.

Inevitably, Marx felt, the impetus for the struggle would have to come from the mass of working people most disadvantaged by the existing relations of production. But this too would not be automatic. Before the struggle could begin, people would have to see through the ideology of rational market forces. They would have to understand the relations of production, and their own position within these relations, and see the potential for change. It would be the role of radical intellectuals to educate working people in these areas. But intellectual revelation alone would not be sufficient. Capitalist contradictions would first have to reach the point where they became part of the immediately experienced reality of the people so that experience and theory would connect. Then the class struggle might seriously begin.

It is human action through class struggle that makes history, but this action is embedded in and structured by material conditions. Marx ([1869] 1935, 13) said that "Men make their own history, but they do not make it just as they please; they do not make it under circumstances chosen by themselves, but under circumstances directly found, given and transmitted from the past."

The concept of class in Marxist theory refers to position in relation to the means of production. It varies with the prevailing mode of production. There are no classes in simple hunting and gathering economies because all people share the same direct access to the common lands on which they depend. Under feudalism, the two great classes are the aristocratic families who control the vast estates and the serfs who work this land. Relatively minor classes in this system include peasants who own and work their own small farms, without any additional tied labour, and the small class of tradespeople and artisans who own their own means of production. Within the capitalist mode of production, the two great classes are the bourgeoisie, who own the means of production, and the proletariat, who have no direct access to any means of production and must sell their labour power for wages.

In any particular historical setting there may be several intermediate classes that are no longer prominent in relations of production. The petite bourgeoisie comprises people who own small amounts of capital and can work for themselves but are not major employers of wage labour. Rentiers comprise a marginal class earning income from rents charged on real estate. Marx predicted that as capitalism developed, the intermediate rentier and petit bourgeois classes would disappear, leaving only the bourgeoisie and proletariat, including a subclass of lum-

penproletariat. The lumpenproletariat comprises unemployed people who have no property. They are the reserve army of capitalism, the poorest people who can only hope to find employment in rare periods of extreme labour shortage.

Within contemporary capitalism, housewives comprise the largest subclass of lumpenproletariat. Normally they have no direct access to any means of production, and they depend upon their husbands' wages for survival. They form a reserve army of labour on which capitalists can draw in time of expanding production and labour shortage and then drop when not needed. Large numbers of housewives, for example, found jobs suddenly open to them during World War II when regular workers were siphoned off into armies. These women found themselves pushed out of the labour market in an equally sudden fashion once the war was over and the soldiers had returned. As Connelly (1978) describes it, women are "last hired and first fired." Their very existence serves to weaken the bargaining power of those who sell their labour power and so keep wages down.

Marx drew a clear distinction between the situation of people as a **class-in-itself** and their conscious realization of their situation as a **class-for-itself**. People who share the same relationship to the means of production constitute a class-in-itself. Only when such people become conscious of this shared class position, and act collectively in their class interests, do they come to form a class-for-itself. This *class consciousness* is a necessary starting point for revolutionary social action.

Contemporary Marxist Theory

Marx is such a complex theorist, and the implications of his work are so far-reaching, that it is simply not possible to sum his theory up in a way that would satisfy all contemporary Marxists. There is no single body of theory, even in the discipline of sociology, that now constitutes "Marxist theory." Marxist-inspired theoretical orientations have developed in several very different directions, especially in recent years, with much internal dissent and debate. Only the flavour of these alternative perspectives can be introduced here.

Marxist Structuralism

The dominant perspective in Marxist theory is inspired by Marx's model of the capitalist system and its internal dynamics and contradictions. It takes from Marx his central observation that all social relations are determined, in the last instance, by the mode of production. The model of the capitalist system thus provides an explanatory framework that can account for specific characteristics of contemporary capitalist societies. This general orientation tends to be loosely referred to as **structuralism** or **Marxist structuralism**. It parallels in some important respects the traditional structural-functional approach that dominates North American sociology. Its power as an approach for analysing contemporary Canadian society is explored in the next chapter.

The Social Construction of Reality and Destructuralism

An alternative theoretical approach developing out of Marxist thought gives greater emphasis to the "humanist Marx" and to his philosophical writings. His model of the workings of the capitalist system provides a useful, practical device that helps to focus questions about what is going on, but it does not itself constitute an explanation for human behaviour. Dorothy Smith, a leading Canadian proponent of this alternative form of Marxist theory, argues that when the model of the capitalist system is imposed as an explanatory scheme, the model itself begins to function as ideology. Taken to its extreme, structuralism comes close to doing what Marx criticized the abstract models of classical economics for doing; that is, giving

causal force to abstract concepts and reducing people to cogs in the system's machinery. Marx himself insisted that we have to begin with what people actually do, in their immediate material situation of trying to make a living, and how they come to account for this experience to themselves. The immediate practical activities of people produce the patterns that social scientists subsequently come to perceive as "the workings of capitalism." According to this perspective, no god is giving orders, no invisible hand is running things. Whatever gets done is done by people.

As noted above, Marx said that it is people who make history, but not in the circumstances of their own choosing. Marxists concerned with the **social construction of reality** or **social constructionists**, would agree that the *actions* of people warrant greater causal emphasis in the creation of history than the *circumstances*, because it is the actions of people over time that create the circumstances in which and against which people formulate responses.

The Marxist historian E.P. Thompson (1978b) has come out strongly against the structuralist, economic determinist versions of Marxism in history. He insists that, in a Marxist approach, class does not constitute a *thing* but a *process*.

> Classes do not exist as separate entities; look around, find an enemy class, and then start to struggle. On the contrary, people find themselves in a society structured in determined ways, . . . they identify points of antagonistic interest, they commence to struggle around these issues and in the process of struggling they discover themselves as classes, they come to know this discovery as class-consciousness (Thompson 1978a, 149).

A case study by Marx himself, *The Eighteenth Brumaire of Louis Bonaparte* ([1869] 1935), is an excellent example of this approach, showing the complex and subtle processes through which class relations began to take on form as people struggled with the immediate political circumstances in which they found themselves.

The economy, like all other aspects of social life, consists only of the actions of people and the actual social relations between them. Dorothy Smith has developed a method of examining in intimate detail, as well as over the broad picture, exactly what people do in their everyday working lives to produce the reality of capitalism in all its dimensions. She illustrates this approach studying the work of newspaper reporters (Smith 1981, 329–34). According to Tuchman (1978), reporters organize their work as follows: an event happens, it is typified as news, and reporters take an appropriate response. If it is *spot news*, they just go quickly to the scene to observe and report the event. On the other hand, if it is *developing news*, they take a series of actions to find out more information about the event and the issues that seem to be associated with it. It seems as though the kind of news event dictates the appropriate response from the reporter.

Smith, however, suggests that we might try to look at this process in the reverse order. It is not the kind of news that dictates what reporters do, but what reporters do that produces the pattern that we subsequently come to recognize as a particular kind of news. It is the reporters' response to an event that makes it news, not any inherent characteristic of the event as such. For example, when events happen late in the day, just before the paper is to be printed, and reporters have no time to contact official sources for additional background information, the event becomes merely spot news. But if the same event were to happen early in the publishing day, and reporters have time to check official sources, get additional information, and interview people for comments, the event would become developing news. The same car accident may be just spot news, one isolated event worth little more than a

paragraph, or it can be made into a major story about road safety, municipal planning and budget priorities, drinking and driving, police checks, car safety equipment, manufacturers' responsibilities, the working of the capitalist profit motive and how it affects the quality of technology, and so on.

Smith suggests that Marx's analysis of the ideological nature of classical economics models can be applied to Tuchman's study of reporters. She argues that Tuchman used the same techniques referred to by Marx: Tuchman collects the data, disembodies them by fitting them into an abstract conceptual model of types of news, and then imposes the abstract model back onto the original behaviour as the explanation for why reporters do what they do. Marx's method, which Smith advocates, works in another way. Researchers collect data by exploring exactly what a reporter does. They then show how the reporter's actual behaviour produces the patterns that we can subsequently talk about as types of news.

The extreme version of this kind of theorizing is coming to be known as **destructuralism**. It begins from the assertion that there are no existing structures beyond the systems of thought through which people represent to themselves what is going on. What we therefore have to explore is just what it is people do such that they come to produce and to maintain their conceptualizations of reality. The social construction of reality and ethnomethodological perspectives nod to each other as perhaps not quite siblings, but close cousins.

Marxist Feminism and Radical Feminism

Marxist feminism constitutes a third theoretical approach developing out of the Marxist perspective. It uses the analytical tools of historical materialism, rather than Marx's actual writings, as inspiration. Marx himself said very little about women.

Mitchell (1972, 24) suggests that if we actually start looking in Marx's work for material under the heading "women," we would probably conclude that Marx was a hopeless male chauvinist. In the presentation of Marx's work in this chapter, we use the inclusive term *people*, but Marx himself uses the term *men*: *men* make their own history. . . ; in the social production of their life, *men* enter into definite relations. . . ; *men* as producers. . . ; and so on. There is little to suggest that Marx ever intended the term *men* to include *women*. He conceives the proletariat to be, essentially, working *men*. Women enter the picture in so far as they themselves sell their labour power in the marketplace. But their work as women, as housewives, as domestic workers, and as mothers, has little place in Marx's analysis of capitalism and the class struggle in history.

Recent feminist theory takes two basic approaches to Marxist theory. The dominant one, represented in the domestic labour debate, which we examine in the next chapter, tends toward a structuralist or Marxist-functionalist approach. It seeks to explicate the position and role of women within the workings of the capitalist system.

An alternative strategy is to try to rework the Marxist concept of class itself not only to incorporate women as proletariat but to give more central attention to a dimension that Marx himself largely ignores. This is the dimension of women's work as reproducers. Marx is held accountable for trying to develop an entire theory without taking into consideration how people themselves are produced. One Marxist, deeply committed to the political economy perspective, admitted that what the feminists were complaining about finally hit him, when it was pointed out that babies don't get produced in factories.

The neglect of reproduction in Marxist theory is a very large omission in the scheme of things. A classical Marxist theorist would probably argue that the question of reproduction has been subsumed under the more general issue of means of subsistence for workers and their dependants. But this does not satisfy feminists. They argue that, in classical Marxism, half the adults in the human race, together with all the children, are left outside the forces of history, along with the family dog.

Eisenstein (1984, 146) suggests that the Marxist version of class should be reworked to incorporate the notion of women as a **sexual class**. This does not mean that they are like the proletariat, defined in relation to the mode of production. Rather they are a sexual class in relation to the mode of reproduction. They are a class in that they perform the basic and necessary activities of society: reproduction, childrearing, nurturing, consuming, domestic labouring, and wage earning. They are a sexual class because what they do as women, the activities for which they are responsible, and the labour they perform are essential and necessary to the operation of society, more important even than the activities of the proletariat.

Eisenstein's conception of a sexual class is not accepted by all **Marxist feminists**, because it moves too far away from the original meaning of class in Marxist theory and tends to separate the sexual from the economic. **Radical feminists**, however, argue that this is a problem with Marxism rather than a problem with feminism. Radical feminists insist that Marxist theory is flawed in not recognizing that the system of male domination over women constitutes a class relation that is as fundamental as that of capitalists dominating labour.

Conclusion

It is not possible to draw any clear conclusions about the contribution of Marxism or Marxist theory to sociology because it is still very much in the process of formulation. Despite the fact that Marx died over a century ago, his ideas are only beginning to be established in mainstream sociology in North America. Marxism came to the fore during the 1960s as a critique of Parsonian functionalism. It is still considered rather avant garde in some sociological circles. The implications of Marxist thought for political economy, for the social construction of reality, and for feminist theory are very much still in the process of being worked out. There is no definitive interpretation of Marx.

You should take the arguments presented here as a point of departure and raise questions for yourself.

The next chapter explores Marxist contributions to understanding contemporary Canadian political economy. The broader implications of Marxism, as they relate to the social relations of family, stratification, education, ethnicity, and modernization, are explored in more depth in later chapters as we present the value of Marxist theory as a critique of traditional functionalism in sociology.

Suggested Reading

The booklet by Ernest Mandel, *An Introduction to Marxist Economic Theory* (1969), provides an excellent and very readable introduction to the model of capitalism as an economic system. Mandel covers the three issues of the theory of value and surplus value, capital and capitalism, and neo-capitalism, showing how contemporary crises of capitalism are managed. Another concise introduction to Marxist political theory is Karl Marx and Friedrich Engels, *The Communist Manifesto*, edited by Samuel Beer ([1948] 1955). This booklet includes an introduction to Marx's ideas, the full *Communist Manifesto*, and selec-

tions from *The Eighteenth Brumaire of Louis Bonaparte* and *Capital*.

Two collections of selected writings by Marx, both edited by Tom Bottomore, give an easy introduction to a variety of Marx's writing. The collection entitled *Karl Marx: Early Writings* (1963) gives selections from his economic and philosophical manuscripts. The second collection, *Karl Marx: Selected Writings in Sociology and Social Philosophy* (1956), covers Marx's materialist conception of history, pre-capitalist societies, the sociology of capitalism, and politics.

Chapter 9

The Political Economy of Canada: "The Main Business"

This chapter is designed to explore and to test Marxist theory concerning the workings of the capitalist mode of production by focussing on the Canadian economy. The fundamental question for political economy theory is whether the contradictions of capitalism foreseen by Marx can be, or have been, overcome by **advanced capitalism**, or whether the crises of capitalism will lead to the overthrow of the system by an alienated and exploited proletariat. The main points of Marx's model, discussed at greater length in the preceding chapter, are outlined below to highlight the questions we need to ask.

Marx and the Contradictions of Capitalism

Marx conceptualized capitalism as based on the private ownership of the means of production in the hands of a small class of capitalists referred to as the bourgeoisie. Others, who do not own any means of production, must sell their labour power in the marketplace to capitalists who use that labour power to run their enterprises and to make commodities. The term *capital* refers to the stock of land, buildings, machinery, goods, and money used in the production of commodities. In practical terms, the critical element of capital is money because it can be used to purchase all other means of production. In capitalist exchange, money is used to purchase the machines, raw materials, and labour power needed to create commodities that can be sold for more money, or profit. The source of profit is surplus value, which comes from the difference between the value of wages paid to workers and the value of the commodities that the workers make. The rate of surplus value provides an objective measure of the rate of exploitation of workers.

Marx argued that the **contradictions of capitalism** stem from competitive pressure to make profits. This pressure drives capitalists to maximize the exploitation of labourers through longer working hours, lower wages, and labour-saving technology to reduce costs. In the long run, this is self-defeating since, as the ratio of machines to labour increases, profits drop and unemployment rises, leading to crises of overproduction as people cannot afford to buy products. Capitalism thus seems prone to continual and ever-worsening cycles of booms and slumps. Falling profits, an insatiable drive for new technology, and bankruptcies among the smaller bourgeoisie lead to unemployment, the polarization of classes, and increasing poverty among workers. The system can be held together by a combination of state domination, **imperialism**, and ideological control by the ruling capitalist class.

These ideas are listed below as a series of predictions that we will test against Canadian data in this chapter.

1. *Increasing concentration of capital.* Marx predicts that giant corporations will control the economy as smaller businesses collapse or are bought out. These corporations will constantly increase in size and decrease in number as they merge or are bought out.
2. *Falling rate of profit.* As more and more money is needed for investment in technology, the returns on investment decline. Surplus value and profits come ultimately from labour power, not from machines.
3. *Polarization of classes.* Capitalists will get richer and richer with the concentration of control over markets. The middle class of small business people and independent commodity producers will collapse into the working class.
4. *Increasing poverty of the masses.* Unemployment continually threatens to undermine wage levels. Labour-saving technology results in more and more people competing for fewer jobs. These workers will eventually be joined by bankrupted former members of the small business class. Basic wages will hover around subsistence levels. The gap between poor workers and rich capitalists will get larger.
5. *Recurrent crises of overproduction.* Due to unemployment and low wages, people lack the money to purchase the goods being produced. Productivity expands faster than markets can absorb the goods.
6. *A treadmill of technological innovation.* When capitalists cannot sell their products, they must drop their prices. They must increase productivity still further to undercut their competitors. Hence they are driven to develop better labour-saving technology, which will enable them to produce more goods with fewer workers.
7. *Recurrent cycles of booms and slumps.* Bankruptcies lead to unemployment and overproduction. Technological breakthroughs such as robotics and computers bring temporary affluence, but competitors catch up and the cycle repeats itself.

The Liberal–Bourgeois Thesis

Within Canadian sociology, the work of political economy has been largely oriented to a debate with the competing **liberal-bourgeois thesis**. This thesis has its roots in the classical economics of Adam Smith, which focus on the key mechanism of competition. Competition in the marketplace regulates profits: if they are too high, other entrepreneurs will rush in to compete and prices will drop; if profits are too low, entrepreneurs will pull out and invest elsewhere. Competition keeps wages fair as workers will change to better-paying jobs if the rate is too low or move into high-wage areas and drive the rates down. Overproduction is similarly regulated because entrepreneurs will shift investments to new products for which there is more demand.

The strongest contemporary advocate of this theory of competition is Milton Friedman, a Nobel Prize winner in economics and long a key advisor to the U.S. government and to its allies in Latin America. Friedman opposes in principle any state intervention in the economy because such interference upsets the delicate balance of supply and demand in the marketplace. He sees the minimum wage as regressive, arguing that it increases unemployment as jobs that might have been viable at lower rates of pay become uneconomical. He argues that the power of huge corporations would be limited by competition if they did not receive state aid and protection (Friedman 1978). Freedom of competition in a capitalist society is, in his view, the main guarantee of democracy and individual freedom.

Research in the liberal-bourgeois tradition points to evidence that advanced capitalism has largely avoided or overcome the contradictions predicted by Marx. The argument is that the expansion of **shareholder capitalism** has led to a democratization of ownership of capital and has promoted a separation of ownership and control through the managerial revolution. The increasing affluence or **embourgeoisement** among working-class people and the rise of the **welfare state** seem to contradict the Marxist prediction of increasing poverty among the masses. The rise of the middle classes, the sector of well-paid professional people, further counters the prediction of a polarization of classes. A political democracy that gives expression to competing interest groups rounds out this picture of a system that enhances the quality of life for the vast majority of people.

In addition to testing Marx's theories on the contradictions of capitalism in this chapter, we will also test the factors that liberal-bourgeois critics see as mitigating capitalism's internal contradictions. These factors are summarized below.

1. *Improved standard of living.* Shareholder capitalism will reduce the concentration of capital. The rise of the welfare state and trade unions will counter the tendency toward the increased poverty of the masses.
2. *Third World exploitation.* Severe poverty will be shifted to the Third World. Cheap labour and cheap raw materials from underdeveloped countries will keep up profit rates for capitalists in Europe and North America.
3. *Constant military spending.* Military expenditures will reduce crises of overproduction. Governments will buy military technology, blow it up or declare it obsolete, and buy more.
4. *High technology.* Technological innovation will outpace declining rates of profit. Productivity goes up exponentially with computers and robotics. Technology itself gets cheaper, so absolute profit levels will stay high, at least in the short run. Hence wages can rise above subsistence levels, especially for skilled labour.
5. *Legitimation.* The system literally delivers the goods. People will be placated by consumer goods, and hence class conflict will be avoided, at least in the short term. Free enterprise will foster democratic institutions that will balance and limit the power of capitalists.

Research from the perspective of a Marxist political economy has sought to challenge many of these predictions, showing how the contradictions of capitalism still persist. Alternative data point to the rise of corporate monopoly capitalism, which spells the end of competition in the marketplace, to the growing polarization resulting from the collapse of the petite bourgeoisie into the working classes, to huge disparities in wealth and poverty within Canada, and to imperialism abroad. Marxist political economy also looks at the character of the state itself and its role in support of ruling capitalist interests. These comparative data will be systematically reviewed below.

This chapter is divided into four major sections, each focussing on a specific aspect of Marxist theory. The first section describes the structure of capitalism in Canada. It begins with evidence of the increasing expansion of **corporate capitalism** and the contraction of smaller businesses. It tests the Marxist prediction concerning concentration of capital against the liberal argument that shareholder capitalism will dilute corporate control over the economy. Subsequently, we explore the particular situation of independent primary producers in Canada. We test the Marxist prediction, that there will be falling rates of profit and bankruptcies among the petite bourgeoisie, against the liberal thesis that free enterprise fosters healthy competition in the marketplace.

The second section focusses on the relationship between capitalism and democratic institutions in Canada. The Marxist thesis holds that the structures of politics, administration, and communications will be dominated by the ideas and the interests of the elite capitalist class. This thesis is tested against the argument that free enterprise fosters democracy, or rule by the people, and that through democratic institutions the mass of people can control and moderate the power of capital.

The third section examines the disparities of wealth between the rich and the poor in Canada. The Marxist thesis holds that most of the wealth generated in capitalist societies will become concentrated in the hands of a small elite class. Meanwhile, there will be an ever-expanding class of impoverished people and a shrinking middle class destined to collapse eventually into poverty. This is tested against the thesis that the welfare state and trade unions will ensure a more equitable redistribution of wealth. We will argue that Marxist predictions fit very closely with the dominant features of contemporary Canadian society, but with two important qualifications. The thesis does not adequately account for the expansion of the middle class of professional people, and it fails to accounts for the situation of women.

The chapter concludes with a section on the feminist challenge to political economy theory. The dynamics of capitalist society seem very different when viewed from the particular standpoint of women as homemakers and mothers. A central argument in the Marxist-feminist thesis is that the focus of traditional political economy theory is too narrow. Political economy mirrors the assumption of classical economics that the "main business" of the economy is to accumulate capital. Consequently the work of women as homemakers is completely ignored.

The Structure of Capitalism

Corporate Monopoly Capitalism

The central point in the Marxist response to liberal-bourgeois theory is the simple but devastating observation that the era of free competition in the marketplace has passed. The competitive market system no longer exists, even though economists still use the rhetoric. It has gone for the very reasons that Marx foresaw. In the competitive drive for better labour-saving technology to push down costs of production, the smaller, weaker, or less ruthless entrepreneurs were eliminated or absorbed by larger, stronger capitalists. A relatively small number of huge corporations now dominates the market and can dictate how it works. These corporations are no longer subject to competitive market forces of supply and demand. They dictate what the supply and price will be and, in large measure, dictate demand through advertising.

It is true that there still is much competition in the marketplace, but this tends to be confined to the weakest sectors of the economy. The competitive sector tends to comprise small firms, such as garment factories, small restaurants, and businesses run by independent tradespeople, which are highly labour intensive and operate on low capital investment. Such firms tend to be unstable. One estimate is that small businesses have a life expectancy of about eighteen months, with a stunning number of bankruptcies every year. New businesses continually enter the market but, in recent years, as many as two-thirds go bankrupt (Veltmeyer 1986, 55). Wages and profits in small business are low.

These small enterprises are up against a market dominated by huge corporations, great behemoths that are capital intensive and have a high level of productivity for labour and consequently have higher base wages. These corporations, along with the state sector of Crown corporations and utilities, are centrally planned. Subsectors of these vast empires are run by managers answerable to corporate directors in terms of their bottom line: profits.

Veltmeyer (1987) provides an excellent review of both the size and the power of these corporations and the processes by which they come into being and grow. He estimates that, in 1983, twenty-five corporations, mostly foreign-owned multinationals, accounted for one-third of all industrial assets, roughly one-quarter of all sales, and one-third of all profits in Canada. One-eighth of one percent of firms accounted for more than half of total sales and two-thirds of assets and profits (Veltmeyer 1987, 18–23).

He also shows the staggering extent of **monopoly** and **oligopoly** throughout major industries in Canada. An **oligopoly** is a situation of shared monopoly, where four or fewer firms dominate the market in a particular industry and can co-operate to control it (Veltmeyer 1987, 25). The tobacco industry, breweries, and motor vehicles are each dominated by four—or fewer—big corporations that control over 90 percent of production. A further twenty manufacturing industries, including petroleum, publishing, iron and steel, and cement, were each dominated by four firms that controlled at least 75 percent of their output. This process of concentration is cumulative, since large firms grow faster than small ones and can accumulate more capital.

The wealth controlled by these firms rivals that of nation-states. World Bank data show that forty-six of the top hundred economies in the world are transnational corporations. The total value of the output of these firms exceeds the gross national product of more than 150 countries, and they are expanding at two-to-three times the national rates of growth (Veltmeyer 1987, 76–79). They expand primarily by buying out or merging with existing corporations.

Horizontal Mergers

The dominant form of takeover in the earlier stages of corporate capitalist growth was through **horizontal integration**, the consolidation of firms in the same industry. This gave the corporation enormous power in setting the terms of labour contracts and fixing prices. The Bertrand Report (1981) on *The State of Competition in the Canadian*

Petroleum Industry estimated that, through price fixing by the "big four"—Imperial, Shell, Texaco, and Gulf—Canadians were overcharged by about $12 billion for petroleum products between 1958 and 1978.

In 1910, the Canadian government passed legislation that provided for the "Investigation of Combines, Monopolies, Trusts, and Mergers" that might lead to the decline of "free competition" and therefore to "unfair pricing" (Veltmeyer 1987, 28). Generally, however, the capacity of the federal government to restrict the formation of monopolies has been very limited. Several royal commissions have documented the continuing problem and expressed grave concerns, but mergers have continued largely unchecked. Several significant mergers and buy-outs occurred in the first month of 1989 alone. Molson's brewery merged with Carling O'Keefe, leaving Labatts as the only other large brewery in Canada. Canadian Airlines made an offer to buy out Wardair, leaving only Air Canada for competition. The buy-out of Consolidated Bathurst by an American company, Stone Container, made the latter the dominant manufacturer of paper products in North America. Imperial Oil bought out Texaco, reducing the "big four" to the "big three."

Vertical Integration

The most important form of takeover is **vertical integration**, the linking of firms that operate at different stages in the development of a product. These firms then have enormous power over primary producers who provide the raw materials for processors and manufacturers.

Potato farmers in New Brunswick find themselves in a situation where everything they need for production—seed, fertilizer, machinery, pesticide—and all stages of food processing, brokerage, wholesaling, and retailing are controlled by the McCain group of companies. McCain owns vast tracts of land on which farmers work as tenants. The corporation controls farm building materials, seeds, fertilizers, and harvesters. It owns the potato-processing factory, storage facilities, the brokerage and pricing firms, even the major truck lines shipping to other parts of the Maritimes and to Ontario and Quebec. No farmer can grow potatoes in New Brunswick without dealing with McCain in some way or another. The result is that the company is in a position to dictate the terms of contracts with potato growers. These terms are frequently very disadvantageous to the grower, who must deliver potatoes to the company at the company's convenience, pay all the storage costs, and make up any shortfall by purchasing additional potatoes. In addition, the company can withhold payment for potatoes to the amount owing to any of the McCain group of companies. Farmers are required to follow specific instructions with respect to type of potato grown, amount and time of application of fertilizer, and time of planting and harvesting. Local banks want contracts signed with processors before they will advance loans to the farmers, as do machinery, seed and feed, and fertilizer dealers (Veltmeyer 1987, 36–38).

Conglomerate Mergers

Conglomerate mergers take the form of links with other companies in fields of production different from that of the parent corporation. Such diversification provides stability as profits in one area can compensate for losses in another. The Thomson empire, for example, controls the big department stores of Hudson's Bay, The Bay, Simpsons, Zeller's, and Fields. There is thus no direct competition between these stores for customers, although managers may be forced to compete with each other for profit ratings. With the takeover of Hudson's Bay, Thomson gained control over significant oil and gas interests, as well as insurance companies and truck lines. Thomson also controls 50 percent of the newspaper market in Canada, his most significant holding being the *Globe and Mail*, plus other papers in the United States and Britain (Veltmeyer 1987, 40). Such conglomerate ownership has criti-cal implications for the control of ideas by the business elites within capitalist society. For example, editors of major newspapers are unlikely to take a critical stand against corporate interests when they are themselves employees of those corporations.

Figure 9-1 The Thomsons' Concentration of Economic Power*

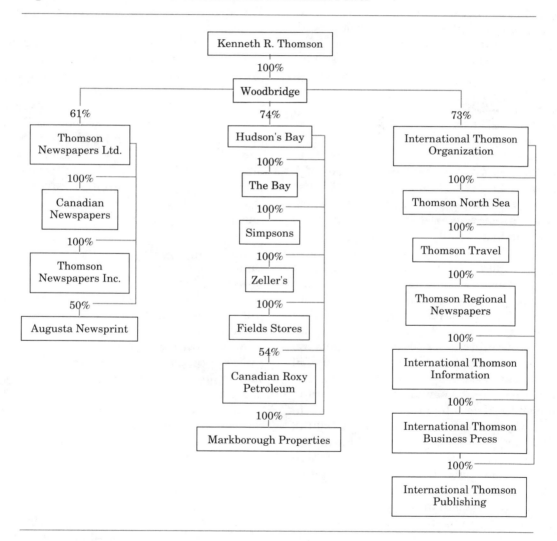

*Percentages indicate the proportion of ownership held by the company that is one step up (i.e., Woodbridge owns 74% of the Hudson's Bay).

Source: Veltmeyer (1987) from *Financial Post 500* (Summer 1986), 208.

Companies of this size have a very lop-sided advantage in dealing with trade unions or non-union labour. A six-month strike by newspaper workers at *The Times* in London cost the Thomson corporation an estimated $35 million in 1980, but the corporation as a whole still increased its profits during that year. In effect, such corporations can afford to ride out a very long strike in one sector by subsidies from other sectors. This gives them a very powerful weapon against workers for whom strikes are a massive drain on economic resources and entail the serious risk of failure.

Intercorporate Ownership and Control

A much cheaper but very effective means of gaining control over other companies is to purchase equity in them in the form of a majority of voting shares, or the largest single block of such shares if share owner-ship is widely dispersed. If a company has its assets divided equally into bonds, non-voting preferred stock, and voting common stock, the purchase of half the voting common stock, or one-sixth of the total worth of the company, will give effective legal voting con-trol. The purchaser can then form a **holding company**, convert its assets into bonds, non-voting preferred stock, and voting common stock, sell everything but a little over half of the voting stock, and still retain voting con-trol over the original company or group of companies. The intercorporate empires con-trolled by two individuals in Canada, Conrad Black and Paul Desmarais and their associ-ates, comprise 350 corporations, plus a further 1500 subsidiaries, with combined assets of $60 billion (Veltmeyer 1987, 53). Three other Canadian families who control giant holding companies are the Thomsons, Westons, and Bronfmans. Apart from these five family empires, the biggest holding com-panies are the chartered banks.

It is almost impossible to keep up with all the ramifications and threads of control of such huge holding companies. Takeover bids and efforts to avoid being taken over com-prise the arena of modern corporate warfare. The burgeoning business section of the *Globe and Mail* reports almost daily instances of companies suddenly finding that their vot-ing stock is being swallowed up. They may not even know who is trying to buy them out because bidding is done through brokers. The targeted company must get cash quickly to buy up its own shares and block the takeover, or it must capitulate. Share prices shoot up because of aggressive buying. The company trying to stop the takeover buys back the shares at inflated prices. In this process, cash flow is critical; firms need access to large amounts of money. Banks play a central role in this game of mergers and takeovers, so much so that Peter New-man (1975, 99–101) described them as the heart of the private intelligence network that keeps top Canadian business people in touch with each other.

Interlocking Directorships

Bank directors are commonly in the position to exert enormous influence over corpora-tions through the mechanism of **interlock-ing directorships.** A *direct interlock* is a situation where a person serves on the board of directors of two different companies. An *indirect interlock* occurs when each of two companies has a director on the board of a third company (Veltmeyer 1987, 60). Cle-ment (1977, 70) shows that there are far fewer elite individuals than there are elite positions. At the time of his study, a mere 274 individuals held a total of 782 positions as directors of big corporations, an average of 2.85 positions per person.

The major interlockers in this system have bank connections. In 1981, 40 directors of the Royal Bank held 431 directorships among them, many in the biggest corpora-tions in Canada. Similarly, 100 top bank directors in Canada held 1110 corporate con-nections. Just 10 individuals held 237 directorships, linking top industrial corporations, foreign corporations, financial institutions such as trust companies and insurance firms, and large family fortunes (Veltmeyer 1987, 60). Newman (1975, 99–101) argues that "the executive board meetings of the five largest banks represent the greatest source of non-governmental power in the country." The power of these bankers is wielded through their ability to withhold favours, to keep those whom they consider unsuitable from joining either their own or any other clusters of influence. In effect, they have virtual veto power over entry into the big business establishment in Canada. Such is the extent of corporate concentration and interlocking networks of power.

A Critique of the Liberal–Bourgeois Thesis

Data on corporate concentration undermine the central pillars of the liberal-bourgeois thesis: free competition, the democratization of capital, and the managerial revolution.

The crucial argument that free competition in the marketplace is the determinant of market forces is decisively refuted. There is nothing but token competition among major retail merchandising chains when they are all part of the same Thomson family empire. Individual store managers may vie with each other for points in the profit-or-perish game, but only frills are involved. "Competing" brand names and "competing" product lines are normally rather than exceptionally manufactured within the same corporate empire. The semblance but not the substance of competition appears on the store shelves. When three or four corporate giants dominate the market, each of them more than likely tied together by interlocking directorates, they are able to dictate market policy. Other companies that do not toe the price line can be rapidly starved out.

The thesis that ownership of capital has been democratized through shareholding is also effectively refuted. While it is true that

thousands, perhaps hundreds of thousands, of individual Canadians do own shares, only a very small minority own sufficient shares in any one corporation to actually sway decisions. People who earn the top 10 percent of all wages and salaries own 72 percent of all shares in Canada. Approximately 1300 wealthy people own 9 percent of all shares, equal to the number of shares owned by the four million lowest income earners. In a one-share-one-vote system, this is not a democracy but a **plutocracy**—rule by the wealthy. Shareholder meetings reflect this plutocracy. They are usually preplanned affairs, in which those present are told what the policies will be. Small cliques of majority shareholders or the directors of holding companies make these decisions.

The third thesis, the separation of ownership from control through the **managerial revolution**, also has little substance. The argument is that a new technocratic group of managers has emerged, hired to run corporations in the shareholders' interests. With a wide dispersal of shareholders, managers may acquire effective power over corporate policy, forming a new social elite of administrators and **technocrats**. The problem with the argument is that, in the vast majority of large corporations, voting control remains within the hands of a single dominant shareholder or clique with majority shares. It is they and not the managers who dictate central policies. The managers may well be in control of the day-to-day operations of the corporation, or their sector of it, but they are answerable to the directors. They run operations, but they do not make key decisions on investments or how assets will be spent. The crucial power to decide what plants to shut down, or where and how to invest economic surplus, is in the hands of directors. Even if managers were able to influence corporate policy, there is no reason to believe that they would in any way change the focus of such policies. They are commonly major shareholders themselves, and their job is to make profits. Those who don't will be fired (Veltmeyer 1987, 65–66).

The Petite Bourgeoisie

Marx's prediction concerning the polarization of classes focussed particularly on the petit bourgeois class, comprising independent producers who own their own means of production but who are not major capitalists. They labour for themselves in small family enterprises, but they are not major employers of labour. Marx predicted that, over time, this small business class would collapse into the proletariat. Unlike corporate capitalists, they would be unable to afford the labour-saving technology that makes possible cheap mass production. Slowly, they would go bankrupt.

Table 9-1   Income of Self-Employed Workers by Sex, April 1986

Income	Male	Female
Less than $ 5 000	12.2	43.7
5 000 – 9 999	14.4	20.0
10 000 – 14 999	14.9	11.9
15 000 – 19 999	12.1	8.4
20 000 – 24 999	10.6	4.6
25 000 – 29 999	7.8	4.2
30 000 – 34 999	7.2	2.3
35 000 – 39 999	5.0	1.3
40 000 – 49 999	6.4	1.2
50 000 – 59 999	2.7	0.0
60 000 and over	6.8	1.7
Self-employed as % all employed	17.1	8.3

Source: Statistics Canada (1988, 74).

In Canada, the petite bourgeoisie comprises independent commodity producers in family-run farming, fishing, and craft enterprises, and another group of small retailers and independent salespeople. The liberal-bourgeois vision of capitalism as founded on entrepreneurship and free enterprise focusses particularly on these small business people. The dream of many workers is that one day they will save enough money to quit their jobs and go into business for themselves. But Canadian data suggest that, as a class, small business people are economically insecure and face a permanently uncertain future. Large numbers of small businesses start up every year, but the majority fail within two years. While self-employed people are much more likely than other workers to say that they would choose the same job again, they are much less likely to say they would recommend it to a friend (Archibald 1978, 129). They are too vulnerable to the whims of corporate buyers and sellers.

Farming

The situation of **independent commodity producers** in Canada has become increasingly precarious in the face of expanding capital, centralized production, and big bankers. There has been a steady decline in the number of farms in Canada as undercapitalized farms have been forced out of business. Between 1931 and 1961, the **capitalization** of farms—that is, the amount of financial investment that the average farmer needs to operate a farm—rose by 450 percent. Over the same period, the number of people working in farming dropped by 50 percent, and output per farm worker doubled. Between 1951 and 1981, fully 80 percent of New Brunswick farms disappeared. In 1951 three million acres were being farmed by 26 000 farmers, but by 1981 only one million acres were being farmed by a total of 4000 farmers (Murphy 1987). In Nova Scotia between 1941 and 1981, 87 percent of farms failed as did 74 percent of farms on Prince Edward Island.

Murphy suggests that the invention of mechanical potato harvesters made possible the expansion of farm size in the Maritimes because of the reduced need for manual labour. But at the same time, it meant that small farmers, who could not afford such expensive equipment, could not compete in the potato market. Others invested in the new machines but could not carry the exorbitant debt.

As small farms went bankrupt, they were bought up by large corporations such as McCain's in New Brunswick. The result of this process was the creation of an underclass of dispossessed rural dwellers, estimated to comprise as many as one-third of the people living in the rural Maritimes during the 1970s (Veltmeyer 1986, 49). These dispossessed farmers and farm workers became dependent upon what wage-work they could find, supplementing their incomes with unemployment insurance and welfare cheques. They swelled the ranks of the poor, socially disorganized, and anomic residents of the rural communities described in chapter 5.

The lot of farmers who have remained in business has not improved either. Despite the doubling of labour productivity, farm incomes generally have fallen and are reflected in declining standards of living. Farmers are largely at the mercy of monopoly processors and distributors. Clement (1983) suggests the term **dependent commodity producers** to refer to the people in this ambiguous class position. Technically they own their own means of production, but they have nevertheless lost their economic independence.

The circumstances of Saskatchewan wheat farmers are similar to those of maritime farmers. Together with small business people in prairie towns, they share what has been called a "companionship of vultures" (*Globe and Mail*, 11 July 1987, D2) as they wait for someone to go bankrupt so that they might survive by buying the farm and thus expanding their holdings. Small business people, who depend on farm families as clientele for their cafes and stores, likewise face bankruptcy as the local population declines.

Between 1956 and 1986, the Saskatchewan farm population shrank by more than half as small farmers abandoned the increasingly corporate industry. The

As prairie farms go bankrupt and are brought up, the local community declines, forcing businesses and schools to close up.

average size of farms increased by 6.4 percent just between 1982 and 1987. Meanwhile wheat prices are dropping. Those who remain in business face mounting debts for their heavily capitalized irrigation, ploughing, and harvesting machinery. As Marx predicted, the rate of profit is falling as an ever-larger percentage of investment goes into machines. In 1987, 8 percent of Saskatchewan farmers were effectively bankrupt and a further 23 percent were unable to prevent their debts from mounting. One farmer projected a year-end loss of $40 000 on his large grain farm. He already had debts that were costing him $100 000. The family survived on the wife's wagework income (*Globe and Mail*, 11 July 1987, D2). Many farm families have already joined the proletariat, with the wife and often the husband working part-time or seasonally for wages, to supplement the farm income.

Farm women have been especially exploited in the process that ties family farms into capitalism. Their exploitation was total because farm wives invariably did not receive wages; they worked for subsistence. A woman could work for a lifetime on the family farm only to find that everything she produced belonged to her husband. This is precisely what happened to Irene Murdoch, an Alberta farm woman. After her husband petitioned to divorce her, the Supreme Court of Canada ruled in 1975 that she had no right to a share in the farm that she had helped to build up during a twenty-five-year marriage. Reaction to this infamous judicial decision spurred changes to family property laws. Today it is more likely that farms are owned jointly by the husband and wife. The woman's situation, however, may not be substantially better. Formerly she worked for the benefit of her husband. Now both work for the benefit of the mortgage company. They constantly run the risk of losing everything, including their family home, if the farm fails.

Only farms with huge outputs of grain can hope to come out ahead of the falling rate of profit on heavy investments at high interest rates. But the crisis of overproduction is now hitting the industry. Wheat prices dropped by 43 percent between 1984 and 1987, and still farmers cannot sell their grain. Canada has enormous stockpiles of grain, so massive that the wheat board is forced to slash prices to sell it. An estimated 500 million people go hungry in the Third World, but they cannot afford to buy our grain. Canada cannot give it away either. If it did, the argument goes, it would promptly bankrupt small farmers in Third World countries by destroying their incentives to grow food for local markets. (We will view this issue further in chapter 15 on modernization.) Meanwhile, everyone connected with wheat production prays for a bad harvest in the Soviet Union.

As small farmers go deeper into debt or are forced out of business, the social costs to rural communities on the Prairies are enormous. Stable, homogeneous communities are torn apart by acrimonious disputes not only between older and relatively debt-free farmers, who inherited their farms, and younger debt-ridden farmers, but also between the specialized grain growers and the mixed producers. Not only farmers suffer. Corporate **rationalization** has killed many small farm-machinery dealerships and bank branches. As grain prices fall and debts rise among farmers, they spend less money, and other local small businesses collapse. People cannot afford to go out so they stay on their isolated farms, and the communities fall apart. Local hockey and baseball leagues collapse as the communities can no longer put teams together. The social anomie that Clark described in the Maritimes has thus hit prairie communities also.

Fishing and Forestry

Independent producers in the fishing industry are suffering the same decline as farmers. They are either unable to compete with huge trawlers operated by fish factories or are reduced to virtual tenant status as dependent commodity producers under contract to fish processing plants, to whom they are indebted for fishing gear.

The stranglehold of big fish packers over fishing communities in the Maritimes has a long history. What has changed in recent years has been the degree of concentration of corporate control in fish factories and the involvement of the state on the side of big corporate capital at the expense of small producers. Sacouman (1985) notes a major shift in maritime government policy towards the fishing industry between 1965 and 1985. This shift began in the 1960s with the forced relocation of outport fishing communities in Newfoundland on the grounds that they were too expensive to service. Then, in the 1970s, the Department of Fisheries gave support to the petite bourgeoisie by financing the production of long-liner fishing boats. The result was indebtedness, as people took out government-backed loans to buy the boats. Moreover, overproduction resulted from the use of so many vessels in the fishing industry. Then, in the 1980s, the state backed large fishing companies in Newfoundland and Nova Scotia. Traditionally, Sacouman notes, there was a roughly equal split in the industry between the small producers and the corporate giants. But this balance has now been broken. The state made huge grants of $100 million to the big companies, while at the same time calling in its loans to small producers. Factory freezer trawlers were licensed to "rationalize" the fishing industry, unifying the catching and processing of fish. The direct result was the loss of 140 worker-years per trawler.

The small inshore fishery is being devastated by this competition from freezer trawlers and foreign fish factories offshore. It has little bargaining power with big fish processors, and the situation is made even more difficult by laws that prohibit unions among entrepreneurs. It took a seven-month strike of Canso Strait fishermen to win the legal right to form a union for the purpose of negotiating contracts with the processors in Nova Scotia. Similar pressures face small fish producers in Prince Edward Island and Newfoundland (Johnson 1972, 151).

The operation of offshore freezer trawlers is also threatening the destruction of what Sacouman refers to as **semi-proletarian production** in the Maritimes. This is a pattern of independent commodity production backed up with wageworking spouses or part-time and seasonal work for the main producer. In the maritime fishing communities, the work that women could find in the fish-packing plants was vital for the survival of their families. It was arduous work, done under appalling conditions for low wages (McFarland 1980), but it met subsistence needs, and in the off season it gave eligibility for unemployment benefits. With the advent of freezer trawlers, however, women have lost these packing jobs. For a variety of reasons, women can generally not go to sea for forty to sixty days at a stretch to work on the boats. As a result, the proletariat becomes almost exclusively male as women are removed from wagework.

Similar changes are happening in the pulp and paper industry. Sacouman (1985) notes that, until recently, there was an equitable split in this industry in the Maritimes: 50 percent of wood was produced by big corporations and 50 percent by small woodlot owners. Again, provincial and federal initiatives, in alliance with large corporations, are changing this balance against the small producers.

The policies advocated by the Nova Scotia Royal Commission Report on Forestry (1984) promise to expand corporate capital production while destroying the small woodlots (Schneider 1987, 117–18). The report recommends establishing uniform government management of private woodlands to ensure a viable market for industries supplying pesticides, fertilizers, and seedlings. This effectively imposes a capital-intensive technology on wood production, with small producers compelled to use expensive inputs in order to compete. They can only afford such inputs with the help of government subsidies, which means that substantial tax dollars flow to multinational companies producing the chemicals and seedlings. Wood producers lose their independence. In order to compete in the tight market for pulp, they must adopt capital-intensive technology. For example, they must use chemical herbicides rather than manual labour to control weeds. The primary beneficiaries of these changes are the foreign-owned pulp companies.

Summary

The liberal-bourgeois vision of free competition in the marketplace, regulating prices, profits, and wages, no longer accurately describes the current structure of capital in Canada, if it ever did. The Marxist thesis, that internal contradictions of capitalism would lead to ever-increasing corporate concentration, and to the collapse of the petite bourgeoisie into the proletariat, finds extensive support.

Through processes of horizontal and vertical integration and conglomerate mergers, once-competitive enterprises have been amalgamated into huge corporations, with subsectors run by managers. Competition among these conglomerates exists only on paper: the big players are able to control the market and to determine both supply and price. Even when individual firms have not lost their identity through outright mergers, the control over major decisions in the investment and transfer of capital is concentrated through intercorporate ownership, holding companies, and interlocking directorships. A handful of family empires and the directors of the major chartered banks in Canada dominate the capital market.

Small businesses continually spring up among these corporate giants, but their survival rate is low. Primary producers in farming, fishing, and lumbering all across Canada are fighting a losing battle against big corporations. They cannot keep up with the pace and the costs of the labour-saving technology of big producers and processors. They survive in ever-smaller numbers, dependent on government subsidies, intermittent wagework and unemployment benefits, and increasingly upon the full-time wagework of some family members, plus the part-time and seasonal wagework of the primary producer.

Capitalism and Democracy

Domination or Pluralism?

The central moral argument of the liberal-bourgeois thesis is that a capitalist system based on free competition in the marketplace, operating with minimal government interference, offers the best protection for individual freedom. It is the pillar of a democratic political system in which competing groups pressure for their distinctive interests. Diverse interest groups within the political arena, much as competing producer groups in the marketplace, are seen as most likely to protect the best interests of the majority of people and to ensure the greatest good for the greatest number.

The alternative Marxist thesis sees the state as organized essentially to protect the interests of the capitalist class and not the interests of all members of society. This is notwithstanding the appearance of multiple parties and competing interest groups. As Marx expressed it in *The Communist Manifesto* ([1848] 1955, 11–12), "the executive of the modern state is but a committee for managing the common affairs of the whole bourgeoisie."

Contemporary Marxist theorist Ralph Miliband (1969) challenges the assumptions of the liberal-bourgeois thesis on its own terms. His central argument is that, while there may be evidence of competition between interest groups, this competition is on very unequal terms. In practice, members of the capitalist class are in a position to shape political decisions decisively in their own interest.

Miliband argues that, far from flourishing in a **laissez-faire system** in which capitalists can operate with minimal interference from the state, advanced capitalism needs, and relies upon, state intervention. The state serves the important function of smoothing out the periodic crises of capitalism, the booms and the slumps that otherwise threaten the stability of the system. The state also serves to control factions within the capitalist class itself—conflicts among industrial, mercantile, and finance capital, for example—so as to safeguard the stability of capitalism as a whole. The state apparatus serves to regulate unions, limit strikes, moderate and deflect potential revolt by the working classes, and soften the effects of unemployment by various welfare measures. A particularly crucial role of the state, as we shall see below, is to legitimize capitalism to the extent that most members of capitalist societies accept the system, even while they suffer from it.

The state itself is not an entity but rather is a process, comprising multiple elements. It includes federal, provincial, and local governments, parliamentary assemblies, the civil service, the military, the police, the judiciary, and a range of other supporting institutions. Miliband demonstrates how the social backgrounds and dominant interests of elites within each of these different sectors have an affinity with those of the business class. Here we will briefly discuss a few of these sectors: elected assemblies, the military, and the judiciary.

Miliband maintains that underneath the appearance of a competing party system in elected assemblies is the reality of a shared commitment to capitalism. Even socialist or left-wing parties still fundamentally support the system; their moderate role is to persuade acceptance of limited reforms. Such parties consistently fail to use popular militancy for radical social change. Rather than inspiring the mass of people to rebel against the capitalist system, they advocate piecemeal reform. In Canada, the New Democratic Party claims to speak out for ordinary people and for social reforms to reduce inequalities, but this is still within capitalism. Business people in the Yukon expressed concern when Tony Penikett's NDP government was elected in 1986, but they need not have worried. By the summer of 1987 business people acknowledged that the NDP had not interfered in any adverse way with business. Penikett himself said that he wished to avoid the mistakes of an earlier NDP government in British Columbia: he wanted to work with business people and not antagonize them.

Within any elected assembly the business elite has massive advantages over all other competing interest groups. Business determines the wages, prices, profits, location of capital investments, level of employment, and rate of economic growth. It also has veto power, or the power of not doing things. Governments fear loss of business confidence if their policies appear anti-business, and with good reason: they depend on international finance, banks, credit, and so on, to function. Labour, on the other hand, has no such power base. Working-class people are internally divided by skill, geography, race, religion, ethnic background, and political ideology. The workers' only weapon is to go on strike, but governments can and frequently do legislate them back to work.

The **military-industrial complex** within North America assures a close affinity of interests among elites in the military, business, and the senior civil service, and there is a frequent exchange of personnel among these sectors. In the United States, for example, an executive of the Ford Motor Company ran the Pentagon for seven years (Miliband 1969). The military is a major supporter of research and development of high technology and a major purchaser of industrial production.

The judiciary is ostensibly an independent body, dispensing justice without regard for special interest groups, yet the existing system of laws upholds and reinforces the interests of corporate capitalism. Moreover, while the judiciary is supposedly independent of government interference, the system of appointment and promotion favours conservative judges whose class of origin, education, and professional tendencies are closely allied to those of the business class.

The following anecdote (*New York Times*, 30 Aug. 1987) helps to illustrate the biases in the legal system. Picture an employee in a widget factory. One day she makes four widgets, tenders cash equal to the cost of the materials and their procurement, reasonable rental value of workspace and tools, apportioned costs of other managerial expenses, and so on, and then leaves, taking the four widgets with her. She plans to sell them and keep the profits. What will happen? She will be arrested and charged with theft. But what are the grounds? Why is the employer not guilty of anything? After all, the employer merely pays the worker a reasonable rent for labour time, keeps the widgets, and sells them at a profit. The answer is that the widgets belong to the employer because the law says they are the employer's property. But there is nothing necessary or inevitable about this arrangement of permitting the employer to rent the worker and keep the widgets. In principle, the relationship could be structured the other way around. It is not this way because the laws are designed to protect the interests of capital more than the interests of workers.

During periods of open confrontation between workers and owners, when strikes are called, the balance of law in Canada comes down clearly on the side of owners. People in Canada have the right of lawful assembly and the right to organize unions, but these are not enshrined in the constitution. Court injunctions can be readily obtained to prevent striking picketers from interfering with the operations of a plant. Strikers can be legislated back to work whenever the government decides a strike is against the public interest, with stiff penalties attached for non-compliance. In the 1987 postal strike, such penalties included banning an elected union official from holding office for five years.

On the other side, there is no federal legislation prohibiting the use of strikebreakers. There are no laws to prevent an employer from depriving workers of jobs or to require the employer to protect workers' interests or to consult with them during technological change. Further, there are no laws requiring profit sharing among employees or requiring that they be represented on boards that make decisions affecting their livelihood. Sweden has many such laws, but moves toward such legislation are strongly resisted in Canada. Canadian law reflects and enforces the core assumptions regarding the relations between employers and employees in the market economy, but this is not a natural or inevitable relation, and it is not immune to re-examination and critique.

Canadian Labour Congress president Shirley Carr talks to media and police at a postal workers' picket line.

Legitimation and Ideological Hegemony

Marx predicted that as the crises of capitalism worsened, the working class would become transformed from a class-in-itself— that is, people in a given relation to the means of production—to a class-for-itself— people aware of their situation and their exploitation under capitalism and ready to take action to transform the system. This critical level of self-awareness has not yet been achieved in most advanced capitalist societies. From the liberal-bourgeois perspective, this is an important indication that the Marxist perspective is flawed. Capitalism provides a relatively high standard of living and access to an ever-expanding array of consumer goods for the working class. The system thus wins legitimation. Capitalism may be geared to profits, but this is not experienced as exploitative when everyone benefits from the expansion of industrial wealth made possible by the competitive drive for profits.

Antonio Gramsci, who wrote many of his works from prison in fascist Italy, challenges the root of these assumptions. He maintains that the apparent consensus in support of capitalism is manipulated by the dominant class. Gramsci develops the central theme of **ideological hegemony**, which refers to the systematic ways in which members of the dominant capitalist class deliberately manipulate and distort the knowledge, ideas, and values of the mass of working people, so as to generate the acceptance or legitimation of capitalism.

Herbert Marcuse, a critical philosopher writing in the United States in the 1960s, argued that this hegemonic ruling process is so successful, and so powerful, that most people find it hard even to conceive of any alternative to capitalism, let alone to advocate such ideas. People, in effect, come to think in one-dimensional terms, to become one-dimensional themselves. In principle, Americans and Canadians have freedom of thought and speech guaranteed in their constitutions, yet in practice they have been rendered virtually incapable of conceiving of alternatives to the status quo. Words have had their meanings truncated. The word *free* becomes synonymous with free enterprise and free competition in the marketplace so that human freedom is identified with capitalism, and all other options with oppression. *Democracy*, with its sweeping sense of "government of the people, by the people, for the people," has become reduced to individuals occasionally exercising their right to vote. The question whether or not America is a democracy, in the deeper sense of the word, cannot even be asked. Revolt against the system is inconceivable when the only perceived options of communism or socialism are regarded in such a pervasively negative way (Marcuse 1964).

How is it possible for this one-dimensional view to take hold so completely?

Mechanisms for Legitimation

Business contributions to mainstream parties far exceed labour's contribution to parties of the left. Members of left-wing parties, oriented toward lower-class and poorer people, have fewer resources of all kinds—money, education, managerial and organizational skills, contacts in high places, and so on—than do traditional parties. Businesses can afford to finance promotional groups and advertising companies to sell products and the business image. In Canada, Imperial Oil employs a full-time staff of professional writers to produce an expensive glossy magazine. It contains first-class photographs, short stories, and articles extolling individual initiative, art, bravery, and intellectual endeavour, all surrounding feature articles on the wonderful enterprise and caring commitment of Imperial. One has to wonder if this is the same caring commitment shown by Imperial's American parent Exxon after the *Exxon Valdez* oil spill that dumped approximately 40 million litres of oil

off the coast of Alaska in March 1989. The company was not only slow to accept responsibility for this enormous environmental tragedy, but its policies reportedly hindered rather than expedited the clean up.

Outside the business elite, other institutions support the capitalist status quo. For example, the church often stands against socialism or communism. In Gramsci's time in Italy, voters were told the choice was between Christ or communism in the 1948 elections. Miliband (1969, 184) notes that many churches found no major difficulty in supporting overtly non-democratic regimes, including the Fascists in Italy, the Nazis in Germany, and collaborators in Vichy France. Some church members were true to their religious convictions and opposed such regimes, but these individuals did not represent the official position of the church. Another force supporting the established order is the nationalism that we learned to value as Cub Scouts and Brownies. It commonly denounces strikes and other challenges to the system as against the national interest.

Education can also be used to support the status quo. The system of education, as Parsons acknowledged, functions to allocate people into positions and to justify such allocation, high or low, as merited. People are perceived to get what they deserve. Universities depend on state financing and heavy government subsidies for research. Business endowments and research are often profoundly conservative and affect what students study. Research of interest to business in the pursuit of profits stands to get substantially more money, and hence more graduate students and researchers, than do left-leaning topics. And it goes deeper than this. In the U.S. during the McCarthy era of the 1950s, universities endorsed the exclusion of "communists" from the faculty. The definition of *communist* was so broad that it came to include almost anyone who openly criticized free-enterprise capitalism, even when that person had no affiliation with the Communist Party. At present, academic economists tend to view Marxist economics as nonsense and so leave it on the margins of the discipline. For students and graduates, nonconformity and rebellion are expensive luxuries when the goal is high-paid employment or, for that matter, any employment at all.

Among the working classes, passivity is created by capitalism because the mode of production appears as a self-evident law of nature. Workers are told that they will lose their means of livelihood in this or that industry because of technological obsolescence, or in the interests of Canada's competitive edge in the world markets, and there does not seem to be any rational basis for argument. Workers must be grateful that unemployment insurance and welfare will help to take care of them.

The Communications Industry

The core mechanism in ideological hegemony is the mass media: newspapers, magazines, books, radio, television, and cinema. The capitalist world prides itself on freedom of the press, a relative lack of censorship, and freedom from government control. It is necessary, however, to look at who owns and controls the media, which directs us straight back to the elite among the corporate class (Miliband 1969, 196–213).

The richest man in Canada, K.C. Irving, estimated to be worth $6.6 billion (U.S.) by *Fortune* magazine, controls a vast corporate empire that includes the major mass media outlets in New Brunswick. According to the *Report of the Task Force on Broadcasting Policy* (Caplan 1986, 634), Irving family members own all the province's English-language daily newspapers. Family members also own the CHSJ radio station and the CHSJ-TV station in St. John. In 1982, the Canadian Radio-Television Commission (CRTC) considered taking action to revoke the Irving family's television licence in order to reduce cross-ownership in the province, but in 1985 the licence was renewed.

The second richest man in Canada, Kenneth Thomson, worth $5.5 billion (U.S.), is a newspaper magnate. In 1980 he expanded his control over English-language newspaper circulation in Canada from 10.4 percent to 25.9 percent by acquiring FP Publications (Kent Commission 1981, 2, 90–91). By the end of 1980, the Thomson group controlled 128 newspapers: 52 in Canada and 76 in the United States. After the acquisition of FP, two conglomerates, Thomson and Southam, controlled almost 60 percent of English-language newspaper circulation in Canada. The two organizations were investigated under the Combines Investigation Act in 1980 when Southam closed the Winnipeg *Tribune* and Thomson closed the Ottawa *Journal*, allegedly to eliminate competition between the two conglomerates in these cities. Newspapers are big business for Thomson. Gross revenues of Thomson Newspapers Limited were over $500 million in 1980, yet even this was less than ten percent of the gross revenue of the entire Thomson group of companies in that year (Kent 1981, 91).

Hot on Thomson's heels is tycoon Conrad Black. He controls the Sterling Newspaper chain, which in 1980 comprised eleven daily and seven weekly newspapers. Again, the newspaper business is only a small part of Black's corporate empire, but it has been expanding throughout the 1980s. Black added the British *Daily Telegraph* to his collection in 1985. He has since acquired twenty small U.S. papers and twenty-eight Quebec dailies and weeklies, notably *Le Soleil* and *Le Droit*, and the Canadian magazine *Saturday Night* (*Globe and Mail*, 25 July 1987, D8). Media ownership in Canada is clearly a game for the corporate elite.

The Kent Commission, set up in 1980 to explore the implications of the concentration of media ownership in Canada, strongly criticized such concentration as against the public interest. It recommended that Irving, in particular, be forced to divest himself of at least some of his newspaper or television channels in order to ensure competition in the media within the Maritimes. The commission's report has quietly gathered dust ever since, with no government prepared to act upon its recommendations.

Clement (1975, chaps. 7–9) points out that the mass media do not provide a two-way exchange of ideas, but rather constitute a mechanism for selecting and screening information from one viewpoint, the viewpoint of corporate elites. The media elite function as **gatekeepers**. This means that they have the power to determine whether or not certain ideas and information will reach a wide public audience. They not only control whether an event is reported but also *how* it is reported. For example, strikes, which are counter to the interests of the corporate elite running the media, are often portrayed as subversive, against the national interest, damaging to the public, irresponsible, unfair, and so on. We are likely to get the same perspective from all branches of the media, except perhaps from small, alternative media outlets. We live in a world of second-hand information regulated by the mainstream media.

Newspaper owners commonly deny that they exercise any direct editorial control over their papers but, as Clement points out, such direct control is unnecessary when they have the power to select their editors. He cites the example of tycoon Paul Desmarais, who took over *La Presse* in Quebec and promptly purged its staff of dissidents. A similar purge took place at the *Globe and Mail* after it was acquired by Thomson in 1980. Changes at the *Globe* that, in the words of its publisher, "better serve the interests of [the paper's] elite audience" include sharp reductions in news space and personnel, dismantling the labour and women's beats while vastly expanding business coverage, reshaping delivery routes to

eliminate "undesirable"—poor—subscribers, and adding glossy magazines to appeal to upscale advertisers. Many columnists, who had contributed to the *Globe's* "mix of voices," departed (Heinricks 1989, 16). In May 1989, for example, the paper dropped the weekly column by David Suzuki, which regularly revealed the damage done to the environment by unbridled industrial expansion, ostensibly because its concerns were too "narrow."

Conrad Black has been particularly outspoken about his interest in owning newspapers. He reportedly has said that he doesn't see much point in owning newspapers if he can't use them to get his point of view across and influence affairs of state (*Globe and Mail*, 25 July 1987, D8). He has apparently agreed not to get directly involved in the editorial policy of the magazine *Saturday Night*, but he has chosen an old friend of his, John Fraser, to run it, and he intends to write regular columns for his newspapers. The potential strength of Black's influence was shown in 1970 when he insisted that his newly acquired paper, the *Sherbrooke Record*, give blanket coverage to the attempt of his junior partner, Peter White, to win a seat in the Quebec election. White's campaign failed miserably. A reporter who worked for the *Record* suggested that this was partly because White was made a laughingstock by the embarrassingly eulogistic coverage provided by Black's paper (*Globe and Mail*, 25 July 1987, D8). The reporter suggested that Black's influence has become more subtle and more persuasive in recent years.

Summary

Miliband's theory of the relations between the state and the capitalist class is not without criticism. Some argue that Miliband's underlying thesis—that the complex apparatus of the state and state policies can be understood simply as the outcome of class-conscious manipulations of the ruling class—is simply inadequate (Gold et al. 1975, part 2, 36). What is going on is far more complicated than this. Poulantzas (1972, 245) argues that the close personal ties and shared family backgrounds between business elites and state officials noted by Miliband are the effect rather than the cause of the affinity between state policies and business interests. He argues that the state is relatively autonomous from the diverse factions of the capitalist class and in fact has to be so in order to be able to protect the interests of capitalism as a whole. It is not the class origins of members of the state apparatus but the relations of production that determine the operations of the state. In principle, members of the state apparatus may come from working-class backgrounds, but it would make little difference to how the state operates because the imperatives of

capitalism remain the same. As we have seen above, the NDP cannot avoid taking into account the fact that much of the revenue of the government, upon which social policies rest, is determined by the operations of big business. Governments cannot afford to undermine corporations unless they are willing to embrace socialism completely.

Despite this qualification, Miliband is essentially accurate when he states that the Marxist perspective has seriously tarnished the liberal image that democratic government is regulated by competing interest groups. There are indeed competing interest groups, but the competition is extremely unequal. Elites within the capitalist system are in a far stronger position to defend and to pressure for their interests, at all levels of the state, than are members of the working class.

The Structure of Classes

The third major area of debate between the liberal and the Marxist theses concerns the structure of classes in capitalist societies. Marx predicted that a steady polarization of classes would occur, with increasing wealth in fewer and fewer hands at one extreme and increasing poverty at the other. The middle group, the petite bourgeoisie, would eventually collapse into the working classes, unable to keep up in the technological rat race.

Proponents of the liberal perspective challenge this thesis on two counts. Firstly, they argue that, under capitalism, the members of the working classes have become increasingly better off, enjoying generally higher standards of living, longer and healthier lives, and access to a vast array of cheap consumer goods. The thesis that the working classes are becoming more like the

bourgeoisie in their styles of life is sometimes referred to as the embourgeoisement thesis.

The second liberal argument is that Marxist theory fails to account for the spectacular expansion of the middle classes—the professional and managerial classes—under advanced capitalism. Even if we discount the argument that managers have actually taken over from owners of capital in the control of corporations, the expansion of the middle class appears to contradict the Marxist notion of class polarization. It is hard to see how these people can fit unambiguously into the working class.

If contemporary Marxist theory is to retain credibility, it needs to account for these conditions. In the following pages, we test the Marxist theory of the polarization of classes against the liberal challenge embodied in the embourgeoisement thesis and the rise of the middle class.

The Rich

The existence of a numerically tiny but immensely powerful class of ultra-rich individuals, who dominate corporate capitalism in Canada and worldwide, supports Marx's prediction of increasing concentration of wealth. In 1987, *Fortune* magazine listed 132 people around the world as billionaires, people whose personal wealth exceeds a thousand million dollars U.S. Topping the world is the Sultan of Brunei ($25 billion) and King Fadh of Saudi Arabia ($20 billion), both oil tycoons. Seven of the 132 billionaires are Canadians. The richest, K.C. Irving and Kenneth Thomson, made their fortunes in oil and in newspapers. Next come the Reichmann brothers and the "supermarket czar" Galen Weston (*Globe and Mail*, 21 Sept. 1987, B14). Conrad Black and Paul Desmarais follow close behind in the multimillionaire category. This handful of men controls more than 1300 companies. Their empires are constantly expanding as they swallow up more and more companies to diversify their holdings.

The business section of the *Globe and Mail* newspaper and its *Report on Business Magazine* keep us informed on the nouveau riche who make their fortunes in the stock market, mastering pyramiding and **leveraged buy-outs**, or "the art of buying companies with little cash and forcing the target to swallow the subsequent debt" (*Report on Business*, Oct. 1987, 27–28). In the process of building his $2 billion empire this way, Gerry Schwartz also built political influence in the federal Liberal Party, taking over as chief party fundraiser in the mid-1980s, replacing an associate of the Bronfman family. Big money and big politics are closely linked.

Hanging on to the coattails of such men are Canada's top executive class, people—

almost always men—who manage the vast corporations that the tycoons acquire. Veltmeyer (1986, 28) describes these executives as men who earn more in one day than most Canadians earn in a year. In 1983, the two top executives of Dome Petroleum received $9.4 million in salaries, equivalent to $37 000 a day; this in a debt-ridden company bailed out by the federal government in 1984 to the tune of $500 million. Several executives in Bronfman's Seagram empire earned over $1 million each in 1983, not counting perks such as stock options.

Estimates of just how many people comprise the corporate elite are hard to make because the relevant information is rarely made public. Veltmeyer puts it at about 3 percent of the population, with a core of perhaps 1 percent and a handful of ruling families.

Welfare for the Ultra Rich

The popular image of welfare is that it goes to the poor. In reality, however, the largest proportion of government handouts, tax breaks, and subsidies goes to the ultra rich, the heads of big corporations.

David Lewis (1972) describes the plethora of grants and subsidies available through the Canadian government to "corporate welfare bums." The Department of Regional and Economic Expansion (DREE) was established to try to promote development in the poorer regions of Canada, but in Lewis's view the department's major practical achievement was to subsidize big companies. Corporations used public money to update equipment in one plant, to close down others, or to relocate at public expense in search of cheaper sources of labour. Among the examples that Lewis gives is Aerovox Canada, a company that was given a grant of $254 000 from DREE to start a new factory in Amherst, Nova Scotia. Aerovox responded by closing down its plant in Hamilton, Ontario, with the loss of sixty-eight jobs at an average hourly wage of $3.32. Ninety new jobs were created in Amherst at an average wage of $2 per hour. The company was thus paid a quarter of a million dollars to reduce its labour costs. Another example is Celanese Canada, which received grants of $279 000 for modernization and expansion of plants in Drummondville, Montmagny, and Coaticook, Quebec. It responded by shutting down its Montmagny plant and laying off 450 workers. DREE then gave $2 477 000 to two other companies to create 412 new jobs in the old Celanese plant. The Newfoundland government heavily subsidized Eastern Pacific Airways, only to have the company move out of the province, with virtually no notice.

Tax concessions to corporations also amount to large government welfare donations. *The Hidden Welfare System* (National Council of Welfare, 1979a) estimates that the total tax deferrals in corporate accounts in 1976 amounted to $7.1 billion, eight hundred million dollars more than the total federal deficit for the 1976–77 fiscal year. Many companies with profits in the hundreds of millions of dollars paid no taxes.

In 1976, federal corporate income tax totalled about $6.7 billion, while federal handouts to business totalled $8 billion. In effect, ordinary people subsidized Canadian businesses by $1.3 billion. Since then, the proportion of tax paid by corporations has dropped steadily compared with personal taxes. Between 1961 and 1986, the proportion of federal tax revenue derived from corporate income tax dropped from 21.6 to 14.3 percent. Estimates suggest that it will comprise 15.4 percent in 1990–91. During the same period, the proportion of federal tax revenue collected from personal income tax rose from 34.0 to 45.2 percent. This could reach over 50 percent by 1990–91 (see figure 9-2) (National Council of Welfare 1986, 44–45). The proposed goods and services tax, due to come into effect in 1991, seems likely to shift the tax burden still further from corporate to individual taxpayers.

Figure 9–2 Federal Tax Revenue by Source, 1961–62 and 1990–91 (Projected)

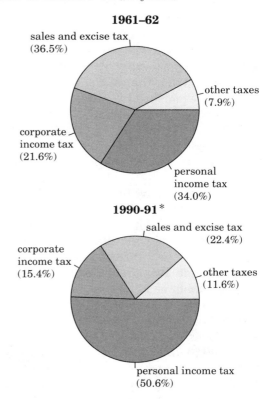

1961–62

sales and excise tax (36.5%)

other taxes (7.9%)

corporate income tax (21.6%)

personal income tax (34.0%)

1990-91 *

sales and excise tax (22.4%)

corporate income tax (15.4%)

other taxes (11.6%)

personal income tax (50.6%)

*Estimated before the announcement of the federal government goods and services tax.

Sources: National Council for Welfare (1986, 45).

Within the personal tax system, the inequalities between the rich and the poor are massive. The National Council of Welfare report notes that the more than sixty deductions, exemptions, credits, exclusions, and preferential tax rates within the income tax system all result in the largest tax savings going to the richest earners in the highest tax bracket. Billions of dollars are involved. At the other extreme, people whose earnings are so low that they are below the tax-paying threshold gain nothing from these concessions. A subsequent report on tax expenditures (1987b) explores who benefits most from a dozen different income tax exemptions. The report notes two clear patterns. In every case, the higher the taxfilers' income, the higher their benefit from the tax expenditure. Taxfilers in the lowest income group get a disproportionately small share of benefits. In 1984, the estimated cost to the federal government of all these tax exemptions was close to $25 billion.

The Poor

It is a harsh jolt to the imagination when one switches from contemplating the lives of the ultra rich to considering those of the much larger groups of Canadians who live in poverty.

Marx made two predictions concerning how capitalism as an economic system produces poverty. The relentless drive toward labour-saving technology in an effort to cut production costs would lead to chronic unemployment. At the same time, the very existence of this class of unemployed people would serve to depress wages to a level at or below subsistence, as people compete against each other for jobs.

Unemployment Figures

For a growing proportion of Canadians in the 1980s, these predictions have become reality. Unemployment hovered around 10 percent of the labour force for most of the decade, with over one million people actively seeking work but unable to find it. The proportions were higher among early school leavers and people living in the poorer regions such as the Maritimes. A report in the business section of the *Globe and Mail* (10 Oct. 1987) notes that the unemployment rate fell to a low of 8.6 percent—still over one million people—in September 1987. Much of the increase in employment, however, has taken the form of minimum wage and part-time work.

The share of total national income going

to wages and salaries fell, and the average wage did not keep pace with price increases during the 1980s. Notwithstanding this, the *Globe and Mail* report expressed concern about the threat of "wage-push inflation." In classical economic theory, high levels of unemployment are seen to weaken the bargaining power of unions and thus the ability of workers to pressure employers for higher wages. Hence, when unemployment falls, and the bargaining power of unions rises, wage settlements are likely to be high, which will push up costs of production and lead to rising prices. As prices rise, unions press hard for even greater wage increases, further pushing up costs of production and fueling the cycle of inflation. In theory, the cycle breaks when high wage costs make industry uncompetitive, so that production is cut back and workers are laid off. The resulting unemployment depresses wage demands. The alternative is for government and business to stand firm against initial demands for wage increases so that the spiral is not permitted to start. The message of the *Globe and Mail* article was that the government should come down hard against teachers and postal workers, or employers and taxpayers would be hurt.

It is important to recognize that the official Statistics Canada unemployment figures seriously underestimate the actual number of people unemployed, because many are excluded by the rigid definition used. The *unemployed*, as defined by Statistics Canada, include only "those actively seeking paid work during the previous week." This excludes all native Indians living on reserves, all people who have given up looking for work because there are no jobs in the region, all women who would like to work but cannot do so because they cannot find day care for their children. People who can find only a few hours a week of part-time work may think of themselves as unemployed, but Statistics Canada does not include them in the jobless rate. The hidden unemployment figure has been estimated as more than double the official rate.

Everywhere workers are finding their jobs threatened by technological innovation. Throughout the 1980s the major concern of unions in contract negotiations was job security. When railway workers went on strike in 1987, their primary demand was job protection, but they lost the fight as the government legislated them back to work. Commentators in the news media openly discussed the necessity of streamlining the railways and cutting up to 50 percent of such jobs in the Maritimes alone in the next few years. Workers in shipyards are facing more than a 50 percent loss of jobs from the combination of supertankers and automated construction. Auto makers can barely protect their jobs against the use of robots on the assembly lines.

The position of bank teller, once a relatively prestigious and fairly well-paid job for women, is being phased out by automatic teller machines. The condescending comments of a bank executive unwittingly support the Marxist prediction of technological unemployment.

> You've got a choice. You can have your two Susy tellers over there, with their vacation days, their sick children, their annual demand for cost of living raises, their desire for promotion; or you can have your two automatic teller machines over here, which can work all night, never get sick or take a vacation, and which only need to be upgraded every five years. It's your choice (Gregory 1983, 100).

Actually, it is not our choice. Automation is commonly forced onto customers whether they like it or not. Many customers prefer to interact with people rather than use machines, but the bank manager's remedy for such customer resistance is simple: "Charge people extra if they insist on seeing a human being; a little pressure helps the public adapt to these new systems" (Gregory 1983, 100). Meanwhile, the customers them-

selves are made to pay for the automation by increased charges for chequing and other services. Job losses in the future are likely to be concentrated in the office-work sector, where the majority of employees are women. Potential job losses to automation are estimated at up to 40 percent by the end of the 1980s. Already fewer and fewer people are doing more and more work (Gregory 1983, 105).

The growing army of unemployed and underemployed workers comprises the lumpenproletariat, most of them desperate to get a job under any conditions. Their need sets worker against worker, breaking the potential power of strike action as they provide a ready source of strikebreakers. In October 1987, while postal workers were on strike to protect their jobs against franchising, hoax telephone calls in Edmonton brought out over one hundred unemployed people to a gathering point in the city. They were hoping for a brief twelve-hour job. One woman, when asked by a CBC reporter why she was willing to strikebreak, said simply that she badly needed a job. She was unemployed and had a young son to support. In Cape Breton in August 1987, a furniture manufacturer, thinking of setting up a factory in the region, demanded that would-be employees pay $10 each for job application forms. Employees would also have to agree to work up to sixty hours a week for minimum wages, with only one week's holiday at the end of the year (CBC News, 11 Aug. 1987). He got hundreds of takers.

Subsistence Wages: The Working Poor

Marx's second prediction, that wages would drop to subsistence level or below, has also become a reality for a growing proportion of Canada's labour force. The Statistics Canada definition of the **poverty line** is based on estimates of the relationship between income and expenditures on necessities (food, clothing, and shelter). The lower the income, the greater the proportion devoted to necessities. Surveys of family expenditure in 1978 and again in 1982 found that families in Canada spend on average 38.5 percent of their income on necessities. The poverty line is defined as the level of income at which families would have to spend 58.5 percent on necessities. The poverty lines vary with size of family and area of residence, since it generally costs more to find housing in towns and cities than in rural areas. The lines are adjusted annually according to the rise in the cost of living. Table 9-2 shows the poverty lines for 1989. They range from $8 901 to $12 037 for an individual and $18 009 to $24 481 for a family of four. There are other measures of poverty, based on different cost-of-living estimates, but this Statistics Canada definition is the most stringent and the most often used.

A National Council of Welfare report entitled *Poverty Profile 1988* (1988a) estimates that in 1986 almost 15 percent of all Canadians, or 3 689 000 people, were living below the poverty line. Provincial figures on those living below the poverty line varied from 10.8 percent in Ontario to 22.8 percent in Newfoundland. It should be noted that most of these poor people have incomes considerably below the poverty line. The gap

between them and the average Canadian is enormous.

Who are the people living below the poverty line? The first myth to dispel is that they are all unemployed. In 1986, over 55 percent of poor families were headed by men and women who were in the labour force (National Council of Welfare 1988b, 78). Over 68 percent of these working poor were working full-time. In other words, more than half of the families living below the poverty line are families whose major breadwinner's income from employment is so low that it pushes them below acceptable subsistence standards.

Throughout the 1970s, the situation of the working poor got worse. According to a National Council of Welfare report (1981), the average cost of living in Canada rose by 43 percent between 1973 and 1977, but the average incomes of people earning the minimum wage rose by only 20 percent. Meanwhile, the average work wage went up by 56 percent. Minimum wage does not keep pace with inflation; both federal and provincial governments have refused to tie it to the cost of living. It is also set so low that in 1989 even a single person earning minimum wage was living below the poverty line. In 1989 the adult minimum wage ranged from $4.00

Table 9-2 Estimates of Low Income Lines for 1989

	Population of Area of Residence				
Family Size	500 000 and over	100 000 – 499 999	30 000 – 99 999	Less than 30 000	Rural
1	$12 037	$11 432	$10 725	$ 9 915	$ 8 901
2	15 881	15 074	14 063	13 048	11 634
3	21 245	20 132	18 815	17 502	15 578
4	24 481	23 266	21 749	20 231	18 009
5	28 526	27 011	25 189	23 469	20 942
6	31 157	29 437	27 516	25 583	22 862
7 or more	34 294	32 473	30 349	28 223	25 189

Source: National Council of Welfare (1989, 9).

to $5.00 per hour, with a typical provincial rate of $4.50. A full-time worker in Nova Scotia earning the provincial minimum wage of $4.50 an hour would earn $9 360 before taxes. After basic taxes, this would drop to $8 305, or $160 a week. This wage is below the poverty line for a single individual living outside a rural area. The 1989 poverty line for an individual living in Halifax, for example, was $11 434 (National Council of Welfare 1989).

Table 9-3 Estimated Welfare Income for a Single Parent with One Child, by Province, 1986

Province	Income
Newfoundland	9 559
Prince Edward Island	9 739
Nova Scotia	9 074
New Brunswick	7 911
Quebec	9 101
Ontario	10 249
Manitoba	8 925
Saskatchewan	9 804
Alberta	9 860
British Columbia	8 861
Yukon	10 303

Source: Adapted from National Council of Welfare (1987c, table 5, pp. 66-69).

For an adult with one child to support, the minimum wage is below the poverty line in every community in Canada. Families with a child to support are better off on welfare than working for minimum wage, especially when working outside the home necessitates additional expenses such as child care, transportation, and clothing costs.

Poverty Among Women and Children

The people worst hit by poverty are women and children. In 1986 women, who made up 50.8 percent of the population of Canada, comprised over 61 percent of unattached individuals living in poverty and over 56 percent of all people living below the poverty line (National Council of Welfare 1988b, 2). In 1986, 33.9 percent of unattached women under the age of sixty-five were living in poverty compared with 28.8 percent of men. Among people over the age of sixty-five, the rates for people living in poverty were 46.1 percent for women and 31.9 percent for men (National Council of Welfare 1988b, 43). While these rates and the gaps between men and women remain high, women have made significant gains since 1980 when the proportion of impoverished elderly women was 65.4 percent. The National Council of Welfare report credits improvements in guaranteed income supplements to pensions and the maturation of the Canada and Quebec pension plans for these gains.

It should be noted that official figures exclude a large but unmeasured class of women who live in poverty in male-headed households. A husband is required by law to feed, clothe, and house his wife in times of need, but he is not obliged to give her any money. A parsimonious husband can make life miserable for a dependent housewife, but this would not show up in Statistics Canada data.

The largest factor in the difference in poverty rates between the sexes is whether families are headed by men or women. In 1986, 56 percent of female single parents were living below the poverty line compared with 22.9 percent of male single-parents and 10.4 percent of couples with children. The blunt reality is that, for a variety of reasons, many women cannot earn sufficient income to support a family (National Council of Welfare 1988b, 31).

Children suffer the most from poverty. Families with children are far more likely to be poor than families without children, and the situation of the former worsened between 1980 and 1986. The poverty rate for families with one or two children in 1986 was double that for families with no children. Families with three or more children have a poverty rate of 21.5 percent, which means that over one in five such families are living in poverty (National Council of Welfare 1988b, 23). Over one million children, or 17.6 percent, lived in poverty in Canada in 1986. Child poverty rates vary by province from a low of 13.4 percent in Ontario to a high of 26.8 percent in Newfoundland. Poverty is the norm for children in female-headed single-parent families. Table 9-4 shows the number of children living in poverty in various types of families in 1986. In New Brunswick, 76.4 percent of children in female single-parent households were poor (National Council of Welfare 1988b, 28–29).

Many low income families find that they do not have sufficient money for food after paying high rents.

Welfare to the Poor

The poorest people in Canada receive proportionately the least from tax concessions and credits. Rich people have been granted proportionately higher tax savings, while payments reaching the poor have declined in relative value. A National Council of Welfare report (1979a) notes that, between 1974 and 1976, the tax savings for dependent children increased by 20 percent, with the richest 10 percent of taxpayers getting 39 percent of the $158 million savings. The lowest income earners, who fell below the tax threshold, got nothing. Family allowances, which actually do benefit poor families, rose by only 10 percent during this period. Tax savings granted to people who could afford to put money in retirement savings plans increased by 56 percent, while old age pension supplements increased by only 29 percent. On all counts, richer taxpayers got more money from the government in tax savings than the poor got in payments. During its first year in office, the Conservative government under Brian Mulroney moved to de-index family allowances and old age pensions so that they would no longer rise automatically with inflation. Public outcry from seniors led to a reversal of this decision for pensions, but not for family allowances.

Quality of Life of the Poor

The stark reality of poverty is that many people in Canada, including the working poor, have insufficient money to meet basic subsistence needs of housing, food, and clothing. The homeless rate in Toronto has been estimated to be between 50 000 and 60 000 people (*Globe and Mail*, 3 Oct. 1987, D1, D8). Many more people are on the verge of homelessness: the cost of housing is so great, relative to their income, that any kind of financial disruption will put them on the streets. A September 1987 survey of eight campgrounds around Toronto showed that about seventy-five homeless families were

Table 9-4 Child Poverty by Province and Type of Family, 1986*

Province	All Families		Couples		Female Single Parents	
	Number	Percent	Number	Percent	Number	Percent
Newfoundland	44 600	26.8	34 500	23.5	7 800	72.9
Prince Edward Island	5 100	15.5	3 500	12.0	1 300	49.8
Nova Scotia	39 000	19.8	20 900	12.4	15 200	70.9
New Brunswick	33 600	20.2	19 700	13.7	12 900	76.4
Quebec	282 100	19.2	181 200	14.1	89 300	64.1
Ontario	268 700	13.4	151 900	8.6	105 500	55.3
Manitoba	58 600	24.3	36 400	17.8	19 700	69.6
Saskatchewan	64 600	25.7	42 200	19.4	19 600	68.7
Alberta	93 600	15.6	55 200	10.7	34 000	51.3
British Columbia	126 300	20.2	65 000	12.3	55 900	70.5
Canada	1 016 000	17.6	610 400	12.2	361 000	61.8

* Children under age sixteen.

Source: National Council of Welfare (1988b, 28).

living in tents. The Canadian Council on Social Development estimated that between 130 000 and 250 000 Canadians needed emergency shelter during 1986.

The problem is simple. A person earning minimum wage—$5 an hour in 1987—in Toronto could earn $800 a month. The average rent for a one-bedroom apartment in Toronto in 1987 was $854, rising to $966 for two-bedrooms. A single person in a bachelor apartment could expect to pay $616 per month, leaving $184 for food, clothes, and heat. Minimum wage in Toronto is so far below subsistence for a family that they cannot even afford to rent a one-bedroom apartment, let alone have money left for food, clothes, and other items that most of us consider essentials, like personal care products, bus fares, school supplies, and furniture. "Luxuries" like a night out once in a while, or a holiday, are out of the question. Families break up and children are put into care because their parent or parents simply cannot find an affordable place to live. Welfare

payments for single people who are deemed employable are set far below the cost of even the cheapest single room in any city in Canada. This is not limited only to Canada. An estimated 40 000 people in the Los Angeles area live in garages. Many of these people work for minimum wage and pay a large part of their income for their substandard housing (*Globe and Mail*, 14 Sept. 1987, A9).

Many low-income people who can afford to pay their rent find that they do not have sufficient money left for food. They rely on food banks, soup kitchens, and hunting through restaurant garbage bins. People who live at this level of poverty pay a high price in self-esteem and in basic nutrition and health. A National Council of Welfare report (1975) cites data on children attending school in Montreal's impoverished East End. It notes that 21 percent of the children were malnourished, 22 percent had retarded height and weight development, and 27.5 percent had retarded physical or mental co-ordination. Poor children are more likely to be born premature and underweight, and they are more than twice as likely as other children to miss a month or more of school a year because of illness. Some children live through prairie winters without winter boots or coats. As a result, they are almost constantly sick.

It is amazing that some of these children actually manage to get passing marks at school. Only a minority do well. Poor children are far more likely to fail in school than those from rich families. Quite apart from nutrition and health problems, they must face the almost daily humiliation of being dressed worse than others, of having teachers criticize what they had for breakfast or for lunch, and of being unable to participate in a multitude of extra-curricular activities because they cannot afford the fees, equipment, or uniforms required. Nor can poor families afford to buy books, to travel, or to participate in cultural activities that stimulate learning.

The mothers of these children suffer too, both the anguish of seeing their children go without things that other children take for granted and also from going without themselves. Poor women are prone to nutritional and vitamin deficiency diseases such as scurvy (O'Connell 1983, 61). Data from a 1987 conference on homeless women show that such women tend to die seventeen to twenty-one years younger than women who have homes (*Globe and Mail*, 23 Sept. 1987).

We have to remind ourselves, when looking at these staggering figures on homeless and hungry people all across Canada and the United States, that these numbers refer to people who are living in the heart of capitalism in countries, that, on average, have the highest standard of living in the world. These data speak of a phenomenal imbalance of wealth. To the obvious questions—why not redistribute some of the wealth? Why not raise the minimum wage? Why not have a guaranteed annual income that would place

everyone above the poverty line?—comes the standard answer that such welfare measures would reduce incentives to work. While nobody suggests that children from rich families will become too comfortable to go out to work, such an argument is used against children from families on welfare (Gregory 1983, 62). Critics maintain that welfare might reduce the pool of cheap labour, or reduce capitalists' incentive to hire people and thus worsen unemployment, or raise corporate taxes and reduce incentives to invest in Canada.

Another example of the poor quality of life of people on welfare is their treatment in the courts. The classist character of the law reveals itself when employed males convicted of drunk driving charges are allowed to serve their sentences on weekends. Middle-class people who fraudulently claimed first-time homeowner grants, amounting to some $9 million in total, went virtually unpunished. Meanwhile, a mother on welfare who did not declare her $200 monthly income from driving a school bus was convicted on twenty-four separate counts of defrauding the government, one for each month involved, and given a four-month prison term (O'Connell 1983, 53–54). There are many other examples of how harshly poor people are treated in comparison with middle-class people in their relations with government agencies.

The Poorest

Bad as are the conditions of poverty experienced by the unemployed and the people living on minimum wage in Canada, they cannot begin to compare to those facing the victims of the American and Canadian capitalist system in the underdeveloped Third World. These countries suffer so badly in world markets against advanced capitalist countries that they survive only by offering their labour at starvation rates and by granting greater handouts and tax concessions to corporations than are found in Canada. The levels of subsistence, and hence the minimum wage rates, in many countries within Africa, Asia, and Latin America fall far below even the level of people living in garages in Los Angeles.

As an example of how Canadian companies contribute to the misery of Third World workers, consider the Bata Corporation, which had set up a shoe factory in the black homeland of KwaZulu in South Africa, about 150 kilometers form Durban. In 1985, Bata paid its black workers about 200 rand a month ($140 Canadian). This compares with a poverty line or "household subsistence level" for the Durban area of about 300 rand. Ottawa's code of conduct for Canadian employers in South Africa set a guideline for wages at nearly 450 rand ($337.50) per month. This would bring wages up to the local "supplemented living level," which

itself was barely above subsistence. Yet Bata payed wages well below even the household subsistence level, which calculates the clothing allowance for an adult woman as one plastic raincoat, one pair of overalls, one sweater, three pairs of stockings, one pair of pajamas, and two headscarves, two brassieres, and two pairs of underpants a year. Household equipment is calculated at one bed for two persons, to last for fifteen years, one table for the entire family for twenty years, one mug, knife, fork, spoon per person to last eight years, and one saucepan, one kettle, and one frying pan per family to last ten years.

The poverty line is more remarkable for what it omits.

It does not allow a penny for amusement, for sport, hobbies, education, medicine, medical or dental care, holidays, newspapers, stationary, tobacco, sweets, gifts or pocket

The worst effects of the contradictions of capitalism are felt in the underdeveloped or Third World.

money, or for comforts or luxuries of any kind . . . or for insurance or saving. It is not a human standard of living (*Globe and Mail*, 16 Feb. 1985, 13).

Bata shoes on sale in Canada may well have been made by people whose income from the Bata factory was only two-thirds of this minimum level.

The reason why people work for such pitifully low wages in Third World countries was pointed out by Marx. The workers can sell their labour cheaply or be replaced by labour-saving technology and so receive no wages at all. Workers have no bargaining power whatsoever. In August 1987, some 300 000 black miners in South Africa participated in a three-week strike for higher wages, but they eventually capitulated with nothing more than slightly improved fringe benefits. They were beaten by the argument that if wages went up, labour substitution technology would quickly follow, with massive layoffs. Unemployment among blacks in South Africa and the surrounding black homelands was so high that, during the miners' strike, the Anglo American Corporation was able to lay off 40 000 employees and hire strikebreakers. Workers are thus trapped in a vicious circle of dependency and low wages, which is very hard to break.

Workers at a Hyundai car factory in South Korea went on strike in July and August 1987 to press for better wages, and the strike quickly spread through 190 other companies. The protest was eventually crushed by state police. Only minimal concessions were granted to the strikers. It was argued that South Korea could only hope to compete on world markets by paying low wages to make cheaper cars and other products. Meanwhile American car manufacturers are pressuring for tariffs and other trade restrictions to reduce competition from foreign auto producers. The alternative strategy, followed by many corporations, is to close down plants in North America and set up factories in the Third World, where they can combine high technology and low wages.

The Affluent Middle Classes

When the two extremes, the super rich and the very poor, are considered, the data clearly fit the predictions derived from the Marxist model. It is with respect to the middle classes, particularly within advanced capitalist countries, that the fit between evidence and model becomes shaky. Marx predicted the polarization of classes into the capitalist elite and the workers at subsistence wages, but he did not foresee the spectacular rise of the middle classes.

This rise of the affluent middle classes is the central focus of the liberal critique of Marxist theory. The core argument is that the wealth enjoyed by the super rich under free-enterprise capitalism provides the fundamental incentive for industrial growth, which has given rise to affluent living standards for the majority of people in developed capitalist societies. The system makes possible enriched lifestyles and the flowering of cultural freedom and democracy, which are constantly being contrasted with the drudgery and mediocre standards of living in communist societies such as the USSR. The poverty of the bottom 10 to 15 percent of the population is not so much denied as downplayed and explained in terms of individual inadequacies that prevent people from taking advantage of real opportunities. Much of contemporary Marxist writing focusses upon the character of the middle class in an attempt to reconcile it with the fundamentals of Marxist theory.

The Embourgeoisement Thesis

The embourgeoisement thesis holds that workers in many industries are becoming more affluent, their wages rivalling the salaried incomes of the professional and managerial class. Car assembly workers are a favoured example for this thesis, together with other skilled tradespeople and skilled industrial workers. Unionized employees can often command high wages, particularly in semi-automated or high-technology industries where labour costs are a declining proportion of overall production costs.

Other theorists argue that a decent standard of living for many workers is bought at the very high price of alienation at work, coupled with the growing threats of automation, deskilling, and job loss. Rinehart, in his powerful study *The Tyranny of Work* (1975), asks whether workers are affluent. For the majority of both blue-collar and white-collar workers, the answer is no. Even those workers who are not close to the poverty line are generally only getting by. They are concerned with meeting car and mortgage payments. Their jobs are becoming increasingly deskilled, with no opportunity for learning or advancement. Covert efforts to humanize work are evident in wildcat strikes, sabotage of the production process, output restrictions, and the permanent struggle against pressures to speed up work.

Those who have skilled jobs find themselves increasingly subject to the threat of technological change and automation, both of which downgrade their skills. Typographical workers in the printing industry once were highly paid, skilled workers in great demand. Now the job has been automated, their skills are obsolete, and their job security is gone. A similar fate befell highly skilled hard rock mining workers at the INCO mines in Sudbury. As all aspects of mine work became progressively more mechanized from the 1960s onward, many of the highly skilled jobs such as drilling and blasting were downgraded to routine semiskilled work easily learned by new employees. Once-powerful workers found their skills obsolete and their job security and high pay gone. Maintenance workers, who look after the new machines, are trained only in narrowly specific skills appropriate for one piece of equipment. This ties workers

to one machine and minimizes the training time required. They are easily replaceable and hence are cheap (Clement 1981, chap. 8).

Office workers also face the mounting pressures of automation. In offices, this process is almost always associated with increased workloads, speed up, and technological supervision of virtually every movement, keystroke, and error. Gregory (1983) describes the alienation of workers in these "electronic sweatshops," confined all their working hours to one spot, doing keystrokes at a tremendous pace, while a computer at the end of the room keeps count.

Productivity increases tremendously with new machines, but this is not reflected in more breaks, more pay, or shorter work-weeks, just more pressure with fewer people doing more work. Meanwhile jobs are devalued, pay is stagnant or declining, and unemployment is rising among secretarial staff. A vice-president of international relations at a Cleveland bank bragged to Swedish researchers that, with the aid of computers, secretaries could handle just about everything while he was away on long trips abroad. When the Swedes asked whether secretaries were being paid more for this extra work, there was a long silence. The answer was no (Gregory 1983, 104).

It is important to recognize that there is nothing inevitable about how new technology is introduced or its effects upon workers. These are matters of conscious choice by those who have the authority to make the decisions. In Sweden the choices have been made very differently from in Canada. Ninety percent of Swedish workers are unionized, and both government and employers have to respond to their proposals. Workers also have guaranteed positions on boards of management of corporations where they work. By contrast, in Canada in 1979, less than 35 percent of paid workers were unionized. This includes 40.1 percent of male and 23.7 percent of female workers (Brisken 1983, 29). Gregory (1983) cites an example of how workers in a Swedish insurance union influenced decisions about technological change. Instead of centralization, speedup, and a decreased labour force doing more work, the union called for the creation of more insurance centres, especially in rural areas, with the objective of reducing customers' travelling time to a service centre. They also wanted increased time with customers to explain services. They argued that, as computers speed up paper work, more time would be available for service, while computer linkups would allow more diverse locations. The problem, then, lies not in the technology itself, but in the manner in which it is used and its purpose. It is a problem, ultimately, of patterns of ownership and control.

Archibald (1978, 174) describes at length the experience of depression, bordering upon mental illness, among many blue-collar and office workers. Work, is, in a literal sense, dehumanizing. Workers are not paid to be creative or to think. They are paid to do as they are told when they are told. As both Archibald and Gregory acknowledge, the result is often passivity and withdrawal, mixed with frustration and covert defiance. People who have no control over their jobs are likely to withdraw from social and political activity. People who have creative jobs, involving decision making and control over their working lives, are far more likely to become involved as leaders in social and political activities as well. Mainstream theory in sociology compares the different levels of apathy and involvement, develops typologies of class culture, and uses them to account for the class character of democracy. It becomes an instance of ideology, of blaming the victims for the results of the dehumanizing experiences of work.

The Professional and Managerial Class

The working lives of people in professional and managerial jobs seem far better in comparison. They earn more money, and their work is not machine-paced. They exercise decision-making responsibilities and have generally higher status than blue-collar and office workers. The term *professional* is associated with notions of autonomy and freedom from external controls. The expansion of this middle class of skilled and well-educated workers is at the core of the liberal thesis of embourgeoisement, which envisions the majority of workers in advanced capitalism coming to share the satisfaction and sense of personal freedom associated with professional work.

Marxist theorists, however, dispute this image of affluence and autonomy. The majority of lower-level supervisors find their jobs almost as tightly circumscribed as do workers, only in different ways. They do not determine the guidelines or objectives of the organizations for which they work but are responsible for ensuring they are carried out. Some suggest that middle-class people working for corporations may be even more alienated than are the working classes. They owe their minds, their thoughts, their whole being to the corporation. They must fit the corporate image. They are paid to think like "corporate men." Workers are paid to do as they are told, but they are free to think as they please. They do not have to accept or believe in what they do, nor need they fit the image desired by the corporation to the same extent that managers must (Smith 1977). The minority of women who enter managerial roles find that they have little if any leeway to change the image. They must conform if they are to keep their jobs or get promoted. Many women managers are finding the demands of corporate conformity so repressive that they are quitting their jobs (Maynard and Brouse 1988). Managers wield considerable power, but that power is borrowed, exercised by proxy from above, and it requires obedience. Essentially their role is to transmit orders from above and to ensure compliance from below.

One supervisor described his job as comprising constant checking on people: checking that they arrive on time, that they do not take too long in the washroom or too long for lunch breaks; checking their work; checking that they are not cheating (Terkel 1974, 400).

For the most part, this is lonely work, with managers separated from the comradeship of fellow workers but too trapped in the hierarchy to have friendships with other supervisors. There is always someone above them trying to find fault, and someone below hoping to push them aside and take their job. Managers thus find themselves caught in a squeeze, subject to scrutiny and control from above and pressure from below (Terkel 1974, 405–06).

In managerial work, the objectives of competition and profits always take precedence over other concerns. The product itself is a matter of virtual indifference. Other professionals who work in industry find themselves constrained by the same priorities of competition and profit, which rob them of their work autonomy. Scientists in industry, for example, find their work subject to bureaucratic controls and their research projects dictated by corporate interests. What autonomy they have is exercised only within strict limits. Research of scientific value may be pushed aside or abandoned if it threatens profitable ventures. Such restrictions may be even harder to bear in some respects than those imposed upon other workers because the education and training of scientists have conditioned them to identify with the image of an autonomous searcher after truth. Industrial reality can be a hard shock.

Workers in the public service sector fare little better. Governments are not geared to competition and profits, but they are geared to restraint and cost cutting, or they risk corporate criticism. Efficiency experts, drawn from management consulting firms to study public sector operations, bring with them the philosophies and loyalties of private business. They also bring the views that the public service is non-productive, even parasitic, and hence that employment in the public sector should be kept to a minimum. Workers find themselves subject to the same work overload, impossible demands, deteriorating working conditions, and drive for labour-saving technology as in industry (Rinehart 1975, 111).

These alienating pressures on managerial, professional, and administrative staff are reflected in growing unionization within this middle-class sector. Managers do not identify with workers or see themselves as members of the proletariat, yet at the same time they feel the need to organize for their own protection. Lower-level managers particularly can find themselves subject to their own programs of efficiency and cost-cutting as computer surveillance techniques and computerized work flow reduces the need for human supervisors (Nichols and Beynon 1977).

Limits to the Traditional Marxist Thesis

The Controversial Character of the Middle Class

Traditional political economy theory has proven a powerful explanatory tool with respect to our understanding of the concentration of capital, the decline of small business and primary producers in Canada, the miserable conditions facing the working poor, and the growing reserve army of unemployed and underemployed people and their children. But it has difficulty classifying the large and growing segment of the labour force employed in technical, professional, and managerial roles, particularly those within the service sector.

Marxist arguments concerning the categorization of the middle classes can only be pushed so far. There are indeed many ways in which managers and professionals are subject to the pressures of capitalism, but then so are the bourgeoisie themselves. The attempt to push everyone who does not own capital into the proletariat only succeeds at the risk of making this class so broad as to be almost meaningless. It also ignores very real gains in affluence and the inequality of working life within the professional, managerial, and technical sectors.

Veltmeyer grapples with these problems in his text on *Canadian Class Structure* (1986, 25) where he debates whether to place the managerial class in the petite bourgeoisie or the proletariat. He acknowledges that the development of capitalism has generated a new form of middle class not envisioned by Marx, a class that falls somewhere between capital and labour. Members of this class sell their labour power but have considerable control over their own conditions of work and often over those of other people. These people are not exploited, strictly speaking, because the wealth that accrues to them from salaries, commissions, or fees is equal to or greater than the value of any wealth or service they create (Veltmeyer 1986, 46–47). Veltmeyer attempts to resolve the ambivalent status of this new middle class in relation to Marxist theory by splitting it into two parts. The lower part, comprising semiprofessionals and office and service sector workers, he places with the proletariat, while the higher sector of managerial and professional workers he places with the business class (Veltmeyer 1986, 25).

While Veltmeyer does not actually cite the classical sociological theorist Max Weber, he comes close to adopting his definition of class as life chances, rather than ownership or non-ownership of capital. Weber acknowledged that ownership of capital was a crucial determinant of life chances for the bourgeoisie at the top of the class hierarchy, and lack of such ownership equally crucial for the propertyless,

unskilled workers at the bottom. But he modified the Marxist model to include skills as a form of ownership that significantly alters people's life chances in the marketplace and hence their class position. He argued that skilled people could not be expected to identify with the unskilled working classes because their actual position within the marketplace was significantly different, as was their style of life, their social status, and the political pressure groups or parties to which they would gravitate (Gerth and Mills 1946, 180–95).

Veltmeyer, in effect, conceptualizes semiprofessionals and office workers as sharing the life chances and therefore the status of the manual working class while professionals and managers share the life chances of the capitalist class. Professionals are thus lumped in with capitalists "parasites" who live on the surplus value created by the producing classes while producing nothing themselves. This surplus class or new petite bourgeoisie encompasses a bewildering variety of occupations. Speculators in the stock market may fit unambiguously into such a category, but when it is expanded to include people working in "insurance, real estate, advertising, finance, as well as those in the ideological apparatus (government, law, military, education, and religion)" (Veltmeyer 1986, 58), one begins to feel uneasy. Veltmeyer goes on to discuss the proliferation of positions requiring professional or advanced technical training, which he describes as "connected to the expansion of reproductive institutions (such as education, medicine, advertising, the media, the professions, research and development, social service, and the welfare state)." He adds further the "independent fee-for-service professionals and managers in the corporate and state sectors of society," who together form "a distinct upper stratum within the new petite bourgeoisie" (Veltmeyer 1986, 58). These are the people who have relatively high incomes and who by definition are not alienated or exploited because they do not produce any surplus value. They do not produce commodities at all and so must live on the surplus value produced by others, although they themselves do not own capital.

Something is seriously amiss with a classificatory system that has such a huge jumble in the middle. A number of Marxist theorists have become embroiled in classificatory nightmares, arguing among themselves where to place boundaries. Such sterile arguments are a sure sign that something is wrong with the model that generates the classifications. Veltmeyer (1986, 61) himself admits that the lines between the managerial stratum of the petite bourgeoisie and the bourgeoisie, and between the bottom rungs of the managerial ladder and the upper parts of the working class, are fuzzy. He cites arguments placing all supervisors and foremen in the petite bourgeoisie on the grounds that they help capitalists dominate, control, and thus exploit workers. Yet the attempt to lump foremen in with the small business class, the original meaning of petite bourgeoisie, is stretching the definitions so wide that Veltmeyer and others reject this and instead place them in with the working class, making the supervisory cutoff somewhat higher up (Veltmeyer 1986, 61).

Ghorayshi (1987) brings up yet another classificatory dilemma when she raises the question of whether Canadian agriculture is capitalist or petit bourgeois. She draws an arbitrary boundary by labelling farms hiring fewer than five person-years of labour as petit bourgeois, and five or more as capitalist. Her main rationale is that non-employer farms do not receive surplus value from the exploitation of labour because they rely solely on their own labour and that of their household members. One is left with the uncomfortable feeling that, by this definition, a male farmer who appropriates all his

wife's labour on the farm, without paying her anything for it, is somehow not exploiting anyone, while if he actually paid her a salary he would be exploiting her.

It is precisely this kind of structuralist Marxism, with its slavish application of abstract categories onto data, that the Marxist historian E.P. Thompson (1978a) challenges. He advocates a conceptualization of class as a process rather than an entity. Classes do not exist with people slotted into them, as in Veltmeyer's approach. Rather, classes emerge as the outcome of processes of struggle around material interests.

The New Middle Class in Marxist Theory

An important alternative analysis emerging within Marxism suggests that the phenomenon of the rising middle class needs to be understood in relation to processes in the development of advanced capitalism. These processes actually require the expansion of an educated middle-class labour force. They also require that capitalists exert less rather than more control over that labour force (Morgan and Sayer 1988, 26).

Morgan and Sayer draw attention to the fundamental importance of innovation to capitalism. Intensification of labour and deskilling are not the only means toward the goal of profit. Product diversification and the cheapening of the machines needed for production are also alternatives. Particularly in the burgeoning field of electronics, product innovation is an essential element in staying ahead of competition in the rate and quality of production. The relations of production that enable capitalists to deskill and control employees are anathema to the flexibility, creativity, and skill needed to be able to develop innovative ideas and to organize, swiftly and collectively, to translate these ideas into commodities. The development of a highly educated, professional sector of the labour force may thus be occurring at the same time that other workers are being deskilled, fragmented, and routinized. Severe shortages of skilled labour can occur at the same time as high unemployment.

Marx himself did not foresee this polarization within the working class between a deskilled lower working class and a highly educated professional working class. Traditional Marxist analysis, which closely follows the model of capitalism proposed by Marx, has tended to be more concerned with explaining away the rise of the middle class than with accounting for it. Morgan and Sayer (1988, 8–9) criticize much Marxist-influenced literature for promoting misleading stereotypes of industry and of the international division of labour. This literature tends to ignore product innovation as a form of competition and to give disproportionate attention to processes of routine mass production when only a minority of employees

in manufacturing still work in such industries.

The argument proposed by Morgan and Sayer is that the seeds of a more adequate account of the rise of the middle class can be found within the Marxist analytical framework. The neglected factor is the compulsion to achieve continual innovation in technological means of production and in products. This compulsion results in a need for a highly skilled and flexible labour force to implement these innovations in order to outpace competitors. This thesis predicts an increasing polarization within the working class, both nationally and internationally, between skilled workers in high technology industries and deskilled workers elsewhere. If this thesis wins general acceptance, it seems likely to generate major changes in Marxist analysis of class relations under capitalism.

The Marxist-Feminist Challenge to Political Economy

Women: The Marginal Topic

It has long been argued that Marxists are unable to deal with the oppression of women because they always subsume it under the oppression of the working classes generally. The Marxist analysis only extends so far. Women who have paid employment can be accommodated on much the same terms as men. They can be classified as capitalists (extremely rare) or workers or placed in the middle-cum-working-class masses as office and service workers, technicians, professionals, and semiprofessionals. The main debate centres around whether to classify office work as middle class or working class, and why women generally are ghettoized into low-paying "women's work."

These are important questions, but they apply to, at most, about half the adult female population of Canada. Statistics Canada data for August 1987 showed that only 52 percent of all women in Canada were listed as employed and, of these, 21 percent worked part-time (Statistics Canada 1987, 45). The problem, then, is what to do with the more than half of all women whose sole or predominant occupation is that of homemaker.

Classical Marxist theory left no place for homemaking within its analysis. People who do such work—virtually entirely women—are relegated to the category of non-productive dependants. Housewives are usually accorded the status of the male to whom they

One of the main questions raised in Marxist analyses of women is why they are ghettoized into poorly paid "women's work."

are attached, either husband or father, suddenly to take on a status of their own, often much lower, when they get a job. Housework as such does not have a clear status. A homemaker who is the wife of a billionaire capitalist is not in the same class as a homemaker married to a propertyless, unskilled, minimum-wage-earner, although even the latter is higher in status than a single-parent welfare recipient.

Until very recently, homemaking was not seen as work at all. It took pioneering studies by feminist theorists in the late 1970s and 1980s to begin to show the amount and the complexity of the work actually encompassed under the label *housework*. Meg Luxton's (1980) study of women's work in the home details just how demanding and how crucial such work is. Homemaking involves all those activities that maintain the house and service its members, including planning and preparing meals, cleaning and maintaining the house and its contents, and obtaining the materials and supplies needed

for that work. It involves financial work of consumption management, ensuring that limited financial resources will cover the subsistence needs of the worker and the worker's family. Shopping for a family on a tight budget, in an era when people are constanty bombarded with advertising concerning the multitude of commodities a family supposedly needs, takes considerable skill. Homemaking further involves all the rhythms of motherwork: coping with pregnancy, birth, infancy, training preschoolers, and supporting school-age children. Often it involves juggling several different schedules to accommodate the demands of baby, preschoolers, school timetables, a husband's work timetable, and the woman's own work. It also includes the emotional labour of tension management, continually repairing the damage done to household members at work and at school. Yet this work still remains a marginal topic, relegated to the sphere outside the labour force or, more usually, outside the economy altogether.

The Domestic Labour Debate

The **domestic labour debate** struggles with questions concerning women's work within the home and its place in the economy. Where and how do domestic workers fit into the capitalist social system? What is it that domestic workers do? What is the function of that work for capitalism? From the answers to these questions, theorists hope to understand why it is that men seem to have power over women in society.

One approach in this debate conceptualizes domestic labour as essentially a remnant of a feudal form of production that has never become integrated into the capitalist system. The relationship between wife and husband within marriage has features in common with the relationship between serfs and nobles under feudalism (Delphy 1984). Women labour within families to produce for the subsistence needs of the unit as a whole under the "lordship" of the husband. This mode of production generates its own internal class struggle between women and men, which occurs independently of the class relations of capitalist production in the wider economy. There seems little reason to expect that such family sex-class relations would disappear with the overthrow of capitalism. The work of housewives is not subject to any of the contractual regulations characteristic of capitalist waged labour. It is not exchanged for wages, and thus has no value within the public market economy (Benston 1969). Benston proposes that these feudal relations of domestic production should be broken by the transfer of all work now done in the home into the public economy. Laundries, restaurants, cleaning services, and day-care centres could theoretically take over all the domestic labour work done by women in private homes. This would draw women into the workforce alongside men, as wage labourers. They would thus escape the feudal bondage of families and have a class status equal to men.

This theory does not explain the persistence of domestic labour as a feudal remnant. If such labour were marginal to capitalism, it should long ago have been swallowed up by capitalist enterprise. Yet domestic labour shows no sign of disappearing.

An alternative approach conceptualizes domestic labour as actively performing a central function for the capitalist system, even as it appears to be outside the market economy. That function is the maintenance and reproduction of labour power (Morton 1972; Dalla Costa and James 1972; Seccombe 1974; 1980). In the language of Marxist theory, domestic labour produces the commodity of labour power for exchange on the labour market. The male wage appears to be exchanged for labour at the work site, but in fact it is exchanged for the labour needed to produce labour power. Women are "paid" at subsistence level to do this work when they are given housekeeping money. This pay is so low that is serves to cheapen the commodity of labour power itself, so that wages can be lower and profits higher (Seccombe 1980). Seccombe suggests that women balance their "average domestic labour time" against the returns they might make from taking wage work and purchasing domestic services from others. Arguing that capital should be required to pay for the labour of producing and reproducing labour power, proponents of this theory demand wages for housework.

This theory does not fully address the problem of why domestic work came to be privatized, invisible, and unpaid (Armstrong and Armstrong 1985, 15). The Armstrongs argue that the privatization of domestic work is fundamental to the workings of the capitalist system. In their view, capitalism is based fundamentally on free wage labour that can be exploited for surplus value. This requires the separation of a public, commodity-production unit from a private subsistence unit. The system of free wage labour itself seems to presuppose that labour is produced at least in part outside the capitalist market, or outside the production process proper. Hence housework, the work that produces labour power, takes place in the privatized and unpaid location of families. Women, not men, give birth to and nurture babies. Hence, women as mothers cannot participate fully in the labour force, at least for a time. Women's subordinate status follows from this enforced separation. Since capitalism values commodities, women's non-commodity work is devalued. Moreover, the position of women as a reserve army of labour is also necessary for the system to function. They even out fluctuating demands for labour because they can be hired when there is a shortage and pushed back into unpaid domestic work at other times. Hence, the relative exclusion and subordination of women appears as a necessary condition for the capitalist system.

The major contribution of the domestic labour debate is that it has at least made housework visible as a topic within traditional political economy theory. But analysis of housework still remains marginal to political economy. When the topic does attract interest, the focus is often on how to minimize domestic labour or to push as much of it as possible onto the public sector in order to free women up to participate more fully in wage labour.

This continuing marginalization of domestic labour is being challenged by radical feminists. Instead of looking at women's domestic work from the standpoint of the dominant capitalist economy, they advocate a new focus that looks at economy from the standpoint of homemakers. It is this emerging perspective that we examine below.

Political Economy from the Standpoint of Women

One of the major theorists to attempt a feminist re-evaluation of political economy is Dorothy Smith. She argues that political economy, as a discipline within social science, is itself embedded in the **ruling apparatus** of capitalism. The problem, she suggests, is that the discipline takes for granted the assumption that the "main business" of the economy is the accumulation of capital. What is left out is, in effect, all the rest of the economy. Smith points out that the precapitalist era made no distinction between production and reproduction. Producing food, shelter, tools, and so forth, met subsidence needs and provided for the children of those who did the work of production (Smith 1987b, 8). There was a unity between the economy and people's lives. Capitalism rent asunder this unity when production was geared to exchange for profit. The focus of political economy retains this distorted view. This is as true for theorists interested in the domestic labour debate as for the field at large. The agenda remains structured by the ruling apparatus because the ruling apparatus predefines what the main business of political economy is, what it talks about, and what it ignores. The result is the marginalization of central aspects of the economy such as reproduction, subsistence, and maintenance of the family and home.

This theoretical critique is still a highly controversial subject within Marxist academic circles. When Dorothy Smith presented a paper entitled "Feminist Reflections on Political Economy" in 1987, it provoked powerful defensive reactions from Marxist theorists present, both women and men. Long-accustomed to taking a critical stand against mainstream economics, the challenge that they themselves might be propounding a conservative, mainstream theory is a bitter pill to swallow.

Smith argues that much feminist work in political economy is still within this mainstream agenda in which the main business is making money. Feminists add topics at the margins of the discipline, but the central focus remains. Smith cites the experience of economist Sylvia Ann Hewlett with the Economic Policy Council in the United States. Hewlett tried to set up a committee in 1980 to study problems of women's work, family, and child care, with a view to making recommendations to the president of United States and to Congress. Virtually no one wanted to serve on the committee because the topics were not seen as the main business of the council (Smith 1987b, 8).

The standpoint of the majority of women is outside the main business of making profits. Most of the work that they do is located in parts of the economy other than where the accumulation of capital takes place. It is this economy that needs to be addressed. What is needed is a redefinition of the term *economy* that does not begin from the accumulation of capital, but from the situation of people in their actual lives. When the main business is redefined as the enhancement of people's lives, rather than the accumulation of profits, then women's work becomes, not peripheral, but central to the analysis.

This change in focus also radically alters the way in which the work of people within the service sector is analysed. Within traditional political economy, such workers are seen as marginal, living upon the wages of productive workers while not producing anything themselves. However, when enhancement of life becomes the definition of the purpose of the economy, people who provide needed services cease to be merely consumers of other people's wages. They actually appear as producers themselves. The dependency relation then appears to work in reverse, with men as a class, as well as children, depending upon the multiple services provided by homemakers, in return for providing a subsistence housekeeping allowance.

A simple example may help to bring this into focus. Consider a Toronto family where the husband works all day for Litton industries, helping to produce guidance systems

for nuclear bombs, while the wife cares for their children and spends her afternoon sitting with her husband's elderly mother who feels lonely and unwell. Whose day's work has produced the most value for the economy? The answer depends on the definition of economy being used. Within the capitalist model, only the worker at Litton has produced surplus value, which contributes to profits, while the wife's work counts for nothing. Within a community benefit definition of economy, the wife has produced a great deal while the Litton worker has contributed nothing.

Marxist-feminist theory advocates a change not only in the definition of economy but also in the methodology used for analysis. It is important to recall that Marx thought that the problem of bias was not in the values of different researchers but in the methods used, methods that obscured what was actually going on. Marx accused the classical economists of his time of using abstract concepts such as *markets* and *exchange of commodities* to explain behaviour, as if people were pawns of market forces. They treated abstractions as concrete entities that do things to people. This is ideological because it obscures the fact that *people* do things, and that actual human relations produce the patterns that economists then use for explanations.

In Marxist-structuralist analysis, the class system tends to take the place of commodities and the market system in explanations. It is viewed as an existing structure that determines people's lives. Veltmeyer (1986, 13) aptly sums up this approach at the beginning of his discussion of the structure of class. He writes:

> To define class in structural terms is to assume the social structure has positions or . . . "empty places" occupied by individuals. The structural analysis of class is primarily the analysis of these places and only secondarily of the actual individuals who fill them.

He goes on to argue that, while it may be important to examine the social conditions of people and their struggle to live within or to change the class structure, the need to understand the positions into which people are sorted has logical priority. It is this commitment to analysing structures that makes the problem of ambiguous classification of the middle classes and women so serious.

Once people are slotted into their places, class position can be treated as a sufficient explanation for whatever happens. The workings of the state in capitalist society can be accounted for by the class of origin of people in different social institutions; the class of origin of newspaper owners becomes sufficient explanation for the content of the papers. Put simply, class position determines behaviour.

Within this framework, the notion of cultural domination of the ideas of the ruling class becomes particularly important to explain the absence of revolt among the working class. The failure of workers to act in accordance with their objective class position is explained in terms of an alienating culture that dopes them into a passive acceptance of their situation. Workers fail to understand that it is private ownership of the means of production in the hands of capitalists that creates and perpetuates their own desperate need to sell their labour power to an employer. Capitalists come to be seen as benefactors because they provide the jobs that workers need. Many workers even side with or vote for their capitalist "benefactors" against other workers. Marx refers to this widespread failure among workers to recognize their true class interest as **false consciousness**. The concept of false consciousness is used to explain why workers are unable to act collectively as a class-for-itself to challenge and overthrow the economic system that oppresses them.

The Marxist-feminist approach advocated by Smith rejects this class determinism. Smith argues that this view of the economy

as a system of predetermined places into which people are slotted is ideological in two respects. First, it adopts the assumptions of the ruling apparatus even as it tries to criticize them. Labour is managed precisely through notions of division of labour and of positions that deserve differential rewards. Such notions are used, for example, to account for the lower average pay of employed women compared with men. They are not underpaid but are simply concentrated in the wrong categories. They need to study science and mathematics to compete for the better jobs that men fill. The questions of whether women's work really is as unskilled as it is held to be, or whether service work such as homemaking, day care, nursing, and teaching actually warrants low pay, disappear from the analysis. The deterministic approach is ideological in a second sense, in that it loses sight of people as active agents in the production of their economic world. *Classes* rather than *people* seem to do things.

What Smith advocates is a shift in focus from the description of class as "empty places occupied by people" to the analysis of active processes, actual things that people do in organizing the relations of production so that the patterns that we see as "class" emerge. The system of classes does not exist all by itself. People actually produce these relations, and they also change them. When questions about class are raised like this, what women do ceases to be a marginal topic and becomes central to the analysis. Women can be shown to be very active in the social construction of class relations through the work they do within the home, as well as in the myriad of offices where secretaries put together the work of their bosses.

This same methodological focus on what people do to put together the patterns that political economists then discover applies equally well to Marxist assumptions about the dominance of the ideas of the ruling class and patterns of class values. People are not preprogrammed robots who automatically think the way they do because of their class position. Class values and ruling ideas do not just happen; they are socially constructed by the actual work that people do. What and how we think results from complex processes of personal experience and how we come to know about the world.

Increasingly in our society this process of learning about our world is organized for us by professionals working in complex organizations. They include teachers, journalists, bureaucrats in all kinds of government agencies, political economists, and writers of sociology texts. Such people gather information, think about it, and organize how it is presented so that others come to view it as they do. Journalists invariably go to the "official" sources in government agencies or other large corporations for background information and comments on current events. These comments are then treated as "the facts of the matter," while what non-officials or ordinary bystanders say is treated as merely opinions. As a result, a great deal of what we think we know about our society is what spokespersons from big corporations decide is relevant to tell us. In Smith's words (1974b, 257), our knowledge is mostly second-hand, already organized by other people. We need to explore the processes by which what we know is produced, in order to understand how and why we think as we do.

It is not possible to summarize all the main points of a political economy from the standpoint of women because the theory is only beginning to emerge. A basic assumption of this approach is that the personal is political: the intimacy of personal relations within families and between colleagues is directly involved in the production of political economy as experienced by women. What is offered below are only suggestions as to the kinds of issues that come into focus when the main business of the economy is defined in terms of the enhancement of the material well-being of people. It challenges the basic value underlying capitalism as a mode of production, namely that profit and accumulation of capital are all that count in economic analysis.

Housework

Homemaking has to be at the heart of a feminist political economy because it is the responsibility of the vast majority of Canadian women, whether or not they are in the paid labour force as well. The standpoint from which women, as women, experience the social world is that of homemaker. Regular housework is described at some length in chapter 11 on the sociology of the family. The focus here is on the hidden economy of social services performed by women at home. There are multiple ways in which the unpaid work of women is appropriated by the state. This appropriation, or exploitation, is especially marked during periods of recession when governments are under pressure from business interests to cut spending. "Savings" in the economy are made through loading more and more work onto women in the home without paying them anything for it and actually firing many who used to do such work for pay.

Armstrong (1984) notes that when governments cut back on hospital services, women take up the slack by doing the nursing at home. They spend far more time in hospitals helping to care for relatives when adequate nursing services are not available. When patients are discharged early to "save" money, women take over their convalescent care at home. When governments cut back on senior citizens' homes and residential homes for the disabled, justifying the financial cuts by arguing that these people are better off within the community, it is women who take over this chronic care nursing for free. Free, that is, to the government. It may often be at great expense to the women themselves who forfeit hours of time, and often paid jobs, to do this care work. When the state cuts back on day-care services and kindergartens, women in the home do the work. When the state cuts back on teachers, homemakers take up the slack, giving their time to supervise lunches and after school activities, and doing the extra coaching and remedial work that teachers no longer have time to do. When youth employment opportunities are cut back, women at home take up the slack by providing homes and care for adolescents who would otherwise be independent. When wages are cut back, women make up the difference with their own labour, trying to substitute for purchases by making do, mending, sewing, knitting, managing with broken appliances. Above all, they double and treble their labour in stress management to absorb and contain the damage done to family members by such cutbacks.

All too often it is women who work in the social service sector who lose their paid jobs when the government cuts back. The government, in effect, defines their work as not in the marketplace, and thus saves all their salaries, while women continue to do the work without pay.

Viewed from the standpoint of women in the home, government restraint programs appear as the most extreme example of total exploitation. Women are driven to perform services without any pay at all and are forced to depend upon others for subsistence. Yet this enormous hidden economy of housework, worth millions of dollars in government savings annually, is invisible to traditional political economy with its focus on capital accumulation. It is treated as nonproductive, as not in the economy at all, and those who do such work are seen as nonentities or idle consumers.

The Formation of Class

In traditional political economy, the class structure can be taken for granted. It exists, it affects people's lives, and it provides a central explanatory framework for what happens in society. From the standpoint of women and women's work, however, class relations do not simply exist. They have to be continually produced and reproduced.

In this production process families, or more specifically homemakers, become the **subcontracted agencies** of corporations. Women work for the corporations without being paid. Without the work of women in the home, workers would not appear for work everyday. The upper echelons of the work world would not maintain their pinstriped image without a host of services to manage the backstage production; alienated workers would not turn up for shifts day in day out, year in year out, without women to keep the pressure up, to control recalcitrant and reluctant labour, to absorb the tensions, repair the damage done, and organize home life around the schedules of the workplace.

Women reproduce the generations of labour power. Motherwork, even more than the work of teachers, serves to reproduce children trained to fit the school system and the demands of corporate careers. The roots of ideological hegemony begin in the home as mothers train their children in what it takes to get by or to get ahead within the corporate capitalist system and motivate them to conform to its demands. They know they will be judged as mothers by how well or how badly their children perform in this world. They also know that the material well-being of themselves and their children and grandchildren depends directly upon such conformity. The price of nonconformity can be too high if it is not themselves, but their children and their grandchildren, who pay.

Women also reproduce class as consumers when they maintain appropriate lifestyle images in their homes. As Smith (1977) points out, these images, especially for middle-class women, are not of their own making but are created for them in the media. Mothers also know that their children suffer humiliation and personal pain when they cannot keep up with the lifestyles of other children in their school, long before the children are old enough to figure out that consumerism is the con game of corporate capital and that one does not have to feel humiliated because one lives in a garage and wears used clothing. Employed women continue this work of reproducing class when, as teachers and school counsellors, they advise children on what they think it takes to be successful in society.

The Ruling Apparatus of Capitalism

From the standpoint of traditional political economy, the ruling apparatus comprises the **military-industrial-political complex**. Corporate bosses are at the centre, wielding influence and dictating policies and laws in the interests of promoting capital accumulation. They are aided by the agencies that enforce these policies. From the standpoint of women, the ruling apparatus looks very different. It is located primarily in the social service sector that directly influences family life.

Donzelot's analysis of *The Policing of Families* (1979) surveys how families have been managed for capitalism. Physicians and psychiatrists worked with middle-class housewives to advise them on appropriate ways of raising children and sanitizing their houses; the social work professions trained educated women to teach uneducated or working-class women new rules of home economics and child care; probation officers threatened women that their children would be removed by the courts if they failed to make them conform to the rules, including rules of compulsory attendance at school. Male doctors broke the control of women over bearing and raising children and destroyed women's independent medical knowledge (Ehrenreich and English 1979). The professions of social psychology and sociology worked to control families, teaching women that the structural-functional model of male and female roles and family forms was biologically and socially necessary and that

any other ways of doing things risked **maternal deprivation**, manifest, of course, in children's failure to succeed in schools and careers (Lasch 1977).

Schools have a **hidden curriculum** that reinforces, above all else, a reliance upon accredited experts. These "experts" are the crucial underpinning of the ruling apparatus over women's lives (Illich 1971). All professions act to weaken rather than empower the working class when they uphold the logic that only people with credentials are experts and that others should rely upon their judgment.

For generations, the professions have been the almost exclusive domain of men. Now more women are entering them, but all the lines of argument and the main beliefs have been set up already. They are very hard to break. When one hears Judith Maxwell, head of the Economic Council of Canada, advocating that food be taxed in the interests of economic efficiency, it becomes clear that being female is not sufficient to change the standpoint of theory. Male professors find it hard enough to get their students to see that law does not simply dispense justice, but *capitalist* justice. There is an additional problem of credibility when the professor is a woman trying to address the issue of capitalist *patriarchy*. When Queen's law professor Sheila McIntyre tried to get students to see that law does not simply dispense capitalist justice, but *patriarchal* capitalist justice, she found herself all but heckled and jeered out of the lecture room by hostile male students. Students even challenged her competence as a lawyer and a professor. At the same time, her colleagues seemed incapable of recognizing that the problem was one of sexism. Only after she went public with a long and very bitter memo to the entire department, excerpts of which were widely circulated in the *Canadian Association of University Teachers' Bulletin*, did they attempt to address the issue of patriarchy at the law school (McIntyre 1986).

Summary

How can women be, in so many ways, at the heart of the system and yet be ignored or treated as a marginal topic? How can the enormity of what they do and their experience of the social reality of capitalism be left out of the picture? How can their work and experience be trivialized, even by women themselves, as somehow outside the main business? Why are they still relegated in sociology texts to a chapter on "the family"?

The problem seems to be that sociology and radical political economy have largely adopted the world view of the owners of big corporations, even as they criticize them. All the issues considered important and relevant are those relevant to corporations. From the viewpoint of business, women are irrelevant because much of their work is done outside the corporation. Capitalism itself dissolved the unity of work and life, of production and reproduction. Now social scientists themselves take the division for granted. Merely hiring more women workers in corporations or having more "female businessmen" will change nothing, because the focus—the consensus as to what the main business is— remains unchanged.

The debate over the place of women in the economy and, indeed, what constitutes the economy has only just begun in sociology, and nobody quite knows where it will go. The main questions have not yet been answered. In fact, some of them have not even been asked!

Conclusion

How well have the predictions generated by the Marxist model of capitalism stood up to empirical testing? The general answer is very well, but there are serious qualifications. The prediction of the tendency toward increasing concentration of capital into a handful of giant transnational corporations has largely been realized. The tendency toward a falling rate of profit is also a reality in traditional industries, especially in agriculture. The polarization of poverty and immense wealth has also largely been realized, especially when viewed on a world scale. Plant closures, unemployment, booms and slumps, crises of overproduction, and under-utilization of capital, are part of the everyday reality in the capitalist world. The harnessing of the state to mitigate these crises, to control labour, to boost the economy with armaments spending, and to defend new markets in Third World countries is similarly very much in evidence.

Marxist predictions have not been borne out with respect to the increasing misery of the masses and the profit margins in high technology industries. The thesis of increasing misery has much truth for the lumpenproletariat, the sectors of declining primary producers, marginalized, underemployed workers, and the deskilled working class. But it has not held true for the burgeoning middle classes. Marxist theory did not predict the spectacular expansion of the sector of highly educated, professional workers who enjoy high salaries and privileged conditions of autonomy in their work. Efforts to explain this sector away are generally unpersuasive. The problem here may lie not in the overall Marxist thesis but in the failure to recognize the consequences of the capitalist compulsion to develop innovative technology, products, and relations of production to win a competitive edge in world markets. The explosion in scientific knowledge in the last generation and the exponential advances in electronics and computers are so far outpacing the predicted tendency toward declining rates of profit. These processes are supporting an affluent middle class whose position depends upon the continuing acceleration of innovation.

The Marxist model also has radical implications for the traditional analysis of democratic politics in capitalist societies. Miliband's structuralist analysis shows the enormous power of the business elites within the political arena and their control over avenues of communication through which capitalism secures its legitimation. But the requirement of a highly educated and autonomous professional class of workers potentially threatens this control. The kind of education that is a prerequisite for innovative work simultaneously generates the capacity for creative questioning that may challenge the systems of legitimation of capitalism. Whether the affluent lifestyles of the professional class are adequate to buy off the critical challenge remains to be seen.

There is another area in which the frantic pace of growth under capitalism may be stemmed. The limits to what the ecology of the planet can bear may be more critical in the long run than the inherent contradictions of capitalism. We explore the relation between the expansion of capitalism and the destruction of the world environment further in chapter 15 on development.

Marxist theory, which focusses exclusively upon relations of production, has been found wanting in the analysis of the position of women and women's work. Relations of reproduction fall outside the Marxist framework. Consequently, relations of patriarchy disappear from view. Developing perspectives in Marxist-feminist theory are only beginning to redress this imbalance.

The future directions of Marxist theory are hard to predict. What seems likely is a move away from traditional structuralist frameworks and toward a focus on the active processes through which relations of capitalism are socially constructed and through which they change.

Suggested Reading

An excellent and very readable source of information on the Canadian corporate economy is Henry Veltmeyer's *Canadian Corporate Power* (1987). Veltmeyer gives a clear and informative overview of Marxist theory on corporate capitalism and includes much valuable information on corporate concentration and monopoly ownership.

Further readings on the decline of small producers are contained in the collection edited by Gary Burrill and Ian McKay, *People, Resources, and Power: Critical Perspectives on Underdevelopment and Primary Industries in the Atlantic Region* (1987). The contributors demonstrate how small producers in agriculture, fishing, forestry, and mining and energy are being crushed by the expansion of corporate capitalism into primary resource industries.

The text by Ralph Miliband, *The State in Capitalist Society* (1969), provides an excellent overview of the relationship between various branches of government and big business within capitalist societies.

For information on the communication industry in Canada, see Wallace Clement, *The Canadian Corporate Elite* (1975), especially chapters 7 to 9. Clement describes the media owners as gatekeepers of ideas, able to include or filter out information as it suits their interests. Useful sources of statistics on media ownership in Canada include Tom Kent, *Royal Commission on Newspapers* (1981), and G.L. Caplan and F. Sauvageau, *Report of the Task Force on Broadcasting* (1986).

An excellent source of theoretical debate and information on the class structure in Canada is Henry Veltmeyer, *Canadian Class Structure* (1986). In the first chapter, Veltmeyer outlines Marxist theory of class. He follows this with a detailed look at the situation of the capitalist class, the middle class, workers, and the poor. The book contains much statistical information in an accessible form.

Other sources of information, especially on poverty and inequality in Canada are the many reports by the National Council of Welfare: *Poor Kids* (1975); *Jobs and Poverty*

(1977); *Women and Poverty* (1979b); *The Hidden Welfare System Revisited* (1979a); *Welfare in Canada: The Tangled Safety Net* (1987c); and *Poverty Profile 1988* (1988b).

An excellent overview of the domestic labour debate is the collection of essays by Armstrong, Armstrong, Connelly, Miles, and Luxton, *Feminist Marxism or Marxist Feminism: A Debate* (1985). Articles by these authors explore how women's work in the home can be incorporated into a Marxist theory of work in relation to the capitalist system. These articles tend to be technical and somewhat heavy reading. Another source of critical debate on the Marxist treatment of feminist issues is the collection of readings edited by Heather Jon Maroney and Meg Luxton, *Feminism and Political Economy: Women's Work, Women's Struggles* (1987).

Part IV

Traditional Theory Under Attack

Chapter 10

Talcott Parsons and Functionalist Theory

Functionalist theory, particularly as elaborated by Talcott Parsons (1902–79) was generally accepted in North America as the orthodox approach to the study of society during the 1950s and 1960s and was claimed by some to be virtually equivalent to sociology as a whole (Davis 1960). It remains the mainstream theoretical approach in the United States. The study of society as a functioning system, comprising interdependent institutions that each perform specialized functions for the social whole, still dominates the format of most introductory texts in sociology. Only in the last decade or so has more critical political economy theory begun to achieve equivalent stature in Canada.

The Analogy Between Biological and Social Systems

The core ideas of functionalism are contained in the analogy that Herbert Spencer drew between social systems and biological organisms. Biological organisms are first and foremost bounded systems; that is, they are distinct entities or bodies that maintain themselves in a state of relative equilibrium or balance. They have built-in self-regulating mechanisms that keep the body in a relatively stable state, continually compensating for environmental changes. The human body, for example, maintains the same basic temperature and has a very narrow range of tolerance for fluctuations in this temperature. If too hot, we automatically begin to sweat, and the resulting evaporation cools us. If too cold, we begin to shiver, our body hair becomes more erect, and body temperature rises. Similarly, a complex enzyme system triggered by insulin keeps the blood sugar level in balance, continually compensating for extra sugar absorbed from food and sugar used up in exercise. Biological sciences explore these balancing mechanisms while medical sciences seek to intervene during extreme situations of illness or injury when the natural equilibrium breaks down.

In order to maintain themselves in a state of equilibrium or health, organisms have basic needs that must be met. We all know that green plants need some minimal access to light, water, and water-soluble minerals in order to survive. The human body, at a minimum, needs food, water, shelter, and a tolerable temperature range for survival. A host of higher-order needs must be met for our bodies to function at full capacity. All organisms are made up of specialized parts that have specific functions for the body as a whole. If any one part is missing or malfunctioning, it has repercussions for the rest. A central concern of biological sciences is to explore these specialized functions and how the various parts work together. Bodies can be conceptualized as made up of numerous subsystems, such as the digestive system, the nervous system, the blood circulatory system, and so on, which are themselves comprised of multiple subparts. All must work together in co-ordinated ways for the organism to function in a healthy way. Most of us are not conscious of these subsystems working, except when something abnormal happens. Then we turn to the medical and biological sciences for explanations.

Functionalism as a social science seeks to analyse societies in ways analogous to the biological study of organisms. The society itself is conceptualized as a bounded, self-maintaining system, comprising numerous specialized parts that must function together in co-ordinated ways. These multiple parts and subparts of societies, such as families, religion, education, and political and economic structures, are analysed in terms of their functions or contributions to the operation of the whole system. Each of these parts can in turn be analysed as a system, with system prerequisites and regulating mechanisms.

Certain operating assumptions in the biological sciences have also been taken over in functional analysis in sociology. The first basic assumption is that organisms are best analysed as **functional unities** rather than as disconnected bits. While it may be very valuable for individual researchers to focus on specialized parts, it is important never to lose sight of the fact that these parts operate only within the environment of the body as a whole.

A second working assumption is **universal functionalism**. Any characteristic of an organism that is constantly found across the species is assumed to have some necessary function that it performs for the body as a whole. Scientists may not yet know what the function of a particular tiny element of a cell or an enzyme might be, but that quest itself becomes a meaningful focus for future research.

The third working assumption, which is closely related to the second, is **functional indispensability**. Each and every element of an organism is assumed to have its own unique and specialized function that the organism would miss if that part were absent or damaged. The argument goes that if organisms did have vestigial or accidental parts that served no useful function, such parts would in all likelihood atrophy and disappear over time. The persistence of certain characteristics is itself an important indication that they serve some useful function.

In functionalist theory in sociology, these same basic assumptions of functional unity, universal functionalism, and functional indispensability guide research questions. A society is analysed as essentially a social system that cannot be reduced to fragmented groups of people. In this sense, the whole is greater than the sum of the parts. Recurrent characteristics of societies are assumed to perform necessary functions, and an adequate explanation for their persistence consists of discovering and explicating what these functions are. They may be obvious or *manifest functions*, which are widely acknowledged by society's members, or *latent functions*, which may not be consciously recognized by many people but which nonetheless meet important societal needs. For functionalists, the value of sociological research lies in disclosing these latent functions, hence increasing our understanding of why certain elements of our society have the characteristics they do.

Durkheim and Erikson's analyses of the latent function of crime in the maintenance of group boundaries and distinctive identities, described in chapter 7, are good examples of the functionalist approach. Coser's (1956) insightful analysis of the social functions of conflict is another example. He shows that, like pain in an organism, conflict gives advance warning of strains within the social system and encourages adaptations or innovations that reduce the conflict and so increase levels of comfort and well-being in society. Two-party or multi-party political systems are especially functional for airing conflicts early and dealing with them in constructive and integrative ways rather than allowing them to build up to an explosive point. The universal characteristic of stratification in societies has also drawn particular attention from functionalist theorists. Their basic explanation is that some system of inequality of rewards meets the essential function of motivating the more able and committed people in a society to strive for the more difficult and socially important jobs. In each of these examples, functional analysis shifts the focus of inquiry from the origins of certain patterns in society to why they persist. The operating assumption for research is that social structures continue because they serve some immediate useful purpose for the society.

The term *useful* itself deserves further consideration since it raises the question, useful for what? Functionalist theorists answer this question essentially the same way biologists do. Different features of society are functional when they help in some way, either manifest or latent, to maintain a stable and integrated social whole, that is, to maintain the state of dynamic equilibrium.

Functionalism promised to provide a truly scientific approach to the study of society. It enabled sociology in a sense to come of age and to join the other natural sciences such as biology, adopting analogous research strategies in the study of social systems. Sociology promised in principle to achieve a unification of all the sciences. The practical value of sociology is that it promised to provide the basic research knowledge required for promoting a harmonious and integrated social order. In a world torn apart by wars and facing the upheavals of the scientific-technological revolution of the twentieth century, such a science was urgently sought and readily accepted.

Parsons' Model of a Social System

Variants of the functional approach had long proven their usefulness in anthropology for the study of small, relatively isolated tribal societies. But it was Talcott Parsons who unquestionably deserves credit for systematizing and elaborating functionalism for application to advanced industrial societies. Parsons is credited, more than any other social theorist, with developing the scientific credibility of sociology. Through his efforts, sociologists began to play an advisory role to governments (Buxton 1985, chap. 7).

Early in his career, Parsons undertook the intellectually enormous task of trying to synthesize major theories of society into a comprehensive framework around the notion of a system of social action. In his book *The Structure of Social Action* ([1937] 1968), he insisted that such a unifying system had to begin with a **voluntaristic theory** of action. People in society are not like cells in a body, preprogrammed to behave in fixed ways. People make free choices. With rare exceptions, people feel that they do what

Talcott Parsons (1902–79).

they do voluntarily, and yet the outcome of these individual actions and choices is a stable social system. How is this possible?

In his second major study, *The Social System* (1951), Parsons formulated a basic model of society, its major parts, and how they are integrated in patterned ways. The model begins with individual actors as the basic building blocks. The critical problem that Parsons grapples with is order. How is order possible in a social system made up of individuals who are capable of making free choices? How can choices be, at the same time, free and yet predictable in an orderly way? The answer, for Parsons, lies in Durkheim's conception of the *conscience collective*: order is produced by moral or normative consensus. Parsons himself criticizes Durkheim for downplaying the central importance of normative consensus in industrial society and for failing to explain the basis of compliance to norms, except through fear of sanctions.

For Parsons, the basis of compliance, and hence the key to the problem of how order is sustained, lies in the internalization of norms. Actors co-operate because they internalize proper courses of action as well as the related values that make them feel shame or loss of self-respect if they fail to live up to these moral values. Knowledge that others share these values and will also react negatively to non-compliance further confirms people in their desire to conform (Heritage 1984, chap. 2). From this perspective, norms are internalized as **need dispositions**. This means that people tend to want to act in conformity with norms and feel dissatisfied if they cannot do so. Norms can be treated as causes of action. Individual actors make choices in the context of particular situations with given means, with ends in view, and with underlying values. These voluntary choices take the form of patterned and predictable behaviour because of the internalization of shared norms at the fundamental level of individual personalities. Ostensibly subjective individual choices become amenable to objective or external scientific analysis in terms of the patterns of values that constrain and determine conduct.

Values can be said to be institutionalized as part of the normative order of society when they are widely internalized. They are institutionalized when the vast majority of society's members choose to conform, feel guilt or shame if they do not conform, expect such conformity of each other, and react negatively with criticisms or punishment when these expectations are not met. We discussed this process, which Berger (1963, 68–78) refers to as "circles of social control," in chapter 2 (see figure 2-1). The innermost circle of control is the internalized desire to conform and internalized guilt, bolstered by approval or disapproval of our friends and close associates. Eventually, economic sanctions come into play as we risk not being hired, losing our jobs, or losing out on benefits when others disapprove of us. Force comes into play only as a last resort.

Roles and the Social System

Shared values alone are insufficient to produce a stable social system of functionally interrelated parts. More detailed sets of behavioural prescriptions are required. These give precise directions for how to behave in different situations and are provided by the institutionalization of typical roles. In the Parsonian model, society comprises a system of roles. Roles are essentially typical ways of behaving in predefined situations and exist independently of any individual in a particular situation. We learn how to behave in such roles, which are predefined for us in varying degrees of detail.

Parsons' voluntaristic theory of action begins with the study of actors and behaviour in typical situations, rather than with the study of total individuals. The social context sets the actor's role.

As we saw in chapter 2, the process by which we learn the behavioural expectations of different roles and the underlying values that motivate conformity to them is termed socialization. Socialization is a lifelong process in which we learn by modelling ourselves on others. As children, we learn first by watching our parents as role models. We later expand our horizons to others whom we want to emulate. As with core societal values, we come to internalize these behavioural expectations and to want to conform to them as part of a basic need to belong and to be approved of. As adults we learn a great variety of different roles, but the process is essentially the same. What society expects of us we come to expect of ourselves. In a sense we become our roles; they become part of us and how we identify ourselves. Hence we feel a sense of duty to fulfil our roles and pangs of guilt if we fail to live up to them.

Individuals perform a series of roles over a lifetime. They also perform a number of distinct and partially connected roles at any one time. Imagine, for a moment, that you are a parent, a classroom teacher, a town councillor, the director of a fund-raising committee, and a member of a local home-owners' association. In some situations, you may find yourself wearing several hats at once. This might occur if there happens to be a petition from the home-owners' association to the town council about where to locate a proposed new school playing field for which you are a fund raiser. All of these roles have to be integrated. According to Parsons, the personality comprises the system that integrates the various roles that one person plays.

Role Theory

A branch of functional analysis loosely referred to as **role theory** (Biddle and Thomas 1966) concerns itself with our interactive behaviour. The study of **role sets** analyses overlapping roles and reciprocal expectations for behaviour in specific situations. The terminology here can be confusing. Sometimes the role set consists of the variety of roles played by one person. More commonly, role sets refer to the variety of roles played by different people that interact or impinge upon each other in a given situation. In either case, the theoretical issues raised are similar.

Different roles are associated with different behavioural expectations that may not always be compatible. A familiar example is that of a school. Overlapping roles include those of students, teachers, parents, head teachers and other administrators, school boards, and support staff such as secretaries, cooks, and caretakers. Sometimes one person may play several of these roles at once, as in the case of a school secretary who is also the parent of a student at the school, or a teacher who may also be a parent and a member of the school board. More commonly, these roles will be played by different people. Each of these positions comprises a set of typical behaviour expectations, and the incumbents of each role have expectations concerning each of the overlapping roles. **Role strain** occurs when incumbents of related roles have differing sets of expectations. For example, parents and teachers may differ in their conception of the teaching role and appropriate classroom behaviour. These potential strains are usually minimized by **role segregation**, a separation in time and space that partially insulates any one role from the others. Parents generally enter classrooms and meet with teachers only at specified and delimited times. School board personnel similarly set policies but do not participate in the day-to-day running of the classroom, unless serious breaches of role expectations occur.

A different kind of role strain occurs within individual actors trying to balance the demands of simultaneous roles that they play in different situations. The role sets of career person and parent, for example, entail different and competing expectations. Again, this potential strain is reduced by segregation of roles in time and space. At certain times of the day, and in certain places, the role demands of the job take precedence; at other times those of parenting are more important. Problems occur only when the role segregation breaks down, as when children are sick and require parenting during the workday or when a parent is trying to work at home. Such strains may be reduced by a subset of rules permitting time off work for extraordinary parenting problems or by the careful segregation of one room in the house for the office. A wealth of detailed case studies in the role theory tradition has documented the reciprocal expectations and rules concerning contingencies of behaviour that permit such complex sets of roles to function smoothly.

Parsons thus bases his model on internalized moral consensus, which guides choices, and internalized expectations for behaviour in typical situations. Both of these are learned through socialization. He then turns his attention to the construction of an elaborate model of the total action system.

The Social System in a General Scheme of Action

Parsons (1978, 18) defines social action as consisting of "the structures and processes by which human beings form meaningful intentions and more or less successfully, implement them in concrete situations." He conceptualizes this action system as comprising four primary subsystems that are hierarchically organized in relation to each other: the **cultural system**, the **social system**, the **personality system**, and the **behavioural organism**. Together they form what Parsons terms "the **cybernetic hierarchy**"; that is, a hierarchy of systems of control and communication in human action. Each of these four subsystems of action are referred to as systems in their own right or as subsystems with reference to the total action system.

The **cultural system** is the broadest of all the subsystems of action. It forms the top of the hierarchy of control. It comprises the system of beliefs, rituals, values, and symbols—including language as a symbol system—through which people confront ultimate questions about reality, the meaning of good and evil, of suffering and death. Culture is thus fundamentally religious. A cultural system is normally broader than any one society. Many societies, for example, share a common Christian culture. In areas containing many societies, distinct cultural systems, such as Muslim and Christian, for example, may intermingle. In his abstract model, Parsons does not consider the possibility that a stable society may encompass more than one cultural system.

The **social system** operates at the second level in the hierarchy of control. It institutionalizes overarching cultural values into structures and processes that collectively organize action. Norms translate cultural values into specific regulations that define the status, rights, and obligations of members. Through such structures, the social system manages the potential for conflict and disorganization between elements in the action system and so maintains social order. The critical function of the social system is to integrate the cultural system with the personality systems of members and the physical requirements of the behavioural organism. The cultural system functions reciprocally to legitimate these societal-level institutions.

A **society** is a particular type of social system, characterized by what Parsons (1978, 22, 29) terms "territorial integrity and self-sufficiency." A society is a large-scale social system that controls behaviour within a given territory, has relatively clear membership status, and is capable of meeting all the life needs of members at all stages of life. In terms of such a definition, Canada can be considered both a society and a social system. A monastery of celibate monks is a social system but not a society because it has to recruit members from outside. The distinction between society and social system is ambiguous in practice. It is unclear whether communities such as a province or a Hutterite colony, for example, constitute a society or merely a social system. The argument tends to focus on relative territorial control, relative self-sufficiency, or relative clarity of membership status. To the extent that Canada is not economically self-sufficient, even its status as a society could be questioned. In practice, these terms are often used interchangeably, although social system is reserved for settings that are obviously not self-sufficient.

The third subsystem in Parsons' scheme of social action is the **personality system**. Individual personalities are in some sense unique, but they are also constrained and patterned by the social and cultural systems in which they develop. Personality is the learned component of the behaving individual, with socialization as the critical process in the formation of personality. The social system integrates the personality system and the cultural system through the organized processes of learning, developing, and maintaining adequate motivation for participating in socially valued and controlled patterns of action (Parsons 1978, 25). Individual value commitments are formed by the shared cultural system while individual motivations are harnessed primarily by internalized loyalties and obligations to the family system. The fundamental function of the personality system within the action system is orientation toward the attainment of goals. The personality system serves the social system through the performance of roles in collectively organized actions.

The fourth subsystem in social action is the **behavioural organism**. The behavioural organism provides the energy for all the higher level systems and also grounds the action system in the physical environment. The social system integrates the behavioural organism into the action system through organizing the processes that meet the basic requirements of food and shelter and the allocation of resources among producers and consumers.

System Prerequisites

The action system as a whole and each of its subsystems are conceptualized by Parsons as meeting a set of four **prerequisites** on which the balance of each system depends. These prerequisites are **latency** or **pattern maintenance**, **integration**, **goal attainment**, and **adaptation**. With respect to the total action system, the cultural subsystem meets the function of latency or pattern maintenance, serving as a reference system of values and meanings in terms of which the other element in the system are patterned. The social system meets the function of integration, organizing and co-ordinating the elements in the system. The personality system meets the function of goal attainment, providing the fundamental motivating drive for action. The behavioural organism meets the function of adaptation, relating the action system to the physical environment that constrains action. These four functions—goal attainment, adaptation, integration, and latency—are often referred to as Parsons' **GAIL model** (see figure 10-1).

Figure 10-1 Parsons' GAIL Model

Goal Attainment set priorities mobilize members	Adaptation get resources distribute where needed
Latency manage tensions motivate performance	Integration co-ordinate activities keep people informed

Each subsystem of the action system has to meet the same set of four **system prerequisites**. Within the social system, for example, the function of goal attainment is performed by political structures, including pressure groups, political parties, and governing bodies such as parliament. It is through such structures that priorities and future directions of the society are sorted out. Economic structures perform the function of adaptation, both developing and distributing resources through such agencies as farms, factories, and the marketplace. The function of integration is provided by law and administration. They serve to co-ordinate activities, regulate contracts, and generally pull the parts of the social system together.

Latency or pattern maintenance is performed by such institutions as schools, churches, and families, which socialize the younger generation, motivate conformity, and support people emotionally.

Within each subsystem there are yet smaller subsystems that have to meet the same prerequisites through various internal structures. The subsystem of a school, for example, needs a governing body to determine goals, including priorities for teaching and budget estimates. Schools also require adaptive mechanisms to get needed funds for salaries, supplies, equipment, and maintenance. This may be primarily from government allocations, private school fees, parental contributions, or fund-raising drives. Schools also need internal administrative structures to co-ordinate activities. Lastly, schools need staff who are committed to the work of latency, instilling in both teachers and students a continuing commitment to the school's educational values and the preservation of school discipline.

Family systems can similarly be analysed in terms of how these four basic needs are met. All families need to have some mechanisms or some person responsible for making key decisions on such matters as major financial investments, where to live, and so on. Someone is every family must also perform the basic breadwinner role, earning the resources on which family members depend for their survival. Someone must co-ordinate activities and ensure that supplies are bought, meals prepared, clothes cleaned, and so on, to be ready as needed by different family members. Families also need to manage the inevitable tensions between the sexes and generations if the family is to continue to hold together as a functioning unit.

Parsons' overarching model is thus a series of systems with subsystems that have sub-subsystems, and so on. They can be visualized as a series of boxes within the larger box of the action system. The social system box contains important institutional subsystem boxes, each of which has to fulfil the same basic GAIL functions (see figure 10-2.

This model looks very impressive in the abstract, but critics complain that the distinctions are very fuzzy in practice. It is far from clear which box specific items fall into. Is the economy purely involved in the adaptation function or is it also part of the goal attainment or pattern maintenance functions? Is family primarily oriented to pattern maintenance or more properly also part of the integration, goal attainment, and adaptation functions? There are no easy answers to these questions. Parsons' theoretical writings tend to be at a high level of abstraction where such question are not raised. Parsons' major contribution to theory lies, perhaps, in his overall vision of social life in terms of interacting systems, rather than in the convoluted abstract models that he builds.

Pattern Variables

The last major dimension of Parsons' overall conception of action systems is his systematization of typical dilemmas of choice in any given role. In any specific behaviour by an individual there are potentially a vast array of orientations toward action that might be adopted. Parsons argues that these can be organized into four options, each associated with one of two opposing sets: traditional or

Figure 10-2   Structure of General Action Systems

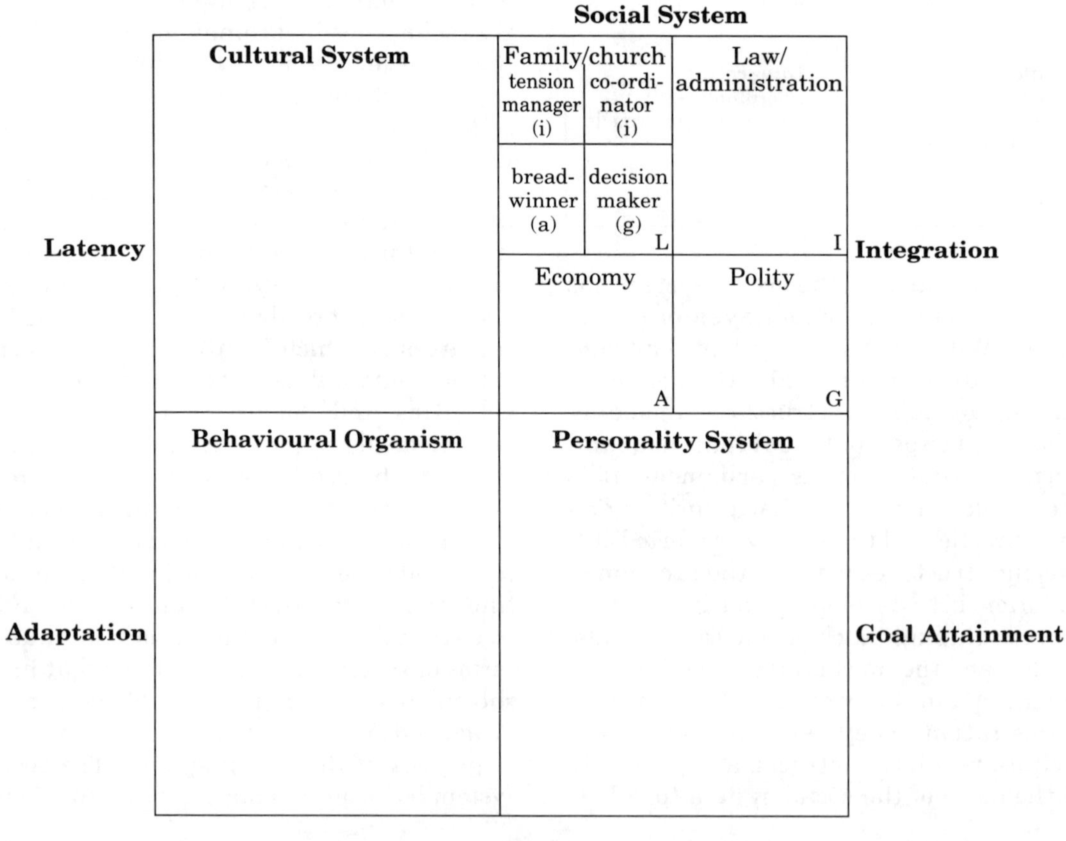

		Social System	
Cultural System	Family/church	Law/
	tension manager (i)	co-ordi- nator (i)	administration
	bread- winner (a)	decision maker (g)	
Latency		Economy	Polity	**Integration**
Behavioural Organism	**Personality System**	
Adaptation			**Goal Attainment**

modern. These patterned sets of dichotomous options are what he terms **pattern variables**. The traditional or family set comprises the orientations of **affectivity**, **particularism**, **ascription**, and **diffuse obligations**, while the modern or occupational set comprises **affective neutrality**, **universalism**, **achieved characteristics**, and **specific obligations**. Parsons conceptualizes any role relationship as analysable in terms of these two sets of action orientations. Table 10-1 shows the two sets of pattern variables.

The first variable is **affectivity** or **affective neutrality**. This concerns the amount of emotion that should properly be displayed in a role. Relations between family and friends are expected to involve some emotional warmth, while relations with clients in a business or professional situation are expected to be formal or affectively neutral. People may rightfully get upset if such expectations are not met in either context.

The second variable concerns whether **particularistic** or **universalistic standards** of evaluation for role performance are appropriate. In relations between friends, subjective standards based on the particular abilities, interests, and effort of one's friends are appropriate, but in the business world, or when hiring a lawyer or going to a medical doctor, objective universalistic standards are appropriate. Professionals are judged relative to the universally defined standards of their profession and not by whether or not one likes the individual personally.

A third variable, closely related to the second, concerns appropriate criteria for assessing an actor, whether by **ascriptive characteristics** or **achieved characteris-**

Table   10-1   The Pattern Variables

Traditional or Family Set	Modern or Occupational Set
Affectivity Show emotional involvement	**Affective neutrality** Remain emotionally neutral
Particularism Judge relative to age, experience, effort, enthusiasm	**Universalism** Judge relative to objective standards of excellence
Ascription Give special consideration to relatives, friends	**Achievement** Consider only specific qualifications
Diffuseness Co-operate, help, and support in as many ways as possible	**Specificity** Strictly limit involvement
Self Give priority to personal interests over what others want	**Collectivity** Give priority to group interests over personal preferences

tics. Ascriptive characteristics are those that we are born with, such as age, sex, appearance, racial or ethnic background, while achievements are those characteristics that we earn by learning special skills or gaining credentials. The first set of characteristics is more important for family or social contacts, the second for business contacts.

A fourth pattern variable concerns the nature of obligations involved in an interaction, whether **diffuse** or **specific**. Obligations toward family and friends tend to be diffuse; friends and relatives call upon each other for a variety of services and support. Business and professional relations are confined to the precise task at hand; neither party to the relationship has any right to ask for or to expect anything more.

A last dimension of role relations is self versus collectivity. This concerns whether the action in question is oriented primarily toward individual interest or toward group goals and interests. Parsons himself accorded this variable less importance in his general model because it was less clearly a dichotomous choice. Individual and group interests frequently overlap, and aspects of both may be involved in any specific role interaction. One does not always have to choose between them.

Parent-child and professional-client relationships are presented by Parsons as polar opposite types of action orientation. Ideally, the relationship of a parent to a child is emotionally affective; evaluations are particularistic with full consideration given to the special situation and abilities of the particular child; assessments are based on ascriptive criteria; role obligations are diffuse. Totally opposite expectations prevail in a professional-client relation such as that between doctors and their patients. Both doctors and their patients are required to maintain a stand of affective neutrality toward each other. One's judgment of a doctor is appropriately in terms of universalistic criteria of the profession and the doctor's professional qualifications and abilities, and not whether the doctor is male or female, an old family friend or a newcomer. Finally, obligations are confined to the specific issue of providing medical advice.

A fundamental assumption made by Parsons, which is explored further in chapter 11, is that the basic pattern variables and their associated action orientations within families and within the world of industry and business are diametrically opposed. Hence, conflict between them is virtually inevitable whenever the two spheres overlap. This potential conflict is avoided in advanced industrial societies by the specialization and segregation of family roles from work roles. This segregation involves not only time and space but also, characteristically, personnel. Men take primary responsibility for work roles while women take responsibility for the diffuse, emotionally charged role of nurturing children. Parsons is not saying that it is impossible for a person to combine the two roles, but that it is difficult and that social norms prescribe in advance which role—family or work—will take primacy when conflicts arise. The segregation of male and female roles found in nearly all societies is thus seen as meeting a basic functional need. Parsons argues that biological differences between men and women, associated with childbirth, breastfeeding, and different average muscular strength, naturally predispose men to specialize in work roles outside the home and women to specialize in child care and homemaking.

A wealth of research in the role-theory tradition has analysed typical patterns of role relations in various situations in terms of Parsons' pattern variables and has examined reactions to violations of these expectations. Parsons himself (1961) did an interesting analysis of the role of elementary school teacher, usually filled by a woman. Parsons argues that a female teacher helps to prepare young children for the transition from the pattern variables appropriate for relations between themselves and their mother at home, to the impersonal pattern variables of the work world. Such a teacher shows affectivity or emotional warmth toward the children and responds to their ascriptive characteristics, and yet at the same time introduces them to universalistic standards of performance and to more limited, specific role obligations than they are used to with their parents.

Modernization

Parsons maintains that entire societies can be analysed in terms of how they meet the basic GAIL prerequisites and the prevailing orientations toward pattern variables. For Parsons, modernization involves a progressive differentiation of structures by which each of the four prerequisites are met. In traditional societies, the kin group is primarily responsible for meeting all of these needs. The **patriarch** or family head tends to set the major goals for the rest of the members. The adaptation function or the economy is embedded in kin and family groups. The family and the patriarch are primarily responsible for societal integration, with power relations organized along age-sex lines. Family socialization is likewise of primary importance in teaching the values and skills that assure the maintenance of established patterns of behaviour from one generation to another.

In modern societies, however, the role of the family has receded to only a partial responsibility for the fourth function. Societal goals are set by specialized role incumbents such as politicians and bureaucrats. Economic activities have moved outside the family circle into factories and corporations. Patriarchs have lost much of their former authority, and societal integration is maintained by specialized legal systems and the civil service. The fundamental teaching roles involved in pattern maintenance have also moved outside the family into the realms of schools, churches, and law-enforcement agencies. Families now specialize in early childhood socialization and tension management through emotional support of members.

Parsons argues further that traditional and modern societies differ in fundamental ways in types of action orientation. Traditional societies, based on kinship, are oriented primarily toward affective, particularistic, ascriptive, and diffuse role relationships. A very different set of pattern variables prevails in advanced industrial societies, characterized as they are by differentiation and specialization of roles. Universalistic standards and evaluation of contacts on the basis of achievement are functional requirements in technologically complex roles. Specialized roles necessarily carry only specific obligations, which in turn promote affectively neutral relationships.

Nowhere are these patterns more apparent than in the realm of public administration. Traditional societies, suggests Parsons, often adopt the formal structures of bureaucracy from advanced industrial societies but not the cultural patterns. The result is nepotism, graft, and inefficiency as personnel selection is made on the basis of family connections and other ascriptive criteria rather than on the basis of skills, and the new role incumbents are then expected to favour friends and family in dispensing patronage from their office. Efficient bureaucracy is functionally necessary for advanced industrial activities. This efficiency requires that appointments be made on the basis of expertise and that operations be impartial. The logical implications of the Parsonian model are thus that the modernization process requires both structural and cultural changes in traditional societies, to promote differentiation and specialization of formal structures and to give primacy to a different set of pattern variables.

It is clear that Parsons developed an extremely elaborate model of the structure of social action. For more than two decades this model has dominated sociological research. It has been so influential that alternative perspectives still tend to identify their own position in opposition to it.

Problems with Functionalist Theory

Serious criticisms have been raised against functionalism, both as a general theoretical approach and with respect to specific elements of Parsons' model. These theoretical issues are addressed here, with particular reference to the alternative approaches of political economy and ethnomethodology.

When sociologists try to explain the existence of certain structures or patterns in society by reference to the functions that these structures perform for the social whole, they are implicitly suggesting that the structures exist because they are necessary. Families perform the basic function of socializing children, thus we have families; stratification performs the function of motivating talented people to strive for important jobs, so we have stratification. This is, of course, an oversimplification of the argument but it helps to reveal the problem, which Merton (1967) calls the *fallacy of functional indispensability*.

Merton points out that there may very well be, and in fact usually are, functional alternatives to these structures. Societies do need some way to socialize children, but there are potentially other ways of doing this than in families. For example, small agricultural communes in Israel experimented successfully with raising children in group homes without having families as we know them (Spiro 1958). Societies do have to motivate people somehow to take difficult jobs, but perhaps there are other motivations besides money. Merton suggests that we can

reasonably expect to find some structures or patterns in society to meet important needs. But identifying these structures is not the same as explaining why we have the specific types of structures—the kind of families or the kind of social stratification—that we find in our society.

Hempel (1970, 127) makes the same point but carries it further. Society may need something, but this does not necessarily mean that it will get it. Durkheim argues, for example, that in order to have social cohesion we need social justice and full employment so that everyone feels they are valued members of the community. But we are a very long way from satisfying either need.

Another problem with functionalist arguments is the difficulty in defining what is necessary for society to function. In biology, it is a fairly straightforward matter to define health and sickness and hence to claim that certain states are necessary for the healthy functioning of the organism. But it is much more difficult to define what a healthy or sick society looks like. One might argue that Canada is sick because we do not have full employment, but there are a great many people in the business community who would not share this opinion. With such uncertainty as to what constitutes a need, the functionalist argument that structures exist because they are necessary becomes untenable.

Hempel points to yet another snag in the argument: the time ordering seems to be wrong. Something exists now because of some effect is will have in the future. Consider the statement, "birds have wings in order to fly." This is a functionalist argument. It seems to imply that birds got together one day, decided flying would be nice, and so started developing wings! The fact that birds have wings enables them to fly, but that does not explain how wings developed. If wanting to fly were sufficient cause for having wings, we would all have them. Functionalism describes the *effects* of certain structures, but it does not go very far toward explaining how or why these structures exist. Biologists delve deep into the structure of genes and genetic inheritance to explain the processes and mechanisms by which complex structures like wings are perpetuated in bird species. This goes a long way beyond explaining wings by showing how they function. Hempel concludes that functionalism is a useful descriptive approach, but it does not explain much about social structures.

It is important not to overstate this criticism. Describing the effects or functions that particular structures have is itself a difficult and useful achievement, particularly when these effects are latent or not recognized by many people. This restricted version of functionalism is valuable, provided we recognize its limitations. Functionalists who are largely content with this level of analysis have produced many insightful studies.

One such study is Merton's (1967, 125–35) analysis of the latent functions of political bosses in America. He asks why political rackets run by party bosses persist. Patronage, bribery, graft, and the protection of criminals clearly violate established moral codes. They persist, Merton argues, because they satisfy subgroups' needs that cannot be met by culturally approved social structures. First, the party boss consolidates what is often widely dispersed power to the point where he can actually get things done. Secondly, he can get around bureaucratic red tape to ensure provision of social services for people otherwise lost in the technicalities. Thirdly, the boss can provide privileges to big business, by acting to control and regulate unbridled competition, without being subject to public scrutiny and control. He is especially important in providing aid to businesses that provide illicit services and hence that are not protected by regular government controls. Fourthly, the party

patronage controlled by the boss provides avenues for upward social mobility for ambitious individuals who lack legitimate avenues to attain success. Hence, political rackets cannot be understood merely as self-aggrandizement for power-hungry individuals who could be cleaned out of the system. Political rackets constitute the organized provision of services to subgroups that are otherwise excluded from or handicapped in the race to get ahead. These are important latent functions that the socially approved political structures cannot adequately meet. Hence, the political rackets persist.

Serious criticisms remain, however, even when the claims for functional analysis are confined to the level of descriptive insights. Merton draws attention to two related problems, which he terms the *fallacy of functional unity* and the *fallacy of universalism*. In biology, the assumption of functional unity holds that every element within a biological organism is functional or useful for the good of the entire organism. The assumption of universalism holds that each and every element found within an organism must perform some necessary function. Merton argues that, however reasonable such assumptions sound in the context of a biological organism, they constitute fallacies when applied to elements within social systems.

The general argument that structures exist because they are functional for the social system assumes that the system operates as a unitary whole. Merton argues that given structures may be beneficial or functional for certain groups in society but not necessarily for others. A high rate of unemployment, for example, is functional for reducing wage demands and so enhancing the competitive advantage of business, but it is not functional for the groups of people who are unemployed or for their family members. Neither is it functional for other small businesses that depend on selling goods to families of unemployed people. At best, one might be able to talk about a net balance of functional advantage. But Merton pushes the criticism further to insist that functionalism should routinely take account of **dysfunctions**; that is, the possibility that some structures have a net balance of negative consequences for a society or for large numbers of its members.

Traditional functionalism begins from the premise that recurrent characteristics in a society, like elements within a biological organism, can be explained by reference to the functions that they perform for the maintenance of the system as a whole. But carried to its logical extreme, this position can lead to what look like absurd claims. One can argue that suicide is functional for relieving tensions; wife battering is functional for enhancing male dominance; war is functional for generating high profits and high employment.

These claims themselves are not false. Suicide, war, unemployment, crime, do have advantages for certain people. The problem lies in the assumption that they benefit the society as a whole. The key question for critics of functionalism is, functional for whom? The corollary, of course, is, dysfunctional for whom? When the issues raised by functionalism are reformulated in this way, important dimensions of power and conflict of interest are introduced into the analysis.

A recurrent criticism of functional analysis, and particularly of Parsons' model of a social system, has been that it does not deal adequately with power. Parsons tends to assume that power generally takes the form of authority, which is used in the interests of system adjustment. Not surprisingly, this formulation has been hard to sustain.

Marxists critics argue that corporate bosses wield enormous power over the economy and over political decisions. The mass of workers may view the exercise of such power as arbitrary and illegitimate, but they are unable to oppose it effectively. The result of confrontations between bosses and workers may be disorder and alienation rather than orderly system adjustment. The power exercised by men over women in families has similarly been challenged by feminists as illegitimate. The exercise of patriarchal powers may lead to family breakdown and divorce rather than to stable marriage.

Functionalism started out with great promise as a unifying scientific approach toward sociological analysis, but it seems not to have lived up to expectations. The major contributions of this perspective lie in two broad areas. First, it recognizes the fundamental interdependence of different parts of society. It increases sensitivity to the fact that change in any one part of society affects all other interrelated structures as well. Secondly, and perhaps more importantly, functionalism has encouraged a wealth of descriptive research that has documented latent or hitherto unsuspected effects of recurrent patterns of behaviour.

The elaborate typologies of system needs and pattern variables worked out by Parsons have, on the whole, not proven particularly useful. System needs are notoriously difficult to establish. Attempts to classify structures as performing one need or another are often not successful. Additionally, each pattern variable is better understood as a continuum rather than a dichotomy and also as varying widely with circumstances rather than as a fixed orientation for given roles.

In summary, the problems associated with traditional functionalist analysis are serious. The system of explanation for the persistence of structures in terms of their functions for the social system is logically flawed. It does not deal adequately with dysfunctions or negative aspects of social structures, nor does it provide an adequate basis for the analysis of power, conflict, and disunity in society. It has thus gained the disrepute of being reactionary and conservative, providing ideological justification for the status quo.

Critical Reformulations of Functionalist Theory

In this section we explore the efforts of theorists, particularly in the Marxist and ethnomethodological traditions, to reformulate functionalism into a potentially more adequate and descriptively useful approach.

A revised model of functionalist analysis proposed by Stinchcombe (1968, 80–100) first addresses the question of the flawed explanatory logic of traditional functionalism. Hempel and others may argue that functionalism cannot go beyond descriptive statements, but the fact remains that most functionalist analysis still aims to do more than describe functions. The tendency is always there to argue that certain structures may exist because they serve certain functions. In other words, some theorists use the functions, or effect, as explanations for the existence of the structures.

Stinchcombe suggests that these logical problems can be resolved if two important changes are made in traditional functionalist analysis. The first change is the explicit recognition and incorporation of intent into the explanation. It makes sense to argue that existing structures are caused by their future consequences if you explain that certain individuals or groups of people intentionally select and reinforce certain structures because they find the effects of such structures beneficial. The second change is that such an explanation needs to examine the mechanisms by which such structures are selectively reinforced and preserved over time. Stinchcombe calls such processes **feedback mechanisms**. In the biological sciences, the exploration of the precise mechanisms and feedback loops by which an equilibrium is achieved is a central part of any explanation of the functions that parts perform for the whole. But to date, functional analysis in sociology has tended to assume equilibrium, without demonstrating the mechanisms through which such effects are

sustained. In short, for Stinchcombe, adequate functional explanations should show that structures exist and are perpetuated over time because they are deliberately reinforced by individuals or groups who find their effects beneficial and who have access to mechanism that are effective in such reinforcement.

Stinchcombe only hints at what some of these mechanisms might be. Some structures may persist simply because no one has any particular interest in stopping them, and because they work sufficiently well that no one has much incentive to seek alternatives. It simply costs too much time and effort to change things. Other structures may be less generally appreciated by all members of the society and hence have to be defended by more overt means. These means might include control over the socialization of young people to ensure that they are instilled with the proper values; access to mass media, which influence how people think and what they know about; and influence over the selection of successors to policy-making situations in society and control of the rules under which successors work.

Marxist Functionalism

Stinchcombe's reformulation of functional analysis directly incorporates notions of power and the unequal ability of different individuals and groups in society to reinforce those social structures that they find beneficial. Stinchcombe (1968, 94) in fact defines the power of a class in terms of its relative effectiveness as a cause of social structures. In this respect, he explicitly relates his ideas to Marxist analysis and to the Marxist assertion that the dominant culture of a society is the culture of the dominant class. The reason why elites are able to perpetuate their values and mode of organization of society is that they have privileged access to and control over all the key mechanisms that reinforce structures. Elites are in a particularly advantageous position to influence the mechanisms that produce the semblance of moral consensus central to the Parsonian model of the social system. They not only control and direct most mass media outlets, they are also able to pay professional people to defend and disseminate appropriate values. Members of the elite are also in the best position to select their own successors and to ensure that their values are perpetuated in the future operation of important organizations in society.

The notion of **Marxist functionalism** proposed by Stinchcombe retains the more insightful aspects of functionalist theory. In particular, he retains both the concept of society as comprising an interrelated system of parts and the mode of analysis that describes and explains the persistence of structures by reference to their consequences. He also emphasizes purposive action as the foundation of his model. The crucial change from the Parsonian model is that Stinchcombe introduces the concepts of class and unequal power. He replaces the notion of society-wide normative consensus with the view that dominant ideas are those perpetuated by the actions of the members of an elite class.

Richard Quinney's analysis of law functioning to protect the interests of the capitalist class, which was outlined in chapter 7, is a prime example of Marxist functionalism. Society is conceptualized as a system of interdependent parts, but it is explicitly a capitalist system. The parts function to protect the elite class and to control and suppress class conflict, which might disrupt this system.

The risk in Quinney's approach is that he repeats earlier logical flaws in functional analysis, namely the fallacies of universal functionalism, functional unity, and functional indispensability. Everything exists because it is functional for the capitalist system—unemployment is functional for profits, welfare is functional for controlling

potential revolt—and the description of some effect provides an explanation for the persistence of such structures. Stinchcombe's reformulation of the logic of functionalism still applies here. An adequate explanation still requires detailed analyses of the feedback mechanisms: who controls them, how they operate, how potential opposition or change is prevented. The capitalist system persists, not because of its own inner momentum, but because people with powerful vested interests take actions to reinforce it on an ongoing basis.

A closely related criticism of functionalism stems more directly from the analytical work of Marx himself than from subsequent political economy theory. When Marx challenged the ideas of the classical economists of his time, he asked a difficult question: what kind of actual social relations must be experienced in order for this kind of economic model to be formulated? Ideas, in other words, do not arise from nowhere. They arise from people's attempts to make sense of their own limited experience. When this same kind of question is asked of Parsons' work, it challenges the claim that his model of a social system is abstract, scientific, and universally applicable. Critics would argue that concepts such as GAIL functions and pattern variables originate within, and refer to the historically specific circumstances of, capitalism. They make sense only in relation to the impersonal capitalist system of commodity production for money.

This criticism can be made clearer if we examine Parsons' analysis of, first, the differences between family and occupational subsystems and, second, the medical profession. Prior to capitalism, there was no clear break between family and work roles for most people. They commonly merged together in household enterprises. Under feudalism, landowners had clearly established personal obligations to provide for the peasant families that were attached to their estates. It was only with the advent of the capitalist wage-labour system that owners of the means of production freed themselves from hereditary obligations toward workers. It was capitalism that segregated production from the home and reduced personal relations to inhuman cash payment in the labour market. It is precisely such a system that is captured in Parsons' concepts of affective neutrality and impersonal and specific role obligations. These concepts cannot be applied universally to all economic systems.

Similarly, there is nothing inevitable about the nature of medicine that would give rise to Parsons' characterization of the doctor-patient relationship as involving affectively neutral, universalistic, achievement-oriented, and specific role obligations. For centuries the opposite was the case. Healing was practised by women whose skills were passed on for generations. The art of healing was integrated into total caring for the person. It was a neighbourly service where the healer knew her patients and their families. She knew about the disappointments, anxieties, and the overwork that could mimic illness or induce it (Ehrenreich and English 1979, chap. 2). Healing was a diverse and creative process that involved many little kindnesses and encouragements and an understanding of the patients' fears and strengths. But under capitalism, the "art of healing" became the "science of medicine," practised by men as a commodity to be sold at a high price. Male practitioners went to tremendous lengths to protect their commodity, undermining the natural healing of women by burning them as witches and by outlawing midwifery and the practice of medicine by those without credentials. Since women were systematically barred from medical schools until late in the nineteenth century, they were effectively prevented from practising medicine. This set of historically specific practices produced the image of doctors described by Parsons.

Parsons' model and the analyses that flow from it are thus faulted for justifying, under the guise of scientific objectivity, a particularly inhuman form of social relations. By treating such relations as universal, abstract truths about society, Parsons glosses over the historically specific and particular social organization that gives rise to the relationships that he encapsulates in his model.

Some have argued that the Parsonian model is, and was intended to be, an important tool in the legitimation and hence perpetuation of the capitalist nation-state (Buxton 1985). Professional social science functions as a powerful mechanism for social control. Parsons defines professionals as a disinterested or affectively neutral class of experts, operating in terms of universalistic standards of science, committed to the specific objectives of research rather than diffuse political obligations, and dedicated to collective societal well-being rather than self-interest. Hence they command authority as impartial advisors to government. Functionalist theorists have advised the business and political elites how to neutralize destabilizing features of change and so bolster the system. Functionalism also provides a means not to see the underlying realities of class, power, and exploitation within the capitalist system. Buxton goes so far as to suggest that Parsons himself might have been aware of the ideological character of his theory, or certainly that many of his followers who adopted and promoted functionalism in social analysis saw it as a means to reduce class tensions.

Psychoanalysis and Socialization

The basic assumption of the functionalist equilibrium model is the internalization of social norms. Individuals, it is argued, come to accept the norms and values of society as their own, and hence they voluntarily regulate themselves in conformity with expectations. The major problem with this perspective is that it does not explain deviance. People appear to conform because they are preprogrammed to act only in conformist ways, much like ants in an anthill.

Dennis Wrong (1961) argues that such reasoning is blatantly naïve. In reality, people can never be socialized to this extent. Human nature is far too complex for that. Wrong draws on **psychoanalytic theories** to suggest that socialization at best achieves only a veneer of conformity over individual self-will, and this conscious self-will is itself only a veneer over much deeper unconscious or semiconscious passions and desires that forever threaten to overwhelm orderly, conformist behaviour.

In psychoanalytic terminology, the **id** comprises the vast reservoir of life forces— sexual passions, drives, and energy—of which the individual is at best only partially aware. The conscious self or **ego** seeks to express and to realize these fundamental drives and passions. They are only superficially held in check by the **superego** of learned social norms and values. This model is illustrated in figure 10-3. Intensive and rigid socialization, such as the kind that puritanical religious sects seek to impose, may succeed in repressing socially unacceptable sexual drives and passions. Socialization may even succeed in pushing them out of the conscious mind altogether, but it can never eliminate them totally. A permanent tension is set up within the individual psyche between repressed drives, guilt, and social conditioning, with the latter continually at risk of being overwhelmed by deep emotional forces. When people are viewed from this perspective, the functionalist vision of societal equilibrium achieved by internalization of norms appears fragile indeed.

The Ethnomethodological Critique

The approach of ethnomethodology—particularly the work of Garfinkel, who was a student of Parsons—offers a different kind of challenge to the functionalist notion of a voluntaristic theory of action. Heritage

Figure 10-3 Model of the Human Mind in Psychoanalytic Theory

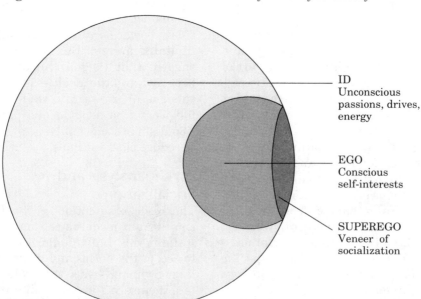

ID
Unconscious
passions, drives,
energy

EGO
Conscious
self-interests

SUPEREGO
Veneer of
socialization

(1984) draws attention to the illusory character of this supposedly voluntary choice. In practice, actors seem to be left with no choice at all because the script is already written. Parsons characterizes people as role players with internalized norms and fixed expectations. These role players are assumed to share their interpretation of the situation and their knowledge of appropriate rules for behaviour. In effect, says Garfinkel, they are "judgmental dopes" (Heritage 1984, 108). They appear to make no judgments of their own. Like mindless robots, they simply follow rules programmed into them.

The alternative perspective of ethnomethodology allows for a much greater fluidity in behaviour. For a start, in real situations we assume that other people are making responsible and meaningful choices in their actions, such that each of us can and do hold ourselves and other people accountable for behaviour. Furthermore, real situations are not predefined. A constant problem in deciding how we should behave or respond to the behaviour of others is in determining what is going on in the first place. Our actions and those of other people define the situation, not the other way around.

Boughey (1978, 171) gives an example of this in his description of cards night at a church. Six rambunctious men were laughing and joking as they played poker. After a particularly raucous outburst, a woman from a nearby table admonished them, "Shshsh! You're in church, you know!" One poker player waved her off with the response, "Naah! But this is cards!" In effect, all the participants in this scene were **defining the situation**. We might conclude that, since the players were so raucous, they must have given priority to the role of "card-playing" rather than to that of "being in church." Conversely, if the men had quietened down after the admonishment, we might conclude that, after a temporary lapse, they followed the behavioural prescriptions appropriate for the role of being in church. The important

point is that a functionalist could only tell after the fact what was going on by the kind of behaviour displayed. Boughey and the enthomethodologists are interested in how people actively choose and create the situation for themselves by choosing how they are going to behave.

Heritage (1984, chap. 5) gives an example of a situation in which one person meets another and greets her. The norm states that greetings should be reciprocated. If the other person does indeed return the greeting, then everything appears normal. But if she is silent, then the situation is not normal, and a chain of guesses as to what else is going on is immediately set off: maybe she didn't hear; she was deep in thought; she deliberately snubbed me; she wasn't who I thought she was; she doesn't remember me; my new hairpiece sure fooled her. There is no passive actor responding in learned ways to a predefined situation. Rather, there is a person actively involved in creating what is happening and what will happen next.

In chapter 4, we saw some examples of the infinitely detailed and careful research that ethnomethodologists carry out in order to explore how people actively make sense of and create the social world and reproduce it as intelligible for each other. What is significant here is the important criticism that this approach raises against traditional functionalist analysis. The basic functionalist assumption of internalized norms and expectations of behaviour is shown to be insufficient as an explanation for social order.

Conclusion

What remains of functionalist analysis when these criticisms are taken into account?

The model of society as a system rather than a collection of disconnected parts remains a central assumption of sociological analysis. Functionalism draws attention to the mutual influence of interdependent elements of society. It also focusses attention on voluntary or purposive action and the importance of typical roles and expectations in guiding behaviour. Functionalism has prompted much valuable descriptive research into the effects of given structures or patterns of behaviour on society.

The weaknesses of functionalism lie in its rigidity, the tendency to assume that existing structures are necessary, because functional, without considering alternatives and especially without considering dysfunctions or damaging effects that given structures may have for less powerful sectors of society. Functionalism typically fails to recognize the essential fluidity and creativity in people's relations with each other. At the system level, functionalism can be faulted for failure to deal adequately with issues of power, conflict, and exploitation in society, except in terms of institutionalized pressure groups. This has marked functionalism as a conservative ideology in the eyes of more critical theorists.

The following four chapters explore the impact of functional analysis on research in a variety of substantive areas, particularly as they apply to Canadian society. These insights are tested against the critical reformulations proposed by Marxist and ethnomethodological perspectives and feminist theory.

Suggested Reading

The most convenient and accessible selection of Parsons' writing is contained in Peter Hamilton's collection, *Readings from Talcott Parsons* (1985). A broadly descriptive article in the collection is "Age and Sex in the Social Structure of the United States." It would be instructive to compare the division of sex roles within different age groups in the 1950s, as outlined by Parsons, with that of the present. In the article "Illness and the Role of the Physician: A Sociological Perspective," illness, particularly mental illness, is treated as a type of deviant behaviour in terms of the sick person's failure to fulfil expectations connected with his or her roles in society. Sickness itself is viewed as a social role in relation to a set of distinctive norms defining appropriate behaviour, such as exclusion from certain normal obligations. The therapist is seen as not just applying technical knowledge to problem cases, but as restoring equilibrium to the social system.

Another broadly descriptive article by Parsons is "The School Class as a Social System: Some of its Functions in American Society" (1961). This article examines the ways in which aspects of the structure of primary and secondary school classes function to adapt young people to adult roles. The students' transformation from family members to members of the wider society is analysed in terms of Parsons' pattern variables.

A brief though demanding exposition of Parsons' scheme of the components of society can be found in his book *Societies: Evolutionary and Comparative Perspectives* (1966).

Chapter 11

The Family: The Site of Love, Exploitation, and Oppression

As we saw in chapter 10, functionalist theory views society as an integrated and self-maintaining system, analogous to a living organism. Like an organism, it is composed of numerous organs or institutions that are structured to meet the specialized needs or prerequisites of the social system as a whole. The system normally exists in a state of dynamic equilibrium. Built-in mechanisms balance change in one part of the system with complementary changes in other parts, so that the order of the whole is maintained despite major changes in structure. Within subsystems of action, or institutions, are individual roles, which comprise typical patterns of action. The entire system is held together by the crucial mechanisms of normative consensus and shared role expectations. These values and expectations for behaviour are internalized by members of society through the complex process of socialization.

The family is an institution that plays a vital part within this functionalist model of society. Functionalists argue that the family is extremely important, indeed indispensable, for the survival of society. For many theorists, society itself can be conceptualized as made up of families linked together. The family is a universal institution; no known society has exited without it. The central integrative process of socialization—the internalization of behaviour patterns and values—occurs primarily within the family. Institutions such as school and church also play a part in the socialization process, but this is generally only after the newborn infant has developed into a socially functioning child. The few documented cases of feral children, or those who have survived in the wild or in extreme isolation without family contact, indicate that these children's behaviour is less than human. Even after they have been intensively trained in clinics, these children have not been able to learn to talk or to think in terms of the symbolic meaning systems that distinguish humans from other animals. Functionalists thus suggest that, without families, there would be no humanity and hence no society. Functionalists accord no other social institution such central importance. For this reason, the study of sociology of the family offers the strongest test of the contributions and the limitations of the functionalist perspective.

Functionalist Theories of the Family

Any institution can be studied from two related perspectives: the contribution of that institution to the functioning of society as a whole or the institution's internal functioning as a subsystem in its own right, with its own set of prerequisites for maintaining a dynamic equilibrium.

The four critical functions that the family unit performs for society are: reproduction of society's members; socialization of new members, especially the newborn and young children; regulation of sexual relations; and economic co-operation to sustain adults and their offspring. The family constitutes the basic emotional or expressive social unit, providing nurturing, protection, and affection for members, controlling their behaviour, and channelling fundamental sexual and reproductive drives into socially acceptable forms. While reproduction and sexual relations can and do take place outside of families, they are only socially legitimated within families. Reiss suggests that this is because the family context best ensures the nurturance of the newborn, with kinship groups on both the father's and the mother's side acknowledging a relationship with, and some responsibility for, the child (Reiss 1976, chap. 2).

The family occurs in a great variety of forms in different societies. There are **extended families**, in which several generations of kin live in the same dwelling, and **nuclear families** consisting of isolated couples with their dependent children. Legitimate sexual relations include **monogamy** (one man with one woman) or forms of **polygamy** (more than one spouse). The more common form of polygamy is **polygyny** (one man having two or more wives), but some societies practise **polyandry** (one woman having more than one husband). Whatever the particular arrangement favoured in a given society, functionalists argue that there is an essential core that is universal. This core was defined by Robert Murdoch (1949, 2):

> The family is a social group characterized by common residence, economic co-operation, and reproduction. It includes adults of both sexes, at least two of whom maintain a socially approved sexual relationship, and one or more children, own or adopted, of the sexually cohabiting adults.

Not all members of a society conform to this pattern of living at any one time, but most people spend a significant part of their lives in a family situation. In Canada, most people marry and have children, and most of these children will do the same when they are adults. Kinship ties remain extremely important to people throughout life, even for those individuals who do not form families of their own.

The nuclear family core of two sexually cohabiting adults of the opposite sex, together with their dependent children, is seen by functionalists a having an essential biological foundation (Goode 1982, 15–32). This thesis incorporates the core ideas of **sociobiology**, a branch of sociology closely associated with functionalism, which studies the biological bases of social behaviour. Functionalist argue that the vital institution of family is rooted in sexual drives and the imperatives of reproduction and in the sociological imperative of transforming the biological organism of a newborn baby into a human or social being. The long helplessness of the human baby, who would quickly die if left without constant care, is another biological foundation for the nuclear family. Unlike many animals, the argument goes, human babies are born with relatively few instincts. They rely upon a complex brain to learn, through symbols and abstractions, the essentials of survival in society. This necessitates a long period of social dependency that lasts until well into adolescence and beyond in complex, industrial society. Because of this, there is a relatively long period during which the nurturing mother depends upon care and support of other adults, usually the husband/father, to meet her economic needs while she is engaged in child care.

Many biological drives predispose humans for male-female pair bonding. Goode suggests that, despite the fact that there is some homosexuality, people are pre-programmed for heterosexuality. The constancy of the human sex drive, far more intense than is needed for reproduction itself, promotes long-term, stable relations between men and women. The biologically based impulse of jealousy reinforces this pair bonding through the urge to regard one's mate as one's exclusive sexual property. Another very general biological drive is territoriality, the natural desire to settle in one location and defend it from others. This is combined with a biologically determined reproductive strategy of having few offspring and caring intensively for them, rather than producing many offspring at once and leaving them to fend for themselves. All these traits create strong impulses in humans to form families.

Functionalists argue that sexual differences promote heterosexual bonding. Only women undergo menstruation, pregnancy, and lactation, and hence they are biologically predisposed to perform the task of caring for children. Breast-feeding intensifies the bond between mother and child. Women are relatively weak during preg-

nancy and just after birth; hence natural choice as well as efficiency dictate that they will stay close to home and children. Males, on the other hand, have greater strength and aggressiveness, which gave them the edge in early hunting societies and hence provided a biological basis for early male dominance. Lionel Tiger (1977) argues that "man the hunter" was preprogrammed for aggression and dominance over females and also for strong male bonding in hunting packs. This predisposition for male bonding gives men an advantage in politics and in business. Tiger argues that women are pre-programmed to be submissive and to be oriented toward their children rather than to form bonds with other women. These biological predispositions favour the sex-role division of labour within families, with women concentrating on nurturing roles within the home while men concentrate on the role of economic provider.

Functionalists posit that sociological factors stemming from the nature of work in industrial societies strongly reinforce this biologically based tendency toward sex-role division of labour within families. As we saw in chapter 10, Parsons argues that family and industry are based on diametrically opposed patterns of action orientation and hence must be separated if both are to function effectively. Family life is based on emotional ties between members; membership is dependent on ascriptive characteristics and not qualifications; individuals are judged by particularistic values as unique family members; and there are diffuse obligations to meet each others' needs in multiple ways. Industry necessarily operates in terms of totally different patterns. Relations between people in industry are emotionally neutral; membership is ideally determined by achievements; judgments are based upon universalistic criteria of standards of performance; and obligations are specific to the particular transaction. The specialization of sex roles, with women concentrating upon the internal affairs of the family while men concentrate upon occupational roles, best serves to minimize confusion of values across the two spheres.

In functionalist analysis, the family constitutes a social system with its own internal needs that must be met if the family is to maintain its equilibrium. Individual families, like society as a whole, must meet the four basic prerequisites of goal attainment, adaptation, integration, and latency or pattern maintenance. Parsons and Bales (1956, chap. 1) analyse how families function internally to divide up critical roles along sex-specific lines. Bales maintains that small groups typically develop two kinds of leaders: an **instrumental leader** who gets tasks done and an **expressive leader** who supports and encourages group members and smooths over tensions. Parsons proposes that, within families, one adult, typically the male, performs instrumental tasks, while the female performs the expressive roles. In terms of system prerequisites, instrumental roles include goal attainment and adaptation. The man typically represents the family to the external social system, making the key decisions that set family goals and earning the resources needed for the family to adapt to its surroundings and survive. Expressive roles are oriented toward the internal needs of the family, meeting the prerequisites of integration and latency by supporting and nurturing people, smoothing over tensions, and teaching the family values and patterns of behaviour to the children. Parsons argues that these functional imperatives reinforce, if they do not totally mandate, sex-role division of labour within families.

Spencer (1976, chap. 11) speculates on what might happen if a particular husband and wife decided to change this pattern. In order to challenge male control over goals and adaptation decisions, she argues, a couple must first acknowledge their present functions. Western societies generally mandate a certain pattern of sex-role specialization, such that the male is obliged to support and defend his wife and children. Thus society penalizes the male if both partners want to stay home. If men and women want equal work opportunities, both must take equal responsibility for support of the family. If the wife were to become the chief breadwinner, Spencer argues, then she would have to have authority within the household. If her job required her to move, then the rest of the family would have to move with good grace. If she pays the bills, she would have to decide the family budget. If she is to be fit and awake for her job, then her dependants would have to protect her health, her mood, her rest, and so on, by obeying her requests. Spencer notes that these are the prerogatives now enjoyed by men and resented by women. She concludes that traditional roles are designed to protect children and hence are functionally necessary, at least to some degree.

Functionalists also argue that the typical nuclear family pattern, consisting of a married couple with their children, is mandated by the requirements of industrial society. Industrialization is founded on free labour markets and a flexible, mobile workforce. Workers and their families must be willing to move as and where the breadwinner's work demands. The nuclear group is much more easily mobile than the extended family group, which is commonly tied to landed property.

In summary, functionalism appears to offer a comprehensive theory that accounts for all the essential features of family as we know it in industrialized society. The heterosexual pair bonding at the core of any family system stems from biological imperatives—not merely the sex drive, but the need for long-term nurturing of newborn infants and children. The sex-role division of labour within families and the segregation of women's domestic nurturing work from male instrumental roles in the work force are rooted both in biological predispositions and in the very distinctive values and behaviour orientations of family life and occupational roles in industrial society. The authority of males in the home in terms of the allocation of money also reflects the imperatives of the breadwinner role that men normally hold. The demands for a mobile workforce account for the predominantly isolated nuclear family residence pattern. The explanation seems complete. It suggests that efforts to change family life or sex roles in any significant way are impractical.

Critique of Functionalist Theory

The functionalist theory of the family has come under considerable attack, primarily for elevating an historically specific form of family into a universal principle. The theory ignores the wide diversity of family forms. Such diversity renders a rigidly defined notion of "the family," such as that proposed by Murdoch, useless. Functionalist views of the family have been challenged, especially by Marxist and feminist theorists, as an ideology that seeks to justify the status quo while ignoring the ways in which family life is arbitrarily constrained by narrowly defined interests associated with capitalism and patriarchy. These are interests that benefit in multiple ways from exploiting the cheap labour of women in the home. Functionalism supports that exploitation by legitimating it as if it were unavoidable and universal. Functionalist theory of the family is criticized for it **monolithic**, **conservative**, **sexist**, and **microstructural biases** (Eichler 1988a, chaps. 1-4). In this section we briefly examine each of these biases in turn.

Monolithic Bias

The **monolithic bias** is inherent in Murdoch's definition of "the family," which functionalists tend to treat as a given. A host of alternative family forms that have existed in other societies, and that are emerging in contemporary industrial societies such as Canada, are simply ignored or treated as problematic deviations. Anthropologists have long been familiar with examples of cultural patterns in other societies that violate some or all elements of Murdoch's supposedly universal family form.

The Nayars of South India had, until the beginning of the twentieth century, a family form that incorporated none of the attributes considered essential by functionalists. Family life was not organized around sexually cohabiting pairs. There was no economic co-operation between women and their sexual partners, and the children of such liaisons had no socially recognized relationship with their biological fathers. They might not even know who their father was. Nayar families were organized around the female line. The joint family comprised the mother, her siblings, and her own and her sisters' children. A brief ceremony took place before girls reached puberty that linked each girl with a man from her own social rank. The ritual functioned only to establish female adult sexual status. From then on, women were free to have sexual relations with whomever they chose. Children lived in their mother's joint family home. Men did not live with their sexual partners; they continued to live in their own mother's household. All property belonging to the joint family was inherited through the mother's line. The mother's eldest brother commonly managed the property, but he did not own it and could not dispose of it. His principle relationship with children was as uncle to his sisters' offspring (Liddle and Joshi 1986, 28, 51–52).

Another family form that violates most of Murdoch's key defining features developed within Israeli agricultural communes or *kibbutzim* (Spiro 1958). There is no formal marriage on the kibbutz. A man and woman "marry" by moving into one room together; to "divorce" they move out. No other ceremonies or obligations are required by the community. Children are raised communally in nurseries. They may visit their parents' room as they choose, but parents are not directly responsible for their support or socialization. Other studies suggest that in Jamaica, and in poor black communities in the United States, nuclear families are also not the norm. The stable relationship is between a woman and her children, while she has only temporary and sequential relations with male partners (Reiss, 1976, 14–15).

In Israeli *kibbutzim*, children are raised communally rather than in traditional families.

Functionalists have responded to these challenges to the universality of "the family" by proposing various redefinitions around the mother-child dyad or, more commonly, by dismissing variations as rare aberrations that prove the general rule (Reiss 1976, chap. 2). The Nayar culture can be viewed as an anthropological anomaly that developed in the exceptional circumstances of extensive migration of males in search of work as soldiers. The fact that this type of family broke down in the early twentieth century during British rule in India indicates that it was not a viable form. The kibbutz is an equally rare example of a very small utopian community, commonly established in an isolated desert area. Critics doubt whether such

a system could work in any larger society. The female-headed households among poor blacks do not represent a cultural ideal so much as the collapse of normal family life in the face of the abject poverty and chronic unemployment of black males. The ideal remains permanent marriage and stable fatherhood.

But charges of monolithic bias cannot be avoided simply by dismissing these family forms as aberrations. Eichler challenges the monolithic bias squarely within the North American society that functionalist theory is designed to explain. She argues that the image of family as the monogamous nuclear group comprising husband, wife, and their biological children applies to only a minority of structures that participants themselves regard as family. The argument that most individuals may have lived in a nuclear family at some time in their lives does not alter the fact that the numerical majority of people in Canada are not now living in such families. Functionalists arbitrarily exclude from their definition of family a multitude of other arrangements: common-law couples (see table 11-1); commuting couples where spouses have careers in different places and meet only on weekends or holidays; couples who do not have children; couples whose children live elsewhere; **reconstituted families** where one or both spouses may have children living elsewhere; single-parent families; homosexual couples; and so on.

Eichler suggests that, if functionalists insist on having one definition to cover all forms of family, it would have to look something like the following: A family is a social group that may or may not include adults of both sexes, may or may not have children born in wedlock, or originating in the marriage, may or may not be living in a common residence, may or may not be sexually cohabiting, and may or may not include love, attraction, economic support, and so on (Eichler 1988a, 4).

Table 11-1 Common-law Partners as a Percentage of all Persons Living as Couples, 1981 and 1986

Age Group	1981	1986
15–19	49.5	59.6
20–24	23.1	32.9
25–29	11.3	16.6
30–34	6.8	10.3
35–39	5.1	7.4
40–44	3.9	5.9
45–49	3.0	4.5
50–54	2.4	3.5
55–59	1.8	2.6
60–64	1.5	2.1
65 and over	1.0	1.5
Total	6.4	8.3

Source: Statistics Canada, Census of Canada.

Eichler proposes that the attempt to define "the family" should be abandoned in favour of an alternative approach that impirically researches the dimensions of family life. The important dimensions that Eichler (1988a, 6) singles out are procreation, socialization of children, sexual relations, residence patterns, economic co-operation, and emotional support. Functionalists assume that members of a family will be high on all dimensions. A husband and wife will have children together, socialize them, have sexual relations with each other, live together, co-operate economically, and give each other emotional support. This global assumption is false. Eichler addresses each dimension in turn, suggesting how it needs to be reconceptualized in terms of a range of behaviour options that vary widely, depending on circumstances.

The dimension of *procreation*, for example, has been radically affected by the number of couples choosing to remain childless and by the high rate of divorce and remarriage. Eichler (1988a, 243) cites evidence that, in Canada in 1985, one in three marriages ended in divorce. The majority of these people remarry, although we do not know how many because Statistics Canada does not record the number of brides or grooms who were previously married. But we can estimate that between a quarter to a third of all Canadian children grow up in reconstituted families where one of the adults with whom they live is not their biological parent.

The dimension of *socialization* is likewise a variable. A child may be socialized by both biological parents together, or by one parent alone, or one parent with one step-parent, or one parent and step-parent in one house and another parent and step-parent in a second house, or some other combination of possible arrangements. It also cannot be assumed that simply because a parent lives in the same house as a child, that that parent is involved in socialization. It is quite possible and probably common for one parent to do most of the socialization work while the other does very little. Similarly, we cannot assume that when parents are divorced, the absentee parent is necessarily not involved in socialization. It may well be that divorced fathers give more time and attention to children than do fathers in two-parent households who take it for granted that the mother will do all the child-rearing work. Even the assumption that socialization gets done by parents can be questioned in a society in which very large numbers of young children spend most of their waking time in child-care centres, or with nannies, and in the company of television.

The notion that *sexual relations* take place only between married or co-habiting partners can readily be challenged. Lifelong chastity in marriage may be the exception rather than the rule. This, in turn, has important implications for procreation. It cannot simply be assumed that all children are the biological offspring of the mother's spouse.

Figure 11-1 Percentage Distribution of Census Families, by Family Structure, 1971 and 1986

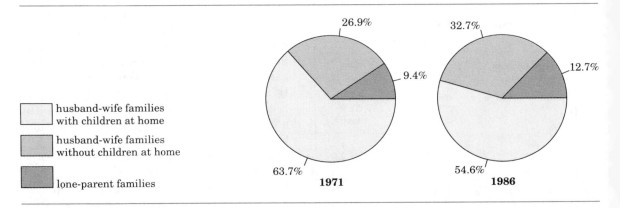

husband-wife families
with children at home

husband-wife families
without children at home

lone-parent families

Source: Statistics Canada, 1971 and 1986 Censuses of Canada

Residence patterns also vary widely. In divorced and reconstituted families, children may have two separate family homes and commute between them. It is possible, although rare in our society, for children to have one residence while the parents rotate. Many two-career families have two or even three separate homes, one near the husband's and/or the wife's work and another family home elsewhere. Many more couples may live in one place during the winter and another during the summer.

Economic co-operation cannot be treated as given within a family. Functionalists conceive of the husband-breadwinner providing economic resources for the homemaking wife and their children, but many other arrangements are common. A sole breadwinner may pool all income for joint family use, or may keep some or most of the money for private use and give only a housekeeping allowance to the spouse. In extreme cases, the non-employed spouse may get no money at all: the breadwinner keeps everything and makes all decisions about what to buy. Two-income families have another set of possible arrangements; this is compounded when there are adult, income-earning children living at home.

The last dimension of family interaction, *emotional relations*, may vary all the way from close, loving, and mutually supportive ties to shallow and detached relations with little emotional involvement. In extreme though by no means uncommon situations, emotional relations may be characterized by abuse, violence, and hatred.

Traditional functionalist theory is not

"Which parent do you want to sign it: my natural father, my step father, my mother's third husband, my real mother or my natural father's fourth wife who lives with us?"

adequate to explore the dimensions of family life because the theoretical structure itself is too rigid. The monolithic bias is so pervasive that most sociology of the family textbooks, even in the 1980s, ignore the huge number of reconstituted families and all other forms of living arrangements not organized around heterosexually co-habiting pairs. All other family forms are predefined as "problem families" regardless of how participants feel about them. We know little or nothing about the internal economies of families, because functionalism does not go beyond treating families as economic units. Most textbooks ignore the issue of family violence entirely or at best treat it as an aberration. This is notwithstanding the evidence of extensive wife battering and the physical and sexual abuse of children. Eichler suggests that, far from being an aberration, emotional stress and violence may be normal occurrences in families. The situation of enforced intimacy between people of different sexes, different careers, different incomes, and markedly different ages would normally be seen as conducive to high stress in any context other than families. Why would we expect families to be immune?

Conservative Bias

Other biases compound the distortions arising from a monolithic focus. Eichler criticizes traditional sociology of the family literature for its **conservative bias**, reflected in a pervasive failure to focus upon changes that are transforming family life. Demographic variables are high on the list of critical changes. People in Canada are having fewer children than in the past and are living much longer. Declining fertility rates mean that most women experience pregnancy only twice in their lives. A full-time mothering role is no longer a lifetime expectation. Over half the adult women in Canada are employed outside the home. Even for the stereotypical family, the period of "Mom, Dad, and the kids" may cover only a limited stage in the

family life cycle. Couples who have one or two children in their early twenties can look forward to twenty to thirty years of working lives after their children have left home. They can also realistically expect ten or more years of life after retirement.

Changes in longevity have been dramatic and are having a profound impact on family life. Eichler (1988a, 42) notes that, in 1931, the average life expectancy for a male at birth was 60.0 years, but this had risen to 70.2 years by 1986. The rise in life expectancy for women was even larger: from 62.1 years in 1932 to 78.3 years in 1986. Thus, women, on average, outlive men by over eight years, and they also tend to marry men who are older than themselves. Data from British Columbia in 1979 indicate that almost three-quarters of the women who had married in the province had husbands who were older than themselves. Only 16.8 percent of marriages were between older brides and younger grooms; in the remainder of marriages, the partners were the same age (Veevers 1986).

The combined effect of women's longer life expectancy and men's older age at marriage leads to very different experiences for women and men (Eichler 1988a, 42–43). The 1981 census shows that 81.3 percent of men aged 65 to 74 were married, as were almost half of those over 85. By contrast, only about half the women in the 65 to 74 age group were married, as were less than 10 percent of those over the age of 85. Figure 11-2 shows the differences in the marital status of elderly men and women. These differences mean that the majority of men can expect to be cared for in their old age by their younger wives, while women of the same age can rarely expect to be cared for by their husbands. It would take a dramatic change in marriage patterns to redress this imbalance, but there is no evidence that this is happening.

Eichler points out that the pattern of long widowhood for women is particularly

Figure 11-2   Marital Status of Elderly Men and Women, Canada, 1986

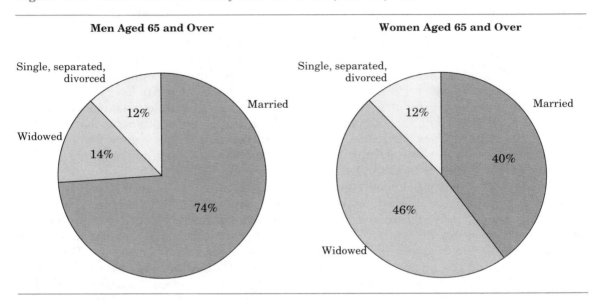

Source: Statistics Canada, 1986 Census of Canada.

problematic because of the uneven distribution of earnings and pensions between women and men. Women who have worked as homemakers all their lives have no individual pension entitlements when their husbands die, other than the universal old age pensions paid by the government. Women generally spend more years outside the paid labour force than men to care for children. Even when they do work full-time, they earn significantly less money than men. Low earnings translate into low pensions. The result is that the majority of widows over age sixty-five live below the poverty line. The 1981 census shows that, for every age group and at every level of education, old women are much poorer than old men.

The rise in average life expectancies also means that a greater proportion of people are living into their eighties and nineties. What this means is that people who are themselves elderly and retired commonly have parents who require care. These responsibilities fall particularly heavily upon women, since it

tends to be women rather than men who do the caring work within families. Many women around sixty-five years of age may find themselves caring for their own very elderly mother, and perhaps their father and in-laws, as well as for their older, retired husband. This is a great deal of work to do at an age when the woman herself might have expected to be able to retire from the obligations of looking after other people.

All of these are very dramatic changes from family life in Canada only a few generations earlier, yet they receive little attention in functionalist theory.

Sexist Bias

The **sexist bias** in family sociology is reflected in the pervasive stereotyping of female and male roles around images of the pregnant woman and man the hunter. Such images are largely irrelevant in an era when few women have more than two pregnancies, and the vast majority of men neither hunt nor have jobs that require hard physical labour. This stereotyping perpetuates the myth that women are only marginally involved in the workforce and that men are marginally involved in homelife and child rearing. Still worse, functionalist theory elevates such myths to the level of functional imperatives, conveying the impression that alternative lifestyles threaten the equilibrium of family and occupational subsystems, and hence threaten society itself.

Microstructural Bias

Lastly, the **microstructural bias** in functionalist theory is reflected in a primary focus on the internal workings of individual family units. Most sociology of the family textbooks give little consideration to the impact of the wider political economy and the nature of government policies as they affect family life. Functionalists tend to discuss family problems as if they arose from inadequacies in the role performance of individual members, rather than from external pressures on people. The microstructural bias is inherent in each of the other biases described above. We cannot understand what is happening to families apart from studying the political economy in relation to which people organize their personal lives.

Marxist Theories of the Family

The Marxist approach to sociology of the family challenges the microstructural bias of traditional functionalist theory. Marxists argue that both the organization of economic production in the wider society and the way people earn their living critically influence the organization of family life. The family form that functionalists assert as universal represents only one historically specific form, prevalent only at a certain stage in the development of capitalism and only for members of a certain social class. Marxist-feminists accept this broad analysis of the relationship between modes of production and family forms but give special attention to the impact of the economy on women's roles within the family. They challenge Parsons' notion of a separation between the **private realm** of family life and the **public realm** of industry. They claim that the demands of capitalism intrude into the most intimate personal relations of family life. Homemakers work for the corporations as much as employees do. The only difference is that the homemakers' work is not acknowledged and is not paid for.

The Marxist Theory of Patriarchy

The Marxist perspective draws its initial inspiration from an early essay by Engels ([1884] 1978), a long-time colleague of Marx. Engels speculates that the earliest form of family was probably communal, based on relatively free sexual relations and organized around matriarchal households, reflecting the known biological relation between mother and child. The family form among the Nayars, described above, closely resembles the model that Engels had in mind.

Engels argues that this original matriarchal family form was probably undermined by two critical factors: the knowledge of paternity and male control over private property. Awareness of the male role in conception represented a profound leap of knowledge, Engels suggests, with important implications for power within the family, especially when combined with control over property. As the means of subsistence changed from hunting and gathering to more settled herding and agriculture, men gained control over land and domestic herds and thus over the economic surplus. As men gained wealth, they wanted to control inheritance through the male line. This necessitated control over women's sexuality and over their offspring. Monogamy and patriarchy emerged together, Engels suggests. Monogamy was strictly required for women; men could still enjoy relative sexual freedom. This inequality gave rise to prostitution. Engels comments that "the overthrow of mother right was the world historic defeat of the female sex. The man seized the reins of the house also, the woman was degraded, enthralled, the slave of man's lust, a mere instrument for breeding children" (Engels [1884] 1978, 736).

Engels suggests that inegalitarian family forms would disappear only under two possible situations. The first was where people were so poor that men would have no property to inherit or pass on. The second was under a system of communal ownership of the means of production and equal employment of women in a socialist society. This would remove forever the basis of male power over women.

Engel's essay, and particularly his theory of the transition from matriarchy to patriarchy, is speculative, based on little anthropological evidence. But his argument concerning the importance of control over property as a determinant of male dominance in the household is widely accepted.

Capitalism and Family Forms in Canada

In a series of essays, Dorothy Smith (1977, 1979b, 1983b) traces changing forms of property ownership associated with the development of capitalism in Canada. She examines how these changes transformed relations between women and men in the home. During the early homesteading period, she argues, a husband and wife shared all property. They depended on each other and worked together to produce everything they needed to survive. There was no separation between domestic and productive work. Men cleared and ploughed land for crops while women maintained gardens, kept chickens, pigs, and cows, helped in the harvest, and preserved the food. Women owned not only what they produced but whatever money they could make by selling surplus vegeta-

bles, eggs, and butter in the market. Thus, a basic economic and social equality existed between wife and husband.

This equality changed in a subtle but significant way with the transition from subsistence homesteading to cash production. Land speculation led to escalating prices, and settlers required heavy mortgages to buy land and equipment. This meant that they were no longer merely producing food for the subsistence needs of their families. Their survival depended on producing cash crops like wheat from which to earn the money to pay bank loans. Laws of property, debt, and credit endowed only the husband with full economic status in a marriage. Land was held as collateral for loans and mortgages made to him. The result, suggest Smith, was drudgery and tyranny for farm wives, who were totally subordinated to their husbands. They laboured on the farms just as they had laboured on the homesteads, but all their labour went to pay off bank loans. When the mortgage was finally paid off, the farm belonged legally only to the husband. Women owned nothing. All the results of their labour were appropriated by their husbands.

The powerlessness of farm wives was underlined by the Supreme Court of Canada decision in 1975 concerning Irene Murdoch. She had worked on the family farm for twenty-five years with her husband but, after their divorce, the court decreed that she had no legal right to any of the farm property. Women who worked with their husbands in other kinds of small business enterprises found themselves in essentially the same situation. They had no assurance of a share in the assets of a business to which they had contributed. It took a national outcry from women's organizations after the Murdoch decision to change the law to give women a share in marital property and family businesses.

As capitalism has advanced, the petite bourgeoisie, or people who earn their living by means of family farms and family-run businesses, has declined. In the current era of corporate monopoly capitalism, the vast majority of Canadian families depend upon employment in large corporations and state bureaucracies. This dependence on wages and salaries from work done outside the home and beyond the control of family members has critical implications for the working lives of those adults who still remain within the home. Typically men were the first to leave the home to work for wages. Women continued to do domestic work and to care for children, but they were cut off from the productive enterprise. Production was no longer centred around the home but took place in factories to which they did not have access. Marxists argue that this historically specific change in the development of capitalism produced the separate role of housewife and the model of the private family segregated from the occupational world. This is the same model that Parsons treats as a universal principal.

Marxist-feminist theorists argue that women's work in the home remains crucial to the productive enterprise. The ties that bind homemakers to the corporations are less immediately visible than those binding employees but, nonetheless, almost all aspects of their working days are dictated by corporate demands. Women's labour within the home is appropriated by corporations in multiple ways, but this relation tends to be covered up by the misleading notion of the homemaker's work as a private service to her breadwinner husband. Smith argues that this "private service" by homemakers for their husbands and children may ultimately be responsible for holding together the entire system of capitalist relations of production. Smith rejects the simplistic version of Marxist theory that claims that class structure determines family structure. She insists that we must examine what people do in their everyday lives to produce the relations that we subsequently come to see as the class

structure. Women's work in the home is an integral part of the processes through which class relations are produced and maintained on a daily basis. It is these work processes that we briefly explore below.

The Social Construction of Class Relations in the Home

Whether or not women work outside the home, they maintain the responsibility for homework. This responsibility and the ways in which women's homework is appropriated by capitalism vary with the social class or occupation of employed family members, which may include the women themselves. A working-class wife has to put a home together, often under conditions of poverty and inadequate housing. Her labour is vital in the struggle for some measure of comfort on a limited income. Her efforts make it possible for people to survive on incomes that may barely meet subsistence needs. Her fundamental work for the corporation is to keep her husband working under these conditions. Corporations know well that married men make more stable workers than single men because of their responsibility to support their families. It is less easy for married men to leave if they do not like the working conditions. The working-class wife supports the capitalist system against her husband because she depends so heavily upon his wages to provide for herself and her children. She cannot let him quit. An unemployed man may commonly be punished by his wife, through nagging, criticism, and humiliation, to pressure him back into the workforce.

Luxton (1980, chap. 3) describes with stark realism the harsh lives of women married to miners in the single-industry town of Flin Flon in northern Manitoba. The working lives of these housewives remain totally tied to the rhythms of their husbands' work. A housewife must get up long before the mine whistle goes, to get her husband up, fed, and ready for work, and she must be there to greet him with his dinner when he returns. When he is working shifts, she must alter her entire schedule to meet his and yet still maintain the school schedules of their children. She must keep the children quiet and out of the way when he is sleeping, do her housework only when it will not disturb him, provide meals when he wants them, and in effect manage the family so that he turns up regularly for work. In a sense, she is as much an employee of the mine as he is, but she does not get paid.

The appropriation of the labour of middle-class women by capitalism takes a different form. In material terms, their lives may be more comfortable and their homemaking responsibilities easier to meet than those of working-class housewives because they do not have to struggle against poverty. But the wives of men who hold managerial and executive positions within corporations may have less personal autonomy as they find themselves more trapped by the demands of the corporation. Smith (1977) argues that, while a working-class man has a job within a corporation, a man in a more senior rank plays a role for the corporation. He must meet the image of a corporation man, and it is his wife's duty to maintain this image and to mould their children to fit it. The family home becomes something of a subcontracted agency of the corporation. The housewife works to produce the image that the corporation wants. The image that is on display is largely set by the media and disseminated in glossy magazines and television advertising; the housewife herself has little control over it. It is subtly but rigidly enforced within the corporate hierarchy. An executive whose personal and family appearance does not conform to the corporate mould tends to be viewed with suspicion and overlooked for promotion.

Middle-class women routinely support the careers of their husbands by relieving them of household and child-care responsibilities. The corporate man is then free to display his undivided loyalty to the corporation by spending long hours of overtime at the office on evenings and weekends and travelling on business whenever requested. In the highly competitive corporate world, such behaviour is often essential for mobility up the corporate hierarchy. The support work that wives do often begins very early in men's corporate careers. A wife may work to support her husband through college. Subsequently, she may help his career by entertaining his business associates and doing unpaid secretarial work. The wife of a professor often helps with the research, sorting, and editing involved in writing, although the resulting work bears only his name. Corporations thus appropriate the labour time of the wives of their executives and professional staff through the support services that wives are routinely expected to provide for their husbands. The competence of wives, especially wives of executives, to perform these support roles can be so important that some corporations have insisted on interviewing not only the male applicants for senior positions, but their wives as well (Kanter 1977).

A middle-class homemaker further serves the corporation through absorbing the tensions generated by the career demands made on her husband. In this there is a catch-22; when she supports and repairs him and sends him back refreshed, she is in fact supporting the external system that oppresses him. But, like her working-class counterpart, she has little choice. To be a good homemaker, she must make her husband's success visible. She cannot afford to let him fail.

Corporations also appropriate the mothering work of middle-class women. Middle-class status is inherited not through property, but through careers, and mothering work is essential to this process. The academic streaming of children begins very early in the education process, and a mother who wants her children to succeed in future corporate careers must groom them even in infancy so that they will perform well from the first days of kindergarten. Her children's failure in school will be seen as evidence that she does not love them enough.

In times of economic recession, women's unpaid labour in the home absorbs the resulting social problems. As unemployment rises, women are disproportionately affected, laid off more frequently, and pushed into part-time work. They bear the increased burden of the emotional stress felt by workers who risk being unemployed or who may be squeezed out in corporate mergers. As we saw in chapter 9, women in the home must absorb the extra work no longer being done by professionals when social services are cut back for the elderly, the handicapped, and the sick. (Armstrong 1984, chap. 7).

In these multiple ways, homemakers work for the corporate capitalist system, work for which they receive no pay and rarely any acknowledgement. The enormity of their exploitation is hidden under the myth of private family life. Until the women's movement began to have some impact, all the work that women did in the home was not even identified as work. It was considered merely "a labour of love" (Luxton 1980).

Research in the Marxist-feminist tradition has documented the processes through which relations of political economy intrude into the most intimate relations of love and marriage. Luxton's study of Flin Flon shows how courtship and marriage are affected by the economy of this single-industry mining town, in which there are few well-paying jobs for women. Marriage is the only viable option for adult women in the town. This reality pervades the dating game and sexual activities. Boys have the chance to earn good money working in the mine while girls do not. Girls therefore trade sexual favours for a good time and economic rewards. Boys pay for the date and expect, sooner rather than later, that the girl will "come across." This same dependency continues after marriage and is made all the more evident if pregnancy has forced a quick wedding. Both the

woman and the man feel trapped by her dependence on his wages.

Luxton (1980, chap. 6) suggests that this economic reality is at the root of much domestic violence. She describes the explosive tensions that revolve around the fact that he earns the money and she spends it. Men who come home drained and exhausted from a day's work at the mine often feel they have a right to control the household because they are responsible for its subsistence. Many of the women whom Luxton interviewed described how they took the brunt of their husband's resentment against his job. One woman summed it up this way: "He puts up with shit every day at work and he only works because he has to support me and the kids. Weren't for us he'd be off trapping on his own—no boss" (Luxton 1980, 70). Women blame themselves, feeling guilty for having induced male hostility and aggression by being a burden. Women absorb the tensions. In extreme cases they absorb violence and beatings. More commonly, they deny themselves even basic needs because they cannot escape the sense of guilt that they are spending "his" money on themselves. This is the reality that is glossed over in the abstract functionalist category of "tension management."

Such dependent relationships may only be marginally improved for most women who take up employment outside the home. Having their own income allows women some independence, but the reality is that few women can hope to earn enough to support themselves and their children above the poverty line. With the exception of a minority of professional women, a male wage is still essential to support an average middle-class family lifestyle.

In summary, Marxist-feminists argue that family relations and domestic work are embedded in the political economy of corporate capitalism. Homemakers are agents of tension management and pattern maintenance for corporations, but their work is not acknowledged and not paid for. They remain outside the corporations and so cannot influence any of the decisions that direct their lives. Smith (1977) sees this as the root of depression and mental illness among women. Women are oppressed in a nameless way by a system from which they appear to be entirely separated and yet which comes to rule the most intimate aspects of their lives. This thesis avoids the monolithic and conservative biases evident in functionalist theory by analysing family structures in their historical and class contexts. Family forms in Canada changed markedly with transformations in capitalism from early homesteading, through cash cropping and small business, to the current form of monopoly capitalism. The thesis also incorporates an analysis of the processes through which people socially construct the realities of family life in the situation in which they find themselves.

The Radical Feminist Critique: Capitalism or Patriarchy?

The radical feminist perspective shares with Marxism an appreciation of the impact of capitalism on family life, but challenges the narrow, deterministic focus on political economy as the cause of family structures. These theorists argue that this tunnel vision of traditional Marxists gives inadequate attention to relations of patriarchy or gender hierarchy that cannot be subsumed under capitalism. They challenge particularly the more deterministic version of Marxist theory, sometimes referred to as Marxist structuralism, that explains family structures by reference to their functions for the capitalist system.

Marxists would argue, for example, that the privatization of women in the home occurs because it is functional for capitalism (Armstrong and Armstrong 1985). Capitalism is based on free wage labour that

requires the separation of a public, commodity-production unit from a private subsistence unit in which free labourers are reproduced and maintained. Hence the subordination of women appears to be a necessary condition for the capitalist system. Structuralist Maxists also describe the position of women as a reserve army of labour, which can be stored cheaply within the home, as necessary for the capitalist system. The implications of this thesis are that the **privatization** of women was not evident in the pre-capitalist era. It arose with capitalism and will decline with the transition to socialism.

Radical feminists argue that the evidence does not support this thesis. In pre-capitalist Europe, the economy may have centred around domestic production in which women were involved, but this did not ensure gender equality, either in family practice or in religious and social ideologies. In many parts of contemporary Asia, in both Hindu and Muslim cultures, the traditions of **purdah**, which include an emphasis on the extreme subjugation and segregation of women within the home, still persist. The origins of the purdah system long predate the emergence of capitalism. If anything, this extreme privatization of women has begun to break down under capitalism, as more women gain access to education and professional employment outside the home. In Soviet society the profit motive has been removed, and free wage labour as a commodity for capitalists to exploit does not exist. The vast majority of adult women are employed full-time in the economy. Yet women have still not achieved equality with men, either outside or inside the home. Women still perform the bulk of all domestic work, and such labour is still denegrated as low status.

The Marxist thesis shows how capitalism accommodates to and uses existing inequalities between women and men in the household, but this is not sufficient to explain why such inequalities developed in the first place or why they persist (Miles 1985). We still need to explain why capitalism developed in such a way as to bolster men's power over women. We need to explain why the sexual division of labour appears as it does. Why is it, almost invariably, women and not men who are engaged in unpaid domestic labour? Marx tends to treat this as the biological nature of things, but it is by no means biologically determined that women must do the domestic work beyond the actual physical acts of giving birth and breast-feeding. Why is it mostly women who bear the double burden of domestic work and a paid job? Why do husbands continue to do so little domestic work in comparison with their wives even when wives are employed full-time? Why is it that the issue of whether a wife should be employed takes on the connotations of a threat to male power and status? Reference to the needs of capitalism does not seem to explain this. Marxist theory would actually predict the opposite response, that men would generally welcome any reduction in the economic burden of a dependent wife.

The prevalence of domestic violence is also not adequately explained within the Marxist thesis. Economic dependence helps to explain the vulnerability of women to male power, but it does not explain why so many wives are battered in the first place (Miles 1985, 47). Nor does economic dependence account for other forms of male violence against women and children, such as rape, incest, and sexual harassment. It cannot explain practices such as burning widows alive on the funeral pyres of their husband, foot-binding, genital mutilation, and **dowry murders**, which are prevalent in some non-Western societies.

Radical feminists assert that Marxist theory describes but does not explain male supremacy inside and outside the home. The exploitation of workers under capitalism and the oppression of women by men are not

equivalent concepts (Eisenstein 1979, 22). Relations of patriarchy have to be addressed directly. In trying to subsume issues of patriarchy under the blanket explanation of capitalism, Marxist theory functions as an ideology. It can serve to legitimate male domination over women by displacing responsibility onto the economy.

This misuse of Marxist theory was powerfully illustrated at a meeting of the Canadian Asian Studies Association in response to a paper describing women's oppression in Pakistan under President Zia's "Islamization" program (Rafiq 1988; Hale 1988). Part of the paper referred to Islamic law concerning rape. A woman who claims she has been raped requires no less than four male witnesses, all of impeccable character, before she can press charges in court. Otherwise, her case will be dismissed, and she herself can be sentenced to public flogging for having engaged in unlawful sex. Men in the audience reinterpreted this paper in terms of the capitalist mode of production, debating how it was in the interests of the capitalist class to keep women at home as cheap labour. In this determinist, structuralist version of Marxism, the men who commit the violence disappear: it is the system that appears to do things. A woman's experience of being raped, with those who violate her not only immune to punishment, but able to have her flogged for even mentioning what they had done to her, was excluded from the debate. It became trivialized as a form of false consciousness, while the concerns of men with their own class oppression took precedence. Radical feminist theory addresses this failure to analyse the oppression of women by placing the issue of patriarchy at the centre of sociology of the family.

The Roots of Male Power

O'Brien (1981) challenges the original thesis proposed by Engels that links male power and control over property. Engels argues that, with the development of settled agriculture and herding, men controlled the means of production and hence the wealth of society. Men sought control over women in order to ensure that their property would be inherited by their own biological children. Thus, the institution of monogamy for women became important. O'Brien suggests that this thesis has too many unquestioned assumptions. Why did men gain control over property in the first place? Why did it have to be inherited through the male line? Why did it have to be inherited individually rather than by the community as a whole? Among the **matrilineal** Nayar in South India, land and animals were communally owned by the mother's joint family and inherited by her children. Men did not have the right to own or to dispose of such property. Why and how did men come to wrest control from the original matriarchal communal families?

O'Brien proposes that the basic causal relationship between control over property and control over women's sexuality should be reversed. Men, she suggests, seek to control property in order to control women's sexual and reproductive powers, not the other way around. The material base of the gender hierarchy is the means of reproduction of children rather than production of material goods. When a woman has sexual freedom, a man has no way of knowing which, if any, of her children he fathered. Paternity is reduced to an abstract idea. O'Brien argues that male alienation from birth, and thus from human continuity through children, is profound. This alienation can only be partially overcome by the institution of monogamy, through which a man asserts an exclusive right of sexual access to a particular woman.

Male power over women is not automatic, but is the result of continual struggle, in which final victory is impossible. Men can struggle to control women, but it is women who control reproduction. Male control over a woman's reproductive powers, and hence male appropriation of her children as his own, is always uncertain. It depends upon absolute faith in her chastity or upon the strictest possible control over her, including her seclusion from other men. It depends also on trust in other men. But such trust is tenuous, especially in the context of war, competition, and hierarchical divisions among men. Male dominance over other men in war is often expressed through sexual violation of the women "belonging" to the enemy.

O'Brien situates the origin of the private family, and the split between the private realm of women and the public realm of men, in this male struggle for exclusive sexual access to women, rather than in the development of capitalism. The economic dependence of women on men and the inability of women to support themselves and their children apart from a man are essential mechanisms for male control over women. The inheritance of property from father to son is also of paramount importance in the social assertion of the principle of paternity over biological maternity. Male control over property and inheritance thus remains central in O'Brien's thesis, but for different reasons than Engels proposes.

The critical difference between the two formulations becomes evident in predicting the behaviour of males who own no property. Engels predicts that when men have no property to control or to transmit to children, they will have no interest in controlling women. O'Brien predicts that such men will still try to control women's sexual and reproductive powers through any other means at their disposal, including sexual violence.

The history of the mother-centred Nayar households gives insight into the nature of the struggle for control over family property and women's reproductive powers. The Nayar family organization did not disappear as an inevitable result of developments in agriculture industrialization. It was deliberately and systematically undermined by the British Imperial government in India.

The British passed a series of laws between 1868 and 1933 that broke up the matrilineal households and imposed a monogamous, male-headed marriage system. The first law held that a man had to provide for his wife and children, a law that had no meaning in the Nayar situation. The next law declared that the wife and children had the right of maintenance by the husband. Again this had little effect because the Nayar did not register marriages. Then followed various Nayar Regulation Laws that decreed that the brief ceremony that took place when a girl reached puberty constituted a legal marriage that could only be dissolved through a legal divorce. The man gained the right to inherit the property of his wife rather than sharing in the communal property of his mother's household. Further laws declared that all property held in common in the matrilineal household could be broken up and inherited and that a man's heirs were no longer his sister's children but his wife's children. The laws were part of a long struggle for supremacy between men and women within the Nayar communities, and they are still bitterly resented and resisted by the Nayar women. Males gained the advantage under the British, both through the laws and through access to an English education, which enabled men but not women to obtain administrative posts in the British colonial service. Men thereby gained personal income and economic independence from the communal household, and they were granted the legal right to dispose of this private property as they wished (Liddle and Joshi 1986, 28–29).

In Canada, male power over women and property was similarly imposed through patriarchal laws. It was not the inevitable outcome of capitalist farming that dispossessed women homesteaders, but specific laws that required a man to have single, unencumbered title to real estate for it to stand as collateral for mortgages and loans. It was only after the Irene Murdoch case in 1975 that these laws were revised to permit and subsequently to require joint ownership by husband and wife of family property used as collateral. Native women were dispossessed by the British North America Act which decreed that any native woman who married a non-native forfeited all her rights to native status and to band property. It was 1984 before this law was changed, and then only after it had been challenged before the World Court.

Given that ownership of property is such an important mechanism in male control over the sexual and reproductive powers of women, it follows that women's paid employment outside the home threatens that control. Radical feminist theory argues that men fear the expansion of income-earning opportunities for their wives, even though this relieves them of the economic burden of a dependent family. The theory predicts that men will strive to minimize the level of economic independence that woman can gain through employment and also that they will strive to reassert control through other mechanisms including domestic violence and medical and legal control over reproduction.

Limits to Economic Freedom for Women

Liddle and Joshi (1986, part IV) argue that class hierarchy in the labour force is built upon and reinforces gender hierarchy. Women are employed but predominantly within low-paid job ghettos. Their incomes supplement their husbands' earnings but do not supercede them. Few women earn sufficient money to provide for themselves and their children at an average standard of living. They still depend on a male wage earner.

The unequal division of domestic labour within the home is cited by Liddle and Joshi as a primary mechanism ensuring the continued economic and familial dominance of men. Even when women are employed in full-time jobs outside the home, they commonly bear almost the entire responsibility for domestic work. Men, by and large, refuse to do this work, or at best contribute only in the least onerous areas. Men appropriate women's labour in the home to restore their own energies. They return to work relaxed and refreshed, while women return to work exhausted from doing three jobs: domestic work, child care, and the work for which they are paid. Then women are penalized in the labour market for having less strength and energy and making slower career progress than men.

Child care outside the home is limited and expensive, so that only women who earn above average incomes can afford it. The majority of women are faced with the choice of taking long periods of time out of the paid labour force to care for young children or working themselves to exhaustion trying to do everything. Women who take such time out, or who begin to develop a career only in their late thirties or early forties, present no competition to men who are far advanced in their positions.

This inequality in the labour force stemming from women's responsibility for domestic work becomes apparent whenever marriages break down. Wives are legally entitled to an equitable share in family property, but husbands take their income-earning capacity with them. All too often, women find themselves left with half a house, but without the income to maintain it.

This artificial separation between the realms of public and private, the world of men and the world of women and children, creates its own dynamic that tends to reinforce male efforts to control and possess women. The public realm is associated with rational and technical concerns of production, and the private family with meeting emotional needs. Men come to depend on women in the home to meet their on-going need for nurturing or mothering, in addition to their need for women to procreate and to nurture their children. This may be especially so in societies where men are discouraged from being nurturing themselves and where they spend their working lives in a public realm, which is characterized by competitive, fragmented, impersonal, and emotionally neutral or non-affective relationships. Long after children have been born and raised, men may still seek to possess women in order to ensure that their own nurturing needs are met. This need for personal nurturing may be so overwhelming for some men that they become jealous of their own children and the attention they are given by the nurturer-mother.

Domestic Violence

The threat and the reality of domestic violence, in all its forms, is another powerful

cathy®   **by Cathy Guisewite**

mechanism for asserting male control over women and children. Until recently, wife beating had both religious and legal approval. The Roman Catholic law of chastisement enjoined a husband to beat his wife for her moral betterment. This injunction was carried over to British common law and Canadian and American law and only began to be challenged toward the end of the nineteenth century. Fathers were also endowed with the religious prescription and legal right to discipline their children using physical force.

In addition to physical battering, children are also victims of sexual abuse. Estimates of such abuse vary widely depending on the measurements used (Badgley 1984, 114). The rate most commonly cited is that one in five girls and one in ten boys have experienced unwanted sexual attention. Guessing rates by pitting the findings of different sources against each other is a largely futile exercise. But the fact that physical and sexual abuse of children occurs in a significant number of families is not in dispute. Why does such behaviour occur?

The Marxist thesis attributes the violence primarily to the frustration experienced by men who are unemployed or are trapped in low-paid, alienating jobs. Radical feminists dispute this explanation as inadequate to account for the extent or the distribution of wife battery and incest. An American study (Shupe, Stacey, and Hazlewood 1987, 22–21) cites evidence that the social background of wife batterers in selected counselling sessions and police records mirrored the population at large with respect to age, education, race, ethnicity, religion, and occupation. The one exception was that the percentage of unemployed men among the batterers was double the national average. Unemployed men seem more likely to batter, perhaps because they have lost the economic basis of their control over their wives, but this does not alter the evidence that men from all strata of the population—including doctors,

lawyers, politicians, ministers, and police officers—beat their wives. Similarly, many of the men who commit incest are "pillars of the community" in other respects.

Various psychological explanations have been put forward to account for wife battering. They include the common argument that it is a symptom of other emotional problems that can stem from trauma from abuse as a child, learned behaviour from watching an abusive father, lack of communication skills with the spouse, low self-esteem, lack of emotional controls, and the need to express repressed anger and frustration (Adams 1988). Radical feminists argue that such explanations only offer excuses for the batterer to continue the behaviour. They also do not account for why the batterer's behaviour is directed at his wife. Batterers rarely assault anyone other than their wives. They do not habitually lose emotional control or lack communication skills in other contexts.

Radical feminists argue that one has to examine the practical gains that accrue to the batterer from his violence; that is, fear and submission in his victim and compliance with his wishes (Adams 1988; Ptacek 1988). Wife battering is essentially a controlling behaviour designed to create and maintain an imbalance of power in the household. Battery and sexual abuse of children are the extreme expressions of male assertion of property rights over women and children. Less extreme forms of such controlling behaviour include verbal and non-verbal intimidation and psychological abuse, pressure tactics like withholding financial support, accusations or threats of infidelity, ultimatums and deadlines that force the woman to comply with her husband's wishes (Adams 1988, 191–94). Such persistent humiliation can be pushed to the point where competent, professional women have their self-esteem destroyed (Forward 1987, 15–85).

Not all expressions of violence are by husbands against wives. Some wives abuse their husbands, but it is currently impossible even to guess at the rate. It would appear that much of the violence directed by wives toward husbands is defensive or retaliatory. The relatively small number of unprovoked attacks on men by female partners seems often to involve jealous ex-wives and ex-girlfriends. Firestone (1971, chap. 6) suggests that many women are so intensely socialized to see their own self-worth in terms of being a sexual partner for a male that, when their relationship breaks down and the male begins to see another woman, their sense of self-worth and identity are shattered. Occasionally these feelings may turn to rage and hatred. Such responses, however, are not equivalent in form or intent to the systematic, repeated brutality that constitutes wife battering. While it may be true that much abuse experienced by husbands goes unreported, the same is true of abused wives. We do know that the overwhelming majority of people who are injured in domestic violence are female. There is a vast body of evidence of systematic, severe, intimidating force used by men against women, while there is no such evidence for women against husbands (Dobash and Dobash 1988, 60–62).

The problems of wife battering and sexual abuse of children are very deep-rooted in our society. They reflect both the identification of masculine sexuality with aggression and the pervasive socialization of males to be aggressive. They also reflect the patriarchal structures of family life that accord authority, power, and control to the father figure. Such power carries with it the inherent risk of corruption. Thirdly, they highlight the emotional shallowness of relations between men, which leaves the family as the only source of human warmth and sensuality. But this source is itself constrained and distorted by the emphasis on exclusivity, possession, authority, and control. Wives and children bear the emotional brunt of these distorted relations.

Custody Battles: Shared Parenting or Patriarchal Control?

Divorce is a fact of life in Canadian society, but its frequency does not lessen the traumatic effect on the parties involved. Divorce invariably means a significant drop in the income of single-parent families headed by women. Divorced fathers who do not want to pay child support face no effective pressure to do so. The default rate on court-ordered support payments has been estimated to be between 80 and 90 percent (Crean 1989, 20). While the court generally awards custody of children to mothers, about half the fathers who contest custody win their case, often in the face of evidence of minimal previous involvement in nurturing and despite evidence of physical or sexual abuse (Chessler 1986). Sexual abuse of children is difficult to prove, and mothers who raise the issue not only risk having their credibility challenged in court, but jeopardize their own custody claims be being labelled as an unfriendly parent who is trying to block rightful access by the father.

Custody battles over children and the demand for mandatory joint legal custody following divorce are forming a new arena of struggle between principles of feminism and patriarchy. Of particular concern to feminists are the threatening implications of seemingly progressive legislation aimed at ensuring the rights of divorced fathers in relation to their children. Mandatory joint custody legislation was passed in thirty-six American states between 1980 and 1988. It became a legal issue in Canada in January 1988 when a private member's bill, which would commit the province to a system of mandatory joint custody, was introduced in the Ontario legislature. Critics of such legislation stress the distinction between shared parenting and joint legal custody. Shared parenting, defined as full involvement in the nurturing and care of children by both parents, has long been advocated by feminists and the **men's liberation** move-

Figure 11-3 Divorce Rate in Canada, 1951–86

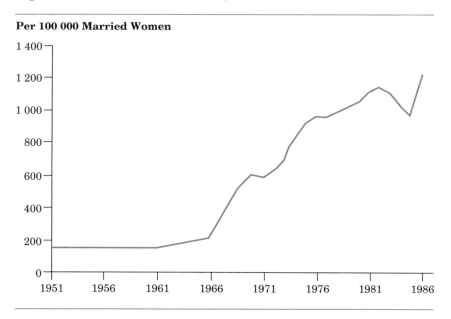

Source: Statistics Canada, Cat. 84-205, and Census of Canada.

ment. Its advocates argue that parents who have shared the nurturing process during a marriage will freely adopt joint custody after a divorce. But such a co-operative experience is a far cry from what happens under mandated joint legal custody.

Despite the public rhetoric, the core of the battle over joint legal custody concerns power and not nurturing. Under joint custody, a father can legally control where and how his ex-wife lives and who she lives with. The father retains legal authority over decisions about religious education, schooling, health care of children, and the like, regardless of whether he is involved in the daily nurturing of the children. Child support payments to the ex-wife may also be cut by as much as 50 percent on the grounds that the father is sharing the costs of maintaining the children in his home. A mother who cannot earn an income equivalent to that of her ex-spouse risks losing custody of her children altogether because she cannot support them

(*Toronto Star*, 19 Feb. 1988). Mothers who raise complaints about how fathers are treating children stand to lose custody on the grounds that they are unfriendly parents. Resolution of these custody battles is rendered all the more difficult because the public rhetoric of share parenting used by fathers' rights groups draws directly upon writings by the feminist and men's liberation movements.

Medical and Legal Control over Reproduction

The struggle for control over women's reproductive power continues in the public arenas of medicine and law. In Canada, the medical profession has almost entirely succeeded in wresting technical control over childbirth from women (Burtch 1988). Formerly, O'Brien suggests (1981, 10), childbirth was an affirmation of sisterhood, a rite shared by the mother-to-be, the midwife, and other women friends who attended the birth in the community. Nowadays child-birth normally takes place in an antiseptic hospital delivery room under the control of predominantly male obstetricians. Until very recently, it was normal for the mother to be drugged into semi-consciousness, her feet tied up in stirrups, while the baby was pulled out with forceps. While some accuse feminists of romanticizing simpler childbirth, O'Brien insists that the issue is male supremacy or, specifically, the supremacy of male doctors over mothers and midwives.

The available evidence indicates that the mortality rate for home births with a mid-wife present is as low or lower than physi-cian-attended births in hospitals. Yet control by the medical profession in Canada is so total that midwifery is illegal. A doctor must be in attendance at a birth. In April 1989, a Montreal doctor was suspended for six months for letting a midwife deliver the baby of one of his patients. Regulations introduced in 1982 require that expectant women in remote Inuit communities be flown thou-sands of miles south to have their babies delivered in Churchill or Winnipeg hospitals (*Globe and Mail*, 10 Nov. 1986, A5). This may entail the separation of a mother-to-be from her family for up to two months. Preg-nant women who want to stay in the com-munity are virtually kidnapped. Inuit women have been delivering their own babies for centuries, but now this ancient knowledge, shared among women, is being systematically destroyed because the younger generation of women can no longer attend community births.

Recent developments in reproductive technology, including test-tube babies, embryo transplants, **surrogate mother-hood**, and artificial insemination, further this process of control over birth by predomi-nantly male scientists. This medico-scien-tific takeover of birth is being combined with increasing legislative controls over the lives of pregnant women. Court-ordered stays in

hospital and cesarean sections against the mother's will have already occurred in Canada (*Globe and Mail*, 1 Aug. 1987, D1-2). A Vancouver lawyer hired to fight one such case commented that one should not underestimate the male fixation on having the perfect son and heir, or what a man might do if a woman pregnant with his child was perceived to be disobeying orders that related to having that perfect baby. The desperation of some men to find a surrogate mother for artificial insemination with their sperm, and the amount they are prepared to pay for this service (around $10 000 U.S. plus expenses) underline how important biologi-cal reproduction is to many men.

The Abortion Debate:
Pro-life or Pro-patriarchy?

The abortion issue is at the centre of the political struggle surrounding reproductive rights in Canada and the United States. In January 1988 the Supreme Court of Canada struck down Canada's existing abortion law as unconstitutional because it was being applied in an arbitrary and discriminatory manner. There were huge geographic disparities in accessibility, and women experienced long and sometimes dangerous delays in having abortions approved. The Supreme Court decision added fuel to the political struggle between the opposing forces.

The outcome of the immediate struggle around the abortion issue is uncertain. It is unlikely that new legislation proposed by the Mulroney government in late 1989 will satisfy all parties. In the context of continu-ing patriarchal and capitalist social rela-tions, any outcome is problematic for women. Lack of access to abortion, in the face of inadequate contraceptive techniques and support services, traps thousands of despe-rate women in situations of oppressive dependency. On the other hand, even the option of abortion on demand may be used as a means for patriarchal control over women's

The abortion issue is at the centre of the struggle for reproductive rights in Canada.

reproductive power. In India, where abortions are readily available after amniocentesis, a procedure that can reveal the sex of the fetus, almost all aborted fetuses are female (Chatterji 1988, 208). Women are under extreme pressure from husbands and in-laws to provide only male heirs. In North America, there is a growing demand for fetal tissue, which is used to treat medical conditions such as Parkinson's disease. Poor women may be pressured to have abortions and sell the fetal tissue.

On the surface, the anti-abortion lobby speaks to a humanistic concern for the sanctity of human life and a reluctance to kill that potential life for motives of convenience. But opponents of the lobby fear that the "pro-life" label obscures a political agenda that is fiercely anti-feminist (Eichler 1985b; Dubinsky 1985). In principle, Eichler argues, the pro-life stand should be consistent with supporting every effort to minimize unwanted pregnancies and to maximize all forms of social support that would encourage pregnant women to keep their babies. But, in practice, the lobby groups fighting hardest to have abortion declared illegal are publicly against most of the policies intended to help women with children.

The anti-abortion movement in the United States campaigned strenuously to bring about the defeat of the Equal Rights Amendment, which would have prohibited discrimination on the basis of sex (Eisenstein 1984). They actively opposed welfare payments to mothers, public day-care programs, and **affirmative action** policies to promote employment for women. A similar lobby group in Canada, REAL (Realistic Equal Active for Life) women, is anti-abortion and is also against welfare and against enshrining equality provisions for women in the Charter of Rights and Freedoms. The REAL women platform opposes abortion under all circumstances; opposes the contraceptive pill as suppressing maternal instincts; opposes

sex education in schools as inciting immorality; opposes welfare and public day care as undermining family responsibilities; opposes affirmative action for women in employment because this creates competition with male breadwinners; opposes feminist counsellors in homes for battered women because they advocate the break-up of the family; opposes the National Action Committee on the Status of Women as anti-family and anti-housewife; and favours the right of a woman to be a full-time homemaker and the obligation of her husband to support her.

This agenda is a clear example of the politics of the "New Right." At the root of the New Right political agenda is a concern with the preservation of the traditional patriarchal family form, centred around the private family home. Women perform the expressive roles of full-time homemaker, mother, and nurturer of the family members, while men are responsible for public instrumental roles as providers. Policies to promote women's employment, state welfare, and public day care are all seen as threatening such families by relieving men of their primary provider role. To the extent that women's domestic work and men's family responsibilities ensure a cheaply maintained, rested, committed, and stable workforce, such policies also threaten capitalist interests. The New Right fears that contraception and abortion rights trivialize the mother role, reduce male commitment or obligation to support mothers and children, and hence undercut the social foundations of a stable family and workforce.

The clash between New Right politics and feminism essentially revolves around the different views of the ideal family. Conservatives frequently claim that feminism leads to the breakdown of the family. The family they have in mind is the traditional patriarchal form that ensures male authority and female domesticity and dependence. The feminist movement advocates a very different form

Table 11-2 Threats to Family as Perceived by Pro-Family Supporters

	Seriousness of Threat					
	Very Serious		Somewhat Serious		Not Serious	
Threat	Percent	Number	Percent	Number	Percent	Number
Declining influence of religion	83	677	15	120	2	15
Undermining of traditional values	81	654	18	143	1	10
Pornography	73	592	23	185	4	32
Spread of secular humanism	68	511	27	212	5	40
Loss of parental control over children	63	511	31	252	6	48
Influences of the gay rights movements	57	462	31	253	12	93
Influences of the feminist movement	54	437	36	289	10	83
Sex education in the schools	43	338	36	284	21	172
Economic hardships facing families today	26	210	44	358	30	243

Source: Erwin (1988, 272)

based on a consensual and egalitarian union that maximizes freedom of choice in the division of roles and responsibilities between spouses.

The National Action Committee on the Status of Women (NAC) is an umbrella organization the represents a broad range of feminist concerns. Its policy platform challenges the economic exploitation of women in the home and in the labour force and challenges the mechanisms of male oppression of women through economic dependence, the domestic burden, family violence, and medico-legal controls over women's reproductive freedom. Specific policies favoured by NAC include affirmative action in employment, universal, affordable child care, transition houses for battered women, income support for women and children to escape the dependency that makes women vulnerable to domestic violence, and protection of women's reproductive choice through safer and more effective contraception, maximum support services for pregnant women, and abortion as a back-up. In this context, abortion rights symbolize the inviolable right of women to control their own reproductive power.

The vision of family at the root of the feminist political agenda is a consensual union between equal partners, free from relations of dependency and without any forced sex-role division of labour between private and public, expressive and instrumental tasks. This vision of family equality presupposes a transformation in the position of women in the labour force and in the ways in which work time is organized. The feminist platform shares with the nascent men's liberation movement a belief that the alienation of men from children can be overcome not through possession of women and children, but through participation as equals in the nurturing process. If men as parents are to assume equal responsibilities with women for domestic and child-care work, then the ways in which men as workers are exploited by capitalism will also have to be transformed.

The abortion debate has become a focal point for struggle around these two very different conceptions of family. Both sides claim to be defending the true interests of women and children. Eisenstein (1984, chap. 7) suggests that the New Right political agenda appeals to many women because it addresses their real material conditions in a patriarchal and capitalist society. The reality is that the mass of women with children are dependent on male breadwinners for their survival. The women's movement, combined with developments in capitalism, has widened opportunities for women beyond traditional domestic roles, but this opportunity is largely illusory. Women predominate in low-paid job ghettos. Rising divorce rates mean that many women must struggle in abject poverty as single parents. The superwoman image of professionals who manage to combine careers and domestic and child-care responsibilities has limited appeal for women who already feel overburdened. Feminism threatens their security without being able to bring about the radical social and economic change needed to provide women with real alternatives.

Limitations of Radical Feminism

The weakness of radical feminist analysis of family life stems from its overly narrow focus. The perspective has drawn attention to widespread and serious problems of violence and abuse within families, which have been overlooked or downplayed by other approaches. But radical feminist research also tends to overstate the case for patriarchy to the extent that the abnormal becomes the norm. Some sources speculate, for example, that as many as one girl in two and one boy in three are victims of incest, an estimate that encompasses virtually every

family in Canada. When concepts are pushed to this extreme, it becomes impossible to make distinctions between different experiences of family life. Radical feminism runs the risk of generating its own form of monolithic bias.

We know that, however pervasive the hidden problems might be, not all people experience family life as abusive. Most people do get married, and most of those who get divorced subsequently remarry. The majority of women and men thus appear to find marriage worth the struggle, or at least feel that it is more rewarding than living alone.

There is evidence of widespread changes in family roles. Husbands and fathers are increasingly getting involved in domestic work and in the nurturing of children, albeit generally not at the same level of responsibility as women. The combination of shorter working hours, free weekends, and changing conceptions of fatherhood means that children and fathers are more closely involved with each other than in the past. The real suffering of many fathers who are separated from their children by divorce cannot by subsumed under the blanket explanations of desire for revenge and legal control over their ex-wives.

The problem for radical feminist theory is to account for these different experiences. The pioneering work of feminist research into family violence means that we can no longer discount the 10 to 20 percent of families characterized by wife battery and other forms of abuse. But neither can we discount the majority of families where couples manage to establish mutually supportive relations and where children can look to both fathers and mothers for nurturance and emotional support. We need more research into the processes that account for this variation.

We are still far from understanding the factors that encourage egalitarian marriages and shared parenting as opposed to patriarchy and rigid role differentiation. Such analysis will need to take into account the context of political economy and the processes that exploit people and help to perpetuate role differentiation and yet simultaneously provide opportunities for women to be financially independent. The analysis will also need to take into account the emotional stress generated by patriarchal family forms and the evidence that men who abuse wives and children were commonly abused themselves when young. Abuse may generate the emotional insecurity that finds expression in the drive for domination and possession in marriage. From this perspective, patriarchy appears less as the expression of male power than of chronic insecurity, powerlessness, and fear. This remains speculation. Feminist theory has opened up the debate by focussing attention on issues that have been ignored by mainstream theories. But the research needed to explain the conflicting patterns of egalitarian and patriarchal families, and nurturing and abusive family relations, is still in its infancy.

Conclusion

Family life may be the most difficult area of sociology to study. It is so familiar and so emotionally charged that it is hard for us to distance ourselves from it. Sociological analysis has moved a long way from the original functionalist view that sex-role divisions within the nuclear family were natural, rational, and efficient adaptations to industrial society. But functionalist formulations still dominate most sociological textbooks. Monolithic, conservative, sexist, and microstructural biases in functionalist analysis of the family are being eliminated only with difficulty. Research in the Marxist tradition shows how different family forms are embedded in economic relations that exploit both women and men and set constraints on their lives. Feminist theory reveals other aspects of the family as the central arena for the struggle between competing principles of gender equality and patriarchy. The processes that influence the outcome of these struggles are still far from understood.

Suggested Reading

An excellent source of statistical information on families in Canada is Margrit Eichler, *Families in Canada Today: Recent Changes and their Policy Consequences*, 2nd ed. (1988a). Eichler takes a very critical approach to traditional sociology of the family and provides quantities of data to back her argument that family life in Canada is diverse and rapidly changing.

For the functionalist perspective, a particularly useful source is the small text by William J. Goode, *The Family*, 2nd ed. (1982). He presents an easily readable account of the critical functions that families perform for the society as a whole.

For the Marxist-feminist approach, an excellent book is Meg Luxton, *More Than a Labour of Love* (1980). Luxton presents an in-depth description of the lives of three generations of women in a small mining town in northern Manitoba. She conveys through the words of the women themselves how deeply their family lives are influenced by the economic reality of their dependence on male wages.

For a radical-feminist perspective, an excellent source book is the collection of articles edited by Yllö and Bograd, *Feminist Perspectives on Wife Abuse* (1988). Articles by Dobash and Dobash, Adams, and Saunders give insight into the experience of wife battery and the difficult problems of doing research and analysis in this area.

Chapter 12

Stratification: Meritocracy as Ideology

Inequality is a pervasive feature of social life. It may be manifested in disparities in access to money and other material resources, in the power to manipulate events in one's own interest, in the prestige enjoyed in relations with others, and in the overall quality of life. The extent of these disparities varies widely across societies. In an industrially advanced economy such as Canada's, very few people are so poor or disadvantaged that their physical survival is threatened by starvation or lack of rudimentary shelter and sanitation. Yet, as we have seen in earlier chapters, Canada does have a visible and growing underclass of homeless and destitute people who rely on soup kitchens and hostels for a meagre survival. At the other extreme, Canada has a class of super-rich, comprising mostly members of the corporate elite, some of whom rank among the richest people in the world.

Various forms of inequality commonly go together, suggesting that there are important causal relationships between them.

Powerful people are often rich, command high prestige, and enjoy pleasurable, even luxurious, lifestyles. The poor are commonly powerless, scorned, and live in misery. Yet there is no inevitable association between these elements. Winning a lottery, for example, may bring wealth and leisure but not necessarily influence or prestige. A large income may not improve the quality of life it if is earned at the expense of chronic anxiety in the high-pressure corporate rat race. In terms of influence, even poor people can exercise power, especially if they are politically united.

Societies vary greatly in the degree of opportunity for **mobility**: that is, the likelihood that people born poor may eventually become wealthy and influential or that people born rich may fall in status. Canadians tend to think of their society as relatively open, offering opportunities for mobility through individual effort and achievement. But we know that social position is very commonly inherited. Children tend to attain a similar social position to that of their parents or to move slightly upwards or downwards. Members of certain groups are disproportionately better or worse off than others. Children from white Anglo-Saxon protestant (WASP) backgrounds have very different life chances on average than children of native Indian or black parents. Why is this so?

Children of native people have very different life chances than do children from WASP backgrounds.

The explanations for inequality offered by different sociological theories reveal core assumptions concerning the nature of social order. Traditional functionalism stresses individual merit. It posits that inequality reflects rewards for individual contributions to the functioning of society. Marxists stress the importance of control over critical means of production for accumulating wealth in industrial society. Variations in income among the mass of working people reflect the relative utility of different workers for the owners of capital. Feminist theory focusses on disparities in wealth, power, prestige, and leisure between women and men, arguing that men, on average, are advantaged in all of these respects. These disparities reflect patriarchy, or the power of men over women, which is distinct from, although associated with, capitalism. Interpretive theory looks within the grand schemes of functioning social systems, capitalism, and patriarchy to explore what people do in their everyday relations to produce the patterns of inequality that we subsequently perceive as merit, class, or gender hierarchies. These theoretical perspectives, and their relative strengths and limitations, are examined below.

Functionalist Theory: Stratification as Meritocracy

The traditional functionalist theory of **stratification** begins from the basic observation that no society is classless. Hence there must be a universal necessity for such stratification. It must perform some function for the social system as a whole, a function so crucial that no society can do without it.

Davis and Moore (1945) provide one of the clearest functionalist explanations for why stratification occurs. Their central concern is with inequality of positions in society, not the characteristics of the individuals in those positions. The basic theoretical question is why roles themselves differ in prestige and rewards. They find the answer in the functional requirement of placing and motivating individuals in any social structure. A social system must distribute members into social positions and must instil in members the desire to perform the attached duties once in the position. This is a continuous challenge because people are constantly being born, aging, retiring, and dying. Competitive systems such as our own stress motives to achieve the positions; non-competitive systems, such as socialist societies, stress motives to perform the duties. Both systems, however, require motivation.

Roles differ enormously in the demands they place on people. If all roles were equally important, and everyone were able to do all of them, then placement would be no problem. However, some jobs are more agreeable, some serve more important social functions, some require more talent and training, and some require that duties be performed more diligently. Therefore, say Davis and Moore, a differential reward system is crucial. These differential inducements form part of the social order and produce stratification. Rewards may include sustenance and comfort provided by economic incentives, self-respect and ego development provided by prestige and power, and recreation and diversion made possible by more leisure time. These rewards are built into positions and constitute the rights that are related to the duties of the roles. Inequality is thus necessary, inevitable, and justifiable.

Two primary factors determine the relative rank of different positions: their importance for the society and the scarcity of personnel for the positions. Important jobs need sufficient rewards to ensure competent performance, but if such jobs are easily filled, great rewards will not be needed. Garbage collector and janitor, for example, are important jobs, but they are relatively easy to fill and so are not highly rewarded. On the other hand, important jobs that require both talent and long training must be well rewarded. No one would go through the training and do the work of a modern medical doctor, the argument goes, unless the position carried great material reward and prestige.

Variations among societies in the income received by the highest- and lowest-paid members are primarily explained by the degree of specialization of roles. Highly industrialized societies such as Canada have an immense variety of specialized occupa-tions, each of them associated with small gradations in income and prestige. Simpler, less industrialized societies have a more limited range of occupations, which tend to require less specialized training. Hence there are fewer gradations of income and prestige. The nature of functional emphasis—whether sacred or secular—also affects rewards. Industrialized societies place greater emphasis on science and technology than on religion, and so scientists and technicians get higher pay. In other societies where science is relatively undeveloped, religious leaders may have far greater influence, prestige, and material rewards than do scientists.

In summary, functionalists argue that stratification is justified on the basis of merit. The critical moral issue for functionalist theory is not equality of rewards, but rather equality of opportunity to compete for them. The true battle is over merit versus inherited advantage.

Critique of Functionalism

Equal Opportunity

Much of the research generated by the functionalist thesis of stratification has focussed on questions of social mobility and differential opportunities for access to positions that carry the highest rewards. Research in the sociology of education has cast doubts on the notion that rewards are based on merit. Tumin (1973) challenges the argument that only a limited amount of talent is available within a population to be trained in appropriate skills for important jobs. He maintains that stratification itself limits the talent pool. We can never know what talents are available among children born to impoverished and disprivileged homes when poverty so pervasively affects their relationship with the school system. Rich children have all the advantages and hence do better in school, get the credentials for better jobs, and in turn give advantages to their own children.

Unequal distribution of motivation to succeed, so important to functionalist theory, is itself a direct product of stratification. Poverty breeds hopelessness. Imagination, curiosity, and aspiration are systematically blunted when children experience powerlessness and humiliation at first hand. It is hard to develop one's full potential under such conditions. The result is low credentials, poorly rewarded jobs, and another generation of children who are stunted and trapped in the poverty cycle.

The argument that conversion of talent into skills requires sacrifices during the training period, and hence merits rewards, again treats the effects of stratification as its cause. Poor families cannot afford to buy books and school supplies or to pay for dance or music lessons, and so on, without cutting back on food money. Poor families cannot afford to keep children in school after the minimum school-leaving age or to send them to university without great sacrifices. The expenses involved are not sacrifices for wealthy parents in the professions. Pay differentials between unskilled work available at school-leaving age and professional careers available to university graduates more than compensate students who defer the gratification of an early job. Tumin estimates that any loss of income is usually regained within

seven to ten years of employment. After this, the lifetime earnings of graduates greatly surpass those of untrained people.

Unequal Importance

The second pillar of the functionalist thesis on stratification is that the most important jobs in society must be the most rewarded, particularly when they require special skills. But, Tumin asks, how is importance to be measured? A typical answer is that importance is calculated in terms of a position's indispensability for society, but it is not difficult to find exceptions to this rule. Farming, for example, is crucial for survival in any society, and it requires skills that take a lifetime to learn, but it is not well rewarded. In terms of industry, during wartime it proved easier to dispense with supervisors than to spare factory workers, but this relative indispensability is not translated into wages.

The real problem is conceptual. Relative importance is a value judgment that is inextricably tied to relative financial rewards. In other words, the argument is circular. Those jobs that are better paid tend to be regarded as more important, regardless of their actual contribution to society or the actual skill levels required for the work.

Women and Stratification

This kind of circularity is especially evident in relation to work habitually done by women. As a sex, women have lower social status than men, so that work identified as "women's work" tends to have low status. The skills and responsibilities involved in such work tend to be downplayed or ignored. Then the lower average earnings of women in the labour force are justified on the grounds that women are concentrated in low-status work. The circle is completed when women themselves internalize such evaluations of what they do, and the low pay associated with it, as justifying the lower status of women generally.

Table 12-1 Average Income by Education and Sex in Canada, 1983

Level of Education	Female	Male
Grade 0 to 8	$ 7 137	$15 923
High School	9 960	18 686
Postsecondary certificate	13 703	24 321
University degree	20 107	33 841

Source: Statistics Canada (1985–86, 51).

The most extreme example of these processes occurs in relation to homemaking. This is a critical, multi-dimensional job that, like farming, takes a lifetime to learn. But it goes unpaid and hence commands such low status that people habitually apologize for doing it. Up until recently, homemaking was not even defined as work.

Within the paid labour market generally, skills associated with women's work are undervalued and underpaid. Nursing is a high-stress, extremely important job that requires a great deal of responsibility. The survival and recovery time of patients often depend more upon the quality of nursing care than on intermittent doctors' visits. The job demands long hours, shift work, and advanced technical skills that require a university degree and years of practical experience. But one would never know this judging from the salary and status that nurses command.

On some university campuses, the starting salary for secretarial staff (virtually all women) is several dollars per hour below that for people who mow lawns (virtually all men). It would be very difficult to argue that lawn mowing is either more important or more highly skilled than the work that secretaries do. The skills of advanced clerical workers are commonly ignored by bureaucratic classification systems that characterize such work as routine delegated tasks.

Women and men might do virtually identical work, but the work done by women tends to be called by a different name and to command lower status and salaries than the work associated with men. Positions like seamstress versus tailor, or cook versus chef, readily come to mind. In Moslem countries, where the work of buying household supplies is habitually done by men, it is seen as requiring important decision-making authority. When the same work is habitually done by women, as in our society, it tends to be thought of as a mundane routine.

Relative Scarcity of Personnel

The functionalist thesis claims that relative scarcity of personnel raises rewards. Jobs that are easily filled need not be paid well. Women who compete with each other for limited jobs in the traditional women's occupations know this well. Tumin (1973), however, points out that scarcity is often artificially constructed in order to protect incomes. For example, predominantly male unions have historically tried to bar women and immigrants from access to unionized jobs, arguing that these groups would lower wages. Women were also barred from entry into universities and hence from any profession that required a university degree. Professions have commonly been in a position to restrict access through their control over accreditation.

First-year admissions into medical schools in Canada have dropped to their lowest level in sixteen years, with only one place for every six applicants (*Globe and Mail*, 11 Aug. 1987). Limitations on enrolments have the approval both of provincial governments and physicians' lobby groups, but for different reasons. Provincial governments hope to reduce the "oversupply" of doctors suggested by some reports on medical personnel and thereby hope to save money on medicare payments. Physicians, on the other hand, have lobbied successfully for cuts in enrolments and for restrictions on the licensing of immigrant doctors in order to limit the number of physicians and thus ensure their continued high salaries. Medical associations can then pressure for a fee schedule increase on the grounds of doctors' stressful work and the long hours they put in. Women doctors are more willing to trade high incomes for shorter working hours in group practices, but the male-dominated profession seems unlikely to encourage this.

Another common practice in limiting access to positions is to raise the qualifications needed to get into a job, thus putting up hurdles to stifle competition from below.

Jobs in business and management, for example, which even a decade ago only required high school graduation, now increasingly require university degrees. This effectively blocks competition from those who have learned their skills from work experience but do not have paper credentials.

Opportunities and salaries available to graduates more than compensate for low incomes earned while at university. Graduates have access to positions closed to those without paper credentials.

Motivation

The last pillar of the functionalist argument is that differential rewards, and hence stratification, are necessary in order to motivate people to fill the more demanding positions. These rewards include money or material goods, leisure, respect, and prestige. Tumin's challenge to this thesis is that there are other kinds of motivators that could achieve the same results. A crucial one is work satisfaction. Positions that require training are usually the most interesting and the least routine. Tumin questions whether such positions need high pay to attract candidates and to ensure competent job performance. Other motives for job performance include the sense of a job well done, prestige from a social duty performed well, or increased leisure hours if the work is particularly demanding or difficult. Women commonly flock to jobs that give them the same time off and holidays as the schools so that they can cope with the extra work and responsibility of having children at home and not have to face the major expense of day care.

Another question is whether money is in fact entirely effective as a reward. In capitalist society, money is emphasized but people attracted by high salaries are just as likely to peddle their services elsewhere to the highest bidder. High salaries do not command loyalty. Senior executives, on average, remain only about four years with any one firm. There is an old joke about people in politics: they are the best politicians that money can buy. The question is whether people who can be bought with money actually do make good politicians or good anything else.

In summary, Tumin's critique points to the fallacies of unity, indispensability, and universal functionalism. Disparities in material rewards may be demonstrably valuable for certain sectors of society, but they can simultaneously be damaging for others. Large differences in income may be useful for motivating people, but they are not indispensable. People can and frequently do commit themselves to doing important work out of a sense of responsibility for others, or for the pleasure and excitement of the work, without demanding high incomes in return. Many persisting differences in prestige, wealth, and power do not serve useful functions for society at all. Functional importance of different positions is a value judgment. Stratification itself limits talent and restricts educational opportunities while other techniques restrict access and cause scarcity to drive up incomes. Training for skilled jobs either is not, or need not be, a sacrifice. People can be motivated to fill positions on the basis of intrinsic job satisfactions and the prestige of the office, without gross inequalities in standards of living.

Marxist Theory: Inequality as Class Exploitation

Marxists agree with traditional functionalists that stratification does perform very important societal functions, but they argue that these functions specifically help to perpetuate capitalism as an economic system. The central Marxist argument is that stratification functions to preserve a system of expropriation of wage labour from the mass of people. Profits from this expropriation accrue to an elite minority of owners of capital. Stratification is at the same time profoundly functional for capitalists and dysfunctional for the interests of the majority of people who must sell their labour. This perspective rejects the **meritocracy thesis** as an ideological distortion that, rather than questioning the structure of the system within which people are forced to compete, blames the individuals who do not get to the top of the reward system.

The Structure of Unequal Opportunities

Marxist analysis begins from the premise that structured inequality of positions in society negates the possibility of equality of opportunity for the masses. Without far-reaching changes in the distribution of wealth, it is structurally impossible to guarantee that all qualified, motivated people can succeed. A simplified model of a social system illustrates the problem (Himelfarb and Richardson 1979, 174). Assume a perfectly closed society in which there are

1000 positions, 10 percent of which are elite and the remaining 90 percent ordinary. Then assume that each of these 1000 role incumbents has one child.

What will happen to these children as they come to take over from their parents? In a society based absolutely upon inherited advantage, the one hundred elite children will take over from the one hundred elite parents, with no elite positions left for anyone else. The nine hundred children of people in the ordinary jobs will remain at the same level.

What will happen in the opposite case, where there is no inherited advantage and everyone has an equal chance to get an elite job? Only 10 percent of all positions, or one hundred jobs are elite. With perfect equality, 10 percent of elite children, or ten children, will get elite positions and the rest will have ordinary jobs. Ten percent, or ninety, of the nine hundred ordinary children will get the remaining elite positions, with the other eight hundred and ten, or 90 percent, remaining where they are. It is clear that, when there are so few really good or elite positions to be had, it makes little practical difference to the masses whether they are filled by inherited advantage or absolute equality. Most people will not get such positions in either case.

Any real change in opportunity for ordinary people will require a change in the structure of positions so that there are many more good jobs to be had. After World War II there were huge increases in the United States in middle-class technical, managerial, and white-collar jobs, as well as pink-collar jobs for women. This expansion is the root of the American Dream, the myth that anyone can achieve upward mobility if they have enough drive and talent. After the war, children whose parents had struggled through the Great Depression found that there were many more well-paying jobs to be had. Children from elite homes enjoyed their usual advantage, but there were still many good positions opening up for others. Subsequently the picture changed. With recession came widespread unemployment and cutbacks in the economy. Fewer jobs meant that more children would not get positions equal to those of their parents, no matter how hard they tried. The structure of the job market and the distribution of wealth have to change in order to turn this around.

How does capitalism as a system function to give rise to the structure of the job market? This structure is largely treated as a given within traditional functionalist theory, so that the only question of interest is why existing jobs are differentially rewarded. But for Marxists, the changing pattern of the job market itself requires explanation. Bowles and Gintis (1976, 10) insist that capitalist production is not simply a technical process, but is also a social process in which the central problem for employers is to maintain a set of social relations and organizational forms that will enable them to exploit wage labourers to extract a profit. The objective of the system is to get the most production for the least wages; that is, to get workers to produce commodities of greater market value than the wages that they receive. Extremes of wealth and poverty are necessarily built into how this system works, and individual differences in abilities or effort count for little.

The critical problem for capitalism as a system is how to prevent revolt. Marxists ask how it is possible to maintain an inegalitarian system in relative equilibrium. What are the mechanisms that minimize the risk of workers forming coalitions to drive up wages or to wrest direct control over the means of production for themselves? The stability of the capitalist system is by no means assured. It has to be actively worked at.

Credentialism as Ideology

An important component assuring the stability of capitalism is force. Capitalists have the power to hire and fire people, and they can also call upon coercive laws to keep labour in line and to weaken unions. But naked force is itself inherently unstable in that it generates hostility and revolt. What is essential to the long-term stability of the system is that workers themselves come to accept the inequalities as just, or at least as inevitable, and therefore become resigned to them, even if they do not actively support them. The system of stratification or differential prestige ranking among workers serves this function, particularly when it is bolstered by the meritocratic ideology of traditional functionalism.

The stratification system, suggest Bowles and Gintis (1976, 81–85), is a direct reflection of capitalist policies of **divide and rule**. Its function is to fragment workers. In its cruder form, ascriptive criteria of race, ethnicity, and sex are manipulated to justify differential rewards. In the United States, older white males, particularly WASPs, are favoured for supervisory positions while immigrants, blacks, and women are given low-paid subordinate jobs. Those in superior positions are encouraged to see themselves as coming from better stock, while subordinates internalize their relative inferiority. The risk of coalitions to form a united front against capitalist employers is thus minimized.

Now that such ascriptive criteria are becoming increasingly discredited as a basis for legitimating inequalities, **credentialism** has come to take their place. This is precisely the meritocratic thesis of functionalism. Marxists agree that motivating people to strive for higher credentials does indeed perform an important function for capitalist society, but it is that of justifying inequality. People with different credentials readily come to see themselves as meriting different rewards. This effectively fragments wage labourers and lessens the possibility of revolt. Those with relatively low credentials come to see themselves as meriting only limited rewards. Bowles and Gintis (1976,

81) argue forcefully that this is not merely a side effect of stratification but is its primary and intended purpose. Capitalists, they argue, will accede to higher wages for certain groups only when this increases social distance between groups of workers and strengthens capitalist control. Capitalists need to cement the loyalty of supervisors to the organization rather than to workers. Hence managers receive higher pay and privileges, regardless of relative scarcity of personnel.

It is important to recognize that Marxism reverses the cause-and-effect relation between credentials and rewards accepted by traditional functionalists. Functionalists, as we saw above, argue that certain jobs need people with higher skills and credentials. Since these people are in relatively scarce supply, the function of higher pay is to attract them to these difficult and important jobs. Marxists argue the reverse. Capitalism requires that workers be fragmented and stratified in order to minimize the risk of coalitions to challenge the controlling position of the capitalist class. Hence largely irrelevant criteria, such as race, ethnicity, sex, and credentials, are used as excuses to reward people differently and so divide them from each other. The function of focussing on credentials is to divide and rule workers by artificially stratifying them.

This is such a turn-around from how we are accustomed to think about credentials and rewards that it deserves further scrutiny. Bowles and Gintis categorically deny that schooling and credentials are actually needed for most jobs that currently demand them. True, there has been an explosion in public education in North America in recent decades, with ever-greater proportions of young people completing high school and seeking postsecondary education. True, on average, there is a **linear relation** between years of formal schooling and economic rewards: the more schooling, the more pay. But, this is not due to any essential requirement that better-paid jobs be filled by people with higher abilities. If such were the case, one would expect a very high correlation between measured intelligence and economic success. We do not find this. When measured intelligence and academic ability are controlled, the relation between years of schooling and pay remains virtually unaltered. It seems to be the piece of paper that counts, not the ability level (Bowles and Gintis 1976, 107).

The Deskilling of Work

Further support for the argument that the function of the growing emphasis on credentials is to fragment workers rather than to meet essential job requirements is that there is little evidence of any major increase in the complexity of jobs in advanced capitalist societies. If anything, the process seems to be working in reverse. Once-skilled jobs are being systematically **deskilled**; that is, they are broken down into simple component operations that can be easily learned. This process has been going on for a long time, dating back at least to the era of **Taylorism**, or **scientific management**, in the last decades of the nineteenth century (Braverman 1974, chap. 4). The expressed goal of Taylor's time-and-motion studies was to break the power that skilled craftsmen wielded through their control over knowledge of the work process. Work was minutely analysed and broken down into component parts, each of which could be assigned to a different worker. Only the boss retained knowledge of the whole process. Taylorism served two functions for capitalism. It fragmented workers and cheapened labour costs. Employers thus deliberately created the mass of repetitive and unskilled jobs that traditional functionalists point to as deserving only low pay and low prestige.

Braverman argues that this deskilling process has continued unabated, with more and more skilled and even professional occupations being degraded into fragmented, repetitive tasks. Workers are continually being replaced by machines, their skills rendered obsolete. Assembly lines and automation have replaced proud crafts. The impetus for deskilling work was not that average workers were unable to learn the jobs. The problem for capitalists has been that skilled workers are harder to control. They can use their knowledge and skills as bargaining chips to get concessions. They also tend to think of themselves as more deserving of rewards. In effect, they threaten profits. People doing simple, fragmented tasks have minimal bargaining power and hence come cheaper.

INCO in Sudbury successfully broke the skills and power of mine workers by introducing new technology to automate work. Highly skilled people, who commanded high salaries and prestige among other workers, found their jobs disappearing (Clement 1981, chap. 10). Children of men who once had skilled jobs at the mine can no longer expect to get similar positions in Sudbury, no matter how motivated and well-educated they might be.

Braverman (1974, chap. 15) documents how the progressive automation of office jobs has reduced once semi-managerial clerical occupations to the level of routine "factory-floor" work. Secretaries become machine operators and key punchers while the knowledge of their work is taken over by a small elite of computer programmers. Another study elaborates on these trends, documenting the devastating effects that microchip technology is having on women's work (Menzies 1981).

This deskilling, fragmenting, and routinizing of work is not an inevitable consequence of modern technology. It is the result of the kinds of technology that owners of capital opt to promote and how they use it. Teams of skilled workers in the steel industry once organized the entire production of steel themselves (Stone 1974). Equipment was rented from owners, and workers contracted to produce given amounts of steel for pay in accordance with market value. There are no technological reasons why steel could not now be produced in this way. Teams of skilled workers can put together entire cars themselves as readily and efficiently as can be done on assembly lines. The president of Volvo in Sweden experimented with precisely such teamwork during a period of relatively full employment when he found he could not keep workers in fragmented assembly-line jobs (Gyllenhammer 1977). The function of job fragmentation is not to ensure greater technical efficiency but to break down workers' power, cheapen their labour, and so raise profits. The reason why the teams of steelworkers were smashed through a lockout, enforced by armed guards, was to enable capitalists to introduce technical innovations without the benefits accruing to the workers.

There is a serious problem for the capitalist system, however, with reducing all jobs to unskilled, repetitive, minimum-wage work: how to prevent coalitions of workers from forming to overthrow the system. The answer in the steel industry was to introduce artificial job ladders. In effect, the owners created a system of stratification to fragment the workers. Petty differences were exploited, linked to credentials such as years of experience and apprenticeship certificates, and used to justify small differences in prestige and piece-rate payments. Workers competed with each other to get the better jobs, and the unions cemented these different pay scales in formal contracts. This was exactly what management wanted. If such petty differences in the job ladder can be linked to race and ethnic differences, so much the better.

Skilled Labour Under Capitalism

Braverman's thesis on the systematic deskilling of work has recently come under strong criticism from some other Marxist theorists (Morgan and Sayer 1988). The challenge is not that Braverman is wrong in principle, but that he oversimplifies what is happening in contemporary capitalism. The overriding objective for capitalists is production for profit in competitive markets. In long-established industries, profits may best be realized by deskilling and therefore cheapening and controlling the workforce. But the strategy spells disaster in industries where rapid product innovation is occurring. Morgan and Sayer refer to high technology sectors such as electronics as "sunrise" industries. Corporations with workers who are highly educated in science and advanced technology, and who have advanced training in management skills essential for directing rapid and complex organizational changes, are likely to beat the competition in developing and marketing innovative products. Traditional firms, which opt for cheap, deskilled labour, will not be able to keep pace with such innovations and so will likely face bankruptcy. Highly skilled workers who are expected to come to up with a stream of innovations cannot be controlled by the tactics of Taylorism. Capitalists may sometimes opt for considerably less control over the workforce if this is the only way to produce a new commodity with strong market prospects (Morgan and Sayer 1988, 26).

One result of a mix of traditional and sunrise industries in a given economy is a simultaneous process of deskilling jobs at one end of the economy and upgrading skills at the other. Despite high unemployment generally, there are still shortages of skilled workers in the electronics industry. These contradictory processes have far-reaching implications for stratification in advanced industrial societies. One probable effect will be increasing income disparities among workers. High unemployment and declining real incomes may be the lot of the mass of workers who compete for deskilled jobs. An elite of university graduates in physical sciences, engineering, applied management, and social sciences are likely to be in high demand in sunrise industries and thus will be able to command high salaries.

Bowles and Gintis recognize that not all jobs could be deskilled, if only because this would make the workforce too inflexible. They note that an effective alternative to deskilling is to create a reserve army of skilled labour. They argue that the function of expanding higher education is to flood the market with skilled workers. Such workers find that oversupply has broken their bargaining power at the same time that their credentials have divided them from other workers (Bowles and Gintis 1976, chap. 8).

But this argument may be too simplistic. The strong interest shown by capitalists in funding applied university research and graduate training in many fields in the 1980s suggests that more is at stake than empty credentialism or a desire to divide and rule the workforce. North American capitalists may just be waking up to the realization that Japanese capitalists are outperforming the Americans in sunrise industries partly because of the greater emphasis on the teaching of mathematics and sciences in schools and universities. The other part of this process, which we discussed briefly in chapter 7, is that Japanese corporations tend to adopt different management strategies. They stress job security, group decision-making, and salaries linked to length of service. The result is much higher loyalty to the corporation among Japanese than American workers. North American companies tend to rely on head-hunting, attracting talented professionals from other companies. This encourages workers who are developing innovative products to try and sell themselves and their ideas to rival companies.

Canada is facing a difficult situation, in that most high technology industries are foreign-owned multinationals. Research and development tend to be concentrated in corporate headquarters, which are mostly in the United States, rather than in Canadian branch plants. This may mean that routine, deskilled work will continue to predominate in Canada, with the exception of the business heartland of southern Ontario. Talented Canadian graduates may have to leave the country in search of high-technology jobs.

The structure of the job market in Canada is likely to be fundamentally altered in the next decade as a result of the free trade agreement between Canada and the United States. Nobody knows how this will work out. The implications of the agreement are discussed in more detail in chapter 15.

Marxist theory sets out to debunk the **technocratic-meritocratic thesis** of stratification as an ideological smokescreen that legitimates and therefore helps to perpetuate inequalities and exploitation. The functionalist theory of stratification legitimates inequality by obscuring the many factors that undermine equality of opportunity and rewards based on merit. Functionalists ignore the processes through which capitalism structures the job market, deliberately deskills many jobs, fragments workers and breaks their bargaining power, and then justifies low pay on the grounds that they are doing unskilled work.

Recent developments in Marxist theory, which focus on the importance of highly skilled workers for product innovation, are narrowing the conceptual gap between functionalist theories of meritocracy and earlier Marxist theories of exploitation of workers in the interests of capitalism. The notion of relentless deskilling of all forms of work, with credentials having no function other than to divide and rule workers, is being challenged. But the core criticism of traditional meritocracy theory still stands. Stratification undermines merit by building in a markedly unequal structure of opportunities for children depending on their ascribed unequal status. Advanced capitalism, organized around multinational corporations, also builds in an extremely unequal structure of job opportunities beyond the control of individual workers.

When functionalism links rewards only to individual efforts and abilities, it totally ignores these larger structural processes that constrain individual life chances.

Much of the Marxist work discussed in this section adopts a structuralist approach: that is, it accepts the model of capitalism as a system and seeks to account for features of society in terms of their functions for that system. Morgan and Sayer's critique of the work of Braverman, and by implication that of Bowles and Gintis, suggests that Marxist structuralism shares some of the conceptual problems associated with functionalism. Braverman does not make the basic functionalist error of assuming that what is good for capitalism must be good for the social system as a whole. But he does tend to assume a functional unity to the capitalist system that may not be warranted. Policies for deskilling and controlling workers may be valuable for the interests of certain capitalists but may undermine the competitive position of others. Braverman tends to assume the functional indispensability of Taylorism for capitalism without exploring the alternative ways in which labour can be managed and exploited for profits.

Not all patterns of stratification evident in North American society are functional for capitalism. Many corporations may be learning that Taylorism, combined with oppressive management practices and head hunting for highly skilled labour, may not be functional for their interests. Such practices may actually be undermining their competitive position. Capitalists and Marxist sociologists still have much to learn about the management of skilled labour.

The Radical Feminist Critique: Gender Hierarchy as Patriarchy

Women as an Underclass

The radical feminist perspective is emerging from efforts to account for the specific character of the subordination of women within the stratification system. This subordination is apparent within capitalism but also in pre-capitalist and socialist systems of economic relations. Data from Canadian society present extensive evidence of the lower economic status of women generally (Armstrong and Armstrong 1984, 18–63). The proportion of adult women in the labour force has more than doubled between 1941 and 1981, to include 52 percent of all women by 1981. But women are heavily overrepresented in a reserve army of part-time, seasonal, and cheap labour. Women are concen-

trated in a small number of occupations—clerical, service, sales, health, and teaching—with three-quarters of employed women in the first three of these categories. When women enter professions, they are heavily overrepresented in low status and low-paid categories. They are dental hygienists, librarians, therapists, and dieticians, rather than dentists, doctors, lawyers, engineers, or university professors (see table 12-2). Between 1960 and 1985, women university professors increased in number from 750 to almost 6000 while the number of male professors increased from 5700 to 29 000

Figure 12-1 Labour Force Participation Rates for Women and Men Over 15 Years of Age, Canada 1911–86*

Labour Force Participation Rate (%)

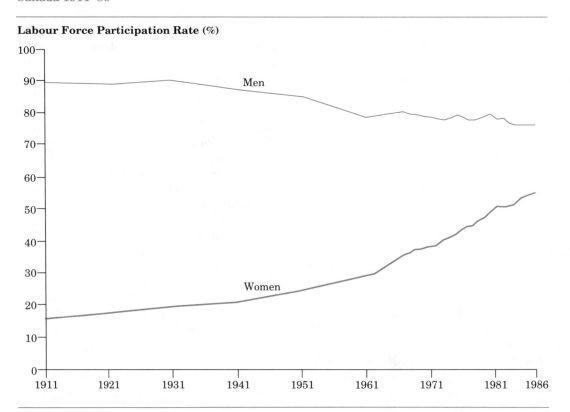

*Figures for 1941 include persons on Active Service on 2 June 1941.

Source: Eichler (1988a, 95) Calculated from Statistics Canada, 1961 Census of Canada, Vol. III (Part 1) Labour Force, table 1, for 1911-61; for 1966–79: Cat. 71-201 Historical Labour Fource Statistics, pp. 151, 153, 158; for 1981–84: Historical Labour Fource Statistics, 1984, Cat. 71-201, p. 220, D767895, p. 225, D768005; for 1985–86, Cat. 71-001.

Table 12-2 Female Workers in Selected Professional and Technical Occupations, 1971 and 1981

Occupation	Female % of Occupation		% of all Female Workers	
	1971	1981	1971	1981
Dental hygienists, assistants, and technicians	76.6	81.1	0.3	0.4
Social workers	53.4	62.6	0.2	0.4
Librarians and archivists	76.4	80.2	0.2	0.3
Physiotherapists, occupational and other therapists	81.6	84.6	0.2	0.2
University teachers	16.7	24.6	0.1	0.2
Physicians and surgeons	10.1	17.1	0.1	0.1
Pharmacists	23.1	41.3	0.1	0.1
Psychologists	47.2	52.0	0.1	0.1
Dieticians and nutritionists	95.3	94.0	0.1	0.1
Lawyers and notaries	4.8	15.1	—*	0.1
Industrial engineers	3.3	12.2	—	0.1
Dentists	4.7	7.9	—	—
Total	29.0	39.4	1.5	2.1

*— means less than 0.1 percent.

Source: Armstrong and Armstrong (1984). Calculated from *1971 Census*, vol. 3.2, table 8; and from *1981 Census, Labour Force—Occupational Trends* (Cat. 92–920), table 1.

(*Globe and Mail*, 28 June 1988, A13). Women are concentrated in the lower professorial ranks, and they earn less than men at every rank, averaging 81 cents to the male dollar.

Reports filed in October 1988 by government-regulated industries, including banks, airlines, railways, telephone companies, and Crown corporations, show that the traditional image of an office as an army of poorly paid female clerical workers answering to a small number of well-paid men still prevails (*Globe and Mail*, 22 Oct. 1988). Women are in the majority of jobs paying less than $25 000 while men predominate in jobs that pay more than $35 000. Women are rarely represented in the very high-paying jobs. Roughly 10 percent of the 13 800 male employees with Air Canada, for example, earn more than $70 000. Only 4 out of the 6300 women working for the corporation earn that much.

The Armstrongs suggest that requiring equal pay for equal work may have served only to increase job segregation in the labour force. The tendency has been for employers to hire only women for certain types of jobs and to pay them low rates. The different concept of equal pay for work of equal value is problematic and has not yet been implemented in nation-wide legislation.

Women have not been displacing male earners, by and large, but have been supplementing their low earnings to prevent severe family poverty. Inflation has undermined the **family wage** system for the majority of families. Conditions of work for lower-class women, especially those in low-prestige sweatshop industries, are generally poor. Women have been joining unions in steadily increasing numbers. They account for half the union growth between 1971 and 1981, but still only 22 percent of employed women were unionized by 1981. The main reason that women gave for joining unions was more often for protection from sexual harassment than for higher wages. Even when women are unionized, their interests are not always well represented. The problem is that men commonly dominate unions and union leadership. Unions themselves have been implicated in enforcing job segregation and unequal pay scales that favour male workers over women.

Perpetuating the Gender–Class Hierarchy

These are the data. The problem is to explain them. The main complaint that radical feminists raise against Marxist theory is that it does not take into account the segmentation of the labour market. The working class is treated as an undifferentiated whole. Class is still defined through the male relation to work. There is still no successful formula for women's analytic and political incorporation into class analysis on equal or complementary terms with men (Brittan and Maynard 1984, 56). Women are simply not included in labour-market theory in any other than a marginal way.

The traditional meritocracy thesis accounts for inequality by reference to individual merit and ability. To account for their subordinate status, we would therefore have to conclude that women are less meritorious, less able, less educated, less competent than male workers. But this conclusion does not stand up to an empirical test.

Marxist theory places the blame not on the abilities of individual workers but upon the workings of the capitalist system. The unequal treatment of women and men in the labour force is a technique used by the capitalist class to divide and to weaken the working class. For feminists, this argument obscures too much. It takes for granted precisely what needs to be explained. Why are women singled out for super-exploitation (Beechey 1977)? How is it that the subordinate status of women was there to be exploited? Why is it that male workers see it as legitimate that fellow workers should be in subordinate, lower paid, and often insecure and temporary work, because they happen to be female? Capitalism could not use women this way if they were not already in family systems in which they were economically dependent upon men. Capitalists may exploit such situations, but the argument that capitalism produced them is less than convincing (Brittan and Maynard 1984, 52–55). Marxists gloss over sexual inequality as merely a divide-and-rule tactic by capitalists, with feminists serving the interests of capitalism by fragmenting and weakening the class struggle.

Brittan and Maynard challenge the **class reductionism** of this version of Marxist theory for leaving out too much. It renders male power and male oppression of women invisible. Cockburn (1981, 54) criticizes Marxist theory by asking some blunt questions:

> Where is the man as male, the man who fills those spaces in capitalist production that he has defined as not [women's], who designs the machines and thereby decides who will use them? Where is the man who decorates the walls of his workplace with pin-ups of naked women and whose presence on the street is a factor in a woman's decision whether to work the nightshift?

Such questions begin to expose relations of patriarchy rather than of capitalism, although the two are very much interrelated. The theory of capitalism can function as the ideology of dominant males. By displacing the causal relation onto the workings of an abstract economic system, this ideology can hide the ways that men practise discrimination against women in the economy.

Hartmann (1979) criticizes both functionalist and Marxist theory for ignoring the role of men—ordinary men, men as men, men as workers—in maintaining women's inferiority in the labour market. She traces the effect of "centuries of patriarchal social relationships" in which men have pushed women into subordinate economic roles. Historically in Europe, when men worked on small farms, women had garden plots for subsistence production. Men were hired as farm labourers while women were displaced. During the early development of factories, women were available as cheap factory labour. Hartmann cites evidence that men resisted factory labour because they did not want to lose their independence, while women and children were described as "more docile and malleable," itself a reflection of long-term subordination to men in agriculture. Men dominated the skilled trades, while women filled less important positions as casual labourers and assistants rather than as master craftsmen. In Canada, women always worked alongside men in developing homesteads and family farms, yet patriarchal laws dispossessed them, vesting ownership rights to the property in the man. Men commonly kept that control even after death by willing all property to their sons, leaving their wives to depend on the charity of their children.

In principle, the expansion of wage labour with industrial capitalism had the potential to break this patriarchal control over women in the family. In principle, pure capitalism promised to bring all women and older children into the labour force as "free"

Historically, male unions took an active role to ensure that women were confined to low-paying, subordinate positions.

labour, independent of men. It would have made all labourers equal, irrespective of sex. So why are women still inferior to men in the labour market? Hartmann leaves no doubt that ordinary working men took a very active role in preventing this equalization and independence from happening. They did it by enforcing a division of labour between the sexes and by using techniques of hierarchical organization and control in labour unions. Women in the labour force, like women with vegetable gardens and chickens, would not threaten patriarchal authority so long as they remained predominantly in subordinate, low-income, and low-power positions relative to men. The potential problem with this arrangement was that the cheap labour of women might undercut men's jobs and wages. This threat had to be controlled, and male unions took active steps to do this.

Initially, as factories expanded, entire families worked together. A male spinner, for example, might hire his wife and children as helpers. Later, when technical changes made this **family factory system** more difficult, male labour organizations lobbied to have children and then women excluded from factory labour altogether. Male workers viewed women as a threat to their jobs because of their lower wages. Their response could have been to join forces in a combined union to pressure for equal pay. Instead, male spinners' unions used their organizational force to eliminate women from factories, even plotting to set fire to a factory in which girls were working at wages below those of male unionists. Hartmann documents the systematic actions of male unions to exclude women from membership and to prevent women from gaining the skills required for equal status jobs. Traditional Marxist theory explains this in terms of animosity toward unskilled labour, which threatened their jobs, but the same men who excluded women from learning these skills offered training to young boys.

Hartmann, among many others, argues that such patterns cannot be explained solely in terms of relations of capitalism. They reflect relations of patriarchy, which capitalism may take advantage of but did not cause. Capitalists can exploit the relations of patriarchy in three ways. They can buy the allegiance of men by using sex status differences to reward males. Secondly, they can threaten to replace men with women and thus weaken labour bargaining power. Thirdly, capitalists can ultimately replace experienced male workers with low-paid women.

But it is by no means obvious that relations of patriarchy always function in the interests of capital. Such relations may actually hamper progress. Is it in the interests of capitalism to pay men a "family wage" so that they can afford to keep wives at home? Is it in the interests of capital that this large, well-educated, potential labour force stays at home? Or that wives do domestic work for free? Domestic work could be done by profit-making service-sector enterprises. Currently, with the flood of women entering the full-time labour force, there has been an enormous expansion in this service sector. Mothers who work outside the home provide a huge market for profitable services in day care, take-out food, domestic cleaning services, and the like. Wage-earning women also expand the market for cars, clothes, holidays, kitchen appliances, and almost everything else. As we saw in chapter 9, the major problem for mature capitalism is finding markets for mass-produced goods. Employed women offer a much bigger market than dependent housewives with housekeeping allowances.

On the issue of employed women, patriarchy and capitalism may well be working at cross purposes. During certain periods, strong male unions have been able to preserve or extend male-dominated strongholds in the labour force, but during periods of expansion, capitalists have been able to overpower male unions. Thus, suggests Hartmann (1979, 228), in periods of economic change, capitalists may be more instrumental in instituting or changing a sex-segregated labour force, while workers fight a defensive battle. In other periods, male workers may be stronger and may be able to drive out women, cheapen female labour, and thus increase benefits to the male sex. Capitalists have indeed used women as unskilled, underpaid labour to undercut male workers, yet this is only "a case of chickens coming home to roost—a case of men's co-optation by and support for patriarchal society with its hierarchy among men being turned back on themselves with a vengeance" (Hartmann 1979, 230).

Eisenstein (1984) carries this exploration of the relations of patriarchy and capitalism in a different direction. She argues that feminism presents a fundamental challenge to liberalism, to the notion of a meritocratic hierarchy based on equality of opportunity. As we saw above, the functionalist thesis of stratification rests on principles of hierarchy and equal opportunity to compete in the race of life. Feminism shows up the contradictions in this thesis. It shows that the ideology of equality of opportunity actually covers up an unequal system that privileges men by their ascribed sexual status.

The meritocracy thesis argues that inequality is necessary to achieve the ideal of human excellence and achievement. It rejects affirmative action, for women or any other disprivileged group, as trying to predetermine the outcome of the competition, to push for equality of results rather than equal opportunities. The liberal thesis, or what Eisenstein calls "liberal individualism," insists that the notion of discrimination applies only to an individual victim, rather than to members of a particular class. The feminist movement, which shows up the situation of women as members of a sexual class, threatens the foundations of the ideology that people are rewarded on the basis of individual merit. Eisenstein points out that men, as men, have a great many advantages over women as childbearers and child rearers, and that all this is obscured under the notion of equal opportunities. She agrees fully with Hartmann that the sexual-class status of women in the economy has much more to do with patriarchy than it does with capitalism.

Prospects for Change and Resistance

Radical feminists argue that true equality between women and men cannot be based on the same opportunity to compete in the labour market. Treatment based on sameness ignores the additional responsibilities of motherhood that women carry. Early feminist writings tended to portray a superwoman image that had women succeeding in full-time professional careers and as mothers and domestic workers as well. The strain proved too much for most women. It led feminist advocates like Betty Friedan (1981) to eschew earlier arguments that housewives were not living up to their potential and to advocate motherhood as a valid career option.

Eisenstein criticized such revisionism as missing the main point that women are a sexual class by virtue of their childbearing and child-rearing work. True sexual equality, and hence true equality of opportunity, must begin from this recognition. True sexual equality will be achieved only when childbearing become politically inconsequential: when it does not restrict women's choices; when it does not mean that women are segregated in the institution of private, domesticated motherhood or forced into economic dependence on men or into secondary wage-earner status; when it does not subject women to restricted notions of sexuality. Such equality implies a far-reaching series of political changes that recognize both the sameness of women and men and the significant difference of childbirth.

What would such a world look like? It would include, among other policies, reproductive freedom, adequate day care, new visions of child care and health care, paternity leave, economic independence, and flexible working time. This is only a beginning: the theory of true sexual equality and what it entails for society has scarcely begun to be developed. The absence, or gross inadequacy, of such policies in most industrial societies attests to how patriarchal our politics are. Patriarchal politics define family as private and insist that day care is a private matter. As feminism begins to win the battle for affirmative action for women as the basis of sexual equality, it threatens the entire logic of liberal individualism and of hierarchy with equal opportunity. For this reason alone, Eisenstein suggests, feminism is an extremely subversive movement in terms of the status quo.

The prospects for change toward such equality are perhaps not as poor as you might think. Women are making slow but noticeable progress in management. Sometimes the price for such progress is too high. An article entitled "Thanks, But No Thanks" (Maynard and Brouse 1988) describes the lives of women who graduated with masters of business administration degrees from the University of Western Ontario. They got good, although not top, jobs as corporate business executives and were "keenly watched and courted [as] the standard bearers in women's drive for equality at work." They found themselves burned out and under extreme stress in the face of inhuman demands to give 110 percent to clients and 120 percent to children, to work from 7:30 a.m. to 6:30 p.m. and on weekends, and to travel for the company. Added to this was the desperate struggle to find and keep adequate day care and the guilt that their children were victims of their mothers' relentless career demands. It was as if the companies were deliberately pushing women beyond human limits to prove they could not be equal to men and should give up and go home. According to the article, many of them did just that, or they started their own businesses.

Another article (Kates 1988) is more optimistic. It gives credit to the Employment Equity Act, which was passed in Canada in 1986. The act requires that all federally regulated companies (banks and transport and communications companies) set up **employment equity** programs and file annual public reports on the demographic composition of their workforce, including data on salaries and promotion for women and minorities. By the spring of 1989, the act was coming under heavy criticism from advocacy groups. Reports produced by federally regulated companies reveal major inequities in pay scales for women and men and restricted employment opportunities for disabled people and visible minorities. But

Cathy copyright 1987 Universal Press Syndicate. Reprinted with permission. All rights reserved.

there are no penalties for failure to practise employment equity. It is up to individual members of disadvantaged groups to challenge these companies in court, using human rights legislation. But such action requires considerable time, money, effort, and legal expertise as well as proof that failure to hire or to promote a particular individual was due to discrimination and not to some other factor. Forcing change in the status quo by this methods promises to be a very long, slow process.

The one section of the act that does appear to have some teeth is the Federal Contractors Program. This program requires every company that has 100 or more employees, and that wants to bid on a federal government contract of more than $200 000, to prove its commitment to gender and minority equity in terms of hiring, training, salary, and promotions. No employee equity plan, no federal contract. What this means is that companies that want large government contracts have to keep women in management positions. To do this, they have had to initiate policies that recognize the sexual particularity or sexual-class status of women.

A decade ago, Kates suggests, a request for maternity leave was an instant ticket to a dead career. Today, Manufacturer's Life Insurance Company has flexible hours, runs an internal course called "Planning for Pregnancy," and has vice-presidents who have taken maternity leaves—on their way up. Esso is trying to recruit on a representative basis from graduating classes and offers a six-month parental leave to either parent of a new baby. The company is no longer demanding that families be able and willing to uproot and move to another city at the drop of a president's hat, a traditional prerequisite for success. It is creating opportunities for employees to advance their careers in the same branch rather than tying promotion to relocation in another city.

Canada still lags a long way behind Sweden in such policies. They still touch only a tiny minority of workplaces. But such examples serve to show up the hitherto largely invisible relations of patriarchy, in which sameness is used to exclude women.

Kates also discusses how the behaviour of men as men, vis-à-vis women, has been and is an integral part of patriarchal politics. Companies that want to hire women managers to enhance their competitive image, and to qualify for government contracts, have actually had to start educating male managers in how to work with women. Kates describes a situation in which a woman was being interviewed for a management position with the Canadian Imperial Bank of Commerce. A male manager, "John," asks if she is married or has any plans and later observes, "She's not all that attractive." The senior manager comments, "John's good, but he's got a problem with women. It will cost him."

Kates shows how women's relative incompetence as managers, compared with men, is socially constructed by how male managers treat them. Such practices are more closely examined in chapter 17. What follows is a brief list of items that give a sense of what sexual equality in the workforce is up against. Women managers experience the veiled hostility of male managers, especially younger ones with whom they are competing more directly, reluctance to include women in the management team, behind-the-scenes barriers to co-operation, the deliberate transfer of a bad worker to their department to foul things up, sexist comments that betray male discomfort at having to work with women, even while this is denied. Women are rated lower than male colleagues regardless of their actual job records; women's promotions are stalled on the unspoken assumption that a women with a family could not do the job; appointments that would give women authority over men are blocked. Women are constantly subjected to scrutiny as tokens. They are left out of the social relations among male managers at the pub, the golf course, and elsewhere. Such relations are actually essential for gaining insider knowledge of what is happening, how to present oneself or one's work, and so on. Women are subjected to insults such as boardroom talk about "tits and ass" or references to a certain woman who would "make a great centerfold for an annual report." They hear men talking about and using secretaries as if they were merely Xerox machines. Female colleagues are fundamentally excluded from information that men share informally, so that women managers find themselves sidelined at meetings.

The greatest impediment to women's success in corporate careers is still the demand for excessively long, sixty-five-hour weeks, a demand that has traditionally been a chief requirement for young executives on the fast track. Most women will not and cannot give up family life for their work. Men have been able to put in such long hours primarily because their wives have absorbed the bulk of their domestic responsibilities. But few women have spouses or other adults at home who can take up most of the domestic and mothering work. Men thus have a significant career advantage over women, but this advantage comes at a high price. Men who value home life and parenting work for themselves, and who want to break out of their stereotyped roles as corporate robots and heart attack candidates, are also disadvantaged in their careers relative to traditional men. The solution may lie in a radical re-organization of labour so that executives work in teams rather than as individuals. Responsibilities could be distributed so that no one employee need work more than a forty-hour week.

The list of socially constructed impediments to women's success in corporate careers is long. None of these impediments are intrinsically essential to running a business. They are relations of patriarchy embedded in relations of business or capitalism. Sociological theory is only beginning to unravel how they work.

The Social Construction of Superiority and Inferiority

In this section, we turn from the broad picture back to the level of relations of everyday life. Grand theoretical schemes of traditional functionalism, Marxism, and patriarchy can all sound very abstract, mechanical, and contrived. Functionalists especially tend to speak in terms of abstract system needs and functions, and individual people appear as little more than cogs in the machine. It is important to realize that these relations of hierarchy, superiority, and inferiority are socially constructed. They are put together by people in their everyday lives and their everyday relationship with others. The special contribution of ethnomethodology is its focus on how people actively construct their sense of reality, how they come to account for and make sense of their lives.

Interpretive theory explores the processes through which people come to see each other as superior or inferior. A good example of these processes can be seen in the position of clerical workers vis-à-vis their bosses. The work of secretaries is taken for granted as routine and unskilled. This is a socially constructed reality, produced by how people talk about what they do, how their work is classified, who takes credit for what, and what opportunities are given or denied to different people to display what they know (Reimer 1987). Clerical staff appear to be doing only routine and delegated work because the creative, non-routine, and managerial work that they do is officially attributed to their bosses. The knowledge on which they draw to organize their bosses' work, collect materials, set priorities, arrange agendas, deal with correspondence, and the like, only becomes visible as their bosses' organizational abilities. When the clerical workers themselves think and talk in terms of the stereotypes and describe their work as merely answering mail, typing, filing, and finding things, they reduce the status of their own work as less skilled than it really is and so help to perpetuate the myth that they lack management skills.

The recognition that people actively produce the stereotypes of gender and class hierarchy does not mean that these stereotypes can readily be dismissed. They do express a real experience, albeit in a distorted form.

Liddle and Joshi (1986, part V) explore how the actual work situations in which people find themselves give rise to gender stereotypes. Their research focusses on women in professional careers in India, but the social processes that they reveal are generally applicable to Canada. Liddle and Joshi note that these professional women accept the stereotype that women are less intelligent and less capable than men. As one women expresses it, boys are intelligent while girls are diligent. How does this stereotype arise and how is it sustained? Liddle and Joshi argue that it is rooted in the fact that men have advantaged access to learning, both on and off the job. They are more likely to have high priority given to their education than are girls, and they are far more likely to be helped informally on the job by senior males and to be involved in the male networks through which they learn about the enterprise. They then appear more competent and informed than the women. Women have less access to resources or to discussions with and advice from colleagues. They may also find themselves pressured to underplay their abilities in front of male colleagues who feel threatened by competent women. Such behaviour feeds the myth that women are less able.

Liddle and Joshi argue that the primary mechanism perpetuating the gender-class hierarchy is the fact that the bulk of domestic work and child care is routinely done by women, whether or not they have other jobs. The class hierarchy presupposes the gender hierarchy. The organization of work and working hours assumes that workers are generally not involved in the performance of domestic labour or child care. Such work is presumed to be done by someone else. The class privileges of professional women similarly depend upon the gender subordination of other women. They rely on these other women for domestic service work and child care at rates so cheap that they absorb only a portion of the money that professional women themselves earn (Liddle and Joshi 1986, 150–51).

Liddle and Joshi (1986, 178–80) describe how professional women act out their subordination to men, both at work and at home. At work they routinely downplay their professional abilities and defer to male views so as not to challenge male authority. At home they hold back their own ambitions so as not to get ahead of their husbands' career, and they are submissive and deferential, especially before any of their husbands' relatives. Why do they do this? It is not by choice but by necessity. Women find that such displays of subservience are essential to gain a minimum of co-operation from male colleagues and to avoid open harassment.

When women refuse to collude with men in sustaining the myth of male superiority, male colleagues become defensive and uncooperative. A common tactic is to denigrate the qualifications or competence of assertive women or to insinuate that they are taking jobs away from men who have families to support. Another common technique is sexual harassment, known in India as Eve-teasing. Women are subjected to gossip and sexual advances. Such harassment is a powerful mechanism by which subordinate men can exert power over women superiors, thus asserting gender privilege over class hierarchy (Liddle and Joshi 1988, 141).

Relations of hierarchy between people are continually reproduced and reinforced through displays of superordination and sub-ordination in intimate behaviour (Archibald 1978). They involve linguistic, gestural, and spatial signs and deference rituals. Actions such as statements of praise or depreciation, or intonation used in talking to someone, convey a message of hierarchy. The way one stands before another conveys insolence or obsequiousness or equality. Who precedes whom through the door, or who sits where, gives similar messages. Which member of the family gets to sit in the most comfortable armchair with the best view of the television, for example, is decided on the basis of family hierarchy.

Archibald (1978, 197) notes that particular forms of body language were a familiar aspect of master-slave relations before the American Civil War. Slaves were expected to display signs of deference, such as tugging at their forelocks, shuffling their feet, grinning, and agreeing with virtually everything the whites said. Similar patterns continue in service jobs such as hotel maid or waitress. Goffman (1959) describes the two-way process of **doing hierarchy** in relations between customers and those serving them in a restaurant. In the dining room the customers were superordinated by servers who treated them with deference and respect and demonstrated demure body language. Once through the doors into the kitchen, however, servers parodied, ridiculed, and criticized the diners. This preserved a sense of dignity and superiority in private that could not be expressed in public.

Asymmetry in familiarity is another form of creating hierarchy. Superordinates have the right to exercise familiarities that subordinates are not allowed to reciprocate (Archibald 1978, 152). Goffman (1967, 64) found that doctors could call nurses by their first names, while nurses generally responded with polite or formal address, "Doctor." In business, a boss may inquire about the elevator operator's family, but it would be impertinent for the operator to ask similar questions of the boss. The subordinate can show appreciation for the concern but not reciprocate it.

In relationships, the superordinate person initiates more interaction, while the subordinate responds more. This is readily apparent in the behaviour of women and men in mixed company. In such situations, women typically display deference toward men. They talk less often and make fewer suggestions than men. They initiate fewer conversations, and they are interrupted more often than men. They agree with others more, but their own suggestions are agreed with less by others. To have their suggestions accepted, they commonly have to get a man to take them up, or have to suggest themselves that what they are saying is the implication of what a man has been saying (Archibald 1978, 199). "Office girl etiquette" still cautions the woman worker not to argue with her male boss, but to agree with him and try to get her own ideas accepted without the boss or other men realizing where they came from (Bernard 1968, 284–87).

Studies of married couples show that when the woman brought up a topic for discussion, it was negatively associated with the amount of time spent talking about it. Couples talk about what the man wants to talk about (Bernard 1968, 125). It is still commonly expected that interaction such as dating, conversation, or sexual activity will be initiated by men. Note how even the common use of the word pairs such as "men and girls" or "man and wife" reflects the hierarchical relationship.

People actively do the work of belittling others, participating directly in the production and reproduction of low social status of certain groups. Archibald (1978) describes this process in relation to both women and to French Canadians. Women as well as men are more likely to accept the content of a lecture or article when delivered by a man rather than a woman. Identical articles, some bearing the name of a female author, others the name of a male, were distributed among students. They consistently voted the articles ostensibly written by men as superior to or more convincing than those with female authors.

Similar disparagement was found in an experiment to test attitudes toward French Canadians. Bilingual speakers recorded a two-minute passage in English and then in French. Judges were asked to evaluate the personality characteristics of speakers using only voice cues. Judges—both French and English Canadian—consistently tended to rate French-Canadian speakers less favourably than English-Canadian speakers (Lambert 1967, 93-94).

The clearly contrived situations in these experiments may have influenced the results, as students might have second guessed what the experimenter was looking for. But they do suggest that people who casually hear advice or commentaries in the mass media will tend to downplay messages from women and minority groups.

Coping with Inequality

What is the price of this socially constructed subordination? Archibald and others suggest that it takes a direct and serious toll on the mental health of those who feel that they are at the bottom of the social hierarchy. Blue-collar workers are more likely than professionals to feel personally powerless over their lives in general. Their feelings of self-depreciation or low esteem can be close to feelings of misery (Archibald 1978, 180). A meter reader described how he had to do his routine job because he had two handicapped children to support, but he added that maybe the real reason why he was a meter reader was that he was no good for anything else (Alderman 1974, 12). Studs Terkel's book *Working* (1972) is full of comments by working people about their jobs. What comes across is their sense of inferiority and even shame; they feel they have to apologise for their jobs to their children. People learn to

daydream on the job, to keep their self-respect by imagining that they are somewhere else. The job becomes bearable when workers dream that one day they will leave and start their own business or that their children will escape the factory.

The psychological price that people pay for the daily experience of subordination can be high. Archibald (1978) suggests that people respond by withdrawing emotionally from their situation, shutting themselves off from those areas of their lives that threaten their sense of self-worth. The symptoms of self-estrangement closely mirror those of reactive depression, including loss of interest in life, decreased energy, loss of concentration, erosion of motivation and ambition, and inability to accomplish tasks (Archibald 1978, 177). This list of symptoms could very easily pass for a psychiatric description of a person suffering from schizophrenia, a mental state in which people feel detached from reality and from everything going on around them (Laing 1965, 42). Archibald draws the conclusion that the social experience of subordination and humiliation at work damages people to such a degree that they can become mentally ill.

Archibald carries the argument further to suggest that the pervasive subordination of women relative to men fosters in women reactive behaviour that borders on mental illness. A study of housewives found that they tend to be "more submissive, less independent, less adventurous, more easily influenced, less aggressive, less competitive, more excitable in minor crises, [had] their feelings more easily hurt, [were] more emotional, and more concerned about their appearance" (Broverman et al. 1970, 6–7). Archibald sees all these behavioural characteristics as typical not specifically of women, but of people in subordinate positions who spend their lives acting out the displays of subservience expected of them. Again, the price they pay for such subservience is borderline mental illness. In the Broverman study, more than half the housewives interviewed complained of feeling restless, grouchy, worn out, tense, and nervous, exactly the same symptoms complained of by ex-mental patients (Archibald 1978, 215).

Similar conclusions on the relationship between subordination and poor mental health were reached in a study of women produced for the Canadian Mental Health Association (*Globe and Mail*, 11 July 1987, A1–2). The report argues that being part of a devalued and oppressed group is detrimental to mental health. It leads to the development of poor self-esteem, low levels of aspiration about one's work and achievement, and the belief that one must accept whatever one is offered. Such feelings, combined with the threat of poverty and family violence, are seen as contributing to depression and anxiety that drive women to attempt suicide in Canada twice as often as men.

Conclusion

This exploration of stratification in capitalist society has taken us a long way from traditional functionalist analysis with its certainty of differential skill requirements and merited differences in prestige and rewards. As the concepts used in analyses change, so also does the nature of the reality being talked about. Where traditional functionalists talk of "stratification," for example, Marxists talk of "class." *Class* essentially refers to power based on relationship to the means of production; stratification is essentially a prestige ranking. For traditional functionalists, stratification is based on innate individual differences in abilities and motivation but, seen from the Marxist perspective, it refers primarily to the relative utility of different positions for the capitalist system at any one time (Boughey 1978, 130). Good jobs can quickly crumble into nothing once they cease to be useful to corporate employers. Members of the prestigious upper middle class of corporate executives have been finding this out to

their cost during the 1980s. Cutbacks in middle management positions have left many unemployed.

The dimension of power or powerlessness is central to the Marxist analysis, not the differences in income or lifestyle that occupy traditional functionalists. It certainly helps to have scarce skills that are in high demand, but it does not alter the fact that shifting labour market demands or new technologies, or just an overabundance of other people with similar skills, can rapidly wipe out any advantage. Distinctions between professional, middle class, working class, and lower class begin to look unimportant under such conditions. What they have in common is insecurity and dependency in the labour market.

Marxists focus on the mechanisms that structure the labour market itself. The development of technology to deskill jobs and replace people and the promotion of a reserve army of skilled labour through mass education serve the function of maintaining the power of the capitalist class to depress wages and to control profits.

To a much more limited extent than traditional functionalists, Marxist theorists acknowledge the need for skills and professional training, and the need to attract particularly able, qualified, and dependable people to certain jobs. But they use different criteria to answer the moral question of what differential rewards should be. Personal need and labour time, rather than importance and scarcity, are the key variables. The well-known Marxist motto is, "To each according to need and from each according to ability." True justice requires equality in power, prestige, and property. People deserve equal power to influence government in their own society, equal dignity as human beings, and equal access to a good standard of living (Boughey 1978, 130). People do not automatically warrant a higher standard of living just because they happen to be born brighter, or with wealthy parents, or because they lucked into an elite job. In theory, people could be rewarded for the labour time they give to their jobs. The time taken to develop skills can be calculated into the amount. So can the extra time involved in doing quality work. Those who support more dependants should take home proportionately more money. These are the principles that underlie current state salary policies in China.

Ethnomethodology introduces a qualitatively different dimension into this analysis of stratification. It insists that both functionalism and Marxism are ideological in so far as they centre the debate on the abstract level of system needs and functions. Ethnomethodology focusses on how people, in their everyday lives, actively construct and reproduce social reality. The legitimation of inequalities, which functions to stabilize the social order, is produced at the level of how people themselves go about "doing hierarchy" or how they act to superordinate and subordinate themselves in everyday behaviour. Both functionalism and

Marxism assume that legitimation of inequality—viewed either as value consensus on merited rewards or as manipulated ideological hegemony to divide and rule—is essential to the equilibrium of the capitalist social system. To the extent that this assumption is correct, it implies that change at the level of everyday interaction, from "doing hierarchy" to "doing equality," could directly threaten the stability of a system based on expropriation for profits. Perhaps that is why the feminist conception of non-hierarchical, co-operative modes of organization rouses such strong opposition in bureaucratic circles. The last chapter of this text looks particularly at this issue.

It should have become apparent throughout this debate that education is related in critical although contradictory ways to stratification. Schools and colleges, with their technological-meritocratic principles, have become central arenas within which relations of stratification are worked out. It is to the analysis of the education system that we now turn.

Suggested Reading

An excellent source of statistical information on inequality in Canada is Henry Veltmeyer, *Canadian Class Structure* (1986). Veltmeyer takes a strong, structuralist-Marxist approach to inequality, showing how capitalism works to create a class of super-rich at the top of the Canadian hierarchy and a class of poor and sometimes destitute people at the bottom.

For a clear presentation of functionalist theory of stratification, the article by Davis and Moore, "Some Principles of Stratification" (1945) is excellent. It is an older publication, but the main argument is very clear, without being hedged or qualified to avoid criticism. The rebuttal by Melvin Tumin, "Critical Analysis of 'Some Principles of Stratification'" (1953) is also very straightforward.

For the Marxist approach an excellent book is Harry Braverman, *Labor and Monopoly*

Capital (1974). This descriptive and readable book presents a strong argument for the importance to capitalism of deskilling workers.

From the perspective of radical feminism, Heidi Hartmann, "Capitalist Patriarchy and Job Segregation by Sex" (1979), presents a ground-breaking study of how male unions systematically limited the job opportunities open to women. A journalistic article by Rona Maynard and Cynthia Brouse, "Thanks but No Thanks" (1988) documents the high stress experienced by women in corporate executive careers.

For the interpretive perspective, any of the studies by Erving Goffman are valuable. They are all very readable descriptions of how everyday life is managed in ordinary interactions. One short book by Goffman is *Interaction Ritual* (1967).

Chapter 13

Education: Does It Moderate or Perpetuate Social Inequality?

Compulsory public schooling for children is a central feature of all industrialized societies. In pre-industrial Europe and Canada, it was normal for families to have primary responsibility for educating the younger generation. Children might be sent to other households to learn to work as servants or to be taught a trade, but there was no separate, publicly financed school system. In advanced industrial societies, the picture is strikingly different.

In Canada, the beginnings of a public school system can be traced back to the early 1840s in Ontario (MacDonald 1988, 102–03). In 1846, a general board of education was set up to examine the state of education in the province and to make recommendations for developing a common school system. In 1850 an act was passed to regulate the classification of teachers and to establish boards of public instruction for each county to certify teachers and to select textbooks. In 1871 free, compulsory education was established. Children between the ages of

seven and twelve had to attend school four months per year. In 1919, the school-leaving age was raised to sixteen. Secondary school fees were abolished two years later. Other provinces slowly followed Ontario's lead.

In contemporary Canada, schooling is compulsory between the ages of six and sixteen, although many children are enrolled in formal educational institutions at an earlier age and remain in school past the legal school-leaving age. Statistics Canada data (1985, 42) for 1984–85 indicate that 431 700 children were enrolled in pre-elementary education, a 9 percent increase since 1977–78. The same data show that 69 percent of seventeen year olds and 20 percent of eighteen year olds were still enrolled in school. Many people continue their formal education in a postsecondary institution. During 1987–88, 12.4 percent of the eighteen to twenty-one age group were enrolled in community colleges and 15.4 percent in undergraduate university programs. Growing numbers of adults attend postsecondary institutions part-time. In total, during 1987–88, there were 427 873 people attending university full-time as undergraduates and a further 257 840 attending part-time. In addition, 94 853 were enrolled in graduate studies. Undergraduate enrolment rose by 61.5 percent between 1971–72 and 1987–88. Enrolment in graduate studies rose by 76 percent during the same period.

Why has compulsory and advanced education achieved such importance in industrial societies like Canada? What forms does education take? What are the explanations for pronounced inequities among different social groups in access to and achievement in education? These are some of the central questions we explore in this chapter.

Theories of education are very closely linked to the theories of stratification explored in the previous chapter. In industrial society, careers have become more important than inherited wealth in determining the standard of living of the majority of people. These careers, in turn, depend on access to education.

As in the previous chapter, we present the traditional functionalist perspective first, followed by the structuralist–Marxist critique. Both of these approaches are challenged by contemporary efforts to reformulate theories of education in less deterministic ways. Such challenges give central attention to the social construction of schooling in everyday interaction in classrooms and to efforts of feminists and others to radically transform the curriculum and teaching methods.

Functionalism: The Liberal Theory of Education

Next to the family, education ranks as the most important institution within the traditional functionalist model of the social system. It is responsible for developing moral or normative consensus, which is at the centre of social integration and pattern maintenance. It is also critical for transmitting essential skills for economic adaptation.

The Ideal of Liberal Education

The nineteenth-century philosopher and reformer John Dewey advocated a free and universal school system as vitally important for democracy and for developing industrial society. He believed that schools have a central role to play in the psychic and moral development of the individual. By helping to develop the cognitive and psychomotor skills of students, schools also offer each individual the chance to compete openly for privileges in society (Boles and Gintis 1976, 20–23). Dewey saw universal education as a powerful mechanism for reducing extremes of wealth and poverty and fostering equality, not merely equalizing opportunities to compete. In his view, universal schooling was not only desirable in itself. It was also an efficient way to train a skilled labour force. Hence it should be eminently compatible with capitalism.

This vision of the education system as democratic, just, and efficient stands at the heart of the functionalist view of stratification in industrial society. Functionalism focusses primarily on the objectives of socializing young people in the skills and moral commitment necessary for them to take over adult roles within the social system. The goal is to ensure the continuity of the system itself. Functionalists define equality of opportunity primarily in terms of meritocracy. In these terms, the desired outcome of schooling is that the more able and motivated students are allocated to the more difficult and important social roles.

The Functions of Schools

Parsons' essay, "The School Class as a Social System" (1961), provides a succinct and candid statement of the basic assumptions underlying the functionalist theory of education. In this essay, Parsons argues that families are not adequate to prepare children for adult roles in advanced industrial societies, primarily because the values and commitments appropriate for kinship roles conflict with those of the workplace. A critical function of schools is to help children to make the transition from the value orientations of family life to the affectively neutral, universalistic, and achievement-orientated values of the work world.

Parsons suggests that it is significant that close to nine out of ten elementary school teachers are women. The nurturing orientation that these teachers provide gives young children some continuity with the mother role and hence absorbs the strain of achievement and differential ranking. Children can relate to their female teacher and try to please her as they do their mothers. They have the same teacher for a whole year in all subjects. This fits the diffuseness of the feminine roles of housewife and mother. At the same time, the teacher is not a mother but is in an occupation. Each year children have a new teacher. This reinforces particularistic role identification. They also learn that the teacher judges them according to their achievements. Parsons further suggest that it is significant that traditionally a high proportion of American school teachers are unmarried. They thus avoid the contradictory demands of maternal and occupational roles for women.

Senior classes are differentiated into specialized subject areas, each taught by a different teacher. The majority of these teachers are men. Specialization by male teachers reduces attachment to any one teacher and promotes and reinforces the masculine image of affective neutrality and specificity. Hence children learn the pattern variables appropriate for adult sex roles.

At the same time, schools socialize children in required commitments and capabilities for adult roles. *Commitment* comprises two broad aspects: societal values and performance of specific roles. The two components of *capabilities* are skills to per-

form the task and role responsibility; that is, the ability to live up to the expectations of others. The school is thus crucial for the allocation of young people into future roles on the basis of achievement. At the elementary level, where cognitive skills appear relatively simple, the moral component of responsible citizenship takes precedence. Students are graded both for achievement and for "responsible good behaviour" such as respectfulness and co-operativeness in class. Parsons sees these as fundamental moral skills, crucial for future leadership and initiative. Stratification on the basis of cognitive skills is translated into college preparatory streaming at grade 9. Parsons admits that the ascriptive characteristics of class of origin influence this streaming, but he concludes that the main focus is still achievement.

Parsons acknowledges that there are tensions in the school system for girls who are placed in the same classrooms as boys but who are constantly reminded that their future lies in marriage and family rather than in specialized occupational roles. Sex segregation commonly found in school playgrounds helps to reinforce a sense of belonging to one's own sex.

Parsons' essay is a masterpiece in displaying the working assumptions of the functionalist approach. The first assumption is *functional indispensability*. Parsons conveys the impression that all aspects of American schools in the 1950s had important functions within the education system and could not be easily replaced. He further accepts the basic assumption of *functional unity*. Any established patterns are regarded as good for the educational system, for society as a whole, and for individual members. There is no question in his model that such practices as the early streaming of children on the basis of behaviour rather than cognitive abilities might not be functional for all sectors of society. The third basic assumption, *universal functionalism*, is evident in Parsons' effort to find a valuable purpose for every detail that he notices. Nothing is dismissed as an irrelevant or useless habit left over from earlier times or from other life situations.

The main problem with this approach is that almost any change in the status quo is problematic. We are left with the impression that any change in the school system, such as using male teachers in elementary grades or married women specialists in later grades, or having mixed playground activities for girls and boys together, would be psychologically disturbing for the students. Contemporary functionalist theories have largely discarded Parsons' assumptions concerning the importance of such details as spinsterhood for elementary teachers, but in other respects his essay still expresses the core ideas of functionalism.

The main functions of the school system, as highlighted by Parsons, can be summarized as follows:

1. to teach the values of achievement, universalistic standards of judgment, and emotional neutrality appropriate for specialized occupational roles;
2. to train in specific skills and knowledge appropriate for occupational roles;
3. to ensure the appropriate selection and allocation of young adults to occupational roles in accordance with merit, as measured by universal standards of achievement;
4. to legitimate inequalities in material rewards in democratic society through principles of merit established in the school grading system;
5. to develop stable social relations with age peers outside the family;
6. to inculcate appropriate sex-role identification.

The functionalist approach to the sociology of education has largely accepted this list of functions defining the roles that schooling plays in society, particularly in preparing children for the job market. The main focus of the debate has been on the extent to which schools are able to meet the moral goals set out by Dewey: to provide equality of opportunity to all children for personal and intellectual development and academic attainment across different social classes, races, and ethnic groups. More recently, the importance of sexual equality has also been recognized. The growing consensus is that, notwithstanding concerted efforts at educational reform, schools are failing miserably with respect to the goal of equality.

Equality and Educational Opportunity

The meaning of *equality* in the context of education is far from clear. One interpretation stresses **equality of condition** or sameness. This implies that a common curriculum should be provided for all children as a standardized, age-graded program of studies without reference to individual differences in interests or abilities. The alternative interpretation stresses **equality of opportunity** for all children to develop their individual potential. This implies that a variety of curricula should be provided so that children with different interests, needs, and abilities would have access to appropriately different education. Differential treatment can be justified on the basis of merit. Specialized and advanced education would be open to all children who qualify on the basis of effort and ability.

Neither principle seems satisfactory when pushed to extremes. Rigid application of the principle of sameness implies that individuals would be stunted and crushed to fit the common mould. On the other hand, rigid application of the principle of differential merit implies that a class of brilliant masters would rule over the mass of stupid drones (Porter, Porter, and Blishen 1982, 5). Historically, the North American school system has struggled to find a compromise. The first stage in the development of the idea of equality in education, associated with the establishment of common schools during the 1840s, assumed that all children must be exposed to the same curriculum in the same school. The second stage is associated with the rejection of the common school ideal in favour of a differentiated curriculum that could be related to the different needs, capacities, and interests of students and to their different occupational futures. Later, the legitimacy of different programs was challenged on the basis that they were a source of inequality of opportunity. Children became trapped in different educational streams that cut off their future options. In the United States the principle of "separate but equal" schools for whites and blacks was rejected on the grounds that segregation itself created inequality. The fourth stage in the development of the notion of equality shifted the focus from equalizing inputs or resources provided in different schools to equality of effects in student attainment. A variety of educational opportunities and resources should be designed to meet the special needs of individual students. The ultimate goal is that all students succeed in school to the best of their innate ability. This change in focus is forcing a new concern with the methods used to produce educational achievement (Porter, Porter, and Blishen 1982, 8).

All sides in the debate try to grapple with the evidence of persistent and marked differences in the formal educational attainment of students from different backgrounds. These differences cannot be accounted for solely by variations in intellectual ability. Porter, Porter, and Blishen (1982) conducted an extensive survey of 2571 Ontario students in grades 8, 10, and 12 to explore the relationship between the backgrounds of students and their aspirations to attend university. The research was initiated during 1971, and the full results were published a decade later. The authors decided to focus on students still in school,

rather than those in university, because they wanted to explore the factors that influenced students not to continue on from school to university. They also focussed primarily on aspirations to go to university, rather than on school performance, as a measure of prospective educational attainment. They argue that the establishment in the 1970s of a policy of open accessibility to postsecondary education for students with a minimum passing grade meant that strong performance in high school was not a useful indicator of long-term achievement. Rather than relying on school grades, the researchers administered their own intelligence test to the students to measure mental ability. The key measure of the social class background of the students was their fathers' occupation. Occupations were ranked on a six-point scale, ranging from higher professions (I) to unskilled work (VI).

The researchers found a direct and strong relation between the father's occupational status and the student's aspiration to graduate from grade 13 and to enter university (see figure 13-1). The higher the occupational status of the father, the more likely the student was to want to complete grade 13. Seventy-six percent of students whose fathers were in the higher professional category intended to go on to university, compared with 46 percent of students whose fathers had unskilled jobs. This gap could only be partially accounted for the different ability levels of students. The researchers found that social class background was a more powerful indicator of aspiration to graduate from university than was measured mental ability (Porter, Porter, and Blishen, 1982, 61).

Among the high-ability boys, 77 percent of those with upper-middle-class backgrounds aspired to graduate from university. The corresponding figure for lower-class boys was 47 percent. At the other extreme, among the low-ability boys, 46 percent of those with upper-class backgrounds aspired to university. By contrast, only 22 percent of low-ability boys with lower-class backgrounds wanted to graduate from university. Thus, there is a 24 to 30 percentage-point difference in proportions of boys aspiring to university that can be accounted for by the effect of social class background. Grade 12 girls show similar differences in aspirations by social class. Among girls with high mental ability, 61 percent of the upper-middle-class girls aspired to university compared with only 36 percent of lower-class girls, a difference of 25 percentage points.

When grade 12 boys and girls are compared, boys have higher aspirations than

girls across most categories of social class and mental ability. The exceptions occur among middle-ability and low-ability students within the upper-middle class where girls equal or exceed boys in aspirations.

These findings concerning the link between social class and aspirations for higher education closely mirror the results of research conducted in the 1950s in the United States by Tumin (1973, 46–54). This similarity suggests that the intervening twenty years of educational reforms had little effect on class bias in educational attainment. However, the differences between the sexes in the Ontario data are significantly

Figure 13-1 Percent Wanting to Graduate from University, by Socio-economic Status, Mental Ability, and Sex, Grade 12

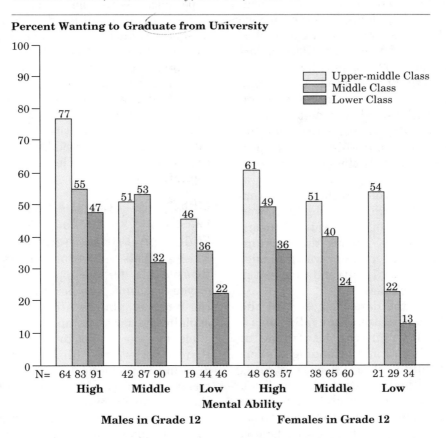

Source: Porter, Porter, and Blishen (1982, 61).

less than in Tumin's data. Tumin found that, in every category of class and mental ability, boys had consistently higher educational aspirations than girls. The rise in aspirations among upper-middle-class girls in the Ontario data is striking.

Porter, Porter, and Blishen studied the correlation between students' aspirations to attend university and several other variables. They found that students from urban areas are more likely to aspire to graduate from university than students from rural areas. Catholics are marginally less likely than Protestants to have such aspirations, which is consistent with the notion that the **Protestant ethic**, favouring business success, would promote education. Both Catholics and Protestants have lower aspirations than Jewish students. Aspirations also drop steadily with an increase in the number of children in a student's family (Porter, Porter, and Blishen 1982, 58, 66, 73, 85).

A follow-up study of the grade 12 students confirmed the predicted relation between social class background and actual attendance at university, particularly among the high-ability students. In this group, 74 percent of the upper-middle-class students went to university compared with 62 percent of the middle-class and 59 percent of the lower-class students. Low-ability students showed similar differences in their rate of attendance by social class. Among the medium-ability group, however, there was an insignificant difference in attendance rates among the three classes.

In summary, the data suggest that the occupational class status of the father has a significant effect on the likelihood of children aspiring to and attending university. The influence of social class exceeds that of mental ability, especially for boys. Students whose fathers are professionals are particularly likely to intend to go to university, even when their mental ability is low. Girls generally lag behind boys in their aspirations to attend university, although

the difference seems to be decreasing, particularly within upper-middle-class families.

When we try to evaluate these data, we should bear in mind that the original survey was conducted in the early 1970s. We cannot assume that patterns prevailing in 1971 will remain unchanged in the 1990s. Statistics Canada data, cited above, indicate that there have been important changes both in the numbers of young adults attending universities and in the proportions of females to males (see figure 13-2).

The value of the research of Porter, Porter, and Blishen lies mostly in the meticulous analysis of relationships between variables to illuminate the causal processes involved and so to give insights into current experiences. While the factual snapshot may rapidly become outdated, the systematic analysis of underlying causal processes gives insight into the character and pace of changes that may be occurring. The researchers utilize the classic survey technique of multi-variate analysis to explore their data. They use statistics to measure the strength of the association between a large number of factors or variables in the lives of the students and the level of educational aspirations expressed by the students.

Functionalist Explanations for Class and Gender Bias in Educational Attainment

Functionalists view education as a system that provides for the appropriate allocation of young people into occupational roles on the basis of ability. How, then, do they explain the large numbers of high-ability students choosing not to attend university? Porter, Porter, and Blishen (1982, 25–29) draw upon the classical functionalist ideas of socialization and self-concept to explore the class and sex differences that are associated with this wasted talent. As we have seen in earlier chapters, socialization is the process through which children learn appropriate social roles and rules of behaviour for the

Figure 13-2 Full-time University Enrolment, by Level and Sex, Canada, 1974–75 and 1987–88

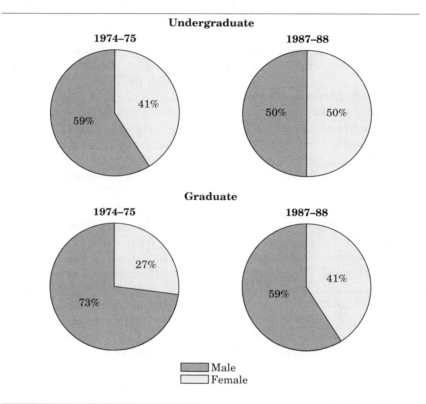

Undergraduate

1974–75

59%

41%

1987–88

50%

50%

Graduate

1974–75

73%

27%

1987–88

59%

41%

Male
Female

Source: Statistics Canada (1985, 59; 1989, 51).

groups in which they find themselves. These rules reflect those of the wider social settings of neighbourhood, social class, and religious group within which families are located. Through interacting with others, children learn to conform to the behaviour that others expect and learn to expect approval and esteem from others for such conformity. Of crucial importance to children is the approval of significant others. These people first consist of immediate family members and later the children's peers and teachers. Porter, Porter, and Blishen predict that the roots of ambition lie in the early socialization process when the influence of parents is likely to be paramount.

Self-concept, the image that we hold of

ourselves, is closely related to socialization. Porter, Porter and Blishen (1982, 117–18) draw on the ideas of symbolic interaction theory, which we explored in chapter 2, to explain the process by which children develop self-concepts of their own abilities. The authors use Cooley's theory of the looking-glass-self; that is, the way in which people reflect on how they appear to significant others and the feelings of pride or shame that such reflections engender. Also significant is Mead's concept of "taking the role of the other"; that is, how children develop a concept of self through trying to see themselves as they appear to others. Porter, Porter, and Blishen suggest that, through such reflexive interaction, boys and girls growing up in different social classes come to develop different conceptions of themselves and their abilities. These self-concepts may not accurately reflect innate mental abilities, but they powerfully influence what children believe they can do, and therefore what they are willing to try.

Porter, Porter, and Blishen devised a series of questions to measure students' self-concepts and to determine who acted as their significant others. Parents seem to be more significant than either teachers or peers in influencing educational aspirations for the majority of children. In every social class, and for both sexes, a greater proportion of students aspired to university when parental influence was high, than when it was low. The high or low influence of peers made relatively little difference. Teachers appeared to have even less influence than peers on future educational plans.

The researchers found large differences between social classes in the amount of direct assistance that parents gave children with schoolwork. At the grade 10 level, they found a difference of 27 percentage points between upper-middle and lower-class boys, and 13 percentage points between upper-middle-and lower-class girls in this regard. By grade 12 these differences rose to 34 and 41 percentage points respectively.

The researchers only briefly considered the possible influence of economic resources and poverty on the aspirations of students whose parents were in the lower class occupational category. They found that a higher percentage of grade 12 students in the upper-income subgroup aspired to attend university than students from poorer households, although this link was also influenced by the number of children in a household. Increasing family size is associated with lower percentages of students aspiring to university. Family income may play some role in encouraging lower-class students to aspire to university, but the researchers suggest that other influences are more significant. They suggest that the socialization effects of linkages with more middle-class family friends or mothers working with middle-class co-workers may best account for the "deviant" cases of aspiring lower-class students (Porter, Porter, and Blishen 1982, 245).

Self-concept of ability seems to be powerfully linked to parental influence and to school performance but minimally linked to measures of mental ability or to teacher's influence (Porter, Porter, and Blishen 1982, 125–29). Self-concept seems to account for the generally lower educational aspirations of girls relative to boys. The researchers found that girls had a lower self-concept of their own ability than boys for every measure used. Their striking finding was that girls achieved consistently better grade-point averages in school than boys for every level of mental ability, and yet they had consistently lower self-concepts of their abilities than boys for every category of ability and performance. Girls, it seems, may be held back by their own low conceptions of themselves.

The researchers link the low self-concept of girls to a combination of socialization and realistic appraisal of the roles they see females perform, both of which are inconsistent with academic success and achievement. Girls, they suggest, are socialized to be overly dependent on the opinions of others and to be submissive. Hence they are more likely to accede to the demands of female teachers and to perform well in school. But because they are not encouraged to be independent, they do not develop confidence in their ability to cope with their environment, and they receive less encouragement from parents to continue their education. They are taught to realize their ambitions through marriage and to passively accept the social status of their husbands.

Boys, on the other hand, are socialized to be independent and autonomous from their mothers, so they resist female teachers in early grades. But, as they near school-leaving age, they are under pressure to qualify for university, as this is linked to future male occupations. They encounter more male teachers in high school and new subjects associated with males in our culture. Hence, boys perform less well than girls throughout school but have higher self-concepts and are significantly more likely to go on to higher education.

If this analysis of the differential socialization and lower self-concepts of girls relative to boys accurately accounts for the 1971 data, it would appear that dramatic changes have occurred in gender socialization in one generation. In 1971, when Porter, Porter, and Blishen did their study, females comprised only 37.7 percent of full-time

undergraduate enrolment. But by 1987–88, they comprised 50.3 percent, plus almost two-thirds of undergraduates enrolled part-time. If the figures for full-and part-time undergraduates are combined, the number of female undergraduates in Canada has marginally exceeded the number of their male peers every year since 1979. These figures suggest that the pattern found by Porter, Porter, and Blishen, that girls generally lack sufficient self-confidence in their abilities to develop high educational aspirations, no longer holds in the 1990s. We need new studies of family socialization to understand what changes have taken place and whether girls are attending university in numbers equal to boys because of, or in spite of, prevailing patterns of socialization.

Figure 13-3 Program by Socio-economic Status, Grade 12

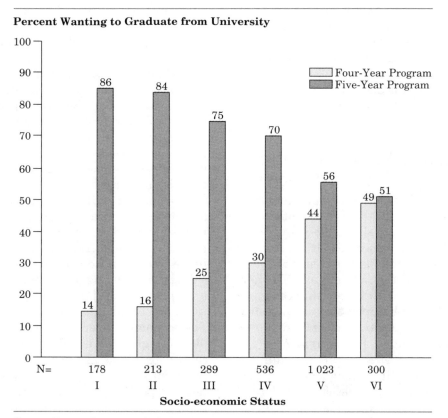

Source: Porter, Porter, and Blishen (1982, 193).

The more general findings of Porter, Porter, and Blishen concerning differential educational aspirations and attainment by social class have not been challenged by any more recent data. The researchers conclude that different patterns of family socialization by social class constitute the primary cause of wasted talents in the education system. Parents are of central importance as significant others for children and are therefore crucial in promoting or reducing educational aspirations. Upper-middle-class parents are more likely to take an interest in, and to help with, their children's schooling and to emphasize success in education as a factor in their approval and esteem. Hence they promote higher aspirations in their children.

Schools may try to develop teaching methods to counter the negative influence of lower-class backgrounds on students, but the real solution seems to lie in changing the norms and values of lower- and lower-middle-class parents. Schools provide an avenue for upward social mobility, particularly with the accessibility of postsecondary education in Canada. But it is up to the students themselves to choose to take advantage of the opportunities provided.

Structuralist–Marxist Theory: Schooling in Capitalist Society

The structuralist–Marxist perspective is rooted in very different conceptions of stratification in capitalist society and of the associated role of education. It promotes a very different kind of research methodology from that of Porter, Porter, and Blishen. Structuralist–Marxist theorists focus primarily on the structure of the school system rather than on aspirations of individual students. Differences in aspirations are regarded as the effects rather than the causes of inequality in education. Functionalists blame lower-class students for not wanting to take advantage of opportunities for higher education and social mobility. In

reality, argue the Marxists, the school system is structured in such a way as virtually to ensure their failure. In focussing on individual aspirations rather than underlying structures, functionalist theory acts as an ideology, a means not to see what is really going on in the school system.

In this section we draw heavily on the work of Samuel Bowles and Herbert Gintis to illustrate the broad outlines of the structuralist–Marxist perspective on education. Their study, *Schooling in Capitalist America* (1976), is widely cited as a seminal work that inspired a decade of Marxist-oriented research in education.

In a summary statement of their theory, Bowles and Gintis (1988b) point to the contradictions between capitalism and democracy. The capitalist economy is driven by imperatives of profit and domination rather than human need. The exploitation of workers for profit presupposes that there are large numbers of people whose sole source of livelihood is selling their capacity to work to capitalists who own the means of production. Capitalism is a totalitarian economic system in the sense that the actions of the vast majority of workers are controlled by a small minority of owners. But this economic system is embedded in a formally democratic political system, which espouses values of equality and justice. The two systems operate from mutually contradictory sets of principles. Political democracy is based on rights invested in the person. The central problems for democracy concern how to maximize participation in decision-making, shield minorities against majority prejudice, and protect majorities against undue influence of an unrepresentative minority. The economic system is based on the principle of rights invested in property. The central problems are how to minimize participation of the majority (the workers), protect a specific minority (capitalists and managers) against the will of the majority, and subject the majority to the will of an unrepresentative minority. Schools are caught in the middle. They are part of the democratic state system, but they are responsible for educating young people to fit into the totalitarian economic system.

Bowles and Gintis (1976, 54) argue that most of the problems in the school system stem from this systemic contradiction between a democratic political system and a totalitarian economic system. The liberal conception of education, first put forward by Dewey, emphasizes three fundamental goals: developing the full potential of individual students with respect to cognitive, physical, emotional, critical, and aesthetic powers; promoting equality through common public schools that would overcome disadvantaged social backgrounds; and ensuring social continuity through preparing young people for integration into adult social roles. Gintis and Bowles argue that these three goals are fundamentally incompatible. Schools cannot promote full personal development and social equality while integrating students into alienating and hierarchically ordered roles within the economy.

The problems are compounded by the compulsion within advanced capitalist economies to develop labour-saving technology that will either displace workers altogether or deskill them in order to cheapen their wage-labour and so raise profits. Bowles and Gintis accept the main theme of Braverman's *Labor and Monopoly Capital* (1974), which predicts that the vast majority of skilled craftworkers, clerical staff, and even professionals will be systematically deskilled and fragmented by technological advances. The resulting class structure will be characterized by a mass of low-skilled workers, controlled by a small class of supervisors and managers, with a very small elite class of highly skilled professionals and executives who run the huge corporations in the interests of the owners of capital. A principle function of schooling in relation to such a system is to prepare the mass of children to fit into a largely deskilled, fragmented, and hierarchical class system. Their natural abilities and desire for autonomy need to be suppressed rather than enhanced to make them comply.

Seen from this perspective, both the evidence of an apparent waste of talented lower-class children who drop out of school, and the lack of fit between mental ability and postsecondary education, take on new meanings. Bowles and Gintis (1976, 8–9, 32–33) note that lower-class children are channelled into dead-end vocational streams in school and drop out early, while less talented upper-middle-class children attain university degrees and highly paid jobs. They argue that such evidence does not imply that schools are failing in their mandate to educate all children equally. On the contrary, schools perpetuate class inequality because this is precisely what they are intended to do, in order to provide workers for the mass of unskilled jobs.

Bowles and Gintis (1976, 82) also recognize that mental ability is not closely linked either to school performance or to postsecondary education and occupational success. This is problematic for the functionalist theory of meritocracy, but Bowles and Gintis argue that there is no compelling reason why they should be linked. High mental ability is not necessary for the majority of jobs within corporate capitalism, including many that ostensibly require credentials. The critical function of credentials, they argue, is to fragment workers and to legitimate status and pay differentials between workers and supervisors, rather than to equip people for skilled work.

Bowles and Gintis (1976, 97–100) cite many examples to back up their argument that the relation between credentials and rewards is largely arbitrary. People who earn credentials, but who lack other attributes of superior status, tend not to get high economic rewards. The economic returns on schooling—average increments in salary for each additional year of formal education—are twice as high for white males as for blacks and women in the United States. White males of upper-class background experience returns on education 66 percent higher than white males of lower-class background. Even when years of experience on the job are identical, white males are likely to have higher earnings than blacks and women. Body image is also important. Bowles and Gintis cite the results of one study that suggested that height was a more important determinant of earnings than either grade point average or a cum laude degree. Another survey of 15 000 executives found that those who were overweight were paid significantly less, the penalty being as much as $1000 a pound.

From the technocratic-meritocratic perspective of traditional functionalism, such patterns are irrational, inexplicable holdovers of ascriptive, particularistic criteria in what should be the impersonal, universalistic, and achievement-oriented bureaucratic world of business. Bowles and Gintis argue, however, that such patterns are far from irrational. They serve important functions for maintaining the equilibrium of the capitalist system. They reinforce the status consciousness that fragments workers. People are much less likely to challenge the prestige, authority, and higher earnings of distinguished-looking older white males, regardless of their actual abilities, than they would if younger, overweight, black women were promoted to supervisory positions.

A mass public education system designed to service this kind of economic order faces serious contradictions. In order to reproduce new workers who will fit smoothly into corporate capitalism, schools must try to teach students to be properly subordinate. Students also must be fragmented to prevent them from uniting to rebel against the inequities. Thirdly, schools must replicate the hierarchical division of labour, preparing appropriate young people for different levels of the corporate order. At the same time that

Figure 13-4 Unemployment Rates by Highest Degree, Certificate or Diploma of Men and Women 15 Years of Age and Over, Canada, 1981

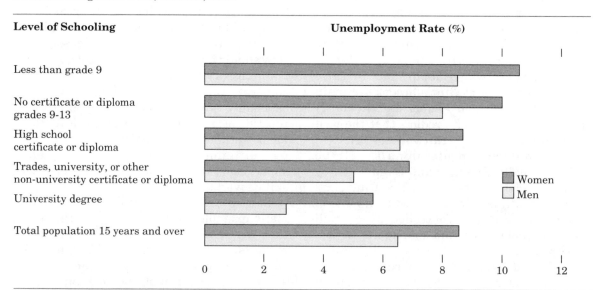

Source: 1981 Census User Summary Tape–SDE81B24.

schools reproduce the social relations of capitalism, they must take care not to appear to contradict the principles of reproducing citizens for the democratic state. Formally democratic political systems, which emphasize equality, participation, and justice, are opposed in almost all principles to the **autocratic** structures of corporations in which an oligarchy of owners of capital dominates decision making. Fitting young people into the world of work thus by no means an automatic extension of cultural norms. It has to be worked at. Bowles and Gintis (1976, 54) argue that the autocratic and oligarchic structures of schools, and the direct parallels between the social relations of classrooms and work situations, function to bridge this gap.

Structural Correspondence Theory

The central argument developed by Bowles and Gintis is **structural correspondence theory**. They argue that schools function to reproduce the social relations of production through a structural correspondence between the form that social relations take in the workplace and in the school. Relationships between administrators and teachers, teachers and teachers, teachers and students, students and students, and also between students and their work, all replicate the hierarchical and fragmented division of labour within corporations (Bowles and Gintis 1976, 131). The content of the curriculum may be designed to teach the values of democratic citizenship, equality, freedom of speech, and so on. But the hierarchical relations within schools teach a very different lesson of submission to a rigid, rule-bound, and autocratic system. The usual liberal argument condoning such patterns is that students are children. They have not reached the stage of adult maturity when democratic rights of free choice would be appropriate.

Schools resemble factories in multiple ways. The architecture of the buildings, with separate rooms, offices, and recreation areas, arranged differently for staff, teachers, secretaries, and students, reproduces in concrete form the division of labour of the school. The seating arrangement in classrooms, with students in rows facing the front area controlled by the teacher, reinforces the hierarchy in which the teacher has authority and the students submit. The lessons of authority and submission are repeated in the routines and rituals of the classroom that require students to speak only when spoken to and to leave and enter classrooms only when bells sound. Through such practices, children become inured to the discipline of the workplace. They develop the types of personal demeanour and self-image that fit them for future occupational roles in factories and bureaucracies. They learn to accept vertical lines of authority. They learn to accept the curriculum package offered. They learn to be motivated primarily through the extrinsic rewards of the grading system rather than the intrinsic pleasures of learning. Students are also fragmented through the insidious emphasis on competition and continual ranking and evaluation (Bowles and Gintis 1988b, 2–3; 1976, 131).

Historical Correspondence Between Schooling and Capitalism

In developing their thesis of a structural correspondence between social relations of schooling and social relations of production, Bowles and Gintis (1976, chap. 6) draw attention to important historical parallels between significant changes in the capitalist economy and developments in the school system. The origin of the common schools in the mid-1830s in the United States coincided with the expansion of the factory system and the widespread labour unrest associated with it. What the factory owners desperately needed was not a skilled labour force, but a disciplined one. People who were used to farming, or to working in their own homes as part of the **putting-out system**, rebelled against factory discipline. Factory owners had to rely heavily upon immigrant labour because abundant land meant that wage labour was scarce. Bowles and Gintis (1976, 152–56) cite data from Massachusetts in the 1860s to suggest that, while the working classes were largely indifferent or opposed to common schools, members of professional and business groups voted in favour of them by a two-to-one margin. What they wanted was not cognitive but moral training, the "hidden curriculum" of character training in the values of order, neatness, politeness, courtesy, and punctuality. What they got in the common schools was enforced military discipline and moral education ideally suited for training a docile and disciplined factory work force.

The subsequent progressive education movement, and greatly increased enrolment in public schools, coincided in the United States with the expansion of corporate capitalism between about 1890 and 1930, another period of pronounced labour unrest (Bowles and Gintis 1976, chap. 7). Corporations had become too large for owners to directly supervise workers. Corporate bosses needed a mass of middle-ranking employees who could be trusted to work without direct supervision in clerical, sales, bookkeeping, and junior supervisory roles. These employees also had to be divided socially from the lower-level workers whom they supervised. More than obedience and punctuality was required. These employees had to internalize an identification with the employer and the corporation. It was this kind of stratified work force that the mass high schools produced. Schools expanded greatly in size and became bureaucratic, hierarchical, and competitive, ousting the once uniform curriculum of the common schools.

Even within a single school, the social relations of the classroom came to conform to different norms. The vocational and general tracks came to emphasize close supervision and obedience to rules. Such training was consistent with the low-level jobs for which these children were destined. Vocational education in schools served the interest of corporate bosses in breaking the power that skilled workers had formerly wielded through the apprenticeship system. College-track classes came to stress a more open atmosphere emphasizing the internalization

Common schools enforced military discipline and moral education well suited for training a docile and disciplined factory workforce.

of norms. Community colleges allowed for independent activity and limited supervision, preparing students for middle-level corporate occupations where dependability and capacity to operate without direct supervision are required. Near the top of the educational hierarchy, four-year colleges came to emphasize social relations more congruent with higher levels of the corporate hierarchy, where internalization of commitment to the enterprise is demanded (Bowles and Gintis 1976, 131–32).

These differences tend to reflect and reinforce the social background from which the majority of students come. Blacks and other minorities in the United States tend to be concentrated in ghetto schools with often repressive authority structures. Working-class schools generally tend to stress behaviour controls, while suburban schools tend to offer relatively open systems that favour greater student participation, more electives, internalized standards of control, and less direct supervision. Such patterns are not accidental. They reflect the work experiences of parents. Working-class parents tend to favour stricter educational methods, directly reflecting their own knowledge that submission to authority is essential to getting and holding a steady job. Professional and self-employed parents prefer a more open atmosphere with greater emphasis on motivational controls rewarding students for achievements rather than for obedience and good behaviour. Such an atmosphere is more consistent with their parents' position in the labour force.

The progressive education movement justified changes from common schools on the grounds that schools would become more responsive to the diversity of individual and community needs. The result, however, was the reproduction of a stratified labour force suited to the requirements of corporate capitalism.

A third phase in the development of the education system, marked by the expansion

of higher education in the 1960s, coincided with the effective domination of the capitalist economy by corporate and state sectors (Bowles and Gintis 1976, chap. 8). Self-employed entrepreneurs were relegated to increasingly peripheral roles. White-collar and professional employment expanded but became more fragmented and compartmentalized. The expansion of community colleges and diploma courses came in response to this shifting job market, producing what Bowles and Gintis refer to as skilled sub-professional white-collar workers. This category includes lower-level supervisors, secretaries, and paraprofessionals in dentistry, law, teaching, and medicine.

Liberal functionalists would largely agree with such an analysis, but structuralist–Marxist theory goes further to draw attention to the changing social relations of higher education. Bowles and Gintis ask why the stress on free inquiry and liberal arts in higher education gave way to an emphasis on vocationalized and compartmentalized packages of credits. Why did the student politicization of the 1960s occur? Why has there been an overexpansion of graduates? The main answer they give is that free inquiry was appropriate for the entrepreneurial class, but not for corporate employees, except at the highest levels. Student radicals were drawn mostly from members of the declining entrepreneurial class who resented the loss of autonomy over their working lives. Mass higher education produced a surplus army of people with bachelors degrees and sub-professional qualifications, and this served to break their bargaining power in the labour market. Corporations thus gained access to a highly skilled workforce, while salaries and other concessions could be held to a minimum. Corporate profits were protected. The training of elites has now shifted further up into graduate and postgraduate education. Free inquiry tends to be stressed only at this heady level.

The pressure on universities to serve industry has now become more overt. It takes the form of cutbacks in public funding to force these institutions into greater direct co-operation with corporations. The result is that university autonomy is undermined, funding of less marketable liberal arts and humanities programs are threatened, and, even in the favoured science and engineering faculties, pure research is subordinated to short-term profit motives. Bowles and Gintis suggest that community colleges have already largely succumbed to pressure to produce the labour force that corporations want. They offer the veneer of higher education for lower-class students but, in reality, they may be little more than "high schools with ashtrays," channelling students into dead-end vocational programs (Bowles and Gintis 1976, 211).

Educational Reform: The Losing Battle?

These outcomes were not what educational reformers wanted. Leaders in the progressive education movement wanted schools to be integrated into local communities and to have a varied curriculum that was responsive to ethnic and cultural diversity. Instead, elite-dominated local school boards control bureaucratic and centralized urban schools that have internal stratification through the tracking and testing systems. Working-class people pressured for higher education opportunities for their children. They got "high schools with ashtrays."

The source of the problem does not lie with the reform goals themselves but with the character of the capitalist economy to which the schools respond. Reformers are to blame in so far as they focus myopically on schools and fail to direct their criticisms at the wider economy that schools mirror. The ideals of spontaneous and independent learning embodied in free schools were relevant for the children of entrepreneurs, but the competitive world of independent capitalists has given way to corporate capitalism. There can be no turning back. For structuralist–Marxists, true educational reform, designed to promote the full creative potential of all children, cannot be achieved within corporate capitalist society. The economic system that schools serve must change first.

It is for these reasons that Bowles and Gintis challenge the radical educational reform goals of Ivan Illich. Illich (1971) draws attention to much that is wrong with contemporary North American education. He argues that, far from enhancing equality, education only forces children to climb a ladder that has no top. Formerly, completing one's education meant graduating from high school. But once the mass of children attained this level, the concept of completing one's education shifted upwards to mean attaining a bachelor's degree. Now, the top rung is shifting up to completion of a doctoral degree. Those who attain doctorates continue to compete over the number and prestige of their academic publications. Education measures how far one gets before one fails or is rejected. Both professionals within the school system and potential employers tend to define those who drop off from lower rungs of the ladder as deserving to lose. Knowledge is a packaged commodity that becomes the private property of those who attain credentials (Illich 1971). Those who do not have formal credentials are predefined as incompetent. Whatever people might learn outside school is treated as not worth knowing. Schoolwork is taught by certified teachers to students incarcerated in classrooms. Students are cut off from the real world. They learn foreign languages from teaching machines in language laboratories, rather than mixing with children from ethnic minorities. Adults are taught to be impotent, not to touch the new technology, and not to trust their own knowledge and experience. They are taught to rely on experts.

Illich (1971) proposes an alternative system of education in which people recover responsibility for their own teaching and learning. Knowledge, he argues, is not a commodity guardedly dispensed by experts. True knowledge requires facilities and access: the opportunity to watch people at work and to learn through intimate access to those with the knowledge one wishes to acquire. This is very different from incarcerating children in baby-sitting institutions.

Illich cites a number of examples to back up his argument that educating people outside schools is a practical goal. Generally, our peers teach us how to drive cars, and few industrial skills are more complex than this. During wartime, five-year apprenticeships were reduced to three months, during which housewives learned to operate machines. Army paramedics found that simple equipment and basic knowledge are enormously helpful. Ehrenreich and English (1979, chap. 2) document how female lay healers informally handed on their extensive knowledge of herbs and healing techniques. They operated within networks of information-sharing and mutual support. Women who emigrated to North America brought this knowledge with them and adapted it to the new land with the help of native Indian healers who knew the medicinal powers of local plants. Women learned the art of healing from each other by going out together to collect herbs and sharing in their preparation and administration to the sick. It was only when male professionals came to dominate that medical knowledge was hoarded by "experts" as a kind of commodity to be sold in the market. Women's networks of mutual help were destroyed, and medicine was established as the prerogative of a social elite. Ehrenreich and English make it clear that this process of converting medicine into a commodity occurred long before it had a credible scientific base. Illich concludes that modern education serves only to foster dependence on experts with formal credentials, to the exclusion of all other forms and sources of knowledge. It perpetuates class distinctions by treating knowledge as a scarce, private property.

For Bowles and Gintis (1976, 255–62), the problem with Illich is that he fails to direct his critique outward to the economic structures that cause schools to function as they do. Illich's vision of a deschooled society in effect treats the socialization agency of the school as the basic explanatory variable. But dismantling schools will not cure the effects of capitalism. Illich tends to argue that individuals are personally responsible for their own deschooling, but Bowles and Gintis deny this. School is, after all, obligatory for ten years and is the major means of access to a livelihood.

Others emphasize the broader implication of educational reform. The critical approach of Paulo Freire (1970) to education for illiterate adults in the slums of Brazil was avowedly political. His goal was to promote among the poorest slum dwellers an awareness of the exploitative nature of the Brazilian social system and then empower them to fight against it. He was so successful that, after a military coup in Brazil in 1964, he was imprisoned and later exiled.

Freire's critique of schooling focusses directly upon the destructive impact of schools on lower-class children and adults. Students in classrooms are treated as objects rather than as acting subjects. They are containers to be filled by the teacher. The more meekly the receptacles permit themselves to be filled, the better students they are. In this system the teacher teaches and the students are taught; the teacher knows everything and the students know nothing; the teacher thinks and the students are thought about; the teacher talks and students listen; the teacher chooses and enforces the choice and the students comply. In the process, schools perpetuate oppression by reinforcing subordination, passivity, and apathy among students. Teachers are created by and in turn reproduce the **culture of domination**. Students learn to respond with fatalism and docility towards authority and to direct their anger against comrades, rather than against their dominators. Their overwhelming aspiration is to take the place of the dominator and to boss others in their turn.

Freire developed a method of educating illiterate adults, which he called **problem-posing**. The method assumes from the start that adults know a great deal through their own experiences of the world. It tries to build on this knowledge by presenting themes and inviting arguments to foster reflection and dialogue. He gives one example of showing adult literacy students a picture of a drunken man being watched by three youths in the street. Students described the drunk as the only productive, useful person in the picture. They described him as returning after work, with wages so low that he cannot support his family. Affluent middle-class kids jeer at him. The students had recognized themselves in the picture and verbalized the connection between low wages, frustration, exploitation, and drunkenness. The original intention of the teacher had been to show them that drinking is wrong and sets a bad example to young people! The probable response to such a lecture would have been silence and withdrawal.

Freire's objections to oppressive schooling may seem far removed from the everyday experience of Canadian university students used to the more open college-preparatory track of Canadian high schools. But for members of socially disadvantaged groups in ghetto classrooms in Canada, the parallels can be only too glaring. The following section, which focusses on an aspect of Canadian Indian school experience, tries to bring this reality closer to home.

Education for Native Peoples
The traditional education of native children took place through total involvement in community life. Children learned through sharing the lives of adults, through watching, listening, and learning by participation in the domestic, economic, political, and ceremonial life of the community. Formal schooling for Indian children in Canada was first provided by missionaries and later by government schools. Attendance at these schools became compulsory. Children from isolated bands were taken away from their communities and placed in residential schools. The explicit goal of residential schools was **assimilation**, or moulding native children into whites. Native parents had no voice in what was taught. The language of instruction was English or French, and children were commonly punished for using their own language in school. This overtly imperialistic form of schooling was later replaced by smaller schools located within the band communities, particularly for the elementary grades. This shift toward educating Indian students within their home communities was an important change, but much of the hidden curriculum of cultural domination remained intact. The description that follows is drawn from two anthropological studies of schools located within two Kwakiutl Indian villages situated along the northwest coast of British Columbia (Wolcott 1967; Rohner 1967). It is supplemented by an overview of formal education in an American Indian community (Wax, Wax, and Dumont 1964).

The hidden curriculum was manifest in the explicit assumption of many white educators in native schools that only what the schools taught was worth knowing. Wax, Wax, and Dumont (1964, 67) refer to this attitude as the **vacuum ideology**. Teachers emphasized what they saw as the meager experience of Indian children outside school and catalogued their multiple deficiencies relative to white children. The Indian children's home experiences, the stories they heard from their parents, the skills of hunting, fishing, and trapping that they learned

The hidden curriculum of the culture of domination was evident in both residential and reserve schools for native children.

from parents were simply ignored because they fell outside the school curriculum and carried no credentials. Teachers generally knew nothing of native culture, values, or language, and had no respect for them either.

Teachers commonly lamented the overwhelming passivity of native children, but this may well have been a symptom of the dehumanizing character of the schools and the breakdown in communication between teachers and pupils (Wax, Wax, and Dumont 1964, 98–99; Wolcott 1967, 92). The older the children grew, the shyer they seemed to become, so that by the eighth grade they were mute to all interrogation. Upper elementary grades were characterized by silent classrooms, the silence providing a shield behind which an unprepared, unwilling student could retreat. The teachers became

ridiculous, futile figures, and they responded by condescension and dislike toward Indian students. Students reduced to objects within the classroom responded by withdrawal into the **non-listening syndrome** (Wax, Wax, and Dumont 1964, 99). Attendance was haphazard. Students would arrive late for school and would drift home at midday, start some task, and not return. They refused any active participation in classroom work. They expected boredom and even asked for highly repetitive work like copying. They had learned to equate the classroom with endless repetition, and they reacted against any variation in routines attempted by a new teacher. Their typical response was, "We didn't come to school for this, we came to do our schoolwork" (Wolcott 1967, 100).

This overt passivity within the classroom was combined with covert, horizontal violence against each other, which Freire observed among the oppressed people in Brazil (Wolcott 1967, 93). Younger children complained of being mercilessly teased, tortured, and bullied by classmates, behind the teacher's back. Some children absented themselves for days in fear. The only advice their mothers could give was to keep out of the way of the bigger children and not provoke them.

The school curriculum seemed irrelevant to the lives of adolescents on the reserves. Not only did it do nothing to prepare them for future jobs in their village, it actually conflicted with their informal education gained through participating in adult activities. Pupils resented attending school when they could otherwise be doing vital things like helping their fathers with fishing and clam digging.

The quality of academic performance in these reservation schools, measured in terms of universalistic grade standards, was abysmal (Wolcott 1967, 111; Rohner 1967, 110). The teachers, trained to respond to universalistic standards, found it almost impossible to adjust. When they administered normal intelligence tests, the native students performed at near idiocy level. It was a hard shock for teachers, despite their knowledge that such tests are culturally biased. Teacher attitudes generally were highly unfavorable toward native people. The village school studied by Rohner (1967, 105) had a turnover of eight teachers in fourteen years. Four of the eight had generated great hostility within the village. One had become so afraid of villagers that he had nailed up all the windows of his home and had refused to let his children play in the village. Another was so hated by the native people that the superintendent had to remove him. Parents were equally intimidated by the teachers and were reduced to silence whenever they attended parent-teacher meetings. They asked only that the school open every day, start on time, and keep the pupils busy.

Discipline problems were to be resolved by the teacher (Wolcott 1967, 86).

Given these kinds of school experiences, it would be miraculous if more than a small minority of native pupils made it through to high-school graduation. Stucturalist-Marxists would argue that they were being educated for failure. The oppressive school system defined all aspects of native culture and traditional knowledge as irrelevant. It judged the students by white cultural standards and found them so ignorant that they were ranked as borderline mental defectives. Pupils learned to expect nothing but boredom and endless repetition in school, an expectation that exactly fits the menial, low-paying jobs that native adults commonly attain in white capitalist society.

Table 13-1 shows that, between 1975–76 and 1988–89, the proportion of native students enrolled in community colleges or

Table 13-1 Native Indian Post-secondary Enrolment, 1975–76 to 1988–89*

Year	Percent
1975–76	0.88
1976–77	0.93
1977–78	1.22
1978–79	1.37
1979–80	1.45
1980–81	1.58
1981–82	1.69
1982–83	2.05
1983–84	2.36
1984–85	2.47
1985–86	3.10
1986–87	3.40
1987–88	3.42
1988–89	3.40

* Combined university and community colleges; full- and part-time; all age groups.

Source: Canada House of Commons. 1989. Based on numbers of Indian students funded under DIAND's postsecondary education program divided by the Indian population as recorded in the Indian registry under the Indian Act.

universities has been creeping up from a low of less than 1 percent to a high of 3.4 percent. This is still far below the proportions for the general population of Canada. The major problem with these data is that they cannot be directly compared with enrolment patterns for Canadians as a whole. Statistics Canada calculates enrolments as a proportion of relevant age groups rather than for the total population. Calculations suggest that approximately 1.6 percent of status Indians (6500 from a total native population of 400 000) were enrolled in university during 1987–88, compared with a national average of about 3 percent.

Notwithstanding the underrepresentation of native students, the federal government announced, in May 1987, its intention to cap the funding available to support status Indians in higher education. This proposal was re-drafted for implementation in April 1989. Aboriginal treaties guarantee free public education to native peoples as part of the agreement for the transfer of Indian lands, but the government claims that this right does not extend to education beyond high school. Such funding, it declared, was a matter of social policy, not legal obligation. Indian leaders and students protested the policy changes throughout the summer of 1989 but won only limited concessions.

As of October 1989, the policies under what is now the Postsecondary Student Assistance Program were still in a state of flux (King 1989). The main principle of the policy proposal still stands, namely to impose a cap on existing funds and to limit the number of months that individual students can receive assistance for given programs. Important interim changes included removing the selection criteria for allocating funds and leaving this to the discretion of the administering organization, either the department itself or the tribal councils. Funding to cover costs of travel to distant universities, and for child care expenses for single-parents and families where both

parents are students, was returned to former levels. The latter provision is especially important in that native students generally tend to be older and are more likely to be supporting children at the same time that they are trying to further their education.

The problem, however, is that the total funding remains capped. Hence bands must choose how to allocate limited funds. Do they help one student with child care costs or support an additional student at university? Do they support several students attending a local community college or meet the higher expenses of one student attending a university many miles from home? The policy allows no appeal mechanism for students who are refused support due to lack of regional funds. The possibility remains open that a separate forum might be set up to debate the contentious question of treaty rights and postsecondary education.

Critics of the cuts argue that restricting funds for higher education is the worst possible form of economizing. Higher education offers one of the few avenues for native people to break out of the welfare trap. Native students are also concerned that special incentive grants and strategic scholarships offered as part of the policy changes direct Indian students into such specialities as commerce, administration, and sciences, but away from law, education, social work, native studies, social sciences, and humanities. Students argue that these latter subjects are as important to native peoples as specialities geared to business and to the exploitation of natural resources.

The problem of capped funding is compounded by the numbers of women who regained their aboriginal status under Bill C-31, passed in 1985. These women had lost their native status by marrying non-status men. Only native men could confer their status on their non-native wives. These reinstated women and their children are eligible for assistance for postsecondary education. But funding for them now directly cuts into limited funding available for other status Indians. Bill C-31 students are ranked lowest of eligible applicants designated under the program. They are the most likely to be cut off if regional funding runs out. The program thus works in an insidious way to divide native peoples while the government continues to hold power.

The Structuralist–Marxist Thesis Reconsidered

The structuralist–Marxist thesis continues to exert a powerful influence over educational theory and research. But since the early 1980s dissatisfaction with the thesis has been growing. Critics argue that aspects of its theory and substantive claims are seriously flawed. Some of this criticism stems from an alternative approach within Marxism, which is sometimes referred to as **cultural Marxism**. This perspective is closely linked in practice with the social construction of reality theory. These approaches challenge structuralist Marxism for being too rigid and deterministic to provide an adequate explanation of the social processes involved in education.

Bowles and Gintis ground much of their thesis on evidence of a historical correspondence between the development of public education and phases in the development of capitalism. In particular, they claim that common schools arose with the expansion of large-scale factory production and the need for a disciplined factory labour force. Several critics dispute this historical concurrence. MacDonald (1988) meticulously analyses the period associated with the expansion of factories in Ontario. He dates this expansion from around 1880, nearly twenty-five years after the development of common schools.

Curtis (1987) notes a similar discrepancy. The Ontario School Act of 1843 actually preceded the expansion of capitalist industrialization in Upper Canada and came well before the Irish famine migration produced the first substantial proletariat in Canadian towns. Curtis argues that the rebellions in Upper Canada in 1837–38 were the primary factor motivating the colonial administration to establish common schools. The objective was to promote a sense of political commitment and duty toward the state. Egerton Ryerson, who was responsible for developing the common school curriculum, avowed that the goal of school reform was to generate self-regulating citizens instilled with affection for the system that controlled them and for the values of patriotism and Christianity. In effect, the objective was to construct citizens for the centralized Canadian state (Curtis 1987, 61). Ryerson adamantly opposed rote learning and physical punishment in favour of a curriculum stressing a humanistic education that would develop moral behaviour and feeling. Ideally, students would behave well, not out of fear or coercion, but because school was intrinsically pleasing to them. Schools would thus create a civil society that would be relatively easy to govern through people's own loyalty to and affection for the apparatus of the state (Curtis 1987, 59).

Egerton Ryerson was responsible for the development of the common school's curriculum in Upper Canada in the mid-nineteenth century.

This thesis does not entirely contradict Bowles and Gintis. The emerging Canadian state was a capitalist state and hence had objectives that were closely compatible with those of the business class. But this is not the same as claiming that state and business interests are identical or that business interests dictate the state school curriculum. It suggests that the school system has a considerable degree of autonomy from the demands of capitalism, an autonomy that structuralist–Marxist theory does not take into account.

A related criticism against structural Marxism is that its exclusive focus on economic relations omits too much. It fails to consider the role of schools in the reproduction of other social relations, including relations of gender, ethnicity, and race (Apple 1988, 117; Moore 1988, 61). The often sexist and racist character of standard school texts is an important element in the reproduction of these social relations. In their own defence, Bowles and Gintis (1988, 236) argue that they did not intend to ignore issues of gender and race, so much as accord causal primacy to class relations. But this assumption of causal primacy needs to be tested: it cannot simply be assumed.

Contemporary critics from within the structuralist–Marxist framework challenge the overly simplistic analysis of the needs of advanced capitalism. Automation and the systematic deskilling of the workforce have played an important role in increasing profits to capitalists in mass-production industries. But, as we noted in the chapter on stratification, Braverman's thesis, on which Bowles and Gintis rely, is seriously flawed when it is applied too broadly to developing industries in the fields of communications and electronics. These industries need a highly skilled workforce capable of generating rapid product innovation (Morgan and Sayer 1988, 26). The expansion of higher education since the 1960s, and the funds that capitalists have donated to certain univer-

sity faculties, cannot be totally dismissed as credentialism. Authoritarian classrooms and standarized curriculum packages are not functional for the production of creative, innovative workers.

The major criticism against stucturalist Marxism, however, goes beyond questions of substantive details or omissions. It questions the conceptual foundation of the approach itself. The central explanatory force in the theoretical model developed by Bowles and Gintis is economic determinism. Schools function to reproduce the social relations of capitalist production. All elements of the school system are explained in terms of their functional utility for the capitalist system (Aronowitz and Giroux 1985, 71, 117; Cole 1988, 7–37; Moore 1988, 58-61; Apple 1988, 124). Ironically, an approach that began as a radical critique of traditional functionalism depends in practice on the same explanatory logic. The structure of parts are explained by their functions for the social system as a whole. The difference is that, in Marxist theory, the system is specifically capitalist. The explanation invokes rigid historical **reductionism**. All changes in the school system since its inception in the 1840s are explained as responses to the needs of capitalism.

The problem with this form of explanation is that it presupposes a passive view of humanity. Human agency plays little part in the analysis. Teachers and students are reduced to mere pawns of the capitalist system (Aronowitz and Giroux 1985, 71). According to structuralist Marxists, schools legitimate inequality and limit personal development to forms compatible with submission to arbitrary authority and aid in the process whereby youths are resigned to their fate (Bowles and Gintis 1976, 266; Coles 1988, 35). There is minimal room for human agency in such a conception of schooling.

Critics point out that, despite the radical Marxist commitment of Bowles and Gintis, the outcome of their theory is politically

reactionary. It supports the status quo in that it leaves no space for individual or collective action to change the situation. The only viable option seems to be resignation or radical pessimism (Aronowitz and Giroux 1985, 79; Cole 1988, 35). More significantly, this ostensibly Marxist argument has been appropriated by spokespeople for the right wing in the United States. Conservatives are in full agreement with the view of Bowles and Gintis that schools are an adjunct to the labour market. They complain only that schools do not do this preparatory work well enough. The left wing seems to have no alternative to offer and therefore seems constrained to silence (Aronowitz and Giroux 1985, 5–6). Aronowitz and Giroux (1985, 128) suggest that, despite their diametrically opposing political values, the philosophies of structuralist Marxism and capitalism share an uncritical acceptance of **scientism**: a reliance on simple cause and effect explanatory models that tend to reduce people to objects at the mercy of structural economic forces.

In this critique, we have referred to structuralist Marxism rather than Marxist theory in general, because there are important developments within contemporary Marxist theory that retain a radical critical perspective while rejecting the deterministic aspects of structuralism. This more flexible cultural Marxism focusses on what people actually do in their immediate material situation and how they come to make sense of their experience. This perspective shifts the focus of research from macrostudies of capitalism to the actual processes of schooling as they are produced by teachers and students as participants in the everyday interaction within the classroom.

With their excessive focus on the macrostructures of capitalism, Bowles and Gintis convey the impression that abstract forces of history produce class relations within the school and the economy. We gain little insight into the actual processes involved.

How is it that capitalists are somehow able to dictate how people should relate to each other within classrooms? How do administrators, teachers, and students make sense of what is happening? How do they respond to such pressures? Why do they put up with them? When and how do they resist? These kinds of questions prompt a very different kind of research from that prevailing in either functionalist or structuralist–Marxist approaches. Rather than mass surveys or sweeping historical overviews, cultural Marxism and the social construction of reality perspective favour research into the intimate details of interpersonal relations within classrooms. It is these relations that we explore below.

The Social Construction of Schooling

Proponents of the social construction of reality do not view classrooms as the effects of social structures. Classrooms are the location within which what we subsequently recognize as social structures of class, gender, or race are produced. The causal processes involved are the meaningful interactions between people in intimate everyday activities. Numerous studies of classrooms are beginning to piece together the mechanisms that produce what Bowles and Gintis identify as the social relations of capitalism.

The Classroom Experience for Students

A classic in this research is the study by Jean Anyon (1980) into how social studies and language arts were taught in five elementary schools located in different communities in the eastern United States. The research describes marked variation in patterns of classroom interaction by the social class background of those attending school. Instruction in the elite school for the children of executives emphasized the development of analytical reasoning and leadership skills. Lessons were creative. Students made presentations to the class and criticized each other's work. In the middle-class school, lessons were very different. Language arts, for example, was reduced to grammar. Teachers checked for right answers rather than for critical understanding of the question. In lower-class schools, children seemed to be taught primarily to follow rules set out by the teacher for completing the exercise. Their work was evaluated not by whether the answers were right, but whether the rules had been followed.

Feminist research is beginning to reveal the mechanisms through which the lower educational aspirations of girls are socially produced within the school system. Russell (1987) cites examples to show how school teachers and counsellors actively and intentionally perpetuate class and sex differences. High-achieving working-class boys are far more likely to be encouraged to join the army or some technical trade than to go to university, because counsellors feel they would be more comfortable with such a class-consistent choice. High-achieving girls are more often counselled into "women's work," such as social work, teaching, and secretarial positions, than into male-dominated, well-paying business and professional positions.

Interaction in the classroom reinforces these messages. Observation sessions in grade 12 classes revealed that teachers directed from one-and-one-half to five times as many questions to boys as to girls. Girls dominated verbal interaction with the teacher in only 7 percent of the classes, while boys dominated in about 63 percent. During the interviews, women teachers spent much more time talking about the behaviour of boys than girls. They found boys more fun and more of a challenge than girls. These schools, in effect, function to perpetuate inequalities on the basis of sex and class of origin, but in such a way that the end result can be justified as merited.

These studies complement other research into how poverty influences the learning experiences of children. Early work on this broad topic tended to stress material deprivation. A study by the National Council of Welfare (1975) documents that poor children are more likely than others to be born premature and underweight, to contract childhood diseases, and to miss one to three months of school in a year because of illness. In 1988 the Vancouver School Board felt compelled to set up a welfare system for hungry school children. With the aid of principals, teachers, and volunteers, the board began feeding some 600 children in 23 schools who appeared to be regularly coming to school without either an adequate breakfast or lunch. The premier of the province, William Vander Zalm, refused to provide even a matching grant to the amount raised by the school board to help subsidize the program. He argued that children who go to school hungry have parents who do not love them enough (*Globe and Mail*, 14 April 1988, A4; 13 May 1988, A5). There were further reports of parents warning their children not to accept the free lunches, even if they were hungry. Vander Zalm had indicated that he would instruct social workers to investigate the family of any child accepting free food, with a view to having the children removed from their parents and put into care.

A municipal inquiry into hunger in Regina, completed in October 1989, reported similar evidence of hungry children in school (*Globe and Mail*, 9 Oct. 1989, A5). In 1987, the Catholic Church began to finance a soup kitchen for children in response to pleas from teachers who said that their pupils were too hungry to be able to learn. By October 1989, the centre was routinely feeding 100 children a day, 60 percent of them natives. Children commonly beg the workers at the centre for extra sandwiches to take home for sisters and brothers. The report on hunger notes that the problem has worsened since 1976 as the economy of Saskatchewan has weakened. Many of the adults surveyed routinely went without food for up to ten days a month.

The report concludes that the indisputable cause of hunger is poverty, "not waste, not laziness, not mismanagement, not bingo, and not neglect, as the stereotypes would have it." The report says that welfare rates and jobs that pay the minimum wage do not provide enough money for nutritious food. "All the best budgeting techniques in the world and all the lessons on nutrition in the world simply won't stretch these inadequate dollars far enough." The report recommends an immediate increase in provincial welfare rates and the minimum wage level. It also stresses the need for transportation allowances and bus tickets for welfare recipients. Many of the desperately poor families cannot even reach the food banks or soup kitchens because they do not have the money for bus fare.

The social effect of poverty on children, and their isolation from others in the classroom, may be less visible than inadequate clothing and ill health, but they are equally damaging to the children's educational aspirations and sense of well-being. Poor children face the humiliation of not being able to bring in money for special school events or excursions. They cannot afford to buy art supplies, sports equipment or uniforms, or instruments for the school band, and so they cannot join in many of the extracurricular activities open to other children. The list of barriers goes on and on (Gabriel 1986). Humiliation fosters withdrawal, defeat, and resentment. It drains them of the motivation to give their best efforts. Poor children lack money for school books and basic supplies, which makes it hard for them to keep up with homework. Cutbacks in school budgets often mean that teachers cannot provide books for all students and cannot permit them to take books home because they must be stored away and used in other classes. Poor children are also more likely to live in inadequate and overcrowded homes where they may have no quiet place to study. Teachers used to be able to supervise quiet study periods after school hours, but with budget and staff cutbacks, such "frills" are eliminated.

Poor children in senior classes may lack the time and energy for schoolwork because they take long hours of employment at minimum wage. If school counsellors suggest they would be better off quitting school to join the army or take a typing job, they are likely to agree. Realistically they see little possibility of mobility into professional occupations when all the people around them only have low-paying semiskilled jobs. **Headstart programs** for children in deprived areas may end up only making things worse because they raise unrealistic expectations, resulting in bitter disappointment for adolescents faced with limited opportunities.

The Social Construction of Teaching

In the above studies, the primary focus is on how teachers construct the social relations of the classroom vis-à-vis the students. Michael Apple's (1986) extensive work on classroom politics shifts the focus to the social relations within which the everyday working lives of teachers are embedded. Apple draws attention to the inherently patriarchal character of the social relations of teaching. The majority of primary school teachers are women and the majority of principals and administrators are men. These men routinely exercise decision-making and disciplinary authority over the work of teachers. School administrators often intervene in the classroom work of teachers in the name of technical efficiency. Teachers are increasingly under pressure to use curriculum packages, with heavy emphasis on the preparation of worksheets and the standardized testing and evaluation of students.

One effect of such packaged teaching, Apple suggests (1986, chap. 2), is to deskill teachers, reducing them to technicians rather than professionals who control their own activities.

Concern with the structuring of the curriculum prompts Apple to look beyond the classroom to the social construction of textbooks. Publishing companies exercise significant control over the content of the texts that are made available to teachers. Acquisitions editors and decision makers in these companies are mostly males with a background in marketing. They focus principally on what they think will sell. The goal is to produce texts with standard content that will be used for years in multiple schools. Apple (1986, chap. 4) stresses the urgent need for detailed research into the routine daily work processes and the politics of publishing companies through which the social construction of textbooks is accomplished.

Apple fears that the growing emphasis upon teaching computer literacy in schools will exacerbate the trend toward standardization and depersonalization of classrooms. Computer manufacturers foist machines onto schools, even offering a free machine for every classroom, in the hope that parents will be motivated to buy school-compatible models for their children to practise on at home. Computers come with standard software packages for classroom instruction. Rarely do these programs incorporate the richness of the professional experience of teachers. Nor do they include the "soft" curriculum of liberal arts. Humanities, ethnic studies, culture, history, politics are all likely to lose out to the mathematical and technical subjects that are readily adaptable to computers. Human interaction in the classrooms declines. Teachers find themselves reduced to technicians running programs. The influx of computers also seems likely to exacerbate class differences between schools. Rich schools can afford multiple machines for personal instruction, and

wealthy parents are able to buy computers for home use. Poorly endowed schools and poorer students are not able to have these advantages. Apple argues too that elite children are more likely to learn the intellectually stimulating aspects of programming, while lower-class children are trained to use computers for drill and practice sessions. The overall result of such curriculum changes, Apple suggests (1986, 142), will be the steady "masculinization" of education; that is, an emphasis on technique and rationality as opposed to concern for human relations, connectedness, and caring, which he sees as feminine values.

Cutbacks in government funding for schools influence the social relations of schooling for teachers no less than for the children from poor families. Dorothy Smith and the Wollestonecraft Research Group (1979) document how cutbacks in school funding affect the everyday work of teachers and produce the classroom rigidities for which teachers are subsequently held responsible. When there is not enough science equipment for all pupils to conduct their own experiments, teachers have to demonstrate the experiments while pupils watch passively. Larger classrooms mean that small-group work and seminars become less and less possible. Children who receive less hands-on experience and less attention get bored and distracted, discipline problems increase, and authoritarianism increases. Teachers do not have time to go through batches of essays or independent projects, so they assign fewer of them and rely more on uniform examinations. Teachers give more and more of their personal time to make up the shortfall in staffing until they burn out and leave the profession or become resigned to lower standards and autocratic methods. The schooling patterns criticized by Bowles and Gintis then take shape. The manifest function of budget cutbacks is simply to save taxpayer's money. The effect is increasingly authoritarian and rigid classrooms.

Proponents of the social construction of reality recognize the striking contrast between the creative teaching in schools for elite children and the uninspired, autocratic styles of teaching in lower-class schools. They argue that this contrast may well have more to do with teachers trying to cope with large classes and minimal teaching aids in lower-class schools than with any deliberate intention by such teachers to reproduce relations of class.

The processes of standardization and control over teaching have now shifted to higher education. In community colleges in particular, overt constraints are placed on teaching in the interest of serving business. Muller (1989) documents how any new programs introduced in community colleges in British Columbia are constrained to conform to local business interests. Standardized forms and procedures govern how new programs are to be presented to the provincial government. These forms require the signatures of relevant employers in the locality of the college, who might be expected to hire students graduating from such programs, to indicate that they have been consulted and have given their approval. Community college management standardizes the curriculum so it is no longer the prerogative of individual instructors. It is even possible for a student to take an instructor to court for breach of contract if the published course curriculum does not appear to have been strictly followed. Student services staff are explicitly directed to guide students towards training for which there are immediate jobs in the local market (Muller 1990). Instructors are also required by college management to keep up with any and all technological innovations, such as computer-designed instruction, that industry wants. Muller concludes that community college management, in effect, works for local industry, while being financed by the state.

Standardized teaching practices are also becoming the norm in undergraduate university programs, although overt controls are less in evidence. Increasing enrolments in the face of limited budgets mean huge lecture halls, oppressive one-way teaching techniques, programmed assignments, and a reduction in individual projects. Students in lower-level sociology and psychology courses are more likely to be tested by multiple-choice examinations, marked by computers, which require rigid conformity to pre-programmed textbook answers. Fighting such trends requires tremendous effort on the part of professors who have to mark several hundred individual essays. Creative undergraduate research becomes progressively less possible as classes of a hundred or more students descend on libraries that can only afford one copy of each book and that have cut journal subscriptions to save money and space. These are the ways in which the social reality of undergraduate education for middle-level corporate conformity is socially constructed.

Reaction and Resistance

Neither teachers nor students are passive objects of pressures to standardize and restrict the social relations of the classroom. They are active participants in shaping their social world. Apple (1986, 48–53) notes the variety of responses by teachers to the introduction of computers and new curricular packages. Some enthusiastically endorse new techniques as symbols of their own expertise in and professional mastery of new technology. Others comply passively with minimum requirements. Still others respond with critical opposition and covert efforts to sabotage the new techniques. Historically, teachers have been active in professional associations that have fought for better working conditions and equitable salaries, for a greater say in what and how teachers teach and who evaluates them, and for control at the level of classroom practice (Apple 1986, 75). Individual teachers, struggling to inspire their pupils in classrooms, usually do not feel that they are functioning to preserve the hierarchical social order. For the best teachers, the opposite is closer to the truth, as they fight to break the hold of inherited disadvantages and push their students to develop inquiring minds and to go on to academic careers. They cannot be seen simply as cogs in the capitalist machine.

Students too are active in shaping the social relations of the classroom. Studies of working-class children are beginning to uncover the ways in which they actively participate in shaping class and gender relations. McRobbie (1978) shows how girls from a lower-class district in England actively resist the efforts of teachers to interest them in school work. When asked what they do during math lessons, they give such answers as "carve boys' names on my desk," "comb my hair under the lid of the desk," "put makeup on, or look in my mirror." Parents and teachers try to encourage them to study more to get a good job, but the girls' own immediate experience of the types of jobs open to women like them does little to induce them to focus on schoolwork. They know that their chance for a decent home and money to support their children depends primarily upon the superior wages of a man. Hence, from as young as thirteen and fourteen years, their preoccupation is with boyfriends and going steady. Success in the classroom consists of asserting their "femaleness" and spending vast amounts of time discussing boyfriends in loud voices that disrupt the class.

This is irrational behaviour from the perspective of the teachers who, at least initially in their careers, are committed to trying to break this pattern and open new options for the girls. But it is fully rational from the perspective of the working-class girls themselves in the face of their expectations for their own future. Actually, it may be the teachers who are being unrealistic and irrational in assuming that they can somehow change the life options for more

than a tiny minority of these girls. It is little wonder that many teachers become more realistic with experience and opt for a more class-biased curriculum to which the girls will respond. In a sense, schools fail the girls but, in another sense, girls fail the schools. The process of class and gender formation is thus mutually constructed within the everyday struggles of the classroom.

It is not only working-class girls who rebel. Willis (1978) documents how "the lads" in working-class schools in Britain also actively resist the efforts of teachers. Their anti-school culture stresses machismo, size, physical strength, and ability to handle oneself. These values mirror the factory-floor culture of working-class men. This culture is both sexist and racist. For these working-class boys, being male means treating women as sex objects and expressing derogatory views of others. Such views are used to justify intimidation of or attacks on Asian and West Indian pupils. The boys' culture is not simply hostile to school per se, but also to women and to ethnic minority groups. Schools participate in the social construction of class, gender, and race relations to the extent that they fail to break this counterculture. The boys' resistance to school turns them into manual labourers. When Bowles and Gintis blame schools for reproducing the class relations of capitalism, they may be attacking the wrong target, blaming teachers for reproducing a culture that they are vainly trying to break.

Limitations in the Social Constructionist Approach

These detailed studies of classroom interaction have brought us closer to understanding the processes through which individuals actively construct their social world. But there remain important flaws or blind spots in the approach. Aronowitz and Giroux (1985) raise three problems that they feel weaken its critical impact.

The first weakness is that the social constructionist approach remains too closely tied to its structuralist–Marxist roots. The dualism of human agency and social structure has not been overcome and, in any struggle between them, structure seems to win. It is only too easy to slip back into the view of teachers and students as victims of the workings of capitalism. Marxists define power in negative terms. They use the word to refer to domination from the top down, with the interests of capitalism commanding the pinnacle. The processes of domination flow downwards from the demands of the market, through the managers of publishing houses and the corporations that produce computers, to school administrators, and onto teachers, with students at the bottom. Social constructionists generally ignore the power of knowledge and the capacity for critical reflection that might emancipate people.

A second, closely related flaw is the conceptual vagueness of the term *resistance*. Almost any kind of reaction to the classroom experience tends to be labelled resistance. Aronowitz and Giroux (1985, 98–104) challenge the value of applying this label to the rejection of schooling by the working-class girls and boys described by McRobbie and Willis. They argue that, in reality, such reactions constitute a slavish copying of the worst aspects of sexism and classism within capitalism. Such withdrawal or dropping out from school is ultimately self-destructive, condemning children to powerlessness in their adult lives. Social constructionism does not consider the possibility that the true rebels may be those working-class children who succeed in school and resist the sexist and classist cultural values that trap others in the social relations of capitalism.

There is actually very little difference between the theoretical approaches of Willis and McRobbie and the classical functionalism of Talcott Parsons. In both cases, people appear as products of their socialization.

True resistance, suggest Aronowitz and Giroux, involves a dialectical process; that is, a process that entails the development of a critical alternative to the status quo and the empowerment of people to struggle toward it.

Aronowitz and Giroux point out that, while the factory-floor culture of Willis's "lads" might once have provided a viable alternative value system to school culture, with an affirmation of manual strength and skills over book-learning, it is rapidly becoming obsolete. The efficacy of this counterculture has been seriously weakened since the mid-1960s by the widespread closure of mass-production factories and the replacement of manual-labouring jobs by machines. Schools have become essential for entry into the labour market on favourable terms. Very high divorce rates, which result in many women raising children alone, and the practical necessity of two-incomes to maintain a reasonable good standard of living, may have rendered the sexist counterculture of working-class girls similarly obsolete.

A third flaw in the social constructionist approach is its tendency to ignore the role of teachers as intellectuals who are actively involved in the creation of what constitutes education (Aronowitz and Giroux 1985, chap. 2). Anyon and Apple come close to this recognition, but both of them slip back into the analysis of teachers as products of their objective structural situation. The irony is that radical thinkers in the cultural Marxist tradition and conservatives who support New Right politics tend to lament that schools are not producing creative, innovative thinkers. Marxists fear that scientific-technical rationality associated with the business of making profits has become so pervasive in western culture that the mass of people have become incapable of thinking any other way. They all parrot the same one-dimensional thought (Marcuse 1964). The very capacity for conceptual thought itself seems to be in jeopardy. Conservatives, on the other hand, fear the North American industry is in crisis because schools are not producing a creative, innovative labour force capable of beating world competition in the race for product innovation.

Both sides in this debate ignore teachers as intellectuals. Teachers are blamed for not producing creative thinkers while they are themselves conceptualized as merely technicians who deliver standard curriculum packages. Aronowitz and Giroux (1985, 167) accuse Marxist theorists of being as bad as capitalists in thinking of people as objects. The thesis that people are reduced to one-dimensional thought by scientific-technical society is conceptually no different from Parsons' view of people as products of their socialization.

Radical Curriculum Theory

One way out of this impasse, suggest Aronowitz and Giroux (1985, chap. 7) is to recognize the repressive as well as the liberating and empowering potential of education. **Radical curriculum** theory must incorporate a language of possibility and not merely a language of criticism. Power cannot be viewed as simply domination from the top. The notion needs to be expanded to include empowerment, with people's capacity to gain power through critical reflection a central element. Structures reflect *meaning*, or the prevailing ways in which we come to understand how societies work. From this, it follows that countercultures, alternative ways of making sense of that reality, can have a radically transforming impact. Resistance to domination involves questioning prevailing ways of thinking and proposing alternatives. Teachers have a potentially critical role in these processes of empowerment and resistance. They are not merely technicians or agents of the state who impose the dominant ideology. They also have the potential to teach their students the capacity for **critical literacy**, a capacity to think and to question what they read, see, and hear. C. Wright Mills (1959) noted this goal in his essay on the promise of sociology. For him the objective of sociology is not to impart more information or facts, but to enhance understanding, or the ability to make sense of this experience.

Feminist Theory as Radical Curriculum: A Language of Possibility

The radicalizing potential of education is a central tenet of feminist theory. Charlotte Bunch (1983) describes how she left university teaching to work full-time in the women's movement but later returned to university because she had become convinced that the development of feminist theory is essential to political action. Theory is not just a body of facts and opinions. It involves the development of explanations that can guide actions.

Bunch proposes a four-part model of theory. The first part is *description*. Changing people's perceptions of the world through new descriptions of reality is usually a prerequisite for changing that reality. In the 1960s, few people would have thought of American women as oppressed, but now the injustices and oppression experienced by women are widely recognized. Feminist work, which described that oppression in a number of different ways, played a critical role in making it visible. The second element of theory is *analysis*. Analysis involves trying to understand why the reality described in feminist work exists and what perpetuates it. The third element is *vision*. The work of envisioning what should exist involves examining our basic assumptions about human nature and relationships. The fourth element of theory is *strategy*. Theoretical understanding of how social relations work is essential to planning ways of changing those relations. Teaching feminist theory thus involves teaching the basic skills of critical literacy—how to read, analyse, and think about ideas—and challenging students to develop their own ideas and to analyse the assumptions behind their actions.

As radical pedagogy, feminism is potentially an agent of change through the process, as well as through the content, of teaching. Feminists widely acknowledge the oppressive hidden curriculum of packaged knowledge and hierarchical instruction that silences children in many classrooms, especially children whose life experiences do not fit the received knowledge.

Belenkey et al. (1986, 4) begin their study of *Women's Ways of Knowing* by asking why it is that women students so often doubt their intellectual competence and feel alienated from formal learning. They suggest that women develop a capacity to learn in spite of rather than because of standard academic instruction that focusses on procedural knowledge and winning arguments. They suggest that women have different educational needs from men. They need "connected teaching"(Belenkey et al. 1986, chap. 10) that emphasizes creative reflection on personal experience and confirms not merely that women can learn, but that they already know something through personal experience. Women need encouragement to find their own authentic voice. They need a combination of freedom and support to enable them to make their own decisions on curriculum. They need to see that theories and models are not divine truths handed down from authority figures, but products of human minds. They need to be made aware that, until recently, most of these minds were male. They need to see that theorizing involves a two-way process of critical reflection between teacher and learner in which they are themselves active creators of knowledge.

These ideas closely parallel the problem-posing approach developed by Freire in his *Pedagogy of the Oppressed* (1970). This similarity suggests that the vision of a non-hierarchical and self-confirming pedagogy is not uniquely appropriate for women but is valuable for all students whose subordinate position in society discourages a sense of competence and mastery in their early lives. Bunch (1983, 258) describes a practical example of problem-posing teaching that has worked successfully with students in her university courses in women's studies. She asks her students to read several articles from feminist and non-feminist magazines, and then encourages them to debate a four-part question: What is the articles's view of reality for women? What does it imply about how, why, or whether that reality needs to change? What are its approaches to those changes? What values does it espouse?

Feminist Teaching and Resistance

Reactions to those teaching feminist theory reveal the contradictory nature of resistance in the classroom. Feminist theory teachers find that, far from resisting the imposition of dominant cultural ideology, students and colleagues often fiercely defend the dominant culture against its critics.

Commonly, feminist work is not taken seriously. Women's studies programs in universities tend to be seen as frills. They are given second-rate status and are generally underfinanced. Even where women's studies exists as a defined part of the curriculum, students aspiring to professional and corporate careers are discouraged from taking such courses. Feminist research falls low on the totem pole in applications for limited grant money. Women professors in general, and feminist professors in particular, are far outnumbered by males, especially at senior and administrative levels where decisions on hiring and funding are made. A recent study at the University of Waterloo concludes that sexual discrimination permeates every corner of life at Canadian universities. It documents widespread use of course materials that include stereotyped views of women, textbook anthologies of literature that contain no writings by women scholars, sexist jokes by professors in classrooms, sexist graffiti, and no fewer than 235 complaints of sexual harassment during the 1985–86 academic year on ten Ontario campuses (*Globe and Mail*, 11 May 1988, A10).

A study by Hall and Sandler (1984) suggests that female students generally face a "chilly campus climate" that is not conducive to learning. This is especially so for women who enrol in the traditional male bastions of physical sciences and engineering faculties. Women students tend to receive less attention and less feedback than male students from the predominantly male faculty. They are more likely to experience disparaging comments about their work or their commitment to studies, or comments that focus on their appearance rather than their performance. They are likely to be counseled into lower career goals than men. As graduates, they are less likely to be included as co-researchers with faculty in academic publications. Women who interrupt their studies, or attend part-time while raising children, tend not to be taken seriously.

Males tend to dominate classroom and seminar discussions. Male styles of communication tend to be highly assertive, combined with physical gestures that express ease, dominance and control. They are more likely to interrupt other speakers and to control the topic of coversation. In laboratory classes, female students routinely complain that men take control over the equipment, relegating female students to note-takers. Females tend to be more personal in their communications, offering more self-disclosure rather than impersonal and abstract styles of speech. This style tends to be disparaged as less intelligent. Women are more reticent in taking over conversations and tend to encourage other speakers. They often feel that they are imposing on advisors rather than that they have a right to ask questions.

The social atmosphere of universities tends to make campuses feel "like male turf." Athletic activities by women tend to get less support and attention than do male sports teams. Women are demeaned when campus organizations screen pornographic movies as fundraisers and when student newspapers publish sexist articles and advertisements.

Women who live in residence face petty hostilities from men under the guise of "fun." At Wilfrid Laurier University, such hostility is evident in a twenty-year tradition of panty raids that were sanctioned by the university administration and organized by residence dons. In September 1989, after one such raid, women's panties were put up on posters in the cafeteria, daubed with ketchup and other substances to represent blood and feces. Crude drawings of female genitalia were emblazoned with obscenities and captions such as "Do you take Visa?" When graduate social work students and faculty started to remove the posters, some students called them "Nazis" or "lesbian radical bitches" and threw garbage at them (*Toronto Star*, 25 Oct. 1989, A1 and 28).

Such behaviour is not limited to Wilfrid Laurier University. In September 1989, women's groups at Queen's University launched a campaign against date rape by putting up posters with captions stating, "No Means No." Some male students in a first-year residence mocked the campaign, putting up their own posters bearing slogans such as "No Means Tie Her Up" and "No Means Kick Her in the Teeth" (*Globe and Mail*, 11 Nov. 1989, D1-2; 17 Nov. 1989). These students were apparently surprised when their posters—intended as a joke—elicited angry reactions.

An article in the *Globe and Mail* suggests that male students generally fail to see sexism on campus because they believe official pronouncements regarding universities' commitment to sexual equality, and they fear that they may be victims of feminists who promote affirmative action policies that discriminate against men. Women experience a different reality, one in which verbal commitments are rarely translated into action unless administrations are pushed by media, human rights commissions, or threats from alumni to withhold financial contributions.

Evidence of a serious backlash against women at universities includes increasing reports of sexual assaults on campus, sexual harassment by male faculty and students, and controversies over sexist student publications. Engineering students' newspapers at Queen's and the University of Alberta, in particular, have been criticized for sexist content "that portrays women in a thoroughly demeaning and abusive manner" (*Globe and Mail*, 13 Dec. 1989, A5).

This backlash against women reached its zenith with the massacre at the University of Montreal on 6 December 1989. This event, which generated horror and fear on campuses across Canada, irrevocably linked the concepts of misogyny, feminism, and violence. A man armed with a semi-automatic weapon entered a classroom in the engineering building and ordered the women students into one corner and men into another. He then ordered the men to leave. Declaring that they were all feminists, he opened fire on the women. Afterwards he roamed through the building, shooting others. He killed fourteen women and wounded twelve other people, including three men, before he turned the gun on himself. A three-page suicide letter found on his body gave the reason for the massacre: women, he wrote, had ruined his life.

In the days that followed the murders, commentators in the media debated how to understand what had happened. On one side were those who insisted that the event was the isolated act of a madman. Others claimed—as did the killer himself—that the massacre was a political act against feminists. They saw it as an extreme expression of the violence men direct at women, and they argued that the denial of this broader context is itself symptomatic of an anti-feminist backlash. In a sense, both responses may be valid. The murderer was insane and was himself a victim of the very misogyny that he expressed. As a child, he had been brutalized, along with his sister and mother, by a father who hated women and viewed them as objects whose function it was to serve men. His son, it seems, learned no other way to be a man. He was driven to hate and, in the end, to murder women whom he could not control.

Women and men came together in vigils on campuses all across Canada to mourn the dead women and to comfort the living. But grief and outrage were not universal. At Queen's, a male student reportedly pointed his fingers like a gun and mimed pulling the trigger at women. At the University of Toronto, seven male students set off firecrackers outside the women's residence, spreading panic. An employee at the same university brought unloaded guns on campus and made favourable comments about the shooting. The Ottawa office of the National Action Committee on the Status of Women received a threatening telephone call from an angry man who said that the killer was not alone in his intense hatred of women. A Catholic priest from Prince Edward Island argued that feminists had brought the massacre on themselves. He believed that the incident was a blessing in that it could teach women a lesson. If women remained in their proper place within the home, caring for their families instead of threatening men, males would not be driven to take such extreme action (CIHI Radio, Norm Foster Show, 15 Dec. 1989).

In such a climate, it is hardly surprising that women drop out of university or lower their academic aspirations during their undergraduate years, while men tend to raise theirs.

This survey of female experiences raises many questions about patterns of change in the social climate of universities. As we noted earlier in this chapter, there has been a steady increase in the numbers and proportions of females enrolling in graduate studies over the 1970s and 1980s. We need more research to understand how so many women have withstood the cool climate at universities and have not permitted it to defeat their aspirations. We need to know if and how feminist women and men are acting collectively to alter this climate. We need to know the extent to which the growing feminist movement is alleviating problems for female students or is generating a backlash that worsens sexism.

Hall and Sandler (1984) draw particular attention to female students' experiences that result from the fact that their professors are overwhelmingly male. The composition of university faculties is changing much more slowly than is the composition of the student body. Female professors are concentrated in low-status short-term positions with little chance of permanent employment. Women comprise only 17 percent of the full-time teaching staff at universities, according to Statistics Canada data for 1985–86, although women currently comprise 37 percent of the pool of doctoral candidates. Those women who are hired are clustered in faculties of nursing, home economics, and social work, which are traditionally seen as female. Very few women are to be found in the engineering and physical science faculties.

Backhouse argues that much-trumpeted affirmative action programs to hire more women professors have been dismal failures (*Globe and Mail*, 30 May 1988, A7). In the fight for limited tenure-track positions, what women tend to do research on, and where they tend to publish their work, does not carry the same weight as traditional malestream topics. Backhouse suggests that the "preference when equal" rule is a policy designed for failure. As we have seen already in this text, appraisal of qualifications and assessment of merit are value-laden tasks.

As Backhouse puts it, "academic hiring committees were unable to recognise female talent before the new rule came in. They are no more likely to assess women as equal to their preferred male candidates under this policy."

Insisting that at least one female faculty member sit on all committees does not help much. For a start it would put an enormous burden of administrative work on the few women faculty available, and even then they would sit as minority members with little control over ultimate decisions. Sexist comments are likely to be curtailed, but this will do nothing to prevent the unspoken and subtle manifestations of sex discrimination.

Backhouse advocates extreme measures such as quotas, the imposition of female hirings on reluctant departments, and the abolition of tenure to break up the "almost impenetrable job security" that it gives to a male-dominated faculty. This could well backfire, however. It is not difficult to guess who would most likely be judged as "not measuring up to adequate standards" in the recurrent blood-lettings that might result. It has been estimated that, at current rates of increase, it would take another hundred years for women academics to achieve numeric equality with males.

Another strategy of resistance to feminist teaching is to sideline feminism (Bezucha 1985, 90). Established professors will support hiring a few women to teach women's studies courses. They then feel that they do not need to change the content of their own courses. Ignorance of feminist theory and research is studiously maintained. This ignorance is not emptiness or mere absence of knowledge. It is an active resistance to knowledge (Aronowitz and Giroux 1985, 159).

Students who are exposed to feminist theory develop their own forms of resistance, as their established frameworks of meaning are challenged. One response is to deny the validity of any evidence that goes against the

Table 13-2 Full-time Undergraduate Enrolment, by Field of Study and Sex, Canada 1983–84 and 1987–88

Field of study	1983–84 Percent male	1983–84 Percent female	1983–84 Total	1987–88 Percent male	1987–88 Percent female	1987–88 Total
Agriculture and Biological Sciences						
Agriculture	62.9	37.1	4 713	62.0	38.0	3 800
Biology	50.2	49.8	9 639	48.8	51.2	15 104
Household science	3.6	96.4	3 513	7.7	92.3	4 478
Veterinary medicine	45.9	54.1	1 053	39.7	60.3	1 145
Zoology	54.4	45.6	781	50.7	49.3	976
Education						
Education	25.6	74.4	27 431	26.5	73.5	29 165
Physical Education	47.7	52.3	12 260	51.8	48.2	14 029
Engineering and Applied Sciences						
Architecture	70.0	30.0	2 220	67.0	33.0	2 142
Engineering	90.2	9.8	37 724	88.2	11.8	35 126
Forestry	88.4	11.6	42 335	86.6	13.4	38 952
Fine Arts	39.7	60.3	13 872	39.8	60.2	14 775
Health Professions						
Dental studies and research	73.8	26.2	1 982	65.2	34.8	1 945
Medical studies and research	58.2	41.8	8 411	55.1	44.9	8 328
Nursing	3.2	96.8	6 634	5.3	94.7	7 021
Pharmacy	32.8	67.2	2 696	36.1	63.9	3 069
Rehabilitation medicine	10.6	89.4	2 510	14.6	85.4	3 132
Humanities						
History	58.6	41.4	4 745	57.5	42.5	7 662
Languages	28.0	72.0	12 757	27.6	72.4	20 096
Other	51.7	48.2	9 858	48.9	51.1	11 159
Mathematics and Physical Sciences						
Chemistry	67.7	32.3	3 052	63.7	36.3	3 947
Geology	79.3	20.7	3 249	75.1	24.9	1 604
Mathematics	64.6	35.4	8 262	63.1	36.9	8 781
Computer science	72.7	27.3	12 250	80.6	19.4	8 165
Physics	88.2	11.8	2 407	86.7	13.3	2 810
Social Sciences						
Business and commerce	58.8	41.2	48 835	55.8	44.2	52 098
Economics	68.8	31.2	10 009	69.1	30.9	12 332
Geography	64.1	35.9	4 466	65.0	35.0	5 041
Law	55.8	44.2	9 892	54.4	47.6	10 433
Political science	63.1	36.9	6 712	59.3	40.7	10 826
Psychology	27.4	72.6	13 187	26.9	73.1	20 037
Social work	18.3	81.7	4 227	19.4	80.6	4 834
Sociology	34.0	66.0	6 157	31.8	68.2	9 928
Grand Total*	52.6	47.4	397 351	49.7	50.3	427 873

* Individual totals will not add up to grand total because certain smaller fields, labelled "other," are omitted from this table.

Source: Statistics Canada (1989, 84–87).

dominant view of reality. Culley (1985, 212) describes the common reactions of students, both female and male, when exposed for the first time to readily available statistics on education, employment categories, and income levels of women compared to men:

> "Who published those statistics?" (US Department of Labor.) "When was that?" (Any time before yesterday is pre-history.) "Those figures must be based on women who work part time." Or, "A lot of women choose not to work, you know, are they in there?" Then soon after, "You can't get anywhere hating men, you can't blame them." And quietly to themselves or to each other, "I heard she's divorced, she's probably a lesbian or something."

Culley suggests that it is important for teachers to let students express these defensive efforts to distance, discount, and deny. Only then can these responses be examined and questioned. Other professors who teach feminist theory describe instances of outright hostility from some students who actively try to disrupt classes by joking, chatting loudly, jeering, and attacking the credibility and professional competence of the professor (Bezucha 1985, 214; McIntyre 1986).

Female professors who adopt a non-hierarchical method of feminist teaching are particularly vulnerable to challenges to their professionalism, because they do not fit the standard image of a professor as a masculine authority figure. Moreover, their teaching techniques violate the prevailing assumption that there should be a clear separation between the public, impersonal, and objective realm and the private, personal, and subjective (Bezucha 1985, 81). Friedman (1985) argues that the prevailing patriarchal culture generally denies women the authority of their experiences, perspectives, emotions, and minds. Feminist teachers who are committed to involving students as equals in the classroom, and who strive to affirm the authority of personal experience as authentic knowledge, risk playing into patriarchal prejudices.

Friedman describes one female colleague who deliberately suppressed her own capacity to synthesize and conceptualize the disparate issues students brought up, in order not to stifle their creative thought. But the unintended result may be that her own competence is diminished in the eyes of students. This approach of treating students as equals in the learning experience violates the patriarchal assumption that competence and authority are displayed through hierarchy. On the other hand, female teachers who adopt tough standards violate the parallel expectations that women should not be authority figures acting in a hierarchical relation over others. Feminist teachers thus tend to lose either way, their authority within the classroom being simultaneously challenged and resented. Students who accept high standards, discipline, and toughness from male teachers often deeply resent the same demands from women teachers.

Feminist teaching generally takes place in patriarchal and hierarchically organized institutions. The clash between the institution and feminist teaching methods comes to the fore at grading time. Whatever their commitment to involving students as equals and affirming the validity of their personal experience, feminist teachers are nonetheless forced to adopt a hierarchical approach and grade students on the basis of classroom performance.

The struggle to establish critical feminist pedagogy is far from won. In 1975, Dorothy Smith analysed at length how women are excluded from the creation of culture. Men predominate in the organizations that govern, administer, and manage society. They vastly outnumber the women in academic rank at universities. They structure the images, vocabulary, concepts, and methods of knowing the world that define the dominant culture. Men attend to and treat as significant only what other men say. Women who want their professional work to be treated as seriously are constrained to write within these established conceptual frameworks. Now, however, the dominance of male perspectives no longer goes unquestioned. Over the last fifteen years there has been an explosion in the production of books by and about women, and the rate seems to be accelerating. Books with feminist titles have become marketable items rather than money-losers. Something in our definition of our gendered reality seems to be changing.

Minority Culture as Critical Pedagogy

Cracks in the armour of dominant capitalist culture may be opening, encouraged at least in part by the fact that half the members of ethnic and racial minorities are women. These women of colour are adding their feminist voices to minority cultural expression. Joseph (1988) describes the radicalizing potential of black feminist pedagogy in schooling in capitalist white society. Her aim it to challenge taken-for-granted interpretations of reality by exposing students to an alternative conceptual system. The standard curriculum, she argues, consists essentially of white male studies, but its capacity to stand as revealed truth is undermined by a reinterpretation of experience from a non-white, non-male perspective. All students need to learn to see their history through the eyes of members of minority groups, such as a Cherokee Indian grandmother, or a black mother in slavery, in order to see the imperialism, racism, and sexism embedded in the dominant culture.

Joseph gives an example of a classroom exercise in which American students were asked to compile a list of words associated with a black ghetto. White students listed such words as overcrowding, drugs, muggings, slum area, poverty, multiple sexual partners, all focussing on perceived defects in the ghetto residents and the need for them to change. Black students put police brutality at the top of the list of ghetto characteristics, followed by exploitation, slum landlords, the worst quality food and highest prices in the neighborhood stores, corruption, and insensitive officials. The class then began to discuss these divergent conceptions. White students responded with uncomfortable, amazed silence. They were taken aback when faced with questions they could not answer because they had never thought that way before. Black students responded with comments to the effect that this was the first time in their school career that they felt comfortable, or felt that the white way of seeing is not the only way or the right way.

The radicalizing potential of women's studies, black studies, or native studies is commonly neutralized by setting up such programs as separate courses of study aimed only at the subgroup concerned. The result is separate education for subgroups, which reinforces segregation. Dominant white male culture remains unchallenged within its own enclave. This is emphatically not what black feminist teachers such as Joseph want to achieve. Joseph stresses that there is no black, native, or women's history that is not also the history of white males. What all students need is to develop the capacity to conceptualize their experience from perspectives other than the prevailing dominant view. The goal is to integrate, not segregate, minority perspectives.

Weatherford (1988) gives a glimpse into what an integrated perspective on history might be like. He asks how the Indians of the Americas transformed the world rather than how the Europeans affected the Indians. He explores the significance for the rise of capitalism of the gold and silver traded by Amerindians, the impact of Amerindian crops, such as the potato and long-fibre cotton, in altering the direction of industrialization, and the contribution of native botanical knowledge to the transformation of modern medicine. In contemporary times, we may have much to learn from native religions that conceptualize the natural world in spiritual terms, rather than as a resource for humans to exploit.

In the present era, when both radicals and conservatives fear that people are being so pacified by mass culture that they are losing their capacity for creative and innovative thought, exposure to a radical pedagogy that challenges prevailing culture seems vital. The question is whether these conflicting perspectives can succeed in radicalizing the dominant ideology, or whether liberal ideology will neutralize them and so remain hegemonic (Gitlin 1980, 256).

Conclusion

Compulsory schooling has a profound effect on children's lives and upon their life-chances after leaving school. This much is beyond dispute. It also seems clear that children with different class, gender, and ethnic characteristics experience schooling and higher education in very different ways, and end up with markedly unequal levels of educational attainment and formal credentials. Different perspectives in sociology struggle with the questions of how and why schooling affects children in these ways.

Functionalist and structuralist–Marxist perspectives agree than schools perform the critical function of selecting and allocating children for adult roles with in the economy, but they focus on very different factors in their analysis of how this selection process works.

Functionalists suggest that, by and large, schools do provide equal opportunities for all children to reach their full academic potential and to strive for social mobility. They locate the causes of unequal attainment by class and by sex primarily in socialization processes that occur within families, largely outside the influence of schools.

Marxist theory, in contrast, locates the causes of low aspirations and unequal attain-

ment in the political economy of capitalism. This perspective largely takes for granted the argument that capitalists seek to standardize and deskill work in the interests of cheapening labour and increasing profits. Scope for creativity seem confined to the elite who direct the huge corporations. This political economy is held responsible for structuring schools in the corporate image. Structuralist Marxists draw attention to the structural correspondence between the social relations within schools and within different levels of the occupational hierarchy in corporations. They argue that there is a fundamental contradiction between the two educational goals of promoting the full academic potential of all children and preparing them for the job market. Whatever the rhetoric of equal opportunity within schools, the form of schooling experienced by the mass of lower-class students stunts their intellectual development and inures them to monotonous routines and oppressive authority. The low educational aspirations of these children and their parents are the effect and not the cause of these structures.

The argument that the structures of corporate capitalism determine the structures and effects of schooling leaves unanswered such critical questions as how these effects are produced and why students and teachers conform. It is these questions that the social constructionist approach tries to answer. This approach begins from the assumption that people, in their everyday interactions, create the social world and give it the patterns and the meanings that we come to see as "the structures of capitalism." Research into intimate interaction within classrooms explores how students react to and against the pressures of school, in terms of how they themselves foresee the utility or irrelevance of education for their future lives. Teachers also struggle to retain some autonomy in their working lives, amid pressures to adopt packaged curricula, textbooks, and technical devices pushed by corporate interests, often acting in concert with school boards and college management.

The central debate within this perspective concerns how far it is possible for people to retain autonomy of thought and action in the face of the established ways of thinking within the prevailing culture. Teachers are criticized by radicals, and increasingly also by members of the business class, for not developing the capacity for creative and innovative thinking in their students. Yet they themselves work in contexts that seem increasingly designed to minimize their own capacity for creative teaching. Feminist pedagogy is one form of teaching that takes seriously the possibility of challenging and changing established social relations through developing in students the power of critical reflection. The question for the future is whether this power will be neutralized and accommodated in the service of greater profits, or whether people will use it to push for more fundamental change.

Suggested Reading

An excellent study of education from the functionalist perspective is by John Porter, Marion Porter, and Bernard Blishen, *Stations and Callings: Making It Through the School System* (1982). Chapter 1 of this book discusses the theory of equality and educational opportunity, exploring the different interpretations that can be placed on the notion of equal opportunity. Chapter 3 outlines in a clear and precise form the basic ideas of socialization and self-concept in functionalist and symbolic interaction theory. The authors then incorporate these concepts into an elaborate explanatory model that guides their research into educational aspirations. The text includes many easily understandable statistical graphs and tables.

The main text that presents the structuralist–Marxist perspective is by Samuel Bowles and Herbert Gintis, *Schooling in Capitalist America* (1976). A briefer introduction to the ideas debated at length in the text is provided in a collection of articles edited by Mike Cole, *Bowles and Gintis Revisited: Correspondence and Contradiction in Educational Theory* (1988). In the prologue and chapter 2 of the collection, Bowles and Gintis summarize their theoretical arguments. In chapters 12 and 13, they address some of the criticisms raised against structuralist–Marxist theory. Chapters 1 and 3 provide a brief but useful overview of criticisms of the work of Bowles and Gintis.

A good introduction to the social construction of reality approach, and one that complements the work of Bowles and Gintis, is by Jean Anyon, "Social Class and the Hidden Curriculum of Work" (1980). She describes in detail the very different teaching techniques that she observed in elementary school classes in working-class, middle-class, and elite school districts. A classic study in the rejection of school values by working-class children is P. Willis, *How Working Class Kids Get Working Class Jobs* (1978). Willis shows how boys have absorbed the shop-floor culture of their working-class fathers, including sexist and racist values, and utilize them to support their rejection of school. A similar study by Angela McRobbie, "Working-class Girls and the Culture of Femininity" (1978) describes how these girls reject the school culture in favour of their paramount concern with sexuality and attracting boyfriends.

Michael Apple's work, *Teachers and Texts: A Political Economy of Class and Gender Relations in Education* (1986), explores the contemporary work of teachers. Apple documents the pressures that threaten to reduce the role of teachers from autonomous professionals to deskilled technicians, constrained to use standardized curriculum packages.

A good overview of the feminist approach to education is provided by a collection of articles edited by Jane Gaskell and Arlene Tigar McLaren, *Women and Education: A Canadian Perspective* (1987). Among other useful updates, the collection includes a reprint of the classic article by Dorothy Smith, "An Analysis of Ideological Structures and How Women are Excluded: Considerations for Academic Women."

Chapter 14

Race and Ethnic Relations: Creating the Vertical Mosaic

The analysis of racial and ethnic relations in society presents a major challenge to functionalist theories of social order, both traditional and Marxist. The subject is very closely tied to conceptions of family, stratification, and education, which we have traced in the previous three chapters. First, the family is clearly implicated in establishing race and ethnic identity through kinship ties and socialization. Secondly, the pattern of stratification in Canada forms what Porter (1968) has called a **vertical mosaic**, with members of different racial and ethnic groups organized vertically with respect to class location. People of white Anglo-Saxon protestant origin prevail at the top of the hierarchy while native Indians are at the bottom. Various other Europeans and non-whites range in between. Thirdly, the system of education, as we saw in chapter 13, reflects and perpetuates this vertical mosaic. The coincidence of ethnicity, race, and class is by

no means peculiar to Canada. It seems to be a recurrent feature of industrial societies, although specific characteristics of the mosaic vary from one country to another.

The critical problem for functionalist theories is to account for the persistence of this vertical mosaic in terms of its functions for industrial societies generally and for the capitalist system in particular. Again, we discuss traditional functionalism first, followed by the structuralist–Marxist approach and the theories that focus on the social construction of reality.

Traditional Functionalism: Consensus or Conflict?

Shared culture or ethnic identity plays a pivotal role in traditional functionalist theory. In the model of a social system developed by Parsons, moral consensus provides the foundation of social order. Such consensus is internalized through early childhood socialization within the family and reinforced through religion and formal education. Components of culture included language, history, symbol systems, values, behavioural norms, expectations, and attitudes—in effect the totality of what Durkheim refers to as the *conscience collective* of a community of people.

In functionalist theory, our cultural community or ethnic group, and not our class, is fundamental to our personal identity. Those whom we identify with as "our people" or "our community," when asked who we are, are typically an ethnic group rather than a class. Membership in such a group is ascriptive, or largely biologically based. Members share unified cultural forms and patterns of communication and interaction. They see themselves and are seen by others as constituting a distinct social category. Membership itself is virtually imperative; opting out of the affiliation is very difficult, especially because it implies renouncing obligations to other members. Offspring of mixed parentage experience some degree of marginality or partial belonging to two exclusive groups. Occasionally, they become a grouping in themselves, like the Métis. If effect, the defining characteristics of an ethnic group are very close to those of a social system as a whole. This closeness is intentional within functionalist theory: this perspective assumes that no social system could function without such a core of common culture.

For functionalist theorists, the presence of immigrants or ethnic minorities within a society is necessarily problematic. By definition, they lie outside the boundaries of the cultural consensus of the majority. They cannot be trusted to have internalized either the appropriate values or the typical behaviours associated with difficult social roles. Predictably, therefore, interaction will be strained and restricted, and social controls will be weakened. Force, rather than the subtle controls of internalized values, will play a grea-

ter role in the maintenance of order. Social interaction will be closest with those who share the same culture. Relations with outsiders will be restricted to those areas where common understanding can be assumed. Interaction will be avoided whenever confrontation or modification of group traditions might take place. The only safe meeting ground for different ethnic groups is the impersonal marketplace.

The concept of **race**, as distinct from **ethnicity**, refers to people's visible and inherited physical differences that are socially noticed. In principle, racial diversity should not give rise to the same interaction problems as ethnic diversity, since race does not constitute any threat to cultural consensus. In practice, however, race tends to be confounded with ethnicity, since members of any given ethnic group tend to see themselves as racially homogeneous. They regard a person of visibly different racial stock as being outside their own ethnic group. Distinct racial characteristics thus heighten the tendency to avoid **out-groups**, or people perceived to be outside one's own cultural group.

A general assumption that derives from traditional functionalist theory is that ethnically and racially mixed societies, such as Canada, are inherently unstable and prone to divisions and conflicts. Metta Spencer (1976, chap. 9) makes explicit these theoretical assumptions in her synthesis of functionalist theories of ethnicity. She predicts that there will always be claims of minority groups for recognition, equality, or freedom, and at least one ethnic group unhappy with its treatment or position within, or rather at the margins of, the society. This prediction is certainly proven correct in present-day Canada.

The functionalist focus on internalization of culture and ethnic identity leads to the assumption that **ethnocentrism** and **prejudice** against other ethnic groups are normal and probably unavoidable attitudes. **Ethnocentrism** refers to an exaggerated

Figure 14-1 Number of Immigrants to Canada, 1852–1980

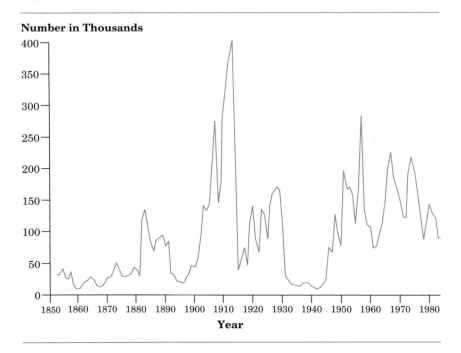

Number in Thousands

Sources: Canadian Employment and Immigration Commission, *Immigration Statistics* (Ottawa: Ministry of Supply and Services), annual issues.

view of the qualities and correctness of the culture of our own group. It is only an extreme form of internalizing the values that define our group vis-à-vis out-groups. **Stereotypes** are simplified versions of other groups, mental cartoons that we form by generalizing too much or by exaggerating the characteristics of ethnic groups on the basis of too little information. **Prejudice** is the logical mirror image of ethnocentrism. It involves prejudging in negative terms the characteristics that we assume are shared by members of other ethnic groups. **Racism** applies such prejudices toward groups that we perceive to be different on the basis of inescapable genetic characteristics. These ethnocentric, stereotypical, prejudiced, and racist attitudes are themselves part of the cultural assumptions of a group, which may be learned through socialization. Socialization also provides us with shared notions of

the relative status of our own and other groups within the society.

In theory, an increased focus on universalistic achievement criteria in industrial societies should bring about a lessening of ascriptive ethnic identifications, but this has not happened. Richmond (1988, 7–9) suggests that heightened feelings of ethnicity, nationalism, and ethnocentrism are the almost inevitable consequences of the rapid pace of modernization. The global character of modern economics creates enormous pressures on people to migrate within and between industrialized countries and from the less developed and poorer countries to those whose economies are expanding. People endeavour to cope with the resulting social upheavals, and their sense of dislocation and stress, by various mechanisms. The form of these mechanisms, suggests Richmond, varies between the dominant or majority group and minorities. Members of the privileged group tend to respond to stress by heightened nationalism and blustering patriotism, often accompanied by racist attitudes. Minority groups tend to respond to stress by closing in upon themselves. Class lines are hardened and ethnic and racial solidarity increases.

Implications for Political Organization

The functionalist analysis of ethnic identification and strained interaction with outgroups has far-reaching implications for political organization. Given the disruptive character of ethnic differences, functionalism posits that the only viable options for the maintenance of social order are **domination**, **separation**, or total **assimilation** of ethnic minorities. The first two options are seen as mechanisms to control and contain conflict. The ideal is full integration because this resolves the source of the tension and so eliminates the need for control.

The first option involves regular and institutionalized **domination** by one group over others. Colonization is the extreme expression of this option. Kuper (1969, 14) argues that, in the absence of cultural homogeneity, the only viable mechanism is regulation through force, which necessitates domination by one cultural section. Van den Berghe (1969, 76–78) similarly concludes that ethnic diversity is intrinsically associated with conflict and can lead to despotic rule. One group manages and manipulates the others and excludes them from access to privileges and opportunities.

In the second option of **separation**, communities live side by side with neither trying to dominate the other, but with little interaction. They remain perpetual strangers and have separate political, economic, and cultural institutions, and minimal intercommunication. This option has the advantage of preserving ethnic diversity, but the political problems are great. To work, separation requires not only tolerance among group members but economic autonomy so that each group controls its own lands and businesses. There must also be legal autonomy, with each group having control over its own members' lives. Ethnic membership must be unambiguous so that everyone knows which legal system applies to whom. Hypothetically, this kind of separation is more viable when the culturally deviant minority is small in number and so does not constitute any great threat to the cohesion and order of the social whole (Kuper 1969, 16; Van den Berghe 1969, 75).

The third option is full participation of all ethnic groups in the same activities, through a process of **assimilation**. *Cultural assimilation* must come first, with groups adopting the lifestyles, language, values, and customs of the dominant group. *Structural assimilation* follows as the immigrant or ethnic minority groups enter the social organization of the dominant group (Gordon 1964). Groups tend to lose language and culture first, but to hold on to religion. Intermarriage is the last to go. The final stage is such total amalgamation that ethnic background is forgotten.

The main value of these three theoretical formulations is that they fully disclose the assumptions of functionalist theory as they apply to the study of ethnic relations, and they carry them to their logical conclusions. The question is how accurate or relevant they are to particular societies. It is possible to test the relevance of all three models using Canadian examples.

Domination

The first model, where one ethnic group exercises institutional domination over another, characterizes the experience of native peoples in Canada. As the fur trade declined and white settlers pushed westward onto the Prairies, the native peoples were driven off their lands onto small reserves. The Indian Act of 1896 established the legal, political, and economic dominance of the federal government over these reserves. The Minister of Indian Affairs had the authority to attend all band council meetings, to veto any bylaws that the bands might pass, to control their finances, to approve all expenditures, and to dictate land sales. Today, Canadian Indians still primarily live on reserves and are still fighting to gain more autonomy and self-government. This essentially colonial situation has been a constant source of resentment and strife.

True to Metta Spencer's prediction, newspapers carry stories of native struggles for better treatment within Canada. Front page news in the *Globe and Mail* on 3 June 1988 was the blockade of a major highway into Montreal by the Kahnawake Mohawk band to protest a police raid on their reserve to seize cigarettes brought in from the United States without the payment of customs duty. The Indians claimed the right to do this as a separate nation within Canada. Also front page news on the same day was the story of Leonard Peltier, an Indian from North Dakota's Pine Ridge Indian Reservation. He had been extradited from Canada and convicted of leading a fight in which two FBI agents were killed on the reservation in 1975. An army of some 200 FBI agents, police officers, and vigilantes had invaded the reservation, ostensibly looking for a suspected criminal. The primary concern of the FBI appears to have been to crush the American Indian Movement, which it perceived as subversive and a threat to the integrity of the American state. Peltier's supporters claim, with considerable evidence, that both the extradition from Canada and the legal case against him were fraudulent. Peltier's situation is a cause célèbre in the Soviet Union where he is viewed as a jailed American dissident. Mikhail Gorbachev raised the subject of Peltier after Ronald Reagen attacked the Soviet record on human rights at a summit meeting between the two leaders.

Native people hold a prayer vigil for Leonard Peltier in front of the Supreme Court of Canada.

The same day that the paper ran the stories about Peltier and the Kahnawake Mohawks, it continued its coverage of the Donald Marshall investigation in Nova Scotia. Marshall, a Micmac Indian, spent eleven years in prison for a murder he did not commit. When he was finally acquitted and freed, he was given compensation of only $270 000, of which $100 000 went to pay legal expenses. The subsequent official inquiry into the case has unearthed considerable evidence of racism at high levels in the justice system, and allegedly also within the Nova Scotia cabinet. One remark, attributed to a representative of the justice system at the original trial of Marshall, was that the Eskasoni reserve near Sydney should be fenced off to prevent the resident Indians from coming into town to cause trouble.

Yet another item in the same newspaper recorded that the chiefs of the Assembly of First Nations in Edmonton had rejected, as merely a vacuous electioneering gimmick, Ottawa's plans for holding talks on native self-government. Native leaders warned Canadians that, if the political situation of Indians in Canada did not soon improve, the younger generation might get so frustrated they would turn on the whites with guns.

From these examples, it is clear that the option of institutionalized domination by one ethnic group over others has not led to stability in Canada.

Separation

The second model, separation, applies in some respects to the situation of French-speaking Quebec within Confederation. The experience of Quebec illustrates the fragility of such an arrangement. Canada seems to be in constant danger of either separating into two autonomous nations or reverting to the first option of quasi-colonial domination.

John Porter (1979, 106) writes enthusiastically of the special relationship of "bi-nationalism of French and English Canada as the founding principle of Confederation." This relationship only makes sense, he suggests, because of very specific historical conditions. The fact that 80 percent of French Canadians live in Quebec gives them a homeland that was conquered. This helps to make sense of, and to give impetus to, the notions of separation and eventual formation of a French state.

In practice, however, the ideal of "separate but equal" status, implied in the separation model, has never been a reality. The French ethnic group, even within Quebec, has until very recently formed a class with deprived status. French elites within the church and the state in Quebec collaborated with the federal government in return for protected status, but the mass of unilingual Francophones occupied the low ranks in the class structure. Professional and business elites in Quebec have been predominantly English Canadians or Americans, and the language of business has clearly been English. The few Québécois who attained professional occupational status had to function in English.

The Royal Commission on Bilingualism and Biculturalism, established in 1963, concluded that either Canada would break up or there would have to be a new set of conditions for Quebec's future existence (Porter 1979, 107). Subsequent policies to institutionalize bilingualism in the federal civil service, together with concessions, especially in social welfare legislation, have moved toward providing special status for Quebec in Canada. But strife continues. In 1976 the Parti Québécois came to power, dedicated to achieving independent nationhood for Quebec. This policy was only narrowly voted down in the 1980 referendum on sovereignty association. While 40 percent of Quebeckers voted in favour of separation, there is evidence that this included 50 percent or more of French-speaking voters.

The problem has not gone away. In 1981, Prime Minister Pierre Trudeau pushed ahead with the patriation of the Canadian Constitution, but Quebec did not join the other provinces in signing the Constitution. The Quebec government feared that its independence of action would be limited too much by federal government powers. Beginning in 1987, there has been a renewed struggle to persuade Quebec to sign the Constitution. An agreement was tentatively worked out between Prime Minister Brian Mulroney and the ten provincial premiers at a meeting at Meech Lake, Quebec, in May 1987. This constitutional accord must be approved by both houses of parliament and by the legislatures of all the provinces before it can be proclaimed into force.

The fundamental provisions of this accord assert the bilingual and bicultural nature of Canada. The opening clause of the agreement states:

1) The Constitution of Canada shall be interpreted in a manner consistent with:

(a) the recognition that the existence of French-speaking Canadians, centred in Quebec but also present elsewhere in Canada, and English-speaking Canadians, concentrated outside Quebec but also present in Quebec, constitutes a fundamental characteristic of Canada; and

(b) the recognition that Quebec constitutes within Canada a distinct society.

The accord also gives Quebec, along with other provinces that so request, considerable powers to control immigration and the reception and integration of these immigrants in the province. The provincial government would receive financial compensation from Ottawa for taking over these responsibilities. Quebec is also guaranteed a proportion of all immigrants, including refugees, coming to Canada in any one year, equal to Quebec's share of the population of Canada, with the right to exceed that figure by five percent for demographic reasons. The intent of these provisions is to ensure that immigrants settling in Quebec will be assimilated into the French language and culture. Quebec can thus increase immigration to compensate for declining birthrates within the province. Other provisions increase provincial powers to nominate candidates for the Supreme Court. Provinces can also choose to opt out of any future national shared-cost program in an area of exclusive provincial jurisdiction if that province undertakes its own programs compatible with national objectives. The province is

guaranteed reasonable financial compensation from the federal government for these programs. Provinces will also be given the right to opt out of any future constitutional amendments that transfer provincial jurisdiction to the federal parliament, again with the guarantee of reasonable compensation. In conclusion, section 16 of the accord states that nothing agreed to within the accord shall affect sections 25 or 27 of the Canadian Charter of Rights and Freedoms. These sections guarantee aboriginal treaty rights and ensure the preservation and enhancement of the multicultural heritage of Canadians.

The accord was enthusiastically endorsed by the Quebec government, but it has subsequently run into trouble. A central concern of many critics is that section 16 of the accord does not include protection of equality rights under section 15(1) of the Charter of Rights and Freedoms. This section guarantees "the right to equal protection and equal benefit of the law without discrimination, and, in particular, without discrimination based on race, national or ethnic origin, colour, religion, sex, age or mental or physical disability." Minority groups fear that their rights might be overridden by Quebec's concern with establishing a distinct French society. The English-speaking minority within Quebec and French-speaking minorities outside Quebec fear that their Charter right are threatened. These fears mounted when the Quebec government used the "notwithstanding" clause in the Charter to override guaranteed language rights when it decreed that all street signs in Quebec must appear only in French.

Women's groups are concerned that the accord does not specifically protect section 28 of the Charter, the section that states, "Notwithstanding anything in this Charter, the rights and freedoms referred to in it are guaranteed equally to male and female persons." Groups such as the National Action Committee on the Status of Women (NAC)

(1987a) argue that, since the accord specifically protects aboriginal and multicultural rights, the absence of specific protection for women's rights is a significant threat.

The governments of the Yukon and Northwest Territories resent being left out of the accord and fear that the amending formula will make it very difficult, if not impossible, for them to gain provincial status in the future. There is also widespread fear that the opting-out clauses in the accord may have gone too far. In an effort to guarantee to Quebec the power to control provincial social services, to aid in the preservation and promotion of the distinct identity of Quebec, the accord threatens the uniformity of federal social services all across Canada. Critics fear that these opting-out provisions may lead to the breakup of Canada into ten or twelve separate state-like entities each with its own separate and unequal services. There remains considerable doubt whether the accord will be ratified and whether, in any case, Canada can hold together as one nation with two distinct societies.

Like the case of Quebec, the survival of other ethnic communities as separate entities within Canada reflects very specific historical circumstances of economy and geography. At the turn of the twentieth century, the Canadian government desperately wanted immigrants to settle the Prairies, and so it promised cultural pluralism (Baker 1977, 117). Ukrainians, Slavs, Doukhobours, and Hutterites were attracted by promises of land and cultural integrity. But they settled in very sparsely populated rural areas in the western provinces where there was little need for assimilation. On occasion, nonetheless, they were pressured to change, to learn English, and to swear allegiance to the British Crown. The general expectation within the government of the time was that all ethnic minorities, French included, would eventually assimilate.

In short, the second political option under traditional functionalist theory, ethnic pluralism in separate communities living side by side, seems almost as unworkable as the first option of colonial domination. Neither domination nor separation of ethnic groups seems to lead to stability. Both seem destined to be associated with continual conflict and stress.

Integration Through Assimilation

Functionalists argue that the third option—acculturation, assimilation, and loss of distinct ethnic identity—is the only one that seems viable in the long run. It promises to remove the basic source of conflict rather than merely controlling and containing it. Porter (1979, 128) advocates this option when he argues that the importance attached to ethnicity in policies of biculturalism or multiculturalism is a regressive step toward a particularistic emphasis on biological descent groups. Any such emphasis on group rights, he argues, militates against principles of citizenship, individual freedom of opportunity, and individual human rights. To Porter, such emphasis is antithetical to the values of the modern state. It would seem to require a focus on affirmative action, positive discrimination, preferential hiring, and the like, to ensure proportional representation within institutional hierarchies.

Porter foresees a potentially nightmarish situation where every large organization, public or private, would be subject to legislative controls dictating precisely what proportion of positions in each rank would have to be reserved for whites or people of colour, males or females, people of English, French, native Indian, or Chinese origin, and on and on. Such practices would constitute a radical departure for a society based on principles of individual achievement and universalistic judgments. The result, suggests Porter, would be forced pseudo-minority group membership, where people would have to identify themselves as a member of an ethnic subgroup in order to qualify for a position under the quota system, even when they had lost any strong cultural or emotional attachment to the group. The enforcement of such a system would depend upon emphasizing visibly distinct group characteristics, passbooks, and the like, and would intensify hostility and rivalry between groups.

Porter concedes that "descent group identification" might be functional as **psychic shelter** in a modern world of bureaucracy and technology and might raise the self-esteem for members of low-status groups and so help them to do better in schools. He is far more worried that the revival of ethnic identities reflects the failure of group members to adopt the universalistic achievement values that are essential to create equal opportunities for individual members to be socially mobile. In short, heightened ethnic identity stifles individual achievement and mobility and may thus perpetuate the vertical mosaic, with ethnic minorities low in the ranking.

Porter acknowledges that **liberal assimilationist values** would require a large measure of conformity to Anglo values on the part of non-Anglo groups. But he argues that this only amounts to conformity to the values of the societies leading in the modernization process, the values of science and technology, universalism and achievement. He concludes that Canada is an advanced industrial society in which the values of rationality and science constitute a universal culture. In such a society, bilingualism might be able to survive, he suggests, but not biculturalism, much less multiculturalism (Porter 1979, 128–33). In effect, Porter offers the people of Quebec a future in Canada in which they might keep the French language alive but cannot hope to retain their distinctive Québécois culture. Staunch defenders of Quebec nationalism, like Marcel Rioux, dismiss such a proposal as "bland bilingual, multicultural pablum" served up on Canada Day (Crean and Rioux 1983, 12).

Limitations of Traditional Functionalism

The first challenge to traditional functionalism is in terms of its use of the concept of *culture*, which it places at the root of ethnic identity. In the functionalist model of a social system, culture encompasses a unified system of values, symbols, technology, lifestyles, language, history, identity, and so on, internalized through socialization. But when we try to apply this unwieldy concept of culture to "dominant Canadians," we cannot make it fit. There is enormous variation on all these dimensions among those who could loosely be lumped together as dominant white Canadians. Consider the variations among upper-, middle-, and lower-class people, elderly, middle-aged, and young people, men and women, those of left, right, and centrist political persuasions, and those holding different religious beliefs. Even language varies so widely that professionals at conferences may as well be speaking Greek as English or French for all the sense that the average person could make of it. We either have to break the concept of culture down into a myriad of subcultures to try to encompass this diversity or, better still, give up the concept altogether.

South African society, with institutionalized apartheid, seems to be the epitome of the functionalist social system prediction that, in the absence of cultural assimilation, some system of segregation will be necessary to contain conflicts. But, if we look closely, we find that the institutionalized segregation in South Africa does not occur along cultural lines. White South Africans of Africaner Dutch and English origins maintain different languages, religions, and customs, yet they work together in political and economic structures. On the other hand, South African coloureds have become culturally assimilated to the language and lifestyles of the dominant group and yet they are kept separate. It is not culture that divides South Africa, but something else. If we abandon the concept of culture as shared beliefs and sentiments, however, then we also have to abandon the functionalist model of social cohesion based upon cultural consensus.

A second critical question concerns whether ethnocentrism and prejudice are necessarily the normal outcome of socialization into one's own group. Functionalist sociologists, along with many liberal thinkers, disclaim that they themselves have ethnocentric attitudes. Yet they are quick to ascribe such ethnocentrism to other Canadians, blaming evidence of conflict between ethnic groups on intolerant attitudes toward cultural diversity. However, it is not difficult to find evidence to support the opposing argument that ethnocentrism is not the prevailing norm in a multi-ethnic, multi-racial community such as Toronto. Each summer the city hosts Caravan, a two-week festival during which members of some

fifty different ethnic groups host pavilions to celebrate their different styles of life. The huge crowds of people who line up for the shows and the ethnic foods belie the functionalist prediction that cultural heterogeneity results in hostility. The predicted state of normless anomie and strife in ethnically mixed communities does not hold either. Toronto as a city is home to, and loved by, too many different people for this model to be true.

As we explored at length in an earlier section of this text concerned with urbanism, the conservative model does not fit. The predictions are false. High-density living and heterogeneous populations do not automatically lead to social anomie. The vertical mosaic of ethnic minorities located at different levels of the social class ranking holds as strongly in Toronto as elsewhere in Canada, and there is also clear evidence of conflict between ethnic groups in the city. But the mechanisms of cross-cultural avoidance and

Table 14-1 Immigrants as a Percentage of the Population of Canada's Ten Largest Metropolitan Areas, 1981

Metropolitan Area	Total Population	Immigrants	
		Number	Percentage of Total Population
Toronto	2 975 495	1 129 340	38.0
Montreal	2 798 045	450 660	16.1
Vancouver	1 250 610	370 240	29.6
Ottawa-Hull	711 920	98 545	13.8
Edmonton	650 895	128 060	19.7
Calgary	587 020	124 105	21.1
Winnipeg	578 625	110 915	19.2
Quebec	569 005	12 255	2.2
Hamilton	537 645	140 240	26.1
St. Catharines-Niagara	301 565	66 280	22.0

Source: 1981 Census of Canada.

ethnocentrism posited by functionalist theory do not seem to be at the root of these problems.

There is evidence that ethnocentrism is not the prevailing norm in a multi-ethnic city such as Toronto.

Brittan and Maynard (1984, 71) question the pivotal role accorded to socialization in fixing attitudes, values, and behaviour. In functionalist theory, the view that socialization remorselessly shapes human personality and conduct is so unquestioningly assumed as to have virtually the status of revealed truth. But, as Brittan and Maynard point out, it is by no means automatic that children will absorb the attitudes and values of their parents. The functionalist model is based on an inaccurate and oversocialized conception of people and an overly rigid conception of rules and role-playing behaviour. Ethnomethodology and social constructionism contend that children drift into adulthood, rather than being programmed into it.

They view culture not as a hard reality but as multiple possibilities. People have the capacity to reflect upon their cultural conditioning, to reinterpret and reconstruct their sense of who they are. Interaction does not follow the rigidly prescribed course of prior expectations but is open to continual renegotiation by all participants. What "ethnic identity" means, therefore, is very much context-dependent. It is flexible and negotiable, depending on the situation and the others with whom one is associating.

Brittan and Maynard push their challenge of traditional functionalism further in their examination of the acquisition of racism. The socialization argument can be reduced to the assertion that children will be prejudiced against out-groups if they grow up in a community in which prejudice is encouraged. If a child is brought up to respect others as equals, and yet turns out to be racist, this tends to be explained by functionalists in terms of inadequate socialization, deviance, or psychological deficiency. Some relate the propensity to racism and ethnocentrism to rigid discipline in childhood and a resulting **authoritarian** personality structure (Adorno et al. 1968). But what of the alternative possibility? How do we explain the many people who grow up in a racist culture, like that prevailing in South Africa, but are not themselves racists? Do they too have deviant personalities or inadequate socialization (Brittan and Maynard 1984, 95–100)?

The major theoretical problem is that socialization is not a sufficient explanation for racism, anti-semitism, or other forms of ethnocentrism. Prejudice and racism have their roots in social structures, not in psychological states, argue Brittan and Maynard. They cannot be eliminated simply by modifying child-rearing practices. The key explanatory variable of traditional functionalist theory—that childhood socialization into the norms and values of one's own group causes ethnocentrism and racism and hence inequality—does not seem to work. It is not just the notion of "oversocialization" that is the problem. The ethnomethodological perspectives, which views ethnic and racial identities as flexible and negotiable, lends itself to the implication that the vertical mosaic of ethnic and racial inequality would disappear if individuals renegotiated their interpersonal relations. This is not very convincing. We have to ask why ethnicity and race are experienced as givens by most people.

The traditional functionalist model of a social system is also open to question in terms of the centrality it accords to cultural conformity and hence to ethnic homogeneity. Durkheim argued that this kind of mechanical solidarity based on sameness would cease to be important in complex industrial societies. The moral basis of social cohesion is interdependence, which is inherent in division of labour. Such interdependence, Durkheim argued, requires tolerance for diversity as its first premise because specialization necessarily generates cultural diversity. There can be no return to homogenization of experience. But interdependence does not automatically ensure social cohesion. There is a fundamental requirement that the division of labour be just and be based on natural inclinations and choices. There cannot be rich and poor at birth, cautioned Durkheim, without unjust contracts and unjust division of labour. From this perspective, it is not so much the ethnic identities and loyalties that create disequilibrium in the social system, but the vertical character of the mosaic, the blatant inequalities and injustices in the ranking of ethnic and racial groups.

Canada's human rights record is one that most of us now would prefer to ignore. Hill and Schiff (1986) document not only a long history of exploiting native peoples and stealing their lands and resources but also a thriving slave trade throughout the eighteenth century. Later, Chinese, Japanese, and East Indian men, exploited as a cheap source of labour for work on canals and railroads and in lumber mills, were denied citizenship rights and subjected to systematic discrimination designed to ensure that they never got out of this cheap labour market. During the Second World War, Canadian-born people of Japanese origin were interned in camps and their property was seized. Jewish people seeking asylum from Hitler's Germany were denied entry into Canada in 1937. During the entire war Canada admitted only 5000 Jewish refugees. Right up until the present, Canada's immigration policies, in effect if not always in formal intention, have favoured white European immigrants over non-whites.

This long history is definitely not the stuff of which organic solidarity, based on justice and equality, is made. The first Fair Employment Act in Canada did not appear until 1951 in Ontario, with federal legislation only in 1967. Comprehensive human rights statutes did not exist in all provinces until 1975. At length, in 1981, the Charter of Rights and Freedoms was passed, guaranteeing "equal protection and equal benefit of the law without discrimination." But there has been some backsliding. The British Columbia government abolished the province's Human Rights Commission in 1983, leaving no staff to investigate complaints or to assist in conciliation or education. The Meech Lake Accord seriously weakens constitutional protection for women and minority groups.

Power and Class Struggle in the Ethnic Mosaic

These diverse critiques of traditional functionalism seem to point ultimately in the same direction. What is missing from functionalist analyses of ethnicity is the dimension of power and its reflection in historical struggles between people. This failure to consider power weakens the focus on socialization and learned attitudes. Attitudes and values do not form in a vacuum. Racism and ethnocentrism are already part of the system in which we live. White children grow up racist not because of mistaken beliefs, but because they discover the presence of racism. Such beliefs are tied into the reproduction of power relations and express where groups are located in society. We learn what ethnicity and race or colour differences mean not merely in terms of stereotypes but in terms of relative power and status. From this essentially Marxist conception of culture, attitudes of ethnocentrism, prejudice, and racism are the effects, not the causes, of location in the vertical mosaic.

The same problem of power limits the conception that ethnic identity is negotiable. Some groups have much greater power to impose their definitions of reality onto others. In Canada, white English settlers, in conjunction with the British government, have held and exercised power (Baker 1977). Their control provided the historical basis for determining both the types of cultural integration, in the broad sense of the shared language, religion, and other values, and how other groups would be structurally incorporated into the class hierarchy of the Canadian mosaic.

Baker suggests that the character of this incorporation was determined by three factors: the historical period in which different groups of settlers came; the extent to which the dominant group needed settlers for economic development; and the power of different groups, based on available resources and how well they could mobilize to use them. Native Indians, he suggests, were relatively useless to the dominant white settlers and so were shunted aside. French Canadians survived as a **siege culture** in Quebec. French elites collaborated with the English and American business class in return for concessions to their religion and language. The men of most other immigrant groups came under strict regulations geared primarily to manpower requirements for the economy. Women were commonly not considered potential recruits into the labour force. They migrated under very different regulations oriented to the perceived need for a larger population base in Canada to support the growing economy.

This major shift in focus, from socialization and conformity needs to power and functions for the economy, is characteristic of structuralist–Marxist theory, to which we now turn.

Structuralist–Marxist Theory

Structuralist–Marxist theory is oriented specifically to the analysis of the functions of race and ethnic divisions for the capitalist social system. The concept of class is pivotal; race and ethnicity are regarded as aspects of class. This model is much better able than traditional functionalism to deal theoretically with the issue of the vertical character of the ethnic mosaic. Far from being an accidental or aberrant feature of ethnic relations, inequality appears as its central function.

Oliver Cox's study, *Caste, Class and Race* ([1948] 1970), is widely cited as a classical Marxist approach to the genesis of racism and its structural significance within capitalism. Cox concedes to traditional functionalism the notion that intolerance or ethnocentrism may be normal features of any community of people, but he argues that racism, as a specific ideology of biological superiority arose with the development of the capitalist mode of production. Cox dates the rise of capitalism to around the beginning of the sixteenth century, although most historians argue that feudalism prevailed until well into the eighteenth century. Cox links colonialism and capitalism and argues that racism arose as a justification for colonialist expansion. It excused the subjugation and exploitation of local people by economically powerful invaders. It continued

Table 14-2 Immigration of Selected Groups into Canada

Group	Date	Major Occupation
Native Peoples	Pre–1600	All occupational roles of self-contained societies
French	1609–1755	Fishing, farming, fur trading and supporting occupations: military, blacksmithing, etc.
Loyalists from U.S.A.: Mennonites, Blacks, Germans, English, Scots, Quakers	1776 to mid-1780s	Farming
English & Scots	mid-1600s on and 1815 on	Farming, skilled crafts
Germans & Scandinavians	1830s to 1850s and c. 1900, 1950s	Farming Mining, city jobs
Irish	1940s	Farming, logging, construction
Blacks from U.S.A.	1850s to 1870s	Farming
Mennonites & Hutterites	1870s through 1880s	Farming
Chinese	1855 and 1880s	Panning gold Railway building, mining
Jews	1890s to WWI	Factory work, skilled trades, small business
Japanese	1890s to WWI	Logging, service employment in city, mining, fishing
East Indians	1890s to WWI and 1970s	Logging, service employment, mining Skilled trades, professions, farm work in B.C.
Ukrainians	1890s to 1914 1940s to 1950s	Farming Variety of occupations
Italians	1890s to WWI 1950s to 1960s	Railway building, other construction, small business Construction, skilled trades
Polish	1945–1950	Skilled trades, factory work, mining
Portuguese	1950s to 1970s	Factory work, construction, service occupations, farming
Greeks	1955 to mid-1970s	Factory work, small business, skilled trades
Hungarians	1956–1957	Professions, variety of other occupations
West Indians	1950s and 1967 on	Domestic work, nursing Factory work, skilled trades, professional service occupations, contract farm labour
Central/South Americans	1970s and 1980s	Professions, factory and service occupations
Vietnamese	late 1970s to early 1980s	Variety of occupations, including self-employment

Source: Cross-Cultural Communication Centre (no date).

thereafter to legitimate the super-exploitation of indigenous peoples as slaves, indentured labourers, and cheap labour for corporate interests. According to Cox, the fight against racism thus entails the destruction of the capitalist system, which produced it.

Subsequent modifications of this structuralist–Marxist thesis retain the basic conceptualization of racial and ethnic minorities as complicating factors or *fractions* in the concept of the working class. The minorities' subordinate position within the economy is explained in terms of class relations under capitalism (Brittan and Maynard 1984, 35–36). *Fractions* refer to stratification within classes, when particular groups, such as migrants, experience systematic economic disadvantage that sets them apart from their counterparts in the dominant white ethnic group. These fractions come to have a particular place in cultural ideology once an ascribed label, such as race, is used to classify and negatively evaluate them (Brittan and Maynard 1984, 45–46).

Some theorists in the Marxist tradition argue that racism is a relatively autonomous ideology that may vary independently of class. But while such complications are acknowledged, the Marxist thesis still argues that categories of race and ethnic group are constructed under certain conditions of capitalist production and are determined in the final analysis by these productive conditions.

The central function of ideologies of ethnocentrism, prejudice, and racism is to divide the working class and thus weaken its potential for unified revolt against the dominant capitalist class. Discrimination against distinctive ethnic and racial groups, the same as against women, serves the dual functions of permitting their super-exploitation in the lowest paid jobs and promoting an aristocracy of labour among the more favoured white ethnic group. Members of this privileged sector then develop their own interests in perpetuating the vertical mosaic, and this facilitates capitalist exploitation of labour in general.

John Rex developed a modified version of this divide and rule theory in which he argues that class struggle and racist ideologies are determined by and reflected in competition over the allocation of scarce resources such as jobs, housing, and educational opportunities. Instead of uniting to fight capitalism for failing to meet their basic needs, people fight each other: locals pitted against immigrants, whites against blacks. In Canada, Francophones compete against Anglophones for coveted civil service jobs. In Britain, Rex suggests, black immigrants fare the worst of all groups and are pushed into high density, decaying areas in the inner cities, where they are subject to super-exploitation by slum landlords who exact the utmost possible rent from black tenants. These tenants have difficulty moving into better and often cheaper accommodation in other neighbourhoods because of discrimination.

Reformulations of Structuralist–Marxist Theory

The classical structuralist–Marxist model described above has a compelling rationale, as does traditional functionalism. But as an explanation for ethnicity, prejudice, and racism, the model has serious shortcomings. The focus on functions for the capitalist system leads in a different direction from the traditional functionalist emphasis on shared culture and social cohesion, but there are similar underlying logical and methodological flaws. Enumerating the functions for capitalism of patterns of racism and ethnocentrism does not establish the cause of these patterns, any more than the argument that "birds have wings in order to fly" explains why birds developed wings and we did not.

Certain critical requirements must be met for structuralist–Marxist theory to provide an adequate explanation of a structure.

First, any functionalist explanation requires a clear statement of intent on someone's part. Structures are perpetuated because they have consequences that are perceived as useful, desirable, or functional for certain people. Secondly, and most importantly, such explanation needs to be grounded in the analysis of the systematic and continuous feedback mechanisms that serve to reproduce, on an ongoing basis, those structures that give rise to the desired consequences. Thirdly, insofar as the patterns in question are not equally in the interests of all members of a given society, it is necessary to show how members of a particular class or group are able to activate those feedback mechanisms that support the structures beneficial to them, against the opposing actions of other groups for whom such structures are dysfunctional (Stinchcombe 1968, 80–100).

This reformulation entails far-reaching changes in the analysis of ethnic and race relations, moving from the passive description of effects to an active analysis of how reality is socially constructed. It entails an analysis in which central importance is given to the relative power of different ethnic and racial groups to influence the variety of mechanisms that structure social relations on an ongoing basis. The outcome of such struggles is never wholly predetermined and is never static.

Brittan and Maynard (1984, 35–70) offer a particularly insightful critique of the structuralist–Marxist model. We will draw on their analysis as we outline some of the major problems and then explore critical alternative approaches. These approaches are developing out of a Marxist tradition but involve a very different methodology and very different assumptions about how the social world that we think of as "capitalist" comes to be put together.

Oliver Cox's early formulation of a Marxist explanation for racism, which reduces it to an ideology developed in the sixteenth century to legitimate colonialism, has been largely discredited. While Brittan and Maynard do not doubt that racism can serve this function, they question whether this explains either its origins or perpetuation. There is evidence that black skins were associated with dirt and evil in Western culture long before colonial expansion began and certainly several centuries before capitalism began to displace feudal relations in Europe. Interracial and intertribal wars, and even genocide, were not unknown in the Americas and Africa before colonialism by Europeans. On the other hand, the refined **biological-genetic theory of race**, which posits that people with different skin colours evolved from distinct subspecies of humans and have innately different levels of intelligence and other attributes, emerged only in the late eighteenth and early nineteenth century, well after capitalism and slavery had become institutionalized. Brittan and Maynard also reject Cox's attempt to distinguish racism from mere "cultural intolerance," within which he includes anti-semitism. It is a serious weakness that Cox's model cannot account for anti-semitism. There are clear problems with the causal analysis of the mechanisms involved in the model.

The modified Marxist thesis subsumes ethnic and racial divisions under variants of working-class status. They are explained as functioning for the super-exploitation of labour for profits. Brittan and Maynard find this model problematic in several respects. It assumes that ethnic and racial identity have no reality other than in terms of class struggle. All minorities and non-whites are lumped together as if they constituted a homogeneous sub-class. Deeply felt group consciousness, reflected in Black Power in the United States, a native Indian cultural revival, or attempts in Quebec to safeguard Francophone culture, are all reduced to aspects of false consciousness: ideologies that weaken working-class solidarity. Traditional Marxists would argue that such group consciousness detracts from the class struggle. Also, according to Marxist analysis, divisions based on ethnicity and race, and the ideologies of ethnocentrism and racism that legitimate them, should not exist in non-capitalist or socialist societies. The ethnic strife in the Soviet Union, which has surfaced under the more open government of Gorbachev, belies such assumptions.

The argument that ideologies like ethnocentrism, racism, and sexism exist because they are functional for capitalism also founders on a serious methodological problem. It relies essentially on a conspiratorial explanation, implying that such patterns represent a deliberately contrived plan on the part of the ruling class. The mechanisms by which racism is produced and transmitted to the working classes remain unspecified. Nor are reasons given as to why whites do not reject such contrived ideas or develop their own. In this deterministic model, members of the working class are portrayed as sheer cultural dopes, incapable of thinking for themselves. Minority group members similarly appear as ignorant pawns in a game over which they have no control.

The theory that racism exists or persists because it is functional for capitalism also exonerates whites from culpability for the deprived status and oppression of minorities. The system produces it, not the white racists themselves. In effect, Brittan and Maynard suggest, Marxist theories of racism, like Marxist theories of sexism, constitute an ideology of dominant white males. Their dominance can be accounted for as functional for capitalism, and at the same time the claims of cultural and racial groups can be dismissed as false consciousness. The concern of white males with their own class oppression takes precedence.

Brittan and Maynard further challenge the assumption that ethnic divisions, ethnocentrism, and racism are in fact as functional for the capitalist system as the Marxist model implies. Capitalism in different locations may well accommodate to and mould existing racial and ethnic divisions, but that is not the same thing as saying that capitalism *requires* such divisions. The reverse may actually be true: such divisions may be dysfunctional for the optimal efficiency of capitalism. A recurrent theme in literature on South Africa is that apartheid is in fact bad for business, and that developments within capitalism may be instrumental in breaking it down (Adam and Moodley 1986).

Ethnicity and Political Struggle

Crean and Rioux's impassioned defence of Quebec nationalism and Québécois culture stands as a strong indictment of the structuralist–Marxist argument that ethnic diversity is the result of efforts by capitalism to fragment workers. They argue firstly that the prevailing corporate capitalist culture of North America promotes anything but ethnic diversity (Crean and Rioux 1983, 74–128). The economies of Quebec and Canada as a whole are dominated by the branch plants of American multinational corporations, and they breed branch-plant cultures propagated through corporate-owned mass media. The cultural industries are big business, worth an estimated six billion dollars in 1980 alone. It is these corporate giants, not childhood socialization, that dictate the culture of our society, extolling individualism, materialism, competition, and a narrow scientific rationalism. It is a culture that imitates what Crean and Rioux see as the "American way of life," dominated by automobiles, televisions, and computers.

Crean and Rioux take seriously the fear expressed by Marxist philosophers like Marcuse (1964) that the pervasive influence of mass media will give rise to one-dimensional people, capable only of uniform thought. People may become so pacified by standardized mass entertainment and simplified television versions of current events that they will lose the capacity to think creatively and independently. The American mass culture industry is governed by a paramount concern with cutting costs through the centralized mass production of standardized items. It is an industry that prizes uniformity and repetition rather than diversity. **Cultural imperialism** is insidious because of its capacity to erode identity and replace the values and customs of the dominated with those of the dominator. It wreaks havoc on smaller and traditional cultures. Against American corporate giants in television, movies, and publishing, Québécois and Canadian artists and cultural outlets need massive subsidies just to survive.

Québécois nationalism and culture form a voice of *resistance* to the homogenizing forces of capitalism. The Québécois retreated into small rural communities after their conquest by the British. They "kept the faith" even as their leaders went to France or collaborated with the English conquerors (Rioux 1978, chap. 3). A local, popular culture was generated through what people did in their villages and neighbourhoods. Such a culture is not just a collection of traits to be enumerated, but the expression of the "innovative, self-creative capacity of people and collective imagination" (Crean and Rioux 1983, 77). For Crean and Rioux (1983, 18), such nationalism is part of the human make-up, a natural expression of responsibility and self-realization.

English-Canadian nationalism and distinctive cultural identity have also been slowly emerging. These too provide a voice of resistance to being swallowed up by American corporate capitalist culture. This resistance is anathema to the corporate vision of continentalism. Its role as opposition became very clear in 1976 with the passage of Bill C–58 or the "Time–Readers' Digest Bill." This bill amended the Income Tax Act to disallow tax deductions for advertising expenses paid to non-Canadian corporations such as border television stations and American *Time* magazine. The objective was to funnel more advertizing dollars into fledgling Canadian magazines. The tumultuous opposition from American business interests to this bill showed just how much was at stake. More recently, concern that Canadian cultural industries will be swamped by American giants was raised in the free trade debate.

When John Porter dismisses this kind of local culture and nationalism as a backward step into particularism and biological descent groups, instead of forward into individualism, universalism, and the values of science and technology, or when structuralist–Marxists dismiss it as the false consciousness of people artificially divided by capitalism, they are dismissing something very important to people. Both approaches, however unwittingly, tend to promote the ideology of multinational imperialism, where diversity is replaced with uniformity and mass production because it is functional for business.

The critical question is whether local culture can survive in the face of the overwhelming force of corporate mass media. At the conclusion of their book, Crean and Rioux seem to be pressing for a vision of an ideal society that is very close to that of Ivan Illich, which we discussed in chapter 13 on education. It is a society based on worker decision making in plants, self-managed enterprise, co-operatives, communes, storefront social services, and so on. Bowles and Gintis suggest that this is the vision of the disinherited entrepreneurial and independent professional class that has been displaced by corporate capitalism and state bureaucracies. Whatever its class of origin, or likelihood of survival against the onslaught of corporate business interests, such ethnic nationalism is clearly related to the capitalist system, but as a dysfunction continually pushing against those structures

Ideologies of ethnocentrism, prejudice, and racism divide the working class and permit the super-exploitation of ethnic and racial minorities.

that promote uniformity in the interest of business. This is an important theoretical shift from the economic determinism of the structuralist–Marxist model, a shift that many theorists argue is much closer to how Marx himself analysed class struggles.

From this perspective, ethnic consciousness is not an entity. It cannot be identified by adding up a set of cultural traits or listing kinship ties. It is a process that emerges in social and political struggle. The classical theorist Max Weber ([1922] 1978, 389) sums this up well when he insists that:

> It is primarily the political community, no matter how artificially organized, that inspired the belief in common ethnicity. This belief tends to persist even after the disintegration of the political community, unless drastic differences in the custom, physical type, or above all, language exist among its members.

In New Brunswick, in September 1989, the newly formed Confederation of Regions Party gave expression to the emerging Anglophone ethnic consciousness. At the root of this consciousness seems to be intense concern with provincial policies for implementing official bilingualism. Monolingual Anglophones fear that such policies restrict their access to senior civil service jobs. They see the members of the minority Acadian population as unfairly advantaged because they are more likely to be fluently bilingual. Ironically, while many Acadians welcome the commitment to provide services in French, some of them fear that the expanding number of bilingual Anglophones may weaken Acadian cultural integrity and political influence.

The "ethnic vote" has long been an integral part of Canadian politics. Far from isolating minorities from mainstream democracy, as traditional liberal functionalist such as Porter have feared, ethnic group consciousness has helped to mobilize people and draw them into provincial and federal politics. An article by Paul Gessell (*Daily Gleaner* (Fredericton), 4 June 1988, 5) describes what he calls the political maturation of Canada's non-Anglophone and non-Francophone groups. During the 1930s on the Prairies, Ukrainians, Poles, and Germans, along with other European groups, began to take control of the political machinery in their communities. Over a thirty-year period this has developed to the point of producing such high-profile politicians as Don Mazankowski, Ray Hnatyshyn, and Jake Epp. Ottawa region contenders for federal party nominations push hard to sign up riding members among Chinese and Urdu speakers. In Montreal area ridings, Italians, East Indians, and Haitians are winning such nominations. People are drawn into politics as members of groups rather than as isolated individuals deciding their vote in front of their television set. Recent emphasis on multiculturalism and affirmative action oriented to groups, rather than to individuals, may well reflect the growing concern of major parties with winning the ethnic vote, particularly the growing voting power of visible minorities.

Traditional functionalism views ethnicity as a holdover of ascriptive kinship ties that are out of place in modern economies. But this perspective cannot account for the active regeneration and cultivation of Québécois and Canadian nationalism and ethnic group voting power. Similarly, structuralist Marxists conceptualize ethnic consciousness as working-class fractions, produced by the capitalist system to divide and rule the mass of people. But this cannot account for the empowerment and resistance evident in such nationalism. Contemporary developments in critical theory, which we explore below, give central focus precisely to these dimensions of power, struggle, resistance, and the active social construction of ethnicity and ethnic consciousness.

The Social Construction of Ethnicity, Gender, and Class

This contemporary approach is inspired by Marxist theory but adopts a methodology and mode of explanation that is very different from the more familiar structuralist Marxism described above. At many points in the following discussion, you will find key words, like *ethnicity* and *class*, in quotation marks to signify that the terms are not being used in their customary sense. They do not denote observable characteristics of people. They refer rather to processes and relations between people.

Ethnicity as a Process

One major difference between structuralist Marxism and social constructionism lies in how the notions of ethnicity, race, gender, and class are conceptualized. The classical approach has been to view them as existing entities that can be observed and measured. The notion of *ethnic group*, for example, is measured through indicators such as descent, common language, common religion, and shared feelings of belonging to the same group. Such a list can be expanded and varied depending on the particular group being studied. *Class*, on the other hand, can be observed through such indicators as occupation, level of income, level of education, and the like. Then research into the relations between the two concepts proceeds by measuring the statistical correlations between the two lists of indicators. Porter's *The Vertical Mosaic* (1968) uses this approach. Gender usually falls outside the realm of analytical relevance altogether for ethnic theorists, or it is categorized as a distinct subset and put in a separate chapter.

For Ng (1988a, 11), the problem is not that such correlations are wrong, but that the approach itself makes it impossible to see the actual connections between the features being measured. Indicators are treated from the start as **independent variables**, to be included as statistically distinct entities. Ng insists that ethnicity, gender, and class are not *things* but *processes*. They are aspects of relations between people, which emerge in the process of struggles over the control of the means of production and reproduction in a given society.

Ethnicity is produced by people in the context of their everyday activities. In order to understand ethnicity, we should begin by looking at how people relate to each other, such that what we subsequently observe as "ethnic differences" actually come about. In much the same way, it would be a mistake to list all the observable differences between women and men, treat them as givens, and then use the differences to explain the resulting social situation of women and men. We know that a major proportion of these observable differences are themselves produced by the social situation of women and men.

In the terminology of ethnomethodology, these observables have already been worked up by social processes that are not immediately visible to us. What we need to look at is not these end products, but the processes that produce them. This approach involves starting at the most basic level of local settings to find out what people actually do in their ordinary, everyday lives to produce these observables. The next step is to explore how this world of immediate experience is structured by social relations beyond it. Smith (1986) refers to this approach as **institutional ethnography**.

The idea that we should try to think in terms of processes, rather than entities, may be easiest to see at first with reference to the concept of class. Braverman (1974, 24) argues that *class* does not refer to a specified group of people but is "an expression for an ongoing social process." This social process involves relations between people and how these relations are changing the way people

have access to the means of production. Skilled professionals in a corporate office, for example, may find their working relations slowly shifting from managerial activities toward machine processing as computers with decision-making functions are introduced. The people involved are the same people, employed in the same office, and with the same job titles, but their class relations have changed. In other words, their situations as workers in relation to processes of production has changed. Their location within the labour market as self-employed entrepreneurs or autonomous skilled workers may change to that of employees hired to do standardized tasks. Their rights and privileges as workers and their relations with employers, co-workers, and clients will also change. Professional social workers engaged in skilled casework and counselling, for example, may find their class relations shifting into that of secretary-bookkeeper as their caseloads expand and standardized forms are introduced to speed up the processing of clients. Conversely, a boy who drops out of high school to take an unskilled job may amuse himself tinkering with his car. When his friends offer to pay him something to fix their cars, his class relations slowly take on aspects of an independent businessman.

Ethnicity is a process rather than an entity in much the same way. The aboriginal peoples of Canada came to be native Indians only through the process of colonization, which "destroyed, re-organized, fragmented and homogenized the myriad tribal groups across the land" (Ng 1988a, 7). The English, Scottish, Irish, and Welsh ethnic groups crystallized into a single British group as they established their dominance in Central Canada with the backing of the British colonial government. Alternatively, the British immigrants splintered into English, Scottish, and Irish in the Maritimes as they struggled for ascendancy over land, tenancies, fishing rights, control over fish processing, and so on. They became so divided that, less than fifty years ago in the Maritimes, they saw themselves as belonging to different races (Ng 1988a, 12). In the 1930s, in the Maritimes, marriages across religious groups, such as Baptists and Roman Catholics, were formally registered as "interracial marriages." Now, with the stress on bilingualism in government service, the main division is between French-speaking Acadians and English-speaking groups in the struggle over jobs.

Relations between ethnicity and class are also best understood as processes. They cannot be studied as sets of variables that can be measured by statistical correlations between indicators. These relations are formed through social processes as a unity. Within the Canadian state, argues Ng, "class" is inherently an ethnic phenomenon. The processes of class and ethnic formation are historically identical. The one simply cannot

be understood except in terms of the other. British immigrants generally came to dominate the Canadian middle and upper classes because this was precisely how the immigration process was organized. This pattern did not simply happen by itself, or come about without human intervention as the result of the functioning of the capitalist system.

Ng (1988a, 8) describes the work of immigration societies set up in most major cities of Canada in the nineteenth century to organize patterns of immigration. Mainly upper-class women reformers actively organized the emigration of working-class girls from Britain to serve as domestics and wives in Canada. The avowed goal of the reformers was to ensure the white character and Christian morality of the dominant group. In the 1890s, peasant farmers of central European stock were encouraged to migrate in large numbers to settle the Prairies, and hence the ethnic class composition of

Figure 14-2 Level of Immigration and Unemployment Rates, Canada, 1946–80

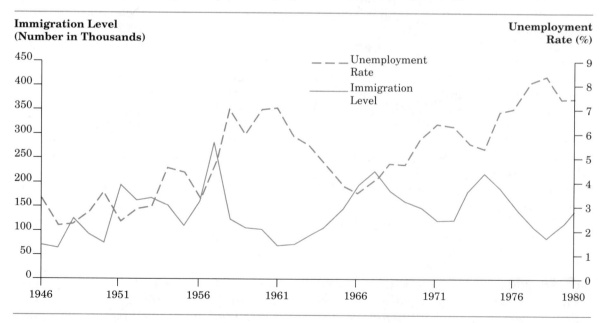

Source: Employment and Immigration Canada, Immigration and Demographic Policy Group, *Immigration Statistics, 1981* (Annual); Statistics Canada, Labour Fource Survey Division, *The Labour Force* (Monthly), Cat. No. 71–001.

that area was formed. Unskilled labourers were encouraged to come to build railroads and canals. They emigrated from countries in which the collapse of the domestic economy had created large pools of destitute people seeking their livelihood anywhere they could find it. So the ethnic-classes of Irish navvies and Chinese coolies were socially constructed.

Subsequent policies were designed to perpetuate these social relations to production for migrating people. Land prices were artificially inflated beyond the means of these migrants so that they remained wage labourers rather than becoming independent farmers. Chinese women were not permitted to immigrate; this helped to ensure a gender-class of temporary Chinese male migrants.

The Immigration Act that came into effect in 1978 divides immigrants into three categories. The **independent immigrant** category, which includes "assisted relatives," comprises people whose entry into Canada is subject to economic requirements and criteria measured by a point system. People gain points according to their level of education, job skills, and ability to meet current labour shortages in Canada. The category of **business-class immigrants** comprises people who have capital to invest in Canadian industries and businesses and can provide guarantees that they will create employment opportunities in Canada. A third category of **sponsored** or **family-class immigrants** includes people who do not accrue enough points by themselves but who are sponsored into Canada by a close relative. In addition, people can apply for **refugee status** and be assessed by a different set of criteria.

Gender Bias in Immigration

This immigration policy is generating a particular form of **gender-ethnic-class** relations within Canada (Ng 1988b, 16). Ng points out that the formal wording of the classifications do not refer to the gender, ethnic origin, or class position of individuals. But the criteria used to determine entry, based on language proficiency, educational attainment, Canadian labour-force requirements, and investment potential, have built-in sexist, racist, and class biases. People from western Europe have a clear advantage in the points system, along with members of the highly educated, English-speaking elite from parts of Asia.

Currently, business people with capital to invest in Canada are in high demand. The migration of Hong Kong Chinese businessmen is encouraged. This has resulted in the formation of an ethnic-class within the Canadian economy very different from that of their Chinese predecessors. A very particular kind of gender-ethnic-class is formed as the wives and children of these businessmen settle in Canada for three-year periods with the intent of qualifying for Canadian citizenship. Their husbands remain in Hong Kong where they can expect to earn huge profits on their investments (Smart 1988). A new class of ultra-rich Chinese women is thus slowly emerging in larger Canadian cities.

At the other end of the vertical mosaic, a different form of gender-ethnic-class is emerging. Black women from the Caribbean enter Canada on temporary work permits as domestics and nannies to care for the children of professional couples. It may be five years or longer before these women gain landed immigrant status and are able to bring their own children to Canada from the Carribean. Their children, often teenagers when they arrive, commonly experience serious problems adjusting to family life in Canada with a mother whom they may not have seen for several years. Many of these children have a limited education, which equips them for only marginal, low-income jobs in Canada. This is part of the process of the social construction of ethnic-class stratification that results in young blacks being especially vulnerable to drug traffickers eager to recruit new customers.

Ng's research focusses on the people who enter Canada as sponsored or family-class immigrants. The majority of these are children and women from the Third World who enter as the dependants of a man who is already residing in Canada. Women are frequently classified as "family class" even when they have been in the paid labour force in their home countries. The husband is classified as the wage earner with the wife as his dependant.

This pattern where males are considered the primary immigrants and females their dependants is particularly pronounced with respect to the admission of refugees. A report on refugees by the National Action Committee on the Status of Women (NAC) (1987, 1) estimates that, during the 1980s, women and children constituted 75 to 80 percent of all refugees and displaced persons in different parts of the world. Women flee their home countries for many of the same reasons as men, but they also face additional persecution as women. In many countries, women may face torture and even execution for such "crimes" as the violation of marital, behavioural, or dress codes specific to women. During wartime, many are widowed and must support their children alone. While fleeing from their homes or surviving in refugee camps, women are also particularly vulnerable to sexual abuse, especially when they do not have the protection of a man. Yet the outstanding feature of Canadian refugee applications is that about 80 percent of them are made by men (National Action Committee on the Status of Women 1987, 2). Most women "refugees" in Canada are sponsored by husbands who have made a previous successful refugee claim. Very few female refugees receive asylum in Canada without the agency of a husband. This means that most of the women who are here are mem-

bers of a relatively small proportion of family units that survive refugee-creating situations intact.

NAC lobbied the federal government to recognize persecution based on sex as just cause for a refugee claim and to agree to accept more female-headed families from refugee camps. In 1988 the Canadian government responded by selecting twenty-five such women, a miniscule proportion of all refugees accepted. For practical purposes, the working definition of "immigrant" and "refugee" is male, with women qualifying only as their sponsored dependants.

The designation of the majority of women entering Canada as family-class or sponsored immigrants has significant consequences for the treatment they receive once they arrive. Sponsored immigrants are not entitled to public assistance, welfare, or any training subsidies. Their sponsor is legally responsible for their welfare, and they can be deported if they are deemed to be a financial burden on the Canadian state. Ng (1988b, 17) points out that this forces many immigrant women into complete dependence on their male sponsors and contributes to their isolation in sometimes unpleasant and even abusive family situations. Their lack of access to government-subsidized language and job-training programs means that they are forced to seek work that is low-paid and marginal.

Arguments about whether race or sex has priority in the oppression of such women are futile. Statistical profiles based on multiple correlations among indicators of country of origin, skin colour, religion, language, and the like, offer little insight into how gender-ethnic-class position within Canada actually gets put together. The vertical mosaic is produced by a combination of immigration policies, the vested interests—both economic and political—that generate such policies, and the way in which these policies are implemented over time. As Ng expresses it, the "ethnic phenomenon" cannot be severed from the relations that give rise to it. Neither can we begin to understand gender, ethnic, and class relations without taking into consideration how they have been and still are being brought about and organized by the Canadian state. The word **state** refers not just to big government, but also to the behaviour of people at all levels of the civil service and related bureaucracies, agencies, departments, and offices. The capitalist system does not function as an entity by itself. It is produced by the behaviour of people.

Institutional Ethnography: The Accomplishment of Gender–Ethnic–Class

Ng (1988b, 15) uses the approach of institutional ethnography in studying immigrant women in Canada. She notes that, technically, the term "immigrant women" refers to all women who are landed immigrants in Canada. These women are concentrated at the top and the bottom of the Canadian occupational hierarchy, either in skilled professional jobs or in unskilled, dead-end positions. But people rarely think of white, educated, English-speaking women in professional occupations as immigrants. What comes to mind when one thinks of an immigrant woman is the image of someone who speaks poor English, who is a member of a visible minority group, usually from the Third World, and who works in an occupation such as office cleaning or garment making. Thus, suggests Ng (1988b, 15), "'immigrant women' is a socially constructed category presupposing, among other things, a labour market relation."

In her research, Ng explores how this observable reality gets produced. How is it that these women come to take on the characteristics and the location in the labour market that others subsequently come to think of as typical of immigrant women? Why is it that one English-speaking, professional woman from India described herself as "never feeling like a stranger in Canada," while others who have been here fifty years still feel like immigrants?

The garment industry employs cheap immigrant labour to compete in international markets.

To help her to answer these questions, Ng (1986; 1988b) studied the work of counsellors in a non-profit employment agency set up for immigrant women. She was concerned with the way in which the counsellors do their work and how this actually produces and maintains a labour market stratified by gender and ethnicity. Agency workers found themselves performing three contradictory roles: assisting immigrant women in finding jobs, acting as agents for employers looking for workers, and socializing women in what was expected of them.

The first stage of the counselling process was the in-take procedure. Job applicants were screened, and anyone not of West Indian, or Chinese-, Italian-, or Spanish-speaking origin was refused service. Initially, the agency had intended to serve all immigrants, with these four groups prominent among potential clients, but the wording of the contract for government funding led to rigidity (Ng 1988b, 36). Later, when the agency asked for additional counsellors to serve a growing number of Vietnamese, Portuguese, and East Indian women, this request was not granted. The formal language of the funding contract thus made membership in a specific ethnic group a determining factor in whether employment assistance would be granted.

The subsequent counselling interview was almost totally constructed by the necessity of filling out the official application for employment forms that the agency used to keep statistics on job placements to justify the funding it received. Any discussion not immediately relevant to the forms was cut off. The counsellors' work involved translating whatever descriptions women gave of previous work experience into a set of categories that fitted job openings supplied by employers.

In the next stage, counsellors screened applicants for employers by matching applicants' skills, as determined by counsellors in the initial interview, with the set of skills specified by the employers. The agency needed a steady flow of job openings in order to function and had a stable network of contacts with employers most likely to hire immigrant women. These were typically large establishments paying minimum wage for repetitive, low-skill work. Women who came to the agency were thus counselled into precisely the kind of jobs with which immigrant women are associated. The possibility of any real diversity of occupation was excluded by the way the agency worked.

In the last stage, counsellors socialized women on the rules of the Canadian labour market, with explicit instructions about the importance of such attributes as punctuality, cleanliness, and so on, and what to say at the job interview. The end result of this work process was the production of "immigrant women" as a special kind of commodity in the labour market. The agency functioned as a subcontracted agency of the state in managing the segregated labour market.

In Ng's words (1988b, 12)

> the agency's operation underwent certain transformations from its inception so that it came to function on behalf of the state apparatus in organizing and producing immigrant women as a distinctive kind of labour, as "commodities," in the Canadian labour market.

Ng alludes briefly to the ways in which this local labour market is itself embedded in a wider set of relations. The Toronto garment industry employs cheap immigrant labour in order to compete in international markets organized around particular patterns of international division of labour. Highly paid, high-technology production is carried on in the capitalist First World, and poorly paid, unskilled assembly work is done in the Third World (Ng 1986). Workers are continually displaced from their means of livelihood in Third World countries. This displacement produces the waves of immigrants coming to Canada to find jobs. There is nothing specifically ethnic about this process. It is not the cultural attributes of the people themselves that account for immigrant women as garment workers. The process is the result of people's activities in a multitude of specific locations such as the employment agency studied by Ng.

In another study, Ng (1981) explores how "ethnicity" for housewives arises from the way in which Canadian society is organized. There is nothing in their everyday lives as homemakers that makes such women intrinsically any different culturally from any other housewives. Their "ethnicity" emerges only in their relations with society when they do not know how to handle Canadian currency when shopping or know how to get around the city on public transit or how to drive the family car. "Ethnicity" is posited as the reason for this incompetence. However, these women managed such activities quite competently in the countries from which they came.

Ng gives an example of a social worker describing difficulties that Portuguese immigrant women have in combining full-time employment with caring for their families. The social worker notes that, in Portugal, mothers usually are the centre of their family world and do not work outside the home. There is nothing ethnic about women finding it hard to cope with a double shift, yet ethnicity is used to account for Portuguese women's problems. Ng suggests that the social worker has learned to use ethnicity as an explanation for experiences. It is part of what one learns in academia, and it is reproduced in research that starts with ethnicity as given.

The "incompetence" that labels housewives as immigrants is itself caused by the way in which Canadian society is organized. It reflects not only state practices with respect to women but also a specific historical form of economy that segregates economic processes from the daily and generational production of the lives of people (Smith 1983, 2; Ng, 1986, 13). Since house-

work is not defined as a job, immigrant housewives are accorded the status of dependants. Hence, they do not qualify for language and job training provided for immigrant breadwinners. Children of immigrants are required to go to school in Canada, but adults can only attend community college programs, for which they must pay fees. Housewives do not earn money and so can only go with the approval and financial support of husbands.

If these women were treated differently when they arrived in Canada, they would not display the kind of behaviour viewed as characteristic of them as types of women. These characteristics are not attributes of the women themselves, but are effects of the treatment they receive. A volunteer agency funded with a different set of criteria, and with different application forms to fill in, could produce a very different reality. One could imagine agencies geared to matching immigrant women with counsellors whose job it would be to teach them basic language, shopping, bus-riding, and car-driving skills. Such coping mechanisms do not imply the total cultural assimilation of basic beliefs and sentiments envisioned in the functionalist model, but merely a practical working knowledge of how the society of the locality in which they live is organized. This itself would alter their characteristics as commodities within the labour force. They would no longer have the credentials typical of workers destined for unskilled jobs in garment factories or as office cleaners. Their credentials, and hence their potential location within the labour market, would be transformed.

The institutional ethnography approach shares with the Marxist perspective the recognition that several classes of people in Canadian society have vested interests in not providing for or requiring education classes for immigrant women. Employers of cheap labour benefit from the production of an underclass of segregated labour. Middle-class ethnic businesses benefit from a captive clientele. Within immigrant families, husbands may benefit from the dependence of wives, which segregates them from the more liberated behaviour of Canadian women. When men decide whether or not to teach their wives to drive the family car, it has direct implications for their own status and ownership rights over the car and where and when the family goes out in it. That men generally are in the position to make such decisions tells us much about the social organization of family economies and car ownership in Canada. The price that immigrant women pay for their high level of dependency in terms of misery, isolation, and at times virtual imprisonment in their homes, can be very high indeed (Wilson 1978).

Research in the social construction of reality tradition draws upon the insights of ethnomethodology into how people use their common-sense understandings to try to make sense of what is happening around them and what they themselves are doing. Concepts such as "race" or "ethnicity" are not facts that can be taken as given. They are the outcomes of social processes through which people interpret what is going on. The social constructionist perspective explores the social processes through which what we subsequently come to perceive as race or ethnicity, gender, and class is produced in everyday interaction. Such concepts are not used to refer to traits that individual people have, but to the outcomes of processes that organize Canadian society in particular ways. Research that treats these observables, and the patterns of social organization, as given, becomes part of the ideological process that legitimates and maintains them.

A further dimension in the social construction of ethnicity, which has been the focus of both ethnomethodological and Marxist research, is the nature of ideological processes themselves and how they come to construct what we think and what we imagine others around us are thinking. We need to explore how it is that members of a society come to view the apparent inequalities along racial, ethnic, and gender lines as somehow legitimate, merited, or at least, to accept them as natural.

The dimension of "public opinion," which functionalists treat as the foundation of social order, is itself a social construction. As Smith has emphasized, our knowledge of society comes to us, for the most part, at second hand. Most of us never see the inner workings of an employment agency dealing with immigrant women, so we have to rely on Ng's description of it for our "facts." Many of us may have no direct experience of immigrants or ethnic minorities, particularly if we live in more homogeneous small towns and villages. We learn what and how to think about minorities from information that reaches us mostly through books, newspapers, radio, and television. Such accounts are put together by professionals: by journalists and academics. Increasingly, social science professionals provide the framework within which people learn to talk about and to account for experience. When we learn to think about members of minority groups in functionalist terms, with such concepts as "culture" as a unitary system of values and beliefs, we also learn to think in terms of "us" and "them." When groups of people running away from a war are described as "illegal aliens" in newspapers, it invokes emotions that set "us" against "them." An alternative choices of words might have evoked empathy.

Sunahara (1981) described how anti-Japanese feeling in British Columbia before World War II made possible the internment of Japanese Canadians, and how a change in popular opinion after the war fostered demands for restitution and apology. What she does not explore is how such popular feelings were socially produced. How was knowledge socially constructed such that people came to think first one way and then another? Before the war, Japan was a rising world power competing with imperialist powers in Europe and North America. After the war, Japan was a potential trading partner of crucial significance to Canada. We need research on how such relations affect the kind of media coverage that prevails and the mechanisms through which the media influence public opinion.

Refugee Status as a Social Accomplishment

A similar process of media-driven panic about immigration occurred during 1987–88 when Bill C-55, a policy to restrict the flow of refugees into Canada, was being debated in the federal parliament. Notwithstanding some dissenting voices, the general impression created by the media coverage was that Canada was being swamped by hoards of bogus refugees pouring in to take unfair advantage of Canada's generosity. A typical newspaper article cited government spokespersons estimating that Canada's system of determining refugees was back logged by 30 000 or more claimants, with new ones coming in at the rate of about 2200 a month (*Globe and Mail*, 3 Feb. 1988, A1–2). An oft-repeated image was that of 174 East Indians, mostly Sikhs, landing at the tiny village of Charlesville, Nova Scotia, in July 1987. People were encouraged to watch the coastlines for "invaders." Dissenting voices from the Canadian Civil Liberties Association and Amnesty International suggested that the refugee system was working, and that all that might be needed was the imposition of visa requirements on travellers to Canada from certain countries. But the media portrayed such voices as the soft response of humanitarian advocates. They contrasted this with stories on the objective and reasoned response of government officials and the majority of Canadians rightly concerned with exploitation of Canada. It

was hard to remind oneself that, even at 2200 people a month, the "flood" of refugees constituted less than two percent of the total number of immigrants that come to Canada annually under the regular immigration policy. The underlying issue seems to have been not concern with how many people come to Canada but rather the Canadian government's desire to regulate what kind of people come, and how they fit labour-force requirements.

When Bill C-55 passed into law in January 1989, it gave government immigration officers the power to deport would-be refugees within seventy-two hours if their claim of persecution in the home country did not seem credible, if they did not have proper identification papers, or if they had arrived from another country deemed to be safe. The way in which *persecution, proper identifications* and *safe third country* are constructed in the initial interview process becomes a critical determinant of the future life chances of claimants.

Would an Asian woman running away from an arranged marriage, where she feared the possibility of being beaten or burned to death for failing to provide an adequate dowry, be considered to have a legitimate claim of persecution? A case cited by the National Action Committee on the Status of Women (1987b, 3) was that of an Islamic woman who was punished for showing too much hair in public. The authorities fixed her veil to her head with thumb tacks. She was also whipped and threatened that, if she were seen unsuitably dressed again, she would be sexually violated and possibly shot. Would such a woman, or multiple other women who fear punishment for disobeying dress codes, be seen as legitimate refugee claimants by Canadian immigration officials? Are such women being persecuted for the non-violent expression of political opinions, or would their dissent be interpreted as personal, not political?

The NAC brief points out that it is extremely difficult for women with children to get to the designated centres in their home countries where they might file a claim for refugee status. The brief also questions whether many women would be able to talk openly about sexual abuse in an immigration hearing. If women do describe such experiences, how might their claims for political asylum compare with claims by members of sports teams visiting Canada from Soviet bloc countries, who hope to escape from communism and play for western teams? More generally, how do we, or how do immigration officials, establish that fleeing from fear of persecution is legitimate, but fleeing from fear of malnutrition and disease is unacceptable? Ostensibly simple procedures, such as the practical interpretation of what constitutes a safe third country also prove complex. For Canadians, the United States is a safe and friendly country, but is it also safe for people fearing persecution in Latin America for voicing left-wing political opinions?

The first deportation under the new refugee rules occurred on 6 January 1989. An East Indian man failed to convince immigration officials that he risked persecution for belonging to a Punjabi student federation. Other members of the federation had been arrested for activities promoting the separate state of Khalistan. How might this claim be compared with those of Chinese students who supported activities in June 1989 to promote greater democratization in China?

Since the passage of the refugee bill, media attention has turned to other issues. We know very little about how the new policies are being put into practice or who is paying what price.

The social construction of reality perspective raises questions about how public opinion is shaped and how people such as immigration officers make decisions in the routine performance of their work. By asking such questions, social constructionists draw attention to the processes through which what we come to see as our daily reality is continually produced and reproduced.

The social construction of ethnic stratification, like all relations of superiority and inferiority, arises in and through the everyday actions of people in relations with each other. It is such encounters that make up the reality of what it means to be black, or native, or otherwise ethnic in Canada. Rose Tanner Brown (1977), a Jamaican woman married to a white Canadian, eloquently describes this reality. It is being singled out for baggage checks at customs every time she travels and having to prove that her battered camera was actually bought in Toronto. It is being stopped on the street by police for spot checks with much higher frequency than her white friends. It is having nervous shop assistants constantly tell her she cannot afford the clothes in their shop; it is regularly being mistaken for the maid instead of a professional woman. It is having an employment agency tell her they have no one on file for household help when she asks, but dozens available when her white husband asks. Afterwards, it is having the Ontario Ombudsman's office tell her that, since she is the prospective employer in this case, there is nothing they can do about it. Above all, it is having white Canadian friends almost invariably deny that such incidents happen, deny that there is racism in Canada, or insist that each of dozens of such incidents was just an isolated case to which she is over-reacting. Brown finds racism in Canada worse than in the United States. At least her American friends react with outrage to such incidents and insist on fighting back to remedy the injustice.

It is in such everyday behaviour that the status of blacks as lower class is socially constructed. When black people are routinely subjected to such humiliating

Events like Black History Week aim to educate people about the culture and contributions of minority groups and to help to modify the social construction of ethnic stratification.

treatment without other people openly objecting, they come to be seen, and perhaps to see themselves, as people whose inferior status warrants such treatment. Poor people, or people dressed in shabby clothes, get similar treatment from police and others. The difference is that a black woman is treated as lower class automatically, even when she is well dressed.

Conclusion

Ethnomethodology forces us to reconsider the role of sociology itself. Sociology is no longer simply an impartial mode of analysis of social reality. It is part of the process that produces that reality. A landlord, an employer, a politician, a police officer, reading the section of this chapter concerned with functionalist theory, will find persuasive and "scientific" grounds for discrimination, segregation, and exclusion of certain kinds of people, lest social cohesion and order be disturbed. Functionalism was, and still is, the dominant theoretical perspective in North American sociology. Texts written from this perspective still structure what most Canadian students learn as sociology of the family, sociology of education, stratification, and ethnicity. Its fundamental concepts of internalized consensus and order, unity, necessity, indispensability, and meritocracy, still provide a powerful and persuasive legitimation for society as we know it.

Structuralist–Marxist theory avoids many of these weaknesses. It focusses directly upon the exploitative character of the capitalist social system and incorporates dimensions of power and inequality into its analysis of class relations. The dysfunctions of the social system for the majority of its working-class members are clearly revealed.

Yet this form of Marxist theory has its

own rigidity and ideological biases. It promotes an explanation for everything in terms of its functions for the capitalist system. In some respects, as Brittan and Maynard suggest, this kind of rigid structuralism constitutes an ideology of dominant white males vis-à-vis women and ethnic minorities. Men are exonerated from culpability when the privatization of women in the home, the designation of domestic work as women's work, and the ghettoization of women in low-paid, low-prestige work are accounted for as functional for the capitalist system. The oppression and exploitation of women is blamed on the system and not on the sexist men who manipulate that system. Similarly, the explanation that racial and ethnic discrimination and ideologies of racism and prejudice exist because they are functional for capitalism exonerates whites in general from responsibility for what happens to ethnic and visible minorities. The women's movement, and separate demands for recognition and equal treatment by native Indians and other ethnic minorities, can be dismissed as false consciousness, as part of a capitalist plot to divide and rule the working class, and so to detract from the main goal of a socialist revolution. The class oppression of white males takes precedence over all other concerns.

A central question for contemporary sociology is how we can retain the positive insights of Marxist analysis while avoiding its oppressive aspects. Theorists who focus on the social construction of reality perspective argue that the problem lies in the preoccupation with abstract models and categories that lose sight of the processes, the actual activities of people in their relations with each other, through which the lived reality of gender, class, and ethnicity are socially produced. Above all, we have to recognize that there is no capitalist system that operates independently of what we ourselves are doing. There is no externalized structure, no entity that does not come from us. Whatever gets done, we do (Smith 1979, 17).

Suggested Reading

The book by Anthony Richmond, *Immigration and Ethnic Conflict* (1988), provides an overview of theoretical and practical issues concerned with ethnic relations in advanced industrial societies. He adopts a mainly structural-functionalist approach to the analysis of structural change and adaptation associated with migration and problems of racism and multiculturalism. The book draws upon Richmond's own extensive survey research on ethnic groups and assimilation in Canada.

The study by Edward N. Herberg, *Ethnic Groups in Canada: Adaptations and Transitions* (1989), provides comprehensive statistical data on the multi-ethnic character of Canada. Herberg draws extensively on Statistics Canada census report from 1871 to 1981 and other published survey research.

The article by John Porter "Ethnic Pluralism in Canadian Perspective" (1979), gives an overview of the traditional liberal-functionalist perspective on ethnicity. He includes a discussion of the "vertical mosaic." Porter also explores the pros and cons of bilingualism and biculturalism from a functionalist perspective.

For a short history of racism in Canada, see D.G. Hill and M. Schiff, *Human Rights in Canada: A Focus on Racism* 2nd ed. (1986). This booklet documents the often discriminatory and exploitative treatment of racial and ethnic minorities in Canada and the slow progress toward establishing a national policy on human rights.

The article by D. Baker, "Ethnicity, Development and Power: Canada in Comparative Perspective" (1977), provides historical evidence of the link between patterns of immigration in Canada and labour force requirements of the dominant group. A short essay by Paul Cappon, "The Green Paper: Immigration as a Tool for Profit" (1978), provides a similar analysis of immigration policy as a tool for capitalist exploitation of cheap labour.

The text by Brittan and Maynard, *Sexism, Racism and Oppression* (1984), provides an insightful critique of the structuralist–Marxist perspective. The authors challenge the argument that race, ethnic, and gender relations can be subsumed under the concept of class or the desire of capitalists to fragment workers. Chapter 2 of this text, concerned with "The Class Problem," is particularly useful. The text as a whole is not easy to read. It assumes a sophisticated grasp of theoretical perspectives and their underlying assumptions.

The essay by Susan Crean and Marcel Rioux, *Two Nations: An Essay on the Culture and Politics of Canada and Quebec in a World of American Pre-eminence* (1983), adopts a cultural-Marxist perspective. They argue strongly that the preservation of minority cultures, with particular reference to Francophone culture in Quebec, is an essential defence against the homogenizing influence of corporate mass media culture.

The article by Roxana Ng, "The Social Construction of Immigrant Women in Canada" (1987), provides an excellent analysis of the experiences of immigrant women from the social constructionist perspective. Ng shows how many of the characteristics associated with immigrant women cannot be adequately understood as attributes of the women themselves. They are effects of how they are treated in Canada.

Chapter 15

Development: Competing Theories of Social Change

Within the world community, there are enormous disparities in standards of living across regions and countries. The world economies can be divided roughly into three blocks. The *First World* comprises affluent capitalist countries in North America, Western Europe, and Japan. The *Second World* is made up of moderately developed, but still poor, centrally planned economies, including the Soviet Union, China, and their satellites. The *Third World* comprises the impoverished and technologically backward regions of Asia, Latin America, and Africa.

The theories proposed to account for this inequality have important practical relevance for the design of national and international development programs. Some theories propose that poverty stems from inappropriate cultural values and a lack of scientific knowledge in the Third World. They assert that the solution to such poverty can be found in education, the transfer of technol-

ogy from the First to the Third World, and the promotion of leaders or role models to inspire more backward people to innovate. Conversely, theories that focus on the exploitation of the Third World by multinational corporations, based in First World countries, see technology transfer and the promotion of capitalist modes of production as exacerbating poverty. Far from alleviating inequalities, such programs are seen as tightening the stranglehold of capitalism over Third World economies so that they can be more severely exploited. Theories that subsume women under men, or that assume that women are the dependants of male breadwinners, foster development projects that worsen both the relative and the absolute poverty of women. Theories that define development only in terms of increasing the total amount of money in an economy foster projects that increase commodities for sale in national and international markets, often to the detriment of local food supplies and at the cost of destroying the environment.

By international standards, Canada is a rich nation, yet there are large disparities in standards of living across regions and communities within Canada. The processes that give rise to such uneven development are similar in many respects to those that link the economies of the First and Third Worlds. Canada's native peoples suffer levels of poverty directly comparable to those of people in the Third World, and they share a common history of colonial exploitation. Canada's national economy is dominated by the **branch plants** of multinational companies, based mostly in the United States. Economic decisions crucial to Canada's future are commonly made by people outside the country. The ties between Canada and the U.S. are destined to become stronger over the next decade with the free trade agreement between the two countries. Theories that link economic progress to capitalism, through the stimulation of private enterprise and expanding trade, predict that the trade deal will generate prosperity for Canada. Other theories that give greater weight to the contradictions within capitalism predict a worsening of regional disparities. Behind the immediate arguments for and against the deal is the broader question of whether the expansionist definition of development is the appropriate model for Canadian or world development. There is mounting evidence that our environment cannot sustain such rapacious industrial growth.

World Development

Functionalist Theory: Modernization as Evolution

The functionalist approach to social change finds its fullest expression in the **theory of modernization**. This theory has its origins in Spencer's model of societal evolution as a systematic and unilinear process of change from simple to heterogeneous structures. This process involves the differentiation and specialization of parts, with increasingly more complex integration through a centralized political order and large-scale organization. Through such a process of change, both biological and social systems achieve progressively more successful adaptation to their physical environment. In societies this is achieved within the economic sphere through the advancement of science and technology, which facilitates ever-more efficient harnessing of energy sources beyond human and animal limitations.

The view of societies as integrated social systems entails the recognition that change in one part will necessarily require adjustments in all other parts. Change within the adaptive or economic sphere cannot occur without corresponding changes in the spheres of goal attainment, integration, and pattern maintenance, that is, within political and administrative structures and especially within culture. Historically, the advancement of science and technology in developed western societies was preceded by far-reaching changes in religious, political, and family structures. As we saw in chapter 6, it has been argued that the Protestant ethic promoted a focus on work as a religious calling and upon success within worldly activities as sign of grace. Such new values were important to the rise of capitalism in Europe.

Parsons' emphasis on a voluntaristic theory of action leads him to focus upon cultural change as a prerequisite for modernization. It is culture that directs the adaptive capacity of societies. Orientations toward action within traditional societies typically focus around kinship systems and give primacy to the pattern variables of affective ties, particularistic loyalties, ascriptive evaluations, and diffuse role obligations. Such values, Parsons argues, are out of place in complex industrial economies. Modern orientations toward action involve affective neutrality, universality, achievement orientation, and specificity in role obligations. Bureaucratic structures and roles epitomize such values. Kinship systems must recede in importance to permit these new values to emerge in response to increasing differentiation and specialization of other social structures.

Cultural Lag

This integrated process of evolution in societal structures and values is held to account for the early modernization of Western capitalist societies, which now comprise the economically advanced First World. This model equally accounts for the much slower rate of development, or the failure to develop, in societies that are now loosely grouped together as "developing" or Third World nations.

Historically, so the functionalist argument goes, Third World societies fell behind because they lacked the preconditions for the emergence of science and technology. Religious values, for example, may have suppressed the free inquiry necessary for science. This particular aspect of the evolutionary process can in principle be circumvented by the transfer of information and technology from advanced to backward societies. The major problem that backward societies have to overcome is **cultural lag**: the failure or excessive slowness of other spheres of society to adapt to the economic changes that technological innovation entails.

This failure to adapt may take any number of forms in different countries. Unstable governments, divided along tribal lines, may fail to provide goal direction. Bureaucracies rife with familistic values may be corrupted by nepotism or hampered by underqualified staff selected on the basis of ascriptive rather than achievement-oriented criteria. Religious values may suppress the orientation toward worldly success values needed for business and for the accumulation of capital. Above all, familism may hamper individual initiative. Individuals may be too closely tied to particularistic family and local loyalties to be either geographically or socially mobile. Hence they fail to take advantage of opportunities available for economic advancement. Familism is also associated with a high birth rate. When this is combined with the transfer of modern medicines from the developed world to reduce the death rate, the result is crushing overpopulation, which leads inexorably to famine.

The Culture of Poverty

This theoretical framework underlies the influential **culture of poverty thesis,** the thesis that a certain constellation of cultural values perpetuates poverty by stifling initiative for change. The same explanation has been applied to account for pockets of poverty within the developed world. It is particularly associated with the early work of Oscar Lewis (1949) and Everett Rogers (1969, chap. 2). Referring to peasants or subsistence farmers in the Third World, Rogers (1969, 19) comments that "they make the economists sigh, the politicians sweat, and the strategists swear, defeating their plans and prophesies all the world over." Their apathy and traditionalism constantly block the implementation of rural development programs.

Reluctance to innovate is associated with a syndrome of cultural traits that includes limited world views and low empathy, familism, mutual distrust in interpersonal relations, dependence on and hostility to government authority, perceived limited good, fatalism, limited aspirations, and lack of deferred gratification. Each of these cultural traits hampers modernization. These traits lead to ignorance, inability to conceive of a future different from the present, and a belief that no one outside the family can be trusted, including government development workers with new-fangled schemes. The trait of perceived limited good refers to the pervasive tendency among peasants to believe that the economic pie is limited and hence that any one who gets ahead must be cheating others out a share. People who do get ahead are viewed with a mixture of envy and scorn, rather than as models to emulate. Peasants display an apathetic resignation to fate because of their limited sense of control over the future. Money is not saved or invested but is spent immediately or borrowed by other family members.

According to this functionalist thesis, the main solution to backwardness lies in continuing to transfer scientific and technological knowledge from the developed world, combined with concerted efforts to change outdated traditional values that block saving, investment, and rational organization of the economies of these countries (Chirot 1977, 3–4). This was the guiding ideology behind the American Peace Corps and Alliance for Progress, which flowered in the U.S. under the Kennedy administration in the early 1960s.

The 1960s were years of optimism sparked by the **green revolution**, a package of scientific developments in agriculture that promised to ameliorate famine. The package included high-yield varieties of wheat and rice, chemical fertilizers and pesticides, and large-scale irrigation projects. Together they had the potential to double or to treble yields. The other avenue for hope was the dissemination of contraceptive technology and aggressive campaigns for population control. It was hoped that, with higher agricultural yields and fewer babies to feed, the battle for adequate worldwide nutrition would be won.

These hopes were only partially fulfilled. The green revolution did raise yields, particularly among large farmers who tended to be more progressive. But the mass of small peasant farmers largely failed to adopt the new technology. The end result was an increase in the gap between rich and poor farmers. The syndrome of attitudes associated with the culture of poverty was widely cited to account for the failure of small farmers to innovate.

The goal of population control similarly met with limited success. Among the wealthier, educated classes, family size did decline, but not among the masses. During the period between 1950 and 1972, the population of Asia rose by an estimated 63 percent, Africa by 72 percent, and Latin America by 91 percent. In contrast, in North America, population increased by only 42 percent and Europe by 26 percent (Kalbach 1976, 11). A report estimated that the world's population reached five billion in July 1987 and is expected to reach six billion by 1999, a rate of increase of 150 people a minute (*Globe and Mail*, 11 July 1987, D1).

Various explanations are offered for continuing high rates of population increase in Third World countries. Improved health care and mass immunization have reduced the infant death rate, but continuing fear of infant mortality makes people reluctant to accept sterilization before the birth and survival of large numbers of children. The medical complications and expense associated with all forms of artificial contraception limit their use, while religious and cultural factors, and especially the desire for sons, favour having many children.

The result is that increases in food production are virtually cancelled out by increases in population. In India, for example, between 1950 and 1970 agricultural yields doubled, but this barely kept ahead of the birth rate. In 1985 the worst happened. Drought in Africa precipitated famine on a devastating scale, with hundred of thousands of people in Ethiopia, Sudan, and Chad starving to death, and millions more barely kept alive in relief camps. Famine struck these regions again in 1987–88. Only massive gifts of food from around the world stood between millions of people and starvation. The only solution, from the perspective of conventional theories, is more of the same: more technology and more cultural change.

In summary, for functionalists the causes of failure to modernize are within the structures and cultures of the backward countries themselves. Research promoted by this theoretical approach has focussed particularly upon technological transfer and aid projects, internal politics and bureaucratic organization within the Third World countries, and the response of local people to small-scale development projects. The long history of frustration and limited results has offered much support for the thesis that deep-rooted structural and cultural changes must precede modernization.

The Modernization Thesis Discredited

Criticisms generated within the functionalist tradition have focussed upon the limited empirical validity of some of the generalizations outlined above. It is not difficult to point to examples of traditional value orientations in developed countries and evidence of modern value orientations in Third World countries, with no appreciable impact on the level of modernization (Frank 1972). The culture of poverty thesis has been challenged on

the grounds that the implied cause and effect should be reversed (Hale 1985, 55). Rather than attitudes causing economic backwardness, it is the condition of economic backwardness that causes the attitudes. Restricted information flow, exploitation, the absolute lack of access to resources needed for agricultural innovation, and the impossibility of saving money in the face of inadequate and irregular incomes are facts of everyday life for peasants in North India, especially small landowners and landless tenant farmers. Such structural factors account both for the failure to innovate and the attitudes that go with such behaviour.

Similarly, with respect to population control, there is evidence that the underlying relation between high birth rates and poverty works in reverse to the usual argument. It is poverty that drives families to have more children, especially male children, to compensate for high death rates and to ensure some means of support in old age. As real economic alternatives emerge for women to support themselves and to raise their standards of living, they choose increasingly to restrict the number of children they have. Attitudes tend to change readily in response to real opportunities for advancement. Functionalism describes the association between attitudes and behaviour, but it does not explain it.

Marxist Theory: Underdevelopment as Capitalist Exploitation

The strongest challenge to the functionalist theory of modernization has come from the perspective of political economy. Ironically, the core of this critique is that functionalism has failed to live up to its own insistence that the functioning of particular elements can be explained only by reference to the wider social system of which they are part.

Functionalism focusses only upon the internal structural characteristics of Third World countries as if they are total social systems functioning in isolation from the determining influence of the world economic system. Political economy challenges this basic starting assumption. It shifts the focus from the internal structures of poor countries to the functioning of the world economic system in which they are embedded. The central argument, which we explore below, is that the wealth of some countries and regions and the poverty of others are, and always have been, systematically related. Frank (1972, 3), rejects outright the notion that somehow Third World societies have not yet developed, or that they lack the required cultural or other prerequisites to copy Western development. The Third World, he argues, is not simply **undeveloped**, continuing to exist in some unchanged, traditional pattern. These societies are **underdeveloped**. Their resources have been, and still are being, plundered, and their internal economies are undermined by processes of a world capitalist economic system.

Historically, most now impoverished Third World societies were subject to the destructive impact of **mercantilism**, **colonialism**, and **imperialism**. The economies of many regions of Africa were devastated by the slave trade, while the indigenous societies of Latin America were crushed by European conquerors plundering the regions in search of precious metals. The economies of conquered regions were directed primarily in the interests of the imperial powers, which focussed upon the extraction of resources to fuel imperial development, while simultaneously retarding and distorting the internal development of the regions themselves. Even now, in many parts of Africa, the main roads go from centres to the ports, rather than to other African centres (Hoogvelt 1976). African interregional telephone lines still link up through Britain.

Imperial governments fundamentally transformed indigenous social structures and often divided up territories with no respect for traditional tribal lines. "Divide and rule" tactics often involved favouring selected local elites or encouraging the immigration of ethnic minorities into the colonies, to act as a buffer group between the colonial power and the local people. East Indians, for example, were used in this way in many of the British colonies in Africa. Such people acted as business middlemen, local administrators, and tax collectors for the colonial governments. Long after the end of the colonial era, the legacy of tribal conflicts and class disparities along ethnic lines still plagues the new nation-states.

Most colonized countries have now gained political independence, but this has not brought effective economic independence. Their economies are still dominated by forces of the world capitalist economic system over which they have little control. This indirect economic control is referred to as **neo-imperialism**.

Capitalism in the Third World

There is a continuing debate among Marxist theorists on the best way to analyse how these processes of economic domination work and whether it is appropriate to focus upon international trade relations, as Frank does, or mode of production, which is the core of traditional Marxist theory. In practice the two processes are intimately related.

Brenner (1977) argues strongly for a focus upon the character of capitalist modes of production for understanding the phenomenal pace of technological change and economic advances in Western capitalist societies. This thesis is explored in depth in chapter 8 on Marxist theory and so will be only briefly reviewed here. Brenner argues that capitalism as a mode of production is unique in promoting a relentless compulsion to invest in new technology to increase productivity, a compulsion rooted in the fact that the mass of people have no direct access to any means for producing for their own subsistence needs.

Classical economists, in the tradition of Adam Smith, stress trade, free competition, and profit maximization for the success of capitalism, but Brenner argues that they ignore the preconditions for such market-oriented and profit-driven behaviour. Peasant farmers, who can provide for their own subsistence outside the market, lack incentives to struggle to maximize profits. They market their surplus for cash to purchase luxury items rather than basic necessities. They have little interest in taking up wagework, except on a temporary basis to provide extra money for luxuries that they cannot produce for themselves. They do not need the wages for their survival. Landowners extract an absolute surplus from labourers under the feudal system and have little incentive to invest heavily to develop additional productive potential. Expanded trade networks within this kind of system of production are likely to result in squeezing more absolute surplus from labourers but not necessarily in the expansion of production.

Hence, argues Brenner, the capitalist mentality of compulsive investment to raise productivity presupposes that direct relations to means of subsistence production for the mass of people have already been broken. People who have to buy or rent land or pay off mortgages, have to be concerned with maximizing returns in the market in order to pay the average rental costs on land or the going mortgage rates. If their level of productivity falls below what is typical for people like themselves, they risk going bankrupt. Owners of productive capital who hire wage labour have to maximize productivity in order to pay competitive wages and so keep their workers. The processes of wagework, capital accumulation, and profit maximization in the marketplace, once started, are self-perpetuating and form the engine of economic growth. Expanded trade relations become important within their context of capitalist relations of production.

In principle, capitalism should have the same effect in the Third World, promoting the accumulation of capital, investment, high labour productivity, and wealth, at least for the bourgeois class. The problem is that it manifestly has not produced such results. Aidan Foster-Clark (1978) rejects the argument that this might be due to resistance from people engaged in pre-capitalist modes of production. The reality is that would-be capitalist developers have been overwhelmed by the all too great potential labour force. People have flooded out of rural areas to swell the slums and shanty towns around all big cities in the Third World. These people have no means of subsistence but wage labour and are desperate to sell that labour at almost any price.

Foster-Clark argues that an "inside-outside" distinction is crucial in understanding capitalism in the Third World. Late capitalism, which is now emerging in the Third World, is essentially **dependent capitalism**, imported from outside in a form already fully developed. Capitalists in the West have had different needs at different times: for raw materials, land, labour, and in times of crises, for markets. Cheap raw materials are perhaps the single most important need. Western capitalists are driven to invest in Third World countries because of their large supplies of very cheap labour and cheap primary products extracted under compulsion from tied labourers. This acts as a balance to the falling rate of profits in advanced, high-technology industries (Laclau 1977, 39).

Toward the end of 1989, major political and economic changes began to occur in many countries in communist Eastern Europe, the so-called Second World. Masses of people demonstrated in the streets demanding that Western-style political democracy replace the one-party communist system. They also pressured for a free market system to replace discredited centrally planned economies. Hundreds of thousands of East Germans flocked to West Berlin to gaze in awe at the consumer goods in the stores. Polish leader Lech Walesa begged American and Western European businesses to invest in Poland. Economists and business people in the Soviet Union, Czechoslovakia, and Hungary swiftly joined the clamour for foreign investment.

People in these countries see the correlation between Western capitalism and high standards of living. Correlation readily becomes interpreted as causation, and capitalism is seen as a potential cure for lower living standards in the Eastern bloc. The hope is that, by opening their economies to Western investors and free market principles, they too will encourage investment, high labour productivity, and the accumulation of wealth.

It is too early to judge the long-term outcome of these new economic policies. But processes that generated economic growth in Western capitalist countries will not necessarily work the same way in the context of contemporary international capitalism. People in the Eastern bloc may find themselves up against the same contradictions of international capitalism that undermine economies in the Third World. India, for example, has been a secular, democratic state with a free market economy since 1947. But this has not brought wealth, or anything approaching Western standards of living, for the masses of Indian people. We explore below some of the major problems with dependent capitalist development in the Third World. These are in many ways similar to the problems that will face the Eastern bloc in the next decade.

Dependency Theory: The Contradictions Within Capitalism

Impoverished Third World countries, struggling to compete in capitalist markets, face all the contradictions of capitalism full blown: the crises of falling rates of profit, the extreme concentration of capital in huge corporate empires, over-production, unemployment, and misery as masses of unemployed people the world over compete to sell their labour to investors at the lowest possible wages.

Table 15-1 Largest 100 Countries and Companies, 1985*

Rank 1985	Rank 1976	Name	GNP/Sales (billion $ US)	Rank 1985	Rank 1976	Name	GNP/Sales (billion $ US)
1	1	USA	3 634.6	16	14	Netherlands	132.6
2	2	USSR	N/A	17	27	Saudi Arabia	109.4
3	3	Japan	1 255.0	18	24	*General Motors*	96.4
4	4	West Germany	613.2	19	17	Sweden	91.9
5	5	France	489.4	20	21	Switzerland	91.1
6	6	UK	425.4	21	23	*Exxon*	86.7
7	7	Italy	348.4	22	42	Korea, Rep of	83.2
8	8	Canada	334.1	23	31	*Royal Dutch/Shell*	81.7
9	9	China	281.3	24	32	Indonesia	80.6
10	10	Brazil	187.3	25	19	Belgium	77.6
11	13	Australia	182.2	26	28	Argentina	76.2
12	20	Mexico	171.3	27	12	Poland	75.4
13	15	India	162.3	28	16	German	
14	11	Spain	160.9			Democratic	
15	18	Iran	157.6			Republic	N/A

Rank 1985	1976	Name	GNP/Sales (billion $ US)	Rank 1985	1976	Name	GNP/Sales (billion $ US)
29	36	Nigeria	73.5	66	57	*Unilever*	21.6
30	33	South Africa	73.4	67	60	*Chrysler*	21.3
31	22	Czechoslovakia	N/A	68	117	*Matsushita*	20.8
32	25	Austria	64.5	69	104	*Hitachi*	20.5
33	41	*Mobil*	56.0	70	—	*Remex*	20.4
34	34	Norway	54.7	71	—	*Shell Oil*	20.3
35	29	Denmark	54.6	72	98	*Elf-Aquitane*	20.1
36	38	*Ford Motor*	52.8	73	69	Chile	19.8
37	39	Finland	51.2	74	75	*Franàaise des*	
38	51	Algeria	50.7			*Petro*	19.3
39	53	*IBM*	50.1	75	55	Portugal	19.1
40	26	Turkey	47.5	76	63	Peru	18.8
41	35	Venezuela	47.5	77	84	*US Steel*	18.4
42	40	*Texaco*	46.3	78	89	Ireland	18.3
43	54	Thailand	41.9	79	106	*Nissan Motor*	18.2
44	47	*Chevron*	41.7	80	114	Singapore	18.2
45	30	Yugoslavia	38.9	81	68	*Phillips*	18.1
46	66	*American Tel &*		82	91	*Siemens*	17.8
		Tel	34.9	83	85	*Volkswagenwerk*	17.8
47	59	Colombia	34.4	84	82	*Daimler-Benz*	17.8
48	49	Philippines	32.8	85	97	*Nestlé*	17.2
49	76	Hong Kong	30.6	86	102	*Petrobas*	16.1
50	61	Libya	30.5	87	130	*United*	
51	71	Egypt	30.1			*Technologies*	15.8
52	44	Greece	29.5	88	118	*Phillips Petroleum*	15.7
53	87	*E.I. du Pont*	29.5	89	88	*Bayer*	15.6
54	72	Malaysia	29.3	90	108	*Tenneco*	15.4
55	74	United Arab		91	80	*BASF*	15.1
		Emirates	28.8	92	120	*Occidental*	
56	58	*General Electric*	28.3			*Petroleum*	14.5
57	64	Pakistan	27.7	93	79	*Hoechst*	14.5
58	67	*Standard Oil*		94	—	*Fiat*	14.5
		(Indiana)	26.8	95	—	*Samsung*	14.2
59	—	*IRI*	26.8	96	112	*Mitsubishi*	14.1
60	95	*Toyota*	26.0	97	—	*Hyundai*	14.0
61	73	*ENI*	24.5	98	—	*General Motors*	
62	65	New Zealand	23.3			*(Canada)*	13.9
63	77	Israel	22.4	99	—	*Imperial Chemical*	13.9
64	86	*Atlantic Richfield*	22.0	100	123	*Sun*	13.8
65	62	Kuwait	21.7				

*Countries are ranked by gross national product (GNP) and companies by sales. Countries are shown in roman type, companies in italic. Deficiencies in the data sources kept this table from being truly complete. The World Bank does not list a few countries, such as Taiwan. Others, such as Romania, Hungary, and Bulgaria were in the 1976 list (they would have ranked 37, 43, and 45 respectively in this table) but were missing for lack of data in 1985; consequently, they are omitted from this table, where they would likely have ranked somewhere in the 50s. Similarly, some very large companies, such as National Iran Oil and Renault, were omitted from the *Fortune* list; others ranked in the top 100 in 1985 but not 1976, or vice versa.

Source: Veltmeyer (1987, 78–79). From World Bank (1986); *Fortune*, 4 Aug. 1986.

Third World countries are in the worst possible position to try to compete with monopoly capitalists. Companies such as Exxon and General Motors command more wealth than the entire economies of most Third World countries (see table 15-1). Veltmeyer (1987) estimated that 70 percent of non-socialist industrial output will be controlled by about 300 such giant corporations by the end of the 1980s. Poor countries, trying to develop their economies, are no match for these giants. The best they can hope for is to compete among themselves to attract what investment they can get, with the carrots of cheap labour, cheap raw materials, minimal taxation, and anything else the giant corporations want. This is not the stuff of which balanced and self-sustaining economic growth is made.

In terms of Frank's **dependency theory**, such poor countries form **hinterlands** for the **metropolis** or centre of capitalism. Hinterlands are the underdeveloped areas that supply cheap labour and cheap raw materials or semi-processed goods to the developed centres. Metropolises are the centres of capitalism, which dominate surrounding regions, extracting their economic surplus. Frank conceptualizes the world capitalist system as hierarchically organized with each smaller metropolis forming a hinterland for yet larger centres.

Frank has been justly criticized for vague use of key terms. It is difficult to pinpoint exactly what he means by a metropolis, particularly when smaller ones are seen as constituting hinterlands for bigger ones, with the ultimate metropolis in New York or Tokyo. In this era of corporate monopoly capitalism, corporate empires, rather than hierarchies of nation-states or regions, constitute the metropolises. The biggest twenty-three corporations in the world have their headquarters in the United States of America, but Canada also is home base to a number of multinationals, as are Japan and many European countries. As we shall see, being home base to a multinational corporation does not guarantee wealth or economic development. Many poorer regions of Canada and the U.S. function as peripheral or hinterland regions, with their productive potential siphoned off by corporate empires.

Frank's major contribution lies in clarifying the mechanisms by which wealth and productive potential are siphoned off. He cites five key mechanisms: control over capital, control over patterns of investment, domination of market relations, decisive bargaining power in the labour market, and political clout, including the use of force as a last resort. We will examine these five mechanisms in turn.

Control over Capital

There has been a net outflow of capital from poorer regions such as Latin America to wealthier regions such as the United States for most of this century. This is despite foreign aid payments, which appear to go from rich to poor nations. This outflow takes many forms, one of the most visible of which is debt repayment. Debts have reached crisis proportions in many Latin American and African countries. Interest payments due on loans are so great that they comprise more than one-third of total national income earned from exports in some of the poorest countries of Africa. The situation is so bad that newspaper articles in June 1988, during an economic summit for leading industrialized nations, speculated on how many babies starve to death for each dollar of interest repaid. These are babies who might not have died if debt repayments could have been spent on clean drinking water or minimal health care in desperately poor countries. The debt repayment problem is made worse by currency devaluations forced on debtor nations by the International Monetary Fund. Governments that, in order to raise revenue, are driven to print more money than they are earning are pushed to the wall by spiralling inflation. The value of their money on world markets drops. The U.S. dollar is the medium of exchange in which most loans are made. Hence, when the currency of a debtor nation is devalued, its debt load increases as more local currency is needed to pay back loans made in dollars.

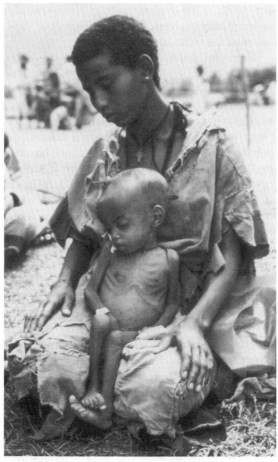

Studies have speculated how many babies die for every dollar of debt repaid by Third World nations.

There is a critical incongruity between the situation of the poorest and the richest debtor nations in this regard. The United States currently ranks as one of the world's largest debtor nations. It has borrowed in the order of three trillion dollars, although this is still relatively small compared with its gross national product. The important point is that such debts have been incurred in dollars. Consequently, as the value of the U.S. dollar has dropped on international markets in recent years, so has its real debt. Raymond calculates that the exchange value of the U.S. dollar has dropped by fifty percent between January 1986 and July 1988 (*Globe and Mail*, 20 July 1988, B5). During this period, the amount of Japanese yen that could be bought for a dollar dropped from 260 to 130, and German marks dropped from 3.4 to 1.7. In effect, Raymond argues, the United States is telling its Japanese and German creditors that it intends to repay only half of what they lent. This represents a greater level of debt cancellation in real terms than Latin Americans and Africans could ever dream of.

The outflow of money from poor to rich nations also occurs in less obvious forms. Cheap exports and overpriced imports, often directly controlled by multinational corporations, generate large profits and dividends that flow back to the corporate home base, together with payments for royalties and financial services of all kinds. Multinational empires often also have close ties to banks and hence have preferential access to large investment loans over struggling smaller companies within the host societies. Multinationals are, in any case, relatively independent of banks because they can use profits from one sector of their activities to finance new investments elsewhere. Their commanding control over access to finance capital gives them effective control over investment policy.

Patterns of Investment

Access to capital gives multinational corporate empires almost total control over decisions about where and how to invest. Such decisions are routinely made in the interests of the corporations themselves and focus on export-oriented production rather than on provision of basic public resources such as roads, railways, and electrical power lines and generators that are needed to promote local industry. Export-oriented production also takes away money and other resources that might have been invested in production geared to the needs of the host societies. Corporations have the power to create boom and bust economic cycles, as they can choose to shift centres of production from one region, or from one country, to another, depending on where the greatest profits might be made. Host societies can do virtually nothing about such decisions. Corporate interests have helped to create a new international division of labour, with many countries specializing in production of one or two goods each. However, this has not brought the host societies increased profits based on the **economies of scale** and efficient production, as envisioned by Adam Smith. The profits have gone to the metropolises, to the handful of huge integrated multinational companies that actually control the market for these specialized products. Host societies are effectively unable to set their own priorities for investment and hence cannot direct their own internal development.

Market Relations

Corporate empires have the capacity to exert decisive control over market relations between poor countries and the world economic system. In the first place, an estimated 30 percent of all world trade is no longer in the marketplace but occurs directly between affiliates of multinational corporations (Martin 1982, 95). Martin concludes that the "open market" is a convenient fiction when applied to international trade. **Transfer pricing**—the price that a parent company sets in selling supplies to its own branch plants or the price at which the parent com-

pany purchases goods produced or assembled by the branch plants—can be manipulated to maximize the outflow of profits to corporate headquarters. Underpriced imports may give a competitive edge to an affiliate over local companies. Alternatively, imports may be overpriced to reduce paper profits and local taxes. Either tactic increases the hidden outflow of money from poor to rich. Martin (1982, 109) estimates that such transfer pricing may account for 82.6 percent of capital returns to headquarters.

Vertically integrated companies also directly control the marketing of products. Six multinationals, for example, control 60 percent of the world production of bauxite and 80 percent of aluminum production (Martin 1982, 100). Sometimes a single corporation controls the export of all bauxite produced in one country to its own plants at home. All the bauxite from the Dominican Republic is sent to Alcoa plants in the United States, while all Haiti's bauxite goes to one Reynolds plant in Texas. The economy of an entire country may be dependent upon the export of one or two specialized products that are under the control of one multinational corporation. The country is thus totally vulnerable to the fluctuations in the market price for these products and to the whim of the corporate directors deciding where and how they will market the products.

Labour Market Relations

In the worldwide labour market, the workers in poor countries provide a vast pool of cheap labour. They have little bargaining power and few rights or benefits. Giant companies shift production to where the labour is cheapest. In 1976, for example, General Electric was negotiating worldwide to build an assembly plant for televisions (Martin 1982, 93). Hourly wages in Taiwan were 37 cents and in South Korea 52 cents. General Electric was negotiating with Indonesia offering 17 cents per hour. Anti-union legislation may also be a part of the bargaining demands of the corporation. Corporations can force or persuade states to enact legislation to ban strikes, picketing, and other union activities as the price for locating a plant in their region.

Force

Should business interests or investments be at risk, large corporations exert substantial political clout. Within the host country itself, the presence of an indigenous capitalist class that benefits directly from foreign capital investments helps to stifle unified opposition. The ultimate back-up for this international system is the military might of the metropolis country. In the early 1970s, when the democratically elected socialist government of Salvador Allende proposed to nationalize the U.S.-owned copper mines of Kennecott and Anaconda in Chile, the corporations were able to mobilize the support of the American government and the CIA to overthrow the regime (Martin 1982, 120–21). International banks, including Canadian banks, co-operated by cutting all credit to Chile. Other international corporations operating in Chile drained their local **subsidiaries** of money and denied supplies of needed resources such as mechanical spare parts, hence grinding the Chilean economy to a halt. International Telephone and Telegraph (ITT) had substantial holdings in Chile and feared nationalization. Corporate directors conspired directly to bring about the downfall of the government through specific forms of armed and funded intervention organized through the American Central Intelligence Agency.

In conclusion, it is important to recognize that dependency theory does not reflect the inexorable working of an invisible hand, with people as mere pawns. It is the result of strategies intended to have specific and foreseen effects. Multinational corporations are oriented toward making profits and increasing their own capital to satisfy large shareholders. Their policies are not designed

to raise living standards for the mass of people in the Third World, and it should not be surprising that this is not their major effect.

Eastern bloc nations, soliciting development aid from Western Europe and North America, may be treated differently from countries in the Third World. An intangible but potentially important advantage may be that Eastern Europeans are generally perceived as members of the same ethnic stock as the people of Western Europe. In November 1989, over one hundred thousand East German refugees flooded into West Germany. Despite initial speculation that they would resent these people for taking jobs and competing for housing, West Germans welcomed them as fellow Germans. They were treated not as refugees, or even as immigrants, but as citizens. The desire to exploit the dependency of Eastern bloc countries for the economic gains of the West may thus be tempered with the political will to promote internal economic development in Eastern Europe.

It is too early to predict the long-term effects of foreign aid in Eastern Europe. But what we have to recognize is that the flow of aid is, in itself, no panacea for economic ills. In the Third World, aid has functioned, not to alleviate poverty and economic dependence, but to exacerbate them. We explore these processes below. They highlight the problems that the Eastern bloc will face in the 1990s.

Foreign Aid: Philanthropy or Commercial Interests?

Carty (1982) begins his discussion of the Canadian International Development Agency (CIDA) with a quotation that defines foreign aid as money you take from poor people in a rich country and give to rich people in a poor country. Over the thirty-year period between 1951 and 1981, CIDA contributed approximately $11 billion to finance thousands of projects in over ninety countries. In addition, it shipped millions of tons of food and other supplies for emergency relief. But, Carty (1982, 150) concludes, the Third World is as impoverished, exploited, and oppressed now as it was three decades earlier. He lays the blame for the lack of improvement on a vision of what constitute Third World problems and their solutions. He argues that this vision is influenced too much by the functionalist theory that failure to develop is the result of lack of appropriate entrepreneurship. According to functionalist theory, foreign aid to support free enterprise capitalism should have produced self-sustained growth. But it has not.

There are several reasons why Canada gives foreign aid: it reflects its philanthropic concern to reduce human suffering, its political aim to win allies and gain international influence, and its commercial objectives to boost export markets for Canadian goods. Carty argues that commercial interests, backed by a very powerful lobby, have taken precedence. He calculates that fully 60 percent of the total CIDA aid budget was spent within Canada on Canadian goods, commodities, and services, creating over 100 000 jobs in Canada. Much aid is unabashedly oriented toward export promotion. The goal is to hook recipients on Canadian inputs in the form of replacement parts, repairs, and services. Development projects also build the infrastructure of roads, railways, and power supplies required by foreign investors (Carty 1982, 168).

The real costs to Canada of CIDA aid may be almost zero once one deducts debt forgiveness on past loans; the transfer of surplus wheat, milk, and rapeseed that we could neither eat nor sell commercially; all the bilateral aid tied to the purchase of Canadian goods and services; loan repayments made to non-governmental organizations based in Canada, which then spend the funds in Canada; and the projected unemployment benefits the Canadian government might have had to pay if these Canadian beneficiaries were not employed (Carty 1982, 171).

Like many other aid agencies, CIDA has its litany of disasters, including projects that imposed totally inappropriate technology on Third World countries and then saddled them with the long-term costs of buying all the spare parts and technical expertise from Canada. In September 1987, Canada gave Thailand a "gift" of five million dollars to develop a commercial-scale food irradiator. CIDA's stated reason for financing the project was to help out an industrializing country by financing expensive technology and expanding potential export markets for Thai produce (*Globe and Mail*, 13 Sept. 1989, A7). However, the Toronto-based environmental group Probe International suggests that the decisive underlying objective was to subsidize Canada's nuclear industry, boost the sales of food irradiation technology developed in Canada, and provide marketing tests for irradiated food in world markets. They support this accusation with reference to an internal document of Atomic Energy of Canada, written before the contract between CIDA and the Thai government was signed. Thai consumer groups fear that they are being used as guinea pigs to test the safety of irradiated food. As of September 1989, five countries, including Japan, Australia, and West Germany, had banned the importation of irradiated food for safety reasons.

While such projects that are potentially beneficial for Canadian exports receive massive financial support, other projects that might help to raise the standard of living of people in poor countries are starved of funds. Commitments for health, welfare, clean water supplies, and education, which might more directly benefit recipient countries, dropped off steadily between 1976 and 1978 in the absence of powerful backers.

Canada's food aid program, while valuable for strictly emergency relief, has been challenged as actually promoting and perpetuating the emergencies its tries to alleviate. In 1976, some 600 000 tons of international food aid was shipped to Bangladesh, yet scarcely 10 percent of it may have reached the destitute. The rest provided cheap, subsidized food for the influential middle classes. Meanwhile it encouraged government complacency about the food crisis and undermined the local markets for the crops of small producers. Many were forced into bankruptcy.

New strategies developed since 1976 are designed in principle to promote "integrated rural development," with more aid going to the less privileged sectors of sharecroppers and small peasant farmers. But Carty suggests that little has changed in practice. By the early 1980s, three quarters of World Bank credit still went to medium and larger farmers for commercial enterprises. In 1978, the World Bank extended $258.5 million to promote non-food crops such as tea, tobacco, jute, and rubber, plus an additional $221 million for food crops for export (Carty 1982, 193). Nothing was done to promote land reforms or any redistribution of income, for fear that it might arouse opposition from powerful sectors within rural communities.

Peasants with medium-sized holdings are often selected as target populations because they have enough land to be integrated into "modernized and monetarized" agricultural systems as good credit risks. On the plus side, productivity increases, but at the price of transforming peasant producers into commercial agriculturalists. They become part of the **agribusiness** system as consumers of agricultural inputs and as producers of crops suitable for further processing. The underlying intent, suggests Carty, is to aid the process of corporate penetration of Third World agriculture and thus to increase dependence on First World agribusiness inputs. Such a claim is consistent with Carty's calculation that the World Bank schemes will generate seven to ten billion dollars worth of sales for multinational corporations over the next few years.

Carty concludes that what the Third World really needs is not foreign aid, but a restructuring of international economic relations. Between 1970 and 1979, CIDA disbursed some $2.4 billion in aid, but in this same period the ten recipient countries experienced a trade deficit with Canada of about $2.4 billion. This trade imbalance wiped out even the nominal value of the aid.

Agribusiness and Famine

It is with respect to food production that the interests of multinational corporations engaged in agriculture diverge most obviously from the interests of the mass of people in Third World countries. Policies to maximize profits have been directly implicated in the causes of famine. Lappé (1971, 16) aptly sums up this relationship when she states simply that "land that grows money can't grow food."

The problem of using land to grow money began during the colonial era when Western powers took over vast tracts of land in subject countries for plantations. Products included tobacco, rubber, tea, coffee, cocoa, cotton and fibres, sugar, and more recently marijuana, for the North American market. All such crops are grown for export only. They cannot be eaten by local people as staple foods. Even crops such as sugar cane are now being grown in Brazil, not for food, but to produce alcohol as a substitute for gasoline.

Many Third World countries depend on these cash crops for their survival. Lappé estimates that coffee alone provides the economic livelihood for forty developing countries. The African country of Rwanda, for example, derived 87.5 percent of its export earnings in 1968 from the sale of coffee. Any fluctuation in the world price of coffee has a major impact on these fragile economies. Beckford (1973, 120–22) cites a long list of countries in Asia, the Caribbean, and Latin America that are primarily plantation economies, with the bulk of their agricultural resources devoted to foreign-owned plantations producing crops for sale to overseas markets. The size of such operations is enormous and is steadily growing as corporations buy more land or push neighbouring farmers out of business. The United Fruit Company in Latin America demanded 5000 acres of the best arable land before it would start a plantation. The company did not use this much land but wanted to hold it in reserve in case they might want to expand in the future. United Fruit controlled 100 percent of the export of bananas from Guatemala in 1966 and 70 percent of banana exports from Costa Rica and Panama (Barnet and Muller 1974). In many instances, the area of land taken over is so vast that it provides the only source of employment for people living in substantial parts of the countries concerned.

Tropical forests in Latin America are clearcut so cash crops can be cultivated.

Feder (1976) describes in some detail how this process of takeover and control occurs. Corporations control production, processing, transport, storage, and financing. They either employ local people directly or extend credits and inputs on a contract basis with prearranged terms of sale advantageous to the corporation. A corporation that grew strawberries in Mexico, for example, enjoyed cheap land rentals and cheap wages. When the soil became depleted from overproduction, the company moved to a new location. Impoverished ex-employees remained behind. Most of the benefits of exports do not go to local people, or to labourers on plantations, but to big companies, which remit profits abroad.

The worst problem is that, as more and more land is taken over for cash crops, there is less available for local subsistence food crops. Farmers are pushed out onto marginal land where yields are low. Food production falls. Food prices rise faster than the prices of export crops, so that foreign exchange earnings are not sufficient to pay for the food imports needed. The problem is worsened by deforestation as local farmers push into what was once forest or grazing land. Poor soils are rapidly depleted.

This process seems to have triggered the massive famine in Ethiopia. Droughts, famine, environmental bankruptcy are not unpredictable acts of god. They are caused by human mismanagement, overcultivation, deforestation, and overgrazing, which have ruined the soil's ability to absorb water. The topsoil blows off and droughts and flash floods result.

Why does this happen? One reason is the desperation of poor countries pushed to the limit to pay off foreign debts through cash crops. The World Bank gives aid to develop cotton for export rather than beans for local consumption because cotton produces money for bank repayments. Cotton replaces food crops and depletes the soil of nitrogen. When it is ready for export, however, countries may

Droughts, famine, and environmental devastation are caused by mismanagement, overcultivation, deforestation, and overgrazing.

run up against trade barriers. Peasants, meanwhile, have been forced onto marginal land, which they overcultivate and destroy. They then face destitution. Ethiopia once had the reputation for being the breadbasket of Africa. Now it is reduced to a soup kitchen. Even at the height of its famine, though, Ethiopia continued to export coffee and meat, largely because it needed the foreign exchange. This export production is supported by the Food and Agriculture Organization of the United Nations and by the World Bank.

Patriarchy: The Underdevelopment of Women

Women, the main producers of subsistence food crops throughout the world, have fared the worst from policies that promote cash crops over local food crops. In the international system of stratification, women are at the bottom. They work the hardest, produce the most, but own and earn the least.

The functionalist model of modern society proposed by Parsons explicitly excludes women from economic development. Women are predefined as specialized homemakers who are or should be financially dependent upon their husbands. They are conceptualized in functionalist development theory as homebound, family-oriented wives and mothers, concerned with socialization and religious training of children, and hence naturally conservative. They are enjoined to behave in accordance with traditional cultural norms, to stress emotions, diffuse and particularistic family ties, and ascriptive values, while men take care of the instrumental roles (Hale 1985, 53).

But the evidence belies this conceptualization of women's lives in the Third World. Women's unpaid labour is estimated to produce one-third of the world's annual economic product. Their work accounts for more than half the food produced in the Third World and as much as 80 percent of food produced in Africa (Sivard 1985, 5). Yet women are largely excluded from agricultural development projects sponsored as part of the green revolution. Only men are defined as farmers; women are farm wives. Projects for women may include some information on high-yielding seeds, but rarely are women taught the business side of farming. Even progressive land reform policies, intended to give ownership rights to those who work the land rather than to absentee landlords, have served to weaken rather than strengthen women's rights to land. Their traditional use-rights are ignored, and land is vested in male household heads (Sen 1985, 27). Western individualistic values are imposed on others. In the Kano River project in Nigeria, communally owned lands were registered only in the name of the "senior owner," almost always a man. Women, along with junior men, lost all their rights (Sen 1985, 35).

Women are systematically disadvantaged with respect to all five of the mechanisms noted by Frank as perpetuating neo-imperialism. First, women have the least access of any Third World group to credit and other financial resources. Because they do not own land legally, they have no collateral (Hale 1985, 58–61). Secondly, investments in agricultural technology are directed toward cash crops, which produce the money to repay loans, rather than toward food that will be eaten locally. Women desperately need appropriate technology to reduce the four to six hours a day needed to search for cooking fuel and to fetch water, but this has a low priority in World Bank objectives. Thirdly, in the markets, women at best scratch out a living in petty trade, which requires minimal capital investment. Fourthly, women also come last in the labour market. As jobs such as weeding and threshing are mechanized, men tend to take them over, leaving even fewer jobs for women. In the growth industries for exports, women tend to be concentrated in the most poorly paid sweatshop work where they have no bargaining power (Sen 1985, 28–29). Lastly, any concerted efforts to raise the status of women tend to be resisted with patriarchal force. Sen (1985, 20) particularly stresses the extent to which fears of sexual aggression manipulate and threaten women's lives, especially in the labour market. Male chauvinism and religious fundamentalism serve to reinforce these processes that keep women in subordinated positions.

Development policies have resulted in the position of women in the Third World being systematically underdeveloped. In many regions, their situation frequently deteriorates from one of independent control over subsistence production to that of unpaid labourers begging for money for food from men who control the expanding cash economy (Rogers 1981, chap. 6; Hale 1981, 152).

A New Vision of Development

Feminists demand fundamental changes in the vision of development. Their goal is to make development more people-centred instead of cash-centred. Sen emphasizes that gender subordination, which is integral to Parsons' model of a modern social system, must be eradicated before people-centred development can take place. Such development must begin with women because their work is central to survival (Sen 1985, 13–16). Women have to be empowered before such changes can take place.

tional and administrative skills needed to run such programs or for being too poorly educated and too focussed upon their family responsibilities to do their jobs adequately. A deeper exploration of exactly what happened

The experience of women who were employed to deliver development projects explicitly designed to improve the living standards of women and children in rural North India demonstrates just how necessary such empowerment is (Hale 1987a; Hale 1987b). The projects largely failed to reach their objectives of providing supplementary nutrition and immunization for children and pregnant women and teaching home economics and adult literacy to women. The women who organized and taught the programs were blamed for lacking the organiza-to these women as they tried to do their everyday work revealed the socially constructed nature of this failure. In critical ways, the work of these women was undermined by the actions of others in the male-dominated development bureaucracy in which they were employed. On a very small scale, the powerlessness of these women in their work mirrored the powerlessness of Third World peoples generally in their relations with foreign development agencies and foreign corporations that control the decisions that influence their lives.

Development In Canada

The growth of industrial society in Canada in many ways reflected Canada's colonial status. This can be seen particularly in the destruction of the economies of indigenous peoples and in distorted patterns of trade and industrialization that have emerged within Canada.

Canadian Development in a World Capitalist System

Canada does not exist in isolation from the world economic system. The development of the Canadian economy has been very closely tied to imperial Europe and later to the United States. It is not the U.S. as such that is the centre of the problem, but the corporate empires that have their home base in the United States and treat Canada as a resource hinterland. Canada as a nation-state is not fully in control of its own economy. Neither, perhaps, is the American government, although this is less clear.

Historically, Canada has benefitted from favorable relations with Europe and the United States and has shared, to a degree, in the spoils of development (Veltmeyer 1987,

77). At the same time, the price Canada has paid for these ties is **dependent development**. Veltmeyer calculates that, almost every year since 1900, Canada has absorbed one-third of all investment capital exported from the United States so that Canada now has the largest **branch-plant economy** in the world. Canada is subject to more foreign ownership than all the other major industrialized countries combined. This is concentrated in resource extraction and high-technology manufacturing industries. The Canadianization policy of the Trudeau government reduced this concentration to some extent, but 84 percent of profits from oil were still in foreign hands in 1983, down from 99 percent ownership in 1974.

The immediate result of concentration of foreign ownership has been the now familiar pattern of capital drain. Over the years, less than 10 percent of American investment in Canada has actually involved the inflow of capital. Most has been in the form of retained earnings—profits made by branch plants operating in Canada—or money borrowed from Canadian banks. Remittances from Canada to the United States in the form of dividends, royalties, licence fees, and so on, have substantially exceeded the inflow of capital almost every year since 1900. Trade between the two countries is increasingly dominated by multinational corporations. Veltmeyer (1987, 86) estimates that, in 1983, between 75 and 80 percent of all imports and exports involved parent-subsidiary transfers by foreign corporations. In such transactions, transfer-pricing arrangement apply, to Canada's net disadvantage.

The distorting effects of this dependent development are revealed in the difference between the types of commodities exported and imported. Canada is near the bottom of the industrially advanced capitalist countries on measures involving manufactured exports. Typically for a branch-plant economy, Canada largely exports raw materials and semiprocessed goods and imports manufactured goods. The one exception is in the automobile industry. Equally typical is Canada's technological dependency. Canada lags far behind other industrialized countries in the proportion of gross national product spent on research and development. The main reason for this is that such research is highly centralized in corporate headquarters. Canada thus relies disproportionately upon labour-intensive, low-technology industry. Such resource-based manufacturing industries are now coming under increasing competition from the Third World. There are numerous examples of corporations closing down assembly plants in Canada to open branches in countries such as Taiwan, South Korea, and Indonesia where labour is vastly cheaper (Martin 1982, 93, 127).

Native Peoples: Development or Economic Imperialism?

Why are Canada's native peoples on the lowest rungs of the capitalist class structure? What are the forces that help to produce the marked disparities between the average standard of living in native communities and in Canada as a whole? To what extent are development projects designed for, and sometimes by, Indians helping to reduce such disparities?

An important part of the answer to the first two questions lies in the brutal exploitation of native peoples, and the plunder of their economic resources by the Canadian colonial government from the time when white settlers began to compete with native peoples for land and other resources. It may well have been inevitable that native hunting and gathering economies would decline with the influx of white settlers (Stanley 1964, 3–5). But there was nothing inevitable about the nature of the treaties imposed upon many native bands or about the fact that, while European settlers were allocated 160 acres of farmland per family, native families were allocated 10 acres or less. Nor was it inevitable that Indian reserves were located on lands unsuitable for agriculture. These conditions were socially constructed by the very uneven bargaining power of the negotiators. In the few instances where Indians settled on good farmland and began to cultivate it, they were pushed off to make way for white settlers. Later, when gold and other minerals were found in the North or when hydro-electric power projects were set up, native lands were expropriated with minimal compensation. Such events reflect the fact that native peoples are not represented within the centres of economic and political control in Canadian society where such decisions are made, and hence that their interest are not taken into account.

Kellough describes how the first Indian Act of 1896 legalized the colonial subordination of native peoples by giving the Minister of Indian Affairs authority over laws and reserve land. The ministry had total authority over what land should be sold for what price. The National Indian Brotherhood estimated that as much as half the original reserve allotment in Canada was lost through land sales to benefit railways, coal corporations, farmers, and recreation developers between 1900 and 1930. All the profits from the sales went to pay the salaries of Indian Affairs personnel (Kellough 1980, 348).

During the late 1960s, the Indian Affairs budget exceeded $62 million per year, but only $1.5 million was spent on economic development. More recently, the rhetoric has changed in favour of promoting such development for native peoples. However, Kellough shows how the failure of potential development projects was social constructed by the actions of officials within the Ministry of Indian Affairs. In one case, Manitoba Indians wanted to develop their wild rice trade. They could not raise a loan directly from a bank because title to Indian lands is vested in the government. They made many requests to the ministry for funding. Finally, a meeting of officials was held to discuss a plan for an Indian-controlled commercial paddy but, significantly, no Indian representative was present. No money was given to Indians. Instead a botanist was hired to research the topic. In the meantime other

commerical enterprises, recognizing the profit potential, entered the trade, using new production methods not made available to the Indians. The predictable long-term result, suggests Kellough (1980, 350), is that wild rice will become a commercial crop dominated by major food chains while Indians lose what little revenue they formerly made from rice gathering.

In 1957, Ontario Hydro built the Cariboo Dam, which raised the waters of the English and Wabigoon Rivers and drowned the local rice crop, worth some $500 000 a year to the people of the White Dog and Grassy Narrows reserves. Yet in the fourteen-year period between 1957 and 1971, the 1400 Indians affected received only $23 000 as compensation. With the rice crop gone, the Indians became dependent upon fish, which were being contaminated with the mercury dumped into the river system by industries located upstream. The long-term result of mercury poisoning was "Minimata disease," a deterioration of the nervous system causing violent behaviour and depression.

Table 15-2   Average Individual Income of Registered Indian and General Populations, Canada, 1985

| Province/Territory | Average Individual Income | | | |
| | Registered Indian Population | | | General Population |
	On Reserve	Off Reserve	Total	
Nova Scotia and Newfoundland	$7 900	$11 200	$8 800	$15 400
New Brunswick and Prince Edward Island	7 500	9 600	8 000	14 700
Quebec	9 900	13 400	10 700	17 100
Ontario	10 100	12 400	11 200	19 500
Manitoba	8 200	9 700	8 700	17 000
Saskatchewan	8 600	9 700	9 000	17 000
Alberta	9 300	10 300	9 700	19 800
British Columbia	9 800	10 800	10 200	18 700
Yukon	8 300	10 800	9 600	20 600
Northwest Territories	8 900	12 300	10 200	21 400
Canada	$9 300	$11 000	$9 900	$18 200

Source: Canada. House of Commons (1989, 74); data based on Census of Canada, 1986.

In October 1989, thirty-two years after the flooding, the White Dog reserve received a compensation cheque from Ontario Hydro for $1.5 million, plus about $900 000 interest. This is equivalent to about three years' income from the old rice crop. A band spokesperson commented that the money will do nothing to give back to the Indians their means of livelihood that were destroyed by the dam (*Globe and Mail*, 19 Oct. 1989, A8). The money will be used for improved housing and job creation. Without a secure economic base, however, the money seems likely to do little more than replace dependence on welfare cheques for a few years.

Another potential development project described by Kellough (1980, 354) was the organization of the Big Bear Gallery in Saskatoon, controlled and directed by local Indians and Métis. Kellough maintains that the staff of the Ministry of Indian Affairs undermined the credibility and effectiveness of the native board of directors from the start by public criticism and by challenging their competence to run the project. The ministry then withheld vital information in early stages of the project. Then it withheld loans and funds at a crucial stage, arguing that the project must prove itself self-sufficient before it could receive funds. Lastly, it offered financial help only on the condition that the project be controlled by ministry staff. When this condition was refused, the project was quashed.

Incidents such as these have been repeated all across Canada. Together they add up to the socially constructed failure of development projects to alter appreciably the economically depressed position of native people. To the extent that the locus of control lies outside the native communities themselves, so does responsibility for the failure of such projects. Empowerment is the necessary first step for true economic development.

The opposition between native economic goals and those of resource extraction companies gained brief public recognition in 1988 when the Lubicon Nation tried to organize a boycott of the Calgary winter Olympics. Since 1940 the Lubicon have been fighting to get a promised reserve, while the federal and Alberta governments stalled over the question of how many acres it should be. Around 1978, oil and gas companies were given permission by the Alberta government to explore in the disputed territory. They wiped out an estimated 90 percent of the local wildlife, bulldozed traplines, and effectively destroyed the Lubicon's traditional way of life. The band members went from 90 percent employment to 10 percent, and their standard of living collapsed. The Indians got none of the benefits or potential jobs associated with oil and gas exploration.

In February 1988 the Alberta government granted rights to a Japanese pulp company to harvest timber and build a pulp mill in the area of the disputed lands. It further granted a $65 million subsidy to support the $500 million investment, which might bring 600 new jobs. The federal government gave a further $9.5 million. The Lubicon were not even informed of the deal (*Globe and Mail*, 11 Feb. 1988, A1–3; 15 Feb. 1988, A6).

In October 1988 the Lubicon appeared to have won their battle for land when the Alberta premier offered to transfer 204.5 square kilometers of provincial Crown land to the band. By the end of the year, however, the parties remained at an impasse. The Lubicon were still trying to block roads in an oil-rich area that the band claims is its hereditary homeland (*Globe and Mail*, 24 Nov. 1988, A1–2).

Regional Disparities and Underdevelopment in Canada

Cultural arguments in the functionalist tradition are still raised to account for regional disparities within Canada. Historically, it is argued that Quebec lagged behind the rest of Canada in economic development because of the stranglehold of the Catholic Church on

French culture. Religious beliefs favoured rural life and large families closely tied to their communities. Catholic education favoured the humanities at the expense of science and technology needed for business. It particularly discouraged the development of entrepreneurial spirit and business ethics that stress individual competition and profit maximization. Only with the Quiet Revolution in the 1960s did this begin to change, but, the argument goes, Quebec still has a cultural millstone around its neck and will take a long time to catch up to the rest of Canada.

Poverty in the Atlantic provinces can similarly be accounted for in terms of rural peasant subsistence values and the backward-looking colonial mentality of the people. People lack the entrepreneurial spirit necessary to take advantage of business opportunities and to get ahead. With a few notable exceptions, such as the McCains and the Irvings, the mass of people remain content with low, subsistence standards of living in quiet rural communities. They are not ready to take risks, to make the investments in education, effort, and entrepreneurial skills to get ahead. They tend to shun or fear the big cities. Many have migrated to Toronto and Montreal looking for work, but few of them, suggests Clark (1978), have had what it takes to succeed. Many Maritimers ended up in the slums among the chronically underemployed of the cities. Many others went back to the Maritimes to survive on welfare, temporary jobs, unemployment insurance, and other government handouts.

Yet some things do not square with this picture of perennial lack of development. Many historical accounts point to thriving commercial enterprises in shipbuilding, manufacturing, and processing for New England markets prior to Confederation. The Atlantic provinces seem to have gone downhill after Confederation with central Canada. Those who see the traditional rural Catholic culture of Quebec as the main

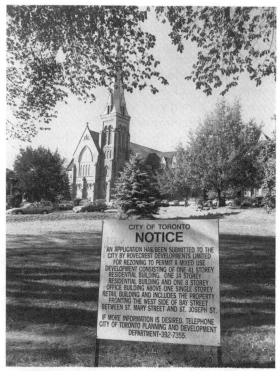

Regional disparities mean that centres like Toronto see massive development while the economies of peripheral areas like the Maritimes collapse.

impediment to economic development fail to take into account Quebec's status as a colony in relation to English Canada and the government policies that sustained this cultural pattern. British businessmen dominated the Quebec economy for their own interests while the provincial government, allied with the Catholic Church, blocked the advancement of the Québécois.

In contrast to functionalists, theorists in the political economy tradition argue that the explanation for regional disparities lies not in cultural differences, but in the contradictions of capitalism itself and its inherent tendencies toward the concentration of capital, the bankruptcy of the petite bourgeoisie, and the increasing poverty of the masses as high technology industries generate unemployment in peripheral areas.

Political economists point to the growing concentration of banking and manufacturing industries in central Canada after Confederation. Once-thriving maritime industries were swallowed up by more powerful competitors and were either run into the ground or closed down following the First World War (Sinclair and Clow 1988, 183–84; Clow 1988). Local banks moved their headquarters to Montreal, and thereafter major investment decisions were made outside the region. Now independent commodity production by family enterprises in farming, fishing, and forestry, the economic mainstay of the peripheral areas of Canada, is collapsing in the wake of concentrated corporate capitalist expansion. In effect, political economists argue, regions such as the Atlantic provinces suffer from precisely the mechanisms of underdevelopment that are at work in the Third World.

Table 15-3 Official Unemployment Rate by Province, August 1989

Province	Rate (%)
Newfoundland	14.3
Prince Edward Island	11.3
Nova Scotia	9.5
New Brunswick	11.1
Quebec	8.5
Ontario	4.8
Manitoba	6.5
Saskatchewan	6.5
Alberta	7.2
British Columbia	8.2
Canada	7.0

Source: Statistics Canada (1989b).

The contradictions of capitalism that underlie regional disparities within Canada are explored at length in chapter 9 on the political economy of Canada. The focus of the present chapter shifts outwards to the context of Canadian development within continental North America. This wider focus has been forced onto centre stage with the implementation of the Canada–U.S. free trade agreement. It is clear that the agreement will change in fundamental ways the economic rules of the game within which Canada's future development will take shape.

The Free Trade Deal and the Future Development of Canada

The free trade agreement between Canada and the United States was signed by both governments in January 1989, after the re-election of Brian Mulroney's Conservative government in November 1988. The election was fought almost entirely around this issue, with the Conservative Party strongly in favour and the Liberals and New Democrats strongly against the deal. The money spent by the government, the Conservative Party, and big business to help push the deal has been estimated at $56 million over two years, about ten times what was spent by those campaigning against the deal (Fillmore 1989, 14). Pro-free trade forces spent $3.5 million during the last three weeks of the campaign alone.

The free trade deal promises to influence fundamentally the future development of Canada. The policy debate that still surrounds the deal is so important and so contentious that it warrants detailed attention. We will be focussing on sociological rather than economic aspects of the debate. But it is hard to grasp the arguments without some understanding of the economic assumptions that underlie them. Hence a simplistic version of the basic economic model is given here. It will then be evaluated within the context of analysis of the uneven character of dependent capitalist development.

From the perspective of classical economics, in the tradition of Adam Smith, the free trade deal appears to offer multiple advantages. Smith argues that the wealth of nations is generated by the expansion of trade relations, which promotes division of labour, specialization, and rising productivity. This in turn makes possible increased employment, higher wages, and lower consumer prices. This notion presupposes that the masses are totally dependent on both the labour market and the commodity market for their survival. This can largely be taken for granted in the North American context.

This model of world trade inspires the policy analysis on free trade provided by Paul Wonnacott (1987) for the Institute for International Economics. The goal, Wonnacott argues, is to eliminate barriers to trade and investment flow between the two countries and so to open up the vast North American market. Much trade between the two countries is already tariff-free, but there remain important barriers in industries such as textiles, clothing, footwear, and furniture, and multiple non-tariff barriers such as quotas, prohibitions on certain imports, preferential government purchasing, and other **protectionist** measures that distort trade. With their removal, Canadian industry will be forced to become more competitive and therefore more efficient. A major factor in efficiency is access to large markets, which makes possible large production runs, specialization, and economies of scale. We will explain these terms in more detail below.

The issue of free trade between Canada and the United States has a very long history. The possibility of reciprocity or bilateral free trade has been discussed by successive Canadian governments since the mid-nineteenth century when Britain repealed the Corn Laws, which had granted privileged access by Canadian grain merchants to British markets. Canada lost its preferential access to British markets and turned toward America as a trading partner instead. A limited Reciprocity Treaty was signed in 1854, but it was abrogated by the U.S. in 1866 in retaliation against the Cana-

dian government for its seeming support of the Confederacy during the American Civil War. The Canadian Confederation was formed in 1867 and, about a decade later, John A. Macdonald's **National Policy** was instituted. This policy established high tariffs against American goods entering Canada. Its primary goal was to pressure American businessmen to invest in Canada in order to avoid tariff barriers. This policy encouraged the development of a branch-plant economy.

Periodic debates on free trade have surfaced ever since. Western farmers wanted free trade to get access to cheaper farm machinery. Manufacturers in central Canada wanted protectionist tariffs to build up their own industries. Others argued that exposure to competition would lead to more competitive and healthier industries and to industrial growth.

From the perspective of classical economics theory, there is much to be gained from the free competition and open markets implied in the free trade deal. In the simplest possible economic model of trade, free trade is efficient because it maximizes competitive advantage. Even if we ignore the benefits of large-scale production, people would benefit because some areas of the continent can produce certain kinds of commodities much cheaper than other areas. Everybody gains when these are freely exchanged. The southern United States produces cotton much more cheaply and efficiently than Canada ever could because of a favourable climate for this crop, while Canada produces softwood more cheaply than the United States can. California also grows grapes better than Ontario, so it makes economic sense for California to specialize in wine production and to sell it to us cheaper than we can produce it ourselves while we produce pulp and paper and sell it to California. Tariff barriers only protect expensive and inefficient industries and make consumers pay more than is necessary.

This particular argument about competitive advantage is not important with respect to the free trade deal because almost all such potential advantages have already been realized. Trade between Canada and the U.S. has been sufficiently free of tariff barriers for so long that both countries freely trade the commodities in which each has the advantage. One significant exception is wine. Canada has long imposed high tariffs on American wines to protect the Ontario wine industry. Ontario grape growers are afraid that, as these tariffs are lifted, they will have such a competitive disadvantage relative to California wines that their businesses will be destroyed.

When this simple model is elaborated to take account of **economies of scale**, the potential gains from free trade become much more significant. This argument assumes that any industry has large overheads and fixed costs. One has to have a factory, machinery, a core of skilled workers, an energy supply, production, storage and transportation facilities, even for very low levels of production. The goal is to expand production to the point where all the means of production are being utilized at their maximum possible levels so that the unit costs of production are minimized.

We can use the example of the Canadian furniture industry to illustrate this idea. A furniture factory producing a specialized line of tables will be able to streamline operations and make its product faster and cheaper than if the same factory varies production among tables, chairs, cabinets, bookshelves, and so on. Long production runs, where the same kind of item is produced, reduce the unit costs of each item, which means that prices can be lower, profits higher, and also wages higher because productivity per worker is higher. Everybody seems to gain.

However, this scenario presupposes very large markets. It is no good to produce hundreds of thousands of tables a month if you cannot sell them. Canadian furniture makers have to confine themselves to inefficient, short production runs because the Canadian market is small and geographically dispersed. Hence, furniture made in Canada for the Canadian market costs more than furniture made in the United States where the market is ten times larger. There has been a double-digit tariff imposed on furniture imported from the United States to prevent their cheaper, mass-produced goods from wiping all Canadian furniture makers out of the market. It would be more efficient in economic terms to have free trade. Canadian manufacturers, like American ones, could then specialize in large production runs—making nothing but maple wood tables, for example—and sell their products all over North America. All that is needed is a transition period in which furniture manufacturers could reorganize themselves and set up specialized production runs in items for which they could find a North American market niche. The free trade deal allows for a variable five-to-ten year adjustment period during which tariffs will be slowly phased out.

The same argument about economies of scale can be made for just about any kind of manufacturing in Canada. Cars made in Canada used to be more expensive than those made in the United States because companies here could only make small numbers of each kind of car. The Auto Pact of 1965 enables the branch plants of the big three automakers to make specialized models and export them duty free to the United States, while other models can be imported duty free. The only stipulation is that the total production in Canada equals at least 75 percent of sales in Canada (Wonnacott 1987, 75).

These, then, are the essentials of the economic arguments in favour of free trade. Tariff barriers prevent full exploitation of **competitive advantage** in certain kinds of goods and protect inefficient and expensive production runs. The result is that consumers pay more, while productivity and wages are lower than they might ideally be. The sudden removal of all such barriers threatens the protected industries but, in the long run, free competition should promote competitive advantage, specialization, and economies of scale to the benefit of everyone.

There is another argument in favour of free trade. Business people are afraid of growing protectionism in the United States. The U.S. imports more goods from abroad than it exports. One way of reversing this, and so protecting U.S. jobs, is to impose tariff barriers to make imports more expensive. Canadian businesses feel very vulnerable to such tariffs, since over 80 percent of our exports go to the United States. Wonnacott notes that several attempts to develop alternative trade with Europe have been dismal failures. Prime Minister Pierre Trudeau tried this policy during the 1970s, but the share of exports to Europe actually declined from 19 percent in 1970 to 15 percent in 1980 to 7 percent in 1985. The argument that we need the free trade deal with the United States so we will not be shut out by protectionism seems very persuasive and was widely used during the free trade debate. There is also a fear that, if Canada were to try and back out of the deal at a future date, American protectionist punishment would be swift.

The Subsidies Debate

From the economics perspective, the only major snag in the free trade debate concerns subsidies. For free trade to work, according to classical principles of competitive markets, it must be truly free and not manipulated by governments. If governments give an industry grants, tax breaks, or special low-interest loans, that industry will be able to sell products at artificially low prices and beat out competitors who do not get such handouts. The Canadian government has been giving many such subsidies to support bankrupt industries and to try to entice new industries to locate in high unemployment areas. Under the free trade deal, the United States government has the right to impose **countervailing duties** on the export of all such goods to counteract the artificially lower prices resulting from the subsidy.

The big stumbling block is how to define a subsidy. When self-employed fishermen can apply for unemployment insurance during the off-season, is this a subsidy? When Nova Scotia offers tax breaks, cheap energy, cheap buildings, and so on, to entice a Michelin Tire plant to set up in the province, how much of this is a subsidy? Is it the total amount? Is it the difference between what Nova Scotia offered and subsidies offered by Ohio? What about subsidies to any other tire plant in the United States? Should the Nova Scotia offer be compared with the maximum or the minimum such subsidy? Or should the net subsidy be calculated by deducting the increased costs of establishing a tire plant away from the prime national location? This is still very contentious. Seven years have been allocated, after implementation of the initial deal, for sorting this out.

So far it sounds as if all the gains are on Canada's side, in its access to a larger market. What do business people in the United States have to gain? They already have the advantage of economies of scale. A ten percent expansion in their potential market will not make that much difference. However, what Canada does have to offer the United States is a secure energy supply. Under the free trade deal, restrictions on American investment in the energy industries, such as oil and gas, are lifted. Also, the United States is guaranteed supplies of energy at the same price that Canadians pay for it. Furthermore, in times of shortage, the U.S. is guaranteed supplies of energy at a level proportional to the amount exported to the United States during the preceding years. This offers security of supply, which balances the security Canadians receive that continental markets will not be closed to them by protectionist tariff barriers.

A second important advantage for the United States is that Canadian markets are opened up for American service industries. The free trade deal is unique in including services as well as manufactured goods. Services include a wide range of activities such as tourism, transportation, communications, insurance, banking and other financial services, and professional consulting firms such as those in construction, engineering, computers, motion pictures, and advertising. During the 1980s, Canada has had a surplus in trade in goods with the United States, but a substantial deficit in services. The United States is becoming a world leader in services and sees this as a way of reducing its overall trade deficit of some $124 billion in 1985. Free trade in services with Canada might help to promote such deals with other countries. In principle, all the arguments of comparative advantage and economics of scale apply to services as well as goods.

The Costs of Economic Rationality: Arguments Against Free Trade

Very simplified versions of economic arguments in favour of free trade have been presented above. They sound so persuasive that it is hard to see why anyone would be against it, except perhaps people employed in the inefficient and unprofitable sectors of the economy that can only survive because of heavy protective tariffs. So why have spokespersons for the Liberal Party, the New Democratic Party, labour groups, and women's groups been so opposed to free trade?

Part of the answer lies in the analysis of the contradictions of advanced capitalism, which we explored with reference to the situation of Third World countries. The economic model of the advantages of free trade presupposes a competitive, free-market economy. Opponents argue that this model is outdated because mature capitalism is characterized by the concentration of ownership of the means of production in huge multinational corporations and by related crises of unemployment, depressed wages, and overproduction. We will explore some of the arguments against the free trade deal from the perspective of critical political economy. The same broad framework used above in Frank's analysis of world trade and underdevelopment in the Third World will be used, focussing on issues of capital control, investment patterns, market relations, labour relations, and force.

Concentration of Capital

An important concern within mainstream economics theory is the potential contradiction between the goals of specialization and economies of scale on the one hand and the fundamental assumption of free competition on the other. When economies of scale are pushed to their limits, the outcome may often be oligopoly—the domination of the markets by a few giant companies, which may act in collusion—or monopoly, where one company controls the market. When this happens, the logic of free competition leading to efficient production and lower prices no longer holds. Prices may rise beyond what is justifiable relative to production costs because there is no competitor to which consumers can turn for cheaper goods. This is why there is a recognized need for governments to oversee the services provided by monopoly utilities such as the telephone company and Canada Post.

This issue of oligopolies and market collusion has important implications for the projected benefits from the free trade deal. Wonnacott (1987, 23, 31) notes that, when some economists have tried to introduce the concept of **imperfect competition** into their models, the estimated benefits to consumers are lower than supporters of the deal claim them to be. However, the analytical complexities involved in adding such assumptions to economic models are such that the simpler model of perfect or almost perfect competition remains very popular.

A sociological study of the Canadian food industry shows how critical such deviations from free competition can be (Winson 1988). A series of mergers since 1986 has resulted in greater efficiency in economic terms: less profitable stores with higher labour costs relative to sales were shut down. But what this has meant for local food producers and processors is a dramatic drop in competitive outlets for their produce. Smaller processors who used to buy from small farmers are being forced out of business by pressure from the retail giants. The bulk of supermarket purchases in Canada are funnelled through only four wholesale buying organizations controlled by the food chains themselves. Consumers who initially benefitted from these economies of scale may soon find themselves at the mercy of two or three integrated food giants that dominate the marketplace.

Free trade seems likely to increase this process of concentration and lead in the long run to worsening crises of capitalism. This is particularly so since the Canadian economy is already dominated by branch plants of larger U.S. corporations. As we noted above, an estimated 80 percent of Canadian trade takes the form of **intercorporate transfers**, under manipulated transfer-pricing arrangements, rather than free market transactions. How does this reality affect the free trade debate?

John Ralston Saul (1988) gives an unusually candid picture of life at the top of these subsidiaries. Branch plant executives speak of their schizophrenic lives, their public status but private subordination, their public authority but private powerlessness, their public support for free trade but private opposition to it. Officially, these men are presidents of their branch-plant companies, but typically they report to divisional managers several levels below the senior management at their parent company. They also generally have little authority over investment budgets. They describe themselves as running "cash cows" for the benefit of the parent company, their role being to remit profits out of Canada undetected by the Canadian government. The typical way is by transfer-pricing arrangements. The apparent profitability of a subsidiary is thus socially constructed by the accounts department, with real profit levels almost impossible to determine.

A classic case of such manipulation of a branch plant by the parent company brought about the collapse of the once-profitable and debt-free Gillette Canada company. It was forced by its parent corporation to buy out another Gillette subsidiary because the parent company needed cash to fight off a takeover bid. The result was that Gillette Canada was saddled with a debt of $269 million and interest payments of $22 million a year. It could not meet the debt load and began to show heavy financial losses. Within a month of the signing of the free trade agreement, this "unprofitable" subsidiary was closed down, its 600 jobs eliminated. The 10 percent tariff barrier on imported shaving products will disappear under the deal, and the parent company will be able to meet Canadian market demands from its plant in Boston (Persky 1989).

Publicly, branch plant spokespersons endorse the ideology of competitive free enterprise, but privately these executives acknowledge that their parent companies frown on competition between a subsidiary and the parent. Hence, Canadian branch plants are inhibited from expanding abroad. This may be a critical part of the explanation why Canadian businesses have seemed so unsuccessful in promoting alternative trade relations with Europe. Branch-plant presidents have no authority to compete in such markets.

Publicly, these executives speak out strongly in favour of free trade. They have to. Their parent companies want it and they risk their jobs by voicing opposition to it. But, under the promise of anonymity, they privately admitted they were against it. The reason is that all the economic arguments, maximized efficiency, international specialization, and economies of scale, point to the rationality of closing Canadian branch plants and servicing the Canadian market from excess capacity already available in parent plants in the United States. Based on an arbitrary measure of majority shareholding, Saul estimates that at least 25 percent of Canadian businesses are branch plants. This percentage rises much higher when one takes into account the fact that a concentrated minority shareholding of 10 to 15 percent may be sufficient to control the board of a company. Free trade thus seems to undermine the long-term future of a very sizable proportion of Canadian operations with their roots outside the country. Branch plants, originally encouraged to establish themselves in Canada by the National Policy, will be encouraged to consolidate operations and close branches with the free trade policy.

There is, however, one plus side to this situation, should the Canadian government ever decide to pull out of the free trade deal. The very fact that so much trade with the United States is through intercorporate transfers serves to reduce the potential threat of protectionist retaliation against Canadian exports. Corporate business leaders have little interest in pushing for a policy of government taxation on Canadian goods that they themselves are importing. The same argument holds with respect to the export of all forms of energy and raw materials. It is not in the long-term interest of American businesses to have to pay higher prices for their imported raw materials. It is only with respect to produce and to finished manufactured goods provided by Canadian-owned businesses that protective tariffs are clearly in the interests of American businesses. This is not a large share of all Canadian exports.

Investment Patterns

Supporters of the free trade deal hope that the removal of all tariff barriers will encourage investment in areas in which each country has a competitive advantage and so will maximize efficiency of production. Those who oppose the deal see the same processes occurring but fear the outcome will mean more concentration in Canada in the areas of resource extraction: oil, gas, and hydroelectric power, mining and minerals, forests and fishing. Foreign investment seems likely to flow into these industries in which Canada has a competitive advantage, leading to increased foreign ownership and control. Supporters have a positive view of such investment, arguing that it will encourage growth in these sectors. Opponents fear foreign control of critically important, nonrenewable sources of energy and raw materials. The fact that, in times of possible future energy shortages, the United States is guaranteed a stable proportion of output, at prices equal to Canadian internal prices, worries many people. We will return to this issue below in the context of ecological concerns.

The negative side to foreign investment and growth in advantaged industries is the fear that less advantaged industries will be squeezed out or pressured into extreme specialization to survive. During the summer of 1988, the grape growers of Ontario had an indication of what might happen: they were refused operating loans by Ontario banks. The banks argued that the grape industry is a poor risk since more costly Ontario wines could not compete with wines from California once all tariff restrictions were removed. Economic efficiency goals are also likely to encourage investment in the manufacturing heartlands of the continent, rather than in the Canadian periphery.

Lifting restrictions on the operation of American banks in Canada means that investment decisions may increasingly be controlled from outside the country, once free trade in services is a reality. Within weeks of the deal being signed, American Express filed notice with the Canadian government that it wanted to set up banking services in Canada. Ironically, Canadian banks will not have the same freedom of action in the United States because U.S. law prohibits interstate banking. This law was designed to avoid the possibility of a nationwide financial disaster, should one huge bank become insolvent.

The Costs of Specialization

Specialization is efficient for corporate capitalist development and is likely to bring lower production costs and higher profits, at least in the short run. But there are problems with the argument of competitive advantage. In the context of world markets, we have already seen the desperate vulnerability of small nations, the bulk of all their exports concentrated in one of two industries, such as coffee and sugar, controlled by one multinational corporation. There are fears that Canada is already vulnerable in this regard because of an overspecialization in staples and limited manufacturing industries. This vulnerability could increase under free trade. Waddell (1988) warns that the auto industry may be Ontario's Achilles heel. In 1987 the transportation industry comprised about 25 percent of Ontario's manufacturing output. A downturn in the market for cars could be disastrous for the provincial economy. Chrysler went to the brink of bankruptcy during a mild recession in 1981 and had to be bailed out by the Canadian government.

Schneider (1988, 122) voices a similar warning against the specialization of maritime forests in softwood trees for pulp. The industry, which is crucial to the maritime economy, could be undermined if new technology makes it cheaper to produce paper from sugar cane residue. Alberta's economy took a nose-dive when world oil prices dropped. Prairie wheat farms provide a classic example of specialization and economies of scale. But the huge wheat farms are also turning into textbook examples of crises of falling rate of profits and overproduction. Farmers are locked in a vicious cycle of increased equipment costs, higher debt loads, ever more efficient production to maximize grain output, falling wheat prices, and the consequent need to expand production still further to keep ahead. They are driven to buy up yet more land at firesale prices as neighbouring farms go bankrupt. Meanwhile, the small businesses and franchises in neighbouring towns collapse as more and more farm families give up and move away. One farm now produces more wheat than fifty farms used to, but one farm family does not buy fifty cups of coffee, or fifty new cars, or fifty pairs of boots. Specialization, economies of scale, and maximizing efficiency have been bought at a very high price in the Canadian prairie economy.

Market Relations

The core of the free trade deal is that it promises to open up continental markets. The goal is a level playing field where all competition will be equal. Supporters argue that possible protectionist barriers to the American market could be catastrophic for Canadian trade and that free trade protects us against such a possibility. Advocates of the deal believe that Canadian business will gain from this continental market and will be able to compete in it as an equal of U.S. business. They argue that, as Canada has been unable to compete successfully in European trade, it needs the U.S. market. The contradiction that Canada is too weak to compete in Europe but is adequate to compete in the U.S. goes unnoticed.

Opponents argue that Canada will be able to compete in the levelled North American playing field only at enormous cost. An emphasis on sameness, without allowing for Canada's particular situation, results in a very unequal formal equality. Canada has a harsher climate and greater geographic dispersal, resulting in higher energy costs, higher transportation costs, and considerable disadvantages in agriculture. When none of these can be compensated for, Canadian businesses may find themselves disadvantaged in continental markets. In the past, Canada has benefitted from cheap sources of energy, but the free trade deal abolishes this. The United States has won the right to purchase energy from Canada at the same price that Canadians pay.

From the point of view of industry, geographic disadvantages may be relatively minor in comparison with the political disadvantages of Canada's much larger public welfare system. Canadian businesses, on average, pay higher taxes than do American businesses to support more comprehensive social programs. Industries may well cry foul if they are expected to compete, unprotected, in American markets, while paying higher domestic taxes. But equalizing taxes means reducing them to American levels and so threatening social services. Social services were not on the table during the free trade talks, but they nonetheless stand to be greatly influenced by the deal.

In March 1989, scarcely two months after the signing of the deal, Laurent Thibault, the head of the Canadian Manufacturers Association, publicly urged the Mulroney government to make deep cuts in social spending because social costs and resulting high taxes affect the competitiveness of Canadian industry (*Globe and Mail*, 2 March 1989). During the November 1988 election campaign, Thibault had strenuously denied the validity of the argument that free trade threatened social programs.

The issue of government taxation also adds an important qualifier to the estimates of cheaper consumer prices that may be gained from the removal of tariffs under the free trade deal. To the extent that such tariffs have been an important source of revenue to the Canadian government, the shortfall will have to be made up elsewhere. The obvious way is higher sales taxes. In the May 1989 federal budget, Finance Minister Michael Wilson confirmed that a federal goods and services tax would be levied, starting in January 1991. The net savings to consumers from the removal of protective tariffs may thus drop to zero. Meanwhile, the artificially protected industries in Canada may go under and, with them, a great many low-income jobs. The purchasing power of these people will clearly not be enhanced by free trade.

The question of regional development subsidies currently dominates the debate concerning the principle of the level playing field versus affirmative action for disadvantaged areas. The theory behind subsidies is that industries need to be compensated for the market disadvantages of locating in peripheral areas. But such practices are declared unfair subsidies under the free trade deal. The huge capital grants given to bail out fishing companies in Atlantic Canada could be cited as promoting an unfair advantage over the fishing industry of the United States. But the abolition of all such regional development grants carries the threat that peripheral areas will never be able to compete on the continental playing field.

Opponents of the free trade deal argue that the U.S. government provides similar regional development subsidies, but it does so under the auspices of military spending. Military spending is explicitly excluded from the free trade deal. This raises the spectre that future regional development subsidies in Canada might increasingly take the form of military spending.

Labour Relations

Many other factors influence how level the playing field can become. Higher minimum wage regulations and stronger union protection legislation in Canada can be seen to put some Canadian businesses at an unfair disadvantage. The classical economics model predicts that capital will relocate to where the labour is cheap and labour laws weak, at least for industries where only a low-skilled workforce is required. It is precisely for this reason that the Nova Scotia government introduced the "Michelin Bill," to strip labour laws of their power in order to attract new businesses such as the Michelin Tire plant.

Labour organizations are worried that Canada may have to copy the United States where labour laws are weaker and minimum wage legislation either nonexistent, as in many southern states, or set at very low levels. The "Mexican connection" is even more worrisome. Goods made by U.S. branch plants located in Mexico can enter the United States—and hence Canada—duty free. The average wage in Mexico is less than $1 per hour (Lynk 1988, 77). In 1988 there were more than 1200 U.S. plants operating in Mexico, including 27 General Motors assembly plants. In April 1988, Chrysler threatened to close a Wisconsin assembly plant and to transfer some assembly work from Detroit to Mexico if the United Auto Workers did not accept an early contract offer from the company (*Globe and Mail*, 28 April 1988, B3). In principle this should not happen in Canada because the Auto Pact stipulates that the value of production in this country must not fall below 75 percent of domestic sales. This is a critical reason why labour leaders did not want the Auto Pact to be on the bargaining table in the free trade negotiations. However, there are strong concerns that the pact may not hold up against free trade and cheaper Mexican-assembled American cars.

It evidently did not occur to Canadian negotiators that minimum wage rates that are set below subsistence level constitute a form of unfair subsidy to American business. Under the free trade deal, Canada has no right to impose countervailing duties against commodities produced by workers who are paid at rates below our minimum wage level.

The classical economics model predicts that, as minimum wage levels drop, unemployment levels also drop, because it becomes more worthwhile for businesses to hire people in marginal jobs. If they had to pay more money, they would not hire them at all. Labour leaders, understandably, do not show much enthusiasm for this line of argument. When the minimum wage falls below subsistence, or below welfare payments, people who otherwise want to work are forced to stay on welfare because they cannot survive without these benefits. People who shift from welfare to bottom-end jobs are no longer eligible for subsidized housing, they pay a rapidly escalating share of child-care costs and contribute to unemployment insurance, health insurance, and the Canada Pension Plan. They have to shoulder the extra costs of going to work and are hit hardest by sales and excise taxes. Minimum wage levels in Canada have not kept up with inflation. Between 1979 and 1986, people on minimum wage lost an estimated 30 percent of their purchasing power. With free trade, this promises to get worse, as minimum wage levels drop to parity with the lowest minimums in the United States or possibly Mexico. The alternative is to maintain higher minimum wage levels and have Canadian firms argue that they cannot compete on the continental playing field . Government-subsidized wages would be subject to countervailing action by the United States.

Force
Few expect that the Untied States would invade Canada with troops to protect multinational corporate interests. But what people do expect is the use of economic force in the disputes settlement mechanism. The fear is that American law will prevail in disputes, and Canadian businesses will be subject to countervailing duties whenever something is construed to be a subsidy or to

be unfair to American business. Some opponents of the deal argue that the definition of a subsidy is so vague that it might include almost anything where American companies feel Canadians have a comparative advantage. Low stumpage fees (the fees that companies pay to the provincial government for the right to cut trees) for British Columbia lumber were cited as justification for countervailing duties on softwood lumber when the trade negotiations were under way. Canadian economists argued that there were multiple reasons why stumpage rates need not be identical with American rates (Wonnacott 1987, 91–93), but they were not persuasive. Opponents of free trade fear that Canada's bargaining power in disputes will be steadily weakened. We will become even more integrated with, and dependent upon, U.S. markets. The Americans will already have gained full investment access to Canadian energy resources and guaranteed supplies at Canadian prices. Canada will be unable to pull out of the deal, except at enormous costs in economic disruption.

The economic arguments against the free trade deal are strong ones. They boil down to the assertion that free trade or market-driven economic development will result in maximizing efficiency and profits for the metropolitan core of giant multinational corporate empires. But this will be at the price of exacerbating the concentration of capital and the related crises of overproduction, unemployment, and declining standard of living of the working classes within peripheral areas of Canada. Consumer gains are unlikely, given monopoly or near-monopoly control over prices and the fact that sales taxes are likely to replace revenue lost with the removal of tariffs.

The Social Costs of Economic Rationality

The most easily recognized social cost of free trade, and perhaps for that reason that most widely discussed, is the inevitable disruption of jobs in uncompetitive industries currently protected by high tariffs. Jobs in these industries, particularly textiles and clothing, are held disproportionately by immigrant women. Their low educational levels, limited skills, and poor command of English make them unlikely candidates for alternative kinds of jobs that might open up under free trade. The potential consumer benefits of free trade for the families of all these women are non-existent. Only massive government-sponsored programs and retraining opportunities would help them. But this presupposes that the Canadian government will change its conception of immigrant women from housewife-dependants, who only earn pocket money in the marketplace, and begin to see these women as the important wage-earners that they are.

In considering these issues, it is important to go beyond the notion that the structures of capitalism work in inexorable ways without human agency. As Roxana Ng's work, discussed in chapter 14, shows, government policies and the working of employment agencies help to produce the gender-class of unskilled immigrant women in the first place. If women had been fully integrated with their husbands into language-training programs and community college trade programs, and had been provided with essential child-care support, they would not have become concentrated in these low-income job ghettos in declining industries in the first place.

The general response to the foreseeable disruptions in these vulnerable industries has been that they can be handled by comprehensive adjustment programs. The related hope, although opponents argue a distant one, is that free trade itself will generate more jobs than it jeopardizes, and hence that displaced workers will be absorbed elsewhere in the economy in the long run.

The implications of the free trade deal for the employment of women go far beyond a concern with women employed in threatened jobs in the clothing industry. Of more general importance are the provisions within the deal for free trade in services. Marjorie Cohen (1987, 1988a, 1988b) gives central attention to what these provisions may entail. Cohen argues that free trade in services was the single most important issue for the United States in the negotiations. Yet the seventy-two volumes of research on free trade prepared by the Macdonald Commission did not examine the effects of free trade on a single service industry. The commission simply assumed that gaining access to the service market would encourage the United States to offer improved access for goods exported from Canada. Cohen argues that this was not a good trade off since two-thirds of all incomes and 70 percent of jobs in Canada are now in the service sector.

The free trade deal is unique in its inclusion of services. The Americans have been trying unsuccessfully for years to have services included in international trade agreements, such as the General Agreement on Tariffs and Trade (GATT), at the urging of the giant service firms like American Express, American Telephone and Telegraph, and Citibank. The reason why it has been so hard is that most other countries do not want free trade in such services because they see it as too great a threat to their autonomy. Yet it has been virtually ignored in public debate and press coverage on the deal.

Left unanswered are major questions concerning the effects of American banks controlling investment funds in Canada, American financial services dominating financial markets, American computers and data-processing industries dominating the flow of information, American consulting firms directing development decisions and dominating high technology research. The agreement prevents any possibility of future national policies in such areas without the prohibitively expensive requirement that American firms be compensated for any potential losses that might follow from such policies.

Special concerns of Canadian cultural industries—publishing, film, broadcasting, and so on—received considerable attention during the free trade debate. In principle such industries are protected but in practice, opponents of the deal argue, this protection is shallow. Salutin (1988) points out that, even prior to the deal, Canadian cultural industries were dominated by U.S. corporations. He estimates that in 1988 Canadian productions accounted for only 5 percent of movie screen time, 2.4 percent of video cassette sales, 2 to 3 percent of prime time television programming, 15 percent of record and tape sales, 23 percent of magazines, and 20 percent of the publishing market. An enormous proportion of the cultural industries in Canada is already American-controlled. The tiny proportion that is still Canadian depends heavily upon government subsidies. Yet U.S. companies can object that subsidies constitute unfair trading practices and damage their market.

On paper, the free trade deal exempts cultural industries from rules prohibiting government subsidies. But there is a catch. The United States has the right to impose countervailing duties on Canadian exports, in any area they choose, to compensate for an American company's loss of income due to Canadian government policies. For example, suggests Salutin, if Canada were to prevent an American corporation such as Coca-Cola or Gulf and Western from buying a Canadian publishing house, the U.S. government would have the right to calculate the financial loss this represented and penalize to the equivalent amount Canadian exports to the U.S. of such items as steel, fish, or agricultural products. If prime time television were to be set aside for Canadian programming, then the U.S. could compute the losses in sales of U.S. programs and impose countervailing duties on some other

Canadian export. Canada cannot even use tax breaks to aid Canadian filmmakers any more because this would constitute a subsidy. Salutin predicts that the Canadian government will never develop or enforce any cultural policy that provokes a complaint from the Americans when the result might be countervailing duties.

Social services such as health, education, and child care are explicitly excluded from the free trade deal, but management services are included. American management consulting firms are increasingly moving into the fields of health and education. Their narrow focus on profits and financial efficiency threatens to lead to the reorganization of social services in ways that have high social costs. A few hospitals in Canada are already run by such management consulting firms. They have introduced multiple cost-cutting measures including patient illness classifications that are fed into computers that then indicate the type and amount of nursing care needed. The effect of such programs on the service labour force can be devastating. The full-time regular nursing force is reduced to a minimum while the majority of nurses are on call, their work confined to part-time and irregular shifts. The quality of care deteriorates as nurses have no discretion to give patients the care they feel they need: this is all predetermined by the computer (Cohen 1988b). A poll conducted for the Ontario Nurses Association in 1988 indicated that around 15 percent of Ontario nurses are planning to leave the profession because of excessive patient loads and demoralizing working conditions (*Globe and Mail*, 15 April, 1988, A4). Under free trade conditions are likely to get worse.

Child care is not included explicitly in the free trade deal, but day-care companies run for profit are included implicitly in the chapter on investment, which gives all service firms, whether or not named in the agreement, the **right to national treatment**. Child-care facilities, too, may soon be run by management consulting firms designed to maximize profits or to minimize costs, with the social service and learning aspects of the work only a secondary consideration. The fact that the Conservative government decided in 1988 to direct child-care funding to mothers, rather than to the establishment of child-care centres, plays into the hands of a profit-oriented system. There is nothing in the agreement to prevent American service firms from sharing in Canadian government funding for social services.

Cohen notes further that the impact of free trade in services is likely to fall hardest on women because they are disproportionately employed within the service sector. It is their jobs that stand to be cut back. Their working lives as nurses and providers of social services are likely to be affected most by profit-oriented, competitive management systems.

Canadian agriculture is also excluded in theory but directly implicated in practice in the free trade deal. Remaining in place are supply management programs, which set limits on agricultural production to prevent the market from being flooded, especially with perishable goods, and thus to protect prices. The problem is that Canadian food processors such as McCain's have indicated that they cannot be expected to pay higher supply-managed prices and at the same time compete with American companies in the production of processed foods such as French fries and chicken nuggets.

Paul Wonnacott argues that Canadian agriculture is inefficient because it is artificially divided into small producer units by government restrictions on interprovincial trade in agricultural products. Eggs, poultry, and dairy products are particularly inefficient, spread among about 2500 independent family farms and protected by a supply management system that allocated quotas to each farmer and regulates product prices (*Globe and Mail*, 6 June 1988, A8). To be competitive, Wonnacott argues, Canadian producers would have to operate on a much larger scale.

In the United States, according to the *Globe and Mail* article, small independent chicken farmers have been forced out of business over the past thirty years by large agricultural conglomerates. About a dozen integrated companies, located almost exclusively in the low-wage southern states, now control most of the U.S. chicken industry. They can produce chickens at 25 percent below Canadian farmers' prices. They do so, however, at a high social and humanitarian price.

Factory farming practices mean that chickens are crammed into battery cages under filthy surroundings and are fed antibiotics and growth hormones.

In the "chicken cities" of the American South, chickens live our their eight-week lives under wretched conditions, crammed in battery cages designed to get as many birds as possible into a limited space and to minimize their movements so that they fatten up quickly. The manure is cleaned out of the chicken sheds only once a year or even once every two years. Canadian chickens face a miserable enough existence on smaller-scale factory farms, but at least they have the relative luxury of having their cages cleaned

out, on average, once every eight weeks, between each batch of chickens. Chickens have to be heavily drugged with antibiotics to kill diseases that they pick up in such filthy surroundings. People who eat them risk building up a tolerance for these antibiotics so that human diseases become increasingly resistant to treatment by regular antibiotics.

The free trade deal will phase out the current 12.5 percent tariff on chicken imports and raise the quotas on imports by about two million more chickens a year. Canadian producers will be under increasing pressure to lower their prices to processors to match American prices. They can only do so by similar economies of scale. Animal rights seem to have no place at all in this philosophy for the future.

Free Trade Reconsidered: Alternatives for Development

The free trade debate, which will for some time be at the centre of the political stage in Canada, has a history that goes back at least as far as 1854. It cannot be discussed definitively in a few pages. The debate itself is only a relatively small part of a much wider concern with world development. The objective of this section is two-fold: to clarify the theoretical assumptions from which competing options arise and to shift the focus of Canada's free trade debate toward the wider issue of world development.

The arguments in favour of some form of free trade agreement are rational and compelling. Proponents foresee large markets, specialization, economies of scale, and the free flow of goods and services across the continent, all of which will maximize the efficiency of production and, hence, the potential for economic growth. The arguments against free trade are also very persuasive. Opponents of the deal predict that it will increase the concentration of capital. Due to this concentration, regional disparities and unemployment and poverty in the peripheral areas will also increase. At the same time the deal will reduce autonomy of political action needed to redress these problems.

When presented in this highly simplified form, the common assumptions that underlie the opposing positions are more striking than the differences. Strong criticisms are raised against specifics of the present deal. Yet the more fundamental question is whether it will really make much difference in the long run if the deal is upheld or torn up. The deal represents a logical continuation rather than a radical departure from processes already under way within the Canadian economy. The deal is likely to speed up these processes but not to change their direction in any fundamental way. Irrespective of the deal, the Canadian economy is primarily a branch-plant economy, subject to increasing corporate concentration and rationalization. Peripheral areas are already substantially de-industrialized and dependent upon transfer payments and seasonal unemployment insurance. Decades of regional development grants, subsidies, and relocation incentives to companies have done very little to change this pattern. The service sector is already shifting toward privatization and the use of management consulting firms to maximize economic efficiency. It is likely to continue in this direction even without granting the right of national treatment to American firms.

What seems to be happening to the political debate in Canada is that the specifics of the free trade deal are determining what is discussed. The critics, in responding to this preset agenda, find themselves constrained by the terms of the model they are challenging. The debate is one-dimensional and leaves too much out. Missing from the public debate on free trade are core questions concerning what visions of modernization we have and whether the continental market-driven form of economic organization can fulfil those visions.

In the middle of the free trade negotiations, in April 1987, the Brundtland Report, entitled *Our Common Future*, was published under the auspices of the United Nations World Commission on Environment and Development. Newspaper coverage of the report argued that "we must be ever mindful of the risks of endangering the survival of life on earth." But for Canadians, the coverage was hidden among other important headlines: "the deepening farm crisis, Canada's multi-billion-dollar military build-up, the free-trade negotiations and the constitutional accord—and another doomsday warning was of only passing interest" (*Globe and Mail*, 20 Oct. 1987, A7).

It is easy to get the impression that free trade and global survival have nothing to do with each other, but the core message of the Brundtland Report is precisely that the model of development assumed in the free trade debate is endangering global survival. It is a form of development driven by corporate concentration and investment decisions geared to maximizing short-term financial returns. Brundtland's stark message is that this path is not ecologically sustainable. It is generating environmental damage of staggering magnitude in the Third World and in industrially developed nations. Ecologically and economically, we can no longer afford it. We need to change course.

The Threatened Environment

The message of the Brundtland Report is that ecologically sustainable development within the Third World needs to be as directly concerned with equitable distribution of development resources as with growth. Agriculture geared to sustainable improvement in food production for local consumption is likely to be cheaper and more profitable in the long run than the current emphasis on cash crops. As we have already seen, the problem with focussing on cash crops is that world commodity prices are unstable. Earnings are rarely sufficient to

A western Guatemalan mountainside is clearcut for corn farming. Soils underlying rainforests can support crops for only a couple of years. Further deforestation results as farmers abandon plots and move on.

satisfy all food needs, particularly when much of the earnings go toward foreign debt repayment. The emphasis on quick profits encourages mining the soil to maximize immediate outputs rather than conserving it as a future resource. The unequal distribution of gains also pushes the large majority of the population of these countries onto marginal land to produce subsistence food crops and to feed local animals. This policy exacts a heavy toll in soil erosion. Rain forests are hacked down for timber and agricultural settlement, but shallow forest soils tend to erode quickly. The watershed deteriorates. Soils low in organic compost have reduced capacity to hold water, and floods and droughts have a steadily worsening impact.

Tropical forests are being reduced at the rate of 7 to 10 million hectares annually; another 10 million hectares are grossly

disrupted. The world's deserts are expanding at the rate of 6 million hectares annually. As habitats are altered, plant, animal, and insect species are threatened. An estimated two-thirds of all plant, animal, and bird species in the world have been lost in the last quarter century. This represents a critical loss of genetic stock for medical and plant-breeding purposes, and an incalculable blow to the quality and variety of life on earth.

In short, the Brundtland Report argues that growth is not enough. We need more concern with quality. A more equitable distribution of resources would help to break the cycle of poverty and ecological destruction in many parts of the Third World. We also need to expand our economic models to incorporate the value of climate control, rainfall, plant and animal preservation, and so on. It makes long-term economic sense to keep the forests, rather than trying to use marginal soil for agriculture that can quickly deplete the soil.

Industrial Agriculture

The Brundtland Report advocates that the industrial world move away from the concept of economies of scale and monocrop agriculture, because in the long run the ecological stress caused by such farming practices is prohibitively expensive. Vast stretches of the Prairies in Canada and the United States are being mined to produce monocrop cereals year after year, with the aid of chemical fertilizers and pesticides. The result is soil reduced to the texture of dust. Soil erosion in Canada alone is costing farmers in the region of $1 billion a year. Over-irrigation is causing the waterlogging, salinization, and alkalization of soils. An estimated 10 million hectares of irrigated land, worldwide, are being abandoned each year due to such problems. Nitrogen fertilizers pollute groundwater, and chemical pesticides threaten human health and endanger fish, birds, and insects, including those that prey on pests. There has also been a great increase in pesticide-resistant pest species. Soils lacking organic materials and bereft of tree-cover cannot retain water. Droughts become a very serious threat.

The report argues that ecology and economics are not necessarily in opposition, but the harmony of these concerns presupposes farming techniques very different from those that now dominate in Western Europe and North America. Mixed farming, crop rotation, and farming along organic principles could be much more profitable in the long run if the costs of ecological deterioration are added into calculations of costs.

Industrial Pollution

Energy consumption has risen exponentially in the industrialized world over the last quarter century, particularly the consumption of wood, oil, gas, coal, and nuclear power. The burning of fossil fuels creates problems of atmospheric pollution, global warming, acidification, and industrial air pollution. Air pollution is damaging vegetation, corroding buildings and vehicles, and killing lakes and fish. Chlorofluorocarbons used in aerosol sprays, refrigeration, and the manufacture of some plastics, especially styrofoam, are known to damage the earth's ozone layer. This is the layer in the outer atmosphere that absorbs ultraviolet light from the sun. The result of its erosion is an increased risk of skin cancer. Mountains of dangerous chemical and nuclear wastes are piling up faster than we can find means to dispose of them safely. A liquid chemical dump polluting the ground water of the communities of Whitechurch-Stouffville, north of Toronto, was implicated in high cancer and miscarriage rates in the locality in the 1980s (Rosenberg 1986). Conditions inside

Chemical dumps can leak into ground water, rivers, and lakes, poisoning fish and contaminating drinking water.

the home are not much better. The average household is a storage site for up to 250 chemicals dangerous to children. One child in the United States is accidentally poisoned every 60 seconds. Currently, impoverished African countries are being pressured by unscrupulous and desperate waste-disposal companies to take hazardous wastes. These nations need money very badly, and they tend not to have enforceable pollution-control legislation.

The burning of fossil fuels, combined with atmospheric pollution, is generating a greenhouse effect, a long-term warming of global temperatures estimated to be between 1.5° and 4.5° Celsius over forty or fifty years. Warmer temperatures threaten to speed up the melting of polar icecaps, which could lead to flooding in low-lying coastal cities and agricultural areas. In other areas it could lead to droughts and crop damage. Canada,

along with many other parts of the world, experienced what might be the beginnings of such fundamental climatic change during the summer of 1988. Extensive droughts damaged the North American wheat and hay crops, while water levels several feet below normal along the Mississippi River disrupted transportation. The drought also dried up prairie potholes, which are the nesting grounds for many species of waterfowl. This severe summer drought added fuel to the debate concerning whether Canada's water resources constitute a commodity under the free trade deal and whether that commodity should or would be diverted south to meet America's growing need for water. Agricultural and industrial uses for water, worth billions of dollars, are at stake. Meanwhile, Torontonians choked on a yellow-brown smog that was a mixture of emissions from coal-fired power plants in the United

Industrial air pollution, and the acid rain that it causes, damage vegetation, corrode buildings, and kill lakes and wildlife.

States and vehicle exhaust fumes, baked by 36° Celsius temperatures.

This kind of industrial development is not only ecologically unsustainable, it is also prohibitively expensive, once the costs of pollution are calculated into economic models. The economics of this form of development change abruptly once the "polluter pays" principle is introduced into the equation. Under this principle, the firms producing the acidic smog in their coal furnaces would have to pay for all the damage to lakes, rivers, vehicles, buildings, and human health, in the areas reached by the polluted air and acid rain. Under such a system, the economics of conservation and pollution control would appear many times more cost efficient than they appear to be now.

Brundtland also notes the staggering costs of urban sprawl created by the concentration of industries in central areas. Urban sprawl, which occurs both in developing and developed economies, results in pollution, housing crises, rising crime rates, and so on. If the industries that locate in urban areas are charged for the full social and environmental costs of urban sprawl, the economics of relocation in smaller centres will look much more appealing. This is particularly true for high-technology service firms where computerized communications systems make geographic decentralization cheap and efficient. In fact, business sections of Canadian newspapers are reporting increasing numbers of businesses that have set up in large, old country houses, to the apparent high satisfaction of management and employees alike.

The Brundtland Report's basic conclusion is that we have to call a halt to the kind of economic development that is endangering the survival of the planet. That does not mean we have to stop development. This is not a viable option in a world where the most

The costs of urban sprawl include overcrowding, traffic congestion, and accompanying air pollution.

basic needs of masses of people are not being met. But it does mean that the form that such development takes must be altered so as to be ecologically sustainable on a long-term worldwide basis.

The toughest challenge in the 1990s will be how to satisfy the newly unleashed demands from the people of Eastern Europe for a standard of living that equals what they see in the West. The risk is that this development will take the form of a massive expansion of Western corporate capitalism eager to exploit the resources of the East, with minimal concern for ecological damage.

A possible compensating factor might be the decline of the Cold War. Resources used to sustain permanent war economies could be redirected to protect the environment. The Brundtland Report estimates that repairing the environmental damage already done to the earth will cost billions, even trillions, of dollars. But such huge sums are only a fraction of current global military spending. Economic forecasters speculate that fundamental restructuring will be needed in the U.S. economy in the 1990s if the Cold War continues to abate. The current system of production, in which an estimated one-third of all economic resources are associated directly or indirectly with war, will become obsolete. The crucial question is what direction and what form such restructuring will take.

Conclusion

Few theorists doubt the ecological disaster warnings contained in the Brundtland Report, or the need for an ecologically sustainable form of development. The major theoretical debate for the future concerns how to get there from here. Is continental free trade one route we might take? On this fundamental question, there is much heated debate.

Mainstream economics, North American style, still has a long way to go to deal with the problems raised in the report. The costs of pollution and pollution controls are not normally incorporated into basic industrial accounting. There is nothing in principle to prevent classical economists from incorporating such costs into their cost-benefit analyses of the losses and profits associated with different systems of production. But in practice, environmental costs, like social welfare costs, are left out of business equations. They form **hidden diseconomies** or real costs that, if actually paid by the companies responsible for the pollution, would greatly reduce their profits, and might well turn these apparent profits into deficits. But such costs are not counted by corporations because normally it is not the corporations that pay them. The people and other creatures whose lives are damaged or destroyed by the pollution pay the price.

In the light of the Brundtland Report, we can begin to see the question of unfair subsidies in a very different light from the perspective of the free trade debate. When North American companies are permitted to operate without practising energy conservation, and without pollution control devices, they are being very heavily subsidized by taxpayers. Trucking companies are being heavily subsidized when taxpayers pay for road repairs and acid rain damage. The economics of using trucks over railways reverses when these hidden subsidies are taken away. Companies locating in metropolitan centres are being heavily subsidized when the costs of urban sprawl are paid by taxpayers. If and when all these hidden subsidies are removed, the economic advantages of relocating in peripheral areas, like Cape Breton or the interior of British Columbia, might be very considerable.

As traditional economists such as Paul Wonnacott have clearly recognized, massive government subsidies do indeed promote inefficient production. The blind spot of such economists lies in the extremely narrow definition of *subsidy* utilized in the equations. The implicit, and sometimes explicit, assumption of mainstream economics in leaving the hidden diseconomies out of their equations is that industry could not pay such costs without destroying all profitability. Hence, they are best ignored.

The political economy critique of mainstream economics directly accepts this assessment of costs but draws different conclusions. While sympathetic to the Brundtland Report, these theorists argue that advanced capitalism is incapable of accommodating any solutions. The structures of capitalism cause the problems and cannot resolve them. Trainer (1985, 217) argues that a capitalist economy obliges us to be affluent and wasteful:

> The tragedy is that ours is an economic system which cannot tolerate significant reduction in the total amount of unnecessary and wasteful production; massive and ever-increasing waste is essential for the survival of our economic system.

If the system were even to try to practise conservation and to cut back on wasteful production, "there would be economic chaos. Factories would close, businesses would go bankrupt, people would be thrown out of work and there would be extensive social and political disruption" (Trainer 1985, 217). The entire system would collapse. Trainer's message is that nothing short of radical social revolution will solve the problems we face. The argument that waste and ecological exploitation are necessary for the system to function constitutes a powerful ideology supporting the status quo. Even the Brundtland Report can be criticized for suggesting there might be viable solutions short of worldwide revolution.

Meanwhile, mainstream critics write articles on such topics as China's acid rain problem (*Globe and Mail*, 22 Feb. 1988, A9) and the desperate pollution problems caused by China's drive for industrialization. Or they focus on the "ecological disaster zone"

around the Aral Sea in the central Soviet Union or on the contaminated beaches, polluted air, and sewage and chemical wastes in rivers and harbours all across the Soviet Union (*Toronto Star*, 10 July 1988, E1–2). The message is that the communist alternative only offers more of the same.

The theoretical circle appears closed. But is it?

Recent publications outlining Swedish policy may present new alternatives. One book, entitled *Saving Lakes* (Melander 1988), documents the success of a ten-year Swedish effort to reverse acidification of lakes. This effort is combined with stringent government policies to control industrial emissions. The liming of lakes was carried out by a Swedish-based enterprise with more than 8000 employees and sales in excess of $1 billion. Pollution control is itself becoming a billion dollar business. It pays for itself in classical economics terms. The economic costs of conservation and prevention are cheaper in the long run than the billions of dollars that pollution damage costs.

Sweden has much more stringent laws than Canada governing forest management. The Swedish multinational Stora Kopparbergs Bergslags, operating in Nova Scotia, practises the worst form of clearcutting with mechanical harvesters. It hires minimal labour and leaves behind environmental damage so severe that forests cannot regenerate. It is essentially a policy of cut and run, supported by a $30 million loan plus grants and leases from the Nova Scotia government. (McMahon 1987, 100–03). However, the same company operates in Sweden on a similar scale but under a totally different set of rules. In Sweden, 15 percent of total woodland cost goes into forest management. Of the 15 000 acres of cut-over land in Sweden, 85 percent were replanted. Natural regeneration occurred on less than 10 percent. Yet, according to the company in Nova Scotia, the majority of new forest could be reproduced by natural regeneration, and replanting took place on only 15 percent of the cut-over land. In Sweden, even after intensive forest management, the cutting cycle is seventy-five years. In Nova Scotia it has been reduced to forty-five years. Harvesting younger and smaller trees means that a much larger acreage has to be cut to yield a given amount of pulp. When this is combined with destructive harvesting practices and limited replanting, the result is a deterioration in the quality of wood products and a steady depletion of forest resources. This kind of forestry is not sustainable in the long term.

The same company is at work in Sweden and Nova Scotia. It is no more intrinsically ecology conscious than any other forest company operating in North America. It operates at an acceptable level of profit in both Canada and Sweden. The difference lies in the fact that, in Sweden, the company has to abide by strict ecological rules. In Nova Scotia it does not.

In July 1988, Sweden passed an Animal Protection Act that governs the conditions of factory farming. To understand how important this is, think back to the description earlier in this chapter of chicken farms in Canada and the southern United States. This kind of inhumane farming is now outlawed in Sweden. Violations of the law are punishable by fines or imprisonment of up to one year. The law includes nine provisions:

1. All cattle are to be entitled to be put out to graze.
2. Poultry are to be let out of cramped battery cages.
3. Sows are no longer to be tethered. They are to have sufficient room to move. Separate bedding, feeding, and voiding places are to be provided.
4. Cows and pigs are to have access to straw and litter in stalls and boxes.
5. Technology must be adapted to the animals, not the reverse. As a result, it must

be possible to test new technology from the animal safety and protection viewpoint before it is put into practice.
6. All slaughtering must be as done as humanely as possible.
7. The government is empowered to forbid the use of genetic engineering and growth hormones, which may mutate domestic animals.
8. Permission is necessary for pelt and fur farms.
9. Doping animals for competition and events is prohibited.

A background statement on the act notes that animal protection and the prevention of cruelty to animals are central ethical issues. It is an essential part of our cultural heritage that animals be guaranteed protection. The act states that battery cages for chickens

> fail to meet even the most basic requirements of the hens—for moving, scratching, flapping, bathing, and preening and for laying. Such a system is unacceptable and must, therefore, be finally phased out over the next ten-year period. In future, no form of animal husbandry which is so insensitive to the needs of the animals will be permitted.

One wonders what it would take to get such an agreement included in the Canada–U.S. free trade deal.

It is important to remember that Sweden is a capitalist country, one that competes reasonably successfully in capitalist world markets. It has a population one-third the size of Canada, and yet it has two successful, world-class automobile production industries. Its standard of living equals that of Canada.

Sweden is by no means immune to the contradictions of capitalism. The critical difference between Sweden and North America seems to be that the former has put the politics back into political economy. Swedish capitalism does not appear to be "rule by nobody." It is rather a way of organizing economic relations that is answerable to wider social concerns. The Norwegian Prime Minister, Gro Harlem Brundtland, may well have had the Scandinavian example in mind when she directed the United Nations Commission on Development and the Environment that produced the Brundtland Report. From this perspective, there is no capitalist system that exists as an entity that does things to us. There is nothing inevitable about "chicken cities" in the southern states, or factory farming, or the destruction of Nova Scotia forests. These things happen because so many political leaders, and the people who vote for them, have come to accept the ideology that such things are inevitable, or that the entire system will collapse if we even try to change things to become more socially or ecologically responsible.

The crucial questions for free trade look very different from this perspective. Will free trade provide a route for moving toward the principles of sustainable development envisioned in the Brundtland Report or toward worsening environmental stress? Will market relations be more open to social and political controls with or without free trade? How might it be used as a vehicle for continental pollution control and ecologically sustainable agricultural and industrial practices? How can such issues be incorporated into public political debate in Canada and the United States on our common future?

There are no easy answers to these questions, but the quality of life for future generations of Canadians and Americans will depend very heavily on how they are addressed. These questions force us to rethink not only how to achieve development but why and in what direction. Is the expansionist, profit-driven notion of development that currently dominates economic and political thinking actually what we collectively need? Or does it offer only the illusion of progress, while covering up a deteriorating quality of life for most of the inhabitants of the planet? We need to look beneath the veneer of economic and technological rationality that drives our society and explore the additional cultural, emotional, and moral dimensions of rational action. Without this wider vision, much of what we call development may be fundamentally irrational.

Suggested Reading

George M. Foster, *Traditional Societies and Technological Change* (1973), gives a sympathetic and perceptive account of problems of development from the perspective of functionalist theory. Foster gives extensive evidence of cultural, social, and psychological barriers to change in traditional societies. He suggests that anthropological analysis of traditional social systems is a valuable aid to promoting technological change.

Everett M. Rogers, *Modernization Among Peasants: The Impact of Communication* (1969), elaborates the concept of culture of poverty in traditional societies. He advocates a top-down model of development through which the better educated and innovative people are first encouraged to adopt new technology, in the hope that subsequently the more backward peasants will copy these role models.

A classic work in Marxist theory of underdevelopment is André Gundar Frank, "Sociology of Development and the Underdevelopment of Sociology" (1972). Frank documents how the economy of Latin America is being systematically plundered by wealthy nations, especially the United States, which take out far more money than they ever put in through loans and investments. An excellent source of information on how Canadian capitalists plunder poor countries is the collection of articles edited by Robert Clarke and Richard Swift, *Ties That Bind: Canada and the Third World* (1982).

A comprehensive study of women and development is Barbara Rogers, *The Domestication of Women: Discrimination in Developing Societies* (1980). Rogers documents how women's interests are damaged by development programs that ignore their needs and give priority to men.

An excellent introduction to the historical and current situation of native Indians in Canada is G. Kellough, "From Colonialism to Economic Imperialism: The Experience of the Canadian Indian" (1980). Kellough documents how Indians were systematically robbed of their resources by the Canadian government, a process that still continues. She also describes several development projects for and by Indians that have been undermined by inept government agencies.

The issue of regional disparities and under-development in Canada is explored in Henry Veltmeyer, "The Capitalist Underdevelopment of Atlantic Canada" (1979). Veltmeyer argues that the relative poverty in Atlantic Canada has been created by corporate capital-ist policies designed to extract profits from peripheral areas and to centralize production.

The economic arguments in favour of the free trade deal are set out by Paul Wonnacott in *The United States and Canada: The Quest for Free Trade. An Examination of Selected Issues* (1987). This is a theoretically sophisticated study that presuppposes some basic knowledge of economics.

Arguments against free trade are explored in two comprehensive collections of short articles. Duncan Cameron, ed., *The Free Trade Deal* (1988), and E. Finn, ed., *The Facts. The Facts on Free Trade: Canada. Don't Trade it Away* (1988). The many articles and commentaries included in these collections explore wide-ranging issues around economic disparities and possible social and cultural costs of free trade.

G.H. Brundtland, *Our Common Future* (1987), documents the extensive destruction of the environment wrought by intensive farming techniques and resource extraction for industry. Brundtland argues persuasively that this form of development is not sustainable in the long term.

Part V

Rationality and Bureaucratic Society

Chapter 16

Max Weber and Rationality in Western Culture

Max Weber (1864–1920) is a monumental figure in the history of the social sciences. He was a historian, sociologist, and philosopher who left an indelible mark on the philosophy of history and on social science methodology. The scope of his scholarship is enormous. He wrote major books on comparative religions of Europe, India, and China, on the economy and political structures of democracy in western Europe, on music and musical forms, the rationality of law, and the structure and function of complex bureaucratic organization.

Background

Weber was born almost fifty years after Marx. Much of his work was a reaction to Marx or, more particularly, to the over-simplified versions of Marxist thought that focussed on economic determinism in social life. The two men wrote within very different cultural settings. Marx and his colleague Engels carried out much of their research and writing in Britain during the early period of industrialization. By this time, the feudal estates had been broken up into grazing pastures. The peasants who formerly farmed these lands had been driven off. Masses of landless and desperately poor people flooded the cities seeking wage work as their only means of survival. They lived under appalling conditions in city slums and worked in the coal mines and expanding textile mills that fuelled the industrial revolution. The emerging merchant-capitalist class effectively challenged the political power and privileges of the declining aristocracy.

Weber lived in Germany during the period when the country was emerging from a collection of divided states into a unified and modernizing country under Otto von Bismarck. Germany's development was based upon centralized administration and the armaments industry rather than on private capitalism. It promoted a different view of the state and different theories of power and administration than those in Marx's work (Lee and Newby 1983, 169). Weber observed the outbreak of World War I and the concurrent collapse of the international socialist movement into nationalist blocs: the European proletariat supported their nation-states rather than the international working-class movement. Weber lived to see the Bolshevik Revolution in Russia in 1917, the collapse of the Spartacist Revolution in Berlin in 1919, and the rise of the Weimar Republic in Germany after the war.

In his personal life, Weber experienced long periods of severe depression. These are reflected in his profound pessimism concerning the future direction of Western civilization. He was intensely aware of the gap between objectives and outcomes of action, between the intended goals and ideals and the often unintended consequences of the means required to attain those goals. Weber himself long defended the ideal of a strong and unified Germany, only to feel contempt for the Kaiser and the policies that led Germany into World War I and eventual military defeat. In his work he argued strongly against any simplified analyses or unitary theories of social change, emphasizing instead the complex multicausality and inherently **probablistic** character of all theories of human action. Human action is the outcome of free will, he argued, and such freedom can never be described through fixed relations of cause and effect.

Weber's Scholarship

Weber struggled to synthesize the very different intellectual traditions that were prevalent in Europe at the time. Among them was **idealism** with its Hegelian emphasis on ideas and values as the distinctive moving force of human history. This was in contrast to Marxist theories of **historical**

Max Weber (1864–1920).

materialism, which contended that class conflict was the driving force of history and the primary determinant of human fate. The idealists emphasized human freedom and uniqueness, which could never be reduced to deterministic rules. Countering them were the **positivists** who sought to apply the methods of the natural sciences to the study of human behaviour, seeking predictive or deterministic laws of action.

Weber tried to reconcile the commitment to notions of individual freedom and religious values with the apparently contradictory commitment to scientific study of human behaviour and to an emphasis on economic materialism in history. He tried also to reconcile the obvious commitment of all researchers to political goals and values with the demand for objectivity in social science research. Lastly, he tried to reconcile the objectives of democracy, with its commitment to representative government based upon participation of an informed population, and the mechanism of **bureaucracy**, which seemed essential to democracy and yet at the same time was its greatest threat. It is the mark of Weber's brilliance that he was largely able to achieve these syntheses in his work.

Weber's Methodological Contribution

Methodology in Social Science

Weber's study of methodology in the social sciences provides the foundations for contemporary ethnomethodology and interpretive sociology. Weber sought to synthesize the objective, empirical methods of the natural sciences with the intuitive aspects of the humanities.

Positivism tries to explain events by reference to laws that describe cause-and-effect relations. It attempts to analyse the social system in terms of causes and effects in the same way that biological systems are analysed. Weber argues that this is impossible. Because people think about what they do, it is inappropriate to apply such law-like, or **nomothetic**, generalizations to human behaviour. People have purposes; their behaviour is meaningful to them. In biology we do not ask chemicals or microbes why they do things. We just account for what happens by reference to the laws of science. But with people, we do have to ask why. Our actions are determined not only by objective conditions and forces, but by the subjective meanings that we attach to our actions, in other words, by our own reasons for doing something.

Weber also wanted to avoid the opposite trap of idealism or the view that all human behaviour entails unique spiritual events that can only be grasped by intuition or empathy. For idealists, the only explanation possible seems to be **ideographic**: unique, subjective, intuitive. The "science" in social science seems to be impossible. We seem to be forced to choose between the view that human action is predictable, which implies determinism, or the view that people have

free will and hence that their actions are not determined by outside forces and so are not predictable.

Weber denies the validity of this apparent dilemma. He argues that meaningful behaviour, or behaviour guided by free will, is not unique and unpredictable or without any pattern or order. Unpredictable or random behaviour would not be meaningful; it would be mindless. Weber resolves the conflict between free will and determinism by arguing that there is no real contradiction between them. Action that is meaningful is, by its very nature, not haphazard, random, or patternless. The scientific study of meaningful behaviour is possible precisely because it is meaningful and therefore organized and predictable. It requires a different kind of explanation from that of the natural sciences, but it is nonetheless amenable to scientific study.

Weber defines sociology as "the science which attempts the interpretive understanding of social action in order thereby to arrive at a causal explanation of its cause and effects" (Ashley and Orenstein 1985, 213). For Weber, then, sociological analysis must do two things. First, it must explore the meaning of actions for the people involved. Secondly, it has to show how this meaning provides a causal explanation for the behaviour. **Social action** is, by definition, any human conduct that is meaningfully oriented to the past, present, or future expected behaviour of others. People relate to each other in meaningful ways, and it is these shared meanings that define our expectations of others and ourselves.

The Study of Meaning

Weber draws heavily upon the work of his friend and colleague, Georg Simmel, who first developed the concept of *Verstehen*, or understanding, as crucial to sociological analysis. Sociologists have to become involved in the process of understanding because the actions that they are trying to explain are actions to which people themselves attach meanings. People do what they do because it is meaningful to them. Hence we can hardly ignore what these meanings are when we try to explain what they do. This does not mean that pure intuition is sufficient for analysis. We still need objective evidence. We need to develop techniques for interpreting meaning so that others can repeat the study and check the results.

The critical methodological question is how we do this. How can we develop an objective, verifiable, repeatable study of meaningful action? We need to remember that meaningful action is not random, but purposive and therefore organized by the people involved. *Verstehen* involves putting ourselves in the position of the people we are studying and trying to reconstruct the interpretations that they might give to their own action (Ashley and Orenstein 1985, 212).

Elliott Leyton neatly sums up this approach to explanation in sociology in a discussion of his study of serial killers and crimes of violence. The ideas for his book, *Hunting Humans* (1986), had one source. "When I can't understand the reasons behind things, when I can't understand the behaviour. That's the genesis of everything I have written. In the act of writing and researching the book, I explain the behaviour to myself" (*Globe and Mail*, 12 Nov. 1987, A15). Explanations must be adequate at the level of meaning and at the level of causality. In other words, the explanation should make sense in terms of the intentions of the actor and should clarify the factors that would predispose someone to want to act in this way.

We feel we have explained the unusual behaviour of serial killers, or the more ordinary behaviour of people in general, when we come to the point where we can say with some assurance that if we had had similar life experiences and value orientations, and had found ourselves in similar circumstances, we could understand how we ourselves might have behaved in a similar way. This is a tall order, but we can do it precisely because we are studying fellow human beings. This is an advantage that we have over the physical scientists. They study objects from the outside, but in social science we study people as subjects engaged in meaningful behaviour, and we can approach an interpretive understanding of that behaviour from the inside.

Direct understanding or reconstruction of action is sometimes possible. It is relatively easy to arrive at a rational understanding of logical relations, such as the reasoning involved in concluding that $2 \times 2 = 4$, or in concluding that certain facial expressions are a manifestation of anger (Giddens 1971, 148). At other times, in order to make behaviour intelligible, we need to understand people's underlying motives. It is relatively straightforward to understand rational means-end selection, as when people have a clearly stated objective with straightforward means to achieve it. In other contexts, the understanding of motives may require much deeper searching. Weber is well aware that human motives are complex. Similar actions may be done for a variety of underlying motives, while similar motives may be related to different forms of actual behaviour (Giddens 1971, 149). People also can waver between conflicting motives.

Given the complexity of human motivation, Weber argues that explanations in sociology must take the form of **probabilities** rather than the absolute predictions characteristic of the natural sciences. We have achieved an adequate explanation when the motive that we understand to be behind the behaviour in question would reasonably, or with some measure of probability, give rise to the kind of behaviour observed.

Such causal relationships or predictions are inevitably subject to qualifications and exceptions. They are not meant to be ahistorical, invariant, or generalizable.

They reflect the particular historical situation in which people find themselves. For example, Weber argued that the Protestant religion was an important causal influence on the rise of capitalism in Europe. Capitalism also flourished in Japan but clearly not because of Protestantism, although there may have been a similar pattern of values in Japanese culture that triggered capitalistic behaviour (Ashley and Orenstein 1985, 214). Marx recognized the historical character of explanations when he criticized the economists of his time for treating concepts such as supply, demand, commodities, labour power, and so on, as universal categories without realizing that they only exist within and because of the very particular and historically situated pattern of organization of economic relations of capitalism.

Human Agency

Weber's demand for adequacy at the level of meaning led him to challenge the utility of holistic or functionalist approaches to the study of human society. Functionalism, he argued, is useful and, in a sense, indispensable in providing a place from which to begin analysis. But the simple analogy between biological systems and social systems soon breaks down. Sociologists need to go beyond functional uniformities to arrive at an interpretive understanding that takes account of the meanings that an action had for the people involved (Giddens 1971, 150).

It is easy for sociologists to be lured into explanations that refer to the social system as a whole, but one must never forget that the conceptual entity *society* is nothing more than the multiple interactions of individuals in a particular setting. Only individual people are agents who actually carry out subjectively understandable action. In functionalist and much Marxist writing, this collection called society tends to take on a reified identity of its own. The word is only a conve-

nient descriptive summary. But it is converted into a thing and then is used in explanations as if it were an acting unit with its own consciousness: society does such and such, or society has certain needs, and so on. This is similar to the complaint that Marx raised against the political economy of his day and its tendency to refer to market forces as doing things to people, while losing sight of the fact that people, and only people, do things.

This is not to say that a sociologist should never use concepts that refer to collectivities such as states or industrial corporations, but, Weber insists, we must remember that these collectivities are solely the result of organized actions of individual people. People may organize collectively to do something, and we may refer to this collective organization as, for example, a corporation, but corporations as such do nothing.

Weber's second demand, for adequacy at the level of causality, led him to reject the opposite extreme of **psychological reductionism** (Giddens 1971, 151). Psychology is certainly relevant to sociological understanding, as are several other disciplines. But we cannot understand how people are organized collectively or analyse these emergent institutions by examining only the psychological make-up of individuals. Psychology is likely to draw heavily upon sociology in understanding the sociocultural influences that mould individuals.

Weber draws a careful distinction between the related disciplines of sociology and history. For Weber, history is concerned with the causal analysis of particular culturally significant events and personalities. Sociology, on the other hand, deals with the observation and explanation of general patterns of behaviour. History may well draw upon such general explanations to account for unique events. Weber saw himself primarily as a historian, but in his major work, *Economy and Society*, he was more concerned with uniformities of socio-economic organization, in effect with sociology.

Causal Pluralism

Weber's concern with adequacy at the level of causality also led him to insist on a strategy of **causal pluralism**; that is, on searching for multiple causes for social phenomena. He rejected as misguided and inadequate the efforts of some theorists, and particularly the approach of oversimplified Marxism, which attempt to explain social phenomena in terms of single factors such as economic determinism. Marx criticized Hegel for trying to analyse ideas without any regard for the social conditions in which they emerged. Weber agreed with Marx's criticism, but he also attacked the opposite fallacy committed by many of Marx's disciples who tried to analyse economic forces without regard for the subjectively meaningful response of individuals to their economic circumstances.

For Weber, sociological explanations have to encompass both objective conditions and subjective forces, for it is through subjective understanding and analysis that these objective conditions come to influence human actions as they do. Ideas and values cannot therefore be dismissed as mere by-products of class position, which can be ignored in explanations. Likewise, the economy is not an entity to which people adjust. It is the outcome of people's subjectively meaningful collective behaviour.

Ideal-Type Constructs

Weber advocated **ideal-type** constructs as a method of inquiry that would be adequate at the level of meaning or interpretive understanding of actions and would at the same time make possible objective and replicable analysis. As we saw in chapter 5, ideal-type constructs are theories that accentuate typical characteristics or elements of action. They are not intended to be literal or accu-rate descriptions of reality, but rather hypothetical models that can be compared with real situations.

Weber argues that this is not so much a new method as a clarification of what social scientists typically do when they try to isolate key elements in a situation. In chapter 5, we examined the model of *Gemeinschaft* and *Gesellschaft* developed by Tönnies to accentuate the distinctive characteristics of pre-industrial and urban societies. In chapter 6 we saw the models of mechanical and organic solidarity developed by Durkheim to accentuate typical forms of social cohesion in undifferentiated and specialized societies. Weber himself developed a series of ideal types of social action that he used as frameworks for exploring distinctive patterns of meaning and action among people in industrial capitalist societies. His ideal-type model of bureaucracy will be described at length later in this chapter.

Objectivity in Social Science

Weber demanded that the study of meaningful action be based upon objectively verifiable and repeatable research. This led to his deep concern with the place of values in research and how objectivity might be possible. Values necessarily enter research as aspects of the subject matter. They also enter as features of the researchers' orientation to the study. Researchers reveal their values by selecting from the infinity of possible subjects those that appear to them to be important or of interest. Nonetheless, Weber insists, the methodology and the outcome of research must be objective; that is, it must be independent of the values of the researcher.

Central to his concern with objectivity is Weber's insistence that science itself cannot pass judgment on values. It is impossible to establish values or ideals scientifically or to decide on a scientific basis what ought to be done. All that science can do is evaluate the adequacy of alternative practical means available for the attainment of given ends, the probable costs of selecting one means over another, and the additional or unforeseen consequences that may arise from particular means.

Weber frequently analysed the struggle for revolutionary socialism in these terms (Lee and Newby 1983, 200). He argued that the very goals of freedom that are part of the ideal of socialism are threatened by the use of force as a means to achieve socialism and by the political repression inevitably associated with the use of force. He also predicted that the consequences of trying to establish a socialist economy within a largely hostile capitalist world would result in multiple difficulties that would undermine the practice of socialism. Thirdly, and most importantly, he predicted that whatever means were used to bring about socialism, the ideals of socialism would be compromised by the organizational means needed to co-ordinate such a society, namely the bureaucratic state. Through his analysis, Weber could show the probable costs and long-term negative consequences of the struggle for socialism but, as he acknowledged himself, such analysis could never answer the ultimate question of whether the struggle would be worthwhile.

The free trade debate provides another example of the limitations of scientific analysis. Social science analysis can add to the debate by showing the probable consequences for various sectors of Canadian and American societies of measures incorporated within the agreement: threatened job losses in some sectors versus the promise of job gains in others; the probable impact upon Canada's cultural industries and social services; and so on. But what such analysis can never determine is whether the end justifies the means, or whether questions of culture or sovereignty should outweigh questions of economic gain, or whether losses to some people count more or less than gains to others. Science cannot answer these ques-

tions, which are based on values. At its best, science can only show what the probable costs will be of various means or actions that may be taken toward the attainment of desired goals.

Weber's powerful essays on "Politics as a Vocation" and "Science as a Vocation" address these ethical dilemmas. Weber distinguishes between two fundamental ethics: the **ethic of ultimate ends** and the **ethic of responsibility** (Gerth and Mills 1946, 120). Neither ethic is in and of itself morally superior to the other. The ethic of ultimate ends is essentially religious. Those who pursue such an ethic are so totally committed to their objective that any means are acceptable if they will further this objective. Such people are not swayed by the consequences, however negative, of their means. When members of the Sons of Freedom sect of the Doukhobours in British Columbia practise arson, they do so in the fervent belief that they are called by God to cleanse the world by fire of idolatry and evil. The immediate negative consequences for themselves or others may be of concern to them, but they do not effect their decision whether or not to commit such an act. The ultimate ethic of purification in the service of God has higher value.

Alternatively, those who accept the ethic of responsibility must take account of the consequences of their actions or means chosen to further their goals. They must calculate at each step the probable consequences of and possible hardships and suffering caused by efforts to obtain their goal. This is particularly true in the face of the recognition that the decisive means for politics is violence. Political authority in any state implies a monopoly of the legitimate use of force. Science cannot answer the question whether, or to what extent, the end justifies the means. Those who imprison Doukhobour women for the crime of arson, and who considering paroling or pardoning them, must weigh the multiple consequences of these actions. They must take responsibility for the probable deaths of the imprisoned women on hunger strike and for the probable property damage in the further acts of arson that may result if the women are freed, and so on.

The recognition that science cannot pass judgment on questions of values led Weber to insist that professors should not teach political positions, any more than religious convictions, to students in the classroom (Gerth and Mills 1946, 145–47). Professors have the same opportunities as other people to air their views in the political arena. They should not use the lecture room for this. Weber was reacting against the practices of the German professors of his day who routinely used their lecterns as pulpits to impose a particular political view of the German state onto students.

Scientific objectivity has nothing to do with ethical neutrality or fence sitting, or taking some middle road. It has to do with commitment to the examination of facts, facts that are often inconvenient for our own or others' opinions. The ultimate questions of values and commitment lie beyond science, in the realms of faith and revelation.

Weber's Substantive Contribution

Types of Action Orientation

Weber's model of types of action orientation outlines four basic kinds of meaningful action or typical orientations that individuals may adopt in relations with each other.

The simplest orientation is **traditional-rational behaviour**, which comprises action based on habit. It involves the least amount of conscious thought. Neither the purpose of the actions nor the alternatives are consciously considered. Traditional-rational actions are done because they always have been done that way.

A second type of orientation, **affective-rationality**, is based on emotions. Actions are expressions of emotions, of passions, and they have an immediacy that involves neither calculated weighing of means or consequences nor commitment to values.

A third kind of orientation is **value-rational**. Here the primary focus is upon an overriding ideal, as in religion. Deeply committed people do not ask the consequences of their actions. They do what they believe is

Tables 16-1   Action Orientation and Legitimate Authority

Types of Action	Types of Legitimate Authority
Traditional Rational (customs)	Hereditary rulers: kings, queens, tribal patriarchs
Affective rational (emotions)	Charisma of people with extraordinary gifts or supernatural powers: Jesus, Gandhi, Hitler
Value-rational (beliefs)	Religious dogma: Bible, Koran, Talmud, authority of church elders
Purposive-rational (practical effects)	Rational legal regulations: bureaucratic rules, formal office, civil law

right, regardless of the outcome for themselves or others. This is the value orientation that underlies the ethic of ultimate ends.

The fourth and most important basis for authority is **purposive-rational action**. This involves the rational selection among alternative means of action that which is the most effective for a given end. It includes rational consideration of consequences in relation to other goals. This kind of rationality is easiest to understand and to analyse and is the basic assumption of theory in economics.

It is important to recognize that all four types of orientation are rational. Action in relation to religious values and emotions are equally rational and equally predictable, as are actions based on custom or habit, once the basic orientation itself is known.

This four-fold model of typical action orientations serves to guide research into the meaning of action from the perspective of the participants' own views of that action. The resulting causal explanation suggests the probability of responses of a certain kind, given the action orientation.

Model of Authority

Weber uses this typology as a basis for his subsequent model of legitimacy of political authority. He draws an important distinction between power that is based on authority and power based on brute force. Authority is legitimate in that the subordinates themselves accept that those in authority have a right to rule, and therefore to expect compliance, even if one might not always agree with particular policies. Weber defines authority in practice as the probability that a given order will be obeyed by a specific group of people. He argues that there are three bases of authority: **traditional**, **charismatic**, and **rational-legal**.

The simplest and historically the most prevalent basis for authority is tradition. Orders are accepted as legitimate when they come from traditional incumbents of hereditary positions. The authority of an elder and patriarch and the divine right of kings rest on such legitimation. Persons exercising power enjoy authority by virtue of their inherited status. Such authority is likely to have force only in relatively stable and unchanging societies.

Authority wielded by charismatic figures is very different. Here legitimation is based on the emotional response of followers to a leader who appears to have extraordinary gifts or supernatural virtue and powers. Great figures in history such as Jesus, Hitler, Gandhi, and Joan of Arc have had such charismatic authority and moved thousand and even millions of people to follow them. E.P. Thompson (1968, 421) described the charismatic power of prophets such as Joanna Southcott whose aura of spiritualism and extraordinary revelation drew a large cult following in England at the turn of the eighteenth century. Charisma means that people are so drawn by the dynamism of the particular person that they are willing to follow that individual without questioning the specifics of policies or direction. The inclusion of Hitler in the list of charismatic figures should be a warning that charisma is a force that can move people for evil as well as for good, or for fleeting goals as well as for critical social movements. It is a powerful force for change, but tells nothing about the direction that such change might take.

Weber saw charisma as the most dynamic and free expression of individual creativity, but also the most transitory of all forms of authority. The rise of charismatic figures is associated particularly with periods of trouble and emergency when people are already predisposed to respond to calls for change. A charismatic leader is always **radical** in challenging established practices and going beyond the rules of everyday life toward new visions.

The problem with authority based on charisma is that it is inherently unstable, lasting only so long as the leader survives and

Charismatic figures can influence thousands, even millions, of people to follow them.

continues to manifest the extraordinary qualities that initially drew the followers. The inevitable death of the leader gives rise to the problem of succession since no successor can hope to command the same charisma. Weber suggests that succession can only take two basic forms. Either it can relapse into hereditary rule based on traditional authority or it can be formalized by elections and rules of organization that shift toward rational-legal authority.

Rational-legal authority is the most important basis for legitimation of power in Weber's model. He saw it is a precondition for the emergence of a modern state and the fundamental legitimation for bureaucratic administration. Rational-legal authority is based on acceptance of the utility of the rules themselves. Orders are obeyed without concern for the personality of the authority figure who sets such rules, because the rules themselves are perceived as rational and purposeful.

The Sociology of Power

In his study of political power, Weber sought to elaborate the insights of Marx on the economic basis of class and class struggle. Weber advocated a wider focus on other bases of group identity and organized political action, and hence on alternatives bases of power, including the power vested in state administration. These relations, Weber argued, are too complex to be reducible to the single dimension of ownership of the means of production within a society. He developed an alternative model of power, which incorporates three distinct, although closely related, dimensions: class, status, and party.

Class

Weber shared with Marx the assumption that ownership or non-ownership of the means of production was a crucial determinant of class position, but he expanded this dichotomy to include other aspects of life chances in the marketplace. He defined **class** as the chance to use property, goods, and services for exchange in a competitive market. The most advantaged group in a capitalist economy is made up of the owners of land, factories, and financial capital, while the least advantaged class comprises people with no property and no skills. In between them are the middle classes. They comprise those who have some property—the petite beourgeoisie—and those, like the intelligentsia, who have some skills. Weber recognized that the proletariat or working class is split by skill differentials. Those with privileged education or professions have very different life changes in the marketplace and very different access to political power than do blue-collar workers who own no property. Such divisions, he predicted, would limit the emergence of class consciousness, since these different life chances would give rise to different values and perspectives upon the world.

Status

Weber agreed with Marxist theorists that economic relations of class are central determinants of individual life chances. But he also insisted that actual life chances are too complex to be reducible to economics alone. **Status** also plays a critical role. Status, for Weber, refers to social prestige and honour and is reflected, above all, in styles of life (Gerth and Mill 1946, 186–94). Attributes ascribed by birth, such as nobility, race, ethnicity, and sex, and religious affiliation may be more immediately influential than objective class position in the development of group identity. The nouveau riche, people who make money in business or in a lottery, may well have the financial attributes of the upper class, such as expensive homes and possessions, but they

may not have the status to gain acceptance from other members of the upper class. They may well be shunned by families with old wealth and breeding. With the passage of time, the offspring of the nouveau riche may gain acceptance within high status circles.

Political action is as likely to reflect status group as class. Historical conflict between Catholics and Protestants in Northern Ireland, for example, cannot be reduced to class conflict. Similarly, in Canada, the struggle for a distinctive identity among the Québécois, native Indians, Doukhobours, and many other ethnic minorities cannot be reduced to relative economic advantage alone. Weber recognized that status is frequently a basis for exclusion or relative disadvantage in the market and that this may well foment group conflict and hostility. But he insisted that religious and ethnic identities exert an independent causal influence on group identity, styles of life, and life chances.

The relation between class and status in Weber's sociology is one of mutual influence. Shared class position within the economy may foster distinctive values and orientations toward life that can draw people together. In his study of comparative religions, Weber draws many parallels between economic experience and religious values. Disprivileged people, for example, are oriented toward other-worldly religions that promise salvation and just compensation for suffering on earth. Nobles are attracted to the view of a god of passion, wrath, and cunning who can be bribed with booty from war. Bureaucrats favour a comprehensive, sober religion such as Confucianism in China, which is expressed in terms of disciplined order and abstract values. Merchants are generally sceptical or indifferent to other-worldly religions that preach salvation, preferring worldly and non-prophetic theology. Shared religious orientation can in turn serve to reinforce separate group identities and loyalties, which may then be reflected in politics. For

Marx, the economy has primacy, but for Weber, status is a related but distinct and powerful force in the political arena.

Party

The concept of **party** for Weber refers to actively organized relations in the political arena. Parties are oriented toward communal action designed to influence policy in favour of specified goals (Gerth and Mills 1946, 194–95). They may represent interests determined through class or through status, or through a combination of the two. Occasionally they represent neither. They differ widely in terms of both the means used to attain power and the kind of community interests that they represent. Above all, the structure and operation of parties reflect the structures of ruling, whether based on hereditary rule, democratic processes, or military coercion or other forms of violence.

A Culture of Rationality

Weber's analysis of the rise of rationality in western European culture, and its formal expression in capitalism and bureaucratic forms of state administration, stands as a major contribution to contemporary sociology. Weber returned again and again in his work to the theme of purposive-rational action and rational-legal authority as embodying the central features of modern industrial society.

Weber saw purposive rationality as the pervasive distinguishing characteristic of Western civilization. Other types of action orientation—toward tradition, emotions, or values—are rational in the sense that they can be understood as organized and meaningful behaviour. But purposive rationality has a distinctly calculated quality. It is oriented toward the efficient use of available means for attaining clearly thought-out goals. Weber considers purposive-rational action a superior form of rationality. Its predominance in Western culture accounts in large part for the spec-tacular progress of Western civilization. Weber found this calculated form of rationality to pervade all aspects of Western culture: religion, law, business, administration, politics, art, music, architecture, education, and formal organization, the ultimate expression of which is bureaucracy.

Weber highlighted worldly rationalism in many aspects of Western culture. Western music, for example, pioneered the development of chord patterns and arithmetical relations. Moreover, the formal writing and timing of music for orchestras developed only in the West. Western art moved toward an emphasis on realism and perspective; architecture was dominated by engineering principles, focussing on straight lines and prefabricated buildings rather than intricate designs. Science promoted emphasis on mastering the world.

Rationality also characterized the development of mass education. Weber suggests that this was intimately tied to the demand for trained experts for newly developing rational-legal administration. The education system was oriented to special examinations by means of which incumbents of official positions could be selected on the basis of merit rather than personal considerations. There was also a demand for regular curricula with standardized content.

Rationality found formal expression at all levels of social organization. It was a central principle in the development of Western legal systems as traditional practices and arbitrary local regulations were replaced by a universal, impersonal legal system. Such a system spread over national and international markets and was essential for the development of capitalism. To do business with people across many different regions and societies, capitalists needed the assurance of a unified and calculable system of laws and regulations governing contracts.

The development of rationality in business was visible in several other areas. Rational bookkeeping was critical since it permitted the calculation of profits and losses in terms of money. Capitalism required wage labourers who were not tied to hereditary obligations to nobles but were free to dispose of their labour power in the market. It also required the absence of restrictions on economic exchange in the market. Capitalism benefitted from the development of technology constructed on rational principles, free from religious or cultural sanctions. Weber suggest that Hinduism may have retarded the development of technology in India by vesting it with religious significance and linking it with hereditary caste occupations. In contrast, the more rational religion of Protestantism was important in promoting the development of capitalism in western Europe.

In *The Protestant Ethic and the Spirit of Capitalism* ([1904] 1930), Weber argued that there was an affinity between the worldly ethic of Calvinism and the rise of capitalism. As we saw in chapter 6, Protestant doctrine held that it was morally proper and a sign of God's grace to amass wealth. But, at the same time, Calvinism discouraged spending money on idle consumption or to aid the poor, whose destitution was a sign of damnation. No other ethic, Weber suggests, could have been more exactly suited to the needs of capitalism. Calvinism provided the rational and emotional motivation for the calculated accumulation and reinvestment of profit.

Weber did not claim that Protestantism caused capitalism, although critics have accused him of this. Rather, he saw the affinity between the two: a mutually supportive relation in which the religious ethic encourages behaviour conducive to business rationality while, at the same time, the experience of capitalism generates a propensity to accept a supportive religious ethic.

Above all, the development of capitalism required rational-legal administration. Bureaucracy, which embodies this principle to its fullest extent, was, for Weber, the most rational form of large-scale organization. An office within a bureaucracy is impersonal, separated from the private life and attachments of the incumbents, and obligations are due, not to the individual, but to the office itself.

Bureaucracy

Weber's ideal-type model of **bureaucracy** is the most famous and the most influential of all his typologies of social action. There are seven elements to this model.

1. Permanent offices guarantee continuous organization of functions, which are bounded by written rules.
2. The rules set out specialized tasks, with appropriate authority and sanctions, so that everyone knows precisely who has responsibility for what.
3. These specialized functions are organized in terms of the principle of hierarchy and levels of graded authority. Lower offices operate under the control and supervision of higher offices.
4. The principle of trained competence ensures that the incumbents of these offices have thorough and expert training, appropriate for their level within the hierarchy.
5. The resources of the organization are strictly separated from those of the individuals who occupy the different offices. This was a critical change from past practice when tax collectors, for example, were required to pay a certain amount from what they collected to the state and lived on the surplus.
6. Administrative actions, decisions, and rules are recorded in writing. The combination of written documents and continuous organization of official functions constitutes the office.
7. These rules guarantee impersonality in the operations of the office, allowing neither favours nor patronage.

The Official

Weber elaborated a further model of the position of the official (Gerth and Mills 1946, 198–204). He stressed that the office is a **vocation**, with performance a duty not exploited for personal gain. Prescribed training and examinations are prerequisites for such employment. These promote the rationality in education noted above. Officers have specified obligations and fixed salaries. They are selected on the basis of their technical qualifications and not favouritism, nepotism, or ascribed characteristics. They are appointed rather than elected. Election, suggests Weber, would compromise the strictness of hierarchical subordination because incumbents would owe loyalties to those who elected them. As appointed officials, they are directly subordinate to the superior who appoints them. Work is a lifetime career, with a fixed salary and the right to a pension. This further serves to reduce susceptibility to bribery or to the temptation to use the office for personal profit. Independence from personal considerations in the discharge of official duties is legally guaranteed by tenure. The result of this form of organization is impartial performance of duties with maximum calculability and reliability.

It should be emphasized that Weber was constructing an ideal-type model of bureaucracy and bureaucratic officials. He was not claiming that any existing bureaucracy would exactly fit all these characteristics. The model is intended to function as a theoretical tool for practical research. It abstracts typical features and their typical interrelations. The extent to which any specific organization conforms to or deviates from this model is a matter for empirical research.

Advantages of Bureaucracy

Bureaucracies have major advantages over other forms of organization, such as honourific administration by courtiers, relatives of the ruler, or amateurs. Bureaucratic organizations have decisive technical superiority. They can operate with precision, speed, and with unambiguous and predictable performance based on rules. They ensure continuity, unity, and strict subordination, which reduces friction between officials. Personal and material costs of administration are reduced to a minimum.

Once fully established, bureaucracy is virtually indestructible. It is *the* means of carrying out community action. It can be made to work for anyone who can control it, because discipline and compliance are built into the structure. The system itself is able to ensure that the staff within the organization cannot squirm out of their responsibilities, for the specialized duties of each office are clearly spelled out. The consequences of bureaucratic power depend on the direction in which it is used. It is at the disposal of varied political and economic interests. As a technical means of organized action, it is vastly superior in effectiveness to any mass action that is not so organized.

Weber argued that bureaucracy was essential to many developments in the modern world. Capitalism needed the precise rules of bureaucracy to organize trade over long periods of time and in foreign countries. A centralized administration was critical for the development of a unified German state. In addition, bureaucracy is indispensable for democracy. As Weber expresses it, the fate of the masses depends on the steady, correct functioning of state administration. It is essential for the equality of treatment implied in democracy. All clients must be treated the same and be subject to the same uniform rules. Such equality presupposes impartial, regulated organization that operates without hatred or passion, without favouritism or prejudice. Weber argued that it is impossible to get rid of bureaucracies, for only such a system provides protection from undependable and amateur administration, favouritism, and corruption.

The Iron Cage

The negative side of bureaucracy lies in its power to compress all human diversity into conformity with its regulations. Bureaucracy threatens to become, in Weber's words, an **iron cage**, imprisoning the human spirit. For Weber, the bureaucratic mode of organization represents the purest expression of purposive-rational action. He never doubted its technical efficiency or its indispensability for rational capitalist enterprise and state administration. Yet he was deeply pessimistic regarding the negative impact of bureaucracy on the quality of modern life. No sphere of social action more completely exemplifies Weber's warning that the means needed to achieve valued ends may have negative consequences that undermine or destroy the very ends themselves. Weber feared that bureaucratic organization threatened the most cherished political goals of the twentieth century: democracy and socialism.

Weber believed that bureaucracy, based on principles of technical expertise and professional secrecy of office, and swollen to millions of functionaries, would come to exercise virtually unassailable power. Democracy, with its goal of social levelling and equality of treatment, could not function without bureaucratic organization, yet this form of administration has the inherent effect of promoting and sustaining a closed group of officials, with the authority of officialdom, raised over public opinion. People would find themselves disempowered against the bureaucratic experts.

Not only ordinary people but their elected representatives would be effected. Efficient bureaucracy rests on technical superiority of knowledge. Inevitably, officials would welcome a poorly informed and hence powerless parliament. There are built-in incentives for officials to fight every attempt of parliament to gain knowledge of bureaucratic affairs. Elected ministers depend on bureaucrats for information on which to base policies.

The loyalty of officials lies not with the general public or the electorate, but with the bureaucracy itself. Their vocation is to serve their official duties. In Canada, as in other Western democracies, it is a criminal offence for civil servants within the state administration to divulge internal policy documents to the public. One official in the Department of Indian Affairs who leaked information about proposed cutbacks to native funding was summarily dismissed.

Socialism, no less than multi-party democracy, is threatened by bureaucratic administration. Socialism may abolish the power of the bourgeoisie through the socialization of the means of economic production, but it cannot abolish the power of the new class of officials. In all probability, Weber thought, officialdom might come to exert even more of a stranglehold on society under socialism because the countervailing forces of entrepreneurs and free enterprise under capitalism would be absent.

Weber argues that it would be illogical to try to control bureaucratic power by making the inner workings of officials subject to the scrutiny of laypeople. This would undermine the efficiency, speed, calculability, and impersonality of the bureaucratic machine itself, and thus undercut the very qualities that make for superior administration.

Weber saw that the inevitable consequence of the smoothly running bureaucratic machine would be the dehumanization of all who come into contact with it. The rigidly defined regulations and responsibilities of an office provide for calculated efficiency but, as a consequence, the individuality of people who must relate to it, either as employees or clients, cannot be admitted. Bureaucracies are oriented toward *formal* rationality: the purposively rational performance of standardized and routine functions. They are opposed in principle to the *substantive* rationality of individual circumstances. A system designed to treat everyone equally inevitably lacks the flexibility to treat individual cases as unique. Those who do not fit the patterns for which the rules are established cannot receive the specialized services they may need. For them the formally rational system becomes substantively irrational.

Those who work as employees within the bureaucracy are even more rigidly subject to its regulations. They operate as cogs in the machine. The major requirement for their position is unquestioning and strict adherence to written regulations within their narrowly defined areas of jurisdiction. Their individuality has no place within such a system, for it would disrupt the calculated order.

Weber believed that the iron cage spread beyond bureaucracy itself, for this mode of organization is only the extreme expression of the purposive rational orientation that dominates all aspects of Western civilization itself. Science brings with it the demythification of the universe. As Weber expresses it, "the fate of our times is characterized by rationalization and intellectualization, and above all, by the 'disenchantment of the world' " (Gerth and Mills 1946, 155).

For Weber there is no escape. "To the person who cannot bear the fate of the times like a man," Weber offers only the retreat into silence and into the old religions. Weber feels that it is understandable that people should turn to religion in the hope of finding a refuge from scientific rationality and an alternative account of the meaning of life. Those who embrace religious doctrine are unable to face reality as it appears in the light of rational, scientific study. They may find comfort in the church, but only at the price of closing their minds to scientific knowledge, an intellectual sacrifice that Weber finds unacceptable. Such a retreat must inevitably fail to satisfy people because they are compelled to recognize their concomitant loss of intellectual integrity. As

Weber sees it, "the arms of the old churches are opened widely and compassionately for [us]," but this emotional escape is only for those who cannot "meet the demands of the day." The iron cage of rationality is the fate of our time.

The Limitation of Weber's Thought

It is not easy to criticize Weber's thought on intellectual grounds for it seems that all the usual criticisms are synthesized or neutralized by Weber himself. The approach of functionalism, which locates people as socialized members of an overarching system, is subsumed and transcended in Weber's work. The Marxist thesis, which seeks to understand human alienation in the exploitative relations of capitalism, is also incorporated. Marxism offers no ultimate escape from the experience of alienation and dehumanization, for socialism is equally an iron cage, albeit of a different sort. Exploitation under capitalism is only replaced by a deeper dehumanization under centralized bureaucratic control. The interpretive focus on individuals as makers of their own social world is, or seems to be, incorporated as well, through Weber's emphasis on meaningful understanding. This understanding is subsumed in his ideal-type model of action orientation.

Weber is his own best critic. He acknowledges that the logical conclusions to his own arguments point to a world that he finds unbearable, dehumanized. For long periods of his life he was profoundly depressed and unable to work. This depression can only be partially accounted for in terms of his personal life and psychological make-up. In part it stemmed from the intellectual hell created by his own ideas.

Rational Action Re-examined

How can we challenge Weber's theory so that we are not condemned to the same disenchantment and despair? A basic problem in Weber's work seems to lie in its starting assumption, in the conceptualization of rationality itself. Weber divides rationality into four distinct types of orientation: traditional, affective, value, and purposive rationality. He claims that Western civilization is characterized by the triumph of the last form as reflected in science, in capitalism, in a worldly success ethic in religion, in rational-legal authority, and ultimately in bureaucratic organizations.

The question Weber does not raise is, how can a civilization, or a mode of organization, be rational if the result is the destruction of the human spirit itself? Weber is deeply aware that the rational choice of means may destroy the intended ends but he does not question the rationality of purposive action dissociated, as it is, from cultural traditions and emotional or spiritual foundations. He sees such separation as necessary for the modern world, whatever its emotional costs.

When Weber separates types of rationality, he is following a long intellectual tradition in Western thought. This tradition commonly draws a distinction between rational and emotional behaviour. Men tend to be thought of as more rational and intellectual while women are conceived of as more emotional and natural or physical. The masculine principle is thus rational, and the feminine principle emotional. It is perhaps for this reason that Weber slips into the easy characterization of those who retreat into religion as people "who cannot bear the fate of the times like a *man*." The assumption seems to be that, in the modern world, retreat into emotions and religious values is inappropriate for men although perhaps acceptable and even normal for women.

Feminist theory, more clearly than other theoretical approaches in sociology, has challenged the separation of rational and emotional, of masculine and feminine, as an injustice to the nature of both women and men. Despite the enormous scope of his scholarship, and the depth of his insight, Weber nowhere explicitly considers the position of women or their role in the development of Western civilization. He does not seem to question their absence from intellectual debate. In his personal life, it is clear that his mother was a central figure in his own intellectual development and that his wife Marianne was the person who held him together during his years of depression and made it possible for him eventually to begin work again. Yet the role of women remains invisible in his intellectual work on the nature of man and civilization. How can this happen?

The feminist critique points to the crucial flaw in his starting assumptions of action orientation. He separates types of rationality such that purposive-rational-legal action—the masculine principle—is separated from the emotional and value-oriented dimensions—the feminine principle. Weber's characterization of Western civilization is, implicitly, a profoundly sexist characterization, although he did not perceive it as such.

The malaise in Weber's work is in essence the malaise of Western civilization itself. Weber sees only too clearly the nature of this disorder: the dehumanization, the demythification, the disenchantment inherent in a civilization that elevates purposive-rational action to the highest form. But he is unable to transcend this view. In Marcuse's terms, he remains trapped in one-dimensional thought, unable to conceive of viable alternatives that do not entail intellectual retreat.

It is the breakdown of the unity of cultural, emotional, and spiritual elements of purposive action that makes possible the colossal destruction wrought in the name of rational modernization in the pursuit of profit. The decision of a capitalist to exploit other people and the environment, to further the goal of short-term profit, is one that has emotional and moral components, whether these are recognized or not. It is also a decision embedded in a habitual or traditional mode of action in Western culture. Weber's artificial division into types of orientation, with only one dimension given recognition, does not hold up. The alternative view, which is reflected in feminist theory, albeit often in confused and half-understood ways, is that no individual, no action, no organization, no civilization can be truly rational if it does not integrate the "masculine" and the "feminine," such that tradition, emotion, and spirituality are integrated into purposive action.

The practical critiques of Weber's thesis on rationality, which we examine in the next chapter, usually have not gone this far, but they reflect the recognition that purposive-rational action, separated from other considerations, is often irrational, particularly in its practical embodiment in bureaucratic modes of organization. Weber's thesis that bureaucracy is the most efficient mode of organization has been challenged precisely because bureaucracy reduces employees to trained robots and clients to standardized cases where their substantively real circumstances cannot be taken into account.

The Marxist critique within organization theory rejects the notion of rationality as the root of bureaucratic structures. It raises the possibility that the very notion of rationality itself is a form of ideological hegemony to legitimate the exploitation of the mass of employees by those who direct the organization. Rationality is an ideology of the most invidious kind because it seems so neutral, so objective, that even to challenge it seems unreasonable.

As we shall see in the following chapter, theorists who have been most influenced by Weber's own methodological concern with interpretive understanding of human action have challenged his thesis as an unjustifiable reification of a system. From the perspective of the social construction of reality, and of ethnomethodology, Weber's model functions as ideology, or as a convenient way of accounting for what people seem to be doing, but not as a causal explanation for behaviour. The model of bureaucracy pays too

little attention to the understanding that individuals themselves have of their relationships with each other. Nor does it pay enough attention to what people actually do, as distinct from what they are supposed to be doing according to the formal plan. The formal model is not a literal description of reality, but rather an accounting procedure, a way in which people have learned to talk about what they do to make sense of it.

Conclusion

The legacy of Weber in contemporary sociology is enormous. His concern with promoting a social science methodology that would have interpretive understanding as its central objective is only just coming to fruition with the development of ethnomethodology, which we discussed in chapter 4.

Weber's substantive and theoretical contribution to sociology was profoundly shaped by his lifelong dialogue with the ghost of Marx. Weber tried to build upon and go beyond the basic conception of the nature of capitalism and class in Marxist theory while rejecting the oversimplified versions of Marxist thought that reduce human behaviour to economic determinism. Weber insisted that emotional life, values, meaning, or culture must be taken into account as critical aspects of all human behaviour, including economic activities. His famous study of *The Protestant Ethic and the Spirit of Capitalism* explores the religious and moral basis of the drive to accumulate wealth, which helped to foster the development of capitalism in Europe. His other historical and comparative studies of religions and sects in Europe, India, and China focus upon the interrelationship between life experiences, based on class position and mode of production, and forms of religious thought. Some of these ideas are explored in the section on religion in chapter 6.

Weber shared with Marx an emphasis on the economic base of life chances in relation to modes of production, but he broadened this focus to explore the diversity of class experience. Weber recognized that, in complex industrial society, skills in themselves constitute a form of means of production. Those who have skills to sell in the marketplace are in a profoundly different class position from propertyless, unskilled labourers. Weber emphasized the importance of status in the formation of social groups. Status is based on ascriptive criteria of ethnicity, race, sex, age, and the like. For Marx, these were merely secondary reflections of economic class position, but for Weber they appeared as important determinants of life chances in their own right. The fact that these variables work at the level of meaning and emotion, rather than material need, makes them no less important as dimensions of human experience. Weber shared with Durkheim an awareness of the importance of social cohesion, which cannot be reduced to dimensions of class. Weber's contribution to the study of class and ethnicity are explored in chapter 9, 12, and 14.

Weber's distinctive contribution to sociology lies in his analysis of rationality in Western culture and its particular expression in the rise of bureaucratic modes of formal organization in business and government. This aspect of his work is the focus of the next chapter. Weber's model of bureaucracy has profoundly influenced the development of organization theory in sociology. Much of the work in the field is either an elaboration or test of his insights or a critical counterproposal to them. In contemporary postindustrial society, characterized by the corporate concentration of capital, multinational corporations the size of nation-states, and centralized state administrations, these bureaucratic organizations are not merely facts of life, but dominant features of human experience.

Suggested Reading

A very readable selection of writings by Max Weber is provided by Stanislav Andreski, ed., *Max Weber on Capitalism, Bureaucracy and Religion: A Selection of Texts* (1983). Andreski provides a brief introduction to Weber's writings, followed by selected excerpts from writings on the uniqueness of Western capitalism, cultural factors that impeded the development of capitalism in the ancient world and in Asia, and the rise of Protestantism and rationalism in the West.

Another useful source is the collection of Weber's writings edited by W.G. Runciman, *Weber: Selections in Translation* (1978). See particularly part 1, The Foundations of Social Theory, with selections on social organization, classes, status groups, and parties, and chapter 18, "The Development of Bureaucracy and Its Relation to Law."

The selection by H.H. Girth and C. Wright Mills, *From Max Weber: Essays in Sociology* (1946), is generally very heavy reading, but it provides an excellent introduction to Weber's theory of bureaucracy in part 8, especially the first two selections "The Characteristics of Bureaucracy" and "The Position of the Official."

Chapter 17

Rationalizing the Irrational: Bureaucratic Conformity or Liberation?

Weber's analytical model of **bureaucracy** has been taken up in diverse ways by different theoretical perspectives in sociology. Traditional structural-functionalist analysis has focussed primarily upon questions of function and efficiency in meeting objective goals or needs of organizations. **Radical structuralism** refocusses the question around deeper issues of power and the apparatus of ruling embedded in the interlocking bureaucratic structures of contemporary society. This approach challenges in fundamental ways the claims to scientific objectivity and neutrality in traditional functionalist models of efficient administration. It explores the central significance of bureaucratic structures as determinants of the hierarchical divisions that we come to recognize as class. Feminist theory has pushed this further to show how bureau-

cracies serve to create the gendered character of society through the job ghettos and limited roles that are made available to women within them.

We follow radical structuralism with a discussion of interpretive theory, which deeply challenges other theories by questioning the taken-for-granted assumption that bureaucratic structures exist as entities that do things or have effects. It suggests an alternative view of bureaucracy as an accounting procedure or a means by which people make sense of what they do. This approach has its roots in Weber's methodological insistence on interpretive understanding and his rejection of holistic concepts that tend to lose sight of the fact that only people are active agents. Bureaucratic organizations are, after all, nothing more than collections of people trying, more or less competently, to get things done. These organizations cannot exist independently of the meaningful understanding of the people involved.

The brilliant and complex work of Michel Foucault is used in this chapter to draw together the radical-structuralist and radical-interpretive perspectives. **Foucault** believes that our social world comes to be known to us, and to have the form it does, through **discourse** about it; that is, through how we talk about it. However, it is also our lived experience of the social world that creates our knowledge and our mode of talking about it. For Foucault, this circle is virtually closed, as the way we talk or think structures our experience, which structures the knowledge expressed when we talk. Very few people can resist thinking and feeling like the mass of people, and those who do tend to be misfits, marginal and powerless people such as those labelled criminal or insane. They may have different things to say, but they are generally ignored or dismissed.

In the last section of this chapter we explore the ideas or discourse of radical feminism, which may have the potential to break the closed circle of thought and experience. This way of thinking begins from the standpoint of people whose central experience of the nurturing children in families is very different from the bureaucratic mode of public life. As women increasingly merge private and public realms in their own lived experience, their emerging knowledge makes possible a radically new discourse. It suggests ways of thinking in which the nature of rationality itself, and with it the entire bureaucratic edifice, is called into question.

This will be a frustrating chapter for people who like their theories in neat packages: functionalism, Marxism, Marxist-feminism, social construction of reality, ethnomethodology, radical destructuralism, radical feminism, and so on. Perspectives are not always clearly spelled out here. And with

good reason. Conflict theory is a kind of Marxism but, if it is so labelled, how do we distinguish it from very different approaches that are in the Marxist tradition? Radical structuralism seems like a convenient label for discussing the analysis of bureaucratic society, but a major contributor to this debate is Foucault, who tends to be called a **destructuralist** because he denies that there are any structures beyond discourse or the ways in which people talk about and make sense of their bureaucratic experiences. Feminism comes in many different colours too. Feminists are closely associated with Marxist structuralism, but also with the social construction of reality approach and interpretive theory. Ferguson's radical-feminist approach is strongly influenced by Foucault's work and does not fit any of the above categories.

The problem of muddled categories, then, cannot be corrected because the categories are, in reality, all mixed up. The business of sociology, except perhaps of the more routine and less inspired versions, is not accomplished in neat theoretical packages. The issue of bureaucracy is so central to our experience of life in industrial society that it has received critical attention from all the various sociological approaches. Contemporary work borrows from, merges with, and modifies earlier works that had approached the topic from a number of different directions.

This chapter takes refuge behind Foucault who flatly refused to let other sociologists assign a label to his work. More than any other in this text, this chapter shows where contemporary sociology is in all its stimulating, maddening muddle. If this discussion helps you to see the different ways in which sociologically meaningful questions might be raised, the different kinds of questions that can be asked, and the multiple ways in which the search for knowledge can proceed, it will have served its purpose as an introduction to the discipline of sociology.

Traditional Functionalism: Bureaucracy as Efficient

Parsons' early essay on "Suggestions for a Sociological Approach to the Theory of Organizations" (1956) aptly summarizes the traditional structural-functionalist perspective. Organizations exist as definite structures designed for attaining specific goals. For Parsons, the question of what constitutes a bureaucracy poses few problems. Organizations are, by definition, formal structures set up for specific purposes, with actions co-ordinated to these ends. Efficiency is measured by success in achieving these ends. The structure of organizations consists of the roles of participants and the values that define and legitimate their functions. Mechanisms for implementing goals consist of the *board*, or top level, which makes policy decisions, and the *line* administration, which makes allocative decisions for optimal use of resources in pursuit of the goals. *Personnel management* is responsible for co-ordination and integration of sub-units, and for ensuring appropriate motivation through coercion, inducements, and therapy. Lastly, the *workers* themselves are responsible for production.

Parsons acknowledges that there may be centrifugal tendencies deriving from the personalities of participants and special interests of individual members, but these are not relevant to the organization itself and are handled by appropriate personnel management. The organization, which interacts with its external environment, is viewed as a single unit with a single goal.

Testing the Model

Empirical research in the functionalist tradition explores the efficiency of bureaucratic structures, as defined by Weber, in meeting explicitly stated organizational goals. A study by Blau (1955) casts doubt on the Weberian model through evidence that bureaucratic procedures actually cause inefficient behaviour. Blau studied four sections of a state employment agency in the United States. The formal goal of the organization was to serve employers seeking workers and workers seeking employment. Employees took telephone calls from potential employers describing job vacancies, screened applicants, and referred them to suitable jobs. They also did employment counselling, especially for the handicapped and for war veterans. The agency had the responsibility of notifying the state unemployment insurance agency of any client receiving unemployment benefits who refused a suitable job without good cause. Bureaucratic measures designed to maximize appropriate employee performance included statistics to measure their performance. These were based on number of interviews per month, number of clients referred to jobs, number of placements, and number of notifications to the unemployment insurance office of fraud.

Blau found that employees of the agency geared their work to what counted. They stopped counselling clients because it took too much time and lowered their performance ratings. They discarded difficult or handicapped clients for the same reason. They also fabricated statistics, such as listing workers who returned to their old jobs after a short-term layoff as new placements. Agency employees also regularly hid job openings from fellow employees to boost their own placement records.

The level of inefficiency created by these practices only came to light by comparison with one section of the employment agency where the employees were all army veterans. Because they were veterans, their jobs were guaranteed. They had no fear of being laid off and so could afford to ignore the rules and performance ratings. They co-operated in their work and shared knowledge of all job openings. They also spent more time counselling applicants because they genuinely cared that these people, many of whom were themselves war veterans, find suitable jobs. The result was that this section actually filled more job openings and placed more people than did the other sections. The bureaucratic rules that controlled the work of employees in other sections of the agency actually created inefficiency because they hampered co-operation.

Blau has not been alone in finding that bureaucratic modes of organization cause inefficiency. Merton (1957) drew attention to the "cogs in the machine mentality" of many career bureaucrats who have learned not to think or to act for themselves but to follow prescribed rules rigidly. Such responses may be functional in routine work but are totally dysfunctional in situations requiring innovation.

Burns and Stalker (1961) highlight the same point in their study of twenty Scottish electronics firms. These firms were struggling to diversify their products in a postwar market where their traditional government defence contracts for radar equipment were declining. Most of these firms were organized in ideal-typical bureaucratic forms, with fragmented, carefully designated jobs in production, sales, and design, co-ordinated through a rigidly defined hierarchy of responsibilities. This formal organization proved disastrous for innovation. Specialized sales personnel went out to get orders, but did not know about production problems and so made impossible promises. They also did not understand design advances and so could not keep abreast of such changes. One department decided to stockpile supplies to be ready for new orders, resulting in bottlenecks at all other stages of production.

Again, the hierarchy of responsibilities that worked well for routine activities stifled new initiative. Everything new was, by definition, outside the jurisdiction of predefined offices. Hence more and more decisions were passed up to the top of the hierarchy while those below refused to do anything until they received direct orders.

The inevitable result was that the manager was swamped and subordinates paralyzed. The typical bureaucratic response was to set up a new role to handle the new problem, but that person's job depended upon the continuation of the problem! This is a typical case of **goal displacement** found in many studies of bureaucracies, where maintaining one's own department takes priority over the total enterprise. The subgoal tends to become that of enhancing the prestige and resources of one's own section at the expense of others.

The few firms in Burns and Stalker's study that did manage to innovate successfully, as measured by developing and marketing a variety of new electronic products, were firms that had largely abandoned the bureaucratic model of organization. The alternative model, which Burns and Stalker label the **organic system**, scrapped the hierarchy and the predefined, fragmented jobs in favour of co-operative teamwork and collective responsibilities. People shared information, made decisions among themselves rather than sending them all to the top of the hierarchy, and then took joint responsibility for the total process. The long-term result was that these few flexible firms successfully innovated while others went bankrupt or limped along.

A study by Dalton (1959, 342–51) documents the perennial conflicts between technical staff and administrators in bureaucracies. The responsibility of technical staff in the firms studied was to develop innovations and suggest improvements in functioning, but these proposals were bitterly resented by administrators, who felt that their own expertise and authority were being challenged. The result was resistance, bordering on sabotage of new ideas. Technical staff, desperate to get at least some of their proposals accepted, resorted to informal bribes and kickback schemes.

These are all relatively old studies and are quite well known. They point to serious inefficiencies in typical bureaucratic modes of organization and suggest that more flexible, co-operative, and less hierarchical systems work better, at least for tasks that are not totally routinized. Yet bureaucracy is more pervasive than ever. Burns and Stalker found that, in many of the electronic firms, the employees themselves actively resisted attempts to break down the bureaucratic system. They seemed to prefer fixed tasks that left no doubt exactly what the workers were responsible for and what they were not responsible for. They preferred to be left alone to get on with their jobs without any further commitment.

The critical theoretical question these studies raise is why there should be such resistance to more co-operative, less hierarchical modes of organization. The Weberian argument that bureaucracy is more efficient is not an adequate explanation.

Conflict Theory: Bureaucracy, Power, and Control

Conflict theory challenges traditional functionalism by asking what segment of society finds bureaucracy functional and efficient. It questions the image of organizations or societies as unified systems with goal consensus and explores instead the dimensions of inequality, class, and power within organizations.

Proponents of conflict theory have pointed out that, historically, factories did not emerge as the result of new technology or concerns with efficient mass production (Marglin 1974). The factories actually preceded the technology. They emerged as the result of the interest of owners of the raw materials in exerting greater control over workers. The older putting-out system, where workers took raw materials to their homes and brought back finished goods, was not conducive to close control over the pace of work. Factories were created so that workers would be under the constant surveillance

and direct control of the bosses. It was very inefficient for the workers, however, because they could no longer integrate child care and other domestic work with production.

It can be argued that all the characteristics of bureaucracy listed by Weber are required, not for efficiency of production, but for surveillance and control over unwilling workers. They reflect and gloss over antagonistic class interests. Gouldner (1952) addresses several questions concerning Weber's model. What kinds of obligations and responsibilities are established in Weber's bureaucratic model? What aspects of behaviour are rendered predictable and calculated? What aspects of organizations are left conspicuously unpredictable? Gouldner answers that the rules defining workers' obligations are the most predictable, while rules defining workers' rights, or management obligations, are the least predictable. Workers have had to form unions to force the establishment of rules concerning seniority, job security, grievance procedures, sick leave, holidays, and the like. Rules defining conformity are the most rigid at the bottom of the organizational hierarchy, where workers are subjected to clocking in and out. Rules are least rigid at the top. Senior managers have much more leeway to arrive late or to take breaks when they want to. The level of impersonality also varies. It is strongest between ranks, defining how subordinates and superiors are to interact, but least rigid among formal equals, especially at the top of the rank. Gouldner concludes that Weber's model does not represent an abstract model of efficiency at all, but rather the narrow perspectives of management experts.

In his major empirical study of bureaucratization in a gypsum factory, Gouldner (1954) traces the actual stages in the development of rigid rules. Initially the factory was anything but bureaucratic. It was located in a small rural community where workers and supervisors grew up together.

The organization was easy-going, with minimal attention to rules so long as the work got done. Job switching was permitted and, when vacancies arose, promotion of local people was favoured over importing outside experts, even if the locals were less qualified.

All this changed when head-office personnel appointed a new boss from outside the factory who was under pressure to improve the organization. Workers resented him. They wanted a local boss and feared the loss of their old privileges. The new boss found himself forced to impose bureaucratic rules to break the resistance of the workers. He could not use the old co-operative relations to motivate workers because he himself was resented by them as an outsider. Hence he relied upon formal rules to back his authority. He displaced their hostility onto superior officers by arguing that the rules came from senior management. Rules were clear and could be rigidly applied to everyone. They permitted spot-checking or supervision at a distance and so lessened the outright expressions of hostility generated by close supervision. Relations between workers and management worsened to the point of a wildcat strike. Ironically, the resolution of the workers' grievances resulted in still more bureaucratization as work roles and responsibilities were even more rigidly defined and delimited. It was clear what workers did and did not have to do, and supervision could become still more impersonal (Gouldner 1965). Gouldner's studies leave little doubt that the main function of bureaucratic rules in the gypsum mine was not to raise efficiency of production, but to impose discipline on reluctant workers. Rules were a symptom of class hostility between workers and bosses.

A historical study into the origins of job structures in the steel industry traces the process of job fragmentation and deskilling of workers (Stone 1974). It was not technical advances, but the class struggle between workers and owners of the Carnegie steel mill, that generated these changes. Before 1892, steel was made by teams of skilled workers with unskilled helpers, using the company's equipment and raw materials. Skilled workers were in complete charge of the labour process. They divided the tasks among themselves, set the pace of the work, and determined pay differentials, with overall pay based on the price of steel. By the 1890s, however, demand for steel was rising, and the owners wanted to raise production and their own profits. A new manager used armed men to close down the plant, lock out the workers, and break their union. New machines were installed, which doubled or trebled productivity while wages went up only marginally. Work was reorganized so highly skilled craftsmen were reduced to semiskilled labourers.

Finally, to break the unified resistance of workers, the owners instituted artificial job ladders. Very minor differences in skill levels were written into distinct job classifications with different pay levels. Workers thus found themselves competing against each other and currying favour with supervisors to get small promotions. Subsequent union contracts cemented these artificial divisions between workers by negotiating bonuses, pay scales, and seniority clauses in line with the new job classifications. The way the work is organized in the steel industry is both produced by the class struggle and used as a weapon in that struggle.

These critical studies change in significant ways the conception of rationality and efficiency on which Weber based his legitimation of bureaucracy. Bureaucratic organizations have been shown in several different contexts to be much less efficient than non-hierarchical, co-operative models, especially when flexibility or innovation is needed. Yet bureaucracy persists. These authors suggest that it persists primarily because it is the most efficient method of controlling reluctant workers while deflecting hostility and opposition. Deskilled, fragmented workers are easily controlled and exploited by managers who monopolize skilled knowledge for themselves. Workers themselves may come to prefer it as a way of minimizing their own commitment to the organization. Bureaucracy is clearly not a neutral mode of organization. It is intimately associated with inequality and power.

Bureaucracy and Oligarchy

Weber did not question the ultimate functional efficiency of bureaucracy for meeting the goals of whoever was in control, and for this he can be justly faulted. But what he did see with stunning clarity was the almost unassailable power that bureaucracy confers upon the elites who control it. Weber likewise did not see job fragmentation as related to a deliberate deskilling process. He was, however, very much aware of the political consequences of the resulting concentration of knowledge and technical expertise in the hands of a bureaucratic elite, and the disempowerment of both functionaries within the bureaucratic machine and the mass of people outside it.

Weber's recognition of the inherent tendencies toward **oligarchy** within bureaucratic organizations, and the threat that these pose to democracy, has powerfully influenced the development of theory in political sociology. Robert Michels ([1911] 1949) drew extensively upon Weber's work to develop the concept of the **iron law of oligarchy** to explain the processes of concentration of power in ostensibly democratic political parties and trade unions. He shared Weber's conviction that organization is essential for the expression of collective will. A disorganized mass of people can rarely accomplish anything. They are easily subject to suggestion by skilled orators and are easily swayed by the emotions of the moment. Sober and disciplined decision making is virtually impossible in mass meetings. Some form of delegation of responsibilities is thus essential, but then the problem of hierarchy

begins to emerge.

In principle, the person who is elected as leader within a democratic organization is the servant of the masses and can be deprived of office at any moment. The ideal is perhaps rotating office bearers. But leadership responsibilities and roles are complex. They require technical knowledge and experience that can only be learned over time. People with legal or technical training have a distinct advantage in such roles. As they develop expertise, however, a gulf inevitably widens between them and the masses who elected them to office. The mass of the people lacks information to make clear decisions, and mass involvement wastes time and limits flexibility of action.

Exactly as Weber recognized, secrecy constitutes a critical source of power. As the gap in knowledge grows between leaders and the masses, more committee meetings are held in secret, and the rank and file get only summary reports. Government bureaucrats welcome a poorly informed parliament because they gain greater freedom of action and freedom from surveillance. Michels recognized that unions could become more oligarchic than political parties because the leaders control the funds and can determine legal strikes. During negotiations they can also claim to know the market better than do members.

In principle, election to office should make incumbents accountable to the electorate and therefore promote democracy. In practice, as Weber pointed out, elections undermine the values of efficiency, impartiality, and expertise in the operation of bureaucracies. A glaring example of this occurred recently in Philadelphia, where more than fifty municipal judges, who are elected to office, were accused of accepting bribes. In 1985, the president of the Composition Roofers and Reroofers Union, Locals 30 and 30B, was caught giving Christmas presents of $300 to $600 to prominent judges in return for leniency when union members appeared in court. The judges were reported to have perpetuated racketeering by having a virtual price list for turning a blind eye to crimes. The chancellor of the Philadelphia Bar Association concluded that such racketeering is almost unavoidable in a system where elected judges receive salaries of $80 000 but where their campaigns cost up to $100 000. It is difficult to prove that bribes were anything more than legitimate campaign contributions. Moreover, there seems to be a great deal of public tolerance for this behaviour. "While it is unclear whether voters are cynical or merely ignorant," every judge who was suspended for accepting bribes was easily re-elected to office (*Globe and Mail*, 31 Dec. 1987, A1–2).

Within political parties and unions, where leaders are elected, the mass of membership tends to become indifferent toward the organization. While a small inner circle allows for speed of action, it means that most members are left out. Michels suggests that when people have electoral rights but no duties, they tend to renounce the rights and are content if someone else takes the trouble to look after affairs. Would-be leaders need to be skilled at making public speeches and controlling information to make themselves appear to be dedicated defenders and advisors of the people. Long-tenured leaders tend to develop an aura of indispensability; the masses feel incompetent to handle their own affairs.

The main threat to the power of a leader is not the masses, but a take-over bid from a new dominant figure. It is difficult to succeed in such a bid because the established elite has the advantage of material resources, time, and support staff. Often elite figures have a full-time, paid staff to develop propaganda, they control the main supply of information, and their high position leads others to emulate them. They may try to co-opt potential new leaders by giving them high level posts and then demanding loyalty, or try to discredit them and label their

followers disloyal. The mere threat of abdication, combined with the threat that the party will lose the next election or the union will lose in negotiations, may be sufficient to get the masses to toe the line. The trump card is to convince the masses that they are incompetent to run affairs without a leader. Hence, Michels concludes, a radical change of leaders can occur, but it is relatively rare and often unstable.

The shortlived leadership change within the United Steelworkers Union of America, Ontario Office, in 1985 seems a classic case of oligarchy at work. A newspaper report (*Globe and Mail*, 9 Nov. 1985) suggests that the union establishment was shocked in 1981 by the election to office of a rank and file member on a platform of union reform. Union staff traditionally had a strong influence on union politics, but the newcomer, a tough militant who led a long strike at INCO in Sudbury two years earlier, broke this pattern. His problem was that, once in office, he was unable to accomplish much reform. He was unable to challenge the political machine of his rivals. He lacked the administrative expertise to crack the entrenched bureaucracy. Four years later his dreams were broken as he was beaten in the elections by an establishment candidate. The union executive reportedly hired a public relations firm to run their campaign. Slick campaign literature was designed for the executive's candidate, and behind him there was the might of the president's office at Steelworkers' headquarters in Pittsburgh.

Michels concludes that the ideal of rule by the masses never occurs and cannot occur. The reality is a circulation of dominant elites. It is perhaps in the face of this level of powerlessness that people come to accept bribery as an effective, if illegitimate, means of exerting influence over officials.

Bureaucracy and Communism
Michels criticizes Marxist theory for failing to take account of administration in theories

of power. Socialism, he argues, is not merely a problem of economics, but also of administration. Large amounts of capital require bureaucracy to organize them, and with this comes hierarchy of control and technical expertise. Hence, the iron law of oligarchy re-emerges. The masses, he argues, will always submit to the minority.

Mosca ([1939] 1960) echoes similar sentiments, arguing that there will always be elites who can monopolize power and advantages through control of political party structures or any large-scale bureaucratic administration. The elite has the advantages of publicity, information control, education, specialized training, and qualifications. Elites also have the advantage of a lifetime of experience that they are able to hand down from one generation to another. Pressure from discontented masses does influence leaders but, whenever established leaders are disposed, another elite minority will have to be elected in their place.

In the final months of 1989, the peoples of many countries in Eastern Europe were struggling with this problem of takeover. Mass demonstrations, protests, and strikes precipitated the resignations of established Communist Party elites. But the difficult task that remained was to select new people to fill the resulting power vacuum. Before free elections could be held, parties had to be organized and leaders found to stand for election. Periodic elections provide a mechanism for the circulation of elites but do not eliminate the need for them. Nor do elections resolve the problem of rigid bureaucratic structures.

The stranglehold of bureaucracy on life in Soviet society has been generally recognized even by the strongest supporters of communism, but widely differing explanations have been proposed for it. Marcuse (1964, chap. 2) suggests that the primary cause of bureaucratic rigidity and authoritarianism lies outside the communist system in the desperate need to establish a strong Soviet Union

in the context of a hostile capitalist world. But while external pressures may have exacerbated the problems, the Marxist argument that a classless society would in principle protect citizens from the ravages of a bureaucratic state clearly has not been sustained in practice.

Barry Smart (1982) argues that two crucial events in Europe in 1968—the popular uprisings among students and workers in France in May of that year and the "Prague Spring"—irrevocably shattered the dreams of European socialists. The protest movements in France formed independently of the trade unions and the French Communist Party, the conventional political institutions of opposition. The generally conservative and unsympathetic response of the Communist Party to these demonstrations revealed the barrenness of the institutionalized and hierarchical forms of political protest. In theory, the Communist Party should have been at the forefront of the uprising, championing the rights and interests of the workers. In practice, the party proved to be out of touch and even hostile to a workers' movement that it did not control. Later that year, the Soviet Union invaded Czechoslovakia to crush the spontaneous social protest movements known as the Prague Spring. Smart argues that this invasion nullified any claim by the government of the Soviet Union to social, economic, political, or moral superiority over capitalist systems.

The massacre of demonstrators in Tiananmen Square in Beijing in June 1989 similarly undermined the legitimacy of Communist Party rule in China. For some three weeks prior to the massacre, several thousand people, led by Beijing University students, camped in the square to pressure for greater democratization in the country. They were denounced as counterrevolutionaries by Communist Party leaders, and the army was ordered to drive them out of the square. Foreign reporters estimate that hundreds of people were shot or crushed by army tanks. The oligarchic structure of the Communist Party was revealed in the power wielded by a handful of old men. It was reputedly one man, the eighty-four-year-old Deng Xiaoping, who ordered the People's Army to disperse the demonstrators. Rumours that Deng might be near death raised speculation that there might be a civil war in China as factions within the elite struggled for supremacy. During the ensuing weeks, it became evident how effectively the bureaucracy could control information so as to present a version of events that minimized the massacre, exonerated the army and the party, and silenced criticism.

In mid-December 1989, an estimated 2000 people were massacred in the central square in Timisoara, Romania. This marked the desperate attempt of Communist Party President Nicolae Ceausescu to crush mass demonstrations against his rule. Within a week of this massacre, the Romanian

The power of bureaucracy in communist countries was shown during the brutal repression of demonstrators in Tiananmen Square and the subsequent information control that silenced criticism.

government collapsed in the face of nation-wide revolt. Ceausescu and his wife were executed on Christmas Day. Subsequent reports indicated that this officially communist country had been ruled for decades by a repressive oligarchy dominated by Ceausescu and his family.

The critical challenge for Marxist theory is to account for the prevalence of Stalinist dictators in communist societies in which theorists had predicted a gradual withering away of state powers. The conventional Marxist response to such repression has been to return to classical texts in an effort to substitute new interpretations of doctrine. In Smart's view, none has yet been able to resolve the crisis of Marxism: the continuing incompatibility between theoretical expectations and patterns of development in Western capitalist societies and the realities in existing communist states.

Reforms instituted under Gorbachev to encourage *glasnost* and *perestroika*—greater openness and restructuring—within the Soviet Union rekindled hopes that a newer, more humane form of communism may yet be achieved. But by the close of 1989, there were signs that the degree of restructuring possible under commuinst rule would not be sufficient to satisfy the Soviet people. An increasing chorus of dissident voices demanded free elections, a free market system run on capitalist principles, and the end to the Communist Party's constitutional monopoly on power. Similar demands were echoed in much of Eastern Europe, particularly in Poland, East Germany, Czechoslovakia, and Romania. Challenges to communist rule throughout Eastern Europe were so sudden and so sweeping that some commentators were led to proclaim that this could be the end of history—the universal triumph of liberal-capitalist democracy (Fukuyama 1989).

These grandiose claims, however, have a hollow ring. In principle, the basic ideology of capitalism, which stresses free enterprise, individualism, and hostitlity to big government and state interference, should have worked against the development of a bureaucratic state in Western societies. But it has not. The iron cage of bureaucracy is not so easily escaped. Weber argued that bureaucratic forms of organization are an essential and unavoidable feature of centralized and industrialized societies, regardless of whether they are organized along capitalist or communist lines. Bureaucratic elites wield power by virtue of knowledge and technical superiority. This power base is far stronger than the raw power of ownership or control over the means of production because it is founded on the legitimating principle of rationality itself. As Weber saw it, purposive-rational organization is inherently bureaucratic and leads inevitably to oligarchy and dehumanization. Neither communist nor democratic procedures would be sufficient to overcome this. New approaches of **radical structuralism** and radical critical theory, in which Foucault is a central figure, have begun the work of pushing beyond classical Marxist and liberal theories, toward a critical analysis of bureaucracy and how relations of power are rationalized.

Radical Structuralism: The Analysis of Bureaucratic Society

Radical structuralism focusses on methods of domination in which, for Foucault, "the increasing organization of everything is the central issue of our time" (Dreyfus and Rabinow 1982, xxii). Foucault uses the metaphor of a **panopticon** to illustrate what he means by bureaucratic society. A panopticon is a circular prison where guards at the centre can see everyone else, without themselves being seen. Foucault uses this image in his discussion of power entering all areas of social life. Foucault viewed power, not as a commodity or possession in the hands of the

state or an elite class, but rather as a process that pervades all levels and all aspects of social life. Networks of disciplinary power are so pervasive as to be virtually synonymous with society itself (Smart 1983, 112).

To understand power in this sense, it becomes necessary to study the mechanisms, techniques, and procedures at the actual point of application. Rather than viewing power as descending from the top down, Foucault conceptualizes it as ascending from the most intimate personal events of life, the everyday methods of observation, recording, calculation, regulation, and training through which individuals are disciplined and normalized in society. The elites within the ruling class may use such mechanisms for their own purposes, but the mechanisms themselves do not originate within the bourgeoisie and neither do they disappear with the overthrow of the ruling elite. The **apparatus of ruling** remains to re-emerge

intact after the political revolution (Smart 1983, 82–87).

The possibility of a **disciplinary society**, a form of power based not on punishment but on intimate knowledge and regulation of individuals, emerged with the development of the human sciences such as psychology and sociology. Rational-technical knowledge and administrative procedures merged in bureaucracies as a tremendously powerful mechanism for controlling people.

This form of power is potentially far more effective than repression or prohibition because it rouses less resistance, costs less, and is directly tied in with the actual services of educational, military, industrial, and medical organizations through which such power is exercised. To challenge it seems like challenging reason itself. Education, for example, is concerned with developing knowledge that can be used to control people. Students of education learn how to manage classrooms so that children conform to what is expected of them. Such power is legitimated in ways that brute force could never be. It appears as productive and positive: it produces well behaved, conformist, normalized people who are productive members of society.

Bureaucratic Society

This section draws heavily on the work of Kathy Ferguson (1984) who in turn bases her analysis of **bureaucratic society** on the work of Foucault. In Ferguson's view, bureaucracy, as an all-pervasive mode of social organization, actually creates the kind of social system that structural-functionalist theory describes: a self-maintaining system that reduces people to sets of fragmented roles. The bureaucratic mode of organization is the experienced practice that makes it possible for society and people to be conceptualized in the mechanistic terms—norms, socialization, roles, role sets, functions, and institutions—of traditional structural-functionalist theory. In this theory, bureaucracy and society become synonymous. The institutionalized sets of roles that bureaucracy makes available to us, together with bureaucratic descriptions of and justifications for these roles or job classifications, structure our social world and shape how we think about it.

Bureaucracy has become so all-pervasive as to leave people with virtually no options. To remove oneself from bureaucracy is to lose almost all important social connections, while to embrace one's role is to lose the dimensions of oneself that do not coincide with organizational roles. The cost of conformity is resignation, while the cost of resistance is disintegration. Whatever course of action one takes is already determined by the organizational environment (Ferguson 1984, 91–92).

For Ferguson (1984, x), the central issue is bureaucracy itself, a mode of organization that hurts, twists, and damages people and limits human possibility. **Bureaucracy** represents "the scientific organization of inequality" through which people are dominated and oppressed. At the same time it legitimates such practices in the name of rationality and efficiency. Conflict-ridden class relations are disguised in the language of administration.

Bureaucracy can be seen as a self-maintaining social system. Whatever the ostensible services that a bureaucracy might have been set up to accomplish, they tend to become secondary to the actual purpose of keeping the machinery running. The central concern becomes the maintenance of a stable environment with predictable behaviour from functionaries within the organization and from clients and customers outside it.

Ferguson's analysis goes far beyond a description of the system. She takes up the challenge that radical structuralism must necessarily examine the mechanisms through which the system is maintained. The primary function of bureaucracy is control, which is maintained in the face of continuing resistance and pressures toward nonconformity. Such maintenance requires the constant renewal of mechanisms that keep the structures intact. These mechanisms include isolating individuals, depersonalizing relations, and distorting communications. The constant appeal to efficiency conceals the control function that hierarchy performs within bureaucracies. Individuals are isolated in their fragmented and delimited roles. Their potential individual contribution is so limited that they are rendered expendable and therefore powerless. The absorption or co-optation of a few key individuals into management creates the illusion of upward mobility and hence promotes loyalty, while supervision, roles, and the hoarding of knowledge control the mass of people.

People interact with others only as role occupants. We come to see each other from the perspective of the organization and the roles we play in it rather than as whole persons. Likewise, in the wider society, people are commonly referred to as if they only existed in terms of standard bureaucratic categories. We come to think of "taxpayers" pitted against "workers" or "citizens" versus "welfare recipients." It is hard to keep sight of the reality that these are not distinct people but common dimensions of experience. The fragmented conception of people in terms of partial and competing roles tends to perpetuate our dependency on the very organizations that cause this fragmentation.

Bureaucratic language further depersonalizes people and reinforces this role fragmentation. The language of **technics** replaces the language of human action: dialogue, debate, and judgment are replaced by feedback, input, and output. Open class conflicts are depersonalized when firing peo-

ple is described as "reductions in force" or "downsizing" (Ferguson 1984, 15–16). Opposition is pacified by the ideological construction of rational administration as neutral, efficient, and effective and by the façade of the ideological neutrality of administration.

Resistance

Opposition may be silenced, muted, or distorted by the conceptions of administrative neutrality and efficiency but, in Foucault's view, it can never be totally destroyed. If people really could be reduced to their roles, to their organizational identities, then the mechanisms of bureaucratic control would no longer be necessary. The intensity of control is itself a measure of the pervasiveness of resistance. In practice, people are never reduced to total conformity.

"I'd like to think of you as a person, David, but it's my job to think of you as personnel."

Drawing by Victor; © 1986 The New Yorker Magazine, Inc.

The exercise of power generates the very resistance to which it responds. Foucault argues that power relations presuppose resistance.

No matter how efficient bureaucracies may be in promoting conformity and passivity, uncertainties remain. Some power must be delegated within organizations, hence opening the way for discretion. No matter how carefully organizations monitor information and select new members, control is never total. People within the organization may filter out or ignore information they receive, or distort information that they pass on, and so produce **intelligence failures** within organizations. People who supposedly direct the organizations fail to achieve intended results because they base their commands on inaccurate and incomplete information. The goals of individual members will never coincide completely with organizational goals. These discrepancies give rise to continual pressures toward resistance.

Bureaucratization is thus not an accomplished entity, but is always a process, a struggle between control and resistance. Mechanisms of control must be constantly reproduced to overcome the opposition that control itself generates. Yet at the same time, bureaucracies must disguise these efforts to deal with conflict in order to maintain the image of administrative neutrality and efficiency upon which their legitimacy and control depends (Ferguson 1984, 17–21). The result is more and more centralization, more standardization of rules and regulations, and ever-increasing ratios of supervisors or managers to actual workers. Ferguson estimates there was one supervisor for every three to four workers in the United States in 1984. Computerized monitoring may reverse this trend in the future by making human supervisors less necessary.

Society as a whole can be conceptualized as a dense network of interlocking organizations that together form a **technical civiliz-ation** penetrating all aspects of social life. Each organization acts as a potential resource for other organizations in an overall collaborative network. Foucault (1980, 106) refers to this as a "closely linked grid of disciplinary coercions" that enforce inequality, normalcy, and control. Unions collaborate with corporations to control workers through contracts. Drug companies make deals with the federal government to change patent laws and gain the co-operation of medical associations by offering lucrative advertising revenues to their publications and career mobility to doctors in drug companies. Clusters of organizations act as suppliers, subsidiaries, distributors, and research organizations for each other. Firms, together with relevant state agencies, provide banking, legal, managerial, advertising, and public relations services for each other. They come together as loose, flexible, very stable networks of interlocking institutions, their minor conflicts contained within a climate of co-operation (Ferguson 1984, 38–42). Increasingly all such organizations come to resemble each other and utilize shared knowledge of techniques of management. Prisons come to resemble factories, schools, barracks, and hospitals, which in turn come to resemble prisons (Foucault 1979, 229).

Normalization

Foucault emphasizes that this bureaucratic, technical civilization cannot be understood in such purely negative terms as repression or constraint. When we think of power in terms of sovereignty, or as imposed by elites from the top down, then we focus on laws, but disciplinary power is not imposed from above. It is exercised through ordinary, everyday activities, and it actually produces how we think of normal reality. It is characterized by **therapeutic intervention** in everything. This intervention is justified in terms of efficiency and technical expertise in the production of **normalized**, productive people. In Foucault's scheme, social work, police, and military become fused. Individual and collective life is controlled through the disciplines of the social sciences and related techniques of administrative law, policy science, social work, public administration, and rational planning.

The most intimate aspects of personal life and social relations are subject to the **cult of rationality** within this therapeutic civilization. Hochschild (1983, 171–77) refers to **emotional labour** in her description of how flight attendants are trained to manage and present feelings and facial and body expressions to produce the required response in the customer. The flight attendant learns the techniques of emotional management with the aid of instruction manuals. The goal is not genuine communication but eliciting appropriate responses from customers, which will raise profits for the airline.

Corporate executives pay up to $75 an hour to learn how to use a well modulated voice (*Globe and Mail*, 24 Dec. 1987, B1–2). "The goal is to develop a 'voice image' that conveys confidence, trust, warmth, and believability to improve the way others respond." The objective is to "help business clients talk their way to success," measured in terms of being persuasive enough to close deals. In Ferguson's terms, people are taught to substitute technique for connectedness, to attach emotions to functions and not to any person. As soon as a new technique is available, it is applied to whatever is at hand. Bureaucracy is the organized expression of this **managerial mentality**.

This cult of rationality in emotion management is never totally successful in reducing all emotions to the plastic responses required. The exercise of such techniques itself generates resistance and withdrawal. Hence, such control requires constant policing and constant repetition, reflected in such practices as annual retraining courses for flight attendants.

The Bureaucratic Construction of Class

Weber's analysis of class in capitalist society modified Marx's thesis in the important respect of shifting the ground of class and class relations from the question of ownership of means of production to life chances within the marketplace. The shift from market capitalism to corporate capitalism has changed the basis of class relations. Ownership of the means of production is no longer a central issue for the vast majority of people. Control over the means of production has become increasingly concentrated in fewer and fewer hands within giant corporate empires and holding companies. Careers within corporate bureaucracies are now the central determinant of class position of the majority of people, with career entry tightly tied to credentials. Location within the bureaucratic hierarchy and the conditions that determine who gets what position are now the key factors in the social construction of class.

Ferguson identifies the layers produced by rigid and fractionalized job hierarchies within this organizational class system. Directors and executives make policy; the new working class of highly skilled technical, managerial, and professional workers administer the implementation of these policies; the industrial and clerical working class with lower educational requirements have highly routinized, fragmented work; the bottom level of marginal workers have casual jobs within the secondary labour market. Casual workers are the people who move back and forth between the roles of workers and clients of unemployment and welfare agencies.

The class system within industrial societies has its origin within such corporate bureaucratic entities. The arrangement of jobs within bureaucracies is very deliberate and is justified in terms of efficiency but perpetuated by the need for control. In this respect at least, the lives of the mass of people in advanced capitalist societies may differ little from the experience of life within state socialist societies.

People who occupy different rungs of the bureaucratic class order have substantially different work situations when measured in terms of income, health and safety, trust, and freedom from close supervision. But they share the same system that de-individualizes them and objectifies their activities and relations (Ferguson 1984, 88). The power that bureaucracy exercises over people is so hard to see because that power becomes so totally part of the activities themselves. It is what people do. If power were always oppressive and negative, it would not be so powerful. It is accepted because it seems productive (Foucault 1980, 119).

Subordination within the bureaucratic hierarchy produces character traits displayed by subordinate, dependent, and powerless people, traits that Ferguson suggests closely resemble the stereotype of femininity. Concern with impression-management is fundamental for subordinates whose well-being depends upon pleasing superiors. Conformity is central to survival within bureaucracies and is produced by close surveillance. Career mobility depends upon pleasing superiors and moulding one's behaviour to fit what superiors want. Career manuals warn aspiring junior managers not to make suggestions that challenge the organization's established ways of doing things. Successful innovations by those who fail to conform to expected bureaucratic patterns of behaviour will be resented rather than welcomed, as they threaten the established order.

The higher up the organizational hierarchy, the more important impression-management and conformity is. As Kanter (1977) has pointed out, social similarity becomes a critical measure of trustworthiness among managers where close surveillance is difficult. As a result, people from cultural backgrounds other than the norm, or people who look different, such as blacks and women, find it extremely hard to break into management ranks, no matter what their competence. They do not fit; they cannot be trusted to conform.

Resistance from within bureaucratic organizations is limited and individualistic. Union radicals and activists at all levels tend to attack individual abuses by particular superiors, or aim at particular policy reforms, rather than attacking the system as a whole. They leave the bureaucratic order intact (Ferguson 1984, 120).

Clients, who seek assistance from social service agencies, occupy the lowest rung on the organizational class structure. Often they are omitted from analyses of organizational hierarchies, and yet they are crucial in the larger class structure of which an organization is part. "There are growing numbers of organizations whose purpose is to process, regulate, license, certify, hide or otherwise control people," and clients are the prime targets (Ferguson 1984, 123). Customers, who purchase goods and services from bureaucracies, have relatively more independence of action than clients, but neither group has much influence over the organizations on which it depends. Advertising, marketing, and sales are concerned with controlling the behaviour and attitudes of customers, much as welfare bureaucracies are concerned with controlling poor people. Ferguson (1984, 123) suggests that the ghettos of big cities that house the urban poor are becoming increasingly like total institutions, subject to administrative controls which define, monitor, categorize, produce, and supervise the inhabitants' behaviour.

The poor, as clients of service bureaucracies, must learn the language of the bureaucracy in order to survive. They must conform to the required image: they must learn to please, to present the appropriate responses, to give recognition to administrative authority, to flatter, and to legitimate the bureaucracy and its rules (Ferguson 1984, 144–46). Ferguson describes the immense strain that this places on poor people. They must learn to treat themselves as categories, to read clues, to control themselves, to anticipate demands, to calculate acceptable responses, and to offer them as signs of deservedness. Even to become clients they must first become cases and pass examinations to demonstrate their eligibility and deservedness. If successful, they are rewarded by becoming the obedient subjects of bureaucratic management. The traits of dependence and passivity help to perpetuate their situation by lowering their self-esteem and ability to assert themselves or to organize collectively. A very few individuals can challenge this by tactics of confrontation but, as Ferguson suggests, such strategies work only because they are rare. It is easier for the administration to give in to the few individual agitators than to fight them, but any organized resistance is likely to be short-lived and easily controlled. Welfare bureaucracies provide financial support to client organizations that then must conform to continue getting support.

The roles available to clients are very limited, and even the ordinary activities of life tend to be redefined in managerial terms. Patients, for example, do not hold dances, they have "dance therapy": they do not play volleyball or cards, they have "recreation therapy" (Ferguson 1984, 137). The most intimate aspects of their personal lives are known to the bureaucracy, while they themselves are not seen as entitled to claim any special knowledge about their situation of poverty, crime, illness, or despair.

Neither Ferguson nor Foucault intend to attack the personal intentions or integrity of caseworkers within bureaucratic agencies. The cause of the problems does not lie in the attitudes, intentions, or personal lack of humanity of these caseworkers, but within the structure of the bureaucracy itself. Both clients and caseworkers are trapped within the same agency and the same fragmented roles. Caseworkers are institutionally constrained regardless of what they think of their clients.

Ferguson describes caseworkers with very different attitudes: some are advocates who care deeply about client rights, some are mediators, and some are narrowly bureaucratic. But these differences in attitudes do not translate into differences in behaviour (Ferguson 1984, 139–40). Their fragmented job responsibilities and the necessity of translating everything in terms of bureaucratic forms and paperwork homogenizes their behaviour. In the end, the differences in attitudes disappear as there is no room for their expression. Work becomes paperwork, with clients ultimately experienced as nuisances in the pressure to complete the forms and get the work done.

In Foucault's terms, power produces the subjectivities. What he means by this is that the very nature of bureaucratic activities produces the attitudes and behaviour of the people—both clients and caseworkers—that in turn perpetuate these bureaucratic activities.

The Bureaucratic Construction of Gender

Bureaucratic practices produce and reproduce **gender class**, the situation of women in relation to men in society, as part of the social construction of class society.

Ferguson (1984, 3–4) suggests that feminism and bureaucracy arose together in Western society. The expansion of managerial and clerical work and the growth of social welfare agencies in the late nineteenth century provided opportunities for middle-class women to move into the paid labour force. New opportunities stimulated rising aspirations. These independent, middle-class women were at the forefront of agitation for suffrage and other reforms that characterized the first wave of feminism.

Ferguson traces the birth of the second wave of the feminist movement to the period after World War II when white-collar work and social service organizations expanded. The growth in job opportunities for women was related to the shift from market to corporate capitalism. This shift was reflected in the rise of large-scale bureaucracies and the resulting need for supervision and record keeping. Moreover, the corporations took over many of the production activities formerly done within the home. New opportunities for women were thus predominantly opportunities to move from work in the home to work in bureaucracies.

Kanter (1977, 3) describes corporations as "people producers." Huge multinationals virtually run the world economy and control most of the jobs. Within this system, women perform clerical services while men manage. Women are in organizations but practically never run them. The human relations school of management theory justifies this practice with stereotypes of men as rational and therefore suited for decision-making positions. Conversely, women are viewed as emotional and thus better suited to work as people handlers in personnel departments and reception areas (Kanter 1977, 25).

In her study of women in the British Columbia civil service, Cassin (1979) explores some of the organizational reasons why affirmative action programs to increase the number of female managers are unlikely to be successful. Men in junior roles in the organizational hierarchy tend to interact far more with male managers and so learn how to present themselves and how to discuss their work in terms of its management or policy implications. When they apply for promotion, they know how to present the right image, and they are well known to those who appoint them. Women, in contrast, tend to be outside this old boys' network. This separation is compounded when they have children and so likely have to restrict their after-hours socializing and overtime work. Women are not taught how to present themselves, and they tend to describe their work in terms of professional and technical competence rather than policy implications. They thus generally sound less like managers in promotion interviews and have less experience and a more limited informal knowledge of organizational policies and practices than do men at junior levels.

Kanter describes at length the patriarchal and patrimonial structure of bureaucratic organizations. By **patrimony**, she means the process by which career ranks and other perks are passed down from male mentors in senior management to junior ranking males with whom they have a fatherly relationship. Management teams are constituted through what Kanter (1977, chap. 3) refers to as processes of virtual "homosexual reproduction" within the old boys' networks. The women who are the secretaries of such men are regarded and treated much as wives. Their primary role is to provide multiple personal services and total loyalty to the boss. They may be promoted along with him, but rarely if ever without him or over him.

The real wives of these male managers are also part of the corporate image, formally outside the organization, paid nothing, and discouraged from visiting the office, but with all aspects of their lives dictated by the corporate image required for their husbands to succeed. As Kanter (1977, 107) puts it, men symbolically bring two people to their jobs, while women are seen to bring less than one, because they are expected to maintain all home commitments.

The very few women who are promoted up the organizational hierarchy function as tokens, their effectiveness undermined by their systematic exclusion from the old boys' networks that sustain men. They are talked about, passed over, and compared in multiple

Bureaucracies are characterized by patriarchal and patrimonial structures within "old-boys" networks.

ways that weaken their effectiveness. Extensive literature on women in management gives advice on how women can function more like men in order to succeed. Such literature blames failure on such weaknesses as emotionalism, fear of success, lack of experience of team sports, and inability to delegate responsibilities or to discipline subordinates effectively (Fenn 1980; Hennig and Jardim 1981; Larwood and Wood 1977). But, as Kanter points out, it is difficult to play on a team if other team members do not want you on it.

Contemporary studies of women in bureaucracies continue to focus largely on how to break this dual labour market through effective programs or training schemes that will facilitate the promotion of women into senior managerial positions in more than token numbers. A plethora of instruction books give advice to women on how to use and to copy male mentors to develop bureaucratic skills to get ahead.

Ferguson rejects this approach as seriously misguided. What she fears most, as we shall discuss further below, is the co-optation of the women's movement into bureaucratic society. Bureaucracy is a means to human oppression and not to liberation. Ferguson hopes for more radical change than this.

The Interpretive Critique

Challenge to Radical Structuralism

There is a serious problem with the deeply depressing picture of bureaucratic society presented above. People appear as cogs in a machine, fractionalized elements within the iron cage. The worst of Weber's nightmare vision of bureaucracy and rationality appears to have come true. We have encountered a similar vision of people as objects within the crushing machine of capitalism in economic determinist aspects of Marxist theory.

The approach of interpretive theory begins from Weber's own methodological emphasis on interpretive understanding, on the meanings that actions have for people themselves. Weber, like Marx himself, insisted that only people do things. Concepts like *bureaucracies* are abstractions that refer to groups of people who are collectively organized to do something. Bureaucracies as such do nothing.

The fundamental critique presented by interpretive theory is that the theories we have examined—both traditional functionalism with its focus on efficient systems, and radical structuralism with its focus on control—reflect a false reification of structures. Both theories tend to take for granted the assumption that organizations are concrete entities that do things to people.

For half a chapter you have read arguments that bureaucracies are all-powerful structures that determine the character of modern corporate capitalist and state socialist societies. It will be difficult for you to set this to one side and consider the argument of interpretive theory that bureaucracies do not really exist.

It may help at this point to recall earlier examples of how the interpretive perspective raises questions. In the discussion of suicide in chapter 6, for example, we saw how "factual" government statistics are derived from coroners' subjective decisions about how to classify ambiguous causes of death. It is clear that the way in which coroners make certain deaths accountable is not necessarily a literal description of what happened. Similarly, references to bureaucracy and bureaucratic structures may also be a way of accounting for what people are doing rather than literal descriptions of what is actually happening. Thus, in our minds we have to separate the account from what might actually be happening.

We have already seen discrepancies in analyses of bureaucratic organizations. Structural functionalists argue that bureaucratic modes of organizing people exist because they are efficient. Conflict theory challenges this by arguing that such organizational practices arose primarily to control people and may actually be very inefficient. Other research is beginning to debunk the argument that bureaucratic modes of organizing people work by deskilling people at the bottom of the hierarchy and concentrating knowledge and hence power at the top. Studies that have looked in depth at what people actually are doing at the bottom show otherwise.

In a study of advanced clerical workers, Reimer (1987) found discrepancies between job descriptions and performance. The job description of clerical workers within the organization chart defines their work as "routine delegated duties" involving limited educational skills or responsibilities. In practice, however, much of the work done by clerical staff requires independent thought, initiative, considerable skills, and comprehensive knowledge of the operations of the organization in which they work. Often, completed tasks are automatically attributed to the manager who delegated the task. The actual skills involved in the routine aspects of clerical work habitually go unnoticed to the extent that even the people doing the work tend to describe what they do in unskilled terms such as "filing" and "sorting." The same work of collecting information done by someone in a more senior rank would be called "researching."

Cassin's (1980) study of women workers in the British Columbia civil service makes similar observations. She points out that many of the clerical staff were actively engaged in managerial work but often without the workers themselves recognizing it. The task of opening and sorting the mail, for example, may sound unskilled, but in practice it requires considerable knowledge and experience. The secretary has to know what must receive immediate attention and what can wait. If a letter contains an inquiry, the secretary needs to know where to find the information to provide the answer and must make it available for the boss. In effect, as secretaries sort mail, they are actually structuring their bosses' jobs, making key prioritizing decisions before the boss even gets involved. If they make mistakes, like putting on the back burner what should have received prompt attention, the ramifications could be serious.

Officially, these managerial skills are non-existent because the job description does not mention them. Yet at an informal level, these hidden skills are acknowledged. This is revealed in the sometimes bitter observations of secretaries that they taught their boss everything he knew, only to see him promoted while they remained behind to run the office and train another neophyte.

Such practices may be little different when the boss is female. They are built into the very pattern of bureaucratic relations. Subordinates are required to take the role of their superior, to internalize it, and to apply it as a guide for their behaviour. One secretary describes how she continually covers up errors made by her incompetent boss, knowing that this supervisor would blame her for things that go wrong while taking all credit for things that go right (Ferguson 1984, 108)

The Documentary Construction of Reality

How does the actual lived experience of people get so distorted that they come to believe the distortions themselves? It is a convenient fiction in job classification that one evaluates jobs and not people, the roles and not the role incumbents. Then anything that does not fit the organization chart—as when both worker and supervisor insist that a junior clerical worker is performing managerial work—can be put down to "person and performance," which is not evaluated because it is defined as not relevant.

A related question raised by Bittner (1965) is, What is the difference between formal and informal organization? The answer is actually circular. Any behaviour

that fits the model or organization chart is formal and all the rest is informal. In other words, anything that does not fit our version of a rational bureaucratic model is simply defined as irrelevant because it is only informal behaviour. It will not appear anywhere in any formal records or minutes of meetings kept by the organization.

What job classification workers do, then, is evaluate the organization chart itself. The reality of what people are actually doing does not enter the picture. So the fiction goes on. A few exceptions can be forced through, under various excuses, but the prevailing fiction, that official job descriptions represent what people do, remains unchallenged.

What can we learn from this? That injustices abound in the hierarchically ordered scale of prestige and differential pay? Yes, certainly. That sexism is rampant, in that it is frequently women whose acknowledged skills are appropriated by their male bosses? This is true as well, but there is more. From the perspective of interpretive theory, what is really important is that we begin to see that the notion of a structured hierarchy of skills and responsibilities itself is only a useful fiction that justifies and mystifies class and power. The organization chart provides an accounting procedure, not a description of what people actually do.

Yet it is precisely these organization charts, these official bureaucratic job descriptions, that provide the descriptive data base from which other people draw their analyses of class structure. Like coroners categorizing deaths, job classifiers in bureaucracies label what they assume people do, or ought to be doing. They thus produce the labour-force statistics on the percentage of professional, managerial, paraprofessional, clerical, and semi- or unskilled workers. Statistics Canada records these convenient fictions in neat tables, which sociologists then use to produce their accounts of the occupational class structure of Canadian society. If the managerial work of people in non-managerial job categories actually gained recognition, along with the non-managerial work that some people in supposedly managerial job categories do, the actual class structure of Canadian society might look very different. The gender-class structure would certainly look vastly different. How different we do not know. Our knowledge of what people do comes to us so totally worked up by bureaucratic accounting procedures, guided by the fiction of organization charts, that what is actually going on is almost impossible to know. We would have to start from scratch.

The issue of unrecognized work goes far beyond the challenge to formal organization charts. As we have seen in earlier chapters, we have good reasons for asking how much teaching housewives do, or how much nursing and social work they do, or how much diagnostic and doctoring work nurses do, how many articles or even doctoral theses are put together by spouses. If we question far enough, our taken-for-granted reality—that housewives do housework and managers manage—may come to seem entirely fictional. The work of exploring behind the social construction of reality has scarcely begun.

Bureaucracies and the Social Construction of Knowledge

Interpretive theory is pushing in the direction of deeper understanding by questioning the ways in which our knowledge of everyday reality actually is put together. How do we come up with the versions of reality that we so readily take for granted? A key element of the answer to this question lies in the behaviour of people within complex organizations. Location within organizations is critical not only in the social construction of class and gender relations but also in the social construction of knowledge itself.

Zimmerman (1974) explores exactly what people in organizations actually do to produce the fact that certain individuals are or are not eligible for unemployment benefits. One requirement is that the potential recipient has been looking for work. How can individuals demonstrate that they have actually looked for work the previous month? Their word is not believable, nor is the word of family members or friends. However, if someone within another organization provides a piece of paper stating that so-and-so applied for such-and-such a post, that will be treated as a fact. While unemployment insurance workers challenge every personal source of proof, they refuse even to consider the possibility that the informant from the other organization might make up the document or statement as a personal favour. The fiction of impersonal role incumbents could not be challenged without the entire fiction of a factual reality coming apart.

Once someone in an organization has declared a person eligible for services like unemployment insurance, that becomes fact for anyone else in any other organization where such information might be relevant. The same goes for proof of birth date. It must be supplied by a piece of paper from a formal organization. People who need any kind of government service soon learn that they must carry such pieces of paper around to every appointment. As Zimmerman puts it, pieces of paper produced by people in organizations become "fact for all practical purposes" for people in other organizations. Statements made by people are suspect, but statements made by impersonal role incumbents are treated as impersonal, unbiased facts.

Tuchman carries this exploration further in her study *Making News* (1978), where she shows that anything said by officials is treated as factual for the practical purposes of newspaper reporters. Information from such sources is reproduced as straight facts while anything said by people who are not officials is presented as conjectures that may or may not be true. It is very difficult for readers to penetrate to the source of these "factual" statements because they are not presented in a way that encourages questioning.

Smith (1979a) has analysed how different accounts of a street riot appear when given by the police rather than by the people in the street. The accounts of bystanders tend to be written in very personal and local ways: "I was saw standing here and saw and heard this and I thought that . . . ." The account attributed to the police, however, tends to be quite different. The distinct observations and thoughts or conclusions of different individuals in different places, who happened to be working as police, all get merged into one official police account, which is impersonal, abstract, and not tied to any one person's observations or location. Again, what people say is just personal opinion while what role incumbents say is fact.

Just how fictional "facts" can be has been demonstrated in a delightful study by Epstein, *The Rise and Fall of Diamonds* (1982). He shows how people in the Debeers corporation, which dominated the diamond market during the 1920s and 1930s, systematically created facts about diamonds so as to generate the fiction that diamonds are good investments and symbols of eternal romantic love. They bribed Hollywood filmmakers and scriptwriters to include scenes of movie idols being presented with diamond rings in romantic scenes. They wrote over a hundred pseudo-news stories about glamourous women in order to include descriptions of the diamonds they wore, diamonds that the company gave them. They even went so far as to set up a Diamond Information Bureau to give the stamp of authority to histories, news releases, and National Geographic feature articles that they wrote about diamonds. They used psychologists to analyse basic human wants such as comfort, longer life, social approval, ability to attract the opposite sex, and freedom from fear, and then manipulated advertising to link diamonds subliminally to these wants. Diamonds became symbols of everlasting love to

be presented at the time of engagement and at all significant wedding anniversaries. This social construction of reality has been so successful that even when people read Epstein's study and realize how the entire myth was put together, they still want a diamond engagement ring (Cassin, personal communication).

Bureaucratic Discourse: Language and Power

One last question remains. How do organizations come to exercise such power over us? They even have the power to create our sense of what is real, including our sense that the organizations themselves are factually real entities. There seems to be a circular process going on. The activities of people whom we refer to as officials in organizations help to create our taken-for-granted factual knowledge about our society, but it is also precisely our taken-for-granted belief in organizations that gives them the power to do so.

Control over the mind is much more powerful than control over the body. Once the way we think is controlled, to the point that we cannot think of any alternative to the present ways of doing things, then we control ourselves. Hence, when Foucault looks for the basis of power in society, he does not look at structures or institutions but rather at knowledge, at how people learn to think. When he refers to knowledge as power, and discourse as political activity, he is referring to how thought controls people.

Education is central to this process. Ferguson suggests that education has come to control and discipline students less through marks than through the definition of knowledge itself, which is tightly tied to careers. In North American universities, a broad focus on liberal arts is losing ground to professional and technical training, such as social work, criminal justice, public and business administration, and so on. These are highly specialized training programs with little focus on the big picture and little critical content. The very activity of learning and the subject matter being absorbed moulds students into their future bureaucratic roles. Such knowledge, like the role itself, is fragmented and discontinuous. Narrowly specialized expertise with appropriate credentials provides a perfect justification for narrowly specialized and hierarchical bureaucratic roles. Ferguson (1984, 45) refers to this as the "lifeboat mentality." All that concerns students is obtaining credentials in order to find a secure organizational niche. Once they find such a niche, they will not need to be controlled from the outside. They will control themselves from the inside, their subjective consciousness meshing with the organizational definitions of their situation.

Foucault connects the two meanings of **discipline**: orderly conduct and a branch of knowledge. From this point of view, social science theories that analyse bureaucratic organizations as efficient and rational systems are political ideologies. In other words, they are part of the domination. When we believe these theories we act accordingly. The discipline of public administration, for example, assumes from the start that organizations are concrete entities, that they are efficient and rational, and that people can be regarded as role incumbents and managed to maximize efficiency. These theories reproduce the viewpoint of managers and give it scientific credibility. At the same time, they reflect how deeply this managerial mentality is rooted in how we think. Conflict theory helps only a little. It draws attention to conflicting class interests in organizations, but we still end up thinking that organizations are efficient, rational systems for capitalists to make profits, and that people are role incumbents.

When we transfer conflict theory to the analysis of Soviet society, the similarities between functionalism and conflict theory become apparent. Organizations that are functional for the capitalist class in western society are functional for the collectivity in a society with collective ownership of the means of production.

Interpretive theory tries to argue that organizations do not exist as entities at all. They exist only in thought as ways of accounting for what people are doing. People are not role incumbents except in so far as they learn to think about themselves in such terms. But language is enormously powerful. As soon as you read the word *organization*, you are likely to start thinking about some entity because that is what the word means to us. I might try to talk about "organizational ways of acting," but you will likely translate this straight back into the familiar word *organization* or *bureaucracy* and wonder why I cannot write plain English instead of jargonese.

It is only a very short step from learning to think in terms of organization language to being controlled by it. Smith (1979a) describes this way of talking as "using the oppressor's language." Think about the situation, described in chapter 2, where a union organization's explanation for why women do not come to meetings is female apathy. In terms of the union's language, a union is a democratic organization set up for the benefit of its members. It is based on voluntary attendance. When we start with this definition, the notion of apathy seems an acceptable explanation for members not bothering to turn up. But when we stop thinking in terms of the organization's language, and start looking at what people are actually doing, the concept of apathy disappears. We see that meetings are organized at times and in places that make it very hard for women to attend. Women are responsible for caring for children, for getting dinner, and for doing housework after work. This fact actually frees men to go to union meetings. We also begin to see that when women do attend meetings, they are shouted down and ignored and their concerns are not treated as very important. What we see is something that looks much more like patriarchy than apathy, but the language a of democratic union organization cannot express this.

It is not organizations as such that control us, but language, knowledge, and the discipline of social science itself. For Foucault it is a closed circle. Language creates our experience; our experience creates the language in which we come to talk about that experience; how we come to talk about it structures our experience, and so on (Ferguson 1984, xiii). The prevailing forms of power and knowledge create the subjective self-consciousness of individuals themselves, including the professionals who create the power and knowledge. There seems to be no way out of this bureaucratic discourse.

Radical Discourse: Feminism and the Possibility of Resistance

For Foucault, this circle of social control through language and experience is never complete. People can never be totally reduced to the sum of their roles. Hence there is always resistance. The exercise of power generates its own resistance. But this resistance is muted and partial. It tends to be expressed by powerless people who live on the periphery of the bureaucratic order. Foucault himself focussed upon the criminal and the insane, the misfits for whom clinics and prisons are invented. These are the people most able to see the gap between their experience and how it is described by officials. But their protest is subdued. It lacks legitimacy; it is not sanctioned. We tend not to consider such people worth listening to.

Ferguson, however, suggests there is another voice of protest and resistance that is less easily dismissed: the voice of feminism. She argues that the different voice of women has the potential to break this closed circle of experience and discourse because women are marginal to these bureaucratic structures and yet at the same time are educated, resourceful, and increasingly visible.

Women have the potential to provide a radical alternative because the traditional standpoint of women has been outside bureaucratic organizations. Women have been more centrally concerned with reproduction and with nurturing children, which provides them with a radically different experience of human relations. Women, as caregivers, nurturers, and providers for the needs of others, are necessarily oriented toward co-operative and non-hierarchical relations. Bureaucratic organizations of hierarchically ordered, narrowly specified roles and responsibilities are anathema to women's primary experience of life as mothers, daughters, and wives. Boys, suggests Ferguson (1984, 160) learn to separate themselves from mothering to identify with the more aloof, separate, and specialized roles of fathers as breadwinners, while daughters never fully make this separation.

As women are emerging from the private life of the home to join public life as employees in ever-increasing numbers, they bring with them the potential for a radically alternative view of collective organization more in keeping with their experience. Ferguson and others (i.e., Gilligan 1982) suggest that radical feminist discourse focusses upon nurturing, concern, and connectedness with others. It incorporates a different definition of rationality in which emotion is viewed as something that people do. Emotion is not the opposite of reason. It is central to reason itself as a way of experiencing the world. An emotionless person is fundamentally irrational. Emotion is a potential avenue to "the reasonable view" (Ferguson 1984, 200). Feminism also calls for a restructuring of the relations between private and public life so that they cease to be defined as opposites and can be integrated. However, this is unlikely to happen without radically changing the character of family or workplace or both. As Parsons' work implies, family-oriented values cannot enter the workplace without changing the bureaucratic model of affectively neutral, universalistic, and specific pattern variables appropriate for fragmented, hierarchically segregated roles.

Ferguson points to an alternative mode of organization in such feminist projects as bookstores, health collectives, newsletters, shelters, crisis centres, and the like, which are able to minimize ties with bureaucratic organizations. There are also occasional glimpses of what might be possible as professional women in law and medicine pool their practices and organize flexible working hours and client-sharing in order to integrate work and child care. Feminist projects are committed to internally decentralized and anti-bureaucratic organization; they rely on personal, face-to-face relations rather than formal rules; and they encourage egalitarian rather than hierarchical relations. They see skills and information as

resources to be shared rather than hoarded (Ferguson 1984, 189–90). Should such modes of organization seem fanciful or inefficient, we should remember that bureaucracies have also been shown to be very inefficient, especially in contexts that require innovation. Bureaucratic structures are oriented more to control and exploitation of a reluctant workforce than to efficiency in achieving other goals.

One outstanding example of feminist principles of organization in action is the Icelandic Women's Alliance or Kvennalistinn. It is a political party committed to fighting for social issues of immediate concern to women. Thornhildur Thorliefsdóttir, one of the party's members of parliament, described the Women's Alliance to Canadian women at a 1988 meeting of the National Committee on the Status of Women (NAC). She referred to Icelandic women's disappointment with its Equal Rights Act of 1971. While the act supposedly gave women equality, it actually gave women an equal

Feminist principles of organization emphasize reliance on personal and egalitarian relations.

opportunity to compete in the men's world on men's terms. It did nothing to recognize women's sexual particularity as child bearers and child rearers. The Women's Alliance took shape in the early 1980s as the conviction grew that it would take a women's party to get women's issues at the centre of the political agenda. The Alliance is committed to radical improvement in child-care facilities and to a significant increase in the minimum wage to raise it above the poverty line, a goal especially significant for single mothers who are overrepresented in the lowest-paying jobs. The Alliance has a women's position on all other social issues as well, including a policy of rejecting heavy industry, with its pollution problems and foreign debts, in favour of small industries. The party won enough seats in the April 1987 elections to hold the balance of power in Iceland's parliament.

The existence of such a party and its electoral success are remarkable enough, but what is more significant is its organizational structure, which is explicitly in accord with the feminist principles described above. The party has no leader; the leadership function is rotated among the members. There is an active mentorship policy, through which large numbers of women are trained to act as representatives for the party in meetings and campaign debates. Often they attend such functions in pairs, one novice with one more experienced woman. This principle of rotation and shared responsibilities makes possible another principle that no office holder serves longer than six to eight years. Through such practices the "iron low of oligarchy" may be broken. As Thorliefsdóttir expressed it, "towers of power isolate people." The task is to ensure that women are never imprisoned in such a tower.

The Alliance operates by consensus, not by majority vote. Members have to work at issues together until some compromise can be found to include all of them. It takes a lot of effort, a lot of meetings, and a lot of time,

but it works. It ensures that individuals cannot dominate or control issues within the party. The party actually refused to join a ruling coalition in 1987 when it became clear that it would have been forced to abandon key principles and so weaken its position as an alternative voice. The party is not entirely sure how it will proceed if it ever becomes the dominant political party, but it is confident it will be able both to govern and to remain faithful to its principles.

Thorliefsdóttir's presentation won a standing ovation from the delegates at the NAC conference. The importance of her message concerning a feminist mode of organizing could not have been more timely, for the same conference was torn apart by dissent over the organization of NAC itself. One of the presidential candidates withdrew from the race, and staff members resigned, criticizing the back-room politics and bureaucratic and hierarchical structures that "leave women feeling battered." Delegates railed against the rigidity of timed agendas and the particular rules of order that seem to reinforce a hierarchical, head-table mode of organizing that silences many women.

NAC is currently going through the agonizing process of organizational review, trying to find ways to incorporate feminist principles into this unwieldy umbrella organization representing hundreds of women's groups across Canada. NAC has a long way to go to reach Kvennalistinn standards. It must work within the difficult context of a bilingual, multi-ethnic, geographically dispersed organization, many times bigger than Kvennalistinn. But perhaps the crisis in 1988 will provide the impetus needed to begin the move toward a more feminist mode of organizing.

Traditional or Radical Marxism?

Measured against such alternative visions, the discourse of the radical left often fails. The goal of socialist revolution, when defined in economic class terms, only promises to repeat the problems in a different form. Smith and Malnarich (1983) hint at the limitations of traditional Marxist thought when they ask, Where are the women in socialist and communist political organizations? Unions have historically regarded women as competitors rather than partners. In contemporary leftist organizations, women comprise about half the membership but are excluded from almost all leadership positions. They are not included in theoretical work. They are absent from political education and propaganda structures and from journal and newspaper editorial boards, and they are rarely involved in political analysis.

Why is this so? Smith and Malnarich reject the organization language that offers apathy as the explanation. They point to the triple workload of women militants. Like men in the movement, women often combine wagework with political work, but they also do housework: the caring and nurturing work; the production and reproduction of people; the financial, material, and emotional maintenance of the family. Smith and Malnarich suggest that militant men are mostly too busy to help out at home, and they almost never share responsibilities fully. Smith and Malnarich root the problem in socialist ideology itself, which defines family and personal life as a private, non-political matter and ignores the interconnection between production and reproduction. In effect, socialists are reproducing capitalist relations in their own organization. They define the working class as those who sell their labour, thus excluding women and children and perpetuating the fragmentation within the working class itself.

The implication of this study is that traditional Marxism needs to merge with feminism before it can hope to offer an alternative that will not turn out to be more of the same with new masters. This, of course, raises the question of the type of feminism with which Marxism should be aligned.

Liberal Versus Radical Feminism: The Risk of Co-optation

In Ferguson's view, the central threat to feminism is the risk of co-optation. She suggests that earlier waves of feminism were defused by the expanding bureaucratic society. The first wave radically challenged the **cult of domesticity**, which rationalized the exclusion of women from the public world. Women argued that their domestic skills and experience provided ideal training for careers in politics, teaching, social services, and other spheres of life. This radicalism, however, became muted into **liberalism** and **consumerism**. The collective movement among women was abandoned in favour of defining female independence in terms of personal fulfillment (Ferguson 1984, 49–51, 179–82). Meanwhile, the demands placed on private life to satisfy all human needs steadily increased as public, bureaucratized life became more emotionally barren.

The second wave of feminism pressured for equality in terms of legal rights. Ferguson suggests that late capitalism's answer to this challenge has been more bureaucracy and the cult of rationality. Feminism raises a radical critique against bureaucracy as an inhuman form of organization, but this critique risks being reduced to a concern with eliminating barriers to women's equal representation in executive positions. This focus on individualism and equality rights for women is important in changing the predominantly male character of bureaucracies, but it promises little real change in the structures that create oppression. The problem is how to be heard in a bureaucratic society when bureaucracy itself appears as the problem.

Ferguson challenges the legal equality approach to feminism on two counts. First, she rejects the belief in individual upward mobility as "the illusion of the epoch"

(Ferguson 1984, 183–92). The message of all the how-to books for women is fundamentally the same: conformity. Women are taught to see their careers in totally bureaucratic images, that is, in terms of hierarchy and fast-track mobility rather than in terms of the intrinsic meaning or value of actions. People are seen as competitors for scarce resources, and co-operation is defined in largely instrumental terms. The price of individual mobility is thus absolute capitulation to the bureaucratic system, with no prospect for change.

The second illusion for Ferguson is the focus on abstract legal rights. On the one hand, this is essential to guarantee access of women to institutions and to legal protection. But on the other hand, it can lead to acceptance of the bureaucratic game. Women are absorbed into the structures rather than fighting against them. The gender-class job ghettos may begin to crack, but the bureaucratic class hierarchy itself remains largely intact.

Lise Gotell (1987) raises exactly this issue when she suggests that the efforts of the Canadian women's movement to attain equality rights in the Canadian Charter of Rights, and to retain those rights against the Meech Lake Accord, may end up distorting the movement itself. She fears that so much effort will go into pressuring for legal equality that the need for more fundamental social reform to make such equality meaningful will be overlooked. Equality risks being translated into empty legal definitions. This analysis has been criticized because legal equality is so important as the basis for everything else. But it is crucial to be aware that the radical feminist critique can slip into liberal feminist concerns for integration on equal terms with men in a system that fundamentally "hurts, twists, and damages people and human possibilities" (Ferguson 1984, xii).

There are signs of this in Canada as women's issues become translated in terms of career equality with men and bureaucratized, institutionalized child care by

experts. In 1987 when the federal government announced small increases in financial support for day care, a strong feminist voice argued that this money should be channelled into training day-care workers and setting up accredited centres. Beneath this important concern for standards and for places is the unspoken assumption that quality care can and should be measured in terms of formal credentials and government-licensed institutions. The natural expertise of mothers who have raised their own children and who earn money by caring for the children of others is discounted in favour of institutionalized credentials. The people who will teach the new credentials come from the disciplines—early childhood education, child psychology, social work—that were so feared by Foucault and Ferguson. The real need for child care might be translated into total bureaucratic control with children required to be placed in day care from very early ages, as they are now required to attend school, unless their parents are trained child care specialists. There is the risk that careers for women and bureaucratized day care for children will silence the last bastion of authentic alternative discourse in this world where "the increasing organization of everything is the central issue of our time" (Foucault in Dreyfus and Rabinow 1982, xxii).

This bureaucratic interference in the lives of people now has the potential to precede birth. A Royal Commission has been called in Canada to examine the implications of issues involving in vitro fertilization or "test tube babies." Scientists now have the technology to screen such embryos genetically before they are implanted in their mothers' wombs. Those whose genes indicate that they will develop inherited abnormalities, such as haemophilia, are discarded. One doctor involved in the development of this technology argues that, in the future, couples who choose not to avail themselves of this screening procedure, and who give birth to disabled children, should be held criminally negligent (Pappert 1989).

Some critics suggest that resistance to the bureaucratic co-optation of feminism itself implies a return to the cult of domesticity and women being limited to the private sphere. It is clear, however, that neither of these options is acceptable. What we need is a more fundamental re-integration of private and public spheres so as to obliterate the artificial barriers between family and productive work, between women and men, between childhood and adulthood. The objective is not to bureaucratize families so as to minimize their interference with traditional careers, but to humanize other spheres of life.

Much of the work to date in women's studies has focussed on making visible women's domestic work. Smith (1987b) urges us to look beyond this traditional focus to recognize that what women are doing is far, far more important than merely domestic work. In this deeply fragmented, irrational culture, what women are doing is nothing less than holding the entire system together.

Men's Liberation

There remains one more potential voice of radical resistance to our bureaucratized world: the voice of **men's liberation**. It is a voice as yet far more deeply subjugated than feminism. In a world so obviously patriarchal, with men in general so obviously occupying superior positions over women in all spheres of life, it is hard even to conceive that men might need liberation. Many men fail to see what else they could want, except perhaps to have their cake and eat it; that is, to retain their dominance within all formal institutions while having richer private lives as well. But the need for men's liberation cannot be so easily dismissed.

The evidence of wife battering and child abuse and the mounting complaints by women that men typically fail to take any responsibility for emotional relationships, plus the evidence of mounting violence on the streets, can be viewed in two not incompatible ways. Women can be seen as victims of patriarchal power, vented increasingly against those women who do not follow traditional roles. Alternatively, such trends can be seen as evidence of the overwhelmingly destructive nature of the bureaucratized world in which most men make their lives. They indicate how severely men are being hurt, twisted, blunted, and dehumanized.

Men's liberation seeks to redefine what it means to be male and to challenge the separation of men from those aspects of life that involve nurturing, caregiving, and reproduction of life itself. It strives for a radical change of structures that now reward competition, aggression, manipulation, and mastery over the material world, and the absence of emotion, at the expense of what it means to be human.

From this perspective, radical feminism and men's liberation have the same goal: the radical demolition of the bureaucratized, hierarchical, specialized, rule-bound, conformist society. Weber's formal rationality has become what he feared it would: an emotional wasteland, an iron cage. The radical critique reveals the fundamental irrationality of western civilization. This critique demands the unity of cultural, emotional, and spiritual elements of purposive action and rejects their segregation into private and public, or feminine and masculine, spheres of life. A social order based on fragmentation does not and cannot provide a meaningful life for the majority of people.

Conclusion

Weber's vision of bureaucracy as an iron cage that imprisons people remains centrally relevant to contemporary industrial society, both communist and capitalist. Bureaucratic organization seems so pervasive that trying to avoid its influence would be tantamount to withdrawing from society itself. Sociological analysis is still far from grasping the full complexity of the processes involved in such organization.

Bureaucratic society has not emerged entirely as Weber conceptualized. Functionalist theory is based on Weber's ideal-type model of bureaucracy as a system of regulations that ensures the efficient co-ordination of specialized activities for given ends. This model has been discredited by evidence that the rigid formal structures associated with bureaucracy undermine co-operation and stifle initiative and innovation. Yet functionalist analysis cannot be easily dismissed. It may be the most popular perspective in sociology precisely because it comes closest to expressing how people feel about themselves in bureaucratic society. The functionalist model of society, which sees individual role incumbents as socialized to conform to expected norms of behaviour, articulates for people their everyday experience of fragmented and ordered lives that bureaucratic processes generate.

Conflict theory is rooted in the structuralist–Marxist tradition that places capitalist relations of production at the centre of analysis. The most important contribution of conflict theory has been to demonstrate that bureaucratic modes of organization have more to do with capitalist control over a reluctant workforce than with efficiency of performance. This strength, however, may also be its limitation. The focus on capitalism has been criticised as too rigid to explore the complexity of bureaucratic power relations that do not stem from ownership of the means of production in the classic sense.

Emerging forms of analysis in the interpretive tradition push this criticism still further. Relations of power and control remain central to the analysis of bureaucratic society, but they are conceptualized in a radically different way from that of Marxist theory. Power is seen as flowing not from the elite down, but from the bottom up. Power is realized in the everyday activities of people at work, in the details of how records are kept and forms filled in, in how language is structured, and in the forms of talk through which we make sense of what people do. Interpretive theory challenges the myth of the machine, the external bureaucratic structure that engulfs people. Yet at the same time, the theory manifests the awesome power of language and bureaucratic thought, through which rationality itself becomes a trap.

The social sciences form part of the relations of power to the extent that their theories legitimate and perpetuate forms of language and thought that trap people. Theories provide accounts of what people do in terms of external structures that are rational and efficient or powerful and inevitable. To challenge such accounts seems to challenge reason. The possibility of resistance lies in new forms of discourse and radically different conceptions of power and human potential. Contemporary sociology is perhaps both part of the problem and part of the solution. It contributes to the iron cage of bureaucratic rationality. At the same time, it offers the capacity to analyse and to question and thus the possibility of resistance and change.

Suggested Reading

A dated but very straightforward statement of the functionalist view of bureaucracy is the article by Talcott Parsons, "Suggestions for a Sociological Approach to the Theory of Organizations" (1956). Parsons presents a short, clear model of how such organizations are supposed to work.

An old but brief and clear critique of Weber's model of bureaucracy from the perspective of structuralist Marxism is by Alvin Gouldner, "On Weber's Analysis of Bureaucratic Rules" (1952). Gouldner shows how the meticulous statement of regulations and duties that characterize the ideal-type bureaucracy applies only to the obligations that workers owe to an organization. The rules specifying the duties and responsibilities of the organization toward the worker are rarely spelled out so clearly. Unions had to fight for these in separate contracts.

Stephen Marglin's article, "What Bosses Do" (1974–75), argues that the rise of factories, where workers were brought together under the supervision of a boss, long preceded the invention of heavy machinery that made collective factory work necessary. He argues that the purpose of factories was to control workers, not to make efficient use of new technology.

The book by Kathy Ferguson, *The Feminist Case Against Bureaucracy* (1984), is an excellent feminist study of Foucault's view of bureaucratic society. This book is very heavy reading and not easy to understand. It is perhaps best used as a reference work for additional information on certain sections of her analysis that are referred to in this chapter.

A more readable and entertaining look at life within a bureaucracy is Rosabeth Moss Kanter's *Men and Women of the Corporation* (1977). Kanter delights in showing up the status games that go on in relations between male bosses and their female secretaries and among male managers vying for prestigious office space. Kanter also provides a very perceptive view of how bureaucracy carries over into the private family lives of employees.

For a view of how bureaucracies help to create what passes as knowledge, see Gail Tuchman, *Making News: A Study of the Social Construction of Reality* (1978). Tuchman describes how reporters rely very heavily upon official spokespersons from bureaucracies to provide much of what they report as factual information.

Epilogue

It is not easy to foresee the directions in which sociology may develop. The only safe prediction is that the sociology of the future will not be the same as the past. The theoretical perspectives of functionalism and structuralist Marxism that have dominated the discipline until recently seem to be in retreat. Contemporary theory is moving away from the analysis of structures and their functions to a concern with processes through which people collectively produce and make sense of their social world. Feminist theory has shattered the myth of scientific objectivity and neutrality and is forcing the re-evaluation of much that has been thought of as fact or revealed truth about human behaviour.

The diversity of theoretical perspectives and the frequently heated debates between sociologists committed to different approaches are indications of the healthy state of sociology as a scientific discipline. As we noted in chapter 1, controversy is a precondition for creative research. The best test of any theoretical explanation is an alternative theory that makes different assumptions and thus generates different kinds of research. In every area of sociology, established assumptions about how social structures function are being challenged and revised by new research prompted by Marxist, feminist, and interpretive perspectives. These competing approaches simultaneously challenge each other. The conceptual barriers between them are breaking down as basic assumptions are modified to accommodate new knowledge.

The central objective of this text has been to introduce these controversies within sociology in an organized way, through exploring the different theoretical assumptions and their implications for research across different social issues. It will have achieved its goal if you come away from the course with a greater critical capacity to question your own experiences of your social world and to participate actively in sociology as critical readers of theory and research.

Glossary

There are many terms in sociology that do not have standard meanings. They are used differently depending on the theoretical perspective of the writer. The definitions suggested below provide a guide to the meaning of terms as they are used in this text. They are not definitive in the sense of specifying how such terms are utilized in all sociological writing. Many theoretical concepts require extensive explanation to capture their full meaning. The best way to understand terms in sociology is to see how they are used in context. There is little value in trying to memorize definitions.

Absolute surplus For Marx, the amount of surplus production available when workers are driven to work as hard as possible and given the lowest possible standard of living.

Abstract labour time Marx uses this term to refer to the average amount of time it takes to produce a given commodity in a society with a given level of technology and knowledge.

Accounting/Accountability In ethnomethodology, these terms refer to the ways in which people use their common-sense knowledge and background understandings to make sense to themselves and to one another of what is going on.

Acculturation The process through which newcomers learn and adopt the prevailing attitudes and values of the group or society that they are entering.

Achieved characteristics Characteristics that one earns by learning skills or gaining credentials.

Actor In functionalism, the conception of a person as a role player within a system of roles.

Adaptation Parsons uses this term to refer to securing needed resources for an activity and distributing them among the people involved.

Adjacency pairs This term is used in conversation analysis to refer to aspects of the structure of typical, orderly conversations. One expects that a certain kind of comment by a participant in a conversation will immediately be followed by a corresponding comment from another participant (i.e., that a question will be followed by an answer).

Advanced capitalism For Marxist theorists, an economic order in which national and international markets are dominated by huge corporations rather than characterized by competition among entrepreneurs.

Advanced communism An economic system where all the important means of production in a society—land, factories, technology—are communally owned. Everyone shares access to them and everyone labours collectively according to their ability to meet the collective needs of the community.

Affective-rational action A term used by Weber to refer to action oriented to emotions.

Affectivity/Affective neutrality Parsons uses these terms to refer to the amount of emotion that should properly be displayed in a given role.

Affirmative action Action taken as part of a policy designed to increase the representation of members of specified groups deemed to be disadvantaged or underrepresented in certain positions relative to their numbers within the population as a whole.

Agribusiness The network of international corporations that controls production, processing, transport, storage, and financing of agriculture.

Alienation Marx uses this term to refer to the dehumanizing character of social relations, particularly under capitalism. The term is used more generally to describe a syndrome or combination of characteristics including powerlessness, meaninglessness, isolation, and self-estrangement.

Altruism Regard for others as a principle of action. Also, a readiness to put the interests of other members of society or those of society as a whole over personal interests.

Altruistic suicide The form of suicide committed by people who are so intensely integrated into their social group or community that they are willing to sacrifice themselves for the good of that community.

Anomic division of labour For Durkheim, a forced specialization that is experienced as unjust or as not regulated by reference to a clear and meaningful system of values.

Anomic suicide The form of suicide committed by people who have lost any clear sense of values that regulate and give meaning to their lives.

Anomie In general this refers to a breakdown in moral order. Durkheim uses the term to refer to the experience of a relative absence or confusion of values and a corresponding lack of meaningful regulations or a clear position and objectives in life.

Anomie theory of crime A theory developed by Merton, which attributes variations in propensity for criminal behaviour to the discrepancy between culturally valued goals and access to socially approved means to achieve them.

Anticipatory socialization The process of imagining future roles and so learning the appropriate behavioural expectations in advance of actually performing the roles.

Anti-semitism Prejudice against Jews.

Antithesis See Dialectic; Dialectical materialism.

Apparatus of ruling A term developed by Smith to refer to the organized activities that form part of the overall mechanisms for control in a society, including the activities of individual people who work in government offices and the forms and regulations that guide their behaviour.

Ascriptive characteristics/Ascription Refers to the characteristics with which we are born, such as age, sex, height, and racial or ethnic background.

Assimilation The process through which individuals or groups of people lose their distinctive ethnic or minority group patterns of behaviour and values and adopt the values and behavioural expectations of the dominant group.

Authoritarian Favouring obedience to authority, rather than individual liberty, as a fundamental value.

Autocracy Rule from above, without democratic participation.

Automation Mechanical or electronic control of a process.

Average labour time For Marx, the typical amount of time it takes a worker to produce a particular commodity with the technology that prevails in a given society.

Background understandings In ethnomethodology, the knowledge that competent participants in an activity or conversation can be expected to have, which allows the activity or conversation to be understandable to them without any further explanation.

Base A term used by Marx to refer to the social relations of production.

Behaviour organism For Parsons, the human biological organism, which provides the fundamental energy and drive for activity and links the social system with the physical environment.

Biological-genetic theory of race The theory that people with different skin colours evolved from distinct subspecies of humans and that they have innately different levels of intelligence and other attributes.

Bourgeoisie Those who own capital, or the means of production, and who hire wage labourers to produce commodities for sale in order to make profits; capitalists.

Branch-plant economy A society in which a significant proportion of all business enterprises are branch plants; that is, subsidiaries of multinational corporations with headquarters in another country.

Breaching experiments A methodological approach in ethnomethodology that involves disturbing what the researcher thinks might be an unquestioned or taken-for-granted rule of normal behaviour in order to test the extent to which that normal behaviour is subsequently disturbed.

Bureaucracy Generally, a formal organization characterized by a hierarchical chain of command and precisely delimited roles and responsibilities governed by written rules. For Foucault and Ferguson, bureaucracy constitutes the scientific organization of inequality through which people are dominated and oppressed. See Disciplinary society; Iron cage.

Bureaucratic discourse Foucault uses the term to refer to a form of talk that translates all human concerns and human interaction into narrow technical language relevant for organizational purposes and for predefined classifications that relate to the specialized work of officials.

Bureaucratic language Description of human interaction in terms of technical jargon referring to regulations defining responsibilities of role incumbents in organizations, often for the purpose of obfuscation.

Bureaucratic society For Foucault, a society in which bureaucracy is the all-pervasive mode of social organization. See Disciplinary society.

Business-class immigrant A category within the Immigration Act that refers to people who have capital to invest in Canadian industries and businesses and can provide guarantees that they will create employment opportunites in Canada.

Calvinism Weber uses the term to refer to the religious doctrine of John Calvin, which advocates a sober, frugal lifestyle and a disciplined obligation to work as a means to serve God. It emphasizes the doctrine of predestination: that salvation is attainable by God's grace alone and that the identity of those who will be saved is known by God from the beginning of life.

Capital The stock with which a company or person enters into business. The means of production. The accumulated wealth used in producing commodities.

Capitalism A system of production in which capital, or the means of production, is privately owned by a small, elite class of people. The mass of people have no direct access to means of producing for their own needs. They depend on selling their capacity to labour to those who own the means of production.

Capitalists Owners of capital or the means of production who hire wage labourers to produce commodities for sale. The bourgeoisie.

Capitalization The expansion in the amount of wealth invested in a business in order for it to remain competitive. Undercapitalized enterprises are those with insufficient investment in technology to remain competitive in the market.

Causal pluralism For Weber, a research strategy that involves searching for multiple causes for social phenomena.

Census/Census data Data obtained through comprehensive surveys of the entire population of a country, carried out with government funding and commonly with the force of law to compel people to answer the questions.

Charismatic authority For Weber, authority legitimated by the extraordinary gifts or supernatural powers that the leader appears to have.

Chicago School A theoretical and methodological approach to urban sociology associated with the University of Chicago during the late 1920s and 1930s. An approach that emphasized the three variables of size, density, and cultural heterogeneity as critical determinants of the character of social life.

Circles of social control The mechanisms by which conformity is produced, including guilt, desire for approval, economic sanctions, and force.

Class Generally, the location in a hierarchically stratified workforce, commonly divided into a set of ranked categories, on the basis of relative income and level of education or skill required. Alternatively, the location within a bureaucratic organization as defined by job classification schemes. Marx defined class as location in relation to the means of production, mostly as owners and non-owners, with some intermediate classes. Weber expanded Marx's definition to refer to differential life chances and the chance to use property, goods, and services for exchange in a competitive market.

Class-for-itself In Marxist theory, the collectivity of members of a class who recognize their shared class position and come together to act in their class interests.

Class-in-itself Marx uses the term as a theoretical concept referring to all people who share the same relationship to the means of production (i.e., capitalists as the class of all owners).

Class reductionism The thesis that inequalities associated with gender, ethnicity, or race can be explained by class interests.

Class struggle The conflict between those who own the means of production and those who do not. For Marx this is a dynamic process of struggle by which working people most disadvantaged by the existing relations of production struggle to change those relations.

Cohort Persons banded together for the purposes of analysis, particularly on the basis of being born during the same period of time.

Colonialism The process of establishing settlements in a conquered territory with the administration of such settlements fully or partially subject to control by the conquering state.

Commodity Anything produced for exchange and not for use by the producer.

Commodity fetishism The tendency to attribute causal agency to commodities exchanged in the marketplace, as if the commodities determined relations between people.

Common-sense understandings Assumptions about how and why things work the way they do, based on immediate, personal experience.

Communism See Advanced communism; Primitive communism.

Community A body of people living in the same locality. Alternatively, a sense of identity and belonging shared among people living in the same locality. Also, the set of social relations found in a particular bounded area.

Competitive advantage Special conditions prevailing in certain areas that enable businesses to produce certain kinds of commodities more cheaply than they can be produced elsewhere.

Conflict theory The study of society, or specific elements of society, conceptualized as made up of parts held together by hierarchical relations of power and dependency. Conflict is seen as endemic.

Conformist A category in Merton's anomie theory of crime. One who accepts socially valued goals and socially approved means to achieve them.

Conglomerate mergers The consolidation of diverse industries within one corporation.

Conscience collective For Durkheim, the totality of beliefs and sentiments common to the average citizens of the same society. The French term is translated into English in two ways. Collective conscience refers to the collective sense of what is morally right and wrong. Collective consciousness refers to a sense of belonging and commitment to a collectivity or community of people.

Consensus In cultural Marxism, a kind of one-dimensional or group thinking manipulated by mass media and the professions to ensure that the values and behaviour expectations of the ruling class will prevail. See Ideological hegemony.

Conservative A vague term used in a variety of ways. Generally, one who is disposed to maintain existing social institutions and to oppose efforts to change or reform them.

Conspicuous consumption Buying and displaying expensive items in order to demonstrate wealth and so enhance one's social status.

Consumerism The high value placed on the ownership or purchase of goods as a means of attaining personal happiness and as a measure of personal success and well-being.

Content analysis A methodological approach that involves the organized counting of content of written materials in relation to predefined categories that are determined by the theoretical hypothesis.

Contradictions of capitalism For Marx, the thesis that the capitalist system of production necessarily works in such a way that it generates problems that become steadily more disruptive for production as the system evolves. Eventually, capitalism is destined to collapse under its own internal problems.

Conversation analysis A theoretical approach within the broad perspective of ethnomethodology that explores the typical ways in which talk is structured by participants.

Core-periphery model A theoretical model of social change that assumes that all innovation occurs in major urban, industrial centres and slowly affects otherwise relatively static and backward rural areas.

Corporate capitalism An economic system in which huge business enterprises are able to dominate the market and substantially influence or determine the supply and price of many commodities.

Correlation A statistical term referring to the degree to which change in one variable is associated with change in another variable.

Correspondence theory This theory, developed by Bowles and Gintis, posits that the pattern of social relations established in one institution (i.e., schools) parallels in critical respects the pattern of social relations established in another institution (i.e., industry).

Counterculture A system of norms and values held by members of a subgroup or class within a society that contradicts or opposes a significant number of the norms and values that prevail within the society as a whole.

Countervailing duties Import taxes that one country imposes on certain commodities from another country to compensate for subsidies that the exporting country has given to producers of the commodities.

Credentialism In Marxist theory, the thesis that formal qualifications are emphasized by capitalists to create artificial division and competition among workers rather than because such qualifications are essential for performance of particular jobs.

Critical literacy The capacity to reflect upon and to question the content of what one reads.

Critical sociology Any sociological theory or research that challenges the legitimacy of the established social order and that seeks to understand the workings of that society as a basis for action to change it.

Cult of domesticity A set of attitudes and values that justifies the segregation of women in the private realm of the home.

Cult of rationality Justification of everything by reference to the supposedly objective principles of scientific and technical efficiency.

Cultural imperialism The practice of one country imposing its cultural values on another. A form of ideological hegemony.

Cultural lag The failure or excessive slowness of prevailing values and norms in a society to adapt to economic changes associated with technological innovation.

Cultural Marxism Closely associated with the social construction of reality perspective, this is a variant of Marxist theory that emphasizes ideological hegemony rather than the determining force of capitalist structures in explaining social relations in capitalist societies.

Cultural system In functionalism, the system of beliefs, rituals, values, and symbols, including language as a symbol system, through which people confront ultimate questions about reality, the meaning of good and evil, suffering and death.

Culture The set of shared ideas about what constitutes ideal behaviour within a given society.

Culture of domination A system of values and behavioural expectations that condones or legitimates subordination of the mass of people to autocratic rule.

Culture of poverty thesis The thesis that poverty is caused or perpetuated by the attitudes and values of poor people, which inhibit them from taking action to ameliorate their situation.

Cybernetic hierarchy For Parsons, a hierarchy of systems of control and communication in human action.

Deferred gratification Foregoing immediate pleasures or rewards in order to work toward greater future rewards.

Defining the situation In symbolic interaction and ethnomethodology, the process of negotiating the meaning of what seems to be going on.

Demography/Demographic The study of vital statistics of a population, including such information as population size, births, marriages, deaths, migration, and so on.

Dependency theory A theory that the poverty evident in the Third World and in poorer regions of developed economies is generated and perpetuated through systematic exploitation by developed capitalist economies.

Dependent capitalism The experience of capitalist development in Third World countries caught in an already highly advanced corporate capitalist world system.

Dependent commodity producers A class of workers who own their own means of production of certain commodities but who are controlled by the corporate monopoly processors and distributors who dominate the market for what they produce. See also Petite bourgeoisie.

Dependent development The restricted pattern of development within a region or country where the economy is controlled externally by capitalist metropolises that develop the locality only as a resource hinterland. See Dependency theory.

Deskilling The process of breaking down a complex operation or activity into simple component operations that can be easily learned.

Destructuralism A theoretical perspective that begins from the assumption that there are no structures in society beyond the ways in which people talk about and account for what they are doing and what is happening. It explores what people do to produce and to maintain the conceptualizations or accounts of reality that they hold.

Determinism Any thesis that sees human activity as caused or controlled by forces independent of human choice or will. See Economic determinism.

Deviance Behaviour that does not conform to behavioural expectations prevailing in a given group or community.

Dialectic Recurrent cycles of thesis, antithesis, and synthesis. Thesis refers to the original idea, philosophy, or system of thought.

Antithesis represents the logical inconsistencies, problems, and anomalies within the thesis. The synthesis is a new system of ideas, thought, or philosophy that resolves these contradictions.

Dialectical materialism The application of dialectical reasoning to the organization of production. Thesis represents the existing organization of production. The antithesis refers to the tensions or problems that impede or shackle the full productive potential of this organization. The synthesis is a new form of organization of production that overcomes these problems and unleashes the full productive potential of the available means of production.

Dialectical method The application of dialectical thinking to a given problem, clarifying the original situation, explicating the contradictions inherent in it, and seeking a synthesis or new approach that will resolve these contradictions.

Differential association theory A theory that attributes variation in propensity for criminal behaviour to relative closeness of involvement with others whose subcultural values condone criminal behaviour.

Differential opportunity theory A theory that attributes variation in propensity for criminal behaviour to the relative availability of legitimate or illegitimate means to achieve valued goals. See Innovator.

Differentiation Generally, the process of becoming less alike as the result of performing more specialized social roles. Spencer uses this term to refer to the breakdown of simple, unspecialized structures into many separate parts.

Diffuse obligations The perceived right of others, such as close family members, to expect a variety of services and support.

Disciplinary society The term is used by Foucault to refer to social order maintained through power based on intimate knowledge and regulation of individuals rather than on punitive sanctions.

Discipline Foucault uses this term to refer both to orderly conduct and to a branch of knowledge.

Discourse For Foucault, how we come to talk about our social world, which determines how it comes to be known to us and to have the form that it does.

Distributive justice The quality of fairness in the distribution of rewards or resources among participants in a situation or activity.

Divide and rule The policy of encouraging schisms within a mass of subordinate people to reduce the likelihood of concerted action by subordinates, thus making them easier to control.

Documentary construction of reality For Smith, a theoretical approach that focusses on how the seemingly neutral language of bureaucratic forms and categories actively structures social relations and what comes to be seen as factual information.

Documentary method of interpretation In ethnomethodology, the active search for patterns in the vague flux of everyday interaction, as a fundamental element of practical, everyday reasoning. This search is based on the premise that there is always an underlying pattern to everyday activity or conversation. Surface appearances are treated as evidence of, or as documenting, this presumed underlying pattern.

Dogmatism An authoritarian assertion of opinion.

Doing hierarchy In ethnomethodology, the actual practices of people in ongoing social interaction that produce and reproduce the experience of some individuals as inferior or superior to others.

Domestic labour debate A body of theory concerned with where and how homemakers fit into the capitalist economic system.

Dominant culture The set of values and behavioural expectations that prevails in a given society and that legitimates and supports the activities that directly benefit the dominant class. In capitalist society, the dominant culture is that which legitimates the activities of the capitalist class in the pursuit of profit.

Dominant values The values of the powerful class that tend to prevail within a society.

Domination In ethnic relations, the state of one ethnic group exerting regularized and institutionalized rule over other ethnic groups.

Dormitory suburbs Suburbs where there are minimal opportunities for paid labour. Members of the paid labour force work elsewhere during the day and return in the evening.

Double standard The standard for behaviour that is applied unevenly within a group or community such that given behaviour will be criticized and condemned if practised by one sector of a community but considered acceptable when practised by others.

Dowry murder A new bride murdered by her husband or his family because the amount of goods or money that the woman brought to the marriage is deemed inadequate. Dowry murder allows the husband to remarry to collect additional dowry.

Dramaturgical model Goffman's theoretical approach that studies how people creatively act out particular social roles in a manner analogous to how actors in a play creatively interpret their script.

Dynamic equilibrium In functionalist theory, the maintenance of balance and order between elements of a society by systematically adjusting for change in one element by complementary changes in other related elements.

Dysfunctions Effects or consequences of any given structure or pattern of behaviour that are damaging for some other element or for people in the wider social system.

Ecological fallacy A logically false or misleading argument that attempts to draw inferences about individuals from aggregate data.

Economic determinism A form of theorizing that reifies the abstract concept of an economic system, such that the system of production is held to cause or to determine all major aspects of social life, without reference to human agency.

Economies of scale A principle of economics that asserts that as the size of a business enterprise increases, the cost of producing any one unit of output decreases.

Ego In psychoanalytic theory, the conscious self that seeks to express and to realize fundamental drives and passions.

Egoism For Durkheim, a value system that places self-interest at the centre. Also, systematic selfishness, reflecting the absence of a sense of social bonds and commitment to other people.

Egoistic suicide The form of suicide committed by individuals who have lost any sense of social bonds linking them to other people.

Embourgeoisement thesis The thesis that, under capitalism, working-class people will become or are becoming steadily wealthier to the point that their lifestyles closely resemble those of professional middle-class people.

Emotional labour The work of managing facial expressions and manipulating the emotional responses of clients as part of one's job.

Empiricism A commitment to and quest for knowledge based on observation and experiment.

Enclosure Feudal landlords' practice of fencing off huge tracts of arable land for sheep pastures thereby depriving serfs of access to land for subsistence crops.

Enumeration In survey research, the process of counting the total membership of a particular set of people from which a sample is to be drawn.

Equality of condition A policy that stresses sameness. In education, it means that a standardized age-graded curriculum be available for all students regardless of individual ability or interests.

Equality of opportunity A policy that, in principle, gives all individuals an equivalent chance to compete for social positions that carry relatively higher rewards. See Meritocracy thesis.

Equilibrium In functionalism, the maintenance of balance and order between elements of a society over long periods of time.

Ethic of responsibility For Weber, moral principles that take account of the probable consequences of actions.

Ethic of ultimate ends A term used by Weber to refer to morality based on obedience to religious doctrine or to what is perceived as the will of God, or some absolute value, regardless of the consequences.

Ethnic/Ethnicity Identity as a member of a distinctive cultural group associated with a particular country or region of origin. Social constructionists argue that ethnicity is used as an ideology that blames differences and inequalities caused by discriminatory treatment of certain people on intrinsic personal characteristics of the victims.

Ethnocentrism A belief that one's culture or way of life is superior to others. An exaggerated view of the quality and correctness of the culture of one's own group. A self-centred view of social life lacking respect for the different perspectives or values of other people.

Ethnomethodology A theoretical approach that focusses on micro-interactions and explores the methods or practical reasoning that individuals use to make sense of what is going on around them. Ethnomethodologists argue that the process of formulating an account of what is happening produces reality for the practical purposes of participants.

Evolution A theory positing that society developed from simple undifferentiated societies into highly complex industrial society in a way analogous to evolution in the natural world where single-cell organisms evolved into complex advanced organisms.

Exchange value For Marx, the amount of human labour time that goes into the production of a commodity. The value of one commodity relative to another is measured by the labour time needed to make the commodities.

Experiment A methodological approach that, ideally, holds constant everything that might influence the phenomenon of interest and then allows one variable to change in a controlled manner. Any subsequent change observed in the phenomenon of interest is then attributed to the influence of the manipulated variable.

Expressive leader One who is primarily responsible for relieving tensions and smoothing social relations in a group.

Extended family A family in which several generations of kin live in the same home.

Extrinsic rewards Payment or other benefits received for doing some activity. The opposite of intrinsic rewards.

Fact Datum. That which is known as the result of empirical investigation conducted according to objective scientific methods of observation and experiment. Also, that which is attested to be correct by an appropriate official within a formal organization. Ethnomethodologists use the term to describe that which a group of scientists agrees to be a plausible way of accounting for particular data. See also Social fact.

False consciousness The condition of some members of the working class who fail to understand their true or objective long-term class interests to the extent that they are predisposed to support a system of production that exploits them.

Familism Particularly close attachment to kin, and high value placed on family membership, combined with generally shallow relations with non-kin.

Family-class immigrant See Sponsored immigrant.

Family factory system The system of production common in the early stages of industrialization whereby all members of a nuclear family were hired together to work in a particular factory.

Family wage The policy of paying male workers sufficient wages to support their wives and children.

Feedback mechanisms The processes through which given structures or patterns of behaviour are selectively reinforced and perpetuated over time.

Feminist movement Collective protest and political action to ameliorate the subordinate situation of women in society.

Feminist theory A perspective that takes as its starting point the situation and experiences of women in questioning the adequacy of any analysis of human behaviour. See also Marxist feminism; Radical feminism.

Fetish An inanimate object worshipped for its supposed magical powers. See Commodity fetishism.

Feudalism/Feudal system An economic system in which land is the primary means of production. Land is owned by a hereditary elite of nobles or lords and is worked by a hereditary class of labourers or serfs who are tied to the land.

Folk society An ideal-type model of isolated rural society.

Fragmentation The subdivision of tasks or responsibilities among workers such that each worker performs highly repetitive and monotonous actions devoid of any intrinsic interest or sense of importance.

Function For functionalists, the basic needs or conditions that must be met by a social system in order to maintain itself in a state of equilibrium. Also, the particular contribution of parts of a social system to the maintenance of the whole system.

Functional indispensability For Parsons, the assumption, borrowed from biology, that every element found within a social system is indispensable for the functioning of that system. Hence, no element can be removed or changed without some negative effect for the system as a whole.

Functional unity For Parsons, the assumption, borrowed from biology, that every element found within a social system has effects or consequences that are good for the entire system.

Functionalism/Structural functionalism The study of society as a functioning system comprising interdependent institutions or patterned relations that are stable over time, and that perform specialized functions for the whole. The central focus is on how order is maintained between elements of society. Any given pattern of relations or structures within society is explained by reference to the effects or functions that such patterns have for the wider whole.

GAIL model See System prerequisites.

Gatekeepers People who are in a strategic position to transmit or screen out information, especially in the media.

Gemeinschaft A theoretical model of a society as a community of people united by relations of kinship, a strong sense of community identification, and shared values and norms. A community.

Gender The socially constructed component of male and female identity as distinct from biological sex differences. In practice, this distinction is frequently blurred because the line between social and biological differences is itself blurred.

Gender-class Socially constructed location of women and men relative to the organization of the activities of production and reproduction. See also Sexual class, which is often used synonymously with gender-class.

Gender-ethnic-class Location within the occupational hierarchy based on the combination of gender, ethnic background, and marketable job skills.

Gender-role segregation Markedly distinct and non-overlapping roles for typical activities for women and men.

Generalized other A group or class of people whose overall responses to us play an integral part in the development of our own sense of self-identity. Similarly, a class or team of people whose reactions we try to anticipate.

Gesellschaft A theoretical model of an association of people related only by transitory and superfical contacts that are formal, contractual, and specified in character. An association.

Goal attainment For Parsons, establishing priorities among competing goals and mobilizing members involved in a given activity to attain them.

Goal displacement The tendency for groups or organizations set up to achieve some specific objective to shift priorities from this original objective to a concern with maintaining the group or organization itself.

Green revolution A package of scientific developments in agriculture that promises to increase yields.

Headstart program A policy of providing enriched learning experiences for young children from economically and culturally deprived families to help them keep up with the achievements of more advantaged children.

Hidden curriculum That which is taught by the form of teaching rather than by the explicit content of lessons.

Hidden diseconomies The costs or negative consequences of economic activities that are not counted in corporate cost-benefit analyses, because members of the wider society, rather than the enterprise engaging in the activities, suffer from, and pay for, these consequences.

Hierarchy Graded or ranked positions within a society or organization.

Hinterland Underdeveloped areas that supply cheap labour and cheap raw materials or semi-processed goods to developed centres.

Historical materialism For Marx, the thesis that the processes by which people meet their basic subsistence needs constitute the foundation of social organization. Hence, the analysis of social life should begin with the study of prevailing modes of production and the relations that these generate between people.

Historical sociology The study of how human actions generate social structures over time.

Holding company A company that holds sufficient shares in multiple other companies to control their executive boards.

Horizontal integration A corporation that owns or controls all or most stages in the production of a specific commodity, including production and supply of all raw materials, manufacturing, distribution, and retail sales.

Human relations school of management A style of management that gives priority to generating a friendly and relaxed social atmosphere in the workplace, on the assumption that contented workers are more productive. The term can be used pejoratively to refer to management styles that manipulate a friendly social atmosphere among subordinates to divert attention from the deeper reality of exploitation.

Humanism For Durkheim, a form of religion or spirituality in which the central value is devotion to humanity rather than to a divinity.

Hypothesis A prediction made on the basis of a theory.

I and Me Terms used by Mead to refer to two aspects of the individual. The I is the impulsive, spontaneous aspects of self. The Me is learned identity, incorporating the common attitutes and meanings of the group to which one belongs.

Id In psychoanalytic theory, the vast reservoir of unconscious and semiconscious drives and passions, especially sexual drives, that underlie and energize our conscious activities.

Idealism A philosophy that emphasizes ideas and values as the distinctive moving force of human history. The view that all human behaviour entails unique spiritual events that can only be grasped by intuition, not by objective scientific method.

Ideal-type model A theoretical model that is designed to highlight the typical characteristics of the kind of social organization being studied.

Ideographic Explanations based on unique, subjective, intuitive accounts.

Ideological hegemony The capacity of the dominant class to rule through control over prevailing ideas or culture. It ensures that the mass of people accept as legitimate the activities that directly benefit the dominant class.

Ideology Systems of values that justify certain kinds of action or ways of life, sometimes to the detriment of other people. Belief systems that strongly influence the way we see social reality. They tend to sensitize us in certain ways and blind us in others. Dorothy Smith uses the term to describe a method of inquiry about society that results in a systematic means not to see and not to know what is actually happening.

Imperfect competition In economic theory this refers to a situation in which a few giant producers or purchasers of a commodity are able to dominate the market and to act in collusion rather than in competition.

Imperialism The practice of one state extending its sovereignty over another by force, usually for the purpose of economic exploitation.

Imperialism of rationality A form of control over, or manipulation of, people. It is exercized by presenting certain kinds of behaviour as consistent with reason or scientific knowledge, such that any disagreement or resistance seems irrational.

Inclusive language Non-sexist language. Gender-neutral language that does not use masculine nouns and pronouns generically to include feminine forms.

Independent commodity producers A class of workers who own their own means of production of certain commodities, generally referring to people engaged in farming, fishing, and the like. See also Petite bourgeoisie.

Independent immigrant A category under the Immigration Act that refers to people whose entry into Canada is subject to economic requirements and criteria measured by a point system.

Independent variable A factor included in research as a possible cause of some phenomenon of interest. It is treated as known or given for the purpose of the research and not as itself requiring explanation.

Indexicality In ethnomethodology, the context-dependent character of the meaning of words or actions. The thesis that words or gestures always stand for or indicate a broader background and that this background understanding is essential for words to have meanings.

Indicator An observable feature that is used in research to measure a particular concept.

Industrial Revolution The period of transiton associated with the eighteenth century in Europe when the primary means of production changed from land to machines located in factories.

Industrialization Mechanization. The transition from dependence on human and animal energy to fossil fuels. Usually associated with a shift in primary means of production from land to machines located in factories.

Inner city A general term referring to the central residential areas within large cities, usually characterized by high density housing.

Innovator A component of Merton's anomie theory of crime. One who accepts socially valued goals but adopts socially disapproved means to achieve them.

Institutional ethnography A theoretical and methodological approach that studies the active processes through which people construct their social reality through their everyday working activities in a local setting (ethnography). It then links these local dynamics to the wider institutional context that shapes them.

Institutionalization The establishment of certain patterns of behaviour as typical and expected to the point that they are generally taken for granted as appropriate by most members of a society.

Institutions Typical ways of structuring social relations around specific functions or needs of a society.

Instrumental leader One who is concerned with and who directs task performance in a group.

Integration Generally, to combine parts into a whole or to combine individuals into cohesive collectivities. Spencer uses this term to refer to the evolutionary process of developing a central co-ordinating agency, such as state administration, to regulate relations between specialized elements of society. Parsons uses the term to refer to co-ordinating the behaviour of different members or role incumbents in a particular activity and maintaining orderly interrelations between role players.

Intelligence failure Loss of effective control in organizations resulting from distorted or inadequate information.

Interactional competence See Background understandings.

Intercorporate transfers The transfer of goods and services between a parent company and subsidiaries or between subsidiaries of the same parent corporation.

Interlocking directorships A situation where one person serves on the board of directors of two or more companies.

Internalization The process of learning group values and behavioural expectations and wanting to conform to them from an inner sense that they are morally right.

Interpretive sociology A paradigm that focusses on micro-interactions and how people present themselves to each other and come to understand the surface and underlying meanings of their interaction. The perspective includes symbolic interaction and the dramaturgical model. Ethnomethodology is sometimes included with the interpretive perspective, although it is distinct from traditional symbolic interaction. See Verstehen.

Intersubjectivity The capacity of knowing what another person actually intended.

Interviewer bias The interviewer's preconceived opinions or personal characteristics that influence the interaction with the respondent and influence in a measurable way the information being sought.

Invisible hand of the marketplace The thesis that the competition between the mass of sellers, trying to get the best price for their commodities, and the mass of buyers, trying to buy commodities at the cheapest price, will produce the best outcome in the long run without external planning.

Iron cage Weber's vision of bureaucracy as an all-powerful system of organization that would regulate all aspects of individual life.

Iron law of oligarchy The process whereby power within any organization comes to be wielded by a tiny elite minority. A process hypothesized to occur regardless of democratic principles or procedures.

Isolation Absence of a sense of social bonds or belonging with other people. Particularly loss of a sense of loyalty or commitment to one's workplace. See Alienation.

Kin universe The average number of kin with whom an individual remains in regular contact.

Labelling theory An approach that focusses on how stereotypes or fixed mental images are applied to certain kinds of people, particularly by officials in positions of power, and the effects that this application has on the self-concepts and future behaviour of the people so labelled.

Labour-saving technology Machines designed to perform work previously done by people.

Labour theory of value For Marx, the theory that the average labour time that goes into the production of a commodity, with a given level of technology, determines the exchange value of that commodity.

Laissez-faire system An economic system that operates without any government control or regulation. Advocacy of such a system.

Latency See Pattern maintenance.

Latent functions Those effects or consequences of any given structure or pattern of behaviour that are important for maintaining social order but that are not directly recognized by people involved in the behaviour.

Leveraged buy-outs The practice of borrowing money to buy a controlling interest in a firm in the hope that assets so gained will generate sufficient profits to pay off the debt.

Liberalism Generally, a belief in the values of free enterprise and equality of opportunity for individuals to compete for social and economic rewards on the basis of merit. Used in a positive sense, it refers to a willingness to help individuals to overcome disadvantages or to open up opportunities for disadvantaged individuals. Critics use the term to refer to people who advocate piecemeal reform of the social system rather than radical or major changes to social structures. Critics also use the term to describe the tendency to blame inequality on personal merit or personal failings without acknowledging the structural constraints that disadvantage many groups.

Liberal assimilationist values Adherence to the viewpoint that members of ethnic subgroups should think of themselves primarily as individuals rather than group members and should assimilate into mainstream society and take advantage of opportunities as individuals. See Liberalism.

Liberal bourgeois theory A theory that emphasizes the positive aspects of capitalism as an economic system. It is considered by Marxists to constitute the ideology of the bourgeoisie. Also, a thesis that associates capitalism with free enterprise and competitive markets that potentially provide opportunities for all people to improve their standard of living. See Liberalism.

Liberation theology A religious doctrine that holds that the call to achieve social justice is central to the Christian message. See Social gospel movement.

Linear relation An apparent relationship between two variables such that any change in the value of one variable is associated with an equivalent change in another variable.

Localism A sense of close attachment to a locality and close involvement with other people living in the locality.

Looking-glass self For Cooley, the way in which people reflect on how they appear to other people who are important to them, how their appearance is being judged by such people, and the effect of such reflection in feelings of pride or shame.

Lord Under the feudal system, one who controls the estate on which serfs work.

Lumpenproletariat In Marxist theory, unemployed workers who form a reserve army of cheap labour power to be used by capitalists as they require additional labour power.

Macrosociology The analysis of large-scale and long-term social processes, often treated as self-sufficient entities such as state, class, culture, and so on.

Macrovariable A variable that cannot be reduced to micro-elements.

Managerial mentality The thesis that organizations are rational and efficient entities and that people can be regarded as role incumbents and managed to maximize efficiency of cooperative activities. Generally, the endorsement of the viewpoint of managers.

Managerial revolution The thesis that ownership of corporations has become separated from control over them. The belief that managers rather than capitalists run corporations.

Manifest functions The consequences of any given structure or pattern of behaviour that are openly recognized and intended by the people involved in the behaviour.

Marginal workers A class of workers who are frequently unemployed or who can find work only in a succession of temporary and low-paid jobs.

Marxist feminism The theoretical perspective that utilizes the model of the capitalist system and its internal contradictions to explicate the position and roles of women within capitalist society.

Marxist functionalism The modification of functionalist analysis to incorporate notions of power and unequal ability of different individuals and groups to selectively reinforce those social structures that they find beneficial.

Marxist structuralism The theory that utilizes the model of the capitalist system and its internal contradictions as an explanatory framework to account for specific characteristics of contemporary capitalist society.

Mass society A society characterized by a standardized aggregate of people who generally lack any sense of special attachment to a local area or to a local group of people.

Maternal deprivation theory The theory that young children require extensive physical and social contact with their mothers in order to become psychologically well adjusted and hence that all evidence for adult maladjustment, particularly delinquent behaviour, can be explained by inadequate maternal attention.

Matrilineal Ancestry and inheritance through the mother's line.

Matriarchy Social organization in which the mother is the head of the family.

Me See I and Me.

Meaninglessness Absence of a sense of involvement in a worthwhile activity. The term refers particularly to fragmented work where one individual's contribution is so small as to seem worthless. See Alienation.

Mechanical solidarity Durkheim used this term to describe a form of cohesion that is based fundamentally on sameness.

Members' competences See Background understandings.

Men's liberation A social and political movement concerned with challenging stereotypes of masculinity and the associated sex roles that confine men to the public occupational realm.

Mercantilism Trade, particularly referring to the historical period when European countries effectively dominated world trade and amassed great wealth at the expense of less developed countries.

Meritocracy Inequality in social rewards based on individual differences in ability and effort.

Meritocracy thesis In functionalist theory, the thesis that hierarchy and social inequality are accounted for by the need to motivate the more talented and competent individuals to occupy the more important and difficult roles in society.

Metaphysical stage A stage in Comte's model of the evolution of societies. Societies in the metaphysical stage are characterized by a prevailing belief in a single deity. Phenomena are explained by reference to abstract forces or ultimate reality rather than to a multiplicity of spirits.

Methodism A puritanical religious doctrine that stresses spiritual egalitarianism, grace through penitance, strictness in religious practice and moral behaviour, and submission to authority.

Methodological holism The principle that social experiences must be explained in terms of forces that operate at the level of the social system as a whole.

Methodological individualism The theory that social experiences can be reduced to the characteristics of individual people. See Psychological reductionism.

Metropolis The centre of capitalism, which dominates surrounding regions, extracting their economic resources.

Microhistory The study of how personal interaction is shaped over time.

Microsociology The detailed analysis of what people do, say, and think in the actual flow of momentary experience.

Microstructural bias A tendency to concentrate on the internal workings of organizations rather than to examine the effects of wider political and economic forces on them.

Microtranslation strategy The attempt to show how large-scale social structures can be understood as patterns of repetitive micro-interactions.

Military-industrial complex The thesis that there is a close affinity between the interests of the elites within the military and industry.

Military-industrial-political complex The thesis that there is a close affinity between the personnel and the interests of elites within the military and industry and senior ranks of the civil service and government ministries.

Millenium The coming of a period of a thousand years of Christ's reign on earth. Symbolically, a period of exceptionally good government, great happiness, and prosperity.

Misogyny Hatred of women.

Mobility Geographic mobility refers to movement from one locality to another. Social mobility refers to a change in relative status, either up or down the social class hierarchy.

Mode of production Marx uses this term to refer to the prevailing way in which a society transforms the material environment to meet subsistence needs.

Monogamy Having only one mate. Marriage between one man and one woman.

Monolithic bias The assertion that a particular phenomenon is uniform throughout, allowing no variation.

Monopoly Exclusive possession of the trade in some commodity by one individual or one corporation.

Morality Durkheim uses the term to refer to the expression of the relationship between individuals and society.

Multinational corporations Business enterprises that operate in one or more countries in addition to the country housing the corporate headquarters.

Multi-variate analysis An aspect of survey research in which statistical techniques are used to see how sets of variables interact in combination.

National Policy The policy instituted by John A. Macdonald in 1878 to establish high tariffs against American goods entering Canada in order to encourage industrialization in Canada. The effect was that American businesses invested in branch plants within Canada.

Natural attitude This term is used in ethnomethodology to refer to people's tendency to assume that social interaction is meaningful, without their reflecting on how such meaning comes to be perceived and sustained.

Natural laws Statement of a causal relationship between physical phenomena, held to be universally true under given conditions.

Need dispositions Parsons uses this term to refer the way people tend to act in conformity with norms and feel dissatisfied when they cannot do so. Individual choices take the form of patterned behaviour because of the internalization of shared norms.

Neo-imperialism The practice of one country exerting effective control over the economy of another country and exploiting its resources even though it has formal independence.

Nomothetic Law-like generalizations. Deterministic cause and effect relations.

Non-listening syndrome A pattern of response to oppressive instruction by withdrawal from active participation and refusal to pay attention.

Normalization Foucault uses this terms to refer to a manipulated conformity managed by rational social science principles and legitimated by reference to models of healthy psychological and social adjustment. See Therapeutic intervention.

Normative consensus In functionalist theory, this refers to a social group's shared acceptance of a set of values and behavioural expectations as legitimate and appropriate. The establishment of normative consensus is considered critical in the maintenance of a stable social order to which members willingly conform.

Norms Typical expectations for behaviour in given situations that are seen as legitimate and appropriate.

Nuclear family A family unit comprising two sexually cohabiting adults of the opposite sex together with their dependent children.

Objectivity The attempt to present and to deal with facts, uncoloured by the feelings, opinions, and viewpoints of the person presenting them. Objective evidence is that which is accepted as factual and independent of the subjective opinions or theories of any observer.

Oligarchy Rule by a few people at the top without democratic participation.

Oligopoly Concentrated possession of the trade in some commodity by a few individuals or a few corporations.

One-dimensional thought The inability to conceive of viable alternative ways of organizing social relations. Acceptance of the status quo and of the prevailing ways of thinking as the only credible option.

Order theory Closely related to systems theory, a perspective in which the central focus is on how a stable balance is maintained between elements of a social system.

Organic solidarity Durkheim uses this term to refer to a form of cohesion based upon specialization and interdependence.

Organic system A form of collective organization that emphasizes co-operative teamwork and collective responsibilities rather than a hierarchy of predefined jobs.

Other For Mead, those people whose responses to us play an integral part in the development of our own sense of self-identity.

Out-group A group of people considered sufficiently different as to be outside one's own cultural group.

Outsiders Nonconformists. People whose lifestyles or characteristics visibly violate at least some of the norms that define membership within a given community. See Symbolic brackets.

Oversocialization The concept of socialization carried to the extreme view that people are nothing but the products of their upbringing and that they lack individual autonomy.

Panopticon A circular prison where guards at the centre can see prisoners without being seen. Utilized by Foucault as a metaphor for bureaucratic society.

Paradigm A broad theoretical perspective that may encompass several more specific but related theories. A pattern.

Participant observation A methodological approach in which the researcher shares as fully as possible in the everyday activities of the people being studied in order to understand their lives through personal experience.

Particularism/Particularistic standards For Parsons, evaluation based on the particular abilities, interests, and efforts of an individual.

Party Weber uses the term to refer to organized relations within the political arena, designed to influence policy in favour of specified goals.

Patriarch Father and ruler of a tribe or family.

Patriarchy A social system based on male dominance and female subordination.

Patrimony Property inherited from one's father. Also used to refer to a system of senior male mentors conferring rank or privileges onto specifically chosen junior males.

Pattern maintenance Parsons uses the term to refer to the mechanisms to manage tensions and ensure that individual role players in an activity have the skills and motivation needed to perform their given role(s) appropriately. Latency.

Pattern variables For Parsons, a patterned set of dichotomous options that systematize typical dilemmas of choice in any given role.

Pay equity Equal pay for equal work means that women and men who do identical work should receive identical pay. Equal pay for work of equal value means that workers in different jobs should receive the same pay when their work involves the same level of skill, responsibility, or difficulty.

Peasant A person who works the land to produce food and other materials for immediate consumption rather than for sale or exchange. In discussions of feudalism, the term is often synonymous with serf. Generally, one who works the land.

Personal troubles Mills uses the terms to refer to the private matters that lie within an individual's character and immediate relationships.

Personality system Parsons uses the term to refer to the learned component of individual behaviour. Socialization is a critical process in its formation.

Petite bourgeoisie Marx uses the term to describe the class of people who own their own means of production and work for themselves but who hire little or no additional wage labour.

Phenomenology A theory of the methods or grounds of knowledge based on the premise that all knowledge constitutes interpretations of basic sense experience. The study of how sensory information becomes interpreted as meaningful.

Piece-rate payment A system of payment based on the number of items or units of work completed, rather than on the length of time worked.

Plutocracy A ruling class of wealthy persons. Rule by the wealthy.

Polarization of classes Marx's thesis that, under capitalism, wealth will become progressively more concentrated in the hands of a tiny elite class of capitalists as the mass of people become steadily more impoverished.

Political economy A theoretical perspective in which the central explanatory framework for analysing society is the Marxist model of capitalism. The dynamics of the capitalist economy are seen as the fundamental determinants of political structures and action.

Polyandry One woman having more than one husband at the same time. Wife sharing.

Polygamy Having more than one spouse at the same time.

Polygyny One man having more than one wife at the same time. Husband sharing.

Positive society The third stage of Comte's model of the evolution of societies. Positive society is characterized by a commitment to scientific rationality. Scientists rather than priests are the intellectual and spiritual leaders, and explanations take the form of regular law-like connections between phenomena based on observation and experiment.

Positivism/Positivist A scientific approach to the study of society that seeks to emulate the methodology of the physical sciences. Emphasis is placed on quantitative, objective data rather than on subjective or impressionistic research. Conclusions are based upon observation and experiments that are assumed to provide factual, objective evidence, independent of the theories or opinions of any observer. Also, the search for deterministic or law-like relations of cause and effect governing human behaviour. The philosophcial assumption that observation and experimentation constitute the only valid form of human knowledge. In ethnomethodology the term refers to an ideology that accords the subjective interpretations of sense experience by scientists more credibility than the subjective interpretations of sense experience by other people.

Poverty line A level of income below which people are defined as poor. Commonly calculated on the basis of the proportion of total income required to meet basic subsistence needs of food, shelter, and clothing in a particular society.

Powerlessness Lack of control over factors directly affecting one's life, particularly lack of control over one's work and fear of unemployment. See Alienation.

Practical reasoning In ethnomethodology, the methods by which ordinary people, in their everyday practical affairs, mutually create and sustain their common-sense notions of what is going on.

Precontractual basis of contract Durkheim uses the term to refer to a collective commitment to shared values that are a moral precondition for orderly contractual relations. It refers, in particular, to a commitment to respect for individual differences and human rights.

Predestination See Calvinism.

Prejudice Prejudging, usually in negative terms, the characteristics that are assumed to be shared by members of another group. Preconceived opinion or bias against or in favour of a person or thing. Commonly used to refer to negative opinions of people regarded as outside one's own cultural group.

Prerequisites Those needs or functions that must be met within any social system for that system to maintain a state of balance or equilibrium.

Presentation of self The image that we try to create for ourselves in the eyes of other people whose opinion we value.

Prescriptive norms Shared behavioural expectations concerning what one should do or how one ought to behave in a given situation.

Primitive communism An economic system characterized by a simple hunting and gathering technology where the means of production—the local plants and animals—are accessible to all, and no one has ownership rights to the terrain or to its resouces.

Private realm In functionalism, the aspects of society perceived as oriented toward personal life, particularly family and leisure activities.

Privatization In the domestic labour debate, this refers to the process of separating domestic work, and the people—mostly women—who perform it, from other productive activities.

Probability The recognition that social phenomena have multiple causes and involve elements of free choice that cannot be predicted with certainty but can be explored with respect to the likelihood of their occurrence.

Problem-posing education Freire uses this term to describe an approach to teaching and learning that assumes that students know a great deal through their own experience of the world. Advocates try to build on this knowledge by presenting themes and inviting arguments to foster reflection and dialogue.

Procedural norms Rules that govern how a particular activity, such as contract negotiations, should proceed.

Profane Durkheim uses this term to describe that which does not belong to the sacred. Mundane, ordinary.

Proletariat Wage labourers who survive by selling their labour power. Those who do not own any means to produce for themselves.

Proscriptive norms Shared behavioural expectations concerning what one should not do or what is unacceptable behaviour in a given situation.

Protectionism The situation where duties are applied to imported goods to raise their sale price relative to the price of equivalent local goods, usually to compensate for higher local production costs.

Protestant ethic Weber uses this term to refer to the moral value accorded to work as a spiritual duty and a sign of God's grace. This value system emphasizes accumulation of wealth as a sign of grace; poverty, laziness, and idle luxury are seen as signs of moral depravity and damnation.

Psychic shelter That which gives emotional or psychological comfort and protection.

Psychoanalysis/Psychoanalytic theory A branch of psychology that conceptualizes the mind as divided into conscious and unconscious elements and investigates the interaction between them.

Psychological reductionism The attempt to explain collective social processes by reference only to the psychological processes within the individuals involved.

Psychologism See Psychological reductionism.

Psychology of domination Personality characteristics generated by the long-term experience of subjugation that tend to promote a fatalistic acceptance of this subjugation.

Public issues Mills uses this term to refer to the broad social forces that affect the life experiences of many people in similar circumstances.

Public realm In functionalism, aspects of society, particularly economic and political institutions, that are perceived to be oriented toward the society as a whole.

Purdah A cultural tradition among East Indians that emphasizes the seclusion of women in the home, as part of a pattern of restrictions on their behaviour. Literally, a curtain, especially one serving to screen women from the sight of strangers.

Puritanism A doctrine that emphasizes extreme strictness in moral behaviour such that frivolity, idleness, and luxury, and sex other than for procreation are condemned.

Purposive-rational action Weber uses this term to describe action based on calculation of the most effective means to achieve a particular desired outcome, balanced against probable costs.

Putting-out system A way of organizing production whereby workers take raw materials home and return finished commodities to the employer.

Qualitative methods Methods that are not based on quantitative procedures. These methods are used to explore small settings in depth with the goal of gaining insight that may form the basis for generalizations.

Quantitive research A methodological approach that counts instances of specified aspects of human behaviour in order to derive broad generalizations about patterns of experience.

Questionnaires A formulated series of questions used in survey research.

Race A concept that refers to people's visible and inherited physical differences that are socially noticed. It is commonly associated with differences in skin colour.

Racism Prejudicial attitudes toward groups perceived to be different on the basis of inescapable genetic characteristics. Feelings of antagonism, commonly associated with hostile and discriminatory behaviour toward people of a different race or visibly distinct descent group.

Radical One who advocates fundamental change that goes to the root of the existing social 'order as distinct from one advocating piecemeal changes.

Radical curriculum An approach to teaching that is committed to promoting social change by developing in students the capacity for critical reflection on their social experience.

Radical feminism A theoretical perspective that focusses on relations of reproduction and patriarchy, rather than relations of production and capitalism, as an explanatory framework in understanding the social experiences of women. It explores the situation of women as a sexual class in the struggle against patriarchy.

Radical microsociology The study of everyday life in second-by-second detail, using such techniques as audio and video 'recordings to permit the detailed analysis of conversations and non-verbal interaction.

Radical structuralism A theoretical approach that focusses on structures of bureaucratic control and power within a society rather than ownership of the means of production.

Rationalization Cost-benefit analysis generally, with both costs and benefits defined primarily in narrow economic and technical terms rather than incorporating all social and emotional costs and benefits. Also, concentrating production in one or a few large enterprises with the objective of minimizing unit production costs. An aspect of the strategy of maximizing economies of scale.

Rational-legal authority Weber uses the term to describe authority legitimated by reference to the practical utility of the rules themselves.

Rebel A category in Merton's anomie theory of crime. One who replaces socially valued goals with alternative goals and who adopts alternative means to achieve these new goals.

Recipe knowledge Awareness of typical patterns of actions, learned through socialization, that provide a basis for interpreting the meaning of particular actions.

Reconstituted family A family produced by combining some members of two previously separate families, usually produced by the second marriage of one or both spouses who bring children from a previous marriage or partnership.

Reductionism The tendency to explain complex phenomena by reference to a single cause. The attempt to explain complex social processes by reference only to some lower level of analysis (i.e., to explain social phenomena by individual psychology). See Psychological reductionism.

Reflexive/Reflexivity In ethnomethodology, the assumption that there is a mutually determining relationship between appearances and underlying patterns. What one notices about an object or event is contingent upon what one assumes it to be. Similarly, what one assumes it to be is contingent upon the details that one notices.

Refugee status Status that can be accorded those fleeing to a foreign country to escape persecution.

Regulations Durkheim uses the term to refer to values and rules that restrain individual self-interest for the good of the social whole.

Reification The tendency to impute causal force or motives to abstract concepts such as society or markets instead of to the activities of people.

Relations of production A Marxist term referring to the prevailing pattern of relationships between people that arises as the result of a given mode of production.

Relative deprivation The subjective experience of poverty or loss in comparison with other people rather than in terms of an absolute measure of penury.

Relative surplus Marx uses this term to refer to the amount of surplus production available after payment of wages, when the productivity of workers is increased through labour-saving technology.

Religion Durkheim describes religion as a unified system of beliefs and practices, relative to sacred things, which unite into a single moral community—a church—all adherents.

Repressive law Durkheim uses the term to refer to law that is essentially religious in character and that is concerned with punishing offenders who have transgressed the shared values of the community.

Reserve army of labour Marx uses the term to refer to those people who can be drawn into the labour market when needed by capitalists but let go, often to return to unpaid domestic work, when no longer needed.

Restitutive law Durkheim uses this term to refer to law that is concerned with the regulation of contracts and the re-establishment of reciprocal obligations between members of a society.

Retreatist A category in Merton's anomie theory of crime. One who rejects or gives up on socially approved goals and who fails to conform to behavioural expectations.

Retrospective interpretation This term is used by advocates of labelling theory to refer to a process of revising one's understanding of the meaning of some previous event or behaviour in order to make it consistent with a subsequent change in one's perception of the people involved.

Right of national treatment Part of the free trade agreement between the American and Canadian governments. Any enterprise based in one country but doing business in the other would be subject to the same regulations as those that apply to local enterprise.

Ritualist A category in Merton's anomie theory of crime. One who rejects or gives up on socially valued goals but conforms to behavioural expectations.

Role A typical pattern of behaviour in a pre-defined situation or status. In ethnomethodology, interpreting behaviour after the fact so as to render it meaningful or accountable, rather than random.

Role distancing Goffman uses the term to refer

to a way of performing a social role so as to convey to onlookers the impression that this is not an activity to which one is wholeheartedly committed.

Role model A person whom others strive to emulate in the performance of a particular role.

Role segregation A separation of roles in time and space, which partly insulates one role from others.

Role set The set of all roles with which a person interacts in the process of playing a specific role. Alternatively, the set of all the different roles that any one person plays simultaneously.

Role strain The conflicting expectations and demands that the person playing a specific role experiences from other people in the wider set of related roles. Also, the conflicting expectations and demands that people experience when playing several different roles simultaneously.

Role taking Mead uses the term to describe the way in which children develop an image of themselves through trying to see themselves as they appear to others.

Role theory In functionalism, the theory concerned with the patterns of interaction established in the performance of typical activities or functions in society.

Ruling apparatus The totality of processes through which the work of governing a society occurs, including the work of employees in local offices and the forms and documents around which their work is organized.

Sacred For Durkheim, that which is set apart by a community of people as the expression or symbol of highest spiritual value. Often, but not necessarily, that which is consecrated to a deity.

Sample A separated part of a population or type of situation being studied, which is used in research to illustrate the qualities of the population from which the part is drawn.

Science A search for knowledge that tries to test tentative assumptions or explanations through the systematic search for evidence.

Scientific management A principle of management of manual work based on the fragmentation of tasks into their smallest component actions, each of which can be precisely regulated through time and motion studies to achieve tha maximum possible speed of performance. Sometimes referred to as Taylorism, after Frederick Taylor, the engineer who first developed the system.

Scientism A reliance on simple cause-and-effect explanatory models that imply that external forces rather than human agency determine human experience.

Secondary analysis Analysis that uses data collected in previous research for some other purpose.

Secondary deviance Used in labelling theory to refer to deviance caused or prompted by the sense of being considered a deviant person by other people.

Self The image of oneself comprising both spontaneous feelings and learned attributes.

Self-estrangement Absence of a sense of personal involvement or pride in what one does and hence a detachment from it. See Alienation.

Semi-proletarianization The situation of people who were formerly self-sufficient producers but who have to take part-time wagework to survive.

Separation In the context of ethnic relations, this term refers to two or more distinct ethnic groups living within the same nation state but maintaining separate political, economic, and cultural institutions and having minimal interaction.

Serf A tied labourer on a feudal estate. A person whose service is attached to the land and transferred with it.

Sets of roles See Role set.

Sex-role socialization The process by which children are taught and internalize behaviour deemed appropriate for their particular sex.

Sex roles Activities that are defined within a particular culture as the typical responsibility only of women or only or men.

Sexism/Sexist bias Stereotyped and usually derogatory attitudes or discriminatory behaviour toward people of one sex, commonly but not necessarly toward people of the opposite sex.

Sexual caste A hierarchical social system in which an individual's life chances and status as superior or inferior are ascribed at birth by the criterion of sex.

Sexual class Location of women and men relative to the organization of the activities of reproduction involving conception, pregnancy, childbirth, nurturing, comsuming, domestic labour, and wage earning.

Shareholder capitalism The thesis that ownership of capital is becoming democratized through large numbers of people owning shares.

Shoptalk The shorthand jargon that can be used in conversations between people who share specialized background understandings.

Siege culture The particular pattern of attitudes, values, and behaviour expectations that develop among people who feel themselves isolated and surrounded by hostile forces.

Significant others People whose relationship to us and whose opinions of us we consider particularly important.

Skilled labour time A concept developed by Marx to refer to the time it takes for a skilled person to produce a commodity. It includes the average time taken to learn the skill, including the teacher's time.

Small-groups laboratories Rooms that, in order to fascilitate experiments, are designed to permit a researcher to control a wide variety of factors that might influence interaction within a small group of people.

Social action In functionalism, the structures and processes by which people form meaningful intentions and, more or less successfully, implement them in concrete situations. Weber used the term to refer to any human conduct that is meaningfully oriented to the past, present, or future expected behaviour of others.

Social construction of reality/Social constructionism A theoretical perspective, loosely associated with Marxist theory, that explores how the immediate practical activities of people in their everyday working lives produce the patterns that we subsequently come to recognize as social structures. Within ethnomethodology, the social construction of reality refers to the taken-for-granted practices and rules for practical reasoning through which people create and sustain their notions of what is going on.

Social facts Durkheim uses this term to refer to social phenomena that are experienced as external to the individual and as constraints on the individual's behaviour.

Social gospel movement A movement that stresses the doctrine of collective social responsibility and the links between Christianity and socialism. Advocates see the call to achieve social justice as central to the Christian message. Concepts of sin and salvation are interpreted in social rather than individual terms.

Social order In ethnomethodology, the active processes of creating and sustaining notions of underlying patterns in the otherwise undefined flux of experience. It is accomplished through practical, everyday reasoning.

Social structures A broad macrosociological term, referring to large-scale and long-term patterns of organization in a society. Roughly equivalent to social institutions. In ethnomethodology, the outcome of practical reasoning processes engaged in by sociologists, and others, to account for what seems to be going on. See Institutions.

Social system In functionalism, the structures and processes that collectively organize action and manage the potential for conflict and disorganization to maintain order over time.

Socialism A political and economic theory that advocates collective responsibility for the well-being of members of a society and hence collective control over economic processes within society.

Socialization The lifelong process through which we learn the values and expected patterns of behaviour appropriate for particular social groups and specific roles. This learning process is particularly intense in infancy but continues throughout life as we change roles and group membership.

Socially necessary labour time See Abstract labour time.

Society Generally, the multiple interactions of individuals in a particular setting. A set of forces exerted by people over one another and over themselves. In functionalism, the term refers to a relatively self-sufficient, functioning social system comprising interdependent parts—polity, economy, family, administration, and so on—that each perform specialized functions for the whole. Parsons uses the term to refer to a large-scale social system that controls behaviour within a given territory, has relatively clear membership status, and is capable of meeting all the life needs of members from birth to death.

Sociobiology The study of the biological bases of social behaviour.

Sociological imagination The capacity to understand the relationships between elements of society and their impact on individual lives. The ability to use information in a critical way to achieve an understanding of what is going on in the world and what may be happening within one's own life experience.

Sociology The scientific study of society. The study of relations of social life. Mills uses the term to refer to the study of the major parts or structures of society (polity, economy, church, family, and so on), how these are interrelated, how they came to be as they appear, how they are changing, and the qualities or characteristics of the people involved. Weber uses the term to refer to the science that attempts the interpretive understanding of social action to arrive at an explanation of its cause and effects.

Solidarity Durkheim uses the term to refer to the emotional experience of cohesion and bonding between individuals so that they feel integrated into a social whole.

Specific obligations The perceived right of others to expect only a narrow range of services confined to the precise task at hand, such as in a business contract.

Sponsored immigrants A category within the Immigration Act that refers to people who are permitted to enter Canada as the dependants of a resident of Canada who agrees to take financial responsibility for them.

State Within the social construction of reality approach, the term is used to refer to the whole spectrum of government, including the behaviour of people at all levels of the civil service and related bureaucracies, agencies, departments, and offices.

Status Generally, the position that one occupies in a society. Weber uses the term to refer to social prestige and honour accruing to a person or office.

Status degradation ceremonies A term used by Garfinkel to refer to rites or actions that publicly signal a drop in social status of a person from a normal member of a group or community to a deviant or stigmatized person.

Stereotypes Simplified versions of other groups of people. Such mental cartoons are formed by generalizing too much or exaggerating people's characteristics on the basis of too little information.

Stigma/Stigmatization Disgrace attaching to some act or characteristic.

Stratification The hierarchical organization of people in occupations that are differentially rewarded in terms of income, prestige, and authority. A general ranking or pattern of inequality in a society, commonly measured in terms of occupation, income, and education.

Structural correspondence theory See Correspondence theory.

Structural functionalism See Functionalism.

Structuralism See Marxist structuralism.

Structure See Social structure.

Structuring The process in time through which actions at any one time set constraints upon subsequent actions.

Subcontracted agency An organization that is used by another to supply goods or to perform work. The term is used figuratively to refer to domestic workers who provide a variety of goods and services for the benefit of corporations, even though not regulated by a specific contract.

Subcultural theory of deviance Growing out of Merton's anomie theory of crime, this theory posits that deviance and crime reflect the values of the subculture of which the deviant is a member.

Subculture A distinctive subset of values and behavioural expectations shared by a particular subgroup within a society.

Subjectivism Any approach that explains human activity solely by reference to individual motivation without considering broader structural forces and constraints.

Subsidiary A company controlled by another company that owns a majority of its shares.

Subsidy Money contributed to an entreprise by the state.

Subsistence Provision of the necessities of life but with little surplus for luxuries or profit.

Subsistence wage The minimum wage required to cover the cost of sustaining workers and reproducing the next generation, given prevailing standards of living and education required by such workers.

Substantive norms Rules that govern what activities should be done (i.e., the responsibilities of participants in a contract).

Suburbs Residential areas in outlying districts of cities, usually characterized by relatively low-density housing.

Superego In psychoanalysis, the veneer of learned values and behavioural expectations that control drives and passions.

Superstructure For Marx, all aspects of culture, ideas, religion, legal, and political institutions, and so on, that are seen as determined by the prevailing mode of production in that society.

Supply-curve demand The relationship between supply of a commodity in the market and the demand for it, mediated by the price.

Surplus value For Marx, the difference between the value of the wages paid and the value of the commodities produced by the worker.

Surrogate mother A woman who becomes pregnant in order to produce a child for someone else.

Survey research A methodological approach that utilizes questionnaires or structured interviews in which a series of questions are asked of a sample of people. Answers are then analysed with the aid of computers to provide broad comparative information.

Survival of the fittest The thesis that those biological organisms and societies that survive and prosper are the fittest or best adapted to their environment.

Symbolic brackets Erikson uses the term to refer to the culturally defined limits of acceptable behaviour that distinguish members of a community from non-members.

Symbolic interaction A theoretical approach within the interpretive perspective. It focusses on micro-interactions and how people use gestures and language to convey typical meanings in interaction with others who share a common cultural background.

Sympathetic introspection An approach within the interpretive perspective. It involves putting oneself in the position of others and trying to explain their behaviour by reflecting on how it might feel to be in that situation.

Synthesis See Dialectic; Dialectical materialism.

System A complex whole. A set of connected parts.

System prerequisites For Parsons, the basic requirements of pattern maintenance, integration, goal attainment, and adaptation found in any on-going social system and subsystem.

Systems theory The study of society as a whole or of specific elements of society as functionally interrelated elements, analogous to a biological organism or an organ within such an organism. The central focus is on how a stable balance is maintained between elements.

Taboo Sacred ban or prohibition.

Taylorism See Scientific management.

Technical civilization A vision of society as comprising a dense network of interlocking bureaucratic organizations penetrating all aspects of social life. See Bureaucratic society; Disciplinary society.

Technics/Language of technics The use of computer terminology to refer to human interaction (i.e., feedback, input, output instead of dialogue, debate, judgment).

Technocracy/Technocrat Organization and management of a country's industrial resources by technical experts for the good of the whole community. A person who advocates this.

Technocratic-meritocratic thesis The theory that hierarchy and social inequality in industrial societies reflect differential competence of individuals with respect to science and technology. See Meritocracy thesis.

Textual analysis A methodological approach that involves the detailed study of particular pieces of writing to reveal how meaning is constructed by the text.

Theological stage A stage in Comte's model of the evolution of societies. In the theological stage, societies are dominated by primitive religious thought, and explanations for phenomena are expressed primarily in terms of supernatural forces.

Theory of exchange In Marxist analysis, the theory that the exchange value of a commodity is determined by the amount of labour that goes into a commodity. Under capitalism, the basis of exchange is money, rather than another commodity.

Theory of modernization A theory originating in Spencer's model of societal evolution. It sees societies evolving toward increased differentiation and specialization in political, cultural, economic, and social areas.

Therapeutic intervention For Foucault, the process of manipulating conformity and consensus in society through technical means developed in the social sciences and justified by reference to efficiency and healthy psychological and social adjustment.

Thesis See Dialectic; Dialectical materialism.

Third World The impoverished and technologically backward regions of Latin America, Africa, and Asia.

Time lags The effect of one variable upon another that occurs after a period of time rather than instantaneously.

Totem Any natural object, especially a local animal or plant, that is recognized as the symbol or emblem of a clan or sometimes of an individual.

Traditional authority For Weber, authority legitimated by custom, such as that of hereditary rulers.

Traditional-rational action Weber uses the term to refer to action that is based on habit.

Transfer pricing The prices charged when goods and services are exchanged between a parent corporation and one of its subsidiaries or between two subsidiaries of the same parent corporation.

Typify/Typifications Sets of shared assumptions concering what is normal behaviour for people in related roles or social positions. See Background understandings.

Typology A theoretical model defining different categories or elements of a phenomenon.

Underdeveloped society A society in which critical economic resources have been and still are being plundered and the internal economy undermined by processes within the world capitalist economic system.

Undeveloped society A society in which the economy continues to function in an unchanged, traditional pattern without benfit of technological advance.

Universal functionalism Parsons uses the term to refer to the assumption, borrowed from biology, that every element found within a social system must perform some function for the whole society.

Universalism/Universalistic standards For Parsons, evaluation based on objective criteria that apply equally to any person performing a given activity.

Unobtrusive measures Measures that avoid the possibility of influencing the phenomenon being measured.

Utilitarian Behaviour or values that give highest priority to practical self-interest.

Utterances In ethnomethodology, sounds made by a person before they have been interpreted as having any meaning.

Vacuum ideology An attitude held by certain teachers that children from minority cultures learn virtually nothing worth knowing outside of school.

Value-rational action For Weber, action that is oriented to an overriding ideal or absolute value, such as religion.

Values The beliefs shared among members of a group or society concerning qualities thought to be desirable or esteemed.

Variable Any phenomenon that has more than one value.

Variable capital For Marx, the labour power purchased by the captialist.

Verstehen The interpretation of behaviour as involving meaningful intentions. A methodological approach that involves trying to reconstruct the interpretations that the people being studied might give to their own actions.

Vertical integration Enterprises that operate at different stages in the production of a particular commodity and are consolidated into one corporation.

Vertical mosaic A pattern of stratification in which members of different racial and ethnic groups are arranged vertically with respect to each other in terms of class position.

Victimless crimes Transactional crimes where the persons involved participate willingly in exchanging goods and services and do not see themselves as either criminals or victims. Crimes against morality where there are no clear victims.

Vocation For Weber, performance of the responsibilities of an office as a duty, not for personal gain.

Voluntarism An explanation for action that refers to the rational and free choice of the actor.

Voluntaristic theory For Parsons, a theory of social action that explains social order by reference to mutual agreement or consensus between actors.

Welfare state A state that provides a range of social services for workers, including such benefits as health care, unemployment insurance, welfare payments, pensions, and the like. Such services ameliorate the effects of cyclical ups and downs in the economy as well as helping workers survive personal crises.

White-collar crime Violations of the law that tend to be committed by professional and business people.

Worked up An expression used by Smith to describe the state of raw sense data having been categorized and organized in terms of an interpretive framework in the process of communicating it.

Reference List

Abrahamson, M. 1978. "Sudden Wealth, Gratification, and Attainment: Durkheim's Anomie of Affluence Reconsidered." *American Sociological Review* 45: 49–57.

Abrams, P. 1982. *Historical Sociology*. Shepton Mallet, Somerset: Open Book Publishers.

Adam, H., and K. Moodley. 1986. *South Africa Without Apartheid: Dismantling Racial Domination*. Berkeley: University of California Press.

Adams, B.N. 1970. "Isolation, Function and Beyond: American Kinship in the 1960s." *Journal of Marriage and the Family* 32 (Nov.).

Adams, D. 1988. "Treatment Models of Men Who Batter: A Profeminist Analysis." In *Feminist Perspectives on Wife Abuse*. Ed. K. Yllö and M. Bograd. Beverly Hills: Sage Publications, 176–99.

Adelberg, E., and C. Currie. 1987a. "In Their Own Words." In *Too Few to Count: Canadian Women in Conflict with the Law*. Ed. E. Adelberg and C. Currie. Vancouver: Press Gang, 67–102.

Adelberg, E., and C. Currie. 1987b. *Too Few To Count: Canadian Women in Conflict with the Law*. Vancouver: Press Gang.

Adler, F. 1975. *Sisters in Crime: The Rise of the New Female Criminal*. New York: McGraw-Hill.

Adorno, T.W., E. Frenkel-Brunswik, D.J. Levinson, and S.R. Nevitt. [1950] 1968. *The Authoritarian Personality*. New York: Norton.

Alderman, T. 1974. "And What Do You Do for a Living?" *Canadian Magazine*, 12 Oct.: 2–13.

Allen, R. 1975. "The Social Gospel and the Reform Tradition in Canada 1890–1928." In *Prophesy and Protest: Social Movements in Twentieth-Century Canada*. Toronto: Gage, 45–61.

Andreski, S., ed. 1983. *Max Weber on Capitalism, Bureaucracy and Religion: A Selection of Texts*. London: George Allen and Unwin.

Anyon, J. 1980. "Social Class and the Hidden Curriculum of Work." *Journal of Education* 162, 1 (Winter): 67–92.

Apple, M. 1986. *Teachers and Texts: A Political Economy of Class and Gender Relations in Education*. London: Routledge and Kegan Paul.

Apple, M. 1988. "Facing the Complexity of Power: For a Parallelist Position in Critical Educational Studies." In *Bowles and Gintis Revisited: Correspondence and Contradiction*. Ed. M. Cole. London: Falmer Press, 112–30.

Archibald, W.P. 1978. *Social Psychology as Political Economy*. Toronto: McGraw-Hill Ryerson.

Archibald, W.P. 1985. "Agency and Alienation: Marx's Theories of Individuation and History." *Studies in Political Economy* 16: 61–75.

Armstrong, P. 1984. *Labour Pains: Women's Work in Crisis*. Toronto: Women's Press.

Armstrong, P., and H. Armstrong, 1984. *The Double Ghetto: Canadian Women and Their Segregated Work*. Rev. ed. Toronto: McClelland and Stewart.

Armstrong, P., and H. Armstrong. 1985. "Beyond Sexless Class and Classless Sex: Towards Feminist Marxism." In P. Armstrong, H. Armstrong, P. Connelly, A. Miles, and M. Luxton, *Feminist Marxism or Marxist Feminism: A Debate*. Toronto: Garmond Press, 1–38.

Aronowitz, S., and H.A. Giroux. 1985. *Education Under Siege: The Conservative, Liberal, and Radical Debate Over Schooling*. Hadley, Mass.: Bergin and Garvey Publishers.

Ashley, D., and M. Orenstein. 1985. *Sociological Theory: Classical Statements*. Boston: Allyn and Bacon.

Atkinson, J.M., and P. Drew. 1979. *Order in Court: The Organization of Verbal Interaction in Judicial Settings*. Atlantic Highlands, N.J.: Humanities Press.

Atkinson, J.M., and J.C. Heritage, eds. 1984. *Structures of Social Action: Studies in Conversational Analysis*. Cambridge: Cambridge University Press.

Atwood, M. 1985. *The Handmaid's Tale*. Toronto: McClelland and Stewart.

Badgely, R.F., chair. 1984. *Sexual Offences Against Children*. Vol. 1. Ottawa: Canadian Government Publishing Centre.

Baker, D. 1977. "Ethnicity, Development and Power: Canada in Comparative Perspective." In *Identities: The Impact of Ethnicity on Canadian Society*. Ed. W. Isajiw. Toronto: Peter Martin.

Barnet, R., and R. Muller. 1974. *Global Reach*. New York: Simon and Schuster.

Baum, G. 1979. "Christianity and Socialism." *Canadian Dimension* 13, 5 (Jan.–Feb.): 30–35.

Baum, G. 1981. "Liberation Theology and 'the Supernatural'." *The Ecumenist* 19, 6 (Sept.–Oct.): 81–87.

Becker, H.S. 1951. "The Professional Jazz Musician and His Audience." *American Journal of Sociology* 57: 136–44.

Becker, H.S. 1963. *The Outsiders: Studies in the Sociology of Deviance*. New York: Free Press.

Beckford, G.L. 1973. "The Economics of Agricultural Resource Use and Development in Plantation Economies." In *Underdevelopment and Development: The Third World Today*. Ed. H. Bernstein. Harmondsworth: Penguin, 115–51.

Beechey, V. 1977. "Some Notes on Female Wage Labour in Capitalist Production." *Capital and Class* 3 (Autumn).

Belenky, M.F., B.M. Clinchy, N.R. Goldberger, and J.M. Tarule. 1985. *Women's Ways of Knowing.* New York: Basic Books.

Bell, Q. 1972. *Virginia Woolf: A Biography.* New York: Harcourt Brace Jovanovich.

Benston, M. 1969. "The Political Economy of Women's Liberation." *Monthly Review* 21, 4 (Sept.): 13–27.

Berger, P.L. 1963. *Invitation to Sociology: A Humanistic Perspective.* New York: Anchor Books.

Berger, P.L., and T. Luckman. 1967. *The Social Construction of Reality.* New York: Anchor Books.

Bergeron, L. 1978. *The History of Quebec: A Patriote's Handbook.* Enlarged ed. Toronto: New Canada Publications.

Berle, A., and G. Means. 1932. *The Modern Corporation.* New York: Macmillan.

Bernard, J. 1968. *The Sex Game.* Englewood Cliffs, N.J.: Prentice-Hall.

Bernard, J. 1972. *The Future of Marriage.* New York: World Publishing.

Bezucha, R.J. 1985. "Feminist Pedagogy as a Subversive Activity." In *Gendered Subjects: The Dynamics of Feminist Teaching.* Ed. M. Culley and C. Portuges. London: Routledge and Kegan Paul.

Biddle, B.J., and E.J. Thomas, eds. 1966. *Role Theory: Concepts and Research.* New York: John Wiley and Sons.

Bienvenue, R.M., and A.H. Latif. 1984. "Arrests, Dispositions and Recidivism: A Comparison of Indians and Whites." *Canadian Journal of Criminology and Corrections* 16: 105–16.

Bierstedt, R. 1966. *Emile Durkheim.* New York: Dell Publishing.

Bittner, E. 1965. "The Concept of Organization." *Social Research* 32, 4 (Autumn): 239–55.

Bittner, E. 1967. "The Police on Skid Row: A Study of Peace-Keeping." *American Journal of Sociology* 32: 699–715.

Blau, P.M. 1955. *The Dynamics of Bureaucracy.* Chicago: University of Chicago Press.

Blau, P.M. 1967. *Exchange and Power in Social Life.* New York: John Wiley and Sons.

Blauner, R. 1964. *Alienation and Freedom: The Factory Worker and His Industry.* Chicago: University of Chicago Press.

Bottomore, T.B., ed. 1956. *Karl Marx: Selected Writings in Sociology and Social Philosophy.* New York: McGraw-Hill.

Bottomore, T.B., ed. 1963. *Karl Marx: Early Writings.* New York: McGraw-Hill.

Boughey, H. 1978. *The Insights of Sociology: An Introduction.* Boston: Allyn and Bacon.

Bowker, L.H., M. Arbitell, J. McFerror, and D. Richard. 1988. "On the Relationship Between Wife Beating and Child Abuse." In *Feminist Perspectives on Wife Abuse.* Ed. K. Yllö and M. Bograd. Beverly Hills: Sage Publications, 158–74.

Bowles, S., and H. Gintis. 1976. *Schooling in Capitalist America.* New York: Basic Books.

Bowles, S., and H. Gintis, 1988a. "Can There Be a Liberal Philosophy of Education in a Democratic Society?" In *Bowles and Gintis Revisited: Correspondence and Contradiction.* Ed. M. Cole. London: Falmer Press, 225–32.

Bowles, S., and H. Gintis. 1988b. "Prologue: The Correspondence Principle." In *Bowles and Gintis Revisited: Correspondence and Contradiction.* Ed. M. Cole. London: Falmer Press, 1–4.

Bowles, S., and H. Gintis. 1988c. "Schooling in Capitalist America: Reply to Our Critics." In *Bowles and Gintis Revisited: Correspondence and Contradiction.* Ed. M. Cole. London: Falmer Press, 235–46.

Brake, M. 1980. *The Sociology of Youth Culture and Youth Subcultures: Sex and Drugs and Rock 'n' Roll?* London: Routledge and Kegan Paul.

Braverman, H. 1974. *Labor and Monopoly Capital: The Degradation of Work in the Twentieth Century.* New York: Monthly Review Press.

Breckenridge, J. 1985. "Equal Pay's Unequal Effect." *Report on Business* (Dec.).

Brenner, R. 1977. "The Origins of Capitalist Development: A Critique of Neo-Smithian Marxism." *New Left Review* 104 (July–Aug.): 25–92.

Briggs, J.L. 1970. *Never in Anger: Portrait of an Eskimo Family.* Cambridge: Harvard University Press.

Brisken, L. 1983. "Women and Unions in Canada: A Statistical Overview." In *Union Sisters: Women in the Labour Movement.* Toronto: Women's Press, 28–42.

Brittan, A., and M. Maynard. 1984. *Sexism, Racism and Oppression.* Oxford: Basil Blackwell.

Broverman, I.K., D.M. Broverman, F.E. Clarkson, P.S. Rosengrantz, and S. Vogel. 1970. "Sex Role Stereotypes and Clinical Judgments." *Journal of Consulting and Clinical Psychology* 34 (Jan.): 1–7.

Brown, R.T. 1977. "Racism in Canada: So You Think It's Just a Few Punks in Subway Stations." *Last Post* (April): 29–37.

Brundtland, G.H. 1987. *Our Common Future.* Geneva: World Commission on Environment and Development. United Nations.

Bunch, C. 1983. "Not by Degrees: Feminist Theory and Education." In *Learning Our Way: Essays in Feminist Education.* Ed. C. Bunch and S. Pollack. Trumansburg, N.Y.: Crossing Press, 248–60.

Burns, T., and G.N. Stalker. 1961. *The Management of Innovation*. London: Tavistock.

Burrell, G., and G. Morgan. 1979. *Sociological Paradigms and Organizational Analysis*. London: Heinemann.

Burridge, K. 1969. *New Heaven New Earth: A Study of Millenarian Activities*. Toronto: Copp Clark.

Burrill, G., and I. McKay, eds. 1987. *People, Resources, and Power: Critical Perspectives on Underdevelopment and Primary Industries in the Atlantic Region*. Fredericton: Acadiensis Press.

Burtch, B.E. 1988. "Midwifery and the State: The New Midwifery in Canada." In *Gender and Society: Creating a Canadian Women's Sociology*. Ed. Arlene Tigar McLaren. Toronto: Copp Clark Pitman, 349–71.

Button, G., P. Drew, and J. Heritage, eds. 1986. *Interaction and Language Use*. Special issue of *Human Studies* 9, 2–3.

Buxton, W. 1985. *Talcott Parsons and the Capitalist Nation State: Political Sociology as a Strategic Vocation*. Toronto: University of Toronto Press.

Calhoun, J.B. 1963. "Population Density and Social Pathology." In *The Urban Condition*. Ed. L. Duhl. New York: Basic Books, 33–43.

Cameron, D., ed. 1988. *The Free Trade Deal*. Toronto: Lorimer.

Canada. House of Commons. 1989. "A Review of the Postsecondary Student Assistance Program of the Department of Indian Affairs and Northern Development." *First Report of the Standing Committee on Aboriginal Affairs*. June.

Canada. House of Commons. Standing Committee on Health, Welfare and Social Affairs. 1982. *Wife Battering: Report on Violence in the Family*. Ottawa: Queen's Printer. May.

Canada. House of Commons. 1989. "A Review of the Postsecondary Student Assistance Program of the Department of Indian Affairs and Northern Development." *First Report of the Standing Committee on Aboriginal Affairs*. June.

Caplan, G.L., and F. Sauvageau. 1986. *Report of the Task Force on Broadcasting Policy*. Ottawa: Ministry of Supply and Services.

Cappon, P. 1978. "The Green Paper: Immigration as a Tool for Profit." In *Modernization and the Canadian State*. Ed. D. Glenday, H. Guidon, and A. Turowetz. Toronto: Macmillan.

Carey, A. 1967. "The Hawthorne Studies: A Radical Critique." *American Sociological Review* 32: 403–16.

Carlson, D.L. 1988. "Beyond the Reproductive Theory of Teaching." In *Bowles and Gintis Revisited: Correspondence and Contradiction*. Ed. M. Cole. London: Falmer Press, 157–73.

Carty, R. 1982. "Giving for Gain: Foreign Aid and CIDA." In *Ties that Bind: Canada and the Third World*. Ed. R. Clarke and R. Swift. Toronto: Between the Lines.

Cassin, A.M. 1979. *Advancement Opportunities in the British Columbia Public Service*. British Columbia Economic Analysis and Research Bureau. Ministry of Industry and Small Business Development.

Cassin, A.M. 1980. "The Routine Production of Inequality: Implications for Affirmative Action." Unpublished paper. Ontario Institute for Studies in Education.

Chance, N.A. 1966. *The Eskimo of North America*. New York: Holt, Rinehart and Winston.

Chatterji, S.A. 1988. *The Indian Woman's Search for an Identity*. New Delhi: Vikas Publishing House.

Chessler, P. 1987. *Mothers on Trial: The Battle for Children and Custody*. Seattle, Wash.: Seal Press.

Chance, N.A. 1966. *The Eskimo of North America*. New York: Holt, Rinehart and Winston.

Chiaramonte, L.J. 1970. *Craftsmen–Client Contracts: Interpersonal Relations in a Newfoundland Fishing Community*. St. John's: Institute of Social and Economic Research.

Chinoy, E. 1955. *Automobile Workers and the American Dream*. New York: Doubleday.

Chirot, D. 1977. *Social Change in the Twentieth Century*. New York: Harcourt Brace Jovanovich.

Cicourel, A.V. 1968. *The Social Organization of Juvenile Justice*. New York: Wiley.

Cicourel, A.V. 1974. *Theory and Method in a Study of Argentine Fertility*. New York: Wiley.

Clark, L.M.G., and D.L. Lewis. 1977. *Rape: The Price of Coercive Sexuality*. Toronto: Women's Press.

Clark, S.C. 1976. "The Issue of Canadian Identity." Lecture at St. Thomas University. 5 Nov.

Clark, S.D. 1966. *The Suburban Society*. Toronto: University of Toronto Press.

Clark, S.D. 1978. *The New Urban Poor*. Toronto: McGraw-Hill Ryerson.

Clarke, R., and R. Swift, eds. 1982. *Ties that Bind: Canada and the Third World*. Toronto: Between the Lines.

Clegg, S., and D. Dunkerley. 1980. *Organization, Class, and Control*. London: Routledge and Kegan Paul.

Clement, W. 1975. *The Canadian Corporate Elite*. Toronto: McClelland and Stewart.

Clement, W. 1977. *Continental Corporate Power*. Toronto: McClelland and Stewart.

Clement, W. 1981. *Hardrock Mining: Industrial Relations and Technological Change at INCO*. Toronto: McClelland and Stewart.

Clow, M. 1988. "Speeding up the De-industrialization of Our Economy: Maritimizing Canada." In *The Facts:*

The Facts on Free Trade—Canada: Don't Trade It Away. Ed. E. Finn. Canadian Union of Public Employees 10, 2 (Spring).

Cloward, R., and L. Ohlin. 1960. *Delinquency and Opportunity: A Theory of Delinquent Gangs.* Chicago: Free Press.

Coch, L., and J.R.P. French Jr. 1949. "Overcoming Resistance to Change." *Human Relations* 1: 512–32.

Cockburn, C. 1981. "The Material of Male Power." *Feminist Review* 9 (Autumn): 41–59.

Cohen, A.K. 1955. *Delinquent Boys: The Culture of the Gang.* New York: Free Press.

Cohen, A.K. 1959. "The Study of Social Disorganization and Deviant Behavior." In *Sociology Today.* Ed. R.K. Merton, L. Broom, and L. Cottrell. New York: Basic Books.

Cohen, G.A. 1980. "Karl Marx and the Withering Away of Social Science." In *Karl Marx's Theory of History: A Defense.* Princeton: Princeton University Press, 326–44.

Cohen, M.G. 1987. *Free Trade and the Future of Women's Work: Manufacturing and Service Industries.* Toronto: Garamond Press.

Cohen, M.G. 1988a. "Services: The Vanishing Opportunity." In *The Free Trade Deal.* Ed. Duncan Cameron. Toronto: Lorimer, 140–55.

Cohen, M.G. 1988b. "U.S. Firms Eager to Run Our Institutions—For Profit: Americanizing Services." In *The Facts: The Facts on Free Trade—Canada: Don't Trade It Away.* Ed. E. Finn. Canadian Union of Public Employees 10, 2 (Spring).

Cole, M. ed. 1988a. *Bowles and Gintis Revisited: Correspondence and Contradiction.* London: Falmer Press.

Cole, M. 1988b. "Contradictions in the Educational Theory of Gintis and Bowles." In *Bowles and Gintis Revisited: Correspondence and Contradiction.* London: Falmer Press, 33–48.

Cole, M. 1988c. "Correspondence Theory in Education: Impact, Critiques, and Re-evaluation." In *Bowles and Gintis Revisited: Correspondence and Contradiction.* London: Falmer Press, 7–15.

Collins, R. 1981. "On the Microfoundations of Macrosociology." *American Journal of Sociology* 86: 984–1014.

Collins, R. 1982. *Sociological Insight: An Introduction to Non-Obvious Sociology.* Oxford: Oxford University Press.

Connelly, P. 1978. *Last Hired, First Fired: Women and the Canadian Labour Force.* Toronto: Women's Press.

Cook, P. 1987. "Losing Often and Losing Badly to Japanese." *Globe and Mail.* 6 July: B3.

Cooley, C.H. 1964. *Human Nature and the Social Order.* New York: Schocken.

Corrigan, P. 1979. *Schooling the Smash Kids.* London: Macmillan.

Coser, L.A. 1956. *The Functions of Social Conflict.* Glencoe, Ill.: Free Press.

Cowie, J., V. Cowie, and E. Slater. 1968. *Delinquency in Girls.* London: Heinemann.

Cox, O.C. [1948] 1970. *Caste, Class and Race.* New York: Monthly Review Press.

Crean, S. 1989. "In the Name of the Fathers: Joint Custody and the Anti-Feminist Backlash." *This Magazine* 22, 7 (Feb.): 19–25.

Crean, S., and M. Rioux. 1983. *Two Nations: An Essay on the Culture and Politics of Canada and Quebec in a World of American Pre-eminence.* Toronto: Lorimer.

Culley, M. 1985. "Anger and Authority in the Introductory Women's Studies Classroom." In *Gendered Subjects: The Dynamics of Feminist Teaching.* Ed. M. Culley and C. Portuges. London: Routledge and Kegan Paul, 209–18.

Culley, M., and C. Portuges, eds. 1985. *Gendered Subjects: The Dynamics of Feminist Teaching.* London: Routledge and Kegan Paul.

Currie, E. 1974. "Beyond Criminology." *Issues in Criminology* 9 (Spring): 133–42.

Curtis, B. 1987. "Preconditions of the Canadian State: Educational Reform and the Construction of a Public in Upper Canada, 1837–1846." In *The Benevolent State: The Growth of Welfare in Canada.* Ed. A. Moscovitch and J. Albert. Toronto: Garamond Press.

Czerny, M.S.J., and J. Swift. 1984. *Getting Started on Social Analysis in Canada.* Toronto: Between the Lines.

Dalla Costa, M., and S. James. 1972. *The Power of Women and the Subversion of the Community.* Bristol, England: Falling Wall Press.

Dalton, M. 1959. *Men Who Manage.* New York: Wiley.

Daly, M. 1973. *Beyond God the Father: Toward a Philosophy of Women's Liberation.* Boston: Beacon Press.

Daly, M. 1978. *Gyn/Ecology: The Metaethics of Radical Feminism.* Boston: Beacon Press.

Daniels, A.K. 1972. "The Social Construction of Military Psychiatric Diagnoses." In *Symbolic Interaction: A Reader in Social Psychology.* Ed. J.G. Manis and B.N. Meltzer. Boston: Allyn and Bacon.

Davis, K., and W.E. Moore. 1945. "Some Principles of Stratification." *American Sociological Review* 10, 2: 242–49.

Day, E.B. 1987. "A Twentieth-Century Witch Hunt: A Feminist Critique of the Grange Royal Commission into Deaths at the Hospital for Sick Children." *Studies in Political Economy* 24 (Autumn): 13–39.

Deffontaines, P. 1964. "The Rang-Pattern of Rural Settlement in French Canada." In *French-Canadian Society*. Vol. 1. Ed. M. Rioux and Y. Martin. Toronto: McClelland and Stewart, 3–19.

Delphy, C. 1984. *Close to Home: A Materialist Analysis of Women's Oppression*. London: Hutchinson.

Dixon, M. 1976. *Things Which Are Done in Secret*. Montreal: Black Rose Books.

Dobash, R.E., and R. P. Dobash. 1979. *Violence Against Wives: A Case Against Patriarchy*. New York: Free Press.

Dobash, R.E., and R.P. Dobash. 1988: "Research as Social Action: The Struggle for Battered Women." In *Feminist Perspectives on Wife Abuse*. Ed. K. Yllö and M. Bograd. Beverly Hills: Sage Publications, 51–74.

Donzelot, J. 1979. *The Policing of Families*. New York: Pantheon.

Dooley, D. 1984. *Social Research Methods*. Englewood Cliffs, N.J.: Prentice-Hall.

Douglas, J. 1967. *The Social Meaning of Suicide*. Princeton: Princeton University Press.

Dreyfus, H.L., and P. Rabinow. 1982. *Michel Foucault: Beyond Structuralism and the Hermeneutics*. Chicago: University of Chicago Press.

Dubinsky, K. 1985. "Lament for a 'Patriarchy Lost'? Anti-Feminism, Anti-Abortion, and REAL Women in Canada." Feminist Perspectives Series. No. 1. Ottawa. Canadian Research Institute for the Advancement of Women.

Duelli Klein, R. 1980. "How To Do What We Want To Do: Thoughts About Feminist Methodology." In *Theories of Women's Studies*. Ed. G. Bowles and R. Duelli Klein. Berkeley: University of California Press.

Durkheim, E. [1893] 1964. *The Division of Labour in Society*. New York: Free Press.

Durkheim, E. [1895] 1964. *The Rules of Sociological Method*. 8th ed. Trans. S.A. Solvay and J.H. Mueller. New York: Free Press.

Durkheim, E. [1897] 1951. *Suicide*. Glencoe, Ill.: Free Press.

Durkheim, E. [1915] 1976. *The Elementary Forms of Religious Life*. London: Allyn and Unwin.

Edgar, J. 1987. "Iceland's Feminists: Power at the Top of the World." *Ms*. (Dec.): 30–32.

Edgell, S. 1980. *Middle Class Couples: A Study of Segregation, Domination and Inequality in Marriage*. London: George Allen and Unwin.

Ehrenreich, B. 1983. *The Hearts of Men: American Dreams and the Flight from Commitment*. Garden City, N.Y.: Anchor Press.

Ehrenreich, B., and D. English. 1979. *For Her Own Good: 150 Years of Experts' Advice to Women*. Garden City, N.Y.: Anchor Books.

Eichler, M. 1980. *The Double Standard: A Feminist Critique of Feminist Social Science*. London: Croom Helm.

Eichler, M. 1985a. "And the Work Never Ends: Feminist Contributions." *Canadian Review of Sociology and Anthropology* 22, 5 (Dec.): 619–44.

Eichler, M. 1985b. "The Pro-Family Movement: Are They for or Against Families?" Feminist Perspectives Series. Ottawa: Canadian Research Institute for the Advancement of Women.

Eichler, M. 1988a. *Families in Canada Today: Recent Changes and Their Policy Consequences*. 2nd ed. Toronto: Gage.

Eichler, M. 1988b. *Nonsexist Research Methods: A Practical Guide*. Boston: Allen and Unwin.

Eisenstein, Z. 1979. "Developing a Theory of Capitalist Patriarchy and Socialist Feminism." In *Capitalist Patriarchy and the Case for Socialist Feminism*. Ed. Z. Eisenstein. New York: Monthly Review Press, 5–40.

Eisenstein, Z.R. 1984. *Feminism and Sexual Equality: Crisis in Liberal America*. New York: Monthly Review Press.

Elias, N. 1970. *What Is Sociology?* London: Hutchinson.

Emerson, J. 1970. "Behavior in Private Places: Sustaining Definitions of Reality in Gynecological Examinations." In *Recent Sociology*. Vol. 2. *Patterns of Communicative Behavior*. Ed. H. Dreitzel. New York: Macmillan.

Engels, F. [1884] 1978. "The Origins of the Family, Private Property, and the State." In *The Marx–Engels Reader*. 2nd ed. Ed. R.C. Tucker. New York: W.W. Morton, 734–59.

Engels, F. [1894] 1959. "On the History of Early Christianity." In *Marx and Engels: Basic Writings on Politics and Philosophy*. Ed. L.S. Feuer. Garden City, N.Y.: Doubleday.

Epstein, E.J. 1982. *The Rise and Fall of Diamonds: The Shattering of a Brilliant Illusion*. New York: Simon and Shuster.

Ericson, R.V. 1982. *Reproducing Order: A Study of Police Patrol Work*. Toronto: University of Toronto Press.

Erikson, K.T. 1962. "Notes on the Sociology of Deviance." *Social Problems* 9 (Spring): 309–14.

Erikson, K.T. 1966. *Wayward Puritans: A Study in the Sociology of Deviance*. New York: John Wiley and Sons.

Erwin, L. 1988. "What Feminists Should Know About the Pro-Family Movement in Canada: A Report on a Recent Survey of Rank-and-File Members." In *Feminist Research: Prospect and Retrospect*. Ed. P. Tancred-Sheriff. Montreal: CRIAW and McGill-Queen's University Press, 226–78.

Falardeau, J.C. 1964. "The Seventeenth-Century Parish in French Canada." In *French-Canadian Society*. Vol. 1. Ed. M. Rioux and Y. Martin. Toronto: McClelland and Stewart, 19–32.

Fassell, M.L. 1987. "Against Women's Interests: An Issues Paper on Joint Custody and Mediation." National Action Committee on the Status of Women. April.

Feder, E. 1976. "How Agribusiness Operates in Under-developed Agricultures." *Development and Change* 7, 4 (Oct.): 413–43.

Fenn, M. 1980. *In The Spotlight: Women Executives in a Changing Environment*. Englewood Cliffs, N.J.: Prentice-Hall.

Ferguson, K.E. 1984. *The Feminist Case Against Bureaucracy*. Philadelphia: Temple University Press.

Feyerabend, P.K. 1970. "How To Be a Good Empiricist: A Plea for Tolerance in Matters Epistemological." In *Readings in the Philsophy of Science*. Ed. B.A. Brody. Englewood Cliffs, N.J.: Prentice Hall.

Fillmore, N. 1989. "The Big Oink: How Business Won the Free Trade Battle." *This Magazine* 22, 8 (March-April): 13–20.

Finn, E. ed. 1988. *The Facts: The Facts on Free Trade—Canada: Don't Trade it Away*. Canadian Union of Public Employees. 10, 2 (Spring).

Firestone, S. 1971. *The Dialectic of Sex*. London: The Women's Press.

Flanders, A., and A. Fox. 1969. "Collective Bargaining: From Donovan to Durkheim." In *Management and Unions*. Ed. A. Flanders. London: Faber and Faber.

Ford, C.S. 1970. "Some Primitive Societies." In *Sex Roles in Changing Society*. Ed. G.H. Seward and R. Williamson. New York: Random House.

Fortin, G. 1964. "Socio-Cultural Changes in an Agricultural Parish." In *French-Canadian Society*. Vol. 1. Ed. M. Rioux and Y. Martin. Toronto: McClelland and Stewart, 86–106.

Forward, S., and J. Torres. 1987. *Men Who Hate Women and the Women Who Love Them*. New York: Bantam Books.

Foster, G.M. 1973. *Traditional Societies and Technological Change*. 2nd ed. New York: Harper and Row.

Foster-Clark, A. 1978. "The Modes of Production Controversy." *New Left Review* 107 (Jan.–Feb.): 47–77.

Foucault, M. 1970. *The History of Sexuality*. London: Allen Lane.

Foucault, M. 1977. *Discipline and Punishment: The Birth of the Prison*. London: Allen Lane.

Foucault, M. 1980. *Power/Knowledge: Selected Interviews and Other Writings 1972–1977*. New York: Pantheon Books.

Fournier, M. 1985. "Sociological Theory in English Canada: A View from Quebec." *Canadian Review of Sociology and Anthropology* 22, 5 (Dec.): 794–803.

Frank, A.G. 1972. "Sociology of Development and the Underdevelopment of Sociology." In *Dependence and Underdevelopment: Latin America's Political Economy*. Ed. J.D. Cockcroft, A.G. Frank, and D.L. Johnson. New York: Doubleday, 321–97.

Frank, B. 1987. "Hegemonic Heterosexual Masculinity." *Studies in Political Economy* 24 (Autumn): 159–70.

Fraser, S. 1987. "Local Journalist Condemns Sexist Bias in Media." *Pandora* (Dec.): 3.

Fraser, S. 1988 "Human Rights: Victim of the Politics of Expediency—The Media: Accessory After the Fact." Lecture given at the Conference on Human Rights and International Co-operation, St. Thomas University, 26 Nov.

Freeman, D. 1983. *Margaret Mead and Samoa: The Making and Unmaking of an Anthropological Myth*. Cambridge: Harvard University Press.

Freire, P. 1970. *Pedagogy of the Oppressed*. New York: Seabury.

French, J.R.P., J. Israel, and D. As. 1960. "An Experiment on Participation in a Norwegian Factory: Interpersonal Dimension on Decision-making." *Human Relations* 13: 3–19.

Friedman, M. 1978. *Capitalism and Freedom*. Chicago: University of Chicago Press.

Friedman, S.S. 1985. "Authority in the Feminist Classroom: A Contradiction in Terms?" In *Gendered Subjects: The Dynamics of Feminist Teaching*. Ed. M. Culley and C. Portuges. Boston: Routledge and Kegan Paul, 203–09.

Fukuyama, F. 1989. "The End of History?" *The National Interest* (Summer).

Gabriel, J. 1986. "School and Stratification." Honours thesis, St. Thomas University.

Gans, H.J. 1962. *The Urban Villagers*. Glencoe, Ill.: Free Press.

Gans, H.J. 1967. *The Levittowners*. New York: Vintage Press.

Gardiner, G.B. 1954. *Witchcraft Today*. London: Rider.

Garfinkel, H. 1956. "Conditions of Successful Degradation Cermonies." *American Journal of Sociology* 61 (March): 420–24.

Garfinkel, H. 1963. "A Conception of and Experiments with 'Trust' as a Condition of Stable and Concerted Actions." In *Motivation and Social Interaction*. Ed. O.H. Harvey. New York: Ronald Press: 187–238.

Garfinkel H. 1967. *Studies in Ethnomethodology*. Englewood Cliffs, N.J.: Prentice-Hall.

Garfinkel, H. 1976. "Manual for Studies of Naturally Organized Activities." Unpublished manuscript. Department of sociology, University of California.

Garfinkel H., M. Lynch, and E. Livingston. 1981. "The Work of Discovering Science Construed with Materials from the Optically Discovered Pulsar." *Philosophy of the Social Sciences* 1: 131–58.

Garigue, P. 1956. "French-Canadian Kinship and Urban Life." *American Anthropologist* 58: 1090–101.

Garigue, P. 1964. "Change and Continuity in Rural French Canada." In *French-Canadian Society*. Vol. 1. Ed. M. Rioux and Y. Martin. Toronto: McClelland and Stewart, 123–37.

Gaskell, J. 1986. "Conceptions of Skill and the Work of Women: Some Historical and Political Isuses." In *The Politics of Diversity: Feminism, Marxism, and Nationalism*. Ed. R. Hamilton and M. Barrett. Montreal: Book Centre.

Gaskell, J., and A.T. McLaren, eds., 1987. *Women and Education: A Canadian Perspective*. Calgary: Detselig.

Gavigan, S. 1987. "Women's Crime: New Perspectives and Old Theories." In *Too Few to Count: Canadian Women in Conflict with the Law*. Ed. E. Adelberg and C. Currie. Vancouver: Press Gang.

Geller, G. 1987. "Young Women in Conflict with the Law." In *Too Few to Count: Canadian Women in Conflict with the Law*. Ed. E. Adelberg and C. Currie. Vancouver: Press Gang.

Gèrin, L. 1964. "The French-Canadian Family: Its Strengths and Weaknesses." In *French-Canadian Society*. Vol 1. Ed. M. Rioux and Y. Martin. Toronto: McClelland and Stewart, 32–57.

Gerth, H.H., and C.W. Mills. 1946. *From Max Weber: Essays in Sociology*. New York: Oxford University Press.

Ghorayshi, P. 1987. "Canadian Agriculture: Capitalist or Petit Bourgeois?" *Canadian Review of Sociology and Anthropology* 24, 3 (Aug.): 358–73.

Giddens, A. 1971. *Capitalism and Modern Social Theory*. London: Cambridge University Press.

Giddens, A. 1979. *Central Problems in Social Theory*. London: Macmillan.

Giddens, A. 1982. *Sociology: A Brief but Critical Introduction*. New York: Harcourt Brace Jovanovich.

Gilligan, C. 1982. *In a Different Voice*. Cambridge: Harvard University Press.

Gintis, H., and S. Bowles. 1988. "Contradiction and Reproduction in Educational Theory." In *Bowles and Gintis Revisited: Correspondence and Contradiction*. Ed. M. Cole. London: Falmer Press, 16–32.

Gitlin, T. 1980. *The Whole World is Watching*. Berkeley: University of California Press.

Goffman, E. 1959. *The Presentation of Self in Everyday Life*. Garden City, N.J.: Doubleday.

Goffman, E. 1961a. *Asylums*. Harmondsworth, Penguin.

Goffman, E. 1961b. "Role Distance." In *Encounters: Two Studies in the Sociology of Interaction*. New York: Bobbs-Merrill.

Goffman, E. 1963. *Stigma: Notes on the Management of Spoiled Identity*. Englewood Cliffs, N.J.: Prentice-Hall.

Goffman, E. 1967. *Interaction Ritual: Essays on Face-to-Face Behavior*. New York: Doubleday.

Gold, D.A., C.Y.H. Lo, and E.O. Wright. 1975. "Recent Developments in Marxist Theories of the Capitalist State." Part 1. *Monthly Review* 27, 5 (Oct.): 29–43; Part 2. *Monthly Review* 27, 6 (Nov.): 36–51.

Gold, R. 1951–52. "Janitors Versus Tenants: A Status Income Dilemma." *American Journal of Sociology* 57: 486–93.

Goldthrope, J.H. 1966. "Attitudes and Behaviour of Car Assembly Workers: A Deviant Case and a Theoretical Critique." *British Journal of Sociology* 27, 3: 227–44.

Goode, W.J. 1982. *The Family*. 2nd ed. Englewood-Cliffs, N.J.: Prentice-Hall.

Goodman, P. 1956. *Growing Up Absurd*. New York: Random House.

Gordon, M.M. 1964. *Assimilation in American Life*. New York: Oxford University Press.

Gotell, L. 1987. "A Helluva Lot to Lose...But Not a Helluva Lot To Win: The Canadian Women's Movement, Equality Rights and the Charter." Paper presented to the Atlantic Political Science Association. York University, 31. Oct.

Gough, K. 1986. "The Origins of the Family." In *Family in Transition*. 5th ed. Ed. A.S. Skolnick and J.H. Skolnick. Boston: Little Brown, 22–39.

Gouldner, A.W. 1952. "On Weber's Analysis of Bureaucratic Rules." In *Reader in Bureaucracy*. Ed. R.K. Merton, A.P. Gray, B. Hockey, H.C. Selvin. New York: Free Press, 48–51.

Gouldner, A.W. 1954. *Patterns of Industrial Bureaucracy*. New York: Free Press.

Gouldner, A.W. 1955. "Metaphysical Pathos and the Theory of Bureaucracy." *American Political Science Review* 49: 496–507.

Gouldner, A.W. 1965. *Wildcat Strikes*. New York: Free Press.

Grabb, E.G. 1984. *Social Inequality: Classical and Contemporary Theorists*. Toronto: Holt, Rinehart and Winston.

Green, B. 1979. "The Christian Left in English Canada." *Canadian Dimension* 13, 5 (Jan.–Feb.): 38–42.

Greenberg, D.F., ed., 1981a. *Crime and Capitalism:*

Readings in Marxist Criminology. Palo Alto, Calif.: Mayfield Publishing.

Greenberg, D.F. 1981b. "Delinquency and the Age Structure of Society." In *Crime and Capitalism: Readings in Marxist Criminology.* Palo Alto, Calif.: Mayfield Publishing.

Greenwood, V. 1981. "The Mythos of Female Crime." In *Women and Crime.* Ed. A. Morris and L. Gelsthorpe. Cropwood Conference Series 13. Cambridge Institute of Criminology.

Gregory J. 1983. "The Electronic Sweatshop." In *Perspectives on Women in the 1980s.* Ed. J. Turner and L. Emergy. Winnipeg: University of Manitoba Press, 99–112.

Griffith, A., and D.E. Smith. 1985. "Feminist Research and Women's Experience: When Mothers Talk." Paper presented to Motherwork conference. Simone de Beauvoir Institute, Concordia University, 4–6 Oct.

Guettel, C. 1974. *Marxism and Feminism.* Toronto: Women's Press.

Guindon, H. 1964. "The Social Evolution of Quebec Reconsidered." In *French-Canadian Society.* Vol. 1. Ed. M. Rioux and Y. Martin. Toronto: McClelland and Stewart, 137–61.

Gyllenhammer, P. 1977. *People at Work.* Reading, Mass.: Addison-Wesley.

Hale, S.M. 1981. Review of B. Rogers, *The Domestication of Women: Discrimination in Developing Societies.* London: Tavistock: 1980. In *Atlantis* 7, 1 (Autumn): 151–52.

Hale, S.M. 1985. "Integrating Women in Developmental Models and Theories." *Atlantis* 11, 1 (Autumn): 45–63.

Hale, S.M. 1987a. "The Documentary Construction of Female Mismanagement." *Canadian Review of Sociology and Anthropology* 24, 4 (Nov.): 489–513.

Hale, S.M. 1987b. *The Elusive Promise: The Struggle of Women Development Workers in Rural North India.* Montreal: Centre for Developing-Area Studies, McGill University.

Hale, S.M. 1988. "Using the Oppressor's Language in the Study of Women and Development." *Women and Language* 11, 2 (Winter): 38–43.

Hall, E.T. 1966. *The Hidden Dimension.* Garden City, N.Y.: Doubleday.

Hall, R.M., and B.R. Sandler. 1984. "Out of the Classroom: A Chilly Campus Climate for Women?" Project on the Status and Education of Women. Washington, D.C.: Association of American Colleges.

Hamilton, P., ed. 1985. *Readings from Talcott Parsons.* London: Tavistock.

Hamilton, R. 1978. *The Liberation of Women: A Study in Patriarchy and Capitalism.* London: George Allen and Unwin.

Hamilton, R., and M. Barrett, eds. 1986. *The Politics of Diversity: Feminism, Marxism, and Nationalism.* Montreal: Book Centre.

Hannant, J. 1988. "The Rise of the New Right in Canada: Implications for the Women's Movement." National Action Committee on the Status of Women. April.

Harper, D. 1979. "Life on the Road." In *Images of Information.* Ed. Jon Wagner. Beverly Hills: Sage Publications, 25–42.

Harris, M. 1986. *Justice Denied: The Law Versus Donald Marshall.* Toronto: Macmillan.

Hartmann, H. 1979. "Capitalist Patriarchy and Job Segregation by Sex." In *Capitalist Patriarchy and the Case for Socialist Feminism.* Ed. Z. Eisenstein. New York: Monthly Review Press, 206–47.

Hartmann, H. 1981. "The Unhappy Marriage of Marxism and Feminism: Towards a More Progressive Union." In *Women and Revolution.* Ed. L. Sargent. Boston: South End Press.

Heap, J.L. "Classroom Talk: A Criticism of McHoul." Unpublished paper. Department of Sociology. Ontario Institute for Studies in Education.

Heath, C. 1981. "The Opening Sequence in Doctor-Patient Interaction." In *Medical Work: Realities and Routines.* Ed. P. Atkinson and C. Heath. Farnborough, England: Gower Publishing: 71–90.

Heinricks, G. 1989. "Whose News? Business Circles the Globe." *This Magazine* (Sept.): 14–21.

Hempel, C.G. 1970. "The Logic of Functional Analysis." In *Readings in the Philosophy of Science.* Ed. B.A. Brody. Englewood Cliffs, N.J.: Prentice-Hall.

Hennig, M., and A. Jardim. 1981 *The Managerial Woman.* New York: Anchor Books.

Henripin, J. 1968. *Tendances et facteurs de la fecondité au Canada.* Ottawa: Statistics Canada.

Henry, J. 1971. *Pathways to Madness.* New York: Random House.

Herberg, E.N. 1989. *Ethnic Groups in Canada: Adaptations and Transitions.* Scarborough, Ont.: Nelson.

Heritage, J. 1984. *Garfinkel and Ethnomethodology.* Oxford: Polity Press in association with Basil Blackwell.

Hill, D.G., and M. Schiff. 1986. *Human Rights in Canada. A Focus on Racism.* 2nd ed. Ottawa: Canadian Labour Congress and Human Rights Research and Education Centre, University of Ottawa.

Himelfarb, A., and C.J. Richardson. 1979. *People, Power, and Process: Sociology for Canadians.* Toronto: McGraw-Hill Ryerson.

Himelfarb, A., and C.J. Richardson. 1982. *Sociology for Canadians: Images of Society.* Toronto: McGraw-Hill Ryerson.

Hochschild, A. 1973. *The Unexpected Community*. Englewood Cliffs, N.J.: Prentice-Hall.

Hochschild, A. 1983. *The Managed Heart*. California: University of California Press.

Hodge, G., and M.A. Qadeer. 1983. *Towns and Villages in Canada: The Importance of Being Unimportant*. Toronto: Butterworths.

Hoebel, A. 1960. *The Cheyennes: Indians of the Great Plains*. New York: Holt, Rinehart and Winston.

Hogg, D. 1988. "Some Lessons that Education Needs Badly." *Globe and Mail*, 17 June, A7.

Hoogvelt, A.M. 1976. *The Sociology of Developing Societies*. London: Macmillan.

Horowitz, I.L. 1968. "'The Life and Death of Project Camelot.*" In *Professing Sociology: Studies in the Life Cycle of Social Science*. Chicago: Aldine.

Horwitz, A.V. 1984. "The Economy and Social Pathology." *Annual Review of Sociology* 10: 95–119.

Hostetler, J.A., and G.E. Huntington. 1965. *The Hutterites in North America*. New York: Holt, Rinehart and Winston.

Huff, D. 1954. *How To Lie with Statistics*. New York: Norton.

Hughes E.C. 1964. "Industry and the Rural System in Quebec." In *French-Canadian Society*. Vol. 1. Ed. M. Rioux and Y. Martin. Toronto: McClelland and Stewart, 76–85.

Humphreys, L. 1970. *The Tearoom Trade*. Chicago: Aldine.

Illich, I. 1971. *Deschooling Society*. New York: Harper and Row.

Ingham, R., ed. 1978. *Football Hooliganism*. London: Inter-Action Imprints.

Inglis, K. 1963. *Churches and the Working Classes in Victorian England*. London: Routledge and Kegan Paul.

Iverson, N. and R. Matthews. 1968. *Communities in Decline: An Examination of Household Resettlement in Newfoundland*. St. John's: Institute of Social and Economic Development.

Jalbert, P. 1984. "'News Speak' About the Lebanon War." *Journal of Palestine Studies* 14, 1 (Fall): 16–35.

Jamieson, S.M. 1968. *Times of Trouble: Labour Unrest and Industrial Conflict in Canada, 1900–1966*. Ottawa: Information Canada.

Janowitz, M. 1967. *The Community Press in an Urban Setting*. Chicago: University of Chicago Press.

Jencks, C., et al. 1972. *Inequality*. New York: Basic Books.

Johnson, H. 1987. "Getting the Facts Straight: A Statistical Overview." In *Too Few to Count: Canadian Women in Conflict with the Law*. Ed. E. Adelberg and C. Currie. Vancouver: Press Gang.

Johnson, L. 1972. "The Development of Class in Canada in the Twentieth Century." In *Capitalism and the National Question*. Ed. G. Teeple. Toronto: University of Toronto Press.

Jong, E. 1981. *Witches*. New York: Harry N. Adams.

Joseph, G.I. 1988. "Black Feminist Pedagogy and Schooling in Capitalist White America." In *Bowles and Gintis Revisited: Correspondence and Contradiction*. Ed. M. Cole. London: Falmer Press, 174–86.

Jungueira, J.C. 1979. "The Re-emergence of the Christian Left in Latin America." *Canadian Dimension* 13, 5 (Jan.–Feb.): 46–49.

Kalbach, W. 1976. "Canada: A Demographic Analysis." In *Introduction to Canadian Society*. Ed. G.N. Ramu and S. Johnson. Toronto: Macmillan.

Kanter, R.M. 1977. *Men and Women of the Corporation*. New York: Basic Books.

Kates, J. 1988. "The Quiet Revolution." *Report on Business Magazine* (July): 58–64.

Keat, R., and J. Urry. 1982. *Social Theory as Science*. 2nd ed. London: Routledge and Kegan Paul.

Kellough, G. 1980. "From Colonialism to Economic Imperialism: The Experience of the Canadian Indian." In *Structured Inequality in Canada*. Ed. J. Harp and J.R. Hofley. Scarborough, Ont.: Prentice-Hall, 343–77.

Kelly, L. 1988. "How Women Define Their Experiences of Violence." In *Feminist Perspectives on Wife Abuse*. Ed. K. Yllö and M. Bograd. Beverly Hills: Sage Publications, 114–32.

Kent, T., chair. 1981. *Report of the Royal Commission on Newspapers*. Hull: Ministry of Supply and Services.

King, P.R. 1989. "Indian Students: Further Interim Changes Announced to PSSAP." *CAUT Bulletin* 36, 8 (Oct.): 10.

Kitsuse, J.I. 1962. "Social Reaction to Deviant Behavior: Problems of Theory and Method." *Social Problems* 9 (Winter): 247–56.

Kitsuse, J.I., and A.V. Cicourel. 1963. "A Note on the Use of Official Statistics." *Social Problems* 12: 131–39.

Kolbenschlag, M. 1979. *Kiss Sleeping Beauty Good-bye: Breaking the Spell of Feminine Myths and Models*. Garden City, N.Y.: Doubleday.

Kuper, L. 1969. "Plural Societies: Perspectives and Problems." In *Pluralism in Africa*. Ed. L. Kuper and M.G. Smith. Berkeley: University of California Press, 7–26.

Kuper, L., and M.G. Smith, eds. 1969. *Pluralism in Africa*. Berkeley: University of California Press.

Kuyek, J.N. 1979. *The Phone Book: Working at the Bell*. Kitchener, Ont.: Between the Lines.

Laclau, E. 1977. *Politics and Ideology in Marxist Theory*. London: New Left Books.

Laing, R.D. 1965. *The Divided Self*. Harmondsworth: Penguin.

Lamb, L., and M. McCall, J. Gossen, and M. Dufresne. 1988. "Fathers' Rights, Mandatory Mediation: The Equality Backlash in Family Law." *Jurisfemme* 8, 3 (Winter): 1–29.

Lambert, W.E. 1967. "A Social Psychology of Bilingualism." *Journal of Social Issues* 23, 2: 91–109.

Landsberger, H.A. 1958. *Hawthorne Revisited: Management and the Worker, Its Critics, and Developments in Human Relations in Industry*. Ithaca, N.Y.: Cornell University Press.

Lapierre, L., and H. Aylwin. 1985. *Canadian Youth: Perspectives on Their Health*. Cat. 82-545E. Ottawa: Ministry of Supply and Service.

Lappé, F.M. 1971. *Diet for a Small Planet*. New York: Ballantine Books.

LaPrairie, C.P. 1984. "Selected Criminal Justice and Socio-demographic Data on Native Women." *Canadian Journal of Criminology* 26, 2: 161–69.

Larner, C. 1984. *Witchcraft and Religion: The Politics of Popular Belief*. Oxford: Basil Blackwell.

Larwood, L., and M.M. Wood. 1977. *Women in Management*. Lexington, Mass.: Lexington Books.

Lasch, C. 1977. *Haven in a Heartless World*. New York: Basic Books.

Lavigne, M. 1986. "Feminist Reflections on the Fertility of Women in Quebec." In *The Politics of Diversity: Feminism, Marxism, and Nationalism*. Ed. R. Hamilton and M. Barrett. Montreal: Book Centre, 303–21.

Lecky, W. 1891. *History of England in the Eighteenth Century*. Vol. 2. n.p.

Lee, D., and H. Newby. 1983. *The Problem of Sociology*. London: Hutchinson.

Lefort, C. 1978. "Then and Now." *Telos* 26.

Lemert, E.M. 1951. *Social Pathology: A Systematic Approach to the Theory of Sociopathic Behavior*. New York: McGraw-Hill.

Lemert, E.M. 1972. *Human Deviance, Social Problems, and Social Control*. 2nd ed. Englewood Cliffs, N.J.: Prentice-Hall.

Leonard, E.B. 1982. *Women, Crime, and Society: A Critique of Theoretical Criminology*. New York: Longman.

Lewis, D. 1972. *Louder Voices: The Corporate Welfare Bums*. Toronto: James Lewis and Samuel.

Lewis, O. 1949. *Life in a Mexican Village: Tepoztlan Restudied*. Urbana: University of Illinois Press.

Leyton, E. 1986. *Hunting Humans: The Rise of the Modern Multiple Murderer*. Toronto: McClelland and Stewart.

Li, P.S. 1979. "A Historical Approach to Ethnic Statification: The Case of the Chinese in Canada 1858–1930." *Canadian Review of Sociology and Anthropology* 16, 3: 320–32.

Liddle, J., and R. Joshi. 1986. *Daughters of Independence: Gender, Caste, and Class in India*. New Delhi: Zed Books.

Lieberman, S. 1956. "The Effect of Changes in Roles on the Attitudes of Role Occupants." *Human Relations* 9: 385–402.

Lipovenko, P. 1987. "Protecting the Fetus: How Far Can the State Go?" *Globe and Mail*, 1 Aug., D1–2.

Littlejohn, J. 1963. *Westrigg*. London: Routledge and Kegan Paul.

Lombroso, C. 1895. *The Female Offender*. New York: Fisher Unwin.

Lorimer, J., and M. Phillips. 1971. *Working People: Life in a Downtown City Neighbourhood*. Toronto: James Lewis and Samuel.

Lucas, R.A. 1971. *Minetown, Milltown, Railtown*. Toronto: University of Toronto Press.

Luxton, M. 1980. *More than a Labour of Love: Three Generations of Women's Work in the Home*. Toronto: Women's Press.

Luxton, M. 1986. "Two Hands for the Clock: Changing Patterns in the Gendered Division of Labour in the Home." In *Through the Kitchen Window: The Politics of Home and Family*. Ed. M. Luxton and H. Rosenberg. Toronto: Garamond Press, 17–36.

Luxton, M., and H. Rosenberg. 1986. *Through the Kitchen Window: The Politics of Home and Family*. Toronto: Garamond Press.

Lynch, M. 1985. *Art and Artifact in Laboratory Science: A Study of Shop Work and Shop Talk in a Research Laboratory*. Boston: Routledge and Kegan Paul.

Lynch, M., E. Livingston, and H. Garfinkel. 1983. "Temporal Order in Laboratory Work." In *Science Observed*. Ed. K. Knorr-Cetina and M. Melkay. London: Sage 183–213.

Lynk, M. 1988. "Our Labour Relations System Faces Americanization: Labour Law Erosion." In *The Facts: The Facts on Free Trade—Canada: Don't Trade It Away*. Ed. E. Finn. Canadian Union of Public Employees 10, 2 (Spring).

MacDonald, P. 1988. "Historical School Reform and the Correspondence Principle." In *Bowles and Gintis Revisited: Correspondence and Contradiction*. Ed. M. Cole. London: Falmer Press, 86–111.

Mackenzie, S. 1986a. "Feminist Geography." *The Canadian Geographer* 30, 3: 268–70.

Mackenzie, S. 1986b. "Women's Response to Economic Restructuring: Changing Gender Changing Space." In *The Politics of Diversity: Feminism, Marxism, and*

Nationalism. Ed. R. Hamilton and M. Barrett. Montreal: Book Centre, 81–100.

Mackenzie, S. 1987a. "Neglected Spaces in Peripheral Places: Homeworkers and the Creation of a New Economic Centre." *Cahiers de géographie du Québec* 31, 83 (Sept.): 247–60.

Mackenzie, S. 1987b. "The Politics of Restructuring: Gender and Economy in De-industrialized Areas." Paper presented to the Canadian Association of Geographers, Hamilton, Ont.

Mackenzie, S. 1989. "Women in the City." In *New Models of Geography*. Ed. R. Peet and N. Thrift. Boston: Allen and Unwin.

Mandel, E. 1969. *An Introduction to Marxist Economic Theory*. New York: Pathfinder Press.

Marchak, P. 1985. "Canadian Political Economy." *Canadian Review of Sociology and Anthropology* 22, 5 (Dec.): 673–709.

Marcuse, H. 1964. *One-Dimensional Man*. Boston: Beacon Press.

Marglin, S.A. 1974–75. "What Bosses Do." *Review of Radical Political Economy* 6: 60–112; 7: 20–37.

Maroney, H.J., and M. Luxton, eds. 1987. *Feminism and Political Economy: Women's Work, Women's Struggles*. Toronto: Methuen.

Martin, D. 1977. *Battered Wives*. New York: Pocket Books.

Martin, D. 1982. "Facing the Octopus: The Transnational Corporation." In *Ties that Bind: Canada and the Third World*. Ed. R. Swift and R. Clark. Toronto: Between the Lines, 87–148.

Marx, K. [1845] 1975. "Thesis on Feuerbach." In *Karl Marx, Frederick Engels: Collected Works*. New York: International Publishers. 5: 3–7.

Marx, K. [1847] 1971. *The Poverty of Philosophy*. New York: International Publishers.

Marx, K. [1859] 1975. "'Preface' to a Contribution to the Critique of Political Economy." In *Karl Marx: Early Writings*. Harmondsworth: Penguin.

Marx, K. [1869] 1935. *The Eighteenth Brumaire of Louis Bonaparte*. New York: International Publishers.

Marx, K. 1967. *Capital*. Vol. 1. *A Critical Analysis of Capitalist Production* [1867]. Vol. 2. *The Process of Circulation of Capital* [1885]; Vol. 3. *The Process of Capitalist Production as a Whole* [1894]. Ed. F. Engels. New York: International Publishers.

Marx, K., and F. Engels. [1847] 1970. *The German Ideology*. London: Lawrence and Wishart.

Marx, K., and F. Engels. [1848] 1955. *The Communist Manifesto*. Ed. S.H. Beer. New York: Appleton-Century-Crofts.

Maynard, R., with C. Brouse. 1988. "Thanks, But No Thanks." *Report on Business Magazine* (Feb.): 26–34.

Mayo, E. [1933] 1960. *The Human Problems of an Industrial Civilization*. New York: Viking Press.

McAteer, M. 1989. "Women in the Clergy: Numbers Keep Growing." *Toronto Star*, 21 Oct., M29.

McCullum,, H., and R. Hatton. 1979. "Project North." *Canadian Dimension* 13, 5 (Jan.-Feb.): 43–45.

McDonald, L. 1989. "First Nations Women and Education." *Women's Education des femmes* 7, 3 (Sept.): 25–28.

McFarland, J. 1980. "Changing Modes of Social Control in a New Brunswick Fish Packing Town." *Studies in Political Economy* 4 (Autumn): 99–113.

McGahan, P. 1982. *Urban Sociology in Canada*. Toronto: Butterworths.

McHoul, A. 1978. "The Organization of Turns at Formal Talk in the Classroom." *Language and Society* 7: 183–213.

McIntyre, S. 1986. "Gender Bias Within the Law School." Memo to all members of the Faculty Board. Queen's University. 28 July.

McMahon, S. 1987. "The New Forest in Nova Scotia." In *People, Resources, and Power: Critical Perspectives on Underdevelopment and Primary Industries in the Atlantic Region*. Ed. G. Burrill and I. McKay. Fredericton: Acadiensis Press, 99–105.

McRobbie, A. 1978. "Working Class Girls and the Culture of Femininity." In *Women Take Issue: Aspects of Women's Subordination*. London: Hutchinson: 96–108.

Mead, G.H. 1934. *Mind, Self, and Society*. Chicago: University of Chicago Press.

Mead, M. 1928. *Coming of Age in Samoa: A Psychological Study of Primitive Youth for Western Civilization*. New York: Blue Ribbon Books.

Meissner, M., E.W. Humphreys, S.M. Meis, and W.J. Scheu. 1975. "No Exit for Wives: Sexual Division of Labour and the Culmination of Household Demands." *Canadian Review of Sociology and Anthropology* 12, 4 (Nov.): 424–39.

Melander, T. 1988. *Saving Lakes*. Trans. C. Thorn. Gothenburg, Sweden: Informator AB.

Menzies, H. 1981. *Women and the Chip: Case Studies of the Effects of Information on Employment in Canada*. Montreal: Institute for Research on Public Policy.

Merritt, M. 1976. "On Questions Following Questions in Service Encounters." *Language in Society* 5: 315–57.

Merton, R.K. 1957. "Bureaucratic Structure and Personality." In *Social Theory and Social Structure*. Ed. R.K. Merton. Glencoe, Ill.: Free Press, 249–60.

Merton, R.K. 1967. *On Theoretical Sociology: Five Essays, Old and New*. New York: Free Press.

Merton, R.K. 1968. *Social Theory and Social Structure.* Englarged ed. New York: Free Press.

Michels, R. [1911] 1949. *Political Parties.* Glencoe, Ill.: Free Press.

Michelson, W.H. 1970. *Man and His Urban Environment: A Sociological Approach.* Reading, Mass.: Addison-Wesley.

Miles, A. 1985. "Economism and Feminism: Hidden in the Household. A Comment on the Domestic Labour Debate." In *Feminist Marxism or Marxist Feminism.* Ed. P. Armstrong, H. Armstrong, P. Connelly, A. Miles and M. Luxton. Toronto: Garamond Press.

Milgram, S. 1974. *Obedience to Authority.* New York: Harper and Row.

Miliband, R. 1969. *The State in Capitalist Society.* New York: Basic Books.

Miller, W.B. 1958. "Lower Class Culture as a Generating Milieu of Gang Delinquency." *Journal of Social Issues* 14, 2: 5–19.

Mills, C.W. 1959. *The Sociological Imagination.* New York: Oxford University Press.

Miner, H. 1939. *St. Denis: A French-Canadian Parish.* Chicago: University of Chicago Press.

Miner, H. 1964. "Changes in Rural French-Canadian Culture." In *French-Canadian Society.* Vol. 1. Ed. M. Rioux and Y. Martin. Toronto: McClelland and Stewart, 63–75.

Misch, C., et al. 1982. *National Survey Concerning Female Inmates in Provincial and Territorial Institutions.* Ottawa: Canadian Association of Elizabeth Fry Societies.

Mitchell, J. 1971. *Women's Estate.* Harmondsworth: Penguin.

Mitchell, J. 1972. "Marxism and Women's Revolution." *Social Praxis* 1, 1.

Molotch, H.L., and D. Boden. 1985. "Talking Social Structure: Domination and the Watergate Hearings." *American Sociological Review* 50: 273–88.

Mooney, J. 1965. *The Ghost Dance Religion and the Sioux Outbreak of 1890.* London: University of Chicago Press.

Moore, R. 1988. "The Correspondence Principle and the Marxist Sociology of Education." In *Bowles and Gintis: Correspondence and Contradiction.* Ed. M. Cole. London: Falmer Press, 51–85.

Morgan, K., and A. Sayer. 1988. *Microcircuits of Capital: "Sunrise" Industry and Uneven Development.* Cambridge: Polity Press.

Morris, A. 1987. *Women, Crime and Criminal Justice.* Oxford: Basil Blackwell.

Morris, R. 1964. "Female Delinquency and Relational Problems." *Social Forces* 42 (Oct.): 82–88.

Morrow, R.A. 1985. "Critical Theory and Critical Sociology." *Canadian Review of Sociology and Anthropology* 22, 5 (Dec.): 771–93.

Morton, P. 1972. "Women's Work Is Never Done." In *Women Unite!* Toronto: Women's Press, 45–69.

Mosca, G. [1939] 1960. *The Ruling Class.* New York: McGraw-Hill.

Muller, J. 1989. "Ruling Through Texts: Developing a Social Service Training Program for a Community College." *Community Development Journal* 24, 4 (Oct.): 273–82.

Muller, J. 1990. "Co-ordinating the Re-organization of Ruling Relations: Management's Use of Human Resource Development for the New Brunswick Community Colleges." In *Political Economy of Community Colleges: Training Workers for Capital.* Ed. J. Muller. Toronto: Garamond Press.

Murdoch, G.P. 1949. *Social Structure.* New York: Free Press.

Murphy, T. 1987. "Potato Capitalism: McCain and Industrial Farming in New Brunswick." In *People, Resources, and Power: Critical Perspectives on Underdevelopment and Primary Industries in the Atlantic Region.* Ed. G. Burrill and I. McKay. Fredericton: Acadiensis Press, 19–29.

National Action Committee on the Status of Women. 1987a. "Brief on the 1987 Constitutional Accord." Presented to the Special Joint Committee of the Senate and the House of Commons on the 1987 Constitutional Accord. 26 Aug.

National Action Committee on the Status of Women. 1987b. "Refugee Women and Bill C-55." Prepared by the NAC Foreign Policy Committee. Sept.

National Council of Welfare. 1975. *Poor Kids. A Report by the National Council of Welfare on Children in Poverty in Canada.* Ottawa: National Council of Welfare.

National Council of Welfare. 1977. *Jobs and Poverty. A Report by the National Council of Welfare on Canada's Working Poor.* Ottawa: National Council of Welfare.

National Council of Welfare. 1978. *Bearing the Burden, Sharing the Burden. A Report by the National Council of Welfare on Taxation and the Distribution of Income.* Ottawa: National Council of Welfare.

National Council of Welfare. 1979a. *The Hidden Welfare System Revisited. A Report by the National Council of Welfare on the Growth in Tax Expenditures.* Ottawa: National Council of Welfare.

National Council of Welfare. 1979b. *Women and Poverty.* Ottawa: National Council of Welfare.

National Council of Welfare. 1981. *The Working Poor: People and Programs. A Statistical Profile Prepared by the National Council of Welfare.* Ottawa: National Council of Welfare.

National Council of Welfare. 1982. *Revised 1982 Poverty Lines*. Ottawa: National Council of Welfare.

National Council of Welfare. 1986. *The Impact of the 1985 and 1986 Budgets on Disposable Income*. Ottawa: National Council of Welfare,

National Council of Welfare. 1987a. *The Hidden Welfare System: Exemptions, Deductions and Credits*. Ottawa: National Council of Welfare.

National Council of Welfare. 1987b. *Tax Expenditures: Who Gets What*. Ottawa: National Council of Welfare.

National Council of Welfare. 1987c. *Welfare in Canada: The Tangled Safety Net*. Ottawa: National Council of Welfare.

National Council of Welfare. 1987d. *What To Look for and Look Out for in Tax Reform*. Ottawa: National Council of Welfare.

National Council of Welfare. 1988a. *Child Care: A Better Alternative*. Ottawa: National Council of Welfare.

National Council of Welfare. 1988b. *Poverty Profile 1988*. Ottawa: National Council of Welfare.

National Council of Welfare. 1989. *1989 Poverty Lines: Estimates of the National Council of Welfare*. Ottawa: National Council of Welfare.

Neill, A.S. 1960. *Summerhill: A Radical Approach to Child Rearing*. New York: Hart.

Neuringer, C., and D.J. Lettieri. 1982. *Suicidal Women: Their Thinking and Feeling Patterns*. New York: Gardiner Press.

Newman, P. 1975. *The Canadian Establishment*. Toronto: McClelland and Stewart.

Neyer, J. 1960. "Individualism and Socialism in Durkheim." In *Essays on Sociology and Philosophy by Emile Durkheim et al.* Ed. K.H. Wolff. New York: Harper and Row.

Ng, R. 1981. "Constituting Ethnic Phenomenon: An Account from the Perspective of Immigrant Women." *Canadian Ethnic Studies* 13, 1: 97–108.

Ng, R. 1986. "The Social Construction of Immigrant Women in Canada." In *The Politics of Diversity: Feminism, Marxism, and Nationalism*. Ed. R. Hamilton and M. Barrett. Montreal: Book Centre: 269–86.

Ng, R. 1988a. "Ethnicity, Gender, Class and Canadian State Formation." Paper presented at Ontario Institute for Studies in Education, 24 Feb.

Ng, R. 1988b. *The Politics of Community Services: Immigrant Women, Class, and State*. Toronto: Garamond Press.

Nichols, T., and H. Beynon. 1977. *Living with Capitalism: Class Relations and the Modern Factory*. London: Routledge and Kegan Paul.

Nicholson, J. 1984. *Men and Women: How Different Are They?* Oxford: Oxford University Press.

Noble, J. 1979. "Social Class and the Under-Fives: Making the 'Differences' Visible." Paper presented to the Canadian Sociological and Anthopological Association, Saskatoon.

O'Brien, M. 1981. *The Politics of Reproduction*. London: Routledge and Kegan Paul.

O'Connell, D. 1983. "Poverty: The Feminine Complaint." In *Perspectives on Women in the 1980s*. Ed. J. Turner and L. Emery. Winnipeg: University of Manitoba Press, 41–65.

Orenstein, D. 1985. *The Sociological Quest: Principles of Sociology*. St. Paul, Minn.: West Publishing.

Panitch, L., and D. Swartz. 1988. *The Assault on Trade Union Freedoms*. Toronto: Garamond Press.

Pappert, A. 1989. "Social Debate Rages Over Unlimited Scope of Test Tube Babies." Part 1 of series The Reproductive Revolution. *Toronto Star*, 7–12 Oct.

Parsons, T. [1937] 1968. *The Structure of Social Action*. New York: Macmillan.

Parsons, T. 1951. *The Social System*. New York: Free Press.

Parsons, T. 1956. "Suggestions for a Sociological Approach to the Theory of Organizations." *Administrative Science Quarterly* (June): 63–69.

Parsons, T. 1961. "The School Class as a Social System: Some of its Functions in American Society." In *Education, Economy and Society*. Ed. A.H. Halsey, J. Floud, and C.A. Anderson. New York: Free Press.

Parsons, T. 1966. *Societies: Evolutionary and Comparative Perspectives*. Englewood Cliffs, N.J.: Prentice-Hall.

Parsons, T. 1978. "The Concept of Society: The Components and Their Interrelations." In *Contemporary Sociological Theories*. Ed. Alan Wells. Santa Monica, Calif.: Goodyear Publishing, 18–31.

Parson, T., and R.F. Bales, eds. 1956. *Family, Socialization, and Interaction Process*. London: Routledge and Kegan Paul.

Pentland, H.C. 1959. "The Development of a Capitalist Labour Market in Canada." *Canadian Journal of Economics and Political Science* 25, 4 (Nov.): 450–61.

Persky, S. 1989. "Capital Offences." Review of E. Kierans and W. Stewart. *Wrong End of the Rainbow: The Collapse of Free Enterprise in Canada*. Toronto: Collins. *Books in Canada* (March).

Philbrook, T. 1966. *Fisherman, Logger, Merchant, Miner: Social Change and Industrialism in Three Newfoundland Communities*. St. Johns: Institute of Social and Economic Research.

Piddington, R. 1965. "The Kinship Network Among French Canadians." *International Journal of Comparative Sociology* 6: 145–65.

Pollak, Otto. 1950. *The Criminality of Women.* Philadelphia: University of Pennsylvania Press.

Pope, W. 1976. *Durkheim's Suicide: A Classic Analysed.* Chicago: University of Chicago Press.

Porter, J. 1968. *The Vertical Mosaic: An Analysis of Class and Power in Canada.* Toronto: University of Toronto.

Porter, J. 1979. "Ethnic Pluralism in Canadian Perspective." In *The Measure of Canadian Society: Education, Equality and Opportunity.* Toronto: Gage, 103–37.

Porter, J., M. Porter, and B.R. Blishen. 1982. *Stations and Callings: Making it Through the School System.* Toronto: Methuen.

Porter, M.R., J. Porter, and B. Blishen. 1973. *Does Money Matter? Prospects for Higher Education.* Toronto: Institute for Behavioural Research.

Poulantzas, N. 1972. "The Problem of the Capitalist State." In *Ideology in Social Science: Reading in Critical Social Theory.* Ed. R. Blackburn. London: Fontana.

Priest, L. 1989. "The Murder of Helen Betty Osborne." *Canadian Dimension* (June): 9–12.

Psathas, G., ed. 1979. *Everyday Language: Studies in Ethnomethodology.* New York: Irvington Publishers.

Psathas, G. 1980. "Approaches to the Study of the World of Everyday Life." *Human Studies* 3: 3–17.

Ptacek, J. 1988. "Why Do Men Batter Their Wives?" In *Feminist Perspectives on Wife Abuse.* Ed. K. Yllö and M. Bograd. Beverly Hills: Sage Publications, 133–57.

Quinney, R. 1975. "Crime Control in Capitalist Society: A Critical Philosophy of Legal Order." In *Critical Criminology.* Ed. I. Taylor, P. Walton, and J. Young. London: Routledge and Kegan Paul.

Rafiq, F. 1988. "Women in Islam with Reference to Pakistan." Paper presented at Canadian Asian Studies Association meeting, Windsor. 9 June.

Rauhala, A. 1988. "Women Alarmed by Male Activists." *Globe and Mail.* 11 March.

Redfield, R. 1930. *Tepoztlan—A Mexican Village: A Study of Folk Life.* Chicago: University of Chicago Press.

Redfield, R. 1941. *The Folk Culture of Yucatan.* Chicago: University of Chicago Press.

Redfield, R. 1947. "The Folk Society." *American Journal of Sociology* 52 (Jan.): 293–303.

Redfield, R. 1964. "French-Canadian Culture in St-Denis." In *French-Canadian Society.* Vol. 1. Ed. M. Rioux and Y. Martin. Toronto: McClelland and Stewart, 57–62.

Reimer, M.A. 1987. "The Social Organization of the Labour Process: A Case Study of the Documentary Management of Clerical Labour in the Public Service." Ph.D. thesis, Ontario Institute for Studies in Education.

Reiss, I. 1976. *Family Systems in America.* 2nd ed. Hinsdale, Ill.: Dryden Press.

Rex, J. 1959. "The Plural Society in Sociological Theory." *British Journal of Sociology* 10: 114–24.

Rex, J. 1961. *Key Problems in Sociological Thought.* London: Routledge and Kegan Paul.

Rex, J. 1973. *Race, Colonialism, and the City.* London: Routledge and Kegan Paul.

Rex, J., and R. Moore. 1967. *Race, Community, and Conflict.* Oxford: Oxford University Press.

Richardson, R.J., and B. Wellman. 1985. "Structural Analysis." *Canadian Review of Sociology and Anthropology* 22, 5 (Dec.): 771–93.

Richmond, A.H. 1988. *Immigration and Ethnic Conflict.* London: Macmillan.

Richmond, A.H., M. Lyon, S. Hale, and R. King. 1973. *Migration and Race Relations in an English City.* London: Oxford University Press.

Rinehart, J.W. 1975. *The Tyranny of Work.* Don Mills, Ont.: Academic Press.

Rioux, M. 1964. "Remarks on the Socio-Cultural Development of French Canada." In *French-Canadian Society.* Vol. 1. Ed. M. Rioux and Y. Martin. Toronto: McClelland and Stewart, 162–78.

Rioux, M. 1978. *Quebec in Question.* Trans. James Boake. Toronto: Lorimer.

Rioux, M., and Y. Martin, eds. 1964. *French-Canadian Society.* Vol. 1. Toronto: McClelland and Stewart.

Rogers, B. 1980. *The Domestication of Women: Discrimination in Developing Societies.* London: Tavistock.

Rogers, E.M. 1968. "Motivations, Values and Attitudes of Subsistence Farmers: Towards a Subculture of Peasantry." In *Subsistance Agriculture and Economic Development.* Ed. C.J. Wharton. Chicago: Aldine.

Rogers, E.M. 1969. *Modernization Among Peasants: The Impact of Communication.* New York: Holt, Rinehart and Winston.

Rohner, R.P. 1967. *The People of Gilford: A Contemporary Kwakiutl Village.* Ottawa: National Museums of Canada.

Rosenberg, H. 1986. "The Kitchen and the Multinational Corporation: An Analysis of the Links Between the Household and Global Corporations." In M. Luxton and H. Rosenberg. *Through the Kitchen Window: The Politics of Home and Family.* Toronto: Garamond Press, 83–107.

Rosenhan, D.L. 1973. "Being Sane in Insane Places." *Science* 179 (Jan.): 250–58.

Rosenthal, R., and K. Fode. 1963. "The Effects of Experimenter Bias on the Performance of the Albino Rat." *Behavioural Science* 8: 183–89.

Ruether, R.R. 1975. *New Woman New Earth: Sexist Ideologies and Human Liberation*. New York: Seabury Press.

Runciman, W.G., ed. 1978. *Weber: Selections in Translation*. Cambridge: Cambridge University Press.

Russell, S. 1987. "The Hidden Curriculum of School: Reproducing Gender and Class Heirarchies." In *Feminism and Political Economy: Women's Work, Women's Struggles*. Ed. H.J. Maroney and M. Luxton. Toronto: Methuen, 229–46.

Sacks, H. 1972. "Notes on Police Assessment of Moral Character." In *Studies in Interaction*. Ed. D. Sudnow. New York: Free Press.

Sacks, H., E. Schegloff, and G. Jefferson. 1974. "Simplest Systematics for the Organization of Turn-Taking for Conversation." *Language* 50: 696–735.

Sacouman, R.J. 1980. "The Semi-proletarianization of the Domestic Mode of Production and the Underdevelopment of Rural Areas in Maritime Canada." Unpublished paper.

Sacouman, R.J. 1981. "The 'Peripheral' Maritimes and Canada-wide Marxist Political Economy." *Studies in Political Economy* 6 (Autumn): 135–50.

Sacouman, R.J. 1985. "Restructuring Conflict and the Question of Class and Gender Alliances in Primary Producer Struggles in the Maritimes, 1965–1985." Lecture at University of New Brunswick. 28 Nov.

Safilios-Rothschild, C. 1969. "Family Sociology or Wives' Family Sociology." *Journal of Marriage and the Family* 31, 2: 290–301.

Safilios-Rothschild, C., and A. Georgiouspoulos. 1970. "A Comparative Study of Parental and Filial Role Definitions." *Journal of Marriage and the Family* 32, 3: 381–89.

Saint Exupéry, A. de. [1943] 1971. *Le Petit Prince*. New York: Harcourt, Brace and World.

Salutin, R. 1988. "What Kind of Canada? Our Culture is not Protected Under this Deal, as Promised." In *The Facts: The Facts on Free Trade—Canada: Don't Trade It Away*. Ed. E. Finn. Canadian Union of Public Employees 10, 2 (Spring).

Saul, J.R. 1988. "The Secret Life of the Branch-Plant Executive." *Report on Business Magazine* (Jan.): 81–85.

Saunders, D.G. 1988. "Wife Abuse, Husband Abuse, or Mutual Combat? A Feminist Perspective on the Empirical Findings." In *Feminist Perspectives on Wife Abuse*. Ed. K. Yllö and M. Bograd. Beverly Hills: Sage Publications.

Schenkein, J., ed. 1978. *Studies in the Organization of Conversational Interaction*. New York: Academic Press.

Schneider, A. 1987. "Underdeveloping Nova Scotia's Forests and the Role of Corporate Counter-Intelligence." In *People, Resources, and Power: Critical Perspectives on Underdevelopment and Primary Industries in the Atlantic Region*. Ed. G. Burrill and I. McKay. Fredericton: Acadiensis Press, 117–22.

Schur, E. 1965. *Crimes Without Victims*. Englewood Cliffs, N.J.: Prentice-Hall.

Schur, E. 1971. *Labelling Deviant Behavior: Its Sociological Implications*. New York: Harper and Row.

Schur, E. 1980. *The Politics of Deviance: Stigma Contests and the Uses of Power*. Englewood Cliffs, N.J.: Prentice-Hall.

Schur, E.M., and H.A. Bedau. 1974. *Victimless Crimes: Two Sides of a Controversy*. Englewood Cliffs, N.J.: Prentice-Hall.

Schwendinger, H., and J. Schwendinger. 1975. "Defenders of Order or Guardians of Human Rights?" In *Critical Criminology*. Ed. I. Taylor, P. Walton, and J. Young. London: Routledge and Kegan Paul, 113–46.

Seccombe, W. 1974. "The Housewife and Her Labour Under Capitalism." *New Left Review* 83 (Jan.–Feb.): 3–24.

Seccombe, W. 1980. "Domestic Labour and the Working-Class Household." In *Hidden in the Household: Women's Domestic Labour Under Capitalism*. Ed. Bonnie Fox. Toronto: Women's Press, 25–100.

Seeley, J.A., R.A. Sim, and E.W. Loosley. 1956. *Crestwood Heights*. New York: John Wiley.

Seligman, M.E.P. 1975. *Helplessness: On Depression, Development, and Death*. San Francisco: W.H. Freeman.

Sen, G. 1985. *Development, Crises, and Alternative Visions: Third World Women's Perspectives*. New Delhi: Development Alternatives with Women for a New Era (DAWN).

Sewell, J. 1985. *Police: Urban Policing in Canada*. Toronto: Lorimer.

Shaw, R.P. 1985. "Humanity's Propensity for Warfare: A Sociological Perspective." *Canadian Review of Sociology and Anthropology* 22, 2: 158–83.

Shulman, N. 1976. "Role Differentiation in Urban Networks." *Sociological Focus* 9: 149–58.

Shupe, A., W.A. Stacey, and L.R. Hazlewood. 1987. *Violent Men, Violent Couples*. Toronto: Lexington Books.

Simmel, G. 1949. "The Sociology of Sociability." *American Journal of Sociology* (Nov.): 254–61.

Simmel, G. 1950. "The Metropolis and Mental Life." In *The Sociology of George Simmel.* Glencoe, Ill.: Free Press, 409–24.

Sinclair, D. 1989. "When Children are Sex Abuse Victims." *United Church Observer* (July): 31.

Sinclair, S., and M. Clow. 1988. "Regional Disparities." In *The Free Trade Deal.* Ed. Duncan Cameron. Toronto: Lorimer.

Sivard, R.L. 1985. *Women: A World Survey.* Washington: World Priorities.

Smart, B. 1983. *Foucault: Marxism and Critique.* London: Routledge and Kegan Paul.

Smart, C. 1977. "Criminological Theory: Its Ideology and Implications Concerning Women." *British Journal of Sociology* 28, 1 (March): 89–100.

Smart, J. 1988. "Immigration and Household Formation: The Emergence of Female-Centred Households Among Hong Kong Business Immigrants." Unpublished paper presented to the Canadian Asian Studies Association. Windsor. June.

Smelser, N.J. 1959. *Social Change in the Industrial Revolution.* Chicago: University of Chicago Press.

Smillie, B.G. 1979. "The Social Gospel." *Canadian Dimension* 13, 5 (Jan.–Feb.): 35–37.

Smith, A. [1776] 1894. *The Wealth of Nations.* London: Macmillan.

Smith, D.E. 1974a. "The Ideological Practice of Sociology." *Catalyst* 8 (Winter): 39–54.

Smith, D.E. 1974b. "The Social Construction of Documentary Reality." *Sociological Inquiry* 44, 4: 257–68.

Smith, D.E. 1975. "An Analysis of Ideological Structures and How Women Are Excluded: Considerations for Academic Women." *Canadian Review of Sociology and Anthropology* 12, 4: 353–69.

Smith, D.E. 1977. "Women, the Family, and Corporate Capitalism." In *Women in Canada.* Ed. M. Stephenson. Don Mills, Ont.: General Publishing, 32–48.

Smith, D.E. 1979a. "Using the Oppressor's Language." *Resources for Feminist Research.* Special publication no. 5 (Spring).

Smith, D.E. 1979b. "Women's Inequality and the Family." Department of Sociology, Ontario Institute for Studies in Education, Mimeograph.

Smith, D.E. 1981. "On Sociological Description: A Method from Marx." *Human Studies* 4: 313–37.

Smith, D.E. 1983a. "No One Commits Suicide: Textual Analysis of Ideological Practices." *Human Studies* 6: 309–59.

Smith, D.E. 1983b. "Women, Class and Family." In *The Socialist Register.* Ed. R. Miliband and J. Saville. London: Merlin Press.

Smith, D.E. 1986. "Institutional Ethnography: A Feminist Method." *Resources for Feminist Research* 15, 1 (March): 6–13.

Smith, D.E. 1987a. *The Everyday World as Problematic: A Feminist Sociology.* Toronto: University of Toronto Press.

Smith, D.E. 1987b. "Feminist Reflections on Political Economy." Paper presented at the Learned Societies. Hamilton, Ont.

Smith, D.E., and G. Malnarich. 1983. "Where Are the Women? A Critique of Socialist and Communist Political Organization." Paper presented at the Conference on Marxism: The Next Two Decades. University of Manitoba.

Smith, D.E., and the Wollestonecraft Research Group. 1979. "Educational Cutbacks and the Workload of Elementary Teachers." *Women in the Educational Workforce.* Status of Women Tabloid. Canadian Teachers' Federation. (Sept.)

Smith, J., and W. Fried. 1974. *The Uses of the American Prison: Political Theory and Penal Practice.* Lexington, Mass.: Lexington Books.

Sorokin, P.A., and C.C. Zimmerman. 1929. *Principles of Rural-Urban Sociology.* New York: Hinney Holt.

Spencer, M. 1976. *Foundations of Modern Sociology.* Englewood Cliffs, N.J.: Prentice-Hall.

Spiro, M.E. 1958. *Children of the Kibbutz.* Cambridge: Harvard University Press.

Spitzer, S. 1975. "Toward a Marxian Theory of Deviance." *Social Problems* 22 (June): 638–51.

Stack, S. 1982. "Suicide: A Decade Review of the Sociological Literature." *Deviant Behavior: An Interdisciplinary Journal* 4: 41–66.

Stanko, E.A. 1988. "Fear of Crime and the Myth of the Safe Home: A Feminist Critique of Criminology." In *Feminist Perspectives on Wife Abuse.* Ed. K. Yllö and M. Bograd. Beverly Hills: Sage Publications.

Stanley, G.F.C. 1964. *Louis Riel: Patriot or Rebel?* Canadian Historical Association Booklet no. 2. Ottawa: Canadian Historical Association.

Statistics Canada. 1984. *Canada's Native People.* Cat. 99-937. Ottawa: Ministry of Supply and Services.

Statistics Canada. 1985. *Education in Canada: A Statistical Review for 1984–85.* Ottawa: Ministry of Supply and Services.

Statistics Canada. 1985–86. *Women in the Labour Force.* Ottawa: Ministry of Supply and Services.

Statistics Canada. 1986. *Canadian Crime Statistics.* Cat. 85-205. Ottawa: Ministry of Supply and Services.

Statistics Canada. 1987. *The Labour Force.* Cat. 71-001. Ottawa: Ministry of Supply and Services.

Statistics Canada. 1989a. *Education in Canada: A Statistical Review for 1987–88.* Cat. 81-229. Ottawa: Ministry of Supply and Services.

Statistics Canada. 1989b. *The Labour Force: August 1989.* Cat. 71-001. Ottawa: Ministry of Supply and Services.

Steedman, M. 1987. "Who's on Top? Heterosexual Practices and Male Dominance During the Sex Act." In *Who's on Top? The Politics of Heterosexuality.* Ed. B. Young, H. Buchbinder, D. Forbes, V. Burstyn, and M. Steedman. Toronto: Garamond Press.

Steinmetz, S.K. 1977–78. "The Battered Husband Syndrome." *Victimology: An International Journal* 2–3: 499–509.

Stillman, D. 1980. "The Devastating Effect of Plant Closures." In *The Big Business Reader.* Ed. M. Green and R. Massie. New York: Pingrim Press, 72–88.

Stinchcombe, A.I. 1968. *Constructing Social Theories.* New York: Harcourt Brace and World.

Stone, K. 1974. "The Origins of Job Structures in the Steel Industry." *Review of Radical Political Economics* 6, 2 (Summer): 113–73.

Straus, M.A., R. Gelles, and S.K. Steinmetz. 1980. *Behind Closed Doors: Violence in the American Family.* Garden City, N.Y.: Doubleday.

Straus, M.A., and R.J. Gelles. 1986. "Societal Change and Change in Family Violence from 1975 to 1985 as Revealed by Two National Surveys." *Journal of Marriage and the Family* 48 (Aug.): 465–79.

Stymeist, D.H. 1975. *Ethnics and Indians.* Toronto: Peter Martin.

Sudnow, D. 1965. "Normal Crimes: Sociological Features of a Penal Code in a Public Defender's Office." *Social Problems* 12: 255–76.

Sudnow, D. 1978. *Ways of the Hand: The Organization of Improvised Conduct.* Cambridge: Harvard University Press.

Sudnow, D. 1979. *Talk's Body: A Mediation Between Two Keyboards.* Harmondsworth: Penguin.

Sunahara, A.G. 1981. *The Politics of Racism: The Uprooting of Japanese Canadians During the Second World War.* Toronto: Lorimer.

Suter, B. 1976. "Suicide and Women." In *Between Survival and Suicide.* Ed. B.B. Wolman and H.H. Krauss. New York: Gardiner Press.

Sutherland, E.H. 1937. *The Professional Thief.* Chicago: University of Chicago Press.

Sutherland, E.H. 1939. *Principles of Criminology.* Philadelphia: Lippincott.

Sutherland, E.H. [1949] 1961. *White Collar Crime.* New York: Dryden.

Sutherland, E., and D. Cressey. 1960. *Principles of Criminology.* Philadelphia: Lippincott.

Suttles, G.D. 1968. *The Social Order of the Slum.* Chicago: University of Chicago Press.

Suttles, G.D. 1972. *The Social Construction of Communities.* Chicago: University of Chicago Press.

Sweezy, P.M. 1942. *The Theory of Capitalist Development: Principles of Marxian Political Economy.* New York: Oxford University Press.

Taylor, I. 1983. *Crime, Capitalism, and Community: Three Essays in Socialist Criminology.* Toronto: Butterworths.

Taylor, I., P. Walton, and J. Young, eds. 1975. *Critical Criminology.* London: Routledge and Kegan Paul.

Teeple, G. 1972. "Land, Labour, and Capital in Pre-Confederation Canada." In *Capitalism and the National Question in Canada.* Ed. G. Teeple. Toronto: University of Toronto Press, 43–66.

Terkel, S. 1972. *Working: People Talk About what They Do All Day and How They Feel About what They Do.* New York: Pantheon.

Thomas, W.I., and F. Znaniecki. [1919] 1971. *The Polish Peasant in Europe and America.* New York: Octagon Books.

Thompson, E.P. 1963. *The Making of the English Working Class.* Harmondsworth: Penguin.

Thompson, E.P. 1975. *Whigs and Hunters: The Origins of the Black Act.* London: Allen Lane.

Thompson, E.P. 1978a. "Eighteenth-Century English Society: Class Struggle Without Class." *Social History* 3, 2 (May).

Thompson, E.P. 1978b. *The Poverty of Theory.* London: Merlin Press.

Thorliefsdóttir, T. 1988. "Iceland's Feminist Party." *Address to the National Action Committee on the Status of Women Annual General Meeting.* Ottawa. 13 May.

Thrasher, F.M. 1963. *The Gang: A Study of 1,313 Gangs in Chicago.* Chicago: University of Chicago Press.

Tiger, L. 1977. "The Possible Biological Origins of Sexual Discrimination." In *Biosocial Man.* Ed. D. Brothwell. London: Eugenics Society, 23–40.

Tompkins, P., and C. Bird. 1973. *The Secret Life of Plants.* New York: Avon Books.

Tönnies, F. [1887] 1957. *Community and Society.* New York: Harper and Row.

Trainer, E.F. 1985. *Abandon Affluence!* London: Zed Books.

Tuchman, G. 1972. "Objectivity as Strategic Ritual: An Examination of Nesmen's Notions of Objectivity." *American Journal of Sociology* 77 (Jan.): 660–78.

Tuchman, G. 1978. *Making News: A Study in the Social Construction of Reality.* New York: Free Press.

Tumin, M. 1953. "Critical Analysis of 'Some Principles of Stratification'." *American Sociological Review* 18, 4.

Tumin, M. 1973. *Patterns of Sociology*. Boston: Little Brown.

Turner, R., ed. 1974. *Ethnomethodology: Selected Readings*. Harmondsworth: Penguin.

Van den Berghe, P.L. 1969. "Pluralism and the Polity: A Theoretical Exploration." In *Pluralism in Africa*. Ed. L. Kuper and M.G. Smith. Berkeley: University of California Press.

Veblen, T. 1928. *The Theory of the Leisure Class*. New York: Vanguard Press.

Veevers, J. 1986. "Age-Discrepant Marriages: Cross-National Comparisons of Canadian–American Trends." *Social Biology* 31, 1–2: 18–27.

Veltmeyer, H. 1979. "The Capitalist Underdevelopment of Atlantic Canada." In *Underdevelopment and Social Movements in Atlantic Canada*. Ed. R.J. Brym and R.J. Sacouman. Toronto: New Hogtown Press, 17–35.

Veltmeyer, H. 1986. *Canadian Class Structure*. Toronto: Garamond Press.

Veltmeyer, H. 1987. *Canadian Corporate Power*. Toronto: Garamond Press.

Waddell, C. 1988. "Ontario's Achilles Heel." *Report on Business Magazine* (May): 25–28.

Warskett, R. 1988. "Bank Worker Unionization and the Law." *Studies in Political Economy* 25 (Spring): 41–73.

Wax, M.L., R.H. Wax, and R.V. Dumont Jr. 1964. "Formal Education in an American Indian Community." *Social Problems* 11, 4 (Spring) Supplement: 1–126.

Weatherford, J. 1988. *Indian Givers: How the Indians of the Americas Transformed the World*. New York: Crown Publishers.

Webb, E.J., D.T. Campbell, R.D. Schwartz, and L. Sechrest. 1966. *Unobtrusive Measures: Nonreactive Research in the Social Sciences*. Chicago: Rand McNally.

Weber, M. [1904] 1930. *The Protestant Ethic and the Spirit of Capitalism*. London: Unwin University Books.

Weber, M. [1922] 1964. *The Sociology of Religion*. Trans. E. Fischoff. Boston: Beacon Press.

Weber, M. [1922] 1968. *Economy and Society: An Outline of Interpretive Sociology*. Trans. G. Roth and G. Wittich. New York: Bedminister Press.

Weber, M. 1949. *The Methodology of Social Sciences*. Trans. E. Shils and A.M. Henderson. Glencoe, Ill.: Free Press.

Weeks, P.A.D. 1982. "An Ethnomethodological Study of Collective Music-Making." Unpublished Ph.D. thesis, Ontario Institute for Studies in Education.

Weeks, P.A.D. 1985. "Error-Correction Techniques and Sequences in Instructional Settings: Toward a Comparative Framework." *Human Studies* 8: 195–233.

Weeks, P.A.D. 1988. "Musical Time as a Practical Accomplishment: A Change of Tempo." Paper presented to the Society for Phenomenology and the Human Sciences, Toronto.

Weir, L. 1987. "Socialist Feminism and the Politics of Sexuality." In *Feminism and Political Economy: Women's Work, Women's Struggle*. Ed. H.J. Maroney and M. Luxton. Toronto: Methuen, 69–83.

Weitzman, L.J., and D. Eifler, E. Hokada, and C. Ross. 1972. "Sex-role Socialization in Picture Books for Preschool Children." *American Journal of Sociology* 77 (May): 1125–50.

Wellman, B. 1978. "The Community Question: The Intimate Networks of East Yorkers." *University of Toronto Centre for Urban and Community Studies and Department of Sociology*.

West, C. 1984. "When the Doctor is a 'Lady': Power, Status and Gender in Physician-Patient Encounters." *Symbolic Interaction* 7: 87–106.

Whyte, W.F. 1943. *Street Corner Society*. Chicago: University of Chicago Press.

Whyte, W.F. 1948. *Human Relations in the Restaurant Industry*. New York: McGraw-Hill.

Whyte, W.F. 1949. "The Social Structure of the Restaurant." *American Journal of Sociology* 54 (Jan.): 302–10.

Whyte, W.H., Jr. 1956. *The Organization Man*. New York: Simon and Schuster.

Willis, P. 1978. *Learning to Labour: How Working-Class Kids Get Working-Class Jobs*. London: Saxon House.

Wilson, A. 1978. *Finding a Voice: Asian Women in Britain*. London: Virago.

Winson, A. 1988. "Shake Ups in Supermarkets Spread Beyond the Shelves." *Globe and Mail*. 30 June.

Wirth, L. 1938. "Urbanism as a Way of Life." *American Journal of Sociology* 44, 1: 1–24.

Wolcott, H.F. 1967. *A Kwakiutl Village and School*. Toronto: Holt, Rinehart and Winston.

Wonnacott, P. 1987. *The United States and Canada: The Quest for Free Trade. An Examination of Selected Issues*. Policy Analyses in International Economics vol. 16. Washington, D.C.: Institute for International Economics.

Wood, E.M. 1982. "The Politics of Theory and the Concept of Class: E.P. Thompson and His Critics." *Studies in Political Economy* 9 (Fall): 45–76.

Woodhouse, H. 1988. "Time To Draw the Line." *Globe and Mail*. 13 May, A7.

Woolf, L. 1969. *The Journey Not the Arrival Matters: An Autobiography of the Years 1939–1969*. New York: Harcourt Brace Jovanovich.

World Bank. 1987. *World Development Report*. New York: Oxford University Press.

Wrong, D. 1961. "The Oversocialized Conception of Man in Modern Sociology." *American Sociological Review* 26 (April): 183–93.

Yinger, J.M. 1957. *Religion, Society, and the Individual: An Introduction to the Sociology of Religion.* New York: Macmillan.

Yllö, K., and M. Bograd, eds. 1988. *Feminist Perspectives on Wife Abuse.* Beverly Hills: Sage Publications.

Young, M., and P. Willmott. 1957. *Family and Kinship in East London.* London: Routledge and Kegan Paul.

Zimmerman, C.C. 1935. "Rural Society." *Encyclopaedia of the Social Sciences* 13: 469.

Zimmerman, D.H. 1974. "Fact as a Practical Accomplishment." In *Ethnomethodology: Selected Readings.* Ed. R. Turner. Harmondsworth: Penguin.

Zimmerman, D.H., and C. West. 1975. "Sex Roles, Interruptions and Silences in Conversations." In *Language and Sex: Differences and Dominance.* Ed. B. Thorne and N. Henley. Rowley, Mass.: Newbury House Publishers, 105–29.

Credits

An honest attempt has been made to secure permission for all material used, and if there are errors or omissions, these are wholly unintentional and the publisher will be grateful to learn of them.

Illustrations

p.6 top: Western Canada Pictorial Index; bottom: The Salvation Army Heritage Centre Canada. p.8 Reproduced with permission of the Regina *Leader-Post*, and Cam Cardow. p.15 Library of Congress. p.21 Excerpt from *An Invitation to Sociology* by Peter Berger, copyright © 1963 by Peter L. Berger. Used by permission of Doubleday, a division of Bantam, Doubleday, Dell Publishing Group, Inc. p.24 Freedom Fest '88, A Festival of Black Culture and Heritage, Courtesy of the Ontario Black History Society. p.28 Courtesy Greenpeace. p.35 Illustration, page 7, from *Le Petit Prince* by Antoine de Saint-Exupéry, copyright 1943 by Harcourt Brace Jovanovich, Inc. and renewed 1971 by Consuelo de Saint-Exupéry, reprinted by permission of the publisher. p.62 Courtesy of the Institute for Intercultural Studies, Inc., New York. p.76 Seneca College. p.85 From *Philosophical Investigations* by Wittgenstein, copyright Basil Blackwell. Reprinted by permission of the publisher. p.93 Courtesy Markham *Economist and Sun*. p.97 Freedom Fest '88, A Festival of Black Culture and Heritage, Courtesy of The Ontario Black History Society. p.109 Courtesy Peter Weeks. p.116 NAC/PA 140823. p.123 Courtesy Peter Weeks. p.124 Courtesy Peter Weeks. p.128 Public Archives of Nova Scotia. p.130 Glenbow Museum. p.167 © Punch/ Rothco. p.169 NAC/C 57365. p.172 Courtesy United Church *Observer*. p.175 Courtesy Canadian Women's Movement Archives. p.180 Photo Features Ltd., Ottawa. p.186 Edmonton *Journal*/Chris Schwarz. p.188 Provincial Archives of Manitoba p.201 Canapress Photo Service/Ray Giguere. p.203 NAC/PA 129838. p.207 Canapress Photo Service/Bloomfield. p.217 Canapress Photo Service. p.229 National Archives, Washington, D.C. p.238 Reprinted by permission of United Electrical, Radio and Machine Workers of America, from *UE News*. p.263 Brandon *Sun*. p.269 Photo Features Ltd., Ottawa. p.280 Canapress Photo Service. p.283 Courtesy Save the Children Canada. p.291 Courtesy Canadian Women's Movement Archives. p.307 Courtesy of the Harvard University Archives. p.330 Courtesy Toronto Jewish Media Centre. p.349 Courtesy Canadian Women's Movement Archives. p.355 Western Canada Pictorial Index. p.359 Western Canada Pictorial Index. p.369 NAC/PA 42949. p.394 Archives of Ontario/RG10-515515. p.339 Glenbow Museum. p.402 The United Church of Canada/Victoria University Archives, Toronto. p.426 Canapress Photo Service/Frank Gunn. p.432 Courtesy Peter Weeks. p.440 Courtesy Cross-Cultural Communication Centre. p.452 The Ontario Black History Society. p.465 Courtesy Save the Children Canada. p.470 Courtesy Dean Nernberg, University of Alberta. p.471 Courtesy Save the Children Canada. p.477 Courtesy Peter Weeks. p.491 Courtesy The Toronto Humane Society. p.493 Courtesy Dean Nernberg. p.494 Courtesy Greenpeace. p.495 Courtesy Ontario Ministry of Transportation. p.505 Library of Congress. p.513 Canapress Photo Service. p.532 Canapress Photo Service. p.534 Reprinted with permission of *The Globe and Mail* (19 December 1989). p.543 Western Canada Pictorial Index. p.549 Courtesy Canadian Women's Movement Archives.

Tables and Figures
Figure 2-4 Statistics Canada, Cat. 81-241; Figure 4–1 and quotes pp.82 and 86–87
Harold Garfinkel, *Studies in Ethnomethodology*, © 1967, pp. 38–39, 42–44, 80–81.
Reprinted by permission of Prentice-Hall, Inc., Englewood Cliffs, New Jersey. Table 5-1
Adapted from J. Henripin, *Tendances et facteurs de la fecondité au Canada* (Ottawa,
1968); Figure 6-1. Statistics Canada, Cat. 84-202, 84-206, and 84-528; Table 6-1 and 6-2
Lapierre and Aylwin, *Canadian Youth: Perspectives on their Health*, Cat. 82-545E;
Figure 7-1 Statistics Canada, *Canadian Crime Statistics*, Annual (Ottawa, 1986), Cat.
85-205; Table 9-1 Statistics Canada (1988), 74; Table 11-1 Statistics Canada, Census of
Canada; Figure 11-1 Statistics Canada, 1971, 1986 Censuses of Canada; Figure 11-2
Statistics Canada, 1986 Census of Canada; Figure 11-3 Statistics Canada, Cat. 84-205,
Census of Canada; Table 12-1 Statistics Canada, 1985–86, 51; Figure 12-1 Statistics
Canada, 1961 Census of Canada, Vol. III (Part 1) Labour Force, table 1, for 1911–61; for
1966–79; Cat. 71-201, Historical Labour Force Statistics, pp. 151, 153, 158; for 1981–84:
Historical Labour Force Statistics, 1984, Cat. 71-201, p.220, D767895, p.225, D768005;
for 1985–86, Cat. 71-001; Table 12-2 Statistics Canada, 1971 Census of Canada Vol 3.2,
table 8 and 1981 Census of Canada, 1971 Census of Canada Vol 3.2, table 8 and 1981
Census of Canada, Cat. 92-920, table 1; Figure 13-2 Statistics Canada, *Education in
Canada. A Statistical Review for 1984–85* (1985); Table 13-2 Statistics Canada,
Education in Canada. A Statistical Review for 1984–85 (1985); Table 13-2 Statistics
Canada, *Education in Canada*, Cat. 81-229 (1989); Table 14-1 Statistics Canada, 1981
Census of Canada; all reproduced with permission of the Minister of Supply and
Services Canada, 1989. Table 7-1 Reprinted with permission of The Free Press, a
division of Macmillan, Inc. from Social Theory anhd Social Structure by Robert K.
Merton. Copyright © 1957 by The Free Press, renewed 1985 by Robert K. Merton. Table
7-3 C. Misch et. al., National Survey Concerning Female Inmates in Provincial and
Territorial Institutions (Ottawa: Canadian Association of Elizabeth Fry Societies,
1982). Reprinted with permission. Table 7-4 Reprinted with permission of Solicitor
General Canada, Correctional Service of Canada, Offender Information System. Figure
9-1 from *Financial Post 500* (Summer 1986), p.208. Reprinted with permission. Table
9-2 National Council of Welfare, *1989 Poverty Lines* (1989), 9. Reprinted with
permission. Table 9-3 Adapted from *Welfare in Canada, The Tangled Safety Net*,
National Council of Welfare, (November 1987), table 5, pp. 66–69; Reprinted with
permission. Table 9-4 National Council of Welfare, *Poverty Profile 1988* (1988), 28.
Reprinted with permission. Table 11-2 Lorna Erwin, "What Feminists Should Know
about the Pro-Family Movement in Canada," in *Feminist Research: Prospect and
Retrospect* ed. Peta Tancred-Sheriff (Montreal: CRIAW and McGill-Queen's University
Press, 1988), 272. Reprinted with permission. Figure 13-1 and Figure 13-3 Porter,
Porter and Blishen, *Stations and Callings* (Toronto: Nelson Canada, 1982). 61, 193; ©
Nelson Canada, 1982, A Division of International Thomson Ltd, 1120 Birchmount
Road, Scarborough, Ontario, M1K 5G4. Reprinted with permission. Figure 14-1 From
Immigration Statistics. Reprinted with the permission of Employment and Immigration
Canada. Table 14-2 Reprinted with permission of the Cross-Cultural Communication
Centre, Toronto. Table 15-1 Reprinted from *Canadian Corporate Power* by Henry
Veltmeyer (Toronto: Garamond, 1987), 78–79.

Name Index

Subject Index